The Palgrave Handbook of Wine Industry Economics

Adeline Alonso Ugaglia
Jean-Marie Cardebat • Alessandro Corsi
Editors

The Palgrave Handbook of Wine Industry Economics

palgrave
macmillan

Editors
Adeline Alonso Ugaglia
Bordeaux Sciences Agro
University of Bordeaux
Gradignan, France

Jean-Marie Cardebat
University of Bordeaux
Pessac, France

Alessandro Corsi
University of Turin
Turin, Italy

ISBN 978-3-319-98632-6   ISBN 978-3-319-98633-3   (eBook)
https://doi.org/10.1007/978-3-319-98633-3

Library of Congress Control Number: 2018964901

This Palgrave Macmillan imprint is published by the registered company Springer Nature Switzerland AG.
The registered company address is: Gewerbestrasse 11, 6330 Cham, Switzerland

Acknowledgments

This book received contributions from economists from Europe, South and North America, Australia, South Africa and China. It describes and examines varying models of wine industry in different countries. Two main models are generally used to describe wine industries, Old and New wine worlds (appellation regimes *vs.* brands and varietals), which are generally discussed and compared with respect to their efficiency. What makes the difference between these models? The industrial organization does. This book therefore proposes a discussion of these models and highlights the key variables of the efficiency of industrial organization in the wine industry worldwide for the first time. This comprehensive volume is essential reading for students, researchers and professionals in the wine industry.

Publishing a book is a long way off and this book would have not been written without the help and encouragement of a lot of people and institutions. This work received a grant from the Excellence Initiative of Bordeaux University (2014–2015) (Initial Support for Exploratory Projects-PEPS Emrgc 2014–2015_Adeline Alonso Ugaglia/MOMAVI/Modeling the wine market in the Traditional Producing Countries (TPC)). Thanks to this grant we have been able to have all the global experts contributing together to this challenging project. It has also received the support of the Bordeaux Wine Economics (BWE) group (bordeaux-wine-economics. com). We would like to thank particularly our Editorial Advisory Board who actively participated in this project since the early beginning and have welcomed our meetings over the years to prepare the book. Of course, this book would not exist without the contributions of all the authors who have kindly accepted to take part to this original work. We thank them for providing high-quality chapters specifically written for the book and to comply with all the requirements we had. During the last months, the first proposal has benefited from the suggestions made by the peer reviewers. We have also been greatly helped by Laura Pacey and Clara Heathcock from Palgrave Macmillan in the editorial preparation, and by Sarulatha Krishnamurthy during the publishing process.

Contents

1   **Introduction**   1
Adeline Alonso Ugaglia, Jean-Marie Cardebat, and Alessandro Corsi

Part I   Structure of the Wine Sectors Worldwide   15

2   **The French Wine Industry**   17
Adeline Alonso Ugaglia, Jean-Marie Cardebat, and Linda Jiao

3   **The Italian Wine Industry**   47
Alessandro Corsi, Simonetta Mazzarino, and Eugenio Pomarici

4   **The Spanish Wine Industry**   77
Luis Miguel Albisu, Cristina Escobar, Rafael del Rey, and José María Gil Roig

5   **The US Wine Industry**   105
James T. Lapsley, Julian M. Alston, and Olena Sambucci

6   **The Australian Wine Industry**   131
Kym Anderson

7   **The Argentinean Wine Industry**   155
Javier Merino

8   The Chilean Wine Industry   177
    G. Marcos Mora

9   The South African Wine Industry   201
    Nick Vink

10 The Chinese Wine Industry   225
    Linda Jiao and Shan Ouyang

Part II   Regulations in the Wine Sector   247

11 Introduction: Regulations in the Wine Sector   249
    Paola Corsinovi and Davide Gaeta

12 International Wine Organizations and Plurilateral
    Agreements: Harmonization Versus Mutual Recognition of
    Standards   253
    Raúl Compés López

13 The European Wine Policies: Regulations and Strategies   265
    Paola Corsinovi and Davide Gaeta

14 Barriers to Wine Trade   291
    Angela Mariani and Eugenio Pomarici

Part III   Diversity of Organization in the Wine Industry   317

15 Introduction: The Diversity of Organizational Patterns in the
    Wine Industry   319
    Adeline Alonso Ugaglia

16 The Organization of Vineyards and Wineries   325
    Douglas W. Allen and Dean Lueck

17   Wine Co-operatives and Territorial Anchoring   339
     Marie-Claude Bélis-Bergouignan and Nathalie Corade

18   Diversity and a Shifting Power Balance: Negociants and
     Winegrowers in Bordeaux   363
     Sofya Brand

Part IV   Backward Vertical Integration   381

19   Introduction: Outsourcing Versus Integration, a Key Trade-
     Off for Wine Companies?   383
     Georges Giraud

20   To Make or to Buy? A Managerial Trade-Off of Winemaking
     Process in the Burgundy Vineyards   389
     Georges Giraud and Abdoul Diallo

21   Vertical Integration and Financial Performance of French
     Wine Farms and Co-operatives   403
     Adeline Alonso Ugaglia and Julien Cadot

22   The Prosecco Superiore DOCG Industry Structure: Current
     Status and Evolution over Time   421
     Eugenio Pomarici, Luigino Barisan, Vasco Boatto, and Luigi Galletto

23   International Perspectives on Backwards Vertical Integration   437
     Alfredo Coelho and Etienne Montaigne

Part V   Efficiency of the Business Models in the Different Wine
     Industries   453

24   Introduction: Does a National Model Exist Which Favors
     Trade Performance?   455
     Jean-Marie Cardebat

25   **Individual and Collective Reputations in the Wine Industry**   463
     Florine Livat

26   **The Chilean Wine Cluster**   487
     Alfredo Coelho and Etienne Montaigne

27   **Producing and Consuming Locally: Switzerland as a Local Market**   507
     Philippe Masset and Jean-Philippe Weisskopf

28   **Conclusion: What's Next?**   523
     Adeline Alonso Ugaglia, Jean-Marie Cardebat, and Alessandro Corsi

Index   531

Editorial Advisory Board

Notes on Contributors

Luis Miguel Albisu is Chairman Scientific Committee, Centro de Investigación y Tecnología Agroalimentaria de Aragón (CITA), Zaragoza, Spain.

Douglas W. Allen is a Burnaby Mountain Professor in the Department of Economics, Simon Fraser University, USA.

Adeline Alonso Ugaglia is Associate Professor of Economics at Bordeaux Sciences Agro, France. She is a board member of the American Association of Wine Economists and takes part to the Editorial Advisory Board of the *Journal of Wine Economics*. She is one of the International Organisation of Vine and Wine (OIV) experts representing France in the group ENVIRO "Sustainable development and climate change".

Julian M. Alston is a distinguished professor in the Department of Agricultural and Resource Economics; Director of the Robert Mondavi Institute Center for Wine Economics at the University of California, Davis; and a member of the Giannini Foundation of Agricultural Economics, USA.

Kym Anderson is the George Gollin Professor of Economics, foundation Executive Director of the Wine Economics Research Centre and formerly foundation Executive Director of the Centre for International Economic Studies at the University of Adelaide, and Professor of Economics in the Crawford School of Public Policy, Australian National University, Australia.

Luigino Barisan works at the Interdepartmental Centre for Research in Viticulture and Enology (CIRVE), University of Padova, Conegliano, Italy.

Marie-Claude Bélis-Bergouignan is Emeritus Professor of Economics at Bordeaux University (GREThA, UMR CNRS 5113), France.

Vasco Boatto is Full Professor of Wine Economics, University of Padua, Italy, member of Interdepartmental Centre for Research in Viticulture and Enology of Padua University and chief of economics center of Prosecco district, Italy.

Sofya Brand is postdoctoral researcher in the Department "Management, Marketing et Stratégie" (MMS), Institut Mines Télécom Business School, France.

Julien Cadot is Associate Professor of Finance at Institut Supérieur de Gestion (ISG) Paris, France, and is an adjunct faculty member of the Wine Executive MBA Hybrid Program of the Sonoma State University, USA. He is in the board of the French Association of Agricultural Economists (Société Française d'Economie Rurale) and of the *Wine Business Case Research Journal*. His research deals with corporate governance in agribusiness, with a focus on the wine industry.

Jean-Marie Cardebat is Professor of Economics at the University of Bordeaux, France, and Affiliate Professor at INSEEC (School of Business and Economics) Bordeaux, France.

Alfredo Coelho is Associate Professor of Management at Bordeaux Sciences Agro, France.

Raúl Compés López has a Ph.D. in Agricultural Engineering awarded from the Universitat Politècnica de València (UPV), Spain. He is a senior professor in the Department of Economics and Social Sciences of the UPV. His areas of expertise are, among others, public policy and markets of the agri-food sector, specialized in wine.

Nathalie Corade is Associate Professor of Economics at Bordeaux Sciences Agro, France, since 1995. Her recent researches focus on short and local food circuits, local food systems and food projects of territories. She is interested in the link between these initiatives and the sustainable development of the territories. She worked previously on the link between the wine sector and the development of territories and was especially interested on the mergers of wine cooperatives and their impact on the territories on which they were historically built.

Alessandro Corsi is Associate Professor of Agricultural Economics at the University of Turin, Italy.

Paola Corsinovi is a Professor at the Hochschule Geisenheim University (Germany) affiliated with the Center of Economics of Geisenheim University. Her research focuses on the European Agricultural Policy with particular to the wine sector and the effects of decision-making and lobby groups.

Rafael Del Rey is General Director of the Spanish Observatory of Wine Markets (OEMV) as well as General Manager of the Foundation for the Culture of Wine, Spain. Graduated in Political Science from the University of Madrid and MA in International Studies at Johns Hopkins' School of Advanced International Studies (SAIS), he teaches in several universities in Spain and other European countries; he writes articles on the economic situation of wine and gives dozens of presentations per year on the economic and legal situation of wine in Spain and the world.

Abdoul Diallo is an Assistant Engineer, Specialist of GIS and data analyst at AgroSup Dijon, France.

Cristina Escobar is a Researcher and a Consultant from CREDA-UPC-IRTA (Centre de Recerca en Economia i Desenvolupament Agroalimentari - Universitat Politècnica de Catalunya - Institut de Recerca i Tecnologia Agroalimentàries), Center for research in Agro-Food Economics and Development, Barcelona, Spain.

Davide Gaeta is an Associate Professor in the Department of Business Administration at the University of Verona, Italy, where he teaches agribusiness, wine firm management and wine policy. He is the co-author of the book *Economics, Governance, and Politics in the Wine Market: European Union Development* published by Palgrave Macmillan. He has managed private and public organizations in the wine sector.

Luigi Galletto is Associate Professor of Wine Economics and Marketing in the Department of Land, Environment, Agriculture and Forestry, University of Padua, Italy.

José María Gil Roig is Professor of Agricultural Economics at the School of Agriculture, Polytechnic University of Catalonia, Spain, and Director of the Center for Research in Agro-Food Economics and Development CREDA-UPC-IRTA (Centre de Recerca en Economia i Desenvolupament Agroalimentari - Universitat Politècnica de Catalunya - Institut de Recerca i Tecnologia Agroalimentàries), Spain.

Georges Giraud is Professor of Agri-food Marketing at AgroSup Dijon, Graduate School of Agronomy, University Bourgogne Franche-Comté, France.

Linda Jiao is a Ph.D. student in Economics at the University of Bordeaux (Larefi), France

James T. Lapsley is Adjunct Associate Professor in the Department of Viticulture and Enology at the University of California, Davis, and academic researcher at the University of California Agricultural Issues Center, USA.

Florine Livat is Associate Professor of Economics at the KEDGE Business School, Bordeaux, France.

Dean Lueck is Director of the Program on Natural Resource Governance at the Ostrom Workshop at Indiana University, where he is also Professor of Economics and affiliated professor at the Maurer School of Law, USA.

Angela Mariani is Professor of Agribusiness and International Trade in the Department of Economic and Legal Studies at the University of Naples "Parthenope", Italy.

Philippe Masset is Assistant Professor of Finance at Ecole hôtelière de Lausanne, Switzerland. He holds a Ph.D. in Financial Economics and his research focuses on wine economics, alternative investments, hospitality finance.

Simonetta Mazzarino is Assistant Professor and Confirmed Researcher of Agricultural Economics in the Department of Economics and Statistics "Cognetti de Martiis", University of Turin, Italy.

Javier Merino is Professor of Economy and Project Evaluation at the Agrarian Faculty, National University of Cuyo, Argentina, and University of Mendoza, Argentina.

Etienne Montaigne is Professor of Agricultural and Food Industry Economics in the Department of Agricultural Economics, Montpellier SupAgro, France.

G. Marcos Mora is Assistant Professor and Researcher in Agribusiness and Food Marketing in the Department of Agricultural Economics, Faculty of Agricultural Science, University of Chile, Chile.

Shan Ouyang works for Beijing Artix Investment Company Co., Ltd, China.

Eugenio Pomarici is Full Professor of Agricultural Economics a the University of Padova (Dep. TeSAF), Italy, affiliate to the Interdepartmental Centre for Research in Viticulture and Enology (University of Padova) and past President of the Economy and Law Commission of OIV, Italy.

Olena Sambucci is a Postdoctoral Scholar in the Department of Agricultural and Resource Economics at the University of California, Davis, USA.

Nick Vink is Professor and Chair of the Department of Agricultural Economics, Stellenbosch University, South Africa, and a Non-executive Director of the South African Reserve Bank, South Africa.

Jean-Philippe Weisskopf is Assistant Professor of Finance at Ecole hôtelière de Lausanne, Switzerland.

List of Figures

Fig. 1.1   The growth of world wine exports 1995–2017 (volumes in thousands of hL). (Source: OIV stats, http://www.oiv.int/fr/bases-de-donnees-et-statistiques)   3

Fig. 1.2   The emergence of the New World in the world wine trade. (Note: Exported volumes in thousands of hectoliters; Source: OIV stats, http://www.oiv.int/fr/bases-de-donnees-et-statistiques)   5

Fig. 2.1   French wine imports and exports (in volume and value). (Source: OIV stats, http://www.oiv.int/fr/bases-de-donnees-et-statistiques)   20

Fig. 2.2   Wine production and consumption in France. (Source: OIV stats, http://www.oiv.int/fr/bases-de-donnees-et-statistiques)   22

Fig. 2.3   Evolution of organic surfaces in France (ha). (Source: Agence BIO 2017)   29

Fig. 2.4   Wine harvest in France by region and color (2015). (Source: DGDDI-CVI Harvest 2005–2015)   32

Fig. 2.5   AOC and PGI and wine color (2010). (Source: Agreste Primeur 2011)   33

Fig. 2.6   Winemaking processing (volume, 2010). (Source: Agreste Primeur 2011)   34

Fig. 2.7   On-farm winemakers' distribution channels by percentage of volume. (Source: RGA 2010)   36

Fig. 2.8   Distribution channels (percentage of volume). (Source: Author's calculation based on RGA 2010)   37

Fig. 3.1   Geographical divisions and main wine-producing Regions   50

Fig. 3.2   Wine consumption flows. (Source: ISMEA, Scheda di settore 2015)   66

Fig. 3.3   Estimable grape flows among operators for total wine, generic wine, GI wine, PDO wine. (Map legend: Grape flows share for **total wine** (generic wine, PGI wine, PDO wine))   69

Fig. 4.1   Evolution of the vineyard area and the production of grapes in Spain. (Source: Own elaboration from Agriculture Yearbooks and Agriculture Statistics. MAGRAMA. Spanish Ministry of Agriculture, Food and Environment (MAGRAMA 2016))   79

Fig. 4.2   Wine vineyard specialization in Spain (2012). (Source: Own elaboration from the Agriculture Yearbook 2013. MAGRAMA. Spanish Ministry of Agriculture, Food and Environment (MAGRAMA 2015c))   80

Fig. 4.3   Distribution of the main grape varieties in Spain (% on total surface) (2014). (Source: Own elaboration from the Inventory of wine-growing potential, 2015. MAGRAMA. Spanish Ministry of Agriculture, Food and Environment (MAGRAMA 2015d))   83

Fig. 4.4   Economic results of the Spanish viticulture holdings (euro). (*[*Preliminary data]* Source: Own elaboration from FADN 2018 (European Commission))   85

Fig. 4.5   The Spanish market for wine (million liters). (Source: OeMv (2018) (Spanish acronym for Spanish Observatory of Wine Markets))   91

Fig. 4.6   Spanish wine exports. (Source: OeMv (2018) (Spanish acronym for Spanish Observatory of Wine Markets))   92

Fig. 4.7   Spanish wine sales structure for the domestic market (%) (e = estimation). (Source: OeMv (Spanish acronym for Spanish Observatory of Wine Markets))   95

Fig. 4.8   Wine consumption at home in Spain (liters per capita). (Source: Own elaboration from MAPAMA. Spanish Agriculture Ministry. Food Consumption Panel (MAPAMA 2018))   97

Fig. 4.9   Place of purchase of wine for at-home consumption in Spain (%). (Source: Own elaboration from MAGRAMA. Spanish Agriculture Ministry. Food Consumption Panel (MAGRAMA 2015e))   98

Fig. 5.1   US wine regions—area, volume, and value of production, 2016. (Source: Created by the authors using data from USDA/NASS 2016a, 2016b, 2017, 2018)   109

Fig. 5.2   Volume shares (%) of tax-paid, domestically bottled wine, by wine type, 2016. (Source: Created by the authors using data from US Treasury/TTB 2016c)   116

Fig. 5.3   Volume and value of US imports and exports of wine, 1966–2015. (Source: Fig. 5 in Alston et al. (2018a). Data are from ITC (2018). *Notes:* Nominal monetary values in these graphs were deflated by the consumer price index (CPI) for all goods taken from USDL/BLS 2015)   120

Fig. 6.1   Bearing area of vineyards, Australia (upper line) and South Australia (lower line), 1843 to 2013 (hectares). (Source: Anderson 2015, Chart 5)   133

Fig. 6.2   Vine area, wine production and wine exports, Australia, 1843 to 2013 (log scale). (Source: Anderson 2015, Chart 9)   134
Fig. 6.3   Share of grape production used for winemaking, Australia, 1939 to 2013 (%). (Source: Anderson 2015, Table 8)   134
Fig. 6.4   Shares of table, fortified and distillation wine in total wine output, Australia, 1923 to 2013 (percentage, three-year moving average around year shown). (Source: Anderson 2015, Chart 31)   135
Fig. 6.5   Average price of winegrapes and of exports (RH axis), and vine area (LH axis), Australia, 1986 to 2017 (A$/tonne, A$/hectoliter, and '000 hectares). (Source: Anderson 2015, Chart 17)   135
Fig. 6.6   Number of wineries in Australia, 1984 to 2016. (Source: Updated from Anderson 2015, Table 21)   137
Fig. 6.7   Share of Australian wineries by crush, 1978, 1996 and 2016 (%). (Source: Updated from Anderson 2015, Table 21)   138
Fig. 6.8   Shares of varieties in Australia's winegrape-bearing area, 1956 to 2012 (%, three-year averages). (Source: Anderson 2015)   146
Fig. 6.9   Exports as percentage of wine production and imports as percentage of apparent wine consumption, Australia, 1843 to 2017 (percentage, three-year moving average around year shown). (Source: Updated from Anderson 2015, Chart 8)   148
Fig. 6.10 Shares of the value of Australia's exports to various regions, 1990 to 2017 (The 2016 data are for the 12 months to September 30). (Source: Updated from Anderson and Nelgen 2013, Table 144) (%)   149
Fig. 7.1   Evolution of cultivated surface area of grapes for winemaking in Argentina (ha). (Source: INV)   156
Fig. 7.2   Variation surface area (1990/2017). (Source: INV)   160
Fig. 7.3   Annual revenues in the viticulture sector (BB AR$ - Dec. 2017). (Source: Area del Vino)   165
Fig. 7.4   Sales price vs. volume. (Source: Area del Vino)   167
Fig. 7.5   Total market in volume (millions of cases), average sales prices (AR$ Dec. 2017/case), and annual revenues of wine (BB AR$ Dec 2017). (Source: Area del Vino)   171
Fig. 8.1   Chile: value chain in the wine industry   190
Fig. 9.1   The flow of product in the South African industry, 1982   206
Fig. 9.2   South Africa's RCA in wine. (Source: Anderson and Pinilla 2018)   218
Fig. 10.1 Evolution of wine consumption and production in China. (Source: Cosllected from OIV annual reports of World Vitiviniculture Situation and OIV Statistics, 2013–2017)   226
Fig. 10.2 Main wine regions in China. (Drawn by author)   229
Fig. 10.3 China wine market share by volume. (Source: MarketLine 2015)   233
Fig. 10.4 Wine market share segmentation by color. (Source: MarketLine 2015 and author's calculation based on Euromonitor International 2011, 2015)   237

Fig. 10.5   Wine distribution in China. (Source: MarketLine 2015 and author's calculation based on Euromonitor International 2011, 2015)   238

Fig. 10.6   Hourglass structure. (Drawn by author)   239

Fig. 10.7   Distribution chain of import wine in China. (Source: Wine Intelligence 2013). Dashed line represents significant relationship but with little volume   243

Fig. 13.1   Policy orientations through the % of budget expenditure. (Source: Author's dataset (elaboration from EAGGF annual expenditures), 2015)   275

Fig. 13.2   National Programme Support 2019–2023: % of budget. (Source: Financial Report, European Commission—DG AGRI (https:// ec.europa.eu/agriculture/sites/agriculture/files/wine/statistics/pro-gramming-2019-2023_en.pdf))   275

Fig. 15.1   Simplified representation of wine industries for Old and New world countries. (Source: Author; Note: The dashed arrows reflect the potential financial contract to buy fresh grapes between pro-ducers and co-operatives or between co-operatives and commercial unions depending of the law status of the co-operative)   320

Fig. 15.2   Diversity of strategies for wine co-operatives. (Source: Corade et Lacour 2015)   322

Fig. 18.1   Bulk wine price fluctuations in Bordeaux. (Source: FranceAgriMer)   374

Fig. 20.1   HAC dendrogram of wine business models in Chablis. (Source: Authors)   393

Fig. 20.2   HAC dendrogram of wine business models in Côte & Hautes Côtes de Nuits. (Source: Authors)   394

Fig. 20.3   HAC dendrogram of wine business models in Côte & Hautes Côtes de Beaune. (Source: Authors)   395

Fig. 20.4   Principal Component Analysis of winegrowers' business models, Burgundy 2011. (Source: Authors)   397

Fig. 21.1   Economic balance by level of vertical integration. (In dark gray, "high balance" on the asset and liabilities, respectively, corresponds to fixed assets and equity. In light gray, the "low balance" to match assets and liabilities, respectively, in WCR and net debt)   411

Fig. 22.1   Conegliano Valdobbiadene Prosecco DOCG: trends in sparkling wine market (bottles), 2003–2016. (*Sparkling: Prosecco Superiore DOCG and Superiore di Cartizze DOCG; Source: Data process-ing C.I.R.V.E., Conegliano, 2018)   423

Fig. 22.2   Conegliano Valdobbiadene Prosecco DOCG: trends in sparkling wine sales on domestic and foreign markets, 2003–2016. (Source: Data processing C.I.R.V.E., Conegliano, 2018)   424

Fig. 22.3 Conegliano Valdobbiadene Prosecco DOCG' supply chains, 2016. (*Prosecco Superiore DOCG Sparkling; ⋯⋯⋯= Production linked to the related own firms; Source: Data processing C.I.R.V.E., Conegliano, 2018.)   427

Fig. 22.4 Conegliano Valdobbiadene Prosecco DOCG: concentration index, 2016. (Source: Data processing C.I.R.V.E., Conegliano, 2018)   430

Fig. 23.1 The 12 leading world wine producers by vine surfaces in 2016 (ha). (Source: Annual Reports, International press)   443

Fig. 24.1 Change in exports in volume between 1995 and 2017. (Source: OIV [Wine International Organization] statistics. Note: the percentages reported correspond to growth rates between 1995 and 2017. (*) For China, the data are from 1995 to 2014)   457

Fig. 24.2 Exportation rate in 2014 in function of origin indicators. (Source: OIV statistics. Note: on the x-axis we find the number of PDOs (for the European countries) or that of simple origin indicators (DO for New World countries). The triangles indicate European countries (except Georgia) and the circles represent New World countries (including Georgia))   458

Fig. 24.3 Trade balance relative to production volume (y-axis) in function of the number of PDOs and DOs (x-axis) for a selection of countries between 1995 and 2014. (Source: OIV statistics. Note: the ratio is calculated on the basis of the trade balance divided by the production of each country, with all the variables expressed in volume. On the x-axis we find the number of PDOs (for the European countries) or that of simple origin indicators (DO for New World countries). The triangles indicate European countries (except Georgia) and the circles represent New World countries (including Georgia). Linear trends are given for the year 2014)   460

Fig. 25.1 Denominations of origin. (Source: Addor and Grazioli 2002, p. 870)   473

Fig. 26.1 An overview of the Chilean wine cluster. (Source: Adapted from Wines of Chile)   493

Fig. 26.2 Establishment dates of grape nurseries and *bodegas* in Chile. (Note 1: new wineries include both the bodegas producing more than 300,000 liters and the bodegas with an export activity. Data includes established wineries until 2011 (Source: INE); Note 2: grape nurseries include the suppliers of *Vitis vinifera* plants and the suppliers of table wine plants. Some of the grape nurseries supplying plants for table grapes may also supply *Vitis vinifera* plants. Data includes established firms in 2015 (Source: SAG))   495

Fig. 26.3 Main joint-ventures and foreign investments in the Chilean wine cluster (1979–2018). (Source: World Wine Data 2018)   499

Fig. 26.4   Evolution of wine grape plantings in Chile (ha) (1994–2014).
            (Source: Elaborated by authors based on data from ODEPA)   501
Fig. 26.5   Exports of bottled wine from Chile per price bracket (US$/case)
            (2014–2015). (Source: ODEPA)   503

List of Tables

Table 1.1	The top ten wine importers and exporters in 2017	3
Table 2.1	Surface, number and average size of grape-growing farms by region (in 2010) (The three top regions, with more than 100,000 ha are in bold)	24
Table 2.2	Areas according to the varietals (%)	25
Table 2.3	Economic size according to the type of wine	26
Table 2.4	Repartition of organic farms and surfaces by region	30
Table 2.5	Four main French wine co-operatives	35
Table 2.6	Turnover of the three main downstream companies—still wine	38
Table 2.7	Cybercommerce in the French wine industry	41
Table 3.1	Number of farms producing wine grapes and vine-bearing area	49
Table 3.2	Italian wine production by type (hl, %)	53
Table 3.3	Total wine production by type of producer (2012)	56
Table 3.4	Shares of total wine production by type of wine, producer, and area (2012)	57
Table 3.5	Bottling unit distribution by capacity	58
Table 3.6	Top 30 wine companies in Italy	61
Table 3.7	Percentage of Italian domestic supply by distribution channels (2017, 155 top wine companies)	67
Table 4.1	Profile of the Spanish wine-exporting company in 2017	87
Table 4.2	Top 25 wineries in Spain according their sales in 2014 (million Euros)	88
Table 4.3	Spanish wine exports by type of wine in 2017	93
Table 5.1	Characteristics of US wine regions, 2016 data	107
Table 5.2	California: total grape area and number of grape-producing farms, 2012	111
Table 5.3	California: size distribution of grape producers, 2012	112

Table 5.4   Characteristics of California winegrapes crushed, 2016   113
Table 5.5   Gallons of bottled wine removed tax paid into US market   116
Table 5.6   Share of all California wineries (2015) and tons crushed (2016) by region   118
Table 5.7   Four largest US alcoholic beverage distributors, 2014   124
Table 5.8   Top ten wine-consuming states in 2016   125
Table 6.1   Share of Australia's wine companies, by year of establishment, 2015   136
Table 6.2   Number of Australian wineries by tonnes crushed, 1998 to 2016   137
Table 6.3   Various attributes of Australian wineries, 2000, 2010 and 2016   138
Table 6.4   Shares of domestic wine sales volume by largest four wineries, Australia and other key wine-producing countries, 2009 and 2015(%)   139
Table 6.5   Ranking of Australia's largest wine companies by wine sales value and other criteria, 2015   141
Table 6.6   Number, vine-bearing area and crush of Australian independent and winemaker grape-growing establishments, by vineyard size range (ha) and state, 2012   143
Table 7.1   Surface area of wine varieties (ha)   159
Table 8.1   Evolution of wine grape acreage by variety (ha)   180
Table 8.2   Cultivated area (ha) with grapevines in irrigated, rainfed and tended irrigation areas   181
Table 8.3   Chile: surface area of vineyards according to conduction system (ha)   182
Table 8.4   Costs and prices of wine grapes at producer level (dollars)   184
Table 8.5   Chile: production of wines by type of wine and market (million liters)   186
Table 8.6   Chile: exports of wines of denomination of origin in volume and FOB value   187
Table 8.7   Concha y Toro Winery: segment, brand and price of their wines   194
Table 8.8   Santa Rita Winery: segment, brand and price   195
Table 9.1   Concentration in the market: a 'new world' comparison, 2014 (%)   210
Table 13.1   The development of European wine policies   268
Table 13.2   Total CMO wine expenditures, 1970–2015   270
Table 13.3   The main traditional terms as referred to EU Reg. 607/2009   284
Table 14.1   Types of tariffs in the international wine trade   293
Table 14.2   EU most favored nations import duties   294
Table 14.3   Non-tariff measures classification   295
Table 14.4   Import measures: technical measures   298
Table 14.5   Key elements in SPS and TBT agreements   300
Table 14.6   Wine exporter's main free trade agreements (FTA)   305
Table 17.1   Co-operative mergers (1968–2006)   340

Table 17.2	Mergers' initial causes and final objectives (number of answers to these items/number of co-operatives studied)	349
Table 17.3	The determinants of a commitment to merger	354
Table 17.4	Similarity, learning processes and success conditions for merger	356
Table 17.5	Observable organizational changes post-merger	358
Table 18.1	Vineyard price in Bordeaux rouge equivalent	371
Table 18.2	Merchants' concentration in Bordeaux	375
Table 18.3	Typology of negociants in Bordeaux: variables	376
Table 18.4	Typology of negociants in Bordeaux: results	378
Table 20.1	Number of wine estates according to the wine-grape-growing area, Burgundy 2011	390
Table 20.2	Efficiency and profitability of wine estates according to size and business model	398
Table 21.1	Number and wine farms' allocation	406
Table 21.2	Size, sales and distribution channel	407
Table 21.3	Economic balance by level of vertical integration	410
Table 21.4	Vertical integration and profitability ratios	411
Table 21.5	Vertical integration and financial risk	412
Table 21.6	Product price and price paid to producers	416
Table 21.7	Margins, obsolescence and leverage	417
Table 22.1	Prosecco Superiore DOCG price differentiation by type of supply chain, wine destination and size on domestic market, 2016	428
Table 22.2	Conegliano Valdobbiadene Prosecco's companies: concentration index, 2008–2016	431
Table 22.3	Prosecco Superiore DOCG producers' distribution by type of supply chain and bottling size, 2016	431
Table 22.4	Prosecco Superiore DOCG industry structure: evolution over the period analyzed, 2010–2016	432
Table 23.1	Concha y Toro: expansion of vineyard surfaces 2002–2018 (ha)	445
Table 23.2	Concha y Toro: expansion of vineyard surfaces in Chilean valleys 2005–2015 (ha)	445
Table 24.1	Average export price in 2017 (in € per liter)	457
Table 26.1	Main wine-related Programs for Modernization and Competitiveness (PMCs)	490
Table 26.2	Concentration of the market shares in the domestic market of the leading wine firms in Chile (% of the total volumes)	496
Table 26.3	Evolution of wine grape plantings in the main regions in Chile (2000–2014) (ha)	502
Table 26.4	Evolution of grape variety plantings, wine production, and exports in Chile (2000–2015)	502
Table 27.1	Consumption, imports and exports (2008–2013)	513

1

Introduction

Adeline Alonso Ugaglia, Jean-Marie Cardebat, and Alessandro Corsi

The Palgrave Handbook of Wine Industry Economics examines varying models of wine industry in different countries and their relevance. The wine industry can be seen as a microcosm of globalization nowadays. It faces the same evolution as other industries in the 1990s: emergence of New producing and consuming countries and rising competition. Over the last 15 years, the international wine market has changed. New competitors appeared on the international scene and joined the top wine producers and exporters. The relatively new hierarchy of wine-producing countries could remain similar for the ten next years, but a process of convergence seems to be under way.

A. Alonso Ugaglia (✉)
Bordeaux Sciences Agro, University of Bordeaux, Gradignan, France
e-mail: adeline.ugaglia@agro-bordeaux.fr

J.-M. Cardebat
University of Bordeaux, Pessac, France
INSEEC Bordeaux, Bordeaux, France
e-mail: jean-marie.cardebat@u-bordeaux.fr

A. Corsi
University of Turin, Turin, Italy
e-mail: alessandro.corsi@unito.it

© The Author(s) 2019
A. Alonso Ugaglia et al. (eds.), *The Palgrave Handbook of Wine Industry Economics*,
https://doi.org/10.1007/978-3-319-98633-3_1

1.1   A Global Panorama of Trade Flows from Leading to Emerging Countries

In recent years, growth in world trade has accelerated and competition has increased. The financial and economic crisis had a deep impact on the world wine industry, both in the producing countries and in the consumer markets. The wine market has to face a globalization process like all the other sectors, following the same phases. Initially concentrated in a small number of countries, the wine trade has opened up to the world, bringing in new competitors. In the process of globalization, it is not only the goods that are traded but also the factors of production. The internationalization of the market therefore also affects direct investment abroad and labor.

But if the globalization of the sector is today very advanced, we can wonder how it will evolve and what the consequences for the wine industries are worldwide. What forms could the future panorama of world trade take? Several scenarios have to be considered.

Globalization comes with phases of emergence of new countries beginning to participate in the exchanges. The wine sector is no exception to this dynamic. After the growth of wine trade within a club limited to a few developed countries, a second phase of emergence has seen the New World countries take over. The leaders of the Old World are competing with the outsiders of this New World, mainly in terms of price competitiveness. A third phase of emergence is at work. It mainly concerns China, whose vineyard is one of the largest in the world. The question is to identify when its exports will compete with those from other producing countries.

1.1.1   First Phase: Trade Growth Between the Developed Countries

Since the 1990s, two remarkable facts have to be noticed concerning the international wine trade. First, the strong growth in trade, since global wine exports have globally doubled between 1995 and 2015. Growth is even more pronounced in value than in volume (see Fig. 1.1), reflecting a rise in the average quality of wine exchanged on the market. This increase in trade highlights the globalization of the sector. We can note that global trade has been growing rapidly and steadily since the mid-1950s and faced a significant decline in 2009 for the first time since the beginning of the decade followed by a rebound in the following years.

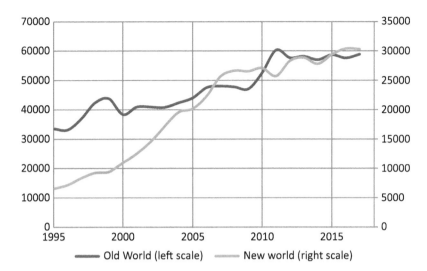

Fig. 1.1 The growth of world wine exports 1995–2017 (volumes in thousands of hL). (Source: OIV stats, http://www.oiv.int/fr/bases-de-donnees-et-statistiques)

Table 1.1 The top ten wine importers and exporters in 2017

Importers				Exporters			
Country	Volume	Value	Euro/ liter	Country	Volume	Value	Euro/ liter
Germany	15.2	2469	1.62	Spain	22.1	2814	1.27
United Kingdom	13.2	3452	2.62	Italy	21.4	5873	2.74
United States	11.8	5190	4.40	France	15.4	8989	5.84
France	7.6	812	1.07	Chile	9.8	1741	1.78
China	7.5	2458	3.28	Australia	8	1727	2.16
Russia	4.5	878	1.95	South Africa	4.5	583	1.3
Netherlands	4.4	1139	2.59	Germany	3.8	926	2.44
Canada	4.1	1653	4.03	United States	3.3	1280	3.88
Belgium	3.1	897	2.89	Portugal	3	752	2.51
Japan	2.6	1388	5.34	New Zealand	2.5	1054	4.22

Note: Volumes are in million hectoliters and values in million Euros
Source: OIV stats, http://www.oiv.int/fr/bases-de-donnees-et-statistiques

Second, the high concentration of trade among six countries is the other feature of wine trade (see Table 1.1). The three largest exporters are traditionally Spain, Italy, and France. In 1995, they accounted for 80% of total exports in volume, just over 66% in 2017. These exports are largely directed to three major consumer countries: the United States, the United Kingdom, and Germany. These countries concentrated 80% of imports in volume in 1995, about 54% in 2017. The international wine trade thus remains very concentrated despite a trend decrease of this degree of concentration.

The disparities in value and volume reflect the positions of the competitors in the wine market. Table 1.1 shows that Spain dominates exports in volume, whereas in value France is in a clear leadership position. These two countries made different strategic choices. Spain has a very aggressive strategy in terms of price on the international market, while France, unable to compete in terms of price, prefers a non-price competitiveness, especially focused on quality, the country, and the region of origin remaining a very important vector of image when a consumer purchases a wine. Italy is halfway between these two competitors in terms of strategic positioning, though it is increasingly moving toward a focus on quality.

The Spanish and French positioning, quite focused on the low or high end, can pose some problems. Of course, a very large diversity of producers exists in all countries, in Spain and France in particular, occupying all segments of the range. It is therefore advisable to remain cautious with the generalizations. Nevertheless, in Spain, the trap would be to devalue the image of the products with prices too low and thus prevent some vineyards to be upgraded. The production of bulk wine at a very low price, which is then exported to countries bottling and marketing it (mainly France), removes for Spain the main part of the added value coming of marketing.

For France, the trap would be to leave the segment of low- and mid-range wines and to promote luxury too much. Obviously, luxury is a segment with very high added value, but gradually abandoning the lower segments would lead to the ruin for many vineyards. Luxury is inherently reserved for a small number of producers. The challenge is to keep a qualitative image for French producers but without offering exclusive wines, which we open only on rare occasions. The large size of the French vineyard indeed requires volume strategies and not only exclusive upmarket strategies moving toward the ultra-premium segments.

From this point of view, and still on a very global scale, the Italian strategy is probably the most balanced between high-volume production with a good added value, as attested, for example, by the international success of Prosecco, and the more exclusive productions from Tuscany and Piedmont.

1.1.2   Second Phase: The Emergence of the New World and the Arrival of Outsiders

Wines from the New World's countries appeared in the international trade of wines at the end of the 1990s. Figure 1.2 reveals the intensity of the increase of exports in volume, while Table 1.1 shows the values of these exports in

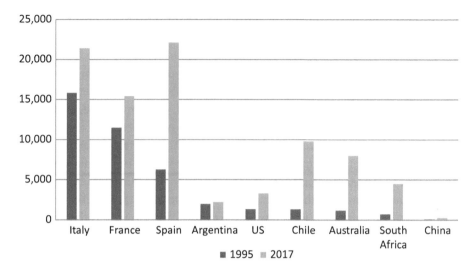

Fig. 1.2 The emergence of the New World in the world wine trade. (Note: Exported volumes in thousands of hectoliters; Source: OIV stats, http://www.oiv.int/fr/bases-de-donnees-et-statistiques)

2015, both in volume and in value. The last column of this table also shows the average price of a liter of wine exported by each country.

The performances of Chile and Australia appear to be the most remarkable. These countries are emerging as the leaders of the New World. Their wine sector is export oriented and very well organized through clusters drawn by leading companies. They have raised their brands to top 10 of the world's leading brands. These countries are at the same time competitive on the costs but with, in addition, products and a marketing strategy very adapted to the Anglo-Saxon consumer. The United States and the United Kingdom are the two main markets targeted by Chile and Australia.

In terms of pure growth, the case of New Zealand is emblematic with exports multiplied by nearly 27 between 1995 and 2015. This performance is all the more remarkable as the average price of wines exported is very high, close to the prices for France. This shows that this wave of emergence induces for the Old World a competition that is not only about volumes. Chardonnays from New Zealand compete with Burgundy wines. This competition is on price but more and more on quality. The example of the United States is also symbolic of this quest for quality and high export prices. This country, and especially California, was the first in the New World to choose constant innovation and a constant search for quality.

The two New World countries that appear slightly behind compared to the others are Argentina and South Africa. In the case of Argentina, it is because the growth of its exports is very low compared to other countries. It is comparable with Germany, a country whose exports of wine are not a priority. Macroeconomic problems in Argentina partly explain these performances. Wine exports contracted considerably during the economic crises of the late 1990s and 2008. In this latter case, restrictions on trade and exchange rate movements are the main reasons for the decline. South Africa is facing a more structural problem. The export performances are good but remain globally associated to rather low-end wines. The price of its exports is struggling to increase and is similar to that of Spain despite lower exports of bulk wine. The trap of low end combined with low added value is very present in this case too.

But the reason why the countries of the New World are particularly remarkable regards their marketing strategies. The creation of strong brands is the main asset of countries like the United States, Australia, and, to a lesser extent, Chile, the three New World countries with the best export performances. These brands capture the added value of marketing while capitalizing on very large volumes and thus achieving massive economies of scale. These brands are therefore a major vector for the competitiveness of these countries. The emergence of major international brands is another indication, together with the emergence of new players, of the entry of the globalization of the wine sector into a phase of maturity.

Argentina and South Africa have so far failed to develop such brands. In addition to quality and price, the sustainability of wine is likely to be a crucial competitive variable that will matter in international trade statistics over time. In this respect, the countries of the New World are clearly ahead of those of the Old World.

1.1.3 Third Phase: The Emergence of a New New World

Other producing countries are gradually becoming part of world wine trade. The countries around the Black Sea in particular, but also China, which increased its exports sevenfold between 1995 and 2015, could be part of the new wave of emergence, that of the "New New World". China is probably the best symbol of the changes at stake on the wine market, being the first country for red wine consumption in the world (the United States being the first one when considering all types of wines).

On one side, the Old Producing countries still count on the global wine market, but they are not dominating this market anymore. They are losing shares and have to make their strategy evolve. On the other side, the big brands are from the United States, Australia, and Chile (New World countries), and compete with the historical champions from the Old World. International trade follows these trends and continues to grow at a steady pace. Wine is also facing a financial globalization by becoming a support for financial investments or even speculation. Wine has finally become a global product since the 2000s.

1.2   Globalization of the Wine Market: Two Models into Question

We often hear about the existence of two main models in the wine industry, Old and New ones (appellation regimes vs. brands and varietals), which are generally discussed and compared with respect to their efficiency. From the three phases described above, we distinguish three groups according to the moment they appeared in the wine industry:

– Old/Traditional producing countries also called the Old World: the countries historically producing wine for centuries as France, Spain, and Italy, plus Portugal, Germany, and Greece if considering the countries still having a significant production (volume and value).
– New producing countries (New World), which have emerged since the 1950s: new producing countries as they began to produce wine far after the countries from the Old World. They had previously no vines and started on the wine market during the second half of the twentieth century. South Africa, Argentina, Australia, the United States, and New Zealand belong to this group.
– New New producing countries (New New World), which appeared on the international wine market in the recent years (twenty-first century) but sometimes had been producing wine for a long time. They include China, India, Brazil, and the countries around the Black Sea. For example, although in Brazil there are a lot of vineyards, only some of them are used for creating wine. The rest produce table grapes, but the share of the wine production is increasing. China has been producing grape wine for a long time, but it wasn't until the late 1890s that the process of true grape winemaking became relevant, and now there are hundreds of varietals produced all over the country.

The book deals with the main ones in each group, respectively France, Italy, and Spain for the Old World; the United States, Australia, Argentina, Chile, and South Africa for the New World; and China for the New New World.

The way the terms Old/New World are commonly used is often close to gross generalizations and also refers to differences in style in the specialized press and media. The differences in Old World and New World wines are described as coming from winemaking practices (tradition) and from the effect of land and climate on the grapes, that is, the terroir. They can also come from rules and regulations that dictate winemaking practices in many Old World regions which could influence a wine's style. Old World is often associated with tradition and history, while New World invokes technology, science, corporations, and marketing. The industrial organization does make a difference as well. The actors involved in the industry, their role along the production process, and the strategies to produce wine in the different countries can also be described as different ones. Considering the actors involved in the chain, in the New wine countries most winemakers are processing and selling wine but do not produce grapes, even if some of them now integrate the grape production to control the supply part of production. The Old World relies more on family estates producing grapes and wines with powerful intermediate bodies to sell the wine on the market. To add value to the wine, they are developing strategies which are often opposed. Old World countries are used to rely on the denomination of origin and appellation regimes, while New World countries focus on developing strong brands and "cepage" or varietal wines. The protected designations of origin (PDO)/protected geographical indication (PGI) system has made the reputation of some famous wine regions as Bordeaux and Burgundy in France with *Grands Crus* and *Châteaux* and a strong reference to the terroir (soil, climate, and know-how).

But the existence of two different and really distinguishable models is very often supposed and implicit. Reality is probably more complex with the coexistence of different strategies within the different producing countries. This is one of the reasons why this book addresses several questions: What are the models of industrial organization in the wine countries? Is it possible to describe them? Are they really different? To go further into the globalization at work for wine production, we intend to describe the industrial organization of the main wine countries according to the international wine trade (France, Italy, Spain, the United States, Australia, Argentina, Chile, South Africa, and China) and analyze the status of these countries. In this competing framework, we wonder about the different strategies and their performance. Regarding the globalization process at work in the wine industry for wine production, we wonder if the different countries will follow a general convergence trend or if different models can and will coexist in the next years. The perspective in this regard is the future challenges that producing countries will face to choose the best strategy for their wine sectors, and this book tends to highlight the key issues that have to be considered.

1.3   Outline

The book is divided into five main parts (apart from the introduction and the conclusion).

Part I aims to identify the different models of wine production in the main wine-producing countries presented above. Based on the description of the industrial organization of each wine country, this part represents a first step to better know and to provide an overall picture of the main features of the wine industry in the nine main wine countries from different regions: the Old World (France, Italy, Spain), the New World (the United States, Australia, Argentina, Chile, South Africa), and the New New World (China). This allows for reasonable comparisons across countries and to discuss the issue of wine industry organization in a context of globalization. The focus is set on the structural features, that is, long-term and not easily changeable character- istics of the sector, rather than on short-term performances. In each chapter, the reader will be able to find many different information on the structural features of the grape-growing/wine-growing sector for the country including geographical distribution of wine-growing farms in the country, proportion of wine-growing farms on the overall agriculture, the average size of wine- growing farms, farm size distribution (small vs. big farms), grape varieties, appellation vs. generic grapes (where applicable), farming techniques (irri- gated vs. rainfed, yields, etc.) and related production costs and revenues, land tenure, family vs. corporate farms. The chapters also include information on the structural features of the winemaking sector (average plant size and size distribution of wineries), types of winemaking firms (on-farm winemakers, wine co-operatives, industrial firms (and shares on total production)), and types of products (appellation vs. generic wines, brand vs. appellation wines, marketing strategies, labeling and communication to consumers, number of brands, price positioning, and volume by segment). Then come the distribu- tion and the relationships along the distribution chain with the contractual arrangements along the chain, the role and relative weight of mass retail, spe- cialized shops, HORECA, and exports as final destinations of the production. What this first part overall shows is that, though some general differences in the structures exist between the Old and the New Worlds, they are not always clear-cut. In particular, the main structural diversities concern the wine farm sizes, the degree of concentration of the sector, and the role of co-operatives. But what also emerges is that different models of organization of the chain coexist. Both winemaker-grape growers and winemakers purchasing grapes exist everywhere, though accounting for different shares of the domestic production. The degrees of concentration are quite diverse, but big firms relying on their brands exist in both the New and Old Worlds. The valorization of specific local characteristics (the terroir and appellation typical model of the Old World) is increasingly utilized in the New World, be it through institutional arrangements or informally through the reputation and the labels.

Part II focuses on the political processes structuring and influencing the wine market worldwide, a perspective that shows that actors in the wine sector act and influence rules and standards. In a context of increasing competition between wines from different countries from all over the world, policies governing the sector are no longer determined at the national level and have a strong influence on the structure of wine industries. Therefore, the analysis focuses here on wine regulations at European and international levels. After the introduction (Chap. 11), Chap. 12 analyzes the international wine organizations and plurilateral agreements, and the dialectic between harmonization and mutual recognition of standards. This chapter focuses on the role of the international organizations such as the International Organisation of Vine and Wine (OIV) and the World Wine Trade Group (WWTG). Through detailed analysis, this section highlights their differences in philosophies and goals of action. Then Chap. 13 focuses on the European wine policy, and its regulations and strategies. It explores the history of the EU wine policies through the analysis of budget expenditure that has characterized the public interventions in 45 years (1970–2015). The objective is to analyze the main drivers that have characterized the EU wine policy from the first CMO in 1962 until the last reform. The authors provide an in-depth analysis of the EU wine policies identifying three main public policy orientations and strategies that occurred in those years such as (1) "price and income support", (2) "quality of wine", and (3) "competitiveness". Finally, Chap. 14 focuses on trade barriers on wine markets as international wine trade, like any other trade, is influenced by barriers which are relevant elements of the global wine market's institutional setting. Trade barriers result from customs tariffs or from policy measures that can potentially have an economic effect on international trade quantity and direction of flows. Wine exporters have actively negotiated preferential trade agreements with importing countries to set lower barriers, and the authors discuss their potential discriminatory effects. Considering the current tensions in international relations, they identify a risk for the rising of trade barriers in the next years and the need to empower an international institution to harmonize the definitions and rules in wine production and trade worldwide.

The next three parts are dedicated to the key variables to analyze industrial organization in the wine sector and its performance: regulation, key actors and the governance of the industries, strategies developed by the players as the vertical integration process.

Part III explores the diversity of business models in the wine industry. It focuses on different key actors in the wine value chain in the Old World: grape and wine growers, wine co-operatives, and negociants/wine merchants. The first chapter of this part (Chap. 15) sets a view of the differences observed in the industrial organization of the wine sector from the actors' point of view, including their strategies. In the Old World, wine industries are more fragmented and atomized. So this chapter focuses on the diversity of grape and wine-growing farms and the variability of their performance, and on the downstream actors as negociants and wine co-operatives. The author shows that it is not all about the size but also on the strategies they develop to better face market demand. Then, the authors of Chap. 16 go deeper into the analysis of vineyard and wineries organization. They use a transaction cost framework to examine the organization of vineyards and winemaking, focusing on three important organizational features of worldwide production: limited contracting, small vineyards producing high-quality grapes, and the separation of wineries from vineyards in the nineteenth century. Then, the part focuses on particular and powerful actors of the Old wine industries: wine co-operatives and negociants with French case studies. Chapter 17 presents the French wine co-operatives and their specific status making them different from wineries in the New World. The authors mainly analyze how the strategies they set to survive on the market (mergers) impact the territorial anchoring which was constitutive of their existence at the beginning. Then Chap. 18 introduces the negociants and *la Place de Bordeaux*, embedded in a complex set of social relationships and governed by various institutions. The author explores this so particular model in the wine sector and shows the diversity and shifting power balance between negociants and winegrowers.

Part IV deals with an important driver of the strategies set by the actors whatever the model and the wine country they are coming from. The challenge of vertical integration is particularly strong in the wine sector because of the interdependence of grape growing and winemaking. Wine companies are facing a process of concentration linked to the search for economies of scale, investment capacities, and bargaining power vis-à-vis retailers. In this context, creating value through downstream integration of production can be difficult for firms, whose financial and human resources are generally limited. This part examines this issue from different points of view according to the actors (wine estates but also wine co-operatives and international companies) and according to the scale (a regional one, concerning Burgundy and Bordeaux wines, but also regional, national, or international). After an introducing chapter (Chap. 19) dedicated to a literature overview on this issue in the wine sector, Chap. 20 provides a cluster analysis to identify the main differences among Burgundy wine estates in terms of winemaking outsourcing vs. vertical integration. The authors show that winemaking integration has a positive effect on wine estates' profitability in Burgundy. Then, Chap. 21 focuses on two levels of vertical integration strategies, first in wine estates and then in wine co-operatives, to explore wine companies' performance in relation to their vertical integration level. The results show that such strategies appear as an efficient way to create value for producers (private cellars and co-operatives members) but that it should not stop at the bulk-wine production stage. The next chapter (Chap. 22) analyzes the evolution and the current structure of the Prosecco Superiore industry at the PDO level, giving qualitative and quantitative evidence of the role of the different models of supply chain. The authors highlight the interaction connecting the different supply chains via the intermediate markets of grape and wine. The intense interrelation among different operators seems to be one of the key factors of enduring success. Finally, Chap. 23 goes up to the international level considering the backward vertical strategies in leading companies, especially in the New World.

The last part finally gives clues to analyze the performance and the efficiency of the wine industries.

Part V addresses the question of the efficiency of the wine industry. Are the strategies developed in the different countries successful or not? To answer that question, this part takes different angles to deal with the results the wine industry got from their different strategies. It first focuses on international trade and the characteristics of the wine industries coming back to their status: Old vs. New World and appellations vs. brands with a simple indication of origin (Chap. 24). The next chapter (Chap. 25) also considers the appellations vs. brand debate, but from a microeconomic point of view. Indeed, the results of wine producers have to be considered at firm level, trying to find out the best way for them to manage reputation, and therefore their sales, either individually through a brand or collectively through an appellation. This idea is to overcome the implicit idea widely retained, about the supremacy of branding in the New World. It starts from the collective reputation model, analyzes its effects as well as its failures, to show that such a categorization might be simplistic. Both coexist more and more frequently on the same label. Then, we chose to present diametrically opposed national case studies of economic success in the wine sector to show that different and opposed strategies can be successful (Chaps. 26 and 27). Indeed, Chile and Switzerland have both enjoyed great success in the wine industry, but by following completely different trajectories. These chapters perfectly illustrate the cautious approach one must take when addressing questions of efficiency, performance, and economic models. The major conclusion to be learnt from this part and probably from the whole book is that there is not one single road to success when talking about industrial organization in the wine sector but that different strategies are possible according to the micro- and macroeconomic characteristics governing the country. Different "models" exist and go against the idea of the homogenization of the wine industry worldwide.

Part I

Structure of the Wine Sectors Worldwide

Coord. by *Alessandro Corsi*

2

The French Wine Industry

Adeline Alonso Ugaglia, Jean-Marie Cardebat, and Linda Jiao

2.1 Introduction

France is a historical wine-producing country, one of the first to have emerged on the wine market, together with Italy and Spain. These three countries define the basis of what is traditionally called the "Old World" in the wine world, including Portugal, Germany and Greece. Rich of a millenary history, wine is inseparable from the culture, heritage, terroirs and economy of France. The wine and spirit sector keeps its position as a large surplus in the French trade balance (11.51 billion Euros, 8.24 only for the wine in 2017) behind aeronautics (17.4 billion Euros) and above perfumes and cosmetics (10.6 billion Euros) (FranceAgriMer 2018a, b). The wine sector is therefore crucial for the French economy, representing the largest surplus in the French agri-food trade balance. It is known as a major asset for France as it generates not only

A. Alonso Ugaglia (✉)
Bordeaux Sciences Agro, University of Bordeaux, Gradignan, France
e-mail: adeline.ugaglia@agro-bordeaux.fr

J.-M. Cardebat
University of Bordeaux, Pessac, France
INSEEC Bordeaux, Bordeaux, France
e-mail: jean-marie.cardebat@u-bordeaux.fr

L. Jiao
University of Bordeaux, Pessac, France
e-mail: linda.jiao@u-bordeaux.fr

© The Author(s) 2019
A. Alonso Ugaglia et al. (eds.), *The Palgrave Handbook of Wine Industry Economics*,
https://doi.org/10.1007/978-3-319-98633-3_2

growth and employment, often in rural areas where jobs are rare (Porter and Takeuchi 2013), but the wine industry also participates in the planning of the territory with an essential landscape function and is, in addition, a well-known supplier of local tax revenues (Cardebat 2017).

France is still one the first wine country in the world for the volumes produced, for the value of exports, for consumption and for the diversity of products. The French wine industry is therefore at a turning point in its history. The evolution of food consumption and lifestyle, the rising of public health and environmental concerns, climate change, but also the success of New Producing Countries and the reform of the Common Market Organization in Europe represent so many challenges for the wine industry in France. To succeed in meeting these challenges for the future, all the actors of the industry have to engage and bring together their efforts for a renewed dynamics based on all its successful assets like terroir, innovation, know-how, PDOs (*Protected Designations of Origin*) and its worldwide reputation.

This chapter seeks to describe the French wine industry and its actors following the process to obtain the final product (grape growing, wine processing and then distribution and commercialization). It begins with a presentation of the wine industry according to its place in the international trade. It then provides details of the winegrowing and winemaking sectors, before presenting the distribution channels. The final sections speculate on how that structure may change in the decades to come and provide a conclusion.

2.2   The French Wine Industry's State and Current Position in the Wine World

About 70% of the French wine production covers 83% of the wine consumption in France and the imported wines the rest. The national market is definitely the main one for French wines for years as only 30% in volumes are exported.

2.2.1   France in the International Wine Trade

After a crisis in 2008, which had seen the collapse of the international market, growth came back in 2010 (+14% in volume and +17% in value) for the French wine industry. In the recent years, on one hand, French wine imports have decreased in 2017 after 3 years of increase (+5% in 2016, +12% in 2015, +23% in 2014) and represents 7.6 billion hectoliters in 2017 (OIV 2018). In value, the imports register a new record with 810 billion Euros (+10%) in 2017. The main part of the wine imported is bulk wine (80%), mainly corresponding to wine without any geographic indication and not mentioning the cepage or the variety. This is the sign of the structural deficit of the French wine industry in low-price wines that the low harvest successions are unable to fill quantitatively. The search for bulk wines at moderate prices leads importers to import wine from Spain for the main part of the volumes imported.

On the other hand, wine trade is largely dominated by Spain, Italy and France, which account for 55% of world market volume in 2017. In value, France and Italy continue to dominate the market with 30% and 19%, respectively, of wine exports in the world (OIV 2018). French wine exports represent 30% of the volumes produced in France and present a steady rise in 2017, staying at a very high level, even being a historical result if considered together with the spirits sector (FranceAgriMer 2018a, b): +5% in volumes (15.4 billion hectoliters) and +9% in value (8.89 billion Euros) (Fig. 2.1). Fifty-four percent of the wines are exported to a European country. The main part (around 50% in volumes) of the wine exported is still bottled wine, mainly to Germany, China, the United Kingdom and the United States. Since 2005, although France has lost its status as the world's largest exporter by volume, it remains largely ahead in value (9.05 billion Euros in 2017—FranceAgriMer 2018a, b). The prices of the wines exported by France are among the highest in the world, reflecting a positioning on well-valued products and even better and better-valued products considering the evolution of the average prices for 15 years (+9%), especially for PDO wines (+20%). These good results were partly pushed by specific plans set by the French government (for the 2008–2013 period, e.g., the plan aimed at increasing the volumes exported on the markets and reinforcing the image and the quality of French wines to increase the value of the products).

It is a little bit different for organic wines which are more exported than noncertified ones (46% of organic wines exported in 2016) (Agence BIO Stats 2017).

The link between wine production and the terroir is worldwide recognized, as AOC (*Appellation d'Origine Contrôlée*, French for PDO) wines account for 39% of French exported volumes and 51% of exported value. PGI (*Protected Geographical Indication*) wines account for 26% in volume and 10% in value. Champagne wines account for only 7% of exported volume, but it generates 29% of total value. The total AOC wines (still wines plus Champagne) account for 46% of export volume and generate 80% of export value.

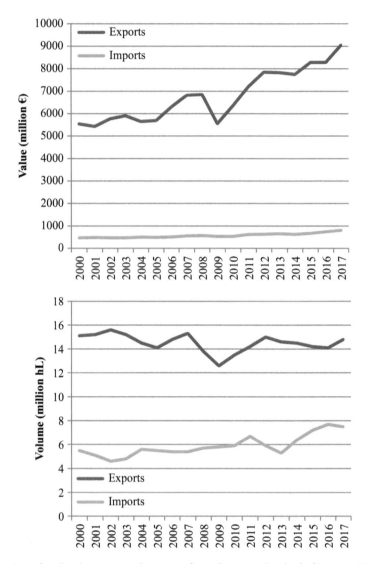

Fig. 2.1 French wine imports and exports (in volume and value). (Source: OIV stats, http://www.oiv.int/fr/bases-de-donnees-et-statistiques)

2.2.2   French Wine Production and Consumption

After years of growth, during the nineteenth century, the area of the French vineyard reached its peak, with 2.465 million ha, in the middle of the 1870s. After this date and because of the *Phylloxera* crisis, the French vineyard has experienced a long period of deceleration. Initially slow, the decline accelerates after World War II, and the surface was divided by two after a century. In the first half of the twentieth century, the production remained relatively stable thanks to an increase in yields. Then, from 1950 to 1990, it increased. Finally, since 1990, it has dropped considerably to fall below the most productive periods of the beginning of the century. Between 2000 and 2011, the vineyard lost 13% of its area. The crisis in the viticultural sector in the 2000s led to major uprooting (together with EU policy). Since the end of the EU program to regulate the wine production potential (2011/2012 campaign), the rate of reduction of the vineyard in France has slowed significantly.[1] The latest available data showed a tendency toward stabilization of the overall area in France around 785,000 ha (OIV 2018), second position right after Spain, representing about 10% of the vines in the world.

France has been historically one of the leaders of wine production around the world. It represents 10% of the vineyards worldwide right after Spain and China and 15% of the wine production (36.7 million hl in 2017—OIV (2018)). However, considering the volumes, wine production in France has fallen sharply in 2017 to the point that—according to OIV—it will be a historically low year but not representative because of extreme climatic events. The production fell by 19% in volume and reached 36.7 million hectoliters.

After the decline following the 2008/2009 economic crisis, world wine consumption has found a positive direction. This upward trend has been observed since 2014. While the United States confirm their position as the world's largest consuming country since 2011 (32.6 million hl), France is the second one (27 million hl in 2017, 11%), followed by Italy, Germany and China (OIV 2018). The decline in consumption in the historically consuming countries—France, Italy and Spain—seems stabilized while consumption in the United States, China and Australia continues to grow. Historically, the French wine market is supported by domestic consumption: France is still the leading wine-consuming country in Europe above Italy, Portugal and Spain, "absorbing" 14% of the wine produced worldwide. France is the first market for French wines (70% of the volumes produced in France, 83% of the wines purchased in France). The imported wines represent 17% of French consumption.

But wine consumption in France has decreased for the last 30 years: whereas in 1975 it was 100 liters per inhabitant per year, it has dropped to 42 liters per inhabitant per year. According to FranceAgriMer (2014), however, there is a decline in nonconsumers of wine for the first time since 1995. The occasional consumption (1–2 once a week or more rarely) takes precedence over regular

---

[1] The annual growth of plantations is limited to 1% in Europe (OIV).

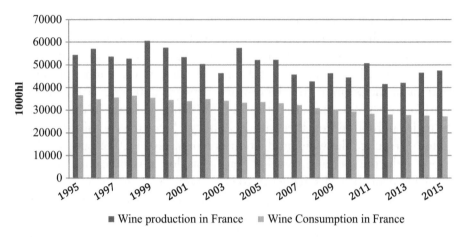

Fig. 2.2 Wine production and consumption in France. (Source: OIV stats, http://www. oiv.int/fr/bases-de-donnees-et-statistiques)

consumption (everyday or almost everyday). As for regular consumers, whose share decreases since 1980, they share stabilized since 2015 (16%). Nevertheless the consumption and the production of wine have been experiencing a long-term decline (since the 1970s) in France (Fig. 2.2).

According to the evolution of its position on wine international markets, France has to face a big challenge. Stuck up over the past ten years between the drop in consumption and the triumphant arrival of the New World wines on the market, French wine producers, as well as other actors in the French wine industry, are actually confronted with an unprecedented commercial context that seems to jeopardize their production practices inherited from the past. While some of them take the opportunity to transform their grape production, make wine and develop marketing practices, many others suffer from the effects of what they perceive as a radical questioning about the way they are making wine. In all cases, they have to perform in order to maintain their competitiveness and to benefit from the favorable global context of increasing demand. In this framework, the complexity of the industrial organization, the high fragmentation of the production and the length of the supply chain constitute real challenges to overcome for the French wine industry.

2.3 The Grape-Growing Sector in France

France is historically one of the leaders of wine production around the world and one of the biggest producers in volume on a surface equivalent to only 3% of the French agricultural area. It represents 85,000 farms dedicated to grape production (20% of the total number of farms), the main part of them (99%) being devoted to wine production.

2.3.1   Ten French Wine Regions

The French wine industry is located in about ten specialized basins. These territories have a strong identity, and each one has its own policy to manage the local industry. For each wine production region, there is an Interprofessional Wine Council mainly in charge of marketing and communication. The marketing and communication department is dedicated to promote the wines in France and abroad. It designs and diffuses the messages to help wine marketing. Especially, it helps in training prescribers (wine merchants, restaurateurs, importers, etc.) and provides the information consumers need. It is also in charge of the registration of transaction contracts, such as the transaction contracts of bulk wine between on-farm winemaking properties and negociants.

They are different according to the type of wine produced and the marketing methods, as well as the size of the farms. Vines are cultivated in different regions, but always under temperate climates, which favor the growth of plants. Together with temperate climates, a large diversity of grape varieties and soils are also favorable to the cultivation of vines on the whole territory. Ten main wine regions have been defined in France, from north to south, or colder to warmer: Alsace-East, Champagne, Burgundy-Beaujolais-Savoie-Jura for continental climate; Loire Valley, Aquitaine, Charentes-Cognac, South-West for the Atlantic climate; Languedoc-Roussillon, Rhone Valley-Provence and Corsica are warmer, covered by Mediterranean climate. Table 2.1 presents the surface, the number and the average size of grape-growing farms for each region and shows that Languedoc-Roussillon, Provence-Alpes-Côte d'Azur and Aquitaine are the main wine regions according to the surface planted with vines and the number of grape-growing farms. The average surface of grape-growing farms in France stands at 9.16 hectares. There are large disparities among wine regions in terms of average size: from the smallest – 2.44 hectares on average for Champagne to the largest – 25.38 hectares for Corsica. Note that three quarter of the vineyards are cultivated by one quarter of the farms with surfaces exceeding 12 hectares on average. The erosion of surfaces mentioned before has affected most basins (HCCA 2017): Languedoc-Roussillon (−19%), Corsica (−14%), Loire Valley Center (−11%), Rhône Valley and Provence (−11%), Bordeaux-Bergerac (−9%), Burgundy-Beaujolais-Savoie-

Table 2.1 Surface, number and average size of grape-growing farms by region (in 2010) (The three top regions, with more than 100,000 ha are in bold)

Wine regions	Grape-growing surface (ha)	Number of grape-growing farms	Average size of grape-growing farms (ha)
Languedoc-Roussillon	**201,500**	**17,423**	**11.56**
Provence-Alpes-Côte d'Azur	**148,500**	**12,924**	**11.49**
Aquitaine	**137,600**	**9533**	**14.4**
Charentes-Cognac	79,900	6047	13.21
Pays de la Loire-Centre	62,100	6289	9.87
Bourgogne-Beaujolais-Savoie-Jura	53,100	8368	6.34
Sud-Ouest	40,400	6037	6.69
Champagne	33,400	13,647	2.44
Alsace-Est	16,200	4462	3.63
Corsica	6600	260,000	25.38
France	779,300	84,990	9.16

Source: Agreste Primeur (2011) and FranceAgriMer (2014)

Jura (−9%) and South-West (−8%) Conversely, certain basins gained surfaces: Champagne (+ 10%), Alsace (+ 4%) and Charentes-Cognac (+ 4%). These are high-valuated wines.

The French vineyard is mainly composed of vines of more than ten years old. The choice for grapes varieties depends on wine production regions. Since the first implantation of the vine in the south of France, and its development in all Gaul by the Romans, the wine growers looked for the plants most adapted to the climate and to the ground to obtain always a better wine. Ranked by planting surface (FranceAgriMer 2014), the top 10 most planted red grape varieties are Merlot, Grenache, Syrah, Cabernet Sauvignon, Carignan, Cabernet Franc, Pinot Noir, Gamay, Cinsaut and Meunier (Table 2.2). For the whites, the top 10 are Ugni Blanc, Chardonnay, Sauvignon Blanc, Semillon, Melon, Chenin, Colombard, Muscat Petit Grain, Viognier and Grenache Blanc. Red varieties represent 72% of the vine area in 2014, and the share of international variety is increasing (42% in 2014).

2.3.2   A Production Segmented by AOCs and PGIs

French wines have an ancient and large reputation based on geographic indications, PDO, still called AOC in France, and PGI. AOC wines are produced in limited areas and subject to strict and precise regulations defined according to "local, loyal and consistent practices". AOC wines are identified with cultural products from a specific region, with its landscapes, history, winemakers and know-how. AOC wines have been very successful in France for a long

Table 2.2 Areas according to the varietals (%)

Variety	Surface in %
Merlot	14
Grenache	11
Syrah	8
Cabernet Sauvignon	6
Carignan	5
Cabernet Franc	4
Pinot	4
Gamay	3
Ugni blanc	10
Chardonnay	6
Sauvignon	4

Source: CNIV/FranceAgriMer (2016)

time. The main part of the production comes from AOC wines, that is, 47% in volume (376 different AOCs in 2017) and from PGI wines, that is, 28% in volume (75 different PGIs in 2017) (GraphAgri 2017), the rest being spirits or wines without any mention of origin. Each AOC or PGI is ruled by an organization called "a defense and management organization" (ODG). It is set up at the initiative of a group of producers and/or processors providing the same production who join forces within a structure to take the step of recognizing a sign of quality, from the elaboration of the specifications to the protection and the valorization of the product. The ODG develops and contributes to the implementation of the product specifications (specificity of the product, production area for AOC, PDO and PGI products whose characteristics are linked to a geographical location), the rules for wine production, wine processing and possibly packaging and labeling. It designates an organization, approved at national level by INAO,[2] to carry out the control of the specifications and gives its opinion on the control or inspection plan drawn up with the inspection body. It participates in the defense and protection of the name of the AOC or PGI, promotes the product and the terroir and develops actions and the economic knowledge of the sector (providing information on volumes, number of operators by category, means of production, product development and outlets).

Ninety percent of the specialized grape farms in France are producing wine under AOC or PGI systems, giving evidence to the importance of mentioning the origin to value the production of this country (Agreste Primeur 2011).

---

[2] INAO is an organization belonging to the French Ministry of Agriculture. It guarantees and protects the denominations of origin, supervises modifications and examines the applications for recognition under official geographical indication.

More than two third of the grape-growing farms are devoted to produce AOC wines, and this part covers around 62% of the vine areas. Alsace-East, Champagne and the Burgundy regions only produce wine under appellation systems (AOC). Great part of the production in Loire Valley (75%), Rhone Valley (67%) and Corsica (54%) is also produced in AOC systems. The production of South-West is more diversified with 41% with AOC (but nearly 100% for the Bordeaux wine region). In Languedoc-Roussillon, the production is mainly produced under PGI systems (59%), with only 26% in AOC. Besides, the regions in the south, Loire Valley, South-West, Languedoc-Roussillon, Rhone Valley and Corsica are characterized by mixed farms—they produce both AOC and other wines. Charentes-Cognac is specialized in grapes for spirits. The majority of wine farms producing AOC wines are bigger than the other ones and the wine farms producing PGI wines are rather small or middle farms compared to AOC ones (Table 2.3).

Producing under appellation system is synonymous of production constraints, the main ones being the limited wine yield per hectare together with a list of authorized varieties (only *Vitis vinifera* for AOCs). Each AOC/IGP area establishes, in contact with INAO, its production conditions. Besides, from an economic point of view, an early assessment of harvest volumes at regional level facilitates the management of the volumes available on the wine market. Some authors also claim for a link between yield limitation and better quality of wines (concentration), but the literature is still too weak on this topic to conclude. In France, vineyards are cultivated by rain-fed systems. Vine irrigation is forbidden but French regulations allow, under certain conditions, exceptional irrigation of vines. The irrigation is strictly forbidden for

Table 2.3 Economic size according to the type of wine

| | Percentage of farms | | | | |
Economic size	AOC wines	PGI wines	AOC and PGI wines	Other wines	Total
Small farms (SGM<25,000€)	27	49	18	47	33
Middle farms (25,000€ < SGM and > 10,000€)	29	35	42	16	29
Big farms (SGM > 100,000€)	44	16	40	37	38
Number of farms	46,600	12,100	3100	6700	68,500

Source: Agreste Primeur (2011)
Note 1: That the economic size of farms is determined thanks to the concept of standard gross margin (SGM) used in Farm Data Accountancy Network (FADN) at European level and expressed of ESU (economic size unit). The value of one ESU is defined as a fixed amount of euros of farm gross margin (FGM)
Note 2: The percentages have to be added up in columns

all wines between 15 August and the harvest. In the case of PGI and wines without any geographical indication, the irrigation is possible after the harvest until 15 August or the ripening (the moment when the color of the grape berries is changing). As for the AOC, by default, the irrigation of vines suitable for the production is forbidden from 1 May up to the harvest and authorized after the harvest until 1 May. However, the irrigation of vines can be authorized, exceptionally, maximum from 15 June at the earliest until 15 August at the latest. This finally explains the low rate of irrigated vineyards according to the importance of the appellation regime in France. These conditions on grape and wine production make a real difference to access natural resources and for production costs/economies of scale.

2.3.3   Characteristics of Grape-Growing Farms

Beyond the size of the farms, the 85,000 French grape farms can be characterized from three important variables: the labor force, the age of the grape growers and the men/women ratio.

Wine farms are characterized by the use of a large wage labor force. Farm specialized in grape-growing use, on average, the equivalent of 1.9 full-time workers seasonal including workers (+0.4 up to other farms). This is why French viticulture is recognized as a sector supplying jobs in the countryside. Nonfamily permanent employees provide 30% of the workload and 18% for seasonal workers. Seasonal work is mainly present in Champagne and Burgundy-Beaujolais-Savoie-Jura because the grape growers harvest by hand more often (Agreste Primeur 2011).

In 2010 (RGA[3] 2010), 6 out of 10 grape growers are 50 years old and over. Among the specialized farm owners of 50 years or older, the majority (60%) does not know who will take over after them or even think the farm will disappear. This could result in a potential loss of nearly 40% of French vineyards. This is a particularly big concern in Gironde, where the share of over 50s among wine growers continues to grow (54%). The demographic succession seems to be less and less easy. Fewer and fewer are generational farms when grape farms used to be family farms (they are dominant in France), and it is more and more difficult to transmit a grape-growing farm.

---

[3] The RGA, or General Agricultural Census, compiles statistics on the number of farms, on the technical and economic orientations, on the agricultural surfaces used, the productions and surfaces concerned, the areas still grassed, and the main grasslands. The RGA (or RA) is organized every 10 to 12 years. The first census took place in 1998, then in 2000 and finally in 2010. They constitute the main data source from the Ministry of Agriculture.

In 2010, 17% of owners are under 40 years of age, compared to 25% in 2000. Almost 61,000 hectares of vines are expected to be transmitted before 2020 (concerning 3000 grape growers over 50 years). For some of them the question of succession begins to arise. The first trends in the census confirm the results of previous surveys, namely, a deterioration in the response rates for the future of the farm but also the correlation between the size of the company and its eventual transmission. In fact, for one in three, the question no longer arises. He already knows his future successor (when it was 50% of them in 2000). Four times out of five, the buyer is part of the family. The farm is smaller (7 ha), when the transmission takes place outside the family because the future owner already owns another exploitation. Thirty thousand hectares are under uncertainty in this region. In 2010, for a future retiree on ten, the question seems resolved: the exploitation will disappear. Either it will be spread in different other companies or the agricultural use of this lands will be lost. For the others, the question has no answer, or they have not yet asked it, or they do not know.

The grape-growing profession is more feminized than in other agricultural professions, as 27% of farm managers are women (23%). This is even more true when we look at the older grape growers (37%) as they often take over from their husbands when they retire.

2.3.4   The Dynamics of Organic Farming

We can observe an interesting dynamics around environmental-friendly and sustainable ones in the French industry in the recent years (organic, biodynamic and natural wines). Official data are available only for organic wines, benefiting from the creation of a dedicated observatory. The organic vineyard has tripled in 10 years. In 2017, the organic viticultural sector in France comprises 5835 grape-growing farms and 78,665 hectares of organically grown vines, representing nearly 10% of the national vineyard in hectares (Table 2.4). The regions which are the most dynamic ones in terms of both volume and number of organic farms are (1) Languedoc-Roussillon as the leading area in France, (2) Provence-Alpes-Côte d'Azur and (3) Aquitaine with Bordeaux wines. Conversions to organic farming experienced a very strong increase between 2008 and 2012 (the conversion lasts three years) and slow down a little bit since then (Fig. 2.3 and Table 2.4).

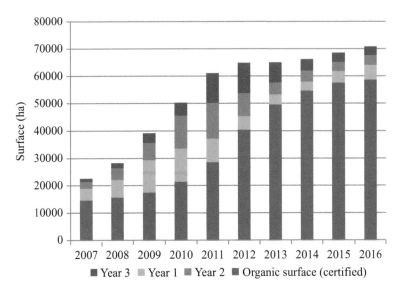

Fig. 2.3 Evolution of organic surfaces in France (ha). (Source: Agence BIO 2017)

2.4 The Winemaking Sector in France

Even if there are many ways for producing wine, the French models for wine production mainly rely on grape growers who are also winemakers, whether in a private cellar or in holding the shares of a co-operative processing and selling the wine. Then, in some French regions, negociants and brokers are very important intermediate actors in the industry.

2.4.1 Wine Production: Yield, Colors and AOC Wines

In France, the average yield is around 50 hl/ha, close to the European one (between 55 and 60 hL/ha depending on the vintage), but this number varies from year to year. For quality and AOC wines, the maximum authorized yield varies between 40 and 60 hl/ha. During the period 2003–2013, the annual yield of AOC was comprised between 42 hl/ha (2013) and 55.8 hl/ha (2005). For less qualified wines, the yield varies from 60 to 80 hl/ha. During 2003–2013, the annual yield of wines other than AOC (Cognac excluded) varied from 63 hl/ha in 2003, 2007 and 2011 to 79.5 in 2004 (FranceAgriMer 2014).[4] There are strong yield differentials between regions, and on average

---

[4] See tables in page 38 and 39 of FranceAgriMer 2014.

Table 2.4 Repartition of organic farms and surfaces by region

Regions	Number of farms		Organic surfaces (ha, certified)		Organic surfaces (ha, conversion) 2017					Total (ha, certified + conversion)		Percentage of organic surface in the whole vineyard
	2017	Evol. /16	2017	Evol. /16	Year 1	Year 2	Year 3	Total	Evol. /16	2017	Evol. /16	
Languedoc-Roussillon	**1466**	**13.6%**	**19,512**	**4%**	**3698**	**1757**	**1136**	**6591**	**67%**	**26,102**	**15%**	**11.2%**
Provence-Alpes-Côte d'Azur	**994**	**8.9%**	**14,088**	**3%**	**1635**	**996**	**734**	**3366**	**30%**	**17,454**	**8%**	**19.1%**
Aquitaine	**826**	**12.2%**	**9097**	**4%**	**1299**	**735**	**533**	**2568**	**60%**	**11,665**	**13%**	**8.2%**
Rhône-Alpes	615	6.8%	4641	6%	388	319	179	885	7%	5527	6%	11.4%
Midi-Pyrénées	333	8.1%	2071	3%	266	198	103	568	43%	2638	10%	7.0%
Bourgogne	322	6.6%	2054	2%	173	469	200	842	40%	2896	10%	8.8%
Alsace	309	6.9%	2203	1%	160	89	99	348	56%	2551	6%	15.9%
Pays de la Loire	264	15.8%	2374	8%	385	442	146	973	39%	3346	15%	10.5%
Centre Val-de-Loire	213	7.6%	2421	1%	224	105	81	410	24%	2831	4%	13.3%
Champagne-Ardenne	158	19.7%	411	15%	128	85	42	256	45%	667	25%	2.1%
Poitou-Charentes	116	20.8%	946	5%	62	153	53	268	18%	1213	8%	1.4%
Franche-Comté	74	8.8%	361	11%	16	56	18	90	-1%	452	9%	18.5%
Corsica	59	5.4%	675	13%	151	153	33	337	5%	1012	10%	15.1%
Auvergne	27	35%	75	4%	22	20	8	50	85%	125	26%	11.5%
Lorraine	25	38.9%	55	6%	43	7	1	52	285%	107	63%	31.5%
Picardie	16	6.7%	36	50%	5	1	2	9	-51%	45	5%	1.8%
Limousin	10	25%	29	160%	4	–	1	5	17%	34	117%	16.6%
Ile-de-France	4	-20%	1	42%	–	–	–	–	-100%	1	37%	2.6%
Haute-Normandie	2	100%	0	–	0	0	0	0	–	0	–	–

(continued)

Table 2.4 (continued)

Regions	Number of farms		Organic surfaces (ha, certified)		Organic surfaces (ha, conversion) 2017					Total (ha, certified + conversion)		Percentage of organic surface in the whole vineyard
	2017	Evol. /16	2017	Evol. /16	Year 1	Year 2	Year 3	Total	Evol. /16	2017	Evol. /16	
Bretagne	1	−50%	C	–	C	C	C	C	–	C	–	–
Basse-Normandie	1	0%	C	–	C	C	C	C	–	C	–	–
Nord-Pas-de-Calais	–	–	–	–	–	–	–	–	–	–	–	–
Outre-Mer	–	–	–	–	–	–	–	–	–	–	–	–
Total France	5835	10.9%	61,048	4%	8660	5588	3369	17,617	46%	78,665	11%	10%

Source: Agence BIO (2017)

they are low compared to competing producing countries in the New World. It impacts production costs compared to countries benefiting from favorable production factors such as natural and human resources less costly. In addition, for many years, there has been a very significant increase in the mortality of vines, which weakens the yields and the productivity of the French vineyards, despite the notable efforts of restructuring and renovating the vineyards, not to mention the National Research Programs on the decline of vineyards in general and on trunk diseases in particular.

In 2010, farms produced 45% of red wines, a production that dominates in France, slightly higher than white wines (43%), far ahead from rosé wines (12%). A large proportion of white wines are detained to spirits (eaux de vie). Figure 2.4 demonstrates the evolution of wine harvest in France by wine region and color.

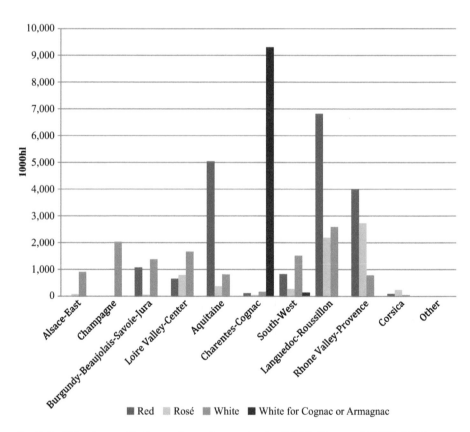

Fig. 2.4 Wine harvest in France by region and color (2015). (Source: DGDDI-CVI Harvest 2005–2015)

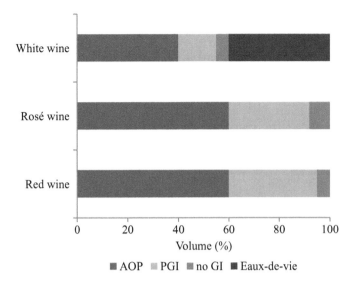

Fig. 2.5 AOC and PGI and wine color (2010). (Source: Agreste Primeur 2011)

AOC and PGI wines value French production since the majority of red and rosé wines are produced under AOC (60%) (Fig. 2.5).

Before 2012, it was not possible to produce "organic wine" but only "wine produced from organic grapes". A European regulation (2012) designed new production specifications defining what an organic wine is and how to produce it (n°203/2012). According to a study by AND-I, commissioned by Agence BIO, nearly 1.82 million hectoliters of organic wines have been sold in 2016. PDOs accounted for 68% of volumes of French organic wines marketed in 2015 and PGIs 25%.

2.4.2 Winemakers

In France, grape-growing farms can deal with their grape harvest in three different wine processing modes:

(i) Using their harvest to make their own wine (on-farm winemakers) in a fully integrated way (from grape production to wine commercialization). In this case, the estates are managing both the grape growing and the wine processing.
(ii) Being co-operative members and delivering the harvest to winemaking co-operatives that process and sell wine on their behalf. There is no contract to sell the grapes between co-operative members and wine co-

operatives (in this sense, it is different from Champagne where the "Maisons de Champagne" buy fresh grapes from grape growers and then process the wine). Grapes and wines remain the property of wine growers until they are sold.

(iii) Selling their fresh grape harvest (rare).

The majority of the grape harvest is processed by on-farm winemakers, representing 55% of the total French harvest, also called private cellars. About 37% of the total grape production is processed by winemaking co-operatives (48% of French wines in volume excluding Cognac in 2016 (FranceAgriMer 2018a, b)). The remaining 8% of the total grape harvest is sold as fresh grapes, grape juices or musts (Fig. 2.6).

In 2010, 53% of the grape-growing farms sent their grapes (partially or totally) to a wine co-operative (39% deliver their whole production to a wine co-operative). Wine co-operatives are typical French structures in the wine industry with a strong link to the terroir and origin of grapes. Their weight remains important in France (606 winemaking co-operatives in 2014). Over 310,000 hectares of vines are cultivated by co-operatives members (and sometimes by co-operatives themselves when they own a small vineyard). The average surface of vines of co-operative members is around six hectares (against nine hectares for the vertically integrated grape and winegrowing farms). Wine co-operatives directly owned by the grape growers on the principle "one man, one voice". They bring together more than 100,000 people, 85,000 associated co-operative partners and 17,353 employees. They achieve a turnover of 5.6 billion Euros and 18,317,022 hL (2014), which accounts for 48% of the total wine production in France (except Charentes-Cognac). More than 50% of the wine co-operatives producing still wines are located in the South-

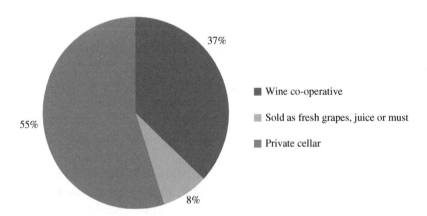

Fig. 2.6 Winemaking processing (volume, 2010). (Source: Agreste Primeur 2011)

Table 2.5 Four main French wine co-operatives

	Turnover 2013 (million Euros)	Wine region
Val d'Orbieu	274	Languedoc-Roussillon
CV Nicolas Feuillatte	210	Champagne
Alliance Champagne	105	Champagne
UDVCR Cellier des Dauphins	100	Rhône

Source: CNIV/FranceAgriMer (2016)

East of France (Languedoc, Valley of the Rhone and Provence). The biggest ones are located in the same region, but also in Champagne (Table 2.5).

Twenty percent of the wine produced in co-operatives is organic wine (FranceAgriMer 2014), representing 27% of the organic wine processed in France. According to the 2015 notifications, 203 wine co-operatives produced wine from organic grapes, up from 70 in 2009 (Agence BIO). They are mainly mixed co-operatives producing both a range of organic and non-organic wines. Nevertheless, to date, wine co-operatives are small businesses or SMEs. Only one has a turnover exceeding 300 million Euros. While size is not in itself a guarantee of success, we must distinguish between what is relevant for the optimization of winemaking tools and what is the case with regard to packaging and marketing. As with other sectors of activity, the rapprochements between co-operatives continue. The number of wine co-operatives has decreased by 40% in the last 20 years.

2.5 Distribution Channels

2.5.1 The Main Distribution Channels Used by Winemakers

Once the wine has been processed, a wine farm (private cellar) or a wine co-operative can sell it through different distribution channels: negociants (also called wine merchants), producer groups, restaurants, wine stores, supermarkets and hypermarkets or directly to consumers (on-farm sale, online sale). An important share of the volumes goes through negociants (64% of the volumes), often via brokers (Fig. 2.7).

For organic wines, sales channels are highly diversified. Of the volumes, 73% are marketed by wine growers and 27% are by wine co-operatives. More than half of the volumes marketed by co-operatives go to negociants. In 2015, 41% of sales of organic wines (in value) concerned direct sales and 23% in wine stores dedicated to organic wines. Direct selling is therefore the main

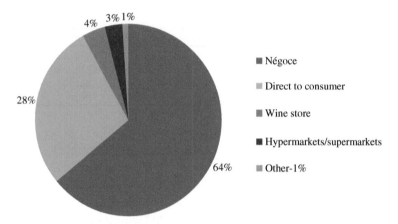

4%   3% 1%

28%

64%

- Négoce
- Direct to consumer
- Wine store
- Hypermarkets/supermarkets
- Other-1%

Fig. 2.7 On-farm winemakers' distribution channels by percentage of volume. (Source: RGA 2010)

channel for organic wines. Forty-six percent of organic wines (volume) have been sold abroad in 2015 (Europe, especially Germany). Fifteen percent of the volumes of organic wines sold in France in 2015 were sold in restaurants or catering services. In 2014, nearly one out of two restaurants had organic wine on their menu (compared with nearly two fifth in 2011). The restaurant owners who have organic wines offered, on average, five different references (CNIV—Panel CHD FACTS). According to Agence BIO, the value of purchases of organic wines by households in France was estimated around 792 million Euros in 2016 (+ 17% between 2015 and 2016). Purchases of organic wines more than tripled between 2005 and 2016. In 2015, organic wine accounted for 12% in value of purchases of organic products by households.

The wine can be sold in bulk, in bottle, or in bag-in-box. Figure 2.8 represents the different distribution channels in France and their share in volumes up to the type of packaging used at the moment of the sale. Bottled wine stands for the majority of direct sales. The main part of the wine sold to the negociants is bulk wine, which they bottle right after and before selling it. On the contrary, when they are selling the wine directly to the consumers, the winemakers bottle and label the main part of their wines.

While the organic wine distribution system appears to be diversified and mobilizes all the classic channels, direct sales and export appear to be of particular relevance. Organic wine growers have to face extra production costs, explained mainly by higher labor costs and partly justified by the higher quality of wines, and typically it results in higher prices for the final consumer. In this case, direct sales could be seen the most remunerative as a producer's

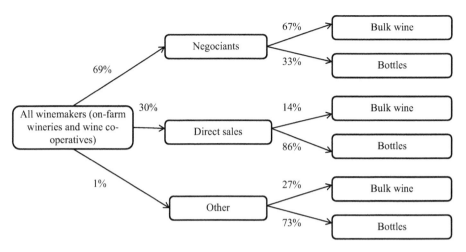

Fig. 2.8 Distribution channels (percentage of volume). (Source: Author's calculation based on RGA 2010)

margins are not squeezed in intermediate transactions. A closer relation between a producer and a consumer also adds value to the product: consumers perceive bio wine primarily as a wine, a cultural product which witnesses the diversity of terroirs (Bouzdine-Chameeva et al. 2013). It explains why the first distribution channel in value is direct sales (41% in value, 28% in volume), followed by organic stores (23% of the market value, 18% in volumes), then the HORECA and finally the large retailers (super and hypermarkets) even if they keep 27% of the volumes (Vignerons bio Nouvelle-Aquitaine 2017).

2.5.2   Negociants as Major Actors in the French Distribution Channels

Negociants play important roles along the wine industry chain from production through wine-maturation and commercialization. FranceAgriMer estimates the number of 1500 wine negociants in France even if it is difficult to identify them according to the diversity of their status and activities. They can buy fresh grapes or grape musts and process their wine (as in the Champagne region) and/or buy the wine in bulk or in bottles (selected via brokers). Then they bottle it if needed and process the distribution step to the final consumer. Growing grapes is the only part they do not manage or rarely. The negociants have a particularly strong position in the Bordeaux wine region. We can consider three types of negociants in the French wine sector:

(i) Negociants who own as well wine estates, or the contrary: wine growers developing a négoce activity. In this case, the negociants can be the producer and distributor of their own wine. They are often big groups and their activities are highly vertically integrated. Such a negociant can also carry out the activities of the two next ones.
(ii) Negociants who buy fresh grapes or grape musts from wine growers for making their own wine. They are in charge of the winemaking, aging, assembling and bottling, and then distributing the wine with their own labels. Such a negociant can also carry out the activities of the next one.
(iii) Negociants only involved in the distribution process. They select wines produced by on-farm winemakers, in bulk or in bottle. If bulk, the negociants can undertake the bottling and labeling in accordance with the regulation at final destination.

In France, the Castel Group, Bordeaux-based international recognized name, dominates the French wine market (Table 2.6). It generates around 12% of the market in volume. Castel Group owns almost 1400 hectares of vineyards in France and another 1600 hectares in Africa. In France, Castel owns 21 winemaking estates in the Bordeaux region and Provence. Their brands occupy the top 3 in the ranking: Roche Mazet, Vieux Papes and Ormes de Cambras, which take a market share of over 2% in volume, followed by La Villageoise, Cambras, Baron de Lestac, Blaissac, Malesan and Boulaouane that stand at leading places in the French market. Les Grands Chais de France takes the second place in the French market with about 3% of the market in volume. Les Grands Chais de France, based at Petersbach in Alsace, is one of the top French wholesale wine and spirits merchants. Its brand JP Chenet, distributed in over 160 countries, claims the title of best-selling French wine in the world. JP Chenet occupies the top market share (0.4% in volume) in the French market as well. Other leading brands of still light grape wine are Cellier des Dauphins (0.5% of the market in volume) that belongs to Union des Vignerons des Côtes du Rhône, Billette and Listel from Domaines Listel,

Table 2.6 Turnover of the three main downstream companies—still wine

Company	Turnover 2013 (million Euros)	Estimated number of bottles (million bottles)
Castel frères group	743	640
Johanes Boubées (Carrefour group)	743	400
Grands Chais de France	693	500

Source: CNIV/FranceAgriMer (2016)

Cramoisay of Maison Noémie Vernaux and Malesan from William Pitters International (MarketLine, Euromonitor and official company websites).

Winemaking firms and negociants are often put in touch thanks to brokers. Wine broker is a profession poorly known to the consumers but well known by experts. They have a great expertise upstream of the distribution channel (quantity produced, quality of the wine, prices on the market) allowing them to connect wine producers with negociants or wine importers. They also develop transaction activities from négoce to négoce. In this sense, they really play an intermediate role in the wine industry. They make each party aware of the conditions of the other. They advise the parties and attempt to reconcile their possibly divergent interests. Then they charge commissions for each transaction. In Bordeaux, they are part of 75% of the registered transactions (100% for the *Grands Crus*). In France, they are in charge of 80% of the AOC production, less for generic wines. Hypermarkets and supermarkets often have their own teams, operating in purchasing centers to deal with wine purchases.

2.5.3   Buying Wine

French consumers buy most of their wine in super and hypermarkets (70% of wine purchases, 9.5 million hl) (FranceAgriMer 2018a, b). Then come hard discount chains (14%), local wine stores (7%), wine stores (3%), direct sales (3%) and sales online (1%) in 2016 (volume) (FranceAgrimer 2017). France counts around 1700 wine stores, mostly owned by 3 chains: Nicolas (450), Inter Caves (224) and Cavavin (120). Gourmet stores and delicatessen remain residual. In terms of price (CNIV/FranceAgriMer 2016) in 2014:

- 29% of purchases of still wines were made at a price lower than 1.49€ per bottle and 7% at a higher price than 5€ per bottle.
- 52% of wines without any geographic indication from France, 55% of non-EU foreign wines (other origins) and 79% of wines without any geographic indication from Europe were purchased at a lower price than 1.49€ per bottle.
- 51% of purchases of AOC wines were made at less than 3€ per bottle and 16% of them at more than 5€ per bottle.

Even if red wines are still the top wines for consumption, the French consumers are more and more interested in rosé wines at the expense of red wines.

2.5.3.1   Mass Distribution (Super and Hypermarkets)

Hypermarkets and supermarkets play leading role in wine distribution. The wine market in these channels represents 4.6 billion Euros per year, or 3% of total store sales (2017). This weight goes up to 4.5% during the period of wine fairs (at least once or twice a year). For several years, wines have been valued by improving the quality of the offer in super and hypermarkets (also true for the other distribution channels). In three years, the number of still wine references has increased in hypermarkets (+39.5) despite a decline in the average linear. In these channels, still wine sales were −1.5% in volume and −0.1% in value compared to 2015. The average selling price (4.49€ per liter) rose by 2.9% compared to 2015. Supermarkets recorded 21.2 additional references of still wines over the last three years. Compared to 2015, sales of still wines in super and hypermarkets decreased by 1.3% in volume and increased by 1% in value, with an average price up by 3.6%, that is, 4.26€ per liter (FranceAgriMer 2017). Growth is better in local wine stores and drive-thru services, although market shares are much more confidential.

The volumes are divided between red wines (54% in value), rosé wines (26%) and white wines (20%) in 2016 according to the same source. Compared to the previous years, the decline in sales continues in volume and in value for red wines (−18% in volume over a ten years period). The market share of foreign wines in the total stills marketed in GD is up, and now stands at 7% in volume and 4% in value. In terms of formats, sales of still wine in bag-in-box continue their growth in supermarkets. These sales accounted for 35% of total sales of still wines in supermarkets in 2014 (CNIV/FranceAgriMer 2016).

2.5.3.2   Focus on Cybercommerce

Cybercommerce doesn't represent a lot in volume, but a huge progression in the recent years. In less than 20 years, wine sales via cybercommerce have become really significant. With 647 players (2/3 dedicated only to wine and spirits), the e-commerce of wines generated an estimated turnover of 430 million Euros in France in 2014. French people are more and more willing to purchase wine online, according to the SOWINE/SSI barometer. We can distinguish different type of cyber players (Table 2.7). Positioned on the diversity of the offer more than local wine merchants, the pioneers face several challenges: recruiting and engaging customers, including technological developments and financing wine storage (expensive). The private sales model is

Table 2.7 Cybercommerce in the French wine industry

Type of Cybercommerce	Examples	Number	Turnover
Pioneers or "pure players"	Millesima, Wine and Co, Vinatis	216 websites	180 million Euros
Private sales	Vente-privee.com, 1jour1vin.com	21 players	75–90 million Euros
Drive thru		13 chains	64 million Euros
Others	Distribution (web)	161 players	10–20 million Euros
	Cross-canal wine stores	203 websites	30 million Euros
	Box, subscriptions	20 players	5–8 million Euros

Source: FranceAgriMer (2017)

driven by the advantages offered to consumers (discounts, famous wine brands, use of luxury codes, etc.). It requires high-tech logistics and specific management of the wine list. Drive-thru services from super and hypermarkets still have a big potential for further development. The type of wine purchased via cybercommerce depends on the player concerned, but it mainly concerns bottled red wine (75cL) priced between 10 and 25 Euros.

2.6   Conclusion and Synthesis: What About the Performance?

The organization of the French wine industry is characterized by the complexity and diversification among wine production regions concerning the actors and their relationship along the distribution chain.

The majority of the grape harvest is vinified by on-farm winemakers, about one third of the production is vinified in wine co-operatives and the selling of fresh harvest takes only a small part of the market. This share varies depending on the region (Exhibit 2.1). The intermediate bodies play important roles in French wine industry. Negociants claim their leadership along the chain, and they can interfere at different steps (rarely for grape production, sometimes to process wine, very often to sell the wine). In addition, the transactions between grape or wine producers and negociants are often linked by brokers. Around 60–70% of the production is commercialized by negociants in the main wine regions. Supermarkets and hypermarkets are dominant channels for the distribution, and the on-trade (restaurants, bars, hotels, etc.) takes about one third of the market. Red wines are the most sold in terms of both volume and value. Whatever the region, wine co-operatives and negociants are the two

arms of the French wine industry. They join in industry groups, either regionally for AOC and PGI wines or nationally for wines with no geographical
indication. They fund efforts to promote their wines and monitor markets,
finance research and development initiatives (FranceAgriMer 2018a, b). We
present in Exhibit 2.1 the main actors and the way they are organized for four
representative wine regions in France: Bordeaux, Burgundy, Champagne and
Languedoc-Roussillon (Exhibit 2.1).

**Exhibit 2.1 Focus on Four Wine Regions and Their Distribution
Channels (Bordeaux, Burgundy, Champagne and
Languedoc-Roussillon)**

Bordeaux

Nearly 80% of the harvest is processed by on-farm winemakers. The transaction of fresh grapes or grape musts is negligible. In addition, this region is characterized by the dynamic and the power of negociants. Over 70% of the Bordeaux wine production is commercialized by negociants (51% for bulk wine and 49% for bottled wine), representing 83% of the wine estates. Brokers are important intermediaries in the Bordeaux wine region. 80% of the transactions between owner-seller and trader-buyer involve brokers.

Burgundy

55% of the harvest is vinified by on-farm winemakers. It is less than in the past due to the development of selling fresh harvest grapes or musts (16% of the crop in 2010 against 10% in 2000), while the proportion of harvest processed by wine co-operative remains stable (29%). The sale of fresh harvest grapes, which can meet the cash requirements, is now practiced by 47% of farms, which is rather rare in the other regions. This is also explained by the increase of sales contracts for the production of sparkling wines. Negociants and wholesalers remain the main destinations (59%). Still, half of the Burgundian wine growers are managing sales through direct selling (40%).

Champagne

On-farm winemakers process less than one third of the harvest (30%), similar for wine co-operatives (28%), while selling fresh grapes or grape musts takes the most important part (42%). Different from other regions, most of the wine produced is sold by direct channels or exported abroad, which presents over 80% of the total transaction volume. Negociants or wholesalers distribute the rest.

Languedoc-Roussillon

In this region, 47% of the farms are small estates, which bring the wine co-operatives to play an important role in winemaking. Nine out of ten operators send all or part of their harvest in wine co-operatives—over 70% of the total harvest. But big properties often process all or almost their whole harvest themselves. Two third of the wine production is commercialized via negociants. The direct sales represent the remaining one third of the total sales.

Source: Authors from the information published on the ODG websites and
Agreste (2011a, b, 2012, 2013)

The production and consumption of wine are inseparable from its circulation and its international trade. We therefore end this chapter providing a synthesis of France's different strengths and weaknesses in relation to its performance on the wine market. Some analyses of the performance of the French wine industry have been published and nearly come to the same conclusions (Porter and Takeuchi 2013; HCCA 2017; CNIV/FranceAgriMer 2016) (Exhibit 2.2).

Strengths of the French Wine Industry

- The wine sector is crucial for the French economy as it represents France's leading sector of the agri-food balance, knowing that public subsidies represent only a small part of the turnover of the sector. Besides, it is worth noted that the Champagne contributes a tiny part in terms of volume but a significant share in this value. It is as well a job-creating sector in rural areas, while unemployment in France is still a major concern.
- At the international level, France is a highly reputed historical wine country. It is still the first wine exporter in the world (in value) and about 30% of the production goes abroad. The European Union is the first destination, and the US and Asian market are the main ones out of Europe. Among the exports, AOP wines account for nearly half of the volume and generate 80% of the value.
- The country is also one of the top producers for wine production (in volume), right after Spain. It offers a high diversity of products. The agroclimatic diversity ensures a high diversity in the combination of climates, grape varieties and soils.
- France, as an Old Wine country, benefits from the know-how of the grape and wine growers, who know the terroir very well. Its image of this industry is strongly linked to "tradition" and to the high quality of the wine produced. The terroir reference must not only be seen as an old traditional notion and policy, invented to protect the production in the Old World, but as a model which determines the life and the future of many producers and people in this industry. It is a collective and long-term construction, authentic by the respect it shows for tradition and local usages.
- With over 300 of AOCs in France, the term "appellation" dominates in grape growing as well as in winemaking. The vineyards devoted to produce AOC wines cover about two third of the areas under vines, and about half of the total wine production is produced in an AOC context. The corollary is that wine yield in the French appellation regime is restricted and submitted

to regulations. For regions such as Alsace-Est, Champagne, Burgundy and Aquitaine, nearly 100% of their production are AOP wines. In terms of economic size, the majority of AOP winegrowing farms or winemaking plants are relatively big compared to others. This segmentation of the market by AOCs and PGIs is an important asset especially since the appellations are well valued, especially for exports.

- It is possible to observe the progressive constitution of powerful private groups or wine co-operatives able to compete at the international level. Some co-operatives, grouped together in co-operative unions are as strong as some negociants. If the appellation regimes dominate the French wine industry, it benefits as well from strong brands integrated in international powerful groups, especially for Cognac (spirits) and Champagne (sparkling). The reputation of the French wine industry also relies on the success of top-end estates and the *Grands Crus* all over the world.

Weaknesses of the French Wine Industry

- However, the domestic wine production and consumption have been experiencing a long-term decline. Facing the challenges from New World wines, French producers need to maintain their competitiveness.
- Some estates are facing economic difficulties due to high production costs for some wines and commercial issues (CNIV/FranceAgriMer 2016).
- Few big French importers and wholesalers focused on emerging markets for wine consumption.
- Although leading brands account for an important market share and have advantages in marketing and communication, the perception of appellation prevails in the French market.
- No French brands in the top 10 of international brands but numerous regions, appellations, farms, brands and intermediaries, unclear for the consumers.
- An involvement for innovation and in research programs hardly recognized by the markets.

Starting from this observation, the stakes for the French wine industry are numerous. One of the main ones is to better adapt the offer to the demand, in particular for the low-end wines. The growth of growing segments is a way to offset the decline in demand. The French sector must also face another major challenge: maintaining its export position and position itself on the best markets. This is an important outlet for French wines, particularly in terms of value, especially when the domestic consumption is declining. The positioning of French wines in the domestic market has also to be the focus of attention, because it remains the major outlet (65% of volumes produced). In France, 75% of wines purchased in 2014 were less than 3€ per bottle. The French sector will therefore have to opt for profitable strategic routes for all its stakeholders. Whenever possible, it is more on valorizing wines with high yields, thanks to an important marketing support. It can also be to value wines produced with limited yields. Or it may be the choice to produce wines at low cost, so high yields, but this strategy is complex in France in the current context.

Exhibit 2.2 Porter and Takeuchi's Analysis About the Performance of the French Wine Industry (2013)

"France's competitiveness has also suffered as a result of changes in the global wine market. Historic price pressure as a result of overcapacity is going away as demand is growing stronger than production capacity. At the same time wine is moving from a regional towards a global product as international trade increases, leading to new competitive pressures for wine growers. France has taken this trend seriously as wine is a key national export for the economy and a key employer for the work force. Overall, performance of the French wine cluster over the past decade is mixed. France wine has a strong position in terms of export values and volumes driven by a higher percentage of exports to non-EU countries. France also has maintained a strong price premium on a per liter basis versus other countries. Despite these positive aspects, the cluster cannot ignore the fact that export growth has not kept pace with other wine-producing countries both in terms of volume and value. France faces particularly strong competition from "New World" producers outside of Europe. The question then begs, how can the French wine cluster remain competitive? The competing clusters in "new world" geographies like Australia, Chile and the United States have gained global export share by adopting the same strategies that made France so successful historically. IFCs that contributed to France's strong performance are now protecting uncompetitive producers and stifling innovation. Producers have been less able or willing to adapt to a changing marketplace, whether due to lack of scale and expertise or an unwillingness to alter owner and worker lifestyles. Going forward, ensuring that national industry organizations and other IFCs drive improvements in productivity will be critical in helping French firms remain globally competitive".

Source: Porter and Takeuchi (2013)

References

Agreste. 2011a. *Premières tendances*, Agreste Données Viticulture Languedoc-Roussillon, Recensement agricole 2010, novembre 2011, 4p.

———. 2011b. *La viticulture en Bourgogne : progression des surfaces et de l'emploi salarié*, *Agreste Bourgogne*, n°125, décembre 2011, 6p.

————. 2012. *La Champagne viticole a maintenu son activité*, Agreste Champagne-Ardenne, Recensement agricole 2010, n°6, septembre 2012, 4p.

————. 2013. *Caves particulières*, Agreste Données Languedoc-Roussillon, Recensement agricole 2010, septembre 2013, 6p.

Agreste Primeur. 2011. *Strong geographical identities*, Recensement Agricole 2010, Wine industry, no. 271, November 2011, 4p.

Bouzdine-Chameeva, T., Briois C. Rames, and P. Barbe. 2013. Les circuits de distribution des vins bio en France. *Economia Agroalimentaire* 15 (3): 103–123.

Cardebat, J.M. 2017. *Économie du vin*. Paris: La Découverte.

CNIV/FranceAgriMer. 2016. Analyse des filières vitivinicoles des principaux pays producteurs dans le monde, France, Décembre 2016, 12p.

FranceAgriMer. 2014. *Les chiffres de la filière viti-vinicole 2003/2013*, FranceAgriMer, novembre 2014, 207p.

————. 2017. *Les synthèses de FranceAgriMer – Vins*, Les achats et les ventes de vin tranquilles – Bilan 2016, 77p.

————. 2018a. *Wine industry*, FranceAgriMer Facts sheets, February 2018, 2p.

————. 2018b. *Les synthèses de FranceAgriMer – Vins*, Vins et spiritueux – Commerce extérieur – Bilan 2017, 28p.

GraphAgri. 2017. Signes de qualité en Europe. *Agreste Alimentation*: 106–109.

HCCA. 2017. La filière viti-vinicole française – consolider les acquis et préaprer l'avenir, Section économique et financière, Décembre 2017, 30p.

OIV. 2018. Conjoncture vitivinicole mondiale 2017.

Porter M., and H. Takeuchi. 2013. *The French Wine Cluster*, Microeconomics of Competitiveness, Harvard Business School, Winter 2013, 33p.

RGA. 2010. *Recensement général agricole, Agreste*. France: Ministère de l'Agriculture.

Vignerons Bio Nouvelle-Aquitaine. 2017. *Le marché des vins bio*. 4p.

3

The Italian Wine Industry

Alessandro Corsi, Simonetta Mazzarino,
and Eugenio Pomarici

3.1 Introduction

Wine production is deeply rooted in the Italian tradition, since viticulture was practiced even before Roman times, and thereafter almost everywhere in the country. Nowadays, Italy is among the main world wine producers, and the Italian wine industry leads the national agribusiness; indeed, although the wine industry is third in the ranking of turnover in the agro-food sector, wine is the true food icon of Made in Italy and the largest contributor to Italian agro-food exports. In particular, viticulture is an important part of Italian agriculture. Vineyards for wine production covered 622,000 ha in 2016, that is, about 5% of the total utilized agricultural area (UAA), but viticulture accounted for 10.2% of the value of agricultural production. With an

---

A. Corsi (✉)
University of Turin, Turin, Italy
e-mail: alessandro.corsi@unito.it

S. Mazzarino
Department of Economics and Statistics "Cognetti de Martiis",
University of Turin, Turin, Italy
e-mail: simonetta.mazzarino@unito.it

E. Pomarici
Department of Land, Environment, Agriculture and Forestry,
University of Padua, Padua, Italy
e-mail: eugenio.pomarici@unipd.it

© The Author(s) 2019
A. Alonso Ugaglia et al. (eds.), *The Palgrave Handbook of Wine Industry Economics*,
https://doi.org/10.1007/978-3-319-98633-3_3

estimated 50.9 million hl in 2016 (Anderson et al. 2017), Italy was the first producer in the world in quantitative terms (about 19% of the world production), although France (which alternates with Italy in the first ranking) outperforms Italy in value terms (Anderson et al. 2017). The Italian wine industry, because of its size and historical evolution, comprises a large number of operators; most of them are professional producers linked to distribution channels, but many only produce for self-consumption or as a hobby. According to the last Agricultural Census, there were 369,000 farms growing wine grapes, but considering only the professional operators, grape production is carried out in about 197,000 farms. Wine-making is carried out in about 55,000 grape-processing plants and bottling in about 8000 plants. These technical production units are linked in various models of production organization, and the Italian wine industry is organized into both integrated and de-integrated supply chains, the latter formed by operators specialized in one or two phases of the wine supply chain.

To describe this complex production system, the chapter is organized as follows. Section 3.2 presents the main features of grape production in Italy. Section 3.3 analyzes the organization of wine production, identifies the technical units involved and their different forms of integration in the supply chains, and discusses the supply concentration and the different typical marketing models of firms. Section 3.4 shows where Italian wine is delivered. Section 3.5 analyzes the relationships and the flows along the chain, presenting the contracts and the main aspects of the sector governance. Finally, Sect. 3.6 contains some final comments on the structure of the Italian wine industry.

3.2 Structural Features of the Wine-Growing Sector

3.2.1 Relevance and Distribution of Viticulture and Farm Size

After a long evolution over 70 years, characterized by a reduction of the total area under vine, the disappearance of mixed cropping in favor of specialized vineyards, and a dramatic reduction in the number of grape-growing farms (Corsi et al. 2018), viticulture is still widespread throughout Italy, although with specific territorial differences. Disregarding farms growing table grapes, in 2010 there were still 369,000 farms growing wine grapes, accounting for 23% of the total number of farms (ISTAT) and covering 626,000 ha (4.8% of total UAA) (Table 3.1). More recent data gathered by a survey carried out

Table 3.1 Number of farms producing wine grapes and vine-bearing area

Territory	Number of farms[a]			Area (hectares)		
	Vineyards for PDO wines	Vineyards for other wines	Total	Vineyards for PDO wines	Vineyards for other wines	Total
Italy	127,970	292,382	388,881	320,859	304,841	625,700
North-West	20,704	19,425	35,174	61,331	10,075	71,406
North-East	46,189	50,286	83,393	116,250	52,099	168,349
Center	17,400	59,850	71,993	65,923	39,553	105,476
South	32,116	113,966	139,346	54,983	102,952	157,935
Islands	8561	48,855	58,975	22,372	100,161	122,534

Source: ISTAT, Agricultural Census (2010)

[a]In the Agricultural Census, the reported number of farms refers to farms where there are predominantly or exclusively vineyards of the mentioned kind. Consequently the overall number of farms is not the sum of partial values. In addition, the overall number of farms also includes farms where there are predominantly or exclusively table grape vineyards and vine nurseries

in 2013 by ISTAT further reduce the number of farms with wine vineyards to just under 310,500 units, while the overall vineyard area estimated for 2017 rises to around 652,000 hectares (ISMEA 2018). These figures consider all farms growing table grapes, including hobby farmers and production for self-consumption.

Notwithstanding the wide diffusion of viticulture, geographical differences are important, both in quantitative and qualitative terms. Consideration of the large-scale territorial division among North-East (NE), North-West (NW), Center, South, and Islands (NUTS1 level in the EU classification) (Fig. 3.1) shows that a large proportion of wine-growing farms are located in the South (36%), while NE (21%) and NW (9%) are less important, and the Center and Islands have 19% and 15%, respectively. However, in terms of vine-bearing area, the share of the South is much smaller (25%), and the share of NE (27%) and of the Islands (20%) is much larger. The differences are more striking in terms of quality, since the South only accounts for 19% of farms producing only Protected Designation of Origin (PDO) wines, while the NE has the largest share of such farms (41%) (Mazzarino and Corsi 2015). Although the issue of "true quality" is much debated, some areas enjoy particular prestige; this is the case of Tuscany, Piedmont, and Veneto for red wines, and Trentino-Alto Adige, Veneto, and Friuli for white ones. Nevertheless, the wines really appreciated by national and international critics come nowadays from vineyards in every part of Italy.

Fig. 3.1 Geographical divisions and main wine-producing Regions

Wine-growing farms in Italy are predominantly small businesses, mostly family-operated. The average size of vineyards is 1.7 ha, and two thirds of wine farms have less than 1 ha of wine grape area, and in the Center and in the South, this share is even larger. Only 7% have over 5 ha of vineyard and 2.6% over 10 ha. The shares of large vineyards are larger in NW, NE, and Islands, where about 10% of wine farms have more than 5 ha of vineyard. The deep historical roots of wine-growing in Italy, along with the general predominance of small and very small farms, are at the origin of this structure. However, while small farms are predominant in number, in terms of area, medium and large farms obviously dominate. Therefore, while only 5% of wine farms are over 5 ha, they account for 54% of wine grape area, with higher shares in NE (60%) and Center (63%). Farms larger than 10 ha of vineyard account for 35% of wine grape area, with a particularly high share in the Center (49.3%). Considering that 35% of the total area under vine represents more than 200,000 hectares, Italian viticulture includes a share of relatively large farms whose overall area is larger than the total area under vine in the USA or in Australia, to cite only the biggest competitors in the New

World. Nevertheless, 12% of wine grape area in Italy consists of farms with less than 1 ha of vineyard, and this share is larger in the South (18%) and in the Center (15%).

3.2.2   Technical Aspects and Land Tenure

On the technical side, an important characteristic of Italian viticulture is the large number of varieties that are grown. According to the national register of vine varieties (MIPAAF 2018), more than 500 wine varieties are grown; most of them are strictly native varieties, not the "international" ones. Though many of them cover small surfaces, even the most widespread variety (Sangiovese) covers a limited share of the total wine grape area (11.4%); all other varieties are below 6% of total area, and the first ten varieties only cover 46% of total wine area[1] (Mazzarino and Corsi 2015). The largest part of vineyards (except for table grapes) are rain-fed, but 21% of the total vine-bearing area is irrigated (Agricultural Census 2010), mostly in the South. Wine-growing is mostly concentrated in the hills (58%), especially in the NW (Piedmont) and the Center (Tuscany), where grape-growing areas are almost totally in the hills. Important parts of the vine area are located on the plains of Emilia-Romagna, Veneto, and the South. Altimetry creates technical differences, since mechanization, especially for harvesting, is difficult on the hills, while it is easier in the plains. This partly explains the differences in the orientation of farms, with the large-scale low-cost wines predominantly produced in the plains, while farms on the hills aim at low-yield, higher-quality grapes, compensating with higher prices for the lower yields and the higher costs. Also the grape-growing agronomic techniques may differ substantially throughout the peninsula because of the different climate conditions, creating diverse landscapes.

Almost all (99%) of wine grape farms are family businesses. Few farms are owned by companies (0.6%), even fewer by cooperatives. In terms of area, the share of family farms is lower but still over 91%, as compared to 6.1% for stock companies. Again, the Center is somewhat different, and the shares are 77.1% and 18.7%, respectively.

---

[1] The most important varieties (over 10,000 ha) are Sangiovese, Trebbiano, Montepulciano, Merlot, Catarratto Bianco, Barbera, Glera, Moscato Bianco, Pinot Grigio, Calabrese (Nero d'Avola), different types of Lambrusco, Cabernet Sauvignon, Chardonnay, Primitivo, and Negro Amaro.

3.2.3   Farmers Classification

The population of grape-growing farms is very heterogeneous in terms of the economic nature of their activity and downward integration. According to AGEA[2] 2012 data, only 197,000 (slightly more than half of the total) engage in a professional business, cropping 550,000 ha (almost 90% of total area under vine). Therefore, the Italian grape-growing sector comprises a large fringe of farms (about 170,000) carrying out viticulture for hobby purposes or self-consumption on small plots or with abandoned vineyards.

It is possible to identify three categories among the professional farmers growing grapes, according to the destination of their production: farmers equipped with wine-making facilities (27%), farmers selling grapes in the intermediate market (31%), and farmers belonging to cooperatives (42%). These categories are important for the analysis of the flows in the chain (Sect. 3.5.1).

3.3   Structural Features of the Wine-Making Sector

3.3.1   Supply Size and Composition

Wine production in volume is variable from year to year due to the climatic conditions that obviously affect vineyard yields. According to ISTAT, it amounts to between 40 and 45 million hectoliters (Table 3.2).

A typical characteristic of the Italian wine supply is the number and importance of wines with recognized geographical origins. Such wines are produced under the EU rules on Protected Geographical Indication (PGI) and PDO. In particular, within the European category of PDO wines, in Italy there are different appellation levels, characterized by increasing and more stringent requirements.[3] The Italian appellation system, modeled on the French one,

---

[2] These figures concerning the professional grape growers come from the AGEA database. AGEA is the Italian agency in charge of the payments of CAP subsidies. According to Reg. 1308/2013, all professional wine grape farmers and all wine-makers have to submit each year a compulsory statement on the quantity of grapes or wines that they produce.

[3] According to Reg. (CE) 1308/2013 and Reg. (CE) 607/2009, EU wines can be marketed as:

• Varietal wines and generic wines, produced with no special restriction on where vineyards, wine-making, and bottling plants are located (in Italy the maximum yield is 50 t/ha). The name of the wine grape variety may be mentioned if at least 85% of the product has been made from that variety.

Table 3.2 Italian wine production by type (hl, %)

	2010	2011	2012	2013	2014	2015	2016
Generic wines	14,996,551	11,978,563	9,692,983	11,917,442	9,916,247	14,257,985	16,761,884
PGI wines	13,953,194	13,592,224	12,546,429	15,787,053	13,451,854	15,423,067	15,345,459
PDO wines	15,743,432	15,060,866	16,025,898	17,339,626	16,373,330	18,954,431	19,508,118
Overall	**44,693,177**	**40,631,653**	**38,265,310**	**45,044,121**	**39,741,431**	**48,638,483**	**51,615,461**
Generic wines	33.6	29.5	25.3	26.5	25.0	29.3	32.5
PGI wines	31.2	33.5	32.8	35.0	33.8	31.7	29.7
PDO wines	35.2	37.1	41.9	38.5	41.2	39.0	37.8
Overall	**100.0**	**100.0**	**100.0**	**100.0**	**100.0**	**100.0**	**100.0**

Source: ISTAT, available at ww.agri.istat.it

started in 1963, but the number of appellations has rapidly and steadily increased since the 1990s. In 2016, the vine area for PGI wines was 149,009 ha, and the corresponding figure for PDO wines was 359,962 ha. Together, PGI and PDO represented 79% of the total vine-bearing area (ISMEA, RETEVINO 2018).

Considering wine production in terms of quality, in the period 2012–2016, Italian wine production in volume (Table 3.2) was almost evenly divided among generic wines (27–28%), PGI wines (32–33%), and PDO wines (39–40%). In terms of value, the shares were obviously different and were estimated (for 2016) at 24%, 18%, and 58%, respectively (QUALIVITA 2018).[4] Wine production is differentiated by type across areas: PDO wines predominate in NW, NE, and Center, NE dominates the production of GI wines, and South has the large majority of generic wines. Production of varietal wines is modest, about half a million hl.

Because of changing consumption patterns and the growing production of sparkling wines (based on white varieties), since the 2011 harvest, white wines have dominated the overall Italian production, accounting in the 2014–2016 period for about 53–54% (ISTAT 2017) depending on the year. In fact, a distribution of this type is more typical of the northern regions, while in the South, Tuscany and Piedmont red wines (including rosé wines) predominate over white ones.

• Wines with a recognized geographical origin, according to the categories Protected Geographical Indication (PGI) and Protected Designation of Origin (PDO). A geographical indication and a designation of origin are names of a region, a specific place, or, in exceptional and duly justifiable cases, a country, used to describe a wine whose quality depends (strictly in PDO case) on the delimited area corresponding to the name, where grapes are cropped and processed according to a recognized set of rules (product specification). In PDO wine production, only varieties belonging to *Vitis vinifera* are admitted, and all grapes must be cropped in the delimited area; in PGI production, also crosses between *Vitis vinifera* and other species of the genus *Vitis* are admitted, and at least 85% of grapes must be cropped in the delimited area.

In Italy PGI wines are presented as IGTs, because "Indicazione Geografica Tipica" is the officially recognized traditional term corresponding to the EU category PGI, and PDO wines are presented as DOC and DOCG wines, because Denominazione di Origine Controllata (Controlled Designation of Origin) and Denominazione d'Origine Controllata e Garantita (Controlled and Guaranteed Designation of Origin) are the officially recognized traditional terms corresponding to the EU category PDO (L. 238/2016). Wines belonging to the DOC and DOCG categories are assumed to be of higher value than IGT wines. Those DOC wines which have achieved particular appreciation by the market can be designated, on the producers' request, as DOCG; in this case producers are obliged to comply with much more stringent production rules concerning not only the grape varieties and the maximum yields in vineyards and wine-making but also the grape selection and the aging. DOC and DOCG wines undergo strict chemical and organoleptic tests at the end of aging and (only for DOCG wines) before bottling; the bottling area can be inside or outside the origin area (depending on the production specification— "Disciplinare di produzione" in Italian).

[4] Estimates on bulk wine at the winery level.

3.3.2   Wine Production Organization

A structural analysis of the wine-making sector must take into account that wine-making is a phase of the wine production chain with several sub-phases, frequently performed by different companies. Given the data availability, the following structural analysis of the Italian wine-making sector considers (i) the technical units[5] operating in the two main sub-phases of wine-making, that is, grape processing (crushing) and bottling and (ii) how such technical units are vertically linked and how they are linked upwards with the grape production phase according to different supply chain models characterized by specific integration patterns.

3.3.2.1   Grape-Processing Technical Units

According to the most recent data made available by AGEA and referred to 2012, crushing is carried out in about 55,000 plants. Processing capacity differs greatly, however, and the largest share of production is concentrated in relatively few plants. About 80% of these plants are estimated to produce less than 500 hl per year, overall representing less than 1% of Italian wine production. On the other hand, about 200 plants, with a processing capacity of over 50,000 hl per year, represent about 60% of Italian wine production.

The grape-processing technical units can be classified into three categories: individual farmers making wine on their farms by processing self-produced grapes; cooperatives, which process mainly grapes delivered by members; and private industrial wineries, which process purchased grapes. Sometimes the borders between categories are not clear-cut, since some wine farmers also buy grapes from other farmers to make their wine and some wineries have their own vineyards. In 2012 individual farmers numbered 52,985 (97%), cooperatives 441, and industrial wine-makers 1414. In terms of the share of wine produced, the cooperatives were the most important and produced 49.6% of the total; industrial wine-makers produced 22.9% and farmers 27.5% (Table 3.3).

Each category comprises technical units that can be very different in terms of size and production orientation. Cooperatives include those with a few dozen members, as well as the main Italian wine firms. Individual farmers range from small producers to large prestigious firms. Also for the industrial

---

[5] The term "technical unit" denotes a single production plant. Several technical units engaged in grape processing may be under the control of the same company.

Table 3.3 Total wine production by type of producer (2012)

	Volume (hl)			%		
	Farmers	Wineries	Cooperatives	Farmers	Wineries	Cooperatives
Italy	12,364,272	10,315,146	22,298,290	27.5	22.9	49.6
North-West	1,674,055	1,250,168	1,270,420	39.9	29.8	30.3
North-East	5,125,387	3,670,548	10,340,461	26.8	19.2	54.0
Center	2,608,629	764,391	1,133,890	57.9	17.0	25.2
South	2,186,493	4,141,579	5,558,374	18.4	34.8	46.8
Islands	769,630	488,460	3,995,145	14.7	9.3	76.1

Source: Based on AGEA data, 2014

wineries, size may differ greatly. However, on average, the largest production capacity by plant is among cooperatives, with an average size of over 50,000 hectoliters, as compared to 7295 for industrial wine-makers and only 233 hectoliters for on-farm producers. The plants with the highest average size are located in the NE (1675 hectoliters) and in the Islands (1456), whereas the lower average sizes are found in the NW (404 hl) and in the Center (430).

The weights of the categories differ among the different kinds (generic, PGI, PDO) of wine (Table 3.3).[6] According to the AGEA data, cooperatives constitute the most important group for all kinds of wine but particularly in the sector of PGI wines, where their share is about 58%. However, industrial wine-makers are also strong in the sector of generic wine, with a share of 38%, against the 45% of the cooperatives. Individual producers are stronger in the sector of GI wines and, above all, for PDO wines, reaching 38% of the total.

The weights of the three categories also differ according to the area and the type of wine. For *generic wines* (Table 3.4), cooperatives are of overwhelming importance in the Islands. There, especially in Sicily, viticulture was traditionally characterized by high yields, high alcohol degree, and low-quality grapes. Hence, wine was mainly exported to be used to raise the alcohol degree of other wines or was used for distillation funded by the EU. Although the average quality of wines in these regions has recently greatly improved, cooperatives, which mainly collected those low-quality grapes, are still dominant. Along with cooperatives, in the rest of Southern Italy, industrial wineries cover the same segment. This outcome is probably also due to the lack of a high-quality wine-making tradition and, hence, on the technical side, to the difficulty for individual farmers to deal with flaws in the grapes and, on the commercial

---

[6] The data presented here are based on AGEA data, which differ, in absolute terms, from the ISTAT data (see Table 3.2) because the production volumes declared to AGEA every year may, for some types of wine and for limited quantities, refer to the previous harvest. Nevertheless, we used them because they are the only data available to estimate the grape flows to the various wine-making operators.

Table 3.4 Shares of total wine production by type of wine, producer, and area (2012)

	Farmers	Wineries	Cooperatives	Total
		Generic		
Italy	17.2	38.0	44.9	100.0
North-West	43.1	38.3	18.6	100.0
North-East	13.2	37.2	49.7	100.0
Center	43.3	43.5	13.2	100.0
South	16.4	45.0	38.6	100.0
Islands	8.3	9.9	81.9	100.0
		PGI		
Italy	29.0	13.2	57.8	100.0
North-West	34.1	19.7	46.2	100.0
North-East	31.3	10.8	57.9	100.0
Center	59.4	11.1	29.6	100.0
South	22.8	22.9	54.3	100.0
Islands	12.3	9.3	78.4	100.0
		PDO		
Italy	37.6	14.5	48.0	100.0
North-West	40.2	29.7	30.1	100.0
North-East	33.3	12.9	53.9	100.0
Center	63.9	7.5	28.6	100.0
South	21.0	8.8	70.2	100.0
Islands	31.0	8.3	60.7	100.0

Source: Based on AGEA data, 2014

side, to adopt appropriate marketing strategies. By contrast, cooperatives are also dominant in the NE for generic wines, but for quite different reasons. Cooperatives there are strong, market-oriented organizations and include the biggest firms in the sector. They have been successful in concentrating the supply and in creating the most popular brands of value wines distributed through large-scale retail.

In the NE, cooperatives are even more dominant for *PGI wines*, but farmers also have more weight (Table 3.4). Using the PGI label more widely has been a recent trend for many producers as a means to improve the quality and reputation of their wines. The possibility to use the PGI label has been much exploited by both farmers and cooperatives also in the South and, to a lesser extent, in the Center.

The share produced by individual farmers is much greater for *PDO wines* than for the other wines, in particular in the NW (especially Piedmont) and in the Center (especially Tuscany) where they account for 40.2% and 63.9%, respectively, of the total of PDO wines. In this segment, the industrial wineries lose weight, since cooperatives maintain their share. This is the result of a self-selection process. Those wine-growers with better-quality grapes and higher wine-making skills choose to make wine on the farm. This is possible due to the strong diversification of varieties and the access to several market-ing channels. In particular, due to the long consumption tradition, consumers prefer local wines, which makes finding local outlets easier. On the other hand, small size makes it more difficult to exploit foreign markets, as well as large-scale retail.

3.3.2.2 Bottling Technical Units

Bottling is the production phase with the lowest availability of specific infor-mation. Nonetheless, bottling technical units are fewer than the number of grape growers and wine-making technical units. A relatively recent study (Malorgio et al. 2011b) estimated that about 8000 bottlers operate in Italy. Also the bottling technical units are very different in size, and the largest amount of wine (about 80%) is bottled by a very small share of bottlers (about 6%) with a relatively high processing capacity (more than 10,000 hl/year) (Table 3.5).

About 20% of the bottling technical units belong to pure (plain) bottlers bottling only wine produced by others. They deliver about one third of the Italian bottled production to the market. The other bottling technical units operate directly in wine-making plants. The majority of them (about 60%) belong to on-farm wine-makers and the rest to both cooperatives and indus-trial wine-makers. Despite the relatively high number of on-farm bottling technical units, most on-farm wine-makers are not equipped with their own bottling line; by contrast, most industrial and cooperative wine-makers are equipped with bottling lines. The absence of bottling lines linked with wine-making facilities has three causes. First, many wine producers (farms, indus-trial wine-makers, or small cooperatives) have neither the sufficient size nor the skills to market bottled wine on their own and therefore sell all their production in bulk to other businesses. Second, several grape-processing tech-nical units may belong to the same firm, which concentrates bottling in a single station. Third, some small wine producers outsource bottling. Indeed,

Table 3.5 Bottling unit distribution by capacity

	Shares on	
Bottling capacity (hl/year)	Units	Bottled volume
< 1000	76	7
1000–5000	15	9
5000–10,000	3	5
> 10,000	6	79

Source: Malorgio et al. (2011b)

many large bottling plants operate as co-packers, and some firms equipped with truck-mounted bottling lines supply the service to small wine producers.

3.3.2.3   Grape Procurement and Supply Chains

The foregoing discussion evidences that the Italian wine industry is based on a complex network characterized by a radical concentration of flows. The grapes originate in a huge number of farms but are crushed by a much smaller number of wine-making technical units, and bottled wine is delivered to the market by a small number of bottling wineries or pure bottlers.

Indeed, it is possible to identify different, though interrelated, supply chains. These are two integrated chains, the Agricultural chain and the Cooperative chain, and two de-integrated chains, the Industrial chain and the pure Bottler chain.

The Agricultural chain and the Cooperative chain can be considered as integrated supply chains because they are headed by bottling firms that deliver to the market wine mostly deriving from self-produced grapes. Firms in these chains can be simple, their technical structure consisting in a wine-making and bottling plant, supplied by one or more vineyards in the immediate surroundings, directly owned (the case of the Agricultural chain); or they can be run by cooperative members (the case of the Cooperative chain). However, firms in this chain can assume a complex network nature. For instance, one or more bottling stations may be supplied by several grape-processing plants belonging to the same firm and by grapes produced by farms directly owned (case of Agricultural chain); or the bottling stations may be functionally linked to wine-making plants via specific agreements among formally independent cooperatives (the case of the Cooperative chain).

The Industrial chain and the Bottlers chain can be considered as de-integrated supply chains because they are headed by firms delivering to the market wine mostly derived from purchased grapes and/or wine. These firms typically have a network of suppliers, in some cases located in the surroundings of the bottling station or, as in the case of larger actors in these chains, spread throughout Italy and in some cases even located abroad. These networks of suppliers can be more or less stable, depending on the nature of the relation between suppliers and supplied (contracts or market; see Sect. 3.5.2).

These four supply chains are anyway interrelated, because exchanges of products may take place among firms belonging to different supply chains. In some cases, grapes or wine produced by firms belonging to Agricultural or

Cooperative chains that exceed their needs are delivered to de-integrated supply chains. In other cases, to enlarge their supply, firms belonging to the Agricultural chain purchase grapes or wine from agents operating mainly in the de-integrated supply chains. All these supply chains are important, in volume and value. Different types of suppliers therefore characterize the Italian wine industry. According to reliable evaluations (Malorgio et al. 2011a), the shares in volume of the four supply chains can be estimated as Agricultural chain, 20%; Cooperative chain, 17%; Industrial chain, 30%; and Bottler chain, 33%. The shares in value are probably different. In particular, the share of the agricultural chain is higher because its share of the more expensive PDO wines in the total supply is larger, and this supply chain includes the producers of the most prestigious Italian wines.

3.3.3   Supply Concentration and Top Players

Even considering that several technical units, also bottling plants, can belong to a single company, wine supply in Italy remains quite fragmented, and the degree of concentration of the industry is modest.

Mediobanca (2018) surveys the 155 main firms (those with a turnover of more than 25 million euros). In 2016, their total turnover was 7.2 billion euros, compared to an estimated Italian total of 13.9 (a share of 51.8%). The four-firm concentration rate is only 13.6%, and the first ten companies only account for 24% of the total turnover.

Two cooperatives (Cantine Riunite and Caviro) are the largest companies, and another two (Cavit and Mezzacorona) are among the first ten companies: cooperatives, though less in number, are absolutely significant in the overall picture of Italian wine-making, both as to volume of wine and turnover (Table 3.6). But also the other supply chains are represented among the top wine firms. In fact, some big companies lead bottler supply chains (e.g. Enoitalia and Italian Wine Brands) and other industrial supply chains (e.g. Mondodelvino Group and Botter). Other companies represent cases of agricultural supply chains, though among these large companies, a minor share of grape and wine is usually outsourced[7] (e.g. Compagnia de' Frescobaldi and Masi Agricola).

All the largest companies have their headquarters in the North (Veneto, Emilia-Romagna, Piedmont, and Trentino) or in Tuscany but with plants or

---

[7] Usually grape or bulk wine destined to low price labels.

Table 3.6 Top 30 wine companies in Italy

Name	Headquarter (region)	2016	2015	2014	2013	Export share 2016 (%)	Governance	Av. Price €/bott
		Turnover (€ millions)						
Cantine Riunite & CIV	Emilia-Romagna	565	547	536	534	66.5	Cooperative	na
Caviro	Emilia-Romagna	304	300	314	321	30.5	Cooperative	0.89
Palazzo Antinori	Toscana	220	202	180	172	64	Family control	7.71
Casa Vinicola Zonin	Veneto	193	183	160	154	86	Family control	3.8
Cavit Cantina Viticoltori	Trentino	178	167	158	153	81	Cooperative	2.38
Fratelli Martini Secondo Luigi	Piemonte	171	162	160	157	90	Family control	2.27
Gruppo Campari (wine dept)	*Lombardia*	*169*	*171*	*209*	*228*	*na*	*Family control*	*3.14*
Casa Vinicola Botter Carlo & C	Veneto	165	154	136	136	97	Family control	2.14
Mezzacorona	Trentino	163	175	171	163	59	Cooperative	3.57
Santa Margherita Gruppo	Veneto	157	118	110	102	69	Family control	6.19
Enoitalia	Veneto	148	135	128	128	74	Family control	1.52
IWB-Italian Wine Brands	Lombardia	146	145	101	101	72	Mixed[a]	3.22
Cantina Sociale Coop. Di Soave	Veneto	117	106	102	103	38	Cooperative	3.03
Gruppo Cevico	Emilia-Romagna	111	113	107	117	28	Cooperative	1.59
Schenk Italia	Alto Adige	106	104	82	80	73	Foreign control	na
Collis Veneto Wine Group	Veneto	106	104	75	78	30	Cooperative	6.3
Compagnia de' Frescobaldi	Toscana	101	95	86	84	62	Family control	8.89
Mondodelvino Group	Emilia-Romagna	101	91	73	66	84	Mixed	1.81
La Marca Vini e Spumanti	Veneto	101	76	60	54	79	Cooperative	2.82

(*continued*)

Table 3.6 (continued)

Name	Headquarter (region)	Turnover (€ millions)				Export share 2016 (%)	Governance	Av. Price €/bott
		2016	2015	2014	2013			
Lunelli	Trentino	96	84	na	na	26.5	Family control	na
Ruffino	Toscana	93	94	81	75	93	Foreign control	3.97
Villa Sandi	Veneto	88	73	na	na	45	Family control	na
Vivo Cantine	Veneto	81	65	na	na	47	Cooperative	na
Cantina di La Vis e Valle di Cembra	Trentino	76	83	na	na	74	Cooperative	na
Contri Spumanti	Veneto	76	79	82	92	39	Mixed	na
Mionetto	Veneto	72	65	na	na	57	Foreign control	na
VS Vinicola Serena	Veneto	68	56	na	na	na	Family control	na
Gruppo Banfi	Toscana	67	70	63	66	57	Foreign control	4.69
Vignaioli Veneto Friulani	Veneto	67	na	na	na	na	Cooperative	na
Quargentan	Veneto	66	68	na	na	na	Family control	na
Masi Agricola	Veneto	64	61	60	65	88	Family control[a]	5.2

Sources: Mediobanca (2016, 2017, 2018) for turnover and governance; average prices are our evaluations
[a]Listed

suppliers in many Italian regions, forming complex supply networks. In particular, firms belonging to the integrated chains directly control a very large area under vine. By way of example, Caviro controls 33,000 ha, Cantine Riunite & CIV 6200 ha, Antinori 3000 ha, Zonin 2000 ha, and Frescobaldi 1350 ha.

Despite the sector's low degree of concentration, the size of the top producers is not small. Indeed, the turnovers of the two major producers (Cantine Riunite & CIV and Caviro) are 565 million and 304 million euros respectively, both comparable to, for example, the biggest Australian and Chilean companies. The weak share of the top producers is rather due to the very large value of Italian wine turnover but also to the absence of truly big non-cooperative firms. Indeed, the big cooperatives are the result of a process of aggregation of medium/small firms; but similar processes have not occurred among family companies. In the recent history of the Italian wine sector, there have been no cases of medium/large firms in financial crisis or gone bankrupt that other firms could easily acquire. The existing large non-cooperative firms have grown only by internal growth without the big jumps that, in the new producing countries, have characterized the evolution of some wine companies (Green et al. 2006; Mariani and Pomarici 2011). As a result, there are no true sector leaders, even if the cooperatives are the most important players.

The analysis of the top 30 players reveals two other characteristics of the Italian wine sector. Wine is the main or the only business of the leading firms (in one case only, that of Campari, wine production is a division of larger group producing beverages and spirits). Foreign capital is rare, since only 4 top companies in the first 30 (and not in the top positions) are owned by foreign capital and only few cases among smaller firms are known[8]; on the other hand, also Italian investments abroad are scarce.

The turnover trends observed since 2011 for larger companies (i.e. those with turnovers above 50 million euros) show that a process of polarization is ongoing within the supply chain (Pomarici 2017). The relative weight of the larger companies is increasing, probably because of economies of scale, which are especially possible for big companies in the *commercial premium* segment. Smaller companies instead exploit niche marketing strategies and special skills, addressing the *super-premium* segment and the local distribution channels. By contrast, medium-sized companies, in the class between 50 and 100 million turnover, show a reduction in their turnover share. This is probably due to their size itself, which prevents either reaching satisfactory economies of scale for intermediate quality segments or achieving a competitive advantage for the top quality segments.

3.3.4 Marketing Strategies

The marketing strategies of individual firms are obviously very different, and it is not easy to give a general assessment. In very general terms, firm brands are not of primary importance for consumers, who are instead more attracted by the appellations and by the region of origin in purchasing (Fait 2010; Corduas et al. 2013).

---

[8] The latest case (2016) is the transfer of the prestigious Biondi Santi winery in Montalcino to the EPI Group (Champagne Piper-Heidsieck).

First, as regards the domestic market, a reason for the limited importance of brands is drinking habits, which are traditionally strongly linked to local wines. Second, with such a large number of producers, it is difficult for consumers to select the information and to check the reputation of the individual producers, and appellations are, albeit imperfect, quality signals (Cacchiarelli et al. 2014). Third, on the producers' side, most firms lack the financial strength and the skills to promote and advertise their products individually, and also among larger firms, the appropriateness of branding activities typical of fast-moving consumer goods is questioned.

In fact, the marketing activities for premium wines are mostly of the push type, with a deep personal involvement of entrepreneurs and oenologists, and addressed to intermediaries, retailers, media, HORECA actors, and selected influential consumers. They also try to benefit from the collective reputation of the appellation and, possibly, from marketing campaigns funded by local public bodies or organizations. On the basic wine side, instead, promotion relies mostly on price promotion and on favorable positions on the shelves.

There are exceptions, however. One is in the segment of very high-quality wines (super-premium, icon), where the winery brand is obviously a strong asset and a marketing tool. Nevertheless, even the most famous producers are usually linked to particular areas and to individual appellations, so that the brand is used in association with the PDO. Very few exceptions are the Super Tuscans and some other similar wines, originally created outside DOC/G regulations, and now still in many cases PGI wines and for which only the brand is a quality signal for consumers.

On the opposite side of the quality scale, brands (but not private labels, unlike in other countries) are used and advertised for generic wines, since this is the only differentiation signal that consumers can receive. For instance, among value wines, mainly sold in supermarkets, Tavernello is the leading brand (Giacomini 2010). It was launched by Caviro, the second cooperative firm by size in Italy, 30 years ago, as the first wine in cartons in Italy.

The marketing style in exports is substantially similar, and firm efforts, depending on their financial resources, are mostly addressed to enlarging and enhancing their relationships with distributors, retailers, media, and HORECA actors, and to influencing consumers, privileging actions below the line (public relations, etc.) instead of above it (advertising). Since 2010 the export promotion of Italian wine firms has been supported by substantial resources provided by the EU Common Agricultural Policy.

In regard to larger firms, the market segments in which they operate and the strategies adopted are quite diversified. In general, cooperatives operate in segments of low- and medium-quality wines, mostly oriented to the mass market, with smaller margins due to the prevailing large-scale retail outlet and to a lower orientation to foreign markets (Mediobanca 2016, 2017, 2018). In terms of types of wine, in 2017 "great wines" (with prices over 25 euros per bottle) were 2.9% of wine labels for cooperatives, compared to 8.2% for private companies. The shares for DOCG and DOC wines were 12.8% and 38.9% for cooperatives and 11.4% and 32.8% for private companies. The shares of PGI were similar (36.6% and 35.8% for cooperatives and private companies, respectively), but the latter had a greater number of generic wines (11.8% vs. 8.8%).

In short, while cooperatives are more concentrated on the medium segment (with the remarkable exceptions of Caviro for basic wines and Collis for super-premium wines), private companies are more dedicated to either the top segment or the lowest one. The comparison of average prices indicates that private companies belonging to the Agricultural supply chain fetch higher prices (especially in the cases of Antinori, Frescobaldi, and Santa Margherita), since they are primarily oriented to super-premium wines, while firms belonging to the other supply chains focus on the basic/premium market.

Analysis of the top players also illustrates the different performances of the Italian companies in terms of exports. Of the first 30 firms, 12 obtain more than 70% of their turnover from foreign markets (up to 97% for Botter and 93% for Ruffino), 7 between 50% and 70%, and the rest below 50% (with a minimum of 26.5% for Lunelli), with no pattern in this respect between cooperatives and private companies.

A special mention should be made of the production of sparkling wines, which has rapidly increased in recent years, up to 610–630 million bottles in 2015[9] (Osservatorio Economico Vini 2016; available at www.ovse.org). The sector is highly diversified in production methods (second fermentation in tanks, i.e. Charmat, 95–96% of the total, and second fermentation in bottles, i.e. Champenoise, for the rest), firm size, appellations (generic, PGI, PDO), taste (sweet, brut, dry, extra dry), and longer or shorter aging. Whatever the segment, big wineries cover the largest part of the production (almost 60%), since the sparkling wine technology is not easily affordable for small farms. The differences in production methods translate into quite different production costs and, in some cases, are conditioned by the level of designation (Zanfi 2009, 2011). Accordingly, sparkling wine can range from the value segment to the super-premium segment, depending on the production method, the aging, and, obviously, the brand. The most important

---

[9] In 2016 the value of the Italian sparkling wines destined for export was 1.2 billion (ISMEA 2018).

production areas are located in the NW and the NE, and are represented by Piedmont for Asti Spumante DOCG (70 million bottles in 2015), by Lombardy for Franciacorta DOCG (top-class region for traditional method, 30 million), by Veneto and Friuli for Prosecco DOC and Valdobbiadene Prosecco Superiore DOCG (470 million), and by Trentino-Alto Adige for Trento DOC (8 million). The production of sparkling wines is expanding out of the traditional areas under several appellations, with an overall share that in 2017 was around 22% of the total.[10]

3.4   The Distribution

In quantitative terms, ISMEA (2015) estimates that of the total available wine (domestic production—95%—plus imports), 45% goes to domestic consumption, 46% to exports, and the rest to distillation and industrial use (Fig. 3.2). Domestic consumption consists in 35% of bulk wine, most of which is sold directly by producers (this part also includes a very small share of self-consumed wine) and in a smaller amount sold on-trade.[11] Wine in bottles or packaged in other containers is estimated at 65% of domestic consumption, of which the largest part (61%) is off-trade.

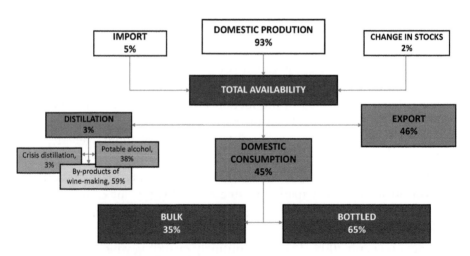

Fig. 3.2   Wine consuption flows. (Source: ISMEA, Scheda di settore 2015)

---

[10] Unpublished information from UIV Wine Market Observatory.

[11] The term "on-trade" means sold for consumption in hotels, pubs, restaurants, and cafes, whereas "off-trade" means sold in supermarkets, stores, food retailers, corner shops, and so on.

Obviously, in the bottled off-trade channel, large-scale distribution prevails, compared to other channels like traditional food stores, wine shops, and direct sales. Nevertheless, no further reliable data on the commercial channels covered by all domestic consumption until the final consumer are easily accessible because they are available only for specific wine categories (PDO, PGI, generic wines). As regards bulk wine, the share of direct sales to final consumers is not small, especially in the case of individual farmers and cooperatives and for some regions because it is still customary for urban consumers to buy wine directly[12] and to bottle it by themselves.

More detailed data on the distribution channels are provided by the above-mentioned Mediobanca surveys (2018), which report the shares of the sales channels used by the top companies, in total and by company category of price segment (Table 3.7).

Among the 155 largest firms, considering their overall supply, the largest share of domestic sales is directed to large-scale retail (38%); and it is bigger for cooperatives (46%) than for private companies (34%). Direct sales (13%) have a relatively lesser importance. The share of HORECA is much smaller for cooperatives (8%) than for companies (22%), since cooperatives prefer to provision other channels such as large-scale retail and wholesalers, probably because of the higher volumes involved. The wholesale channel remains an important channel for all firms, because it is a way to reach consumption areas far from those of production. In short, the main difference between the big firms and the farmers is that the farmers sell more through direct sale and local supermarkets or wine shops, and less on-trade, especially through large-scale retail.

Table 3.7 Percentage of Italian domestic supply by distribution channels (2017, 155 top wine companies)

Distribution channels for domestic supply	Supply of the top Italian wine companies					
	All wines			Great wines		
	All firms	Private	Coop	All firms	Private	Coop
Direct sale	12.6	14.4	10.6	18.8	23.6	12.1
Large-scale retail	38.2	33.9	45.5	3.3	3.4	2.1
HORECA	16.5	21.7	8.2	37	37.1	38
Wine shops and wine bars	8.1	10	4.5	23.6	26.3	16.7
Wholesalers and intermediaries	16.8	14.6	20.5	8	3.7	17.2
Other channels	7.8	5.4	10.7	9.3	5.9	13.9

Source: Mediobanca (2018)

---

[12] It is also customary for farms and cooperatives to deliver bulk wine to consumers' homes.

The destination of the great wines (those with a price of more than 25 euros) of the largest firms is rather different and suggests the different orientation of distribution channels in terms of type of wine. HORECA and small shops (wine shops and wine bars) have the largest share (respectively, 37% and 24%) of consumption of great wines, followed by direct sales (19%), while large-scale retail has a very low weight (3%). The main difference between cooperatives and companies is that the latter use more direct sales and small shops and rely less on trade.

Distribution outlets are reached in Italy in almost the same way by all firms. Firms are connected with small outlets like wine shops, restaurants, bars, and wholesalers through a network of sales representatives, which can be larger or smaller according to the firm's size. The purchase platforms of large-scale retailers or restaurant chains are reached via specialized intermediaries. Distributors (i.e. operators that have the monopoly within an area of the sales of the products of a winery and that promote its brand) have a quite limited role in Italy, especially in the case of great wines.

The exported wine is shipped mainly in bottles; indeed, bottled still and sparkling wines account for 75% of total exports in volume.

Most wine firms reach the foreign markets through local importers abroad, possibly supported, in the case of smaller firms, by specialized intermediaries (Mediobanca 2018). Larger companies may have various importers in the same country, one to reach large retailers and others to reach wine shops and restaurants. The 155 larger companies too mostly export through foreign importers (75% of their exports), less through their own networks (10%), though cooperatives have a larger weight in the latter (14%). Indeed, only few firms, private or cooperative, have established controlled distribution companies in some importing markets. Among the great wines, the share of importers is slightly larger (78%), especially for private companies (88%).

3.5   Relationships Along the Chain

3.5.1   The Flows Along the Production Chain

The Italian wine production chain is based on different supply chains differently integrated. The flows of grapes originate from a very large number of farms, but an increasingly smaller number of operators control the flows of wine in the subsequent phases of the chain.

The available data enable detailed analysis of the flow in the first step of the wine production chain, from grapes to bulk wine, showing how grapes

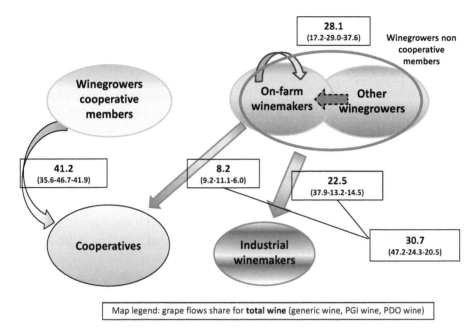

Map legend: grape flows share for **total wine** (generic wine, PGI wine, PDO wine)

Fig. 3.3 Estimable grape flows among operators for total wine, generic wine, GI wine, PDO wine. (Map legend: Grape flows share for **total wine** (generic wine, PGI wine, PDO wine))

produced by the three types of professional farmers already identified (Sect. 3.2.3) move to the three types of wine-makers (Fig. 3.3). Farmers who are cooperative members and farmers who make their own wine do not sell grapes on the market for a price. The grapes passing through a sale are those purchased by cooperatives from nonmembers and by industrial wineries. They can be estimated at about 8% and 22.5% of the total volume of grapes[13] (Mazzarino and Corsi 2015). According to the latest available data, referring to the 2012 harvest, the provision of grapes to cooperatives by their members accounted for 41% of the total production, and the share of on-farm wine-makers was 28%. Hence, the share of grapes passing through a formal market is about a third of the total output (31% in 2012). The formal market therefore strongly concentrates the flow, because about 60,000 farmers deliver their grapes to only 1400 industrial crushing plants. This adds to the concentration operated by the cooperatives, as 441 cooperative plants process the grapes produced by 83,000 cooperative members.

---

[13] This estimate does not consider the flows of grapes produced by other farmers to farmers making wine; moreover, grapes possibly sold to cooperatives and industrial wineries by farmers making wine, when exceeding their processing capacity, are aggregated to the grapes sold by "other farmers".

The flows are different for the different categories of wine. For the grapes destined for generic wine, the part provided by cooperative members is 36%, the part processed on the farm is 17%, that purchased by cooperatives is 9%, and that purchased by industrial wineries is 38%, so that the share of the formal market (47%) is relatively high. The corresponding share for PGI grapes is only 24% (11% purchased by cooperatives, 13% by industrial wineries), while the share processed by cooperatives from their members is 47%, and the amount self-provided by farmers is 29%. Finally, for PDO wines, the share of the formal market is about 20% (6% purchased by cooperatives, 14.5% by industrial wineries), while 38% is used for on-farm wine-making, and 42% is provided to the cooperatives by their members.

The analysis of flows in the second step of the wine production chain, from bulk to bottled wine, cannot be supported by detailed data, but it can nevertheless be based on a reliable evaluation (Malorgio et al. 2011b). This second step involves about 70% of the wine produced, as about 30% is marketed in bulk for domestic consumption or export.

In analyzing this second step, it is convenient first to consider that the wine produced on-farm and by cooperatives is only partially bottled by the same operators. The shares of their own wine directly bottled by farmers and cooperatives are about 45% and 20%, respectively. Therefore, on-farm wine-makers and cooperatives, net of internal exchanges, deliver to the intermediate wine market over 50% of the wine volume. Indeed, on-farm wine-makers typically either bottle their entire wine production or sell it totally in bulk. On the contrary, most cooperatives are equipped with a bottling line, but they typically bottle only a share of their wine and supply bottlers in Italy or abroad, especially in the last period of development of an international bulk market (Mariani et al. 2012).

The industrial wineries buy on the intermediate market and bottle bulk wine for about 30% in addition to the wine that they produce directly. Of course, pure bottlers buy the totality of the wine that they bottle on this market. Also this intermediate market strongly concentrates the flows, as the wine produced by about 45,000 wine-making technical units is delivered to fewer than 3000 bottling stations.

Summing up, the structure of Italian wine industry, as based on both integrated and de-integrated supply chains, includes two intermediate markets, grapes and wine. Although smaller in volume than 30/40 years ago, these markets are still important in quantitative and functional terms and are structurally necessary for the functioning of the de-integrated supply chains but also give flexibility to the functioning of the integrated supply chains.

3.5.2   Intermediate Markets and Contracts

In the past, there existed big local markets where intermediaries and wine-makers traded a very large proportion of grapes. These markets are now reduced in size because they handle only one third of the grapes, given that most of the grapes are processed either by the farmers themselves or by their cooperatives. Moreover, when wineries produce higher-quality wines, they tend to have stable purchase relationships with wine-growers—so as to ensure a supply of good-quality grapes—on the basis of formal or informal contracts.

Price setting differs according to the different flows. Of particular importance is the mechanism used by cooperatives. Since the Italian law imposes strong constraints on the destination of profits of cooperatives, in practice profits are distributed to members as higher prices for the grapes that they deliver. Members (who generally are bound to provide their total production to their cooperative) therefore receive a first price as an advance. When the cooperative accounts are closed, profits are distributed as an additional price (balance). Hence, the real price that cooperative members receive depends on the overall wine market and on the cooperative's efficiency rather than on the market for grapes. Similarly, for wine-growers that are also on-farm wine-makers, the real price that they receive for their grapes depends on the overall wine market and on the wine-making efficiency rather than on the market for grapes. Of course, for on-farm wine-makers, also the quality of the grapes (and, hence, their skills in growing the grapes) matters. The same applies to the cooperative members, since cooperatives usually pay their members according to the quality of their grapes. In the long term, cooperatives and on-farm wine-makers have acted as powerful indirect regulators of the market of grapes, over which wholesalers and industrial wine-makers traditionally exercised market power. Partly, growers provide grapes to industrial wineries under contract, so that prices are set in advance. This also concerns some on-farm wineries, which increase their wine production by buying other grapes, and it mainly happens when they aim at quality wines. When costs are the main concern, wineries buy on the spot, have no long-term relationship with the sellers, and choose mainly according to the price. The prices on these markets are not easy to detect but mainly depend on the supply of grapes and/or on the existing wine stocks of previous harvests. However, the market for grapes based on spot prices is a minor market, because it concerns a minor part of the processed grapes. However, the share of the spot market is larger for the grapes for generic wines or for some large-volume PDO/PGI wines.

In some cases, collective agreements are signed between the associations of the wine-growers and those of the industrial wine-makers, setting prices and other conditions. This concerns some wines where almost the totality of grapes is processed by industrial wineries, typically in Piedmont and Sicily. In Piedmont the most important agreement concerns the Moscato grapes for Asti and Moscato d'Asti DOCG wines, but others deal with Brachetto grapes for Brachetto d'Acqui and Piemonte Brachetto wines, Cortese grapes for Gavi wines, and Chardonnay and Pinot noir grapes for Alta Langa sparkling wines. In Sicily, they concern the grapes for Marsala and Pantelleria DOC wines. For example, the agreement for Moscato sets the grape price yearly, within the limits of established yields (possibly lower than those that are allowed by the PDO regulation). Some small price increase is possible for particularly good-quality grapes. The payments are usually in two installments, of which the first at the end of the year, for 50–75% of the total amount. In Sicily, the agreements on grapes for Marsala and Pantelleria DOC wines set the minimum price for the "basis" grape (20° Babo). To this, further payments, directly agreed upon by the seller and the buyer, can be added in the case of higher sugar content or good conditions of the grapes; these payments may substantially increase the minimum price (CIA 2012).

The intermediate wine market is of some significance. In this market some important geographical delimitations may exist because, for most PDO wines, the area where bottling is possible corresponds to the grape-growing area. Such limits do not exist for PGI and generic wines. Also in the intermediate wine market, exchanges are regulated by contracts or spot transactions. The prices of wines destined to be sold as PDO or PGI are mainly influenced by local factors, while the prices of generic wines are increasingly influenced by international markets, as Italian large bottlers are now also procuring wine abroad.

3.5.3 Interbranch Organization and Sector Governance

The Italian wine industry lacks a unitary governance because the actors are represented by many organizations. Farmers are represented by three general farmers' unions, and cooperatives are represented by two main unions plus some minor ones. Moreover, two wine producer organizations (Unione Italiana Vini and Federvini) are also active; many farmers or cooperative members of these bodies are also members of their general association. As a matter of fact, this fragmentation often hampers the development of efficient and shared policies for the sector.

Also other bodies have a role in the governance of the Italian wine industry. Among them, the association of oenologists (Assoenologi), the association for wine tourism, the association of wine cities, and, in particular, the interbranch organizations constituted among producers of one or more PDO/PGI wines (Consorzi di Tutela) according to the EU and national regulations[14] to pursue the interests of their members—in particular to promote their wines, to improve knowledge about production techniques and market conditions, to regulate the supply, and to prevent the unlawful use of the name of the wine. In Italy about 110 Consorzi di Tutela are active and are recognized by the Ministry of Agricultural, Food and Forestry Policies; these bodies at the regional level negotiate local wine policies, while their national association (Federdoc) takes part in the negotiations concerning the national wine policy.

Research and technical innovation are carried out mainly by research centers of the network of the Ministry of Agricultural, Food and Forestry Policies (Consiglio per la ricerca in agricoltura e l'analisi dell'economia agraria—CREA) and by several university departments, which also train the oenologists.

3.6   Conclusions

The overall picture that can be drawn is a multifaceted one. However, some main structural elements emerge.

A first aspect is the diversity of the operators included in the structure of the Italian wine sector (Sardone 2014). This applies to grape-growing as well as to wine-making and distribution.

The wine-growing sector extends throughout Italy but with specific territorial differences. Its core lies in Veneto, Tuscany, and Piedmont for quality wines and Emilia-Romagna, Veneto, and Apulia for mass consumption wines, even if also other regions produce wine grapes. It is mainly composed of small family farms, growing a large number of varieties and with a large number of PDO and GI wines.

The wine-making sector, too, comprises a variety of operators with different specializations and different relations for grape procurement, defining two integrated supply chains (Agricultural and Cooperative) and two de-integrated ones (Industrial and Bottler), each of which is highly diversified. In the overall system, cooperatives are the most important players, both as leading firms and

---

[14] EU: Reg. 1308/2013, art. 157, 158, 167; Italy: L. 238/2016, art. 41.

as widespread organizations of wine-growers. Historically, the fragmentation and the small size of wine-growers rendered them subject to the market power of wholesalers and industrial wine-makers. Cooperatives, supported by a legislation favoring them and by farmers' unions, have been the reaction to that situation, with greater or lesser success depending on many factors, particularly social capital and human capital. Differences in social capital and historical heritage are at the origin of the differences within the cooperative sector, of which the stronger and more market-oriented part is located in the North. Some are leading firms and have succeeded in adding value to the mass production of their members.

Private companies are also among the leading firms, but within this group, firms belong to different supply chains, and their strategies are rather diverse, both as to the orientation to the internal or the export market, and to the market segment and to the production organization.

In this regard, on-farm wine-makers are part of the trend changing the relationships within the industry, that is, the trend toward quality. This has been a consistent trend of the Italian wine industry in recent decades, as shown by the constant increase in the number and share of PDO and PGI wines and, more significantly, by the success in keeping up with the competition of the new producing countries on the export market and in increasing the average export price (Corsi et al. 2004, 2018). On-farm wine-makers have been deeply involved in this trend, and their share of PDO wine production is particularly large. Given the average small farm size, they have had a strong incentive to upgrade the quality and to try to gain larger margins by exploiting the consumption trends to decreasing consumption but to higher-quality wines.

For the largest part of the sector, the differentiation strategies are mainly based on appellations rather than on brands. Brands are important marketing tools in three segments: (i) the value wine segment, mainly occupied by big cooperatives; (ii) the sparkling wine segment, dominated by private companies; and (iii) the quantitatively small but economically important segment of some icon and super-premium wines. Appellations are an important marketing tools especially for the growing sector of on-farm wine-makers striving to enhance the quality of their wines but not big enough to afford marketing strategies of their own. However, they are also largely used by big firms and big cooperatives, and even producers of super-premium and icon wines are generally complying with appellation regulations, since their wines are linked to a particular *terroir*.

The present situation, although so varied, is nevertheless consistently the result of a long process toward vertical integration; and therefore the role of intermediate markets and intermediaries has decreased relatively to the past, though it remains important in some areas. Wineries have a strong incentive to have their own vineyards, since if the majority of the grapes that they use come from their own vineyards, they are classified as agricultural firms, and the fiscal regime in that case is much more favorable. On the other side, farmers have a strong interest in adding value to their products either by controlling the processing directly or through their cooperatives. Within this trend, an obvious selection process is ongoing, since technical and marketing skills are required for the single wine-makers and managing skills are required for the cooperatives. The final outcome is unclear, but it is doubtful that a single organization model will prevail. It seems much more likely that a variety of solutions will survive by exploiting specific assets and skills.

References

Anderson, K., S. Nelgen, and V. Pinilla. 2017. *Global wine markets, 1860 to 2016.* Adelaide: University of Adelaide Press.

Cacchiarelli, L., A. Carbone, M. Esti, T. Laureti, and A. Sorrentino. 2014. Prezzi e qualità del vino: un confronto fra regioni. *AgriRegioniEuropa* 10 (39): 13–18, Dic. 2014.

CIA. 2012. *Siglato l'accordo interprofessionale sul prezzo dell'uva DOC Marsala.* CIA di Trapani. Available at: www.viniesapori.net

Corduas, M., L. Cinquanta, and C. Ievoli. 2013. The importance of wine attributes for purchase decisions: A study of Italian consumers' perception. *Food Quality and Preference* 28: 407–418.

Corsi, A., E. Pomarici, and R. Sardone. 2004. Italy. In *The world's wine markets. Globalization at work*, ed. K. Anderson. Cheltenham: Edward Elgar.

———. 2018. Italy Post–1938. In *Wine globalization: A new comparative history*, ed. Kim Anderson and Vicente Pinilla. Cambridge: Cambridge University Press.

Fait, M. 2010. Brand-landequity nei territori del vino. *Mercati e competitività* (3): 119–140, Milano, Franco Angeli.

Giacomini, C. 2010. "Tavernello" il vino più bevuto nelle famiglie italiane: un caso di successo. *Mercati e competitività* (2): 145–155, Milano: Franco Angeli.

Green, R., Zúñiga M. Rodríguez, and Pinto A. Seabra. 2006. Imprese del vino: un sistema in continua evoluzione. In *Il mercato del vino: tendenze strutturali e strategie dei concorrenti*, ed. G.P. Cesaretti, R. Green, A. Mariani, and E. Pomarici. Milano: Franco Angeli.

———. 2015. Scheda di settore. Settore vino. Aggiornata al 21/10/2015. Ismea, Rome.

————. 2018. Scheda di settore. Settore vino. Aggiornata ad aprile 2018. Ismea, Rome. Available at: http://www.ismeaservizi.it/flex/cm/pages/ServeBLOB.php/L/IT/IDPagina/3525#MenuV

ISMEA, Sezione RETEVINO DOP-IGP. 2018. Ismea, Rome. Available at: http://www.ismeamercati.it/flex/FixedPages/IT/VinoDati.php/L/IT

ISTAT. 2010. 6° Censimento Generale dell'Agricoltura, data warehouse. Available at: http://dati-censimentoagricoltura.istat.it/?lang=it

————. 2013. 9° Censimento dell'Industria e dei Servizi. Roma.

Malorgio, G., C. Grazia, and C. De Rosa. 2011a. Forme organizzative e scelte strategiche per la valorizzazione dei vini a denominazione di origine. *Economia agroalimentare* (1–2): 367–390, Franco Angeli.

Malorgio, G., E. Pomarici, R. Sardone, A. Scardera, and D. Tosco. 2011b. La catena del valore nella filiera vitivinicola. *Agriregionieuropa* (27): 14–19, Dic. 2011.

Mariani, A., and E. Pomarici. 2011. Strategie per il vino italiano. Edizioni Scientifiche Italiane, Napoli.

Mazzarino, S., and A. Corsi. 2015. I flussi dell'uva verso la vinificazione: un'analisi comparata per regioni e macroaree. *Economia agro-alimentare* 20 (1): 29–58.

Mediobanca. 2016. Indagine sul settore vinicolo. Mediobanca, Milano, Aprile 2016. Available at: www.mbres.it/sites/default/files/resources/download_it/Indagine_vini_2016.pdf

————. 2017. Indagine sul settore vinicolo. Mediobanca, Milano, Aprile 2017. Available at: https://www.mbres.it/sites/default/files/resources/download_it/Indagine_vini_2017.pdf

————. 2018. Indagine sul settore vinicolo. Mediobanca, Milano, Aprile 2018. Available at: https://www.mbres.it/sites/default/files/resources/download_it/Indagine_vini_2018.pdf

Osservatorio Economico Vini. 2016. Produzione nazionale di vini spumanti 2015–2016. Available at: http://www.ovse.org/mercati-e-consumi/avvio.cfm?idContent=198

Pomarici, E. 2017. Le grandi imprese del vino italiano: dinamica e peculiarità. *AE Agricoltura/Alimentazione/Economia/Ecologia* (2): 56–69.

QUALIVITA. 2018. Rapporto 2017 ISMEA-QUALIVITA, XV. *I Quaderni Qualivita* 35–39. Available at: www.ismea.it/flex/cm/pages/ServeBLOB.php/L/IT/IDPagina/10226

Sardone, R. 2014. I numeri del vino italiano. *Agriregionieuropa* 10 (39): 9–13.

Zanfi, A. 2009. *Atlante degli spumanti di Italia, vol. Metodo Classico*, Carlo Cambi Editore, 7–35.

————. 2011. *Atlante degli spumanti di Italia, vol. Metodo Italiano*, Carlo Cambi Editore, 20–76.

4

The Spanish Wine Industry

Luis Miguel Albisu, Cristina Escobar, Rafael del Rey, and José María Gil Roig

4.1   The Importance of the Wine Sector in Spain

Worldwide, Spain usually has ranked third among wine producer countries after Italy and France. However, it is the most important country in terms of land allocated to vineyard, accounting for 12.7% of the world's surface (967.000 ha of 7.6 million ha). Furthermore, it has recently become the largest world exporter in volume, with 22.1 million hl in 2017, which represented 20.5% of the world's wine exports (OIV 2018).

———————————————

L. M. Albisu (✉)
CITA, Zaragoza, Spain
e-mail: lmalbisu@cita-aragon.es

C. Escobar
Center for Research in Agro-food Economics and Development UPC-IRTA (CREDA), Castelldefels, Spain
e-mail: cristina.escobar@upc.edu

R. del Rey
Spanish Observatory of Wine Markets (OeMv), Madrid, Spain
e-mail: direccion@oemv.es

J. M. Gil Roig
Technical University of Catalonia, Catalonia, Spain
Center for Research in Agro-food Economics and Development UPC-IRTA (CREDA), Castelldefels, Spain
e-mail: chema.gil@upc.edu

© The Author(s) 2019
A. Alonso Ugaglia et al. (eds.), *The Palgrave Handbook of Wine Industry Economics*,
https://doi.org/10.1007/978-3-319-98633-3_4

The vineyard is a key crop for sustainable development in most territories in Spain. It contributes to the economy, to territorial balance and to landscape maintenance, and offers a product linked to the Spanish history, culture and diet. Moreover, the Spanish wine has significantly contributed to enhance the image of the country abroad (OeMv 2015a). Some regions of Spain could not be understood without the vineyard, such as Castilla-La Mancha, where, for some municipalities, wine and vines have contributed to structure the territory, to create social cohesion and to preserve the environment and the biodiversity (JCCM 2011). Spain produces a wide range of wines, including well-reputed wines that have been able to compete internationally. In fact, there are 91 protected designations of origin (PDOs[1]) and 41 protected geographical indications (PGIs).

The value of wine and must production is not stable, as it depends on the yearly harvest conditions, among other factors. The contribution of wine and must in Spain to the value of total crop production, and to the value of the primary sector as a whole (agriculture, livestock and fish), reached its maximum in 2013—the best year since the last 25 years—due to a very good harvest (MAGRAMA 2015b). The production of wine and must accounted that year for 1868.5 million euros, which represented 7.09% of the total agricultural output and 4.23% of the total primary sector output. For the last ten years (2005–2014), the average weight of wine and must production was of 4.62% and 2.80% from the total agricultural output and the primary sector output, respectively. Moreover, in spite of the traditional volatility, there is an upward trend along the analyzed period.

Grape output volatility has to do mainly with yield variation, but total output shows a positive trend on average, despite reduction of the planting area. As the total area allocated to vineyards has been continuously decreasing over the last decade, increasing production has been due to yield increases as a consequence of the transformation of dry land into irrigated land, the introduction of higher-yielding varieties and other technological and agronomic improvements. In 2015 vineyards accounted for 941,000 of hectares, which means a decrease of 18.9% in the last ten years (Fig. 4.1).

A singular characteristic of the Spanish wine sector used to be that vineyards were located in nonirrigated land; however, recent and large investments have changed that situation. Only 21.6% of the total area was irrigated in 2004. Ten years later, irrigation has been extended to 37.2% of total vineyards,

---

[1] PDO is equivalent to the French term AOC, *Appellation d'origine contrôlée*.

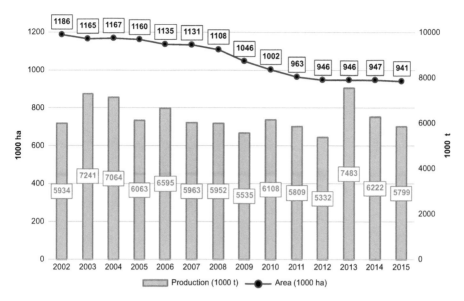

Fig. 4.1 Evolution of the vineyard area and the production of grapes in Spain. (Source: Own elaboration from Agriculture Yearbooks and Agriculture Statistics. MAGRAMA. Spanish Ministry of Agriculture, Food and Environment (MAGRAMA 2016))

with higher percentages in Navarra (61.5%), Balearic Islands (54.3%), La Rioja (50.8%) and Castilla-La Mancha (46.6%) (MAGRAMA 2015a).

The value of grape production, as mentioned, follows the same pattern than the total output, indicating also that prices have been quite stable along the analyzed period. Higher yields are observed in 2013 giving a total production of 7,635,000 of tonnes, while the average harvest (2002–2015) was a little bit higher than 6,200,000 of tonnes (Fig. 4.1).

Spain enjoys a variety of agro-climatic conditions, soil heterogeneity and grape varieties, generating a wide range of different wines. Spanish weather and agronomical conditions make wine grapes able to grow all over the country. However, there are some regions which are more specialized in vineyard (Fig. 4.2):

• La Rioja and the province of Alava (the southern province of the Basque Country). Both are included within the most known and important Spanish wine regions (QDO La Rioja[2]).

---

[2] QDO: Qualified Designation of Origin.

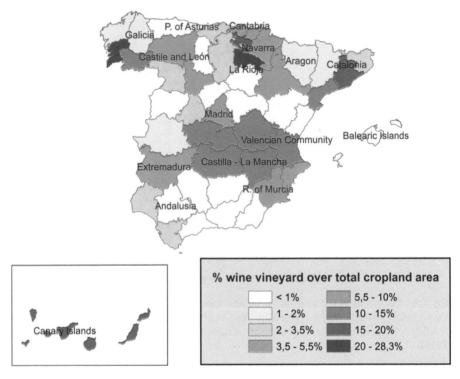

Fig. 4.2 Wine vineyard specialization in Spain (2012). (Source: Own elaboration from the Agriculture Yearbook 2013. MAGRAMA. Spanish Ministry of Agriculture, Food and Environment (MAGRAMA 2015c))

- The southern provinces of Galicia (NW of Spain), which are mainly known for their PDO Rias Baixas and Ribeiro.
- The Canary Islands: They represent a small proportion of the total vineyard in Spain. However, this crop is one of the few that bears their agro-climatic circumstances, and, thus, the region is highly specialized on it.
- The provinces of Barcelona and Tarragona, in Catalonia. They account for more than 90% of the cava (sparkling wine) produced in Spain (PDO cava).
- Some of the provinces of Castilla-La Mancha and southern Extremadura. This big land extension includes 17 PDOs, among them La Mancha and Valdepeñas, two of the largest PDOs in Spain.

The most important region in terms of area of vineyard is Castilla-La Mancha, which gathers 46.6% of the total area in Spain. This is because of its big extension and its high crop specialization. Next, we find Extremadura, Castilla and León and the Valencian Community, with similar percentages over the total (8.7%, 7.8% and 7.5%, respectively). La Rioja and Catalonia rank in the fourth and fifth places, with 5.8% and 4.7% of the surface, respectively (MAGRAMA 2015c).

4.2   Structural Features of the Wine-Growing Sector

4.2.1   Farm Size

Agricultural holdings (AHs) with vineyard in Spain are relatively small with an average utilized agricultural area (UAA) of 6.57 hectares. There is, however, a high heterogeneity among the different regions. Among specialized wine regions, larger holdings are located in Extremadura and Castilla-La Mancha, while the smallest are concentrated in the Canary Islands, Castilla-León and Aragón. In relation to farm size, 39.8% of the holdings have from 1 to less than 5 hectares (accounting for 8.6% of the total vineyard UAA), while 33.6% have from 5 to less than 20 hectares (28.2% of the total vineyard UAA), being the latter the most important segment. Holdings between 20 and less than 50 hectares of UAA (14.1% of the total number of vineyard holdings) represent the second most important segment in terms of surface (26.8% of the vineyard area) followed by the segment with 100 hectares of UAA or more (4.2% on the total holdings) and accounting for 20.5% of vineyard UAA (Agricultural Census 2009, INE).

4.2.2   Land Tenure

The land tenure of the vineyard holdings is primarily the private property, representing 73.2% of their UAA. The rest is basically rented (20.0%), with a small percentage of sharecropping or other systems (6.8%). If we segment vineyard holdings taking into account their total standard output, it can be observed that, in general terms, the smaller the total standard output, the higher the share of land in property. Rented land accounts for over 25% in larger holdings, while sharecropping is relatively more important in intermediate holdings (Farm Structure Survey 2013, INE).

4.2.3   Employment

In 2013, the employment in AHs oriented to viticulture was 57,609 annual working units (AWU), which represented 7.1% of the total employment of the primary sector (812,199 AWU) (INE, Spanish National Statistics Institute, Farm Structure Survey 2013). Apart from direct employment, viticulture generates a significant amount of indirect employment in the food industry and the service sector, which is difficult to quantify (PTV 2012). In 2013, the average AWU per holding was 0.83, very close to the average figure for the whole Spanish agricultural sector which was of 0.84 AWU. The labor force comes mainly from family work, accounting for 61.2% of the total AWU. From this percentage, the head of the holding provides 36.9% of the total AWU, while other family members participate with the remaining 24.3%. Stable workers and temporary workers account for 18.4% and 20.4% of the total AWU, respectively.

4.2.4   Legal Entity

According to the last available Agricultural Census (2009), AHs in Spain are basically owned by natural persons (94.2% of the AH with UAA), not enterprises. The grape-growing sector does not differ significantly from this figure (95.8%). Moreover, this model of family enterprise/farmer manager is quite homogeneous across the different Spanish regions although some slight differences can be observed. Among the most important wine producer regions, in Catalonia and Navarra, the percentage of commercial firms is relatively higher (Farm Structure Survey 2013, INE).

4.2.5   Crop Specialization

Grape production in Spain is mainly used for the production of wine (95.7% of the vineyard holdings allocate grape production to wine). Among these holdings, approximately 50% are registered to produce wine with either a PDO or a PGI indication, even though final sales under a quality indication may depend on the needs of the market. Furthermore, the production of quality wine is concentrated in larger holdings. In fact, the average size of holdings oriented toward quality wines is 8.36 hectares, while it is only 4.64 hectares in the case of holdings producing table wines. In the case of holdings oriented to produce table grapes or raisins, the average surface is 2.30 and 1.26 hectares, respectively (Agricultural Census 2009, INE).

4.2.6   Grape Varieties

In Spain there are 66 grape varieties that are relevant in surface. However, only a few represent a high proportion of the Spanish vineyards (in relative numbers). The most importance grape variety in Spain is Airen, which occupies 22.5% of the surface. Airen is a white grape variety, very abundant in the South Spanish plateau, especially in Castilla-La Mancha (Fig. 4.3). The second most important grape variety is Tempranillo, which occupies 21.4% of the Spanish vineyard. It is a red grape variety extensively grown to produce red full wines. Its origin comes from the Spanish region of La Rioja, being, therefore, the most produced grape within this region. The third position in the ranking, further down in significance from the previous two, is occupied by the grape variety Bobal (6.7%), which has its origin in the Valencian Community. It has been traditionally linked to bulk wine production, although there is a growing interest in this variety to produce quality wines.

Grenache occupies the fourth position with 6.6% of the surface. This Mediterranean variety is one of the most widely planted red wine grape varieties in the world. Its origin is in Aragon but has spread rapidly across other regions. It has a special relevance in the production of red and rosé wines. Monastrell occupies 4.7% of the total surface and has also an important presence worldwide. These five varieties account for 61.9% of the total Spanish vineyard. The remaining 38.1% is shared by a large amount of grape varieties,

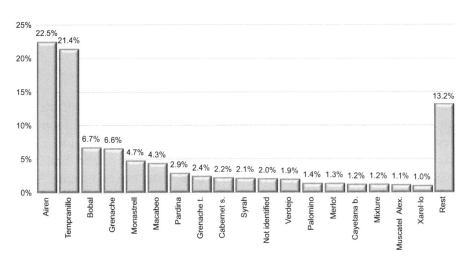

Fig. 4.3 Distribution of the main grape varieties in Spain (% on total surface) (2014). (Source: Own elaboration from the Inventory of wine-growing potential, 2015. MAGRAMA. Spanish Ministry of Agriculture, Food and Environment (MAGRAMA 2015d))

such as Macabeo, Pardina, Grenache tintorera, Cabernet Sauvignon, Syrah, Verdejo, Palomino, Merlot, Cayetana blanca, Muscatel from Alexandria and Xarel·lo as the more relevant.

Since the introduction in 1999 of the "grubbing-up" and "restructuring and conversion of vineyards" measures in the Common Market Organization for wine, grape varieties in Spain have suffered some important changes. Most of the older varieties have experienced a progressive loss of their relative importance during the last 15 years (MAGRAMA 2015d). It is worth noting the significant decrease that was experienced by the grape variety Airen, which has reduced its surface in almost in 100,000 hectares (−30.7%). On the opposite side, among the traditional varieties, only three have increased their surface: Tempranillo (28.8%), Macabeo (10.3%) and Grenache tintorera (7.0%). Foreign varieties have become more relevant, especially Syrah, Chardonnay and Cabernet Sauvignon. Verdejo has received an increasing attention during the last years while the success of Palomino has to do with its resistance to drought, being highly appreciated in the south of Spain and base for the famous Sherry wine.

Spanish vineyards have a considerable age: 41.6% of the vineyard area is more than 40 years old (MAGRAMA 2009). As it is expected, traditional varieties tend to be older than most of the modern varieties. Therefore, Syrah, Cabernet Sauvignon and Merlot are the three youngest grape varieties. As it was mentioned, however, the grape variety Tempranillo, which is a traditional one, remains also planted in recent years, probably due to its prestige and notoriety in the country.

4.2.7   Farm Net Income

Farm Net Income (FNI) is obtained by adding to the total output the balances of the subsidies and taxes (also those related to investments). From this result, the total costs are deducted. Total costs encompass the total intermediate costs (plants, fertilization, crop protection, machinery and buildings' maintenance, energy, etc.), depreciation and the total external factors (rent, interests and wages). In general terms FNI represents the compensation for the use of the owner fix production factors (land, capital and work), plus the business' risk (benefits or losses). Data in this section come from the Farm Account Data Network database (FADN 2018, European Commission). Long trends have to be interpreted with some caution, as there have been some changes both in the sample size and in the methodological framework. In any case, results in Fig. 4.4 provide a good orientation about the economic performance of vineyard holdings.

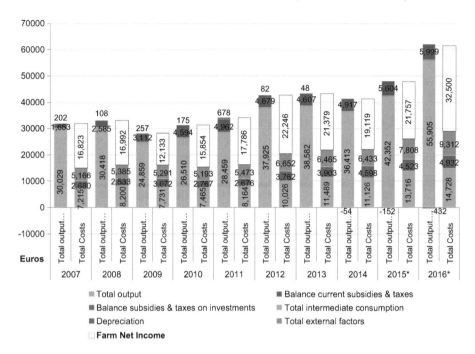

Fig. 4.4 Economic results of the Spanish viticulture holdings (euro). (*[*Preliminary data]* Source: Own elaboration from FADN 2018 (European Commission))

The FNI for viticulture holdings in Spain shows an upward trend from 2007 to 2016, with an average of 19,659€ per holding. The result from 2016 is especially high (32,500€). Conversely, minimum is found in 2009 (12,133€) (Fig. 4.4). The variation on the FNI follows closely the variation on the total output, which mainly comes from revenues from the production of wine and grapes. On the other hand, total costs show a steady rise on the studied years, with a higher rise in 2012 (25.3%). This last rise is experienced in the three main cost types: intermediate consumption, depreciation and total external factors, which raised 22.8%, 40.6% and 21.5%, respectively.[3]

The poor economic performance of grape production is a major challenge to overcome. Low farm revenues may threaten the future sustainability of small farms and provoke an increasing abandonment of vineyards. Low farm prices per kilogram have stimulated grape production in volume to maintain farm income in many Spanish wine regions, generating wine surpluses which, in turn, have push prices down particularly for basic wines. Finally, the increasing international market competition has accentuated this problem, especially in nowadays economic crisis context (PTV 2012).

---

[3] Considering the ten years globally, the total intermediate consumption represents the highest cost, accounting for 49.0% of total costs, followed by external factor costs (31.0%) and depreciation (17.4%).

4.3   Structural Features of the Wine-Making Sector

4.3.1   Plant Size and Size Distribution of Wineries

In 2013, it was reported that there were 4,036 wineries in Spain (down to 4,024 in 2014), which accounted for 14% of the total number of enterprises in the agrifood sector. The average size was small as 84% had less than 10 workers and only 66 of them (1.6% of the total) had more than 50 workers and 9 had more than 200 workers. This structure defines the scope of their commercial activities although things are changing due to the recent crisis. Some years ago the small size of most wineries encouraged them to focus primarily on local markets, where there are strong emotional linkages between producers and consumers; the recent crisis in domestic consumption has forced a great number of companies to look at international markets. According to ICEX's profile of the export wine company (see OeMv 2015c), in 2014 there were 3897 Spanish wineries exporting to international markets. If we compare this figure with total number of wineries reported by the Spanish National Institute of Statistics (INE) (INE 2015), such number would mean that 96.8% of total registered wine companies have some international sales activity.

Actually, this profile of the exporting Spanish wine firm reinforces the idea of many small companies in the wine sector but with a relatively high degree of concentration of sales. As shown in the table, 65.3% of total exporting companies sell less than 50,000€ of wine in international markets, and they account for 1% of the total export value, whereas only 2.4% of total companies (the 93 largest ones) account for more than two thirds of total export value (Table 4.1).

In total, all the wine enterprises occupied 23,743 persons, which accounted for 6.7% of the total employment in the agrifood sector. However, that is the direct employment as many more people were employed in other related enterprises. Again, despite the existence of a large number of firms, there is quite a big concentration of total sales among a small number of wineries. It is estimated that five enterprises cover more than a quarter of the total sales in the Spanish market and that the largest eight wineries in Spain—the only selling above 100 million euro—account for almost half of total sales (Castillo 2015a). Some cooperatives are large, and they collect their grapes from their cooperative members close to where their elaboration plants are. In the case of the most common small cooperatives, the grape production area is in the village or nearby villages. The top 25 wineries in Spain are listed on Table 4.2.

Table 4.1 Profile of the Spanish wine-exporting company in 2017

Company's export value	Number of firms	Exports (1000 €)	Percentage of firms	Percentage of exports
<5.000 €	1,364	1,822	33.5	0.1
From 5.000 to 25.000 €	846	11,062	20.8	0.4
From 25.000 to 50.000 €	366	13,227	9.0	0.5
From 50.000 to 500.000 €	953	168,073	23.4	5.8
From 500.000 to 5 mill €	439	671,451	10.8	23.0
From 5 mill to 50 mill €	102	1,376,136	2.5	47.1
>50 mill €	6	680,911	0.1	23.3
Total	4,076	2,922,680,0	100.0	100.0

Source: OeMv (2018) with data from Instituto Español de Comercio Exterior (ICEX)

In 2014, four companies stand out with more than 200 million euros in sales. These companies are the Freixenet Group, J. García Carrión, Félix Solís Avantis and the Codorníu Group. Spain is a country with a large vineyard area which is widespread all over the country although the cultivation intensity is different among regions. The top wineries by volume are located in the areas where the production is the greatest such as Castilla-La Mancha (large cooperatives and the firms Félix Solís, García Carrión and others) or nearby regions. There is not far distant grape transportation in the country. However, there are some commercial flows among wineries for cheap wines or to reinforce shortcoming due to climatological effects, varietal compositions to reach wine balances and price differentials.

On the other hand, some medium to large wineries are fully related to quality wines and are located in the most famous PDOs. Their margin is usually greater than the one for larger-volume wineries. However, during the last 20 years, there has been a wide distribution of companies of all sizes in different regions in order to produce different wines. The largest ones have had a tendency to invest in well-known PDOs in order to improve their margins and provide higher-quality wines. Medium and even some small companies traditionally linked to famous wine regions have also invested in other PDOs or non-PDO areas to elaborate different wines (e.g. whites or sparkling) as well as to elaborate products at lower cost. A special case should be considered for cava wines, mostly located in the Catalonian region and concentrated around two big firms (Freixenet Group and Codorníu Group), who have also entered into the production of other types of wines in several Spanish PDOs.

Table 4.2 Top 25 wineries in Spain according their sales in 2014 (million Euros)

	Company name	Sales 2014 (million Euros)
1.	Grupo Freixenet	535.0[a,b]
2.	J. García Carrión, S.A. (wines)	334.4
3.	Félix Solís Avantis, S.A.	253.0
4.	Grupo Codorníu	218.0[a,c]
5.	Grupo Miguel Torres	182.4
6.	United Wineries Iberia, S.A. (Gr. Arco)	160.0[a]
7.	Grupo González Byass (wines)	150.0[a,d]
8.	Pernod Ricard Winemakers Spain	120.0[a,c]
9.	Grupo Barón de Ley	86.9
10.	Grupo Faustino	80.0[a]
11.	Cia. Vin. Norte España, S.A. (CVNE)	77.6[e]
12.	Grupo Marqués de Riscal, S.A.	55.0[a]
13.	Grupo Vivanco	50.0
14.	Grupo Osborne (wines)	50.0[a,f]
15.	Grupo Vinos & Bodegas	47.5
16.	Reserva de la Tierra S.L.	47.5
17.	Grupo Hijos de Antonio Barceló	45.0[a]
18.	Juan Ramón Lozano, S.A.	43.4
19.	Grupo Bodegas Gallegas	42.0
20.	López Morenas, S.L. (wines)	40.0
21.	Cherubino Valsangiacomo, S.A.	40.0[a]
22.	Bodegas Ontañón, S.A.	39.9[c]
23.	Vicente Gandía Pla, S.A.	36.0
24.	Grupo Bodegas Muriel	35.0
25.	Viñedos de Aldeanueva, S.Coop.	34.5

Source: Castillo (2015a)

Notes: [a]Authors' estimation; [b]Closing date of the balance sheet in April 2014 and 2015, respectively; [c]Closing date of the balance sheet in June 2013 and 2014, respectively; [d]Closing date of the balance sheet in August 2013 and 2014, respectively; [e]Closing date of the balance sheet in March 2014 and 2015, respectively; and [f]Closing date of the balance sheet in January 2014 and 2015, respectively

4.3.2   Types of Wine-Making Firms

According to Langreo and Castillo (2013), wine-making firms can be differentiated by the degree of vertical integration between grape-growing and wine-making processes. Thus, the main types are:

- Firms that produce their own grapes, elaborate their wine and, after aging, bottle it. They are mostly small and medium firms that sell high-quality wines with prices above average.
- Cooperatives that gather grapes from their members and produce bulk or bottled wines. These enterprises account for around 60% of total wine production, although a smaller portion of sales.

– Wine firms that buy grapes and elaborate wine which is sold on bulk or bottled. They operate with contractual arrangements. Some of them mix with their own grapes as well.
– Wine firms that occasionally buy wine, mature it and bottle it. They can mix with their own wine depending on their business strategies.

There are wine-making firms that have intermediate situations and cannot be located in any of those groups. Altogether it can be said that, in a country with large wine production, and with wineries located in many different regions, all sort of wine-making firms can be found. It is also necessary to point out that cooperatives and private firms have usually different approaches due to their entrepreneurial circumstances. Generally speaking, cooperatives concentrate their efforts on volume, whereas many private firms are small. It does not mean that the opposite can also be found.

4.3.3   Types of Products

Spain has all sorts of wines (whites, reds and rosés) and many other kinds like cavas (sparkling), fortified wines and wines with low alcohol content. Reds are the most important corresponding to the traditional taste of the Spanish consumer, which exist in many different regions.

Quality wines have been commonly identified with designation of origin (PDO) wines, and top wineries are usually located in one or several of the PDOs. This means that Spanish consumers relate quality wines to those coming from PDOs, although perceptions vary for each one of them. Some PDOs have limited or local markets, whereas others sell a great part of their production in international markets.

QDO Rioja stands above all of them, and it has been able not only to have a wide distribution in the Spanish market but to achieve leadership in many geographical areas. Its system of young, "crianza" and "reserva" wines has been widely used by many other wineries all over Spain. The main difference is the amount of time needed to age wines and to follow certain technical specifications. Nowadays, international markets are not so prone to accept those categories, and they specify their own conditions, which creates some tensions among members of the PDO regulatory councils.

4.3.4   Marketing Strategies

Although changing very quickly in recent times, traditionally Spanish wineries have not been so concerned about marketing, and they have concentrated their efforts on producing grapes and wines of good technical quality. They have had an understanding that mainly technical measurable parameters are essential to reach quality wines. There is a great amount of brands in the market, estimated in more than 25,000. Distribution brands account for more than a third of total sales, and the first entrepreneurial group covers 16.8% of total sales, and the second only reaches 5.2%, which is another sign of the limited impact of big wineries and the spread of wine businesses in this country (Castillo 2015a).

Although a vast majority of companies have recently experienced some exposure to international markets, most of the smaller ones primarily reach local markets where either their brands or the PDOs in which they are located support their market penetration. Mid to large wineries have totally different approaches looking for national and international distribution. Some of their brands do not have much strength, and they rely either on PDO brands or on country recognition. Most recent marketing trends, however, are pushing wineries to heavily invest in recognized brands, which only since 2013 are allowed to identify wines from different regions. In Europe PDOs have certain impact especially for the most important ones but faraway countries, like the United States and China, rely more on the image of the country of origin. Unfortunately, most Spanish wines reach low-segment prices, and therefore their image is low. In the last decade, there has been a great increase of wine volume exports, but growth in terms of value has been slower.

4.4   The Distribution

Sales of Spanish wine—in volume—have been increasing for a long while and keep on growing in a continuous upward trend (Fig. 4.5). However, if we divide the total wine market into domestic and international markets, we can observe that there is a clear difference between them: while the export market keeps growing continuously, even showing a more pronounced boost in recent years, the domestic market, conversely, recedes in a continuous slope down. The continuous drop of the domestic market—which is of a great concern— has pushed the wine sector to a deeper internationalization, also encouraged by the increase in production. From 2003, the volume of exports has surpassed the domestic consumption reaching a new maximum every year since then. Fortunately for the wine sector, the exports growth rate has generated a positive upward trend in the Spanish wine market as a whole. Nevertheless, these major trends are recently changing. Since the end of the economic crisis in 2015, the domestic market experiences certain recovery after years in which

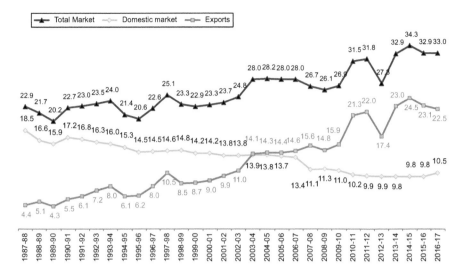

Fig. 4.5 The Spanish market for wine (million liters). (Source: OeMv (2018) (Spanish acronym for Spanish Observatory of Wine Markets))

the downfall was stabilized. At the same time, the strong need for urgent international markets to sell excessive production is now less dramatic. Although still very dependent on the size of the harvest, international sales of Spanish wines do not seem to grow much more in liters while showing certain signs of improvement in value terms.

Wine consumption in Spain, as in other traditional producing countries, has been steadily declining. This downfall of consumption is mainly related to a cultural change of habits, partly associated with the behavior of younger generations showing a greater detachment from wine and its culture. Traditionally, wine consumption used to be a daily routine (for lunch or dinner at home). However, over the last 20 years, there has been a progressive substitution of wine by other drinks such as beer and nonalcoholic drinks. Nowadays, the consumption of wine has become more sporadic, linked to more special meals (with friends, business, etc.) and more focused on higher-quality wines. In fact, the consumption of quality wine has increased, but it has not compensated the decrease of non-PDO wines, as it will be shown later.

On the other hand, in other traditionally non-producing countries, wine consumption is growing, and consumers understand it differently than in the Mediterranean producing countries (Albisu and Zeballos 2014). Therefore, it would be helpful to fully understand why some of the formulas used in non-producing countries are not working in Spain and, conversely, which formulas should be used in Spain in order to reverse this trend or, at last, to stabilize current figures. Some hints could be to dissociate wine and food consumption, make wine consumption an easy practice—not too sophisticated—and bring it closer to the youth, among other measures (Albisu and Zeballos 2014).

4.4.1 Spanish Wine Exports

Spanish wine exports have been experiencing a continuous growth both in value and in volume (Fig. 4.6). In 2012 the value of wine exports represented 69.5% of total production. This percentage is higher than that in Chile and Australia (63%), which are known as paradigms of wine-exporting countries in the world. Furthermore, it indicates the determined commitment of the sector to international markets, mainly as a way to counterbalance the already mentioned decrease of domestic consumption which, on the other hand, has been negatively affected by the economic crisis since 2010 (Compés et al. 2014). In 2014 the difference in volume between production and domestic consumption reached 28.2 million hectoliters, which became the largest world difference, above the 24.3 million of Italy, and second largest in relative terms (72.4% of production) just behind Chile's 74.1% (OeMv 2015b). This desperate need to export in Spain counterbalances also the decrease in wine distillation due to changes in the European legislation, which used to be very important for Spain.

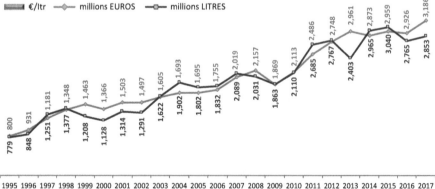

Fig. 4.6 Spanish wine exports. (Source: OeMv (2018) (Spanish acronym for Spanish Observatory of Wine Markets))

Table 4.3 Spanish wine exports by type of wine in 2017

	Value (million Euros)	Value (%)	Volume (million l)	Volume (%)	€/l
Bottled wine	1713.0	58.6%	803.0	34.1%	2.13
PDO	1268.3	43.4%	369.3	15.7%	3.43
Others	444.7	15.2%	433.7	18.4%	1.03
Bulk	588.0	20.1%	1263.9	53.6%	0.47
Sparkling wine	458.7	15.7%	181.9	7.7%	2.52
Vermouth and semi- sparkling wines	98.1	3.4%	91.0	3.9%	1.08
Fortified wines	64.8	2.2%	17.5	0.7%	3.70
Total wines	2922.7	100.0%	2357.2	100.0%	1.24

Source: OeMv (2018) (Spanish acronym for Spanish Observatory of Wine Markets)

The positive trend of the Spanish wine exports can be associated to the competitive prices, which have been quite stable during the last decade with the only exception of 2013, when prices increased because of a harvest shortage on the previous year. Spain has become the most competitive wine exporter in the world, especially in relation to non-PDO bulk wine at very low prices. In 2017, bulk wine prices were as low as 0.47 €/l, after growing due to a new relatively short crop that year. Therefore, exports of bulk wines account for 53.6% of the volume exported while only contributing to 20.1% of the total export value (Table 4.3). On the opposite side, bottled wines[4] including those commercialized in bricks account up to 58.6% of the value of the Spanish export although only represent 34.1% of the total volume.

This situation has generated some controversy among some stakeholders who have questioned if this was the best strategy for the Spanish wine sector (Del Rey 2015; de la Serna 2013; among others), encouraging a better market positioning to achieve higher export prices. In this context, there is a generalized idea that Spain has to progressively move away from exporting "unspecialized bulk wine" to varietal higher-priced bulk wines and increase exports of branded and bottled wines to final international consumers.

However, the current situation has to be understood within a historical perspective. Spain has had a long tradition in exporting wines which goes back to the eighteenth century with the Jerez/Sherry wines (Maldonado 1999) and even to the Roman and Phoenician times. More recently, exports of Spanish wines recovered after the establishment of many good wine professionals in the North of the country, while phylloxera attacked French vines.

It was during the second half of the nineteenth century and the early twentieth century when the production of quality wines started to attract attention, mainly focused in La Rioja (red wines) and Penedès (sparkling wines).

---

[4] Bottled wines refer to wines sold in containers of up to a maximum of two liters.

However, most of the domestic population continued to demand table wines. By the 1970s and the 1980s, significant changes took place in consumption and export patterns in Spain. In fact, the international demand for bulk wines had a first increase until the 1970s, which also can explain the delay in the adoption of a generalized new strategy of producing quality wines (Fernández and Pinilla 2014) and anticipated the larger growth experienced by exports of this type of wine in the twenty-first century.

More quality wines were produced and started to be exported worldwide, from the most famous regions. Companies started to grow, driven by a higher demand, to face new challenges. While domestic consumption in all producing countries including Spain started to decrease sharply, wine began to be a popular beverage in non-producing markets, pushed by new research and comments on its health properties and the lifestyle it represents. Initially, France and Italy were the best-placed producers to take advantage of these new trends, but Spain has followed quickly.

Nowadays, when the Spanish wine sector is characterized by a highly diversified supply, with modern business networks able to innovate (PTV 2012), and when the international reputation of Spanish wine has been widely recognized through the concession of many international awards (Compés et al. 2014), it is of paramount importance to make an effort to communicate the reality of the Spanish wine industry and to reshape the image of Spanish wines among international consumers. It is also the time to make Spanish wines easily available to consumers all around the globe by improving global distribution.

Improving competitiveness is a challenge that requires creating competitive advantages—public and private—that enable companies to increase quality, differentiation and innovation all over the food chain (Compés et al. 2014). At the company level, however, strategies are conditioned by structural and organizational characteristics of the industry. Some of the companies are big enough and keep on growing to improve their commercial efficiency. Many others are small wineries who need to develop joint strategies in order to internationalize their products (PTV 2012).

4.4.2   Wine Distribution Channels in the Domestic Market

As it was mentioned before, the wine domestic market has been shrinking continuously during the last decades although it seems to be more stable in recent years. This reduction has been worsened during the economic crisis since 2008, which, among other effects, has strongly hit the HORECA (HOtels, REstaurants and CAfeterias) sector (Fig. 4.7). According to official figures—not always reliable particularly in this sector—wine consumption in Spain in HORECA decreased by 53.4% between 2006 and 2017 (from 616 to 287 million liters) (OeMv 2018). This is linked to overall decrease of the HORECA business during the economic crisis since 2010. However, the later recovery from the hardest years of economic crisis shows positive change rates for on-trade wine sales in 2016 and 2017. The decrease is also related to cultural and socioeconomic changes, the rise of blood alcohol level controls, the great diversity of wine references and a low product rotation (Castillo 2015b) as well as due to legislation against smoking in public places.

In order to cope with this dramatic downfall, wineries have been working to find other channels that could be a way out for their productions and that would compensate the uninterrupted drop of domestic consumption. Some companies started to increase sales on the off-premise channel to big distributors, which appeared as a challenging shift in their commercial development. But a further search for other channels, especially for small and medium firms previously relying on the HORECA sector, also responds to a strategy of diminishing the strong dependence on big retailers and improving producers' positioning in the food chain (PTV 2012).

Therefore, in the last recent years, there has been an increase of sales that go through non-traditional channels of distribution, such as (1) wineries' direct sales, especially through wine tourism; (2) online sales and E-commerce, sup-

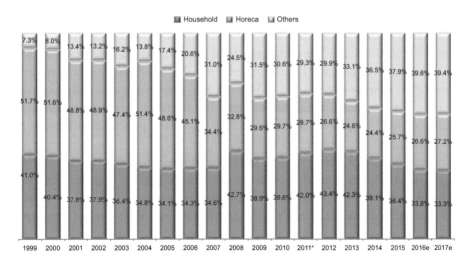

Fig. 4.7 Spanish wine sales structure for the domestic market (%) (e = estimation). (Source: OeMv (Spanish acronym for Spanish Observatory of Wine Markets))

ported by social networking, as sales diversification and direct communication with the consumer; (3) pop-up caterings and (4) the so-called self-consumption or direct distribution to associates mainly in cooperatives. The search for other channels is supposed to grow in the upcoming years (OeMv 2015a; Castillo 2015b).

4.4.3 Household Consumption

The main drinks consumed in Spain are mineral water and soft drinks and soda. Mineral water consumed was 52.36 liters per capita in 2013, followed closely by soft drinks and soda with 45.90 liters per capita. However, both have experienced opposite trends since 2008[5]: while the consumption of mineral water is declining, that of soft drinks has increased. Among the alcoholic drinks, beer is clearly preferred over wine; beer consumption reached 16.54 liters per capita in 2013 (following an upward trend), while the consumption of wine only arrived at 9.23 liters per capita, with a clear declining trend also for consumption at home. Table wines accounted for a higher percentage of this reduction, while the consumption of quality wines has experienced a slight but continuous upper trend (Fig. 4.8).

4.4.4 Place of Purchase

In Spain, wine for consumption at home is mainly purchased in supermarkets and self-service stores. In YoY[6] June 2017, this type of retail outlets accounted for 50.2% of total wine sales. Their relative importance has increased over the last decade. If we add hypermarkets, total share increased up to 64.6%, but their relative importance has decreased since 2005. Discount stores are also important in wine distribution (15.0% in YoY June 2017) although, as in the case of hypermarkets, their market share has decreased. Therefore, the wine sector depends highly on big retailers that push their prices down because of their strong market power (PTV 2012) (Fig. 4.9).

Traditional wine shops occupy the fourth place. This type of retail outlets has also reduced its market share although, since 2012, the negative trend has turned to be slightly positive. It is noteworthy to mention the limited relevance of internet sales although with a significant increase in the last two years.

---

[5] Methodological changes introduced in 2008 would explain a small break on data series.

[6] YoY = year on year.

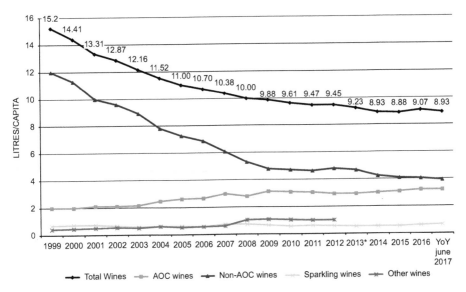

Fig. 4.8 Wine consumption at home in Spain (liters per capita). (Source: Own elaboration from MAPAMA. Spanish Agriculture Ministry. Food Consumption Panel (MAPAMA 2018))

4.5   Relationships Along the Chain

4.5.1   The Role of Different Operators

The structure of the supply chain determines the role of the different operators (Langreo and de Castillo 2013). Thus, there is a direct market from grapes to wines, which account for 15–25% of total production with private firms taking the lead; the cooperatives that have an important role on bulk wines; and the distributors, at wholesale level, which gather wines coming from many small and medium enterprises to sell bottled wines.

Cooperatives look for immediate benefits as they are caught with requests from their members to achieve high prices for their grapes, whereas private companies can have longer perspectives. It does not mean that this behavior always happens because small- and medium-sized firms, which are the most common types, do not have enough capital to face long-term strategic decisions. Family wine firms have also their own difficulties, especially for second and third generations, as it is difficult to meet agreements among many family members.

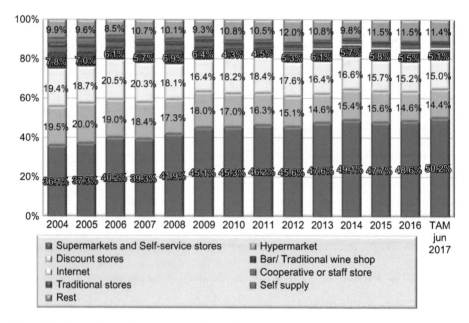

Fig. 4.9 Place of purchase of wine for at-home consumption in Spain (%). (Source: Own elaboration from MAGRAMA. Spanish Agriculture Ministry. Food Consumption Panel (MAGRAMA 2015e))

4.5.2   Contractual Arrangements

Two stages can be differentiated. The first is between wine growers and wine plants to transform grapes into wines. Nowadays, strong links exist among farmers and their cooperatives because they have norms to compulsorily supply all the grapes they produce, which was not the case years ago. The price settlement is open to final results, and they might get a small part a few months after delivering the grapes. However, the final monetary compensation is arranged once the cooperative has received the full amount. This creates difficulties to farmers because the span between delivering the grapes and getting the final compensation could last more than one season.

Unfortunately many cooperatives do not have quality specifications, or they still have too weak requirements. This approach has negative consequences because oenologists are not able to reach the quality standards they would like to have for their wines. On the contrary, there are cooperatives that specify many technical conditions, such as the distinction between grape varieties, grape harvesting period, technical care needed along the season and all sort of technical standards when the grapes reach the wineries.

These different situations depend on the final products cooperatives sell in the market. Thus, cooperatives interested in selling bulk wines at cheap prices to be blended by other distributors are not so interested in requiring strict quality conditions, and they are more concerned on the quantity and the price. On the other extreme, there are cooperatives which sell their wines in more competitive worldwide markets and have to accomplish requirements set by their clients, and consequently they transmit to their farmers all the needed requirements.

Private firms have different arrangements. Some of them have contracts for each season under detailed specifications, but it is becoming more common to establish contracts covering several seasons in order to assure quality and controlled supply to meet market needs in the medium term. This kind of arrangement is the norm for those wineries that want to produce quality wines or/and wineries producing wine in denominations of origin where it is not easy to find a great amount of farmers producing quality grapes, so it is important to establish long-term contracts. Nevertheless, the existence of a myriad of small wineries with their own production areas transforms the entire enterprise in a compact decision-making agent of which grapes and wines to produce.

More recently, the release of a new legislation in August 2013 makes compulsory for private wineries (not for cooperatives) to establish written contracts with their suppliers and make payments within a 30-day period after delivery of grapes.

4.5.3   Leadership Along the Chain

Retailers, like in many countries, take the leadership along the chain. Three features reinforce their role in Spain: (1) the excess supply existing in the market, (2) the need of many wineries to find a place on the shelves to sell their wines and (3) the small size of most of the wineries. Specialized or gourmet shops have a determinant role for small wineries as they are for them the most important channel of distribution. Internet has not yet reached selling significance, but it is the most important information channel for both the national and foreign markets.

PDOs take the reference lead among consumers, and the diversity of brands is compensated by the leadership that QDO Rioja and to a lesser extent PDO Ribera del Duero have nationwide. Other PDOs are known locally or not so widespread. Very few brands are distributed all over Spain, and some of them do not have a great impact because it is quite common, among wine firms, not to use the same brand in food shops and the HORECA channel of distribution. One of the reasons is the high markup that restaurants apply to their wines and the contrast, on prices, consumers might have when comparing different channels of distribution, which is a cause of continuous misunderstanding.

Only a limited number of large wineries exert their power along the supply chain. They mostly sell cheap wines although they are also entering into the market of high-quality wines in different PDOs. Large cooperatives are taking an important role because large distributors need big suppliers and cooperatives are able to attend their requests especially in export markets. Their transformation from bulk wine sellers to bottled wine sellers has reinforced their role in the supply chain.

4.6   Conclusions

The Spanish wine sector is characterized by its prominent position in the world. It is the most important country in terms of land allocated to vineyard area as well as one of the top wine producer countries, competing in the last years with Italy for the first rank. It is also the largest wine exporter. However, it is generally considered to have cheap wines in the market due to a big, recent, disequilibrium between restructured and more irrigated vineyard supply and lower domestic consumption and distillations. This recent unbalance has pushed large amounts of Spanish wines in bulk, mainly to other and more experienced exporting countries like France, Italy, Portugal and Germany. At the same time, stakeholders are increasingly concerned with the effect that such unbalance may also have in the distribution of low-price bottled wines, which may erode the image of the whole category. On top, the best wines from the most prestigious regions occupy low- to medium-segment prices in international markets expanding the idea of a country with a global supply of low-price and somehow medium-quality wines. However, large investments in reinforced distribution capacity and the expansion of the number of exporting firms, jointly with better knowledge of international markets, may improve the value of Spanish wine exports.

There are vineyards in many regions, but Castilla-La Mancha gathers close to 50% of the total area. It is distinguished by having more than 130 quality geographic indications differentiated by its origin, either PDO or PGI, and the PDO Rioja stands well above the rest, but there are several of them who have increased their quality in the last decade and are making great efforts to reach better positions on international markets.

Water scarcity is one of the main determinants of traditional low and volatile yields which, in turn, generate a lack of homogeneous quality, reducing the competitiveness of the Spanish wines in international markets. To compensate for this shortcoming, some wine trade flows among regions have usually taken place, lowering prices significantly. The recent restructuration of around 300,000 hectares of new plantations (partially financed by the Common Agricultural Policy) has allowed increasing yields generating positive expectations of production increases during the next decade which have already been noticeable in the last years.

Grapes are cultivated in small holdings. To compensate the low competitiveness of the small size of vineyards, the strategies have been focused on creating large cooperatives or producing high-price wines. There are two grapes widespread over the country, which distinguish their wines: Airen for basic white wines and Tempranillo for red wines. However, there are many other local varieties not fully exploited to sell wines in international markets and, so far, only known in local markets.

Despite the fact that the average winery size is also small, their degree of internationalization has increased sharply in recent years due to demand limitations in the Spanish market. The proliferation of brands characterizes the Spanish market, and there are few brands with a real national impact. The largest wineries are not ranked among the top in the world. Private wineries have put more emphasis on bottled wines than cooperatives although some of the latter have placed their brands in the most competitive markets all over the world.

One of the most intriguing questions is why wine consumption has been so low in Spain and how to stop the downward trend. Young people do not consider it a fashionable drink, and beer is more popular. Women have not been incorporated as new consumers, and many efforts should be made to create new products and images. Due to several reasons, consumption at hotels and restaurants, at least until mid-2015, was suffering more than consumption at home. This creates constant market tensions, as supply is continuously increasing, forcing wineries to make efforts to export their wines. However, Spanish wines are poorly positioned in international markets in terms of both price and image. There is a real need to significantly increase investments to reverse this global situation. The good news, though, is that such investments have been made in recent years and may have consequences in the short run.

It is possible to find all sorts of wines, but red wines are prevalent over the rest for bottled wines although the vineyard area for whites is larger. Cavas or sparkling wines have particular significance for their penetration in international markets, and their production is concentrated in Catalonia. Distillation of wines has been decreasing during the last years, whereas must production is on the increasing trend.

Apart from being a very important economic sector, wine is a significant component of the Spanish culture, and the country's landscape cannot be understood without its vineyards. There is no other crop in Spain which is able to represent the huge diversity of the Spanish geography. There are so many different varieties and geographic conditions that there is an extreme diversity of wines not well known not only outside the country but also within Spain. The Spanish wine sector is in a continuous transition from the traditional culture to an opening to new markets. During the last years, considerable efforts have been done to adapt Spanish wines to different consumers' appreciations in international markets but without losing its original identity. The strategy is clear, but the road is long and new investments should be carried out.

References

Albisu, L.M., and G. Zeballos. 2014. Consumo de vino en España: tendencias y comportamiento del consumidor. In *La economía del vino en España y en el mundo*, ed. J.S. Castillo and R. Compés, 99–140. Spain: Cajamar Caja Rural.

Castillo, M. 2015a. *Vino: Buscando atraer a un consumidor global*. Alimarket. November 20. http://www.alimarket.es/noticia/196298/Vinos%2D%2DBuscando-atraer-a-un-consumidor-global. Accessed 20 Nov 15.

———. 2015b. *Lineal de vinos: El consumidor pide calidad*. Alimarket. March 26. http://www.alimarket.es/noticia/179033/Lineal-de-vinos%2D%2DEl-consumidor-pide-calidad. Accessed 22 Sept 15.

Compés, R., C. Montoro, and K. Simón. 2014. Internacionalización, competitividad, diferenciación y estrategias de calidad. In *La economía del vino en España y en el mundo*, ed. J.S. Castillo and R. Compés, 311–350. Spain: Cajamar Caja Rural.

De la Serna, V. 2013. El desafío de Castilla La Mancha. *El Mundo Vino*, October 28.

Del Rey, R. 2015. *Oral communications of the OeMv*. Observatorio Español del Mercado del Vino.

FADN. 2018. Farm Accounting Data Network. European Commission.

Fernández, E., and V. Pinilla. 2014. Historia económica del vino en España (1850–2000). In *La economía del vino en España y en el mundo*, ed. J.S. Castillo and R. Compés, 67–98. Spain: Cajamar Caja Rural.

INE. 2009. Spanish National Statistics Institute. Spanish Agricultural Census.

———. 2013. Spanish National Statistics Institute. Farm Structure Survey.

———. 2015. Directorio Central de Empresas: explotación estadística (DIRCE). http://www.ine.es/jaxi/menu.do?type=pcaxis&path=/t37/p201/&file=inebase. Accessed 21 Sept 15.

JCCM. 2011. Junta de Comunidades de Castilla La Mancha. Department of Agriculture, Environment and Rural Development from Castilla-La Mancha. Estrategia regional del vino y los productos derivados de la uva de Castilla-La Mancha. Horizonte 2020. http://www.castillalamancha.es/sites/default/files/documentos/20120511/portada20e20introduccion203.pdf. Accessed 2 July 2015.

Langreo, A., and J.S. Castillo. 2013. Estructuras, organización y modelos empresariales en el sector. In *La economía del vino en España y en el mundo. Cajamar Caja Rural*, ed. R. Compés and J.S. Castillo, 141–174 Spain.

MAGRAMA. 2009. Spanish Ministry of Agriculture, Food and Environment. Basic Vineyard Survey.

———. 2015a. Spanish Ministry of Agriculture, Food and Environment. Surface and Crop Yields Survey.

———. 2015b. Spanish Ministry of Agriculture, Food and Environment. Economic Accounts of Agriculture.

———. 2015c. Spanish Ministry of Agriculture, Food and Environment. Agriculture Yearbooks and Agriculture Statistics (2002–2014).

———. 2015d. Spanish Ministry of Agriculture, Food and Environment. Inventory of wine-growing potential.

———. 2015e. Spanish Ministry of Agriculture, Food and Environment. Food Consumption Panel.

———. 2016. Spanish Ministry of Agriculture, Food and Environment. Surface and Crop Yields Survey.

Maldonado, J. 1999. La formación del capitalismo en el marco de Jerez. De la vitivinicultura tradicional a la agroindustria vinatera moderna (siglos XVIII y XIX). eds. Huerga y Fierro pp 434.

MAPAMA. 2018. Spanish Ministry of Agriculture and Fishery, Food and Environment. Food Consumption Panel.

OeMv. 2015a. Observatorio Español del Mercado del Vino. Spanish Observatory of Wine Markets.

———. 2015b. Observatorio Español del Mercado del Vino. Spanish Observatory of Wine Markets: Spain seventh largest world wine consumer and 33rd in per capita consumption.

———. 2015c. Observatorio Español del Mercado del Vino. Spanish Observatory of Wine Markets. March 10, 2015: "Según informe de ICEX España Exportación e Inversiones, 3.897 empresas exportaron vino en 2014".

———. 2018. Observatorio Español del Mercado del Vino. Spanish Observatory of Wine Markets.

OIV. 2018. International Organisation of Vine and Wine. Elements de Conjoncture Mondiale. April.

PTV. 2012. *Agenda Estratégica de Innovación*. Plataforma tecnológica del vino. http://www.ptvino.com/phocadownload/general/Agenda_Estrategica_Innovacion_PTV.pdf. Accessed 2 July 15.

5

The US Wine Industry

James T. Lapsley, Julian M. Alston, and Olena Sambucci

5.1   Introduction

Among countries, the United States is the world's fourth largest producer of wine and the largest consumer and importer (Wine Institute 2015a, b; ITC 2017). Consequently, the structure of the US wine industry is of interest, not

The work for this project was partly supported by the University of California Agricultural Issues Center and the National Institute of Food and Agriculture, US Department of Agriculture, under award number 2011-51181-30635 (the *VitisGen* project). The authors are grateful for this support and for excellent research assistance provided by Jarrett Hart. Views expressed are the authors' alone.

J. T. Lapsley (✉)
Department of Viticulture & Enology, University of California, Davis, Davis, CA, USA
University of California Agricultural Issues Center, Davis, CA, USA

J. M. Alston
Department of Agricultural and Resource Economics, University of California, Davis, Davis, CA, USA
Robert Mondavi Institute Center for Wine Economics, University of California, Davis, Davis, CA, USA
Giannini Foundation of Agricultural Economics, Berkeley, CA, USA
e-mail: julian@primal.ucdavis.edu

O. Sambucci
Department of Agricultural and Resource Economics, University of California, Davis, Davis, CA, USA
e-mail: sloan@primal.ucdavis.edu

© The Author(s) 2019
A. Alonso Ugaglia et al. (eds.), *The Palgrave Handbook of Wine Industry Economics*,
https://doi.org/10.1007/978-3-319-98633-3_5

just to Americans but also to wine producers and consumers in many other countries. This chapter describes the salient features of this fascinating industry throughout the marketing chain from the vineyard through to the final consumer from an economics perspective and, where possible, in quantitative terms.

The first main section (Sect. 5.2) describes the winegrape-producing industry—which is predominantly located in California and two other West Coast states, Washington and Oregon—in terms of the total number and size distribution of firms, patterns of prices, and production. This section draws heavily on Alston et al. (2015, 2018a, b). Winegrape production is somewhat vertically integrated with winemaking, but many firms specialize at least to some extent in either grape production or wine production, as we document. Section 5.3 documents details of US wine production and consumption, including the significant roles of exports and imports. The winemaking industry is mostly located close to where the grapes are grown, although each of the 50 states claims a wine industry. Details are provided on the total production and the mixture of sizes and types of firms. Next, Sect. 5.4 describes the unique US wine distribution system, from the producer (winery) through to the final consumer, created by the hodgepodge of laws and regulations governing the market as an aftermath of national Prohibition (1920–1933). Section 5.5 concludes the chapter.

5.2   Winegrapes

In 2016, the United States produced 4.4 million tons of grapes crushed for wine, with a farm value of $4.1 billion (Table 5.1), and it has accounted for about 10% of the world's wine volume in recent years (e.g., Wine Institute 2015a). Of the US total winegrape area of some 250,000 hectares in 2016, four states accounted for over 94%: California (CA), 80.3%; Washington (WA), 8.6%; Oregon (OR), 3.8%; New York (NY), 1.9%.[1] Of these, only New York is not on the West Coast. The total value of all US farm production in 2016 was $357 billion from a total of 370.1 million hectares, including $194 billion worth of crops produced using 157.7 million hectares of cropland (USDA/ERS 2018; USDA/NASS 2012b). Hence, the wine industry contributed 1.1% of the total value of farm production value (2.1% of crop value), but it did so using only 0.07% of all land in agriculture (or 0.15% of cropland). Winegrapes are more important in California, accounting for 8.9% of the value of farm production and 2.3% of all land in agriculture (or 6.3% of cropland).

---

[1] Areas of vines and cropland for 2016 in this paragraph are estimated based on areas in 2012, the most recent census for which data are available at the time of writing.

Table 5.1 Characteristics of US wine regions, 2016 data

Region	Crush district	Total acreage	Volume (tons)	Crush price ($/ton)	Value ($ millions)
Napa-Sonoma (NS)	3	59,675	226,442	2590	587
	4	45,339	153,045	4686	717
	Total	**105,014**	**379,487**	**3435**	**1304**
Central Coast (CC)	7	48,128	268,688	1386	372
	8	49,817	224,584	1656	372
	Total	**97,945**	**493,272**	**1509**	**744**
Southern Central Valley (SCV)	13	77,239	1,265,648	306	388
	14	20,980	283,335	298	85
	Total	**98,219**	**1,548,983**	**305**	**472**
Northern Central Valley (NCV)	9	7218	62,690	584	37
	11	74,072	802,122	612	491
	12	31,162	372,947	444	165
	17	22,087	168,592	621	105
	Total	**134,539**	**1,406,351**	**567**	**798**
Other California (OC)	1	17,250	77,951	1542	120
	2	9420	46,528	1684	78
	5	3824	21,281	910	19
	6	6858	30,565	1148	35
	10	7158	21,467	1371	29
	15	684	425	689	0.3
	16	1732	4839	1754	8
	Total	**46,926**	**203,056**	**1434**	**291**
California (CA)		**482,643**	**4,031,149**	**895**	**3609**
Washington (WA)		**52,000**	**270,000**	**1160**	**313**
Oregon (OR)		**23,000**	**67,000**	**2140**	**143**
New York (NY)		**11,684**	**54,000**	**626**	**34**
United States (US)		**569,327**	**4,422,149**	**927**	**4099**

Sources: Appendix Table 5A in Alston et al. (2018a). Created by the authors using data from USDA/NASS (2016a, b, 2017, 2018)

Notes: Average weighted prices per ton in California are calculated using total tons crushed, by crush district. Acreage of winegrapes in NY was calculated by applying volume of winegrapes as a percentage of total volume to total grape acreage, as data on winegrape acreage were not available

5.2.1   Production Regions and Varieties Grown

California differs from the other major producing states, and itself contains several distinct wine production regions that differ in terms of their terrain, climate, soil types, mixture of varieties grown, and quality of grapes and wines produced. Data on production and prices of winegrapes in California are available in some cases by county (of which there are 58, not all of which grow winegrapes) and in others by crush district (of which there are 17). Some crush districts contain several counties or parts of counties. Alston et al. (2015) organized these data into five regions, defined such that each county fits entirely into one of the five regions. Treating each of the other significant wine-producing states (i.e., WA, OR, and NY) as a region, we have eight primary US wine-producing regions comprising these three plus the five in California.

Table 5.1 includes some detail on the salient features of the eight main US wine-producing regions we have identified as they stood in 2016. Several distinct patterns are apparent in this table, as illustrated in Fig. 5.1. First, California dominates the national total area, volume, and value of wine production. Second, the regional shares differ significantly among measures of area, volume, and value of production. In particular, the Southern Central Valley has a much larger share of volume compared with area and especially value of production, while the Napa-Sonoma region has a much smaller share of volume compared with area and value of production. These patterns reflect the relatively high yield per acre (and correspondingly low price per ton) of grapes from the Southern Central Valley and the conversely low yield and high price per ton in Napa-Sonoma. In 2016 in Napa County the average yield was 3.5 tons/acre and the average crush price was $4686/ton, about 15 times the average crush price in the Southern Central Valley where the average yield was 15.8 tons/acre. The other regions were distributed between these extremes with higher yields being generally associated with lower prices per ton.

Within the United States, in 2016 five varieties (Chardonnay, Cabernet Sauvignon, Merlot, Pinot Noir, and Zinfandel) accounted for over 50% of the total volume and 60% of the total value of production from the five states included in Table 5.1. As discussed in detail by Alston et al. (2015), these five varieties predominate in several of the main production regions—in particular in the premium price regions within California, as well as in Washington and Oregon—but the emphasis varies among the premium price regions and some regions are quite different. In particular, the hot Southern Central Valley (dominated by French Colombard and Rubired used to produce grape juice concentrate as well as bulk wine) and New York (dominated by non-*vinifera* American varieties, Concord and Niagara) are quite unlike the other regions climatically and in terms of their grape varietal mix.

Chardonnay is the most important variety in terms of total bearing area nationally and is highly ranked throughout the premium regions, but the

Area by Region

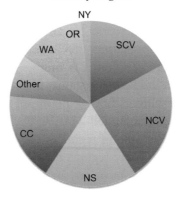

Volume by Region

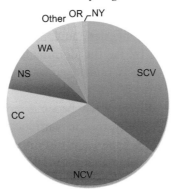

Production Value by Region

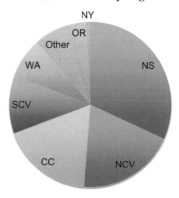

Fig. 5.1 US wine regions—area, volume, and value of production, 2016. (Source: Created by the authors using data from USDA/NASS 2016a, 2016b, 2017, 2018)

Napa-Sonoma region is especially known for its Cabernet Sauvignon, which is its most important variety and increasingly so, and likewise in Washington. The cooler coastal regions—in particular Oregon and the Central Coast of California—are relatively specialized in Chardonnay and Pinot Noir and other cool climate varieties. Zinfandel is more significant in the Northern Central Valley and other mid-price regions, and these patterns reflect this variety's dual roles in serving as both a premium red varietal wine and as lower-priced "blush" (white zinfandel) wine.

Prices vary systematically among regions—the Napa-Sonoma region has generally higher prices than other regions for all varieties, and the Southern Central Valley has generally lower prices. In addition, prices vary systematically among varieties—among the higher-quality (higher-priced) varieties grown in significant quantity, Cabernet Sauvignon generally is ranked higher than Chardonnay, and Zinfandel generally is ranked lower. But the sizes of the premia, and even the rankings of varieties, vary among regions. For example, Pinot Noir ranks above Cabernet Sauvignon almost everywhere, but not in Oregon where Pinot is by far the dominant variety, nor in the Napa-Sonoma region; Chardonnay is ranked above Cabernet Sauvignon in the Central Coast region.

Because grape-growing location has become recognized as an important element of perceived wine quality, the vineyard location is often identified on the wine label. Prior to 1983, wineries could only use geopolitical locations, such as counties or towns, on labels. In 1983 the Federal Government responded to industry desire to place more precise vineyard locations on wine labels by creating a new type of location, the so-called American Viticultural Areas (AVAs—see US Treasury/TTB 2013). AVAs are defined geographic areas that may be quite large and cross state or county lines, or may be quite small and lie within a county or, in some cases, another AVA. The Napa Valley AVA is, for instance, a large AVA located within Napa County. The Oakville AVA is a much smaller AVA that is located within the Napa Valley AVA. In contrast, the Carneros AVA is a defined AVA in the southern portion of Napa and Sonoma Counties. Today, wineries may identify the grapes used in a wine as coming from an AVA if 85% of the grapes were grown in the AVA.

5.2.2   Size Distribution and Nature of Firms

Equivalent data are not available for every state, but some detailed data on the size distribution and nature of grape-producing firms are available for California, which accounts for four-fifths of US winegrape production

Table 5.2 California: total grape area and number of grape-producing farms, 2012

Geographic area	Total grape area		
	Farms	Acres	Acres/farm
Napa-Sonoma	3148	113,128	35.9
Central Coast	1286	131,448	102.2
Southern Central Valley	3141	463,380	147.5
Northern Central Valley	1489	176,826	118.8
Other CA	2398	54,819	22.9
California State Total	11,462	940,177	82.0

Source: Table 2 in Alston et al. (2018a). Created by the authors using data from USDA/NASS (2012a)

(Table 5.2). In 2012, California had 11,462 farms that grew grapes. The total area (including nonbearing vines) was 940,177 acres planted to grapes, an average of 82 acres per farm. These statewide average figures mask some variation among regions, and they also include grapes intended for grape juice, table grapes, and (dried) raisin production—all in the Southern Central Valley. Of the total of 463,380 acres of vines in the Southern Central Valley, an estimated 128,449 acres would have been devoted to wine production.[2] In the Central Valley—with its higher yields and lower prices per ton—winegrape production generally is conducted at a larger scale compared with the Coastal regions, especially Napa-Sonoma, with an average of 36 acres of winegrapes per producer. Not surprisingly, growers in California's Central Valley have mechanized, adopting mechanical pruning and harvesting at a higher rate than coastal growers, who generally continue to rely on hand labor for many operations. Over 80% of California's winegrapes are harvested by machine. Machine pruning is less widely adopted (Dokoozlian 2013).

Table 5.3 contains more information on the size distribution of grape producers in terms of area planted to grapes—again, including all end uses of grapes, not just wine. As is typical of farm-size distributions, this distribution is heavily skewed to the right. The vast majority of grape producers have relatively small vineyards and, while the average area is 80 acres of vines, the median is closer to 15 acres. Reflecting this skewedness, the roughly 50% of growers who had less than 15 acres of vines collectively accounted for less than 2% of the total vineyard area, while the 89 (less than 1%) growers who had 1500 acres or more were responsible for almost 30% of the total area. More than half the total vineyard area is on farms with 500 or more acres of vine-

---

[2] The percentage of winegrape acreage for the Southern Central Valley region in 2012 was estimated using the California acreage report (USDA/NASS 2012d) and applied to the total acreage for 2012 from Table 2 in Alston et al. (2018a).

Table 5.3 California: size distribution of grape producers, 2012

Size range	Total bearing and nonbearing vines		Cumulative total	
	Farms	Acres	Acres	%
0.1–0.9 acres	1357	450	450	0.05
1.0–4.9 acres	2509	5525	5525	0.59
5.0–14.9 acres	2165	18,345	18,345	1.95
15.0–24.9 acres	1374	25,673	25,673	2.73
25.0–49.9 acres	1340	47,004	47,004	5.00
50.0–99.9 acres	1094	75,613	75,613	8.04
100.0–249.9 acres	907	139,156	139,156	14.80
250.0–499.9 acres	359	123,336	123,336	13.12
500.0–749.9 acres	122	74,500	74,500	7.92
750.0–999.9 acres	71	60,783	60,783	6.47
1000.0–1499.9 acres	75	91,412	91,412	9.72
1500.0 acres or more	89	278,382	278,382	29.61
All Farms	11,462	940,177	940,179	100.00

Source: Table 3 in Alston et al. (2018a). Created by the authors using data from USDA/NASS (2012c)

yard. Of course, and as noted above, these distributional figures for the state-wide industry as a whole will not be equally representative of all segments. In particular very large vineyards are much more likely to be found in the Central Valley than in the premium coastal valleys where land values are very much higher.

California includes a diverse mixture of production models. A vineyard may be vertically integrated with a winery, in a single enterprise, or the two enterprises may be entirely separate. In some cases a winery may crush and bottle only estate-grown fruit while, next door, a vineyard sells all its production to a winery somewhere else. Because grape growing and wine production are often separate businesses in California, most wineries contract with grape growers. Goodhue et al. (2003) reported that 90% of California growers sold grapes under contract and that 10% of contracts were pre-planting contracts in which the winery contracted to purchase grapes from a not-yet-established vineyard. Production models vary from region to region within California, and Table 5.4 provides details, district by district, of the balance between purchased, custom crush, and own tons crushed by wineries. For the state as a whole, only 15% of tons crushed were own-grown, the vast majority were purchased. This pattern was even more pronounced in the Southern Central Valley where only 5% of the crush was own fruit. In the premium coastal regions, the share of own-grown fruit was closer to 40% of the total crush.

Some wineries may have a cellar door from which they sell at retail whereas others may leave the retailing to others. Reflecting this diversity, California has an active market for winegrapes—whether under contract or for spot sales—as well as markets for bulk wine and bottled wine. Particular sizes of vineyards— depending on the location and market segment to be served—are more or less appropriate for these different business models. Some wine businesses in California are engaged in every aspect, growing grapes, making wine, offering custom crush and winemaking services, importing and exporting bulk or premium wine, and providing cellar door experiences at boutique winery estates.

5.3   Wine Production and Consumption

The quantity of wine consumed in the United States has increased every year for the past 20 years, almost doubling from 464 million gallons in 1995 to 949 million gallons in 2016 (Wine Institute 2018). This expansion is a result of both population growth and an increasing rate of adult per capita con-

Table 5.4 Characteristics of California winegrapes crushed, 2016

Region	Crush district	Total tons crushed	Tons purchased	Custom crush	Own tons crushed	Own tons/ total tons crushed
Napa-Sonoma	3	226,442	144,846	1618	79,979	0.35
(NS)	4	153,045	89,402	3190	60,453	0.40
	Total	**379,487**	**234,248**	**4807**	**140,432**	**0.37**
Central Coast	7	268,688	172,141	787	95,760	0.36
(CC)	8	224,584	158,251	10,011	56,322	0.25
	Total	**493,272**	**330,392**	**10,798**	**152,082**	**0.31**
Southern	14	283,335	268,317	59	14,959	0.05
Central	13	1,265,648	1,210,224	213	55,211	0.04
Valley (SCV)	**Total**	**1,548,983**	**1,478,541**	**273**	**70,170**	**0.05**
Northern	9	62,690	35,429	1037	26,224	0.42
Central	11	802,122	729,455	3314	69,353	0.09
Valley (NCV)	12	372,947	274,361	1096	97,490	0.26
	17	168,592	148,460	991	19,141	0.11
	Total	**1,406,351**	**1,187,705**	**6438**	**212,208**	**0.15**
Other	10	21,467	14,714	447	6306	0.29
California	15	425	152	110	164	0.38
(OC)	16	4839	2145	221	2473	0.51
	1	77,951	53,736	9627	14,588	0.19
	2	46,528	33,919	3660	8949	0.19
	5	21,281	18,077	587	2617	0.12
	6	30,565	20,359	960	9246	0.30
	Total	**203,056**	**143,102**	15,612	**44,342**	**0.22**
California (CA)		**4,031,149**	**3,373,988**	**37,928**	**619,233**	**0.15**

Source: Created by the authors using data from USDA/NASS (2016a)

sumption. Both trends are expected to continue and the volume of US wine consumption is predicted to increase by 50% by 2030 from a 2010 base (Lapsley 2010). US growth trends stand in marked contrast to declines in volume of wine consumed in France, Italy, and Spain (OIV 2015). It is no surprise that many suppliers, both domestic and foreign, are focused on the US market.

5.3.1   Domestic Production and Consumption

In the United States, wine is defined as the product of the fermentation of fruits, predominantly grape, into an alcoholic beverage. Because alcohol is taxed in the United States, wine production is regulated at the Federal level by a bureau of the Department of the Treasury, the Alcohol and Tobacco Tax and Trade Bureau, generally known by its last three initials as the "TTB." The TTB licenses alcohol producers, including wineries, receives tax payments from producers and importers, approves wine labels, and publishes monthly and annual production statistics. Wine producers file reports of production and sales and make tax payments to the TTB. The frequency of such reports depends upon the amount of tax liability, but every producer files at least once a year. The information from producers is summarized each month by the TTB, along with an annual report. These reports are available online at http://www.ttb.gov/wine/wine-stats.shtml. Much of the data presented in this section is derived from TTB annual statistics. Wine producers are also licensed by the states in which they operate, and state requirements for production and licensing differ from state to state, a topic that is covered in greater detail in Sect. 5.4.

Wines are taxed at different rates, depending upon wine type, alcohol concentration, and volume of production. Still wines are defined as wines containing less than 0.392 grams of carbon dioxide per 100 milliliters. Still wines with 0.5–16% alcohol by volume pay a Federal tax ranging from $0.07 per gallon for production volumes below 30,000 gallons up to $1.07 per gallon for volumes over 750,000 gallons. Wines with alcohol concentration of 16–21% pay $0.57 per gallon for production below 30,000 gallons and $1.57 per gallon for production over 750,000 gallons. Wines with alcohol concentrations over 21% but under 24% incur a tax of $2.15 per gallon when produced in volumes under 30,000 gallons up to $3.15 per gallon for production over 750,000 gallons. Wines containing carbon dioxide above the limit for still wines are referred to by the TTB as "effervescent" and are grouped into two categories: Artificially carbonated, which pays a tax of between $2.30 and

$3.30 per gallon, and naturally carbonated, which is taxed between $2.40 and $3.40 per gallon (U.S. Treasury/TTB 2016a) depending upon volume produced. These tax rates are for calendar years 2018 and 2019 and may change depending upon Congressional action (or inaction).

The TTB figures for production of still wines include wines made from fruits other than *Vitis vinifera* and from non-*vinifera* grapes. "Wine" produced from apples is called "hard cider" and is taxed between $0.164 and $0.226 cents per gallon depending upon the volume produced. Hard cider is listed separately from other still wines in TTB reports, but non-*vinifera* wine is not reported separately. Although we have no way of knowing the exact volume of non-*vinifera* wines, we do know that wines produced in California are made from *Vitis vinifera* and represent about 85% of all wine produced in the United States.

Still wine accounts for the vast majority of domestically produced and bulk imported wine that is bottled and consumed in the United States, although smaller volumes of other types of wine are produced, and about 10–11% of production is used for distillation. According to 2016 TTB data, over 604 million gallons of still wine were bottled and removed after payment of tax for domestic consumption. This represented 82.6% of the approximately 708 million gallons of domestically bottled wine.[3] Cider accounted for 6.5% of total volume, effervescent wine was 3.9%, flavored wines, such as vermouth, and wine coolers totaled 3.4% and 3.5%, respectively (Fig. 5.2).

In the past decade, the volume of domestically bottled wine (including cider) tax-paid into the US market has increased by almost one-third, from just over 527 million gallons in 2005 to over 700 million gallons in 2016. Cider consumption increased more than eightfold, growing from 4.8 million gallons to 47.5 million gallons. Still wine grew by almost one-third during the same period, while wine cooler volume declined. Table 5.5 shows volumes by type of wine removed tax-paid in 2005 and 2016, and the percentage change. We assume tax-paid bottled wine is intended for the US market because exported wine does not pay Federal tax.

The vast majority of wine produced in the United States is produced in California. In 2016, the TTB reports approximately 806.4 million gallons of still wine produced in the United States, with California responsible for 680.3 million gallons, or 84.3%. New York State, with 27.9 million gallons, and Washington State, with 40.7 million gallons, are second and third

---

[3] The term "removed" here refers to removal of the product from a bonded warehouse, as it enters commerce and, if it is destined for domestic sale, incurs excise tax.

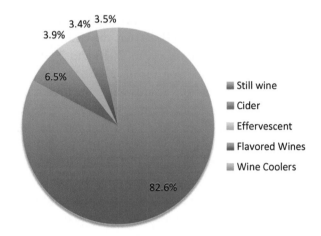

Fig. 5.2 Volume shares (%) of tax-paid, domestically bottled wine, by wine type, 2016. (Source: Created by the authors using data from US Treasury/TTB 2016c)

Table 5.5 Gallons of bottled wine removed tax paid into US market

Wine type	2005	2016	Percentage change
	Millions of gallons		Percent
Still wine	457.2	604.2	32.2
Cider	4.9	47.5	867.3
Effervescent	19.4	28.6	47.4
Flavored wines	15.8	25.0	58.2
Wine coolers	30.3	25.8	−14.9
Total taxable removals	527.6	731.0	38.6

Source: Table 7 in Alston et al. (2018a). Data are from Treasury/TTB (2005, 2016c). Percentage calculations by authors

in production. All of California's and Washington State's wine production is from *V. vinifera* grape varieties, while New York State's production includes fruit wines and wines produced from native grape species and hybrids.

The increase in US demand for wine is reflected in an increase in the number of wineries, which has more than doubled in the past decade. In 2004 there were 4325 wineries in the United States, with 2059 located in California, but by 2014 the number of US wineries had increased to 10,417, with 4285 located in California. Other major states with wineries are Washington State, 989; Oregon State, 580; and New York State, 481. However, every state has a few wineries and produces some wine (U.S. Treasury/TTB 2016b).

Although over 10,000 wineries are operating in the United States, a handful of large wineries dominate production and distribution of wine. Over the past 20 years, the largest US wine producers have become marketers of wine as well as producers, importing bulk wine to be bottled under their own brands, and importing and distributing bottled wines from foreign producers. It is estimated by industry analysts that in 2014, the three largest US wine producers, *E & J Gallo*, *The Wine Group*, and *Constellation Brands*, together produced or imported approximately half of all wine sold in the United States. The top ten producers accounted for over 80% of US sales, and the top 30 are estimated to be responsible for approximately 710 million gallons of the 769 million gallons of wine consumed in 2014, or 92% of sales (Wine Business Monthly 2015; Wine Institute 2018), leaving 59 million gallons to be supplied by the remaining smaller firms. These indicative figures impart a sense of the concentration within the US industry.

Since the TTB does not release production data at the firm level, it is not possible to report precise figures of production volume by wineries. However, given that there were more than 10,000 wine producers in 2014 and having estimated that US total wine consumption, after subtracting sales by the top 30 wine firms, was approximately 59 million gallons (which includes imported bottled wine not sold by the largest firms), it follows that the typical US winery is very small, perhaps producing 5000 gallons of wine. This conclusion is reinforced by an examination of wine production by region within California. Using TTB data of California wine producer and blender permit holders at the end of 2015, we sorted wineries by production region. Then, for each region, we computed its share of California's total grape tonnage in 2016 and its share of the total number of California wineries in 2015. Results are shown in Table 5.6.

As noted in Sect. 5.2, California's Northern and Southern Central Valley vineyards (crush districts 9, 11, 12, 13, 14, and 17) produce approximately 70% of California's winegrapes. However, this productive grape-growing region has only 9% of California's wineries. Central Valley wineries are quite large and efficient, processing almost 3 million tons of grapes in 2016 and producing inexpensive wine retailing at under $8 per bottle, which accounts for a large share of all table wine sales. More than 70% of California's wineries are located in coastal areas (crush districts 1–8); yet, collectively, these areas produced just 26% of all California winegrapes in 2016. For the most part, these coastal wineries, along with wineries in California's Sierra Nevada foothills, are quite small, each producing small quantities of more expensive wines.

Wines consumed in the United States retail at a variety of prices and labels often bear information on varietal content as well as where the grapes used to

Table 5.6 Share of all California wineries (2015) and tons crushed (2016) by region

Region	Crush district	Volume (tons)	Number of licenses (number)	Share of tons crushed (percentage)	Share of licenses (percentage)
Napa-Sonoma	3	226,442	785	5.6	20.3
(NS)	4	153,045	959	3.8	24.7
	Total	**379,487**	**1744**	**9.4**	**45.0**
Central Coast	7	268,688	106	6.7	2.7
(CC)	8	224,584	719	5.6	18.6
	Total	**493,272**	**825**	**12.2**	**21.3**
S. Central Valley	14	283,335	16	7.0	0.4
(SCV)	13	1,265,648	52	31.4	1.3
	Total	**1,548,983**	**68**	**38.4**	**1.7**
N. Central Valley	9	62,690	112	1.6	2.9
(NCV)	11	802,122	141	19.9	3.6
	12	372,947	14	9.3	0.4
	17	168,592	17	4.2	0.4
	Total	**1,406,351**	**284**	**34.9**	**7.3**
Other California	10	21,467	255	0.5	6.6
(OC)	15	425	39	0.0	1.0
	16	4839	224	0.1	5.8
	1	77,951	115	1.9	3.0
	2	46,528	49	1.2	1.3
	5	21,281	24	0.5	0.6
	6	30,565	248	0.8	6.4
	Total	**203,056**	**954**	**5.0**	**24.7**
California (CA)		**4,031,149**	**3875**	**100.0**	**100.0**

Source: Data from USDA/NASS (2016a), US Treasury/TTB (2015). Percentage calculations by authors

produce the wine were grown. Price and varietal information is generally derived from UPC (bar code) labels that are scanned by retailers, who then sell their data to consumer research firms such as IRI or Nielsen, which then collate and clean the data for resale to producers and others. Scanner data represent perhaps 50% of US wine sales by volume and do not include information from major retailers such as Costco or Walmart, or from restaurants and bars, which retail approximately 25% of all alcoholic beverages by volume.

Although scanner data do not represent the entire universe of wine sales in the United States, they do provide information on the US marketplace for wine. In 2014, according to Nielsen data, 70% of all table wine tracked by Nielsen, both domestically produced and imported, sold for under $8 per bottle, while approximately 4.7% retailed at above $15 per bottle (Penn 2015). These numbers differ somewhat from those supplied by industry analyst, Jon Fredrikson, who focuses on California wine sold in the United States. Fredrikson (pers. comm. 2016) estimates that in 2015, 52% of California wine retailed for under $7 and that 15% retailed at above $14 per bottle. The discrepancies are probably the result of comparing different years, different data sources, and the inclusion of imported wine in the Nielsen data.

Wines sold in the United States may bear a varietal designation on the label if 75% or more of the wine was produced from the named grape variety. Nielsen data for table wine sales for the 52 weeks ending in October 2015 show that approximately 85% by value carried a varietal label. Chardonnay, at 19%, and Cabernet Sauvignon, at 16%, were the two most popular varieties, followed by Pinot Grigio, Pinot noir, Merlot, and Sauvignon blanc, which collectively accounted for 28% of the value of table wine sold in the United States. In 2015, red wine represented just over 50% of Nielsen tracked wine sales by value, followed by white wines at 43% of value, and rose or blush wines at 6% (Wine Business Monthly 2016).

5.3.2   Imports and Exports

The United States consumes more wine than it produces, but even though a net importer, the country exports significant quantities of wine: For the past decade approximately 100 million gallons each year, a bit over 10% of its total production in 2016, if distilling material is included. Hence, the United States is a major importer of wine, and for the past decade, approximately one-third of all wine consumed in the United States has been imported. Figure 5.3 shows the volumes and values of imported and exported wine of all types by year.

The share of imported wine in total consumption has increased slightly over the past decade, but the increase in import volume has been primarily in inexpensive bulk wine, rather than in bottled wine. In 2005, US wineries imported 10.3 million gallons of wine in containers larger than 4 liters, a volume that represented approximately 6% of all imported wine. By 2016 bulk wine imports had grown to 70.5 million gallons, accounting for almost 25% of all imported wine volume. During the same period, bottled wine imports increased by 31%, from 176 million gallons in 2005 to 240 million gallons in 2016 (ITC 2017).

The growth in volume of imported bulk wine has become an issue for winegrape growers in California's southern Central Valley. Their concern has centered on a trade policy referred to as "drawback," which allows an importer to recapture up to 99% of taxes paid on imported goods when goods defined as "interchangeable" are exported. In 2003, the US Bureau of Customs and Border Protection allowed drawback on imported wine for the first time and

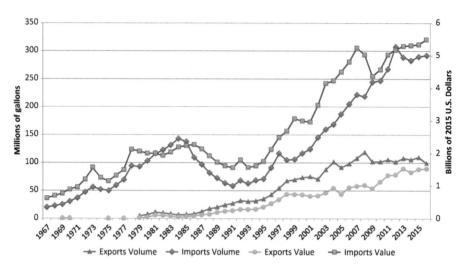

Fig. 5.3 Volume and value of US imports and exports of wine, 1966–2015. (Source: Fig. 5 in Alston et al. (2018a). Data are from ITC (2018). *Notes:* Nominal monetary values in these graphs were deflated by the consumer price index (CPI) for all goods taken from USDL/BLS 2015)

defined interchangeable wine as wine under 14% in alcohol, of the same color, and within 50% of value. Such tax refunds could be as high as $1.60 per gallon for wines imported in large containers from countries without free trade agreements. Since prices of bulk wine imported into the United States have ranged around $3.80 per gallon for the past decade, the incentive is strong and the potential drawback is significant. Some Central Valley grape growers fear that drawback encourages California wineries to import increased quantities of bulk wine, rather than to purchase California grapes. However, Sumner et al. (2012) concluded that when imports exceed exports, the drawback policy encourages exports, which should increase demand for California grapes. Bulk import volumes have exceeded bulk export volumes since 2011.

The United States exports both bottled and bulk wine. While the volume of exports increased by just 8.5%, from 91.0 million gallons in 2005 to 98.7 million gallons in 2016, the value of exported wine increased by over 130%, from $606 million dollars in 2005 to $1.5 billion in 2016. The United Kingdom is the single largest importer of US wine and took 32% of all US wine exports by volume. However, most of the UK import volume is shipped in bulk and at a low price of $11 per gallon. By value, Canada is the most important importer of US wine, buying bottled wine at an average price of over $21 per gallon and receiving more than 18% of US wine exports by volume in 2016. Over the past decade, China has emerged as a major market for US wine, growing from just over 1 million gallons in 2005 to over 6 million gallons in 2016. Most of this is bottled wine at an average price of over $27 per gallon (ITC 2017). Although volume and value of wine exported have increased in the past ten years, it seems that most US producers are focused more on the expanding domestic market than on export opportunities.

5.4   Distribution

In 2018, the United States was the largest national wine market in the world in value and in volume. Yet, despite its name, as a market the United States is hardly "united" and from a wine marketing perspective is better considered as 51 different entities consisting of 50 states and the Federal District of Columbia. As a legacy of the American experiment with Prohibition from 1920 to 1933, each state has the constitutional power to regulate the production, importation, and sales of alcoholic beverages within its borders. This has resulted in significantly different systems of distribution and sales from state to state. For instance, in Utah, the State acts as the sole importer and retailer of alcoholic beverages. In contrast, other states license private importers, wholesalers, and retailers to distribute and make retail sales.

Other differences among states abound. Some states, such as New York, do not allow sales of alcoholic beverages in stores that sell foods. Other states, such as Oregon, allow private licensed distribution of beer and wine but act as distributors of distilled beverages sold in the state. Some states, such as Ohio, require that suppliers post wholesale prices with the state prior to selling to an Ohio distributor. This price posting, along with mandated markups for distributors and retailers, results in no discounting or price competition among retail stores. Other states, such as Colorado, allow only one license per business entity, which precludes chain retailing of alcoholic beverages. Because of these differences among states, wine suppliers, whether domestic producers or importers, must treat each state as a separate sales environment. For this reason, a uniform system of wine marketing and distribution across the United States is essentially impossible for wine producers and importers.

National Prohibition, which prohibited the commercial production, distribution, and sale of alcoholic beverages, was enacted by Congress in 1917 as the 18th Amendment to the US Constitution. As with all Constitutional amendments, after approval by two-thirds of Congress, it required ratification by three-quarters of the states. The 18th Amendment was ratified in January 1919, and Prohibition became effective a year later, on January 16, 1920 (Seff and Cooney 1984). By the late 1920s, many observers believed that national Prohibition was a failure, having led to illegal alcohol sales and the rise of organized crime. However, the overturning of the 18th Amendment required a new Constitutional amendment, which needed both a two-thirds approval by Congress, and ratification by 36 of the then 48 states. At the time, more than 12 states opposed the repeal of Prohibition, which effectively blocked repeal. In 1932, a compromise was reached.

The 21st Amendment was passed by Congress in February 1933 and ratified by the states in December of that year. The political price of the compromise is found in section two of the 21st Amendment which states that "The transportation or importation into any State, Territory, or possession of the United States for delivery or use therein of intoxicating liquors, in violation of the laws thereof, is hereby prohibited." The 21st Amendment thus essentially grants to each individual state the ability to control the sale of alcoholic beverages however it wishes, up to and including the prohibition of sales, although states cannot discriminate between alcoholic beverages produced in state or out of state, as such discrimination violates the "Commerce Clause" of the Constitution.

In 1933, following Repeal of Prohibition, each state had to determine how it would tax and control the production, distribution, and sales of alcoholic beverages. At Repeal, the main concerns for state governments were to collect state alcoholic excise taxes and to encourage "temperance" by controlling who could enter the new marketplace, by regulating the hours and locations of sales, and by separating production and distribution from retailing (Mendelson 2009). Approximately 20 states became what are referred to as "control" states, where the state became the importer and retailer for alcoholic beverages. Today, following a policy change in Pennsylvania in June 2016, Utah remains as the only control state where all wholesaling and retail sales are performed by the state. Most of the other original control states have retained some form of state wholesaling and sales for spirits but now allow wine and beer to be imported, distributed, and sold by companies licensed by the state. The majority of the states at Repeal did not choose the control model but rather created state governmental agencies, often referred to as Alcoholic Beverage Commissions (ABCs), which set conditions for retail sales and licensed producers, wholesalers, and retailers.

Regulation of production, distribution, and sales varies greatly among states. California, the major wine-producing state, allows licensed wine producers to act as producers, wholesalers, and retailers, although limiting the number of retail locations allowed to a wine producer. Over the past two decades, as wine production has expanded in other states, state governments have encouraged domestic wine production by amending laws to allow their in-state wineries, under restricted conditions, to sell directly to retailers and consumers. However the general case is that, in most states, out-of-state wine suppliers (either domestic producers or importers of foreign wines) must acquire licenses from the state ABC and then must sell to in-state wholesalers licensed by the state ABC. These wholesalers pay state excise taxes for wine imported into the state and maintain inventory for sale to state licensed retailers. Licensed retailers then sell to consumers. This system is referred to as the "three-tier" system, with the first tier being the supplier, the second tier being the wholesaler, and the third tier being the retailer.

The three-tier system places at least two business entities between a supplier and the end consumer. The system also requires that, in most instances, suppliers must have a business relationship with at least one wholesaler in every state in which the supplier desires to sell wine. A cursory examination of the listing of wholesalers at the TTB web site (U.S. Treasury/TTB 2015) shows over 19,000 licensed wholesalers across the 50 states. But this number is quite misleading, as each wholesale location requires a separate license, and the 19,000 licensees are not distinct firms. Most wholesalers are quite small businesses that serve a limited geographic area within a state, but in every state and nationally, distribution of alcoholic beverages is dominated by a handful of large wholesalers.

Industry analysts indicate that in 2017 the four largest wholesalers of alcoholic beverages accounted for approximately 55% of all wholesale sales (Wines and Vines 2017). Wholesaler consolidation is an ongoing trend that will probably continue because distribution of alcoholic beverages exhibits economies of scale. Table 5.7 lists the top four wholesalers in the United States, all of which are multibillion dollar companies and all the result of recent mergers. The top wholesaler, *Southern Glazers*, was created in 2016 when *Southern*, the largest distributor, merged with *Glazers*, then the fourth largest. *Breakthru Beverage* had been created a year earlier when *Wirtz Beverage* merged with New York-based *Chalmers Sunbelt*. *Republic National Distributing Company* was the result of a 2007 merger of *Republic Beverage Company* and *National Distributing Company*. Most recently in November 2017, the numbers 2 and 3 wholesalers, *Republic National* and *Breakthru Beverage*, announced their intention to merge operations in 2018 (Marsteller 2017) although as of this writing, the merger has not yet occurred.

When a domestic wine producer or importer has distribution with a company such as *Southern Glazers* or *Republic National Distributing Company*, the supplier can be assured of geographic reach for its products. However, the supplier will also be one of hundreds, perhaps thousands, of suppliers, each vying for attention from the large distributor. In a national sales environment with over 9000 domestic producers, the reality is that most individual suppli-

Table 5.7 Four largest US alcoholic beverage distributors, 2014

Company	Estimated revenue ($ billions)	Market share by revenue (%)	Total states covered (number)
Southern Glazers	16.5	29.0	41
Republic National	6.5	11.4	22
Breakthru Beverage	5.4	9.4	16
Young's Market Co.	3.0	5.2	11

Source: Wines and Vines (2017)

ers are not in a position to choose a distributor in a given market. Rather, the distributor chooses the supplier. Without a licensed distributor, it is difficult for a supplier to sell more than a few cases of wine in a given market.

Because of the inherent difficulty in securing distribution in every state, some suppliers might decide to focus on one or two states or metropolitan markets rather than to pursue national distribution. States differ greatly in total population as well as rates of per capita consumption; hence the volume of wine consumed varies tremendously from state to state. Table 5.8 lists the top ten wine-consuming states in 2016, showing each state's wine consumption in thousands of gallons and as a share of total US wine consumption. In 2016, the top five wine-consuming states consumed 42% of all wine consumed, and the top ten states almost 60% of all wine sold in the United States. Collectively, in 2016 these top ten states consumed 526 million gallons, which, if they were a country, would put them in fifth place, behind Germany and ahead of the United Kingdom (Wine Institute 2015b). Clearly, a wine supplier does not need to pursue national distribution in order to sell significant volumes of wine in the United States. But it is equally true that most suppliers focus on states with high volumes of wine consumption, making those markets quite competitive.

State laws also affect where wine is sold, making it less meaningful to speak of national trends. In those states where wine can be discounted and can be sold in chain grocery stores, large retailers such as Costco and Walmart have gained market share. These retailers use their purchasing power to negotiate lower purchase prices, and this, combined with efficient store management and scale, which allow lower operating margins, enables them to offer lower prices to consumers. But some state sales environments are not conducive to large chain retailers. The states of New York and New Jersey, the third and fourth largest wine markets by volume in the United States, do not allow wine to be sold in grocery stores. Retailers in these states must choose between sell-

Table 5.8 Top ten wine-consuming states in 2016

State	Gallons (thousands)	Share (%)
California	148,347	16.5
Florida	71,538	8.0
New York	67,598	7.5
Texas	59,177	6.6
Illinois	35,041	3.9
New Jersey	34,027	3.8
Massachusetts	28,934	3.2
North Carolina	28,085	3.1
Pennsylvania	27,230	3.0
Virginia	26,246	2.9
Top ten total	526,223	58.6
US total	898,700	100.0

Source: Haughwout et al. (2018)

ing groceries and selling alcoholic beverages. Some states, such as Ohio, do not allow distributors to offer price discounts to retailers based on volume purchases, thus negating the purchasing power inherent in chain retailing, at least for alcoholic beverages. Other states, such as Colorado and Massachusetts, limit the number of retail locations per license holder, thus reducing the potential for chain retail sales.

The reduction of costs in supply chains has been a major force in business modernization for at least two decades. However, the current alcoholic beverage supply chain in the United States is entrenched in state law and efforts to bypass the three-tier system have met with little success, although there have been some changes. In 2005, the US Supreme Court reviewed Michigan and New York laws that allowed in-state wineries to make direct shipments to in-state consumers, but disallowed that privilege to out-of-state wineries. In a 5 to 4 decision in *Granholm v. Heald*, the Court found that states could not discriminate between in- and out-of-state producers, thus opening the door for direct shipments from winery to consumer (Mendelson 2009).

Although this decision has legalized the possibility of direct shipments to many states, the reality is that states can legally require registration fees, payment of excise taxes, and reporting requirements that, while in aggregate are reasonable expenses for in-state wineries with significant volumes of direct sales, become prohibitively expensive for an out-of-state winery that is shipping only a few cases per month to a particular state. Shipping costs for a few cases are also significantly higher than for truckloads of wine. Although direct shipping of wine and the bypassing of the three-tier system may widen the range of consumer choice, direct shipping still represents a very small percentage of wine sales in the United States. In 2014, nine years after the Granholm decision, approximately 4 million cases were direct shipped to consumers, which represents just over 1% of wine consumption in that year (Gordon 2015; Wine Institute 2018).

The United States is an attractive market for wine producers because it is large, lucrative, and still growing with a significant demand for premium wines as well as lower-priced wines. However, the effect of America's experiment with Prohibition is still felt in the marketplace in the form of the three-tier system of distribution. The sale of more than a few cases of wine in a state functionally requires that a supplier have an agreement with an in-state wholesaler. Consolidation of distributors coupled with an increasing number of suppliers makes distribution one of the key challenges for domestic and foreign wine producers desiring to sell wine in the United States.

5.5   Conclusion

This chapter has reviewed winegrape growing and wine production, distribution, and consumption in the United States. The industry is concentrated in the western United States, dominated by California, which produces four-fifths of the total. Nationally, winegrape growing is relatively unimportant when compared with commodities such as corn or soybeans, and winegrapes are best understood as a high-value specialty crop, whose high prices are driven by an increasing demand for wine on the part of American consumers. This increased demand has been met by expansion of vineyard acreage across the United States, by increased importation of bulk and bottled wine, and by a doubling of the number of US wineries over the past decade. Although the experiment with Prohibition has left a legacy of patchwork laws throughout the nation, making wine distribution cumbersome and costly, increased consumer demand for wines of all types is forcing changes in distribution. These changes, coupled with increased rates of per capita consumption and population growth, should insure that the United States remains the world's major wine-consuming country for the first half of the twenty-first century.

References

Alston, J.M., K. Anderson, and O. Sambucci. 2015. Drifting towards Bordeaux? The evolving varietal emphasis of U.S. Wine regions. *Journal of Wine Economics* 10 (3): 349–378.

Alston, J.M., J.T. Lapsley, and O. Sambucci. 2018a. Grape and wine production in California. In *California agriculture: Dimensions and issues (in process)*, ed. R. Goodhue, P. Martin, and B. Wright. Berkeley: Giannin Foundation of Agricultural Economics.

Alston, J.M., J.T. Lapsley, O. Sambucci, and D.A. Sumner. 2018b. United States. In *Wine's evolving globalization: Comparative histories of the old and new world*, ed. K. Anderson and V. Pinilla, 410–440. Cambridge: Cambridge University Press.

Dokoozlian, N. 2013. The evolution of mechanized vineyard production systems in California. *Acta Horticultura* 978: 265–278.

Goodhue, R.E., D.M. Heien, H. Lee, and D.A. Sumner. 2003. Contracts and quality in the California winegrape industry. *Review of Industrial Organization* 23 (3): 267–282.

Gordon, J. 2015. DtC Wine Shipments Grow 15% in 2014. *Wines and Vines,* January 15. Available from: http://www.winesandvines.com/template.cfm?section=news&content=144614. Accessed 16 Dec 2015.

Haughwout, S., M. Slater, and I. Castle. 2018. *Apparent per capita alcohol consumption: National, state, and regional trends, 1977–2016.* National Institute on Alcohol Abuse and Alcoholism. Surveillance report #110. Available from: https://pubs.niaaa.nih.gov/publications/surveillance104/CONS14.htm. Accessed 24 May 2018.

International Organization of Vine and Wine (OIV). 2015. *World vitiviniculture situation.* Available from: http://www.oiv.int/oiv/info/enpublicationsstatistiques. Accessed 16 Dec 2015.

Lapsley, J.T. 2010. Looking forward: Imagining the market for California wine in 2030. *Agricultural and Resource Economics Update* 13 (6): 12–15.

Marsteller, D. 2017. SND: Republic and Breakthru Join Forces. *The Wine Spectator,* November 20. Available from http://www.winespectator.com/webfeature/show/id/Republic-and-Breakthru-Join-Forces. Accessed 5 April 2018.

Mendelson, R. 2009. *From demon to darling: A legal history of wine in America.* Berkeley: University of California Press.

Penn, C. 2015. Industry outlook and trends. *Wine Business Monthly.* February.

Seff, J., and J. Cooney. 1984. The legal and political history of California wine. In *The University of California/Sotheby Book of California Wine*, ed. D. Muscatine, A. Maynard, and B. Thompson, 412–446. Berkeley: University of California Press.

Sumner, D.A., J.T. Lapsley, and J.T. Rosen-Molina. 2012. Economics of wine import duty and excise tax drawbacks. *Agricultural and Resource Economics Update* 15 (4): 1–4.

United States Department of The Treasury/Alcohol and Tobacco Tax and Trade Bureau (U.S. Treasury/TTB). 2005. *Monthly statistical report–wine*, January 2005–December 2005. Available from: http://www.ttb.gov/statistics/05winestats.shtml. Accessed 17 Dec 2015.

128 J. T. Lapsley et al.

———. 2013. *American Viticultural Area (AVA).* Available from: https://www.ttb. gov/wine/ava.shtml. Accessed 12 July 2016.

———. 2014. *Monthly wine statistics.* Available from: http://www.ttb.gov/wine/ wine-stats.shtml. Accessed 17 Dec 2015.

———. 2015. *List of permittees.* Available from: http://www.ttb.gov/foia/frl.shtml. Accessed 22 Mar 2016.

———. 2016a. *Tax and fee rates.* Available from: http://www.ttb.gov/tax_audit/ atftaxes.shtml#Wine. Accessed 6 Apr 2016.

———. 2016b. *Bonded wine producers: 1999-Sept. 30, 2015.* Available from: http:// www.ttb.gov/foia/frl.shtml. Accessed 6 Apr 2016.

———. 2016c. *Statistical report–Wine, January 2016–December 2016.* Available from https://www.ttb.gov/statistics/2016/final16wine.pdf. Accessed 24 May 2018.

United States International Trade Commission (ITC). 2017. *International trade centre international trade statistics 2001–2017.* Available from: http://www.intracen. org/itc/market-info-tools/trade-statistics/. Accessed 20 May 2018.

United States International Trade Commission (ITC). 2018. *Trade database.* Available at: https://dataweb.usitc.gov/.

United States Department of Agriculture/Economic Research Service (USDA/ERS). 2018. *Farm income and wealth statistics database. US farm sector financial indicators.* Available from: http://www.ers.usda.gov/data-products/farm-income-and-wealth-statistics/data-files-us-and-state-level-farm-income-and-wealth-statistics. aspx. Accessed 20 May 2018.

United States Department of Agriculture/National Agricultural Statistics Service (USDA/NASS). 2012a. *Census of Agriculture.* Available from: http://agcensus. usda.gov/Publications/2012/Full_Report/Volume_1,_Chapter_2_County_ Level/California/st06_2_031_031.pdf. Accessed 18 Feb 2016.

———. 2012b. *Census of Agriculture Highlights: Farms and farmland.* Available from: http://www.agcensus.usda.gov/Publications/2012/Online_Resources/Highlights/ Farms_and_Farmland/Highlights_Farms_and_Farmland.pdf. Accessed 18 Feb 2016.

———. 2012c. *Census of Agriculture.* Available from: http://www.agcensus.usda.gov/ Publications/2012/Full_Report/Volume_1,_Chapter_1_State_Level/California/ st06_1_039_039.pdf. Accessed 18 Feb 2016.

———. 2012d. *Historical acreage reports.* Available from: http://www.nass.usda.gov/ Statistics_by_State/California/Publications/Grape_Acreage/index.asp. Accessed 18 Feb 2016.

———. 2016a. *Historical crush reports.* Available from: http://www.nass.usda.gov/ Statistics_by_State/California/Publications/Grape_Crush/index.asp. Accessed 20 May 2018.

———. 2016b. *Historical acreage reports.* Available from: http://www.nass.usda.gov/ Statistics_by_State/California/Publications/Grape_Acreage/index.asp. Accessed 18 Feb 2016.

————. 2017. *Noncitrus fruits and nuts*. 2016 Summary. Available from: http://usda.mannlib.cornell.edu/usda/current/NoncFruiNu/NoncFruiNu-06-27-2017.pdf. Accessed 20 May 2018.

————. 2018. *Statistics by state*. Available at: https://quickstats.nass.usda.gov/. Accessed 22 May 2018.

United States Department of Labor/Bureau of Labor Statistics (USDL/BLS). 2015. *Consumer price index detailed report*. December. Available at: http://www.bls.gov/cpi/cpid1512.pdf. Accessed 15 Oct 2016.

Wine Business Monthly. 2015. WBM 30 list. *Wine Business Monthly*, February.

————. 2016. Retail sales analysis. *Wine Business Monthly*, January.

Wine Institute. 2015a. *World wine production by country*. Available from: http://www.wineinstitute.org/files/World_Wine_Production_by_Country_2015.pdf. Accessed 20 May 2018.

————. 2015b. *World wine consumption by country*. Available from: http://www.wineinstitute.org/files/World_Wine_Consumption_by_Country_2015.pdf. Accessed 18 Feb 2016.

————. 2018. *Wine consumption in the U.S.* Available from: http://www.wineinstitute.org/resources/statistics/article86. Accessed 24 May 2018.

Wines and Vines. 2017. Top U.S. Wine Distributors. *Wines and Vines*, September. Available from https://www.winesandvines.com/features/article/189047/Top%2010%20U.S.%20Wine%20Distributors. Accessed 5 Apr 2018.

6

The Australian Wine Industry

Kym Anderson

6.1 Introduction

Vines were planted in Australia as soon as Europeans first settled in 1788, but
for the next 50 years they were used to produce table grapes and wine mostly
for family, friends, and neighbors. During that time rum and other spirits,
plus beer, were the dominant alcoholic beverages. Commercial wine production only began in the 1840s, but it accelerated when a gold rush led to the
trebling of Australia's non-aboriginal population in the 1850s.

Despite having favorable wine-growing conditions, Australian wine exports
were insignificant before the mid-1860s, net export status was not achieved
until the 1890s and it took until the 1970s before annual per capita domestic
consumption of wine exceeded 10 liters. Even that represented only one-fifth
of national alcohol consumption; and barely 2% of Australia's wine production was being exported in the 1970s and early 1980s. The country's index of
revealed comparative advantage (the share of wine in the value of Australia's
exports of all goods divided by wine's share of global merchandise exports)
was always below 1 before 1990, but by 2005 it reached 11 (when it was

K. Anderson (✉)
Wine Economics Research Centre, University of Adelaide, Adelaide, SA, Australia
Crawford School of Public Policy, Australian National University,
Canberra, ACT, Australia
e-mail: kym.anderson@adelaide.edu.au

© The Author(s) 2019
A. Alonso Ugaglia et al. (eds.), *The Palgrave Handbook of Wine Industry Economics*,
https://doi.org/10.1007/978-3-319-98633-3_6

131

exceeded only by Moldova and Georgia) before falling to less than 4 by 2014. By then, Australia's index was also below that of New Zealand, Chile, France, Portugal, Italy, Spain and South Africa (Anderson 2018).

Over that 150-year period of long-run growth, the industry went through four boom-slump cycles before beginning its fifth boom in the latter 1980s. During the next two decades per capita consumption trebled, wine production quadrupled, and the share of production exported rose to two-thirds—by which time Australia accounted for almost one-tenth of global wine exports. That latest boom peaked just as the global financial crisis hit in 2008, following which the industry saw profits slump once more for a decade. Considerable structural adjustments were made over that decade as wineries positioned themselves to a return to another growth phase.

This chapter seeks to explain why the industrial organization of Australia's wine industry has changed over those 17 decades of growth and cycles to what it is currently. It begins with a brief outline of the industry's emergence and how it has evolved through those past cycles around its long-run growth path. It then provides details of the industry's current structural organization and how it developed. The final sections speculate on how that structure may change in the decades to come and provide a synthesis.

6.2   The Australian Industry's Emergence and Cyclical Growth

Grapes are perishable, and vines are perennial; planting such a crop involves a large up-front investment with no yield for the first three years, and full production of quality fruit requires at least four more vintages. Furthermore, the future demand for winegrapes is uncertain. Hence the decision as to whether, when and how much to expand or contract the area and varieties of grapevines is a complex one, depending as it does on expected product prices, costs and capital appreciation or depreciation. Since producers vary in their expectations, if an expansion or contraction is to occur, it will tend to happen only gradually as more and more would-be investors become convinced that a change in profitability will persist long enough to be worth responding to (Dixit and Pindyck 1994). Meanwhile, in the open Australian economy, the market price of grapes will move away from its trend level while this slow supply adjustment is occurring, and then gradually move back to trend as the last of the adjustment occurs. Should there be excessive exuberance on the part of investors in response to a period of high grape prices, and if firms have incomplete information on the extent of new investments by other firms, there is a risk of overshooting in aggregate. If that happens, there will then be a sharper fall in grape prices three to five years later once that excessive planting transposes into excessive output ready for sale.

Vine-bearing area provides a better indicator of the trend supply of grapes than the actual quantity of grapes harvested, because the latter is influenced by seasonal yield fluctuations. Figure 6.1 reveals the five cycles in the expansion of Australian vineyards since the 1840s and also the dominance of the state of South Australia.

The price for grapes is a function of both supply and demand, the latter coming from various sources: As fresh table grapes, for drying or for making wine. Up to the latter 1920s, vine area and wine production expanded in parallel, but thereafter wine production grew considerably faster than the area of vines (see upper two lines in Fig. 6.2). The share of grape production used for winemaking grew from just 10% at the end of the 1930s to more than 90% from the turn of this century (Fig. 6.3). This reflected only partly a faster growth in demand for wine than for table or drying grapes; it also reflected an oversupply of grapes which would be wasted if not converted into wine. Since there was no growth in wine exports from Australia between the 1930s and 1980s (Fig. 6.2), half of that wine was subsequently distilled and a further

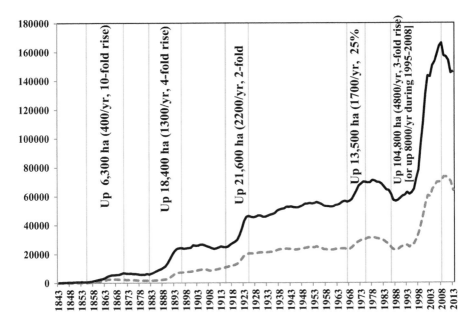

Fig. 6.1 Bearing area of vineyards, Australia (upper line) and South Australia (lower line), 1843 to 2013 (hectares). (Source: Anderson 2015, Chart 5)

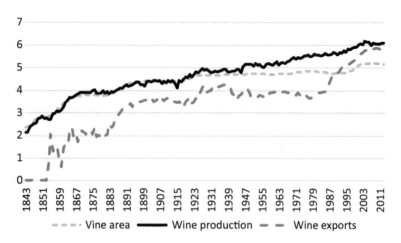

Fig. 6.2 Vine area, wine production and wine exports, Australia, 1843 to 2013 (log scale). (Source: Anderson 2015, Chart 9)

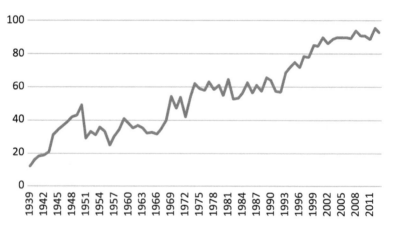

Fig. 6.3 Share of grape production used for winemaking, Australia, 1939 to 2013 (%). (Source: Anderson 2015, Table 8)

one-quarter was fortified (Fig. 6.4). Only since the 1980s has (mostly still) table wine regained the dominance it had in the nineteenth century.

The latest cycle began with the rise in the local price of exported wine when the Australian dollar slumped in the mid-1980s. That export price got reflected in the price of winegrapes, but it took until the mid-1990s before the area of bearing vineyards began to rise as potential investors adjusted their expectations—especially following the release of a 30-year strategic plan by the

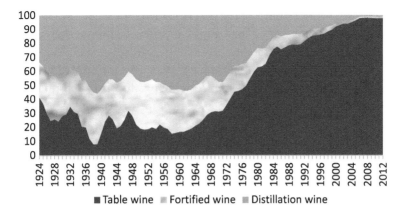

Fig. 6.4 Shares of table, fortified and distillation wine in total wine output, Australia, 1923 to 2013 (percentage, three-year moving average around year shown). (Source: Anderson 2015, Chart 31)

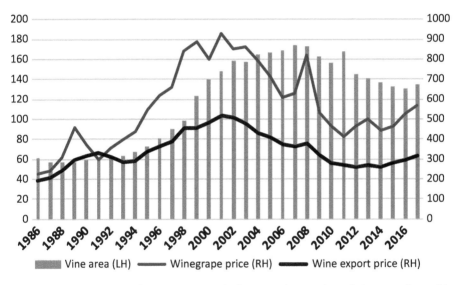

Fig. 6.5 Average price of winegrapes and of exports (RH axis), and vine area (LH axis), Australia, 1986 to 2017 (A$/tonne, A$/hectoliter, and '000 hectares). (Source: Anderson 2015, Chart 17)

industry (AWBC and WFA 2007). That bearing area continued to rise for a dozen vintages until 2008—even though the average prices of exported wine and of winegrapes peaked at the turn of the century (Fig. 6.5). Between 2001 and 2011, the export price halved and the winegrape average price fell by 60% in nominal Australian dollars, and they remained at those low levels through to the 2014 vintage.

A key reason for the slump of the past decade has been a boom in Australia's mining sector, thanks to China's rapid industrialization. That caused the Australian real exchange rate to double in value between 2001–02 and 2012–13. However, during the subsequent two years it returned halfway back to its 2001–02 level, which has enabled wine producers to sell much of their excess wine stocks. As a result, average winegrape prices rose slightly in 2015 and somewhat more in 2016 and 2017 (Fig. 6.5).

Many winegrape growers, unable to recover even their variable costs during recent years (WFA 2015), decided to replace their vines with more profitable crops. As a result, by 2015 Australia's total bearing area of grapes was one-fifth below the peak in 2008.

6.3   The Structure of Australia's Wine Industry

Just 2% of wine firms operating in Australia today began commercial life prior to 1900, only 6% began prior to 1970, and all but one-fifth have been operating for less than three decades (Table 6.1). The number kept growing every year until 2013 but fell in 2014 and remained lower the next two years (Fig. 6.6).

Most of those new wineries are very small though. During 2010–16, around one-fifth crushed less than 10 tonnes and another one-third or more crushed between 10 and 50 tonnes (Table 6.2). The proportion below 100 tonnes has fallen only slightly over the past two decades, and the proportion above 1000 tonnes has been below 5% since 1996—compared with more than 15% in 1978 (Fig. 6.7).

Table 6.1 Share of Australia's wine companies, by year of establishment, 2015

Period of establishment	Share (%)
Pre-1860	0.9
1860–79	0.6
1880–99	0.7
1900–19	0.2
1920–49	1.1
1950–69	2.5
1970–79	7.6
1980–89	14.0
1990–99	39.8
2000–14	32.5
	100.0

Source: Anderson (2015, Table 26)

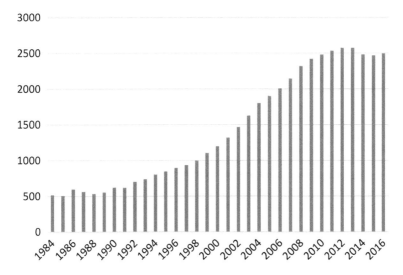

Fig. 6.6 Number of wineries in Australia, 1984 to 2016. (Source: Updated from Anderson 2015, Table 21)

Table 6.2 Number of Australian wineries by tonnes crushed, 1998 to 2016

	1998	2000	2002	2004	2006	2008	2010	2012	2014	2016
<10 tonnes					277	390	459	543	548	526
10 to 19 tonnes					324	376	412	449	391	365
<20 tonnes	293	337	418	582						
20 to 49 tonnes	211	259	331	414	481	512	527	553	506	472
50 to 99 tonnes	145	180	212	254	303	337	346	316	328	306
100 to 249 tonnes	142	157	189	211	242	257	259	235	229	235
250 to 499 tonnes	50	78	88	106	126	150	158	147	146	144
500 to 999 tonnes	31	40	61	72	74	76	85	85	81	85
1000–2499 tonnes	44	45	54	45	69	61	58	52	61	58
2500–4999 tonnes	19	29	36	40	27	37	38	36	27	29
5000–9999 tonnes	16	20	23	24	28	23	22	16	12	10
10,000+ tonnes	34	41	41	43	41	28	28	31	27	123
Unspecified	13	11	12	7	16	73	85	109	125	141
Total	998	1197	1465	1798	2008	2320	2477	2572	2481	2494

Source: Anderson (2015, Table 21), updated from http://winetitles.com.au/statistics/

In 2000, 80% of wineries had a 'cellar door' (meaning they sell direct to retail customers from the winery itself or a separate retail outlet they own), and 40% were exporting (though mostly to just four English-language destinations). By 2016, there were twice as many wineries, but only two-thirds had a cellar door, and the share exporting had already peaked and then fallen to 47%. While virtually all make table wines, a declining share is making forti- fied wines (less than 30% in 2016) and a rising share (42% by 2016) produces

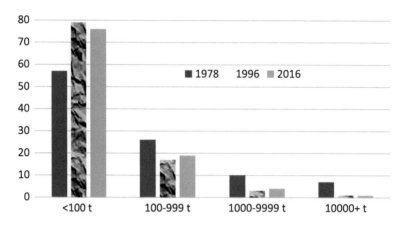

Fig. 6.7 Share of Australian wineries by crush, 1978, 1996 and 2016 (%). (Source: Updated from Anderson 2015, Table 21)

Table 6.3 Various attributes of Australian wineries, 2000, 2010 and 2016

	2000	2010	2016
Total no. of producers	1197	2420	2468
Share (%) of producers...			
Making table wine	99	99	98
Making fortified wine	33	29	29
Making sparkling wine	28	35	42
Making organic wine	na	5	4
Making wine on site	63	52	53
With a website	25	84	90
With a cellar door	78	68	66
Who export wine	41	51	47
Who export to the United Kingdom	28	27	21
Who export to the United States	26	27	18
Who export to Canada	11	24	19
Who export to NZ	14	8	8
Who export to Japan	12	12	13
Who export to Hong Kong	8	19	21
Who export to Singapore	7	25	22
Who export to China	2	23	30

Source: http://winetitles.com.au/statistics/wineries_numbers.asp

sparkling wines; 4% are making organic wines and only half are making wine on site (down from two-thirds prior to 2000). All but one-tenth now have a website. Around half export wine, but in 2016 only one in five or six exported to what had been Australia's two largest markets, the United Kingdom and the United States, with a larger proportion exporting to the fast-growing markets in Asia, especially China (Table 6.3).

The 1% of Australian wineries that crush more than 10,000 tonnes account for all but one-seventh of the national crush, with around half crushed by the three biggest wineries. By contrast, those firms crushing less than 1000 tonnes account for no more than 4% of the national crush and of the wine produced in Australia.

This very strong concentration of firms in Australia's wine production is not uncommon among New World wine-exporting countries. In 2009 Australia at 62% was second after Chile in the share of domestic sales accounted for by the country's four largest wineries. That share had fallen to 41% by 2015 though, as several large firms consciously moved away from producing large-volume but low-priced/low-profit lines. This compares with Chile at 91%, Argentina at 60% and the United States at 56% in 2015. By contrast, in Western Europe the highest national four-firm concentration in 2015 was 20% (Spain), followed by Italy (18%, up from 10% in 2009) and France (16% in 2009)—see Table 6.4.

Table 6.4 Shares of domestic wine sales volume by largest four wineries, Australia and other key wine-producing countries, 2009 and 2015(%)

	Largest firm		Largest four firms	
	2009	2015	2009	2015
Australia	23	16	62	41
Other New World				
New Zealand	24	23	48	53
Canada	21	12	42	34
United States	21	23	56	56
Argentina	29	27	61	60
Chile	33	31	>86	91
South Africa	34	31	37	36
Western Europe				
France	11	na	16	na
Italy	6	8	10	18
Portugal	8	3	25	10
Spain	12	11	21	20
Austria	5	6	13	10
Germany	1	1	4	4
C/Eastern Europe				
Bulgaria	13	12	40	38
Hungary	8	9	15	19
Romania	11	11	32	38
World	**13**	na	**28**	na

Source: Anderson and Nelgen (2013, Table 33), compiled and updated from Euromonitor International (2016)

While the biggest wineries in Europe tend to be producer cooperatives, in Australia (and most other New World countries) the largest ones are either listed on the stock exchange or are large family firms or private equity groups.

Certainly cooperatives operated in Australia in earlier decades, but they were either converted to or absorbed by other private companies. The country's biggest winery by volume today (Accolade) was purchased in 2003 as BRL Hardy, which was a merger of the Hardy family business (founded in 1853) with the former Berri and Renmano cooperatives (founded in 1922 and 1914, respectively).

Mergers and acquisitions tended to occur during boom periods or as 'fire sales' when the industry had been depressed for some time. A large number of multinational, multiproduct firms purchased Australian wineries during the 1965–76 boom, for example, but many of them soon divested of those assets once the boom subsided. The best of their brands have become part of what are now the country's three biggest wineries (Anderson 2015, Table 23). Each of those three firms depends on independent growers for the majority of their winegrapes in Australia, but they also now make wine in other (especially New World) countries. As a consequence, they are in a stronger bargaining position when they negotiate price and other supply conditions with those independent grapegrowers than was the case during the vineyard expansion boom in Australia in the 1990s.

The largest Australian wineries in terms of the value of wine sales in 2015 are listed along with various additional criteria in Table 6.5. What is clear from that table is the relatively low-rank correlations across those criteria. Some grow a large share of the grapes they crush, others a small share; some also buy wine from other processors; some have a single processing plant, others have several large or smaller plants (in different locations); some sell mostly in the domestic market, others mostly export; some export low-value wines, others high-priced ones. Only four of those 18 firms were not already operating by 1980.

The biggest exporting firms have been able to produce large volumes of low-end premium wines that use grapes from several regions, so as to ensure little variation from year to year in wine style and quality. That type of homogenous product suited perfectly the customers of large British supermarkets. By the mid-1980s, those supermarkets, dominated by Sainsbury's, Marks and Spencer, Waitrose and Tesco, accounted for more than half of all retail wine sales in the United Kingdom (Unwin 1991, p. 341).[1] Given also Australia's

---

[1] The introduction of commercial television in the 1980s strengthened the market power of large supermarkets. See the special issue on the history of commercial television in Europe in *VIEW Journal of European Television History and Culture,* Volume 6, Issue 11, 2017.

Table 6.5 Ranking of Australia's largest wine companies by wine sales value and other criteria, 2015

	Wine sales value	Wine prod'n volume	Owned or leased vine area	Owned or leased vines (ha)	Wine export value	Wine export volume	Earliest year of brands
Treasury Wine	1	3	1	9133	1	2	1843
Pernod Ricard	2	4	5	1662	3	4	1828
Accolade	3	1	9	1002	4	1	1836
Casella	4	2	2	2891	2	3	1969
Australian Vintage	5	5	3	2700	5	5	1938
McWilliam's	6	11	10	980	10	10	1877
De Bortoli	7	7	11	845	8	7	1928
Warburn	8	8	8	1017	14	13	1959
Brown Brothers	9	18	13	787	12	18	1889
Yalumba	10	13	12	820	7	8	1849
Tahbilk	11	19	21	421	17	15	1860
Angove	12	15	na	na	15	12	1889
Kingston Estate	13	6	6	1500	9	na	1979
Qualia	14	10	14	690	18	17	2009
Wine Insights	15	na	17	508	na	na	1930
Andrew Peace	16	12	16	565	6	6	1995
Littore	17	14	4	1850	19	14	2008
Zilzie	18	9	15	587	20	19	1999

Source: http://winetitles.com.au/statistics/wineries_numbers.asp

close historical ties with Britain, its firms were able to dominate that market in the final decade of the twentieth century.

Not all of Australia's oldest wineries are the largest. Among them are the dozen so-called First Families of Wine, which between them have 1200 years of winemaking experience (www.australiasfirstfamiliesofwine.com.au). These are all family-owned private businesses, some of them several generations old. They formed an alliance in 2009 to tell the world about the heritage of Australia's premium wines, to share the stories behind them, to celebrate the things they have in common and the differences that make them unique and occasionally to travel together on sales missions abroad.

In terms of quality of wines produced in Australia, as of 2009 about one-eighth were non-premium, half were commercial premium (between US$2.50 and $7.50 per liter wholesale pre-tax), a bit over one-quarter were super premium still wines and one-tenth were sparkling wines. Domestic consumption and imports were more biased toward higher quality, while exports were more biased toward the lower-quality range in 2009 (Anderson and Nelgen 2013, Section VI). Since then, however, the quality of Australian wines produced, consumed domestically and exported have all risen somewhat. In the case of red wines, for example, the share of off-trade domestic sales at less than AUD6 per liter fell from 35% to 25% between 2009 and 2016 while the share above AUD13.50 per liter rose from 27% to 33% and the share between those two extremes rose from 38% to 42% (Euromonitor International 2017).

6.4   Features of Grape Growing in Australia

There are more than twice as many independent grapegrowers as winemaker-grapegrowers in Australia, and their vine area and winegrape crush also are about twice that of winemaker-grapegrowers. This varies by state though, with South Australia having a disproportionate share of independent grape-growers (see bold columns of Table 6.6). Many of those independent growers would have been members of processing cooperatives (as in Europe) before those organizations were absorbed by private companies. The average vine-yard size was 23 hectares nationally in 2012, but that of independent grape-growers was only two-thirds the size of that of winemaker-grapegrowers (20.5 vs. 30.4 hectares). The latter have lower yields per hectare though, at 8.6 tonnes compared with 12.3 tonnes for independent grapegrowers in 2012, according to the data reported in Table 6.6. It is not clear whether the average size of vineyards and their average yields will rise or fall over the coming years, given the wide dispersion in vineyard area around the average size.

Australia's regions can be classified as hot, warm and cool. Hot regions in 2008 accounted for 61% of the volume of winegrapes produced but just 44% of their value, while cool regions accounted for 9% of the volume and 16% of the value. Yields are particularly high in the hot regions because of irrigation, averaging 17.5 tonnes/ha in 2012 while cool regions averaged 5.6 tonnes and warm regions only a little higher at 6.2 tonnes. Winegrape prices are more than commensurately lower in the hot regions, however, at three-fifths of the national average compared with 70% above that average in warm regions and 110% above in cool regions (Anderson 2015, Tables 55, 57, 61, 72 and 73). During 2012 to 2015, more than 85% of the growers in hot regions suffered financial losses, whereas in Australia's other regions less than half the produc-ers suffered losses in those painful years when grape prices were at their lowest (WFA 2015).

Table 6.6 Number, vine-bearing area and crush of Australian independent and winemaker grape-growing establishments, by vineyard size range (ha) and state, 2012

Number	Independent grapegrowers					Sub-total	Winemaker-grapegrowers					Sub-total	Total
	<10	10–25	25–50	50–100	>100		<10	10–25	25–50	50–100	>100		
South Australia	1158	585	261	117	55	2176	161	145	95	50	58	509	2685
New South Wales	430	244	124	65	53	916	204	66	21	16	29	335	1252
Victoria	568	190	63	39	25	885	348	89	50	29	17	532	1417
Western Australia	214	70	21	11	6	323	168	79	16	18	17	298	620
Tasmania	51	2	2			56	61	10	1	3	3	79	134
Australia total[a]	2458	1096	472	232	140	4398	994	394	187	116	125	1815	6213

Area (ha)	Independent grapegrowers					Sub-total	Winemaker-grapegrowers					Sub-total	Total
	<10	10–25	25–50	50–100	>100		<10	10–25	25–50	50–100	>100		
South Australia	5844	9018	9033	8192	11,596	43,683	761	2437	3395	3453	16,242	26,287	69,970
New South Wales	1853	3870	4423	4315	13,194	27,654	872	977	671	1075	7114	10,709	38,363
Victoria	2333	2876	2167	2565	4272	14,213	1465	1347	1688	2124	3876	10,500	24,713
Western Australia	799	1069	733	760	860	4222	766	1281	494	1206	2349	6095	10,316
Tasmania	105	28	71			205	213	125	41	204	442	1024	1229
Australia total[a]	11,045	16,934	16,427	15,833	29,921	90,160	4254	6229	6399	8144	30,196	55,222	145,382

(continued)

Table 6.6 (continued)

Crush (tonnes)	Independent grapegrowers					Sub-total	Winemaker-grapegrowers					Sub-total	Total
	<10	10–25	25–50	50–100	>100		<10	10–25	25–50	50–100	>100		
South Australia	67,291	119,257	121,043	83,905	150,648	542,143	3525	14,816	20,897	22,529	165,008	226,776	768,918
New South Wales	15,801	42,393	57,528	54,819	177,313	347,854	2312	3356	2279	8156	96,844	112,948	460,802
Victoria	26,215	38,323	32,406	35,426	55,704	188,074	5681	7861	11,218	17,344	47,576	89,680	277,754
Western Australia	3557	6781	6138	4601	5450	26,528	3490	7419	3409	9184	17,992	41,493	68,021
Tasmania	455	147	155			757	971	638	136	1503	1375	4622	5379
Australia total[a]	113,534	206,947	217,269	178,752	389,115	1,105,618	16,311	34,240	38,172	58,717	328,992	476,431	1,582,049

Source: WGGA (2013)

[a]Total includes Queensland, the Australian Capital Territory and the Northern Territory, where winegrape growing is very minor

Since the demise of cooperatives, growers have sought contracts with wineries. These have varied from a handshake to a written legal document. Typically they specify an area of vines by variety and certain quality criteria or proxies such as a maximum number of tonnes per hectare. In the 1990s as the industry was expanding and wineries were keen to secure grape supplies, contracts as long as ten years were not uncommon. But as the oversupply situation emerged in the new century, those contracts were often renewed with much shorter time frames. In some cases they were not renewed at all, leaving the grower to either sell on the spot market or get the grapes produced into wine for later resale in the wholesale bulk market or for retail sale under their own new label.

Despite the rapid expansion of Australia's wine industry over the two decades to 2008, vineyards still account for less than 1% of the country's area under crops, and even less than was the case in the first globalization wave in the latter half of the nineteenth century. In 2015 its share was 0.55%, which is not much above the global average of 0.45% of total crop area—and barely one-tenth the fraction in the key wine-producing countries of Western Europe.

Winegrapes in Australia are grown in more than 60 legally defined regions or geographical indications, covering a spectrum from cool (similar to Burgundy) to hot (similar to some Mediterranean regions). A little over two-fifths of the bearing area is located in hot regions, a similar proportion is in warm regions and the remaining one-eighth is in cool regions. Almost half the vineyards are in the state of South Australia, which has all three types of climate zones. The vineyards on the island of Tasmania, by contrast, are virtually all classified as cool climate. Irrigation is essential in the hot regions, so their vineyards are mostly located along the sides of major rivers. In cool regions, by contrast, irrigation is rarely used once young vines are established.

In sharp contrast to the European Union, there are relatively few regulations controlling the winegrape production process in Australia. In particular, blending of wines from any combination of grape varieties is allowed, as is blending from any number of regions. There is therefore no distinction in Australia of the sort made in Europe between appellation and generic wines. Australian producers have made a point of marketing their wines with varietal labeling and have only recently begun to also emphasize regional (and even single vineyard) origins of the grapes. Meanwhile, France is beginning to add varietal names to the labels of some of its wines. Hence the Old World and New World are converging toward both using both attributes in their marketing.

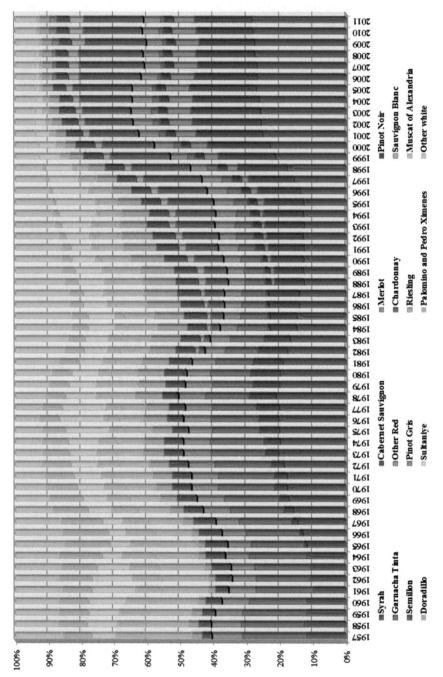

Fig. 6.8 Shares of varieties in Australia's winegrape-bearing area, 1956 to 2012 (%, three-year averages). (Source: Anderson 2015)

Australia has changed its winegrape varietal mix enormously during the past six decades. Figure 6.8 reveals the expanded share of bearing area of reds through the 1960s and 1970s before whites emerged with a new preference for Chardonnay, and then reds re-emerged with the expansion of both Cabernet Sauvignon and Syrah (Shiraz) plus Merlot. Accompanying the growth of these varieties was the demise in popularity of grape varieties such as Garnacha Tinta (Grenache), Muscat of Alexandria, Doradillo, Sultana, Palomino and Pedro Ximenes. Those declining varieties had been the mainstay of fortified wines and/or served well as multipurpose grapes able to be directed to drying when that was more profitable than their use in winemaking (Fig. 6.8).

These trends in winegrape-bearing areas mean there have also been great changes in the country of origin shares of the nation's winegrape varieties, as defined by Robinson et al. (2012). Australia's mix has become more 'international' or, more accurately, more French than most countries. In the 1950s, 20% of the national vineyard was planted to French varieties while 40% was planted to Spanish varieties and another 10% to Greek varieties. Only small shares were from Italy and Germany, and the shares from other countries were tiny. By contrast, by the early 2000s all but 10% of the bearing area was planted to French varieties, and Spanish and German varieties filled half of the remainder. In this second decade of the present century, there has been new interest in planting varieties from warm parts of southern Europe (especially Italy) in anticipation of further global warming, but they still comprise only a small fraction of the national area (Anderson 2016, Table 2).

The main reason for Australia's varietal mix becoming more French has to do with Shiraz, or Syrah as it is called in most parts of the world. The popularity which Australia brought to Syrah in the 1990s has led to many other countries expanding their plantings of this variety. In 1990 there were barely 35,000 bearing hectares globally, making it 35th in the area ranking of all winegrape varieties in the world. But by 2000 there were 102,000 hectares, and by 2010 that had risen to 186,000, bringing Syrah to the 6th position on that global ladder and less than one-third below the global areas of the two now-most-widespread varieties, namely, Cabernet Sauvignon and Merlot (Anderson 2013).

Over the decade to 2010, the Syrah area globally grew more than either Cabernet or Merlot—in fact only Tempranillo expanded faster. Certainly Australia contributed to that expanding area of Syrah, but expansion was even greater in France and Spain. There were also large plantings in other key New World wine countries, and in Italy and Portugal. As a result, Australia is no longer as globally dominant in this variety: Its share of the global Syrah area dropped from 29% in 2000 to 23% in 2010—even though Syrah increased its share of Australia's own vineyards over that decade, from 22% to 28%.

Varietal differences also are more muted between regions within Australia than is the case within other countries—notwithstanding the very large differences in growing conditions between cool, warm and hot regions across Australia. In 2010, of the three most similar regions in the world to each of Australia's 94 regions and sub-regions, less than 7% were non-Australian regions. In New Zealand, by contrast, more than two-thirds of the three most similar regions to each of its ten regions were in other countries (Anderson 2016).

6.5   The Changing Structure of Australian Wine Distribution and Retailing

During Australia's first export boom in the three decades to World War I (see Fig. 6.9), virtually all its wine was shipped bulk, in hogsheads (large wooden barrels). Exports were generally of extremely low quality prior to that (mostly dry red, shipped only weeks after the grapes had been crushed), with little invested in marketing and distribution arrangements in the (almost sole) destination country of Britain. While strong prejudices against New World wine remained throughout that first globalization wave, a firm reputation for

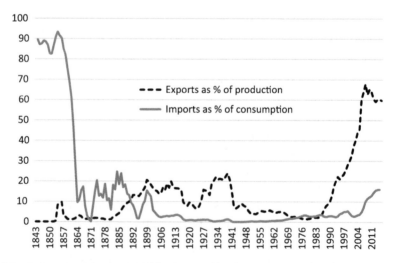

Fig. 6.9 Exports as percentage of wine production and imports as percentage of apparent wine consumption, Australia, 1843 to 2017 (percentage, three-year moving average around year shown). (Source: Updated from Anderson 2015, Chart 8)

Australian dry wines began to be established in Europe by 1914 in the generic sense at least, even though varietal, regional and winery brand labeling was still absent (and would be until the 1950s).

In the first half of the most recent three-decade export boom, by contrast, most wine was exported in labeled 750 ml bottles revealing regional details along with the winery brand. In addition, as mentioned above, Australian producers chose to differentiate themselves from those in Europe by clarifying on their labels the winegrape variety or varieties (or cultivars) used to produce each wine.

Since 2000, however, the share of Australian wine exported in bulk has risen rapidly, from less than 15% to 57% by 2014 (in volume terms and to 22% in value terms), although it fell slightly to 53% by 2017. That bulk wine is typically transported in 24,000-liter bladders that fit exactly into 20-foot containers for shipping to the northern hemisphere. Only some of it is low-quality surplus wine destined for blending into non-premium wine at its destination; an increasing share of it is bottled and labeled on arrival by or for the winery that produced it or for a retailer seeking to label it under its own brand. That is especially so of exports to the United Kingdom, all but one-fifth of which is shipped bulk.

The destination of Australia's exports has changed dramatically in the past two decades. The United Kingdom and New Zealand were initially the main destinations, and then gradually the United States and Canada became more important. But in the most recent decade, East Asia has also become very significant such that by 2017 it had a far larger share (46%) than either Europe

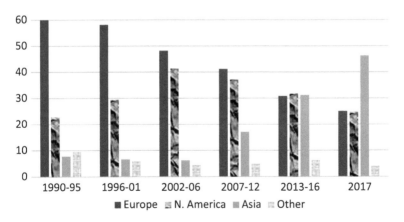

Fig. 6.10 Shares of the value of Australia's exports to various regions, 1990 to 2017 (The 2016 data are for the 12 months to September 30). (Source: Updated from Anderson and Nelgen 2013, Table 144) (%)

or North America, both at 25% (Fig. 6.10). The average price of Australia's exports to Asia are about twice as high as exports to the rest of the world, and most sales are now in bottles. This plus proximity ensures the region's importance to Australia relative to other wine-exporting countries will grow as Australia continues to raise the average quality of its wine exports and as the three bilateral trade agreements recently signed by Australia with China, Japan and Korea are implemented—and the United Kingdom's withdrawal from the EU is likely to contribute to that trend (Anderson and Wittwer 2015, 2018).

In the Australian domestic market (where 35–40% of production is sold), supermarket dominance has been on the rise. Today just two supermarket chains (Coles and Woolworths) account for the majority of domestic wine sales, with Aldi supermarkets a distant third but rapidly expanding. Each of them is developing their own 'home' brands, with perhaps more than one-fifth of their wine sales now under their own labels. Since consumers find it very difficult to distinguish those brands from traditional winery brands, they are in direct competition with the latter on the same supermarket shelves.

It is this dominance of supermarkets at home, as well as abroad, that has encouraged takeovers and increasing concentration among wineries and their corporatization. The aim of those developments has been partly to raise the enormous amounts of capital required for expansion: The capital intensity of winegrape growing is about 50% above that of other agriculture, and that of winemaking is more than one-fifth higher than that of other manufacturing in Australia. Larger size and greater diversity of offerings also improve the negotiating position of wineries vis-à-vis supermarket retailers and the financial muscle to market abroad.

The latter is more important for wineries in the antipodes than in the northern hemisphere, because of the long distance and travel costs associated with developing and maintaining those export markets. True, relative distance is becoming less of a handicap for Australia as markets in Asia grow. Nonetheless, breaking into and servicing those emerging markets is very time-consuming, so economies of size of export-focused wineries will continue to play a role there as well.

Online sales are becoming more important in Australia as elsewhere. In Australia in 2016 they accounted for 10% of the volume of off-trade wine sales (and 4.4% of the value of all alcohol sales in 2014, up from 0.9% in 2009). However, the supermarket chains are at least as actively engaged in online sales as other retailers, and this channel may even be adding to their overall market dominance. Indeed one of the two large Australian supermarkets is exploring the option of establishing a physical and online presence in

China, which will mean Australia's exporters to that expanding market will not have escaped that retailer's influence.

One indication of that increasing dominance is the declining share of the five top wineries' brands in the volume of Australia's domestic sales. In 2008 those five brands accounted for 65% of the still wine market in Australia, but by 2016 their share was just 48% (Euromonitor International 2017).

6.6   What of the Future?

Recovery from the Australian wine industry's recent difficulties won't be easy, as major adjustments are required by many participants. To the extent there is a willingness to continue to invest for the long term (rather than just focusing on quarterly returns to shareholders), and if the earlier spirit of collaboration and unity within the industry can be reinvigorated, a return to at least normal levels of profitability should be possible before long. Growth in domestic sales will be sluggish because of slowing income and population growth and a strengthening anti-alcohol lobbying; but with the ending of the mining investment boom, the Australian dollar depreciated by more than one-quarter during 2013–17 which has boosted Australia's competitiveness in export markets and lessened the competition from imports in the domestic wine market.

As well, adjustments are under way in generic export marketing. The earlier emphasis on 'Brand Australia', of providing 'sunshine in a bottle', has switched to a marketing strategy that places far more emphasis on higher-quality wines and exploits the scope to differentiate through building regional, varietal and style reputations. This new emphasis is certainly needed, given the increasing competition from lower-wage Southern Hemisphere countries in the commercial premium category. Chile may have already surpassed Australia in offering the world the best value wine in that category, hence the switch in emphasis to making the point that Australia also offers excellent value for money with its finer wines.

Getting that message across in not only Australia's traditional markets but also in Asia will require a larger generic marketing budget than the industry has had in the past, which was trivial relative to the value of national production and the extent of expenditure by European competitors. In 2011–12, for example, Australia's expenditure on generic promotion was barely 0.7 cents per liter of wine produced. That same year, Bordeaux alone spent 3.3 cents per liter. The European Union supplements regional and national promotion expenditures of its member states, and during 2009–13 it provided 522 million Euros for wine promotion, the equivalent to 0.6 Australian cents per liter of EU wine produced. Moreover, that EU promotion expenditure is to be raised to 1156 million Euros for the period 2014–18 (European Court of Auditors 2014). That is around 1.3 cents per liter, or double the rate recently spent in Australia—and that is just the supplement from Brussels, which adds to what will be spent by national governments and EU wine regions themselves.

Fortunately for the Australian industry, the national government announced in 2016 that it would provide a one-off grant of AUD50 million over the four years to 2020 to boost the industry's competitiveness and thereby reboot profitability. More specifically, this Export and Regional Wine Support Package is to focus on wine promotion internationally and domestically and is designed to help regional wine producers, wine-related tourism and export-focused businesses.

As for grape and wine research, less than 1% of the value of grape and wine production has been invested in R&D in the past, despite the returns from such investments being very high. Returns in the next two decades are likely to be even higher, bearing in mind rapid marketplace changes (the need to produce better quality rather than quantity of grapes and wine) and long-term uncertainties such as climate change and global economic growth.

Wine consumer tax policy reform could contribute to the transition to higher-quality wine production. If Australia were to switch from its current 29% ad valorem wholesale tax to a volumetric tax on domestic sales, that would encourage the transition to finer wines while weakening the case by anti-alcohol lobbies and the beer and spirits producers for a higher *rate* of tax on wine. Such a switch would make it easier for small fine-wine producers to sell all their production on the domestic market, thereby avoiding the high fixed costs of breaking into new export markets.

6.7   Synthesis of Structural Features

This chapter makes it clear that Australia's wine industry structure is very different from that of traditional wine-producing countries of Europe. Specifically, in Australia:

- Winegrape production faces relatively few regulations and so growers are free to choose their variety of grapes, yields, how much to irrigate and so on.

- Wineries too face relatively few regulations and so can blend wines from various regions, blend whatever varieties they wish and label their bottles with as much varietal, regional and vineyard information as they wish.
- Since the industry's take-off in the 1990s, the focus has been on export markets, since the domestic market has been growing very little in volume terms at least.
- The importance of Asia, and especially China, to Australian wine exporters is already very strong and will become even more so in the next few years as Australia's new bilateral trade agreements with Northeast Asian countries are implemented.
- The average quality of wine will keep rising as the share of production in the warmest regions, where quality is lowest, shrinks in response to global warming and rising prices of irrigation water.

References

Anderson, K. 2016. Evolving varietal and quality distinctiveness of Australia's wine regions. *Journal of Wine Research* 27 (3): 173–192, September.

———. 2017. *Australia's wine industry competitiveness: Why so slow to emerge?* Wine economics research centre working paper 0317, University of Adelaide, November.

Anderson, K. (with the assistance of N.R. Aryal). 2013. *Which winegrape varieties are grown where? A global empirical picture.* Adelaide: University of Adelaide Press. www.adelaide.edu.au/press/titles/winegrapes.

———. 2015. *Growth and cycles in Australia's wine industry: A statistical compendium, 1843 to 2013.* Adelaide: University of Adelaide Press. www.adelaide.edu.au/press/titles/austwine.

Anderson, K., and S. Nelgen. 2013. *Global wine markets, 1961 to 2009: A statistical compendium.* Adelaide: University of Adelaide Press. www.adelaide.edu.au/press/titles/global-wine.

Anderson, K., and G. Wittwer. 2015. Asia's evolving role in global wine markets. *China Economic Review* 35: 1–14, September.

———. 2018. *Cumulative effects of Brexit and other UK and EU27 bilateral FTAs on the world's wine markets.* Wine Economics Research Centre Working Paper 0118, University of Adelaide, January.

AWBC and WFA. 2007. *Wine Australia: Directions to 2025.* Adelaide: Australian Wine and Brandy Corporation and Winemakers Federation of Australia. www.wineaustralia.com/Australia/Default.aspx?tabid=3529.

Dixit, A., and R.S. Pindyck. 1994. *Investment under uncertainty.* Princeton: Princeton University Press.

Euromonitor International. 2017. *Passport: Wine in Australia*. London: Euromonitor International, June.

European Court of Auditors. 2014. *Is the EU investment and promotion support to the wine sector well managed and are its results on the competitiveness of EU wines demonstrated?*, Special report no. 9, Luxembourg: Publications Office of the European Union.

Robinson, J., J. Harding, and J.F. Vouillamoz. 2012. *Wine grapes: A complete guide to 1,368 Vine varieties, including their origins and flavours*. London: Allen Lane.

Unwin, T. 1991. *Wine and the vine: An historical geography of viticulture and the wine trade*. London/New York: Routledge.

WFA. 2015. *2015 production profitability analysis*. Adelaide: Winemakers Federation of Australia, December.

WGGA. 2013. *National winegrape grower booklet*. Adelaide: Wine Grape Growers' Association, November.

7

The Argentinean Wine Industry

Javier Merino

7.1 Introduction

In the last three decades, the Argentinean wine industry has experienced a dramatic change in its value-added chain. In the 1990s it opened its economy, and very important foregoing investors came to the wine sector. At the beginning the most important change took place in the vineyards. A special situation in the exchange rate then allowed the wineries to go to export markets and introduce the wine successfully in the most sophisticated markets. At the same time, some wineries introduced Malbec, which was welcomed by consumers. This caused a drastic change in the Argentinean wine sector that became a competitive player in the wine market worldwide. The recent years have been very difficult for the Argentinean economy, and many wineries have had to adapt the business to new conditions, especially in the domestic market. Nowadays the Argentinean wine sector structure is very different, and the wineries and producers have the challenge to grow in a very competitive market with opportunities and very strong threats.

J. Merino (✉)
Cuyo National University, Mendoza, Argentina
University of Mendoza, Mendoza, Argentina
e-mail: jmerino@areadelvino.com

© The Author(s) 2019
A. Alonso Ugaglia et al. (eds.), *The Palgrave Handbook of Wine Industry Economics*,
https://doi.org/10.1007/978-3-319-98633-3_7

7.2   Structural Features of the Vinegrowing Sector

7.2.1   Evolution of Vineyard-Planted Areas

Argentinean viticulture has experienced a major transformation process over the last two decades, showing a substantial increase in wine quality and establishing a firm foothold in the international markets. This transformation began in the vineyard, back in the 1980s, when a maximum of 315,000 ha (777,000 acres) were planted (Fig. 7.1), a large portion of which were low-quality grapevines that had been planted almost exclusively for the domestic market. With little to no international placement, the consumption of low-quality grapes soon began to decline.

The first half of the 1980s was witness to a vine-uprooting process, the aftermath of successive crises, production surpluses, and low prices subsidized by the national government. When combined with a variety of political interventions, from strict regulation policies to grape purchases by the State, none of these events contributed to a profitable activity. Soon after the uprooting of almost 100,000 ha of vineyard-planted areas (250,000 acres), in the year 2000, only 188,000 ha (465,000 acres) remained, despite an ongoing process of planting newer and higher-quality vineyards in order to improve wine quality for export purposes.

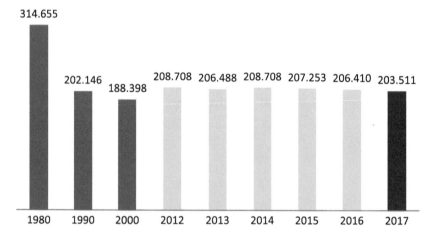

Fig. 7.1 Evolution of cultivated surface area of grapes for winemaking in Argentina (ha). (Source: INV)

From 1990 to the present day, the cultivated surface area of high-quality varieties has increased by almost 4600 ha (11,300 acres). However, when analyzing the nine most purchased varieties for export (Malbec being the leader), their growth in particular has increased to more than 77,000 ha (190,000 acres), while other varieties have fallen by more than 72,000 ha (178,000 acres).

7.2.2   Regional Distribution

Traditionally located on the west of Argentina, wine-producing regions are strewn along the foot of the Andes mountain range, a feature that has translated into a unique and special prestige associated with the grapes and wines coming from the said regions. Although wine grapes are grown in 17 out of 24 provinces in Argentina, Mendoza ranks first in terms of wine production, representing more than 71% of the country's total vineyard-planted surface area and stretching over four oases from north to south. Argentina is one of the countries with the highest latitude dispersion of vineyards. Mendoza is followed by San Juan and La Rioja provinces in terms of wine production. In the last few years, new provinces added to the list, notably Neuquén in the Argentine Patagonia.

7.2.3   Growth of Wine Provinces

Argentina's switch in grape varieties went hand in hand with the adoption of new technologies in the irrigation systems, which additionally expanded the planted surface area-inadequate vinegrowing regions where traditional irrigation methods were otherwise not possible. This spurred Argentine viticulture to extend to high-altitude areas and regions where the combination of thermal amplitude and soils offered the possibility of growing higher-quality grape varieties, very much demanded by international markets.

Between 2001 and 2013, the provinces of Mendoza, Neuquén, and Salta revealed the largest area expansion. In the first one, Mendoza, new regions began being cultivated. Neuquén, the newest of the Argentine winemaking regions, expanded due to private investments, financial support from the local government, and optimal agricultural conditions given its latitude, sun exposure, and the presence of wind year-round. In Salta, the vinegrowing region with the highest altitude in the country, the surface area expanded in an attempt to increase thermal amplitude for the production of red varieties.

Observing the change in planted surface area and the variations of more than 5000 ha (12,500 acres) alone hides the fact that 11 regions still managed to increase their planted surface area by 26,000 ha (64,000 acres) between 2001 and 2013. Luján de Cuyo, Argentina's most traditional winegrowing region, with the largest Malbec-planted surface area, led this change by expanding to the south and west. This area is home to some of the oldest wineries in the country, along with those founded in Maipú.

7.2.4   The Switch in Varieties

The most cultivated variety today is Malbec (Table 7.1), due to international and national demands. While the total cultivated surface area has been increasing 0.02% annually over the last 25 years, red varieties have expanded 3.7% per year. Beyond Malbec, varieties such as Cabernet Sauvignon and Syrah, among red grapes, and Chardonnay and Sauvignon Blanc, among white varieties, have increased their cultivated surface area. Malbec proved to be the main catalyst behind this process. Back in 2017, Malbec boasted Argentina's largest cultivated surface area, even after having suffered from the drastic, low-price-driven vine-uprooting process that took place in the 1980s.

Eleven varieties were responsible for boosting this expansion. Almost all of them were red, but Chardonnay and Sauvignon Blanc played a major role as well. Closely behind Malbec, the next largest expansion was evidenced by Cabernet Sauvignon, which grew more than 12,650 ha (31,000 acres). Before the acceptance of Malbec, primarily in international markets, the most appealing vine to investors was actually Cabernet Sauvignon, mainly because it had been leading worldwide preferences since the beginning of varietal wine phenomenon in the United States. In fact, from 1990 to 2000, during the first phase of Argentinean viticulture modernization, the cultivated surface area of Cabernet Sauvignon grew almost 10,000 ha (25,000 acres), that is, two thirds of total growth, while Malbec only grew 6000 ha (15,000 acres).

Syrah ranks third when it comes to investments. With respect to this variety, investors, especially in the 1990s, focused on two signs. The first one was the considerable growth that, for some time, positioned this variety in the sphere of foreign markets, following the success of Australian exports. The second was the possibility of taking advantage of a number of tax breaks, especially in San Juan, where this variety had proven to adapt very well.

Bonarda has shown a very interesting growth period on the grounds of two notable characteristics: its easy adaptability to blend, especially with Malbec,

Table 7.1 Surface area of wine varieties (ha)

	1990 (1)	2000 (1)	2010 (1)	2017	Variation 1990/2017	CAGR 1990/2017
Red						
Malbec	10,457	16,347	28,481	41,301	30,844	5.2%
Bonarda	12,186	14,989	18,748	18,708	6522	1.6%
Cabernet Sauvignon	2347	12,199	17,672	14,997	12,650	7.1%
Syrah	687	7915	13,086	12,470	11,783	11.3%
Tempranillo	5659	4335	6563	6015	356	0.2%
Merlot	1160	5513	6937	5510	4350	5.9%
Sangiovese	3015	2491	2230	1713	−1302	−2.1%
Pinot Noir	232	1047	1675	2045	1813	8.4%
Tannat	42	136	578	835	793	11.7%
Cabernet Franc	76	207	578	1043	967	10.2%
Barbera	958	1061	732	426	−532	−3.0%
Other red varieties	5562	3808	5497	8496	2934	1.6%
Red surface area	**42,381**	**70,048**	**102,777**	**113,559**	**71,178**	**3.7%**
White						
Pedro Giménez	20,647	15,101	13,378	10,713	−9934	−2.4%
Torrontés Riojano	8625	8181	8480	8171	−454	−0.2%
Chardonnay	908	4625	6584	6207	5299	7.4%
Muscat of Alexandria	10,184	5539	4034	2637	−7547	−4.9%
Chenin Blanc	4031	3591	2851	2045	−1986	−2.5%
Sauvignon Blanc	278	827	2297	2061	1783	7.7%
Torrontés Sanjuanino	4914	3166	2527	1820	−3094	−3.6%
Ugni Blanc	2229	2846	2425	1495	−734	−1.5%
Semillón	1255	1028	956	728	−527	−2.0%
Other white varieties	7326	4530	4225	3551	−3775	−2.6%
White surface area	**60,398**	**49,432**	**42,906**	**39,428**	**−20,970**	**−1.6%**
Pink-skinned						
Cereza	43,100	31,666	29,934	27,971	−15,129	−1.6%
Criolla Grande	36,837	24,641	20,749	14,842	−21,995	−3.3%
Muscat Rose	15,503	10,656	8691	6185	−9318	−3.3%
Other pink-skinned varieties	3927	1956	1908	1526	−2401	−3.4%
Pink-skinned grape surface area	**99,367**	**68,918**	**55,101**	**50,524**	**−48,843**	**−2.5%**
Total surface	**202,146**	**188,398**	**200,784**	**203,511**	**1365**	**0.0%**

Source: INV

and its high yields in certain regions. For a long time now, many wineries have been trying to position this grape internationally as the second most important variety from a.

Chardonnay, on its part, fifth in the expansion of cultivated surface area, shares a similar story as that of Cabernet Sauvignon. Implanted because of its international popularity, Chardonnay can be used in producing sparkling wines, which experienced an impressive growth in Argentina, following the worldwide trends set by younger generations (Fig. 7.2).

In Argentina, Merlot suffered the same fate as that on the world stage. A once prestigious variety suffering depreciation from consumers, its extension in our country went from about 1000 ha (2500 acres) in 1990 to more than 7400 ha (18,200 acres) in 2006, to ultimately decline in 2017 to less than 5500 ha (13,500 acres).

Fascinating stories concern the rest of the varieties that expanded in the last quarter of this century, since all of them constitute modern phenomena. In

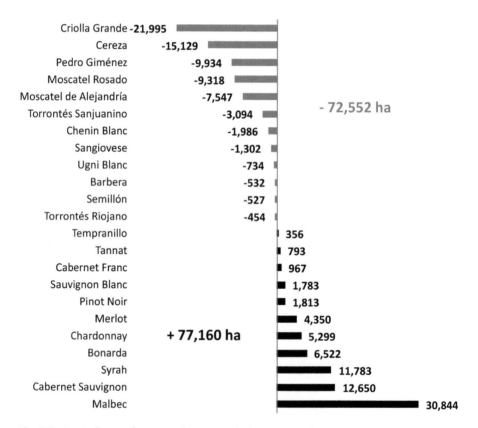

Fig. 7.2 Variation surface area (1990/2017). (Source: INV)

the case of Sauvignon Blanc, its expansion reflected the formidable acceptance it was getting from New Zealand, which led it to expand to new regions, such as Chile. Consequently, given its international popularity, many Argentinean wineries began growing this variety, contributing to expand its cultivated surface area during the first decade of this century.

Pinot Noir, on its part, has been growing uninterruptedly since 1990 for a variety of reasons, including the demand for sparkling wines in medium-to-high price ranges as well as its exceptional adaptation to regions in Valle de Uco and Patagonia. Additionally, the growing international demand for still red wines from Burgundy, France, resulted in the creation of new wine styles from the regions of Sonoma and Oregon in the United States and, more recently, New Zealand.

The decreasing cultivated surface area experienced by some varieties has been attributable to the inability to adapt to a number of consumers' demands, such as price and quality.

7.2.5   The Expansion Cycle of the Main Varieties

As mentioned before, several vineyard investment stages took place that matched the different market incentives and the existing surface area each variety covered when modernization began. Essentially, the said expansion process was the natural corollary to the newly acquired maturity and knowledge regarding the viticulture industry. Three periods can be identified at this stage:

1. An introduction period (1990–2000): this is the time when Argentina held an open economy policy and sought to attract investors to the activity. Export expertise was not abundant, and world market trends remained yet unclear as to how to define viticulture in the country. Incentives were in place to motivate the planting of new varieties, such as reduced prices of land and the availability of irrigation technology.

   Throughout this first period, varieties may be defined as those "internationally in demand" that did not cover a large implanted area—except for Malbec, Bonarda, and Tempranillo, whose expansion rates ranged between 10% and 25% annually. The Malbec phenomenon had yet to start, although this variety already covered more than 10,000 ha (25,000 acres) at a time when other varieties, such as Cabernet Sauvignon, barely extended to 2000 ha (5000 acres), and the rest remained well below these figures.

2. The expansion period (2000–2010): worldwide sales of Argentine wine spiked on currency exchange conditions that proved favorable to foreign markets. This triggered a powerful process that entailed a change in wine consumption trends, switching from formerly demanded lower lines all the way to the higher price ranges. This period was also characterized by the primary role assigned to consumers' preferences, which were becoming increasingly knowledgeable about wine as well as more selective and focused.

   This period additionally evidenced a change in the behavior with respect to the rest of the varieties. Firstly, their surface area expansion substantially reduced, as if anticipating to a maturation period. A few varieties remained the exception, notably Sauvignon Blanc, perhaps influenced by its success in New Zealand; Tannat, very much adapted to some regions alone; or Cabernet Franc, whose behavior resembled Tempranillo's when its cultivated surface area dramatically reduced in some places but experienced increase in others. All the while, Malbec continued to expand to a considerable total area of 16,000 ha (39,500 acres).

3. Maturation period (2010–present): the world market signs and Argentina's economic scenario played a decisive role in investment decisions, as companies had gained considerable commercial experience by now. The only variety to outgrow the others during this period was Malbec, reaching almost 41,000 ha (101,000 acres) in 2017 despite its uprooting process back in the 1980s. Furthermore, the expansion occurred despite Argentina's ongoing macroeconomic context as from 2010, when inflation edged up and a process of domestic currency depreciation ensued that immediately had an impact on exports, the main driver for growth. Because of low market demand, the surface area of some varieties reduced, such as Cabernet Sauvignon, Merlot, Sauvignon Blanc, and, to a lesser extent, Chardonnay. In a number of cases, these hectares have been replaced with Malbec vines. The phenomenon in Argentina is not an isolated event, and this is why it followed the tendency established between 2000 and 2010.

   Cabernet Franc and Tempranillo constitute, perhaps, the two exceptions to the rule. The former, covering a relatively small implanted surface area, was a variety widely used at the beginning in plenty of French-style blends, until some wineries decided to produce it as a single varietal, something that had quite a favorable reception. Tempranillo, on the other hand, was gaining worldwide recognition because of its success in Spain, but it remained almost unknown in the New World. This, however, did not hold true for Argentina, where Tempranillo already covered a large cultivated surface area when compared to other red varieties.

The rest of the varieties showed a similar evolution, supported by the "globalization" of viticulture and the rapid adoption of innovations. A comment should be made by now regarding Malbec: although a roaring success in the United States in the few last years, Malbec has not been used to leverage the other varieties previously examined. Consequently, Malbec could be used to showcase other red and even white varieties in the future.

7.2.6   Size of Properties and Changes in Technology

The switch of planted varieties was further accompanied by changes in the production systems. One of the most striking phenomena behind the transformational process of Argentinean viticulture from 1990 to the present days has been the arrival of investment in the sector, largely attributable to a prospect of profitability. The vineyards covering large surface areas now expanded even further, to more than 100 ha (250 acres), while those covering less than 10 ha (25 acres) were soon uprooted. This, in turn, increased the average cultivated surface area from 5.8 ha (14.3 acres) in 1990 to 9.2 ha (22.7 acres) in 2017, which contributed to and improved productive efficiency.

The number of vineyards has increased by 1.2% annually since the year 2000, in a context where larger estates evidenced higher growth rates than the smaller establishments. A survey conducted in 1990 revealed the existence of 36,000 estates. In 2017, however, slightly more than 24,000 estates remained, showing a 30% decrease and, consequently, the concentration of vineyards among fewer estate owners. Many of the wine producers who abandoned the activity did so because their small-scale production, based on growing table-wine grapes, was no longer profitable.

Besides the increase in size, Argentinean vineyards experienced a change in technology as they began incorporating modern irrigation and protection systems (especially against hail) as well as new vine training systems. Today, most vineyards resort to the pergola-training system, currently used in more than 121,000 ha (300,000 acres), although the last few years witnessed the expansion of the trellis system, now covering more than 79,000 ha (195,000 acres)—a similar figure as that of high-quality wine grape expansion.

Across certain warmer areas of Argentina, the vine pergola-training system is the preferred option to improve grape protection, even though higher-quality vineyards will typically make use of the trellis system.

7.2.7   Raw Material Market

Argentina's raw material (grape or bulk wine) market is very well developed. In the last decade, about 25% of the grapes intended for wine production were sold to independent producers. In addition, about 8% of the total represented bulk wine sales from wineries that were not able to bottle their production on their own. In other words, the raw material market accounts for one third of the total number of bottled wines. Given the type and quality of raw materials, the bulk wine market is intended for low-price wines, while the grape market aims at medium- to high-end wines. The former market involves estate owners who have made large investments in their production in order to meet the large wine producers and bottlers' requirements. Lastly, it should be mentioned that high-quality grapes, intended for high-end wines, are generally grown by the same wineries that make and bottle the said wines.

The grape market is typically managed by means of agreements between wineries and producers. Some have been able to maintain their commercial relationship to this day, after many years of business. The larger wineries will regularly visit the vineyards and make suggestions on vineyard management. Great trust is developed in this type of relationship, since most grape prices will be defined after the harvest, once the wineries have already crushed the berries. In the case of bulk wine, many wine agents will offer the product to different potential buyers and receive a commission upon closing the deal. Finally, some producers who do not bottle their own production will normally grow their grapes in wineries and ultimately sell their wine to them.

7.2.8   Revenue in the Primary Sector

The total revenue of the viticulture sector has been calculated taking into account the figures for grape sales and the considered value of the finished product owned by the wineries. Over the last 15 years, oscillations in grape prices and the sector's strong transformation process have been two important factors affecting revenue (Fig. 7.3). In its early stage, the participation of red grapes was nowhere near the levels it would reach between 2004 and 2009. In these years, red grapes were able to maintain their revenue due to productivity expansion and stable prices. In 2010 and 2011, wine producers' turnover increased because of the price spike due to the scarce availability of grapes, the grim result of two consecutive poor harvest seasons. At that time, the demand for red grapes shifted to regions where prices were lower.

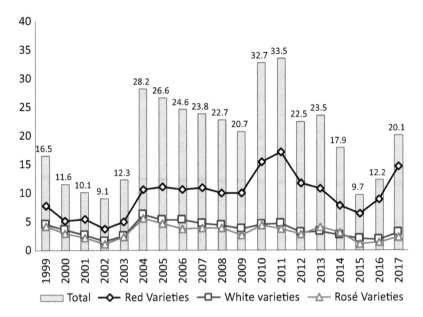

Fig. 7.3 Annual revenues in the viticulture sector (BB AR$ - Dec. 2017). (Source: Area del Vino)

As from 2004, the demand for varietal wine exports grew significantly. This, in turn, increased the sector's profitability and boosted expansion given the advantageous exchange rate in place.

The decline in pinked-skinned grape production has been independent from economic transformations and is rather the result of opposite international and domestic demand trends.

When calculating the average revenue per hectare across different varieties, Malbec comes across as the outright winner, outperforming every other variety given its greater expansion process. Pinot Noir ranks second, although it should be noted this variety is much more developed in certain regions.

7.3   Structural Features of the Winemaking Sector

7.3.1   Average Winery Size

A study conducted by the Argentinean Viticulture Observatory (Observatorio Vitivinícola Argentino) classified different companies operating in the viticulture market. The indicator used was the companies' commercialized volume for each establishment in the country. A "domestic market profile" or "export market profile" was created and assigned depending on the companies' main line of work. The study did not include wineries selling bulk wine alone, as they were considered to belong to a niche market that sells wine to the same wineries that will later on commercialize it as a finished product.

Additionally, the wineries were classified according to the size of their annual volume production into the following categories: small (less than 1 million liters), small/medium (1–4.99 million liters), medium/large (5–9.99 million liters), and large (more than 10 million liters). In Argentina, there are 719 establishments, 62% of which (477 establishments) showed a domestic market profile, while the remaining 272 tended toward the export profile.

Mendoza played a significant role in terms of total figures, especially in the ratio of total export production, which is clearly different from that in other provinces. Out of the 568 establishments registered in Mendoza, 58% fall within the domestic market sphere while 42% exhibit an export profile. When analyzing them by size, most of the establishments with an "export profile" (216 out of 239) are small (with a production volume below 1 million liters per year). Twenty wineries fall within the intermediate range, and only three have been described as large (producing more than ten million liters per year). The large establishments with an export profile manage 72% of the total volume, whereas the small ones participate in only 8% of overall production.

The majority of cases in Mendoza, 329 establishments in 2013, have a domestic market profile. When classifying them by size, small companies, once again, comprise 87% of the total. At the other end of the continuum, 15 wineries fall under "large companies", while only 29 are intermediate. The other vinegrowing provinces offer a very different panorama, predominantly oriented to the domestic market, except for the province Neuquén, which shows almost even proportions between domestic and external profiles. The provinces of Salta, Catamarca, and Río Negro all show a strong predominance of domestic market wineries (more than 80% in the total number of companies and more than 95% in terms of volume). San Juan, the second largest vinegrowing sector in Argentina, features 75% of its wineries with a domestic profile (45 establishments) that makes up for 96% of the province's total volume. San Juan also features 15 companies with an export profile (25%) that accounts for 4% of the province's total volume. In the case of La Rioja, figures reveal a small number of overall participants: only eight establishments, five of which have a domestic profile and, three, an export profile.

A comparison between the results found in 2013 and those in 2005 reveals a tendency toward reducing the share of domestic-market-profile companies while favoring that of export-market-profile companies. This is evident in the cases of

Mendoza, San Juan (showing a drastic change in this respect), La Rioja, Río Negro, and Neuquén. Salta and Catamarca, on the other hand, displayed altogether an opposite situation. With respect to the company distribution according to size, no significant differences were observed between 2005 and 2013.

7.3.2   Strategic Focus

The Argentinean viticulture industry operates with different strategic focuses, partly influenced by the favorable export market that has been in place for the last two decades. Actually 350 companies devote themselves to export, while only 190 operate at a purely domestic scale. Large macroeconomic changes have caused a certain turmoil for wineries' strategic positioning, which today require a more competitive focus.

Figure 7.4 illustrates a focus group composed of 91 wineries (chosen by Área del Vino Consulting Group) representing more than 75% of Argentina's

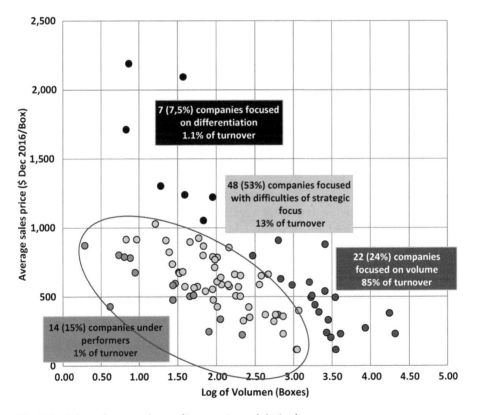

Fig. 7.4   Sales price vs. volume. (Source: Area del Vino)

wine total revenue and showing a traditional representation of price quantity. Based on the said diagram, the following conclusions can be made:

- 7.5% of companies focus on elevated prices.
- 24% of companies focus on high volume.
- 68% of them lack competitive focus—increased competition will affect them considerably.
- Companies focused on differentiation need to work actively on marketing and inventory control.
- Companies with strategies in volume need to work on consolidating their position by means of an active price policy.

7.3.3   Origin of Capital

Today, 31% of viticulture companies in Argentina constitute foreign investment operations, whereas 69% correspond to Argentinean capital. The arrival of foreign investors occurred mainly during the 1990s and ended between the years 2000 and 2005.

Among Argentinean companies, 65% are corporations, 30% constitute family-owned businesses, and 15% are cooperatives. It should be noted that the smaller cooperatives have joined and merged into the Argentine Federation of Viticulture Cooperatives (FECOVITA), currently positioned as one of the largest companies in terms of total sales. With respect to family-owned wineries, some have been operational in the country for more than 100 years, with the vast majority of them tracing back their roots to Italian or Spanish origins.

Lastly, the main foreign investors who own wineries in Argentina are from Chile (32%), France (21%), Austria (11%), the Netherlands (7%), and Portugal (7%). The last few years have also seen the arrival of investors from countries such as the United States, who have purchased small wineries.

7.3.4   Internal and External Variables Affecting Profitability

1. **Consumer preference**: transformations in the global and domestic demand for wines have been intimately connected to changes in consumers' preferences. This is true of many countries, especially in the New World, where varieties that can adapt to these preferences are often created. Vineyards in Argentina experienced a restructuring process, especially between 2000 and

2010, similar to that experienced worldwide. The expansion of Malbec accounts for a striking difference and one that may largely explain the success of Argentinean wines. Argentinean wines constitute a local phenomenon whose promotion to other winegrowing regions took a relatively longer time. However, the demand for Malbec will continue to grow in the years to come, although perhaps not at the same rate as before.

2. **Production cost**: Argentinean viticulture faced a marked tendency toward increasing costs in the last few years, due to the rising labor cost relative to wine and grape prices. This, combined with the increasingly difficult management of human resources, especially temporary workers, resulted into the considerably widespread mechanization of harvest.

3. **Fall in demand of export wines**: Argentinean wines experienced double-digit growth rates until 2010, when the consequences of several macroeconomic changes pushed up inflation. Policies seeking to change foreign exchange rates as from 2010 have delayed exchange rate adjustments, making export operations difficult. Consequently, low-price wines lost competitiveness and were left outside export operations, an event that had a negative impact on the price of the raw material that was acquired largely by the grape-producing wineries.

4. **Fall in domestic demand**: grape varieties covering large acreage were intended for medium- and high-end wines, both in the global and domestic markets. In recent years, recession in Argentina has taken a heavy toll on consumers' income, bringing the demand for wine and grapes to a grinding halt.

For a few years now, the volume of wine sold in the Argentinean winemaking sector has been declining. A decade ago, 40 million extra wine cases were sold with respect to today. However, the domestic and export markets reported a dramatic decrease five years ago, and, in 2017, the total number of wine cases sold was 125 million.

With sporadic variations, Argentina's domestic market has been declining over the past 30 years. It finally reached a plateau in 2008, making any price changes directly dependent on price movements experienced by the products placed at the lower half of the wine pyramid, especially regarding Tetra Brik wine shipments. In parallel, the foreign market has shown a reduction in volume, both for bulk and bottled wines. In 2016, in total, this number has hit its lowest mark in the past decade.

The combination of smaller volume and lower prices led the industry's total revenue to a sum below that obtained in 2006 and 18% below its all-time high, recorded in 2011. The industry has been suffering consecutive decline in sales for five years in a row, resulting in very serious effects on several fronts, including:

The Fall in Grape Price The price of raw material is one of the main items affected when revenues decline. An asset with no alternative use in the current economy, its value is flexible, unlike that of other goods and services consumed by the industry. As a consequence of low prices, winemakers have had to cope with a very harsh reality in the past few years, sometimes working despite evident losses, which resulted in disinvestment and lesser quality. Smaller wineries, however, were less likely to transfer this adjustment to vinegrowers as they have a larger proportion of their own grapes for winemaking.

Disinvestment Between 2010 and 2015, according to information provided by wineries and collected by the Wine Division from Banco Supervielle, the industry's total assets fell about 19%, while fixed assets fell by 33%. This means that the industry today shows one third less competitive capacity in terms of investment operations in vineyards, machinery, and other fixed assets.

Concentration As with every economic process subject to adverse external conditions, the sector tends to concentrate on the stronger companies that show a better capacity to resist these conditions. Five years ago, companies whose sales worth was above ARS 500 million per year represented more than 78.7% of sales of the Argentinean viticulture industry, whereas now they represent 81.3%.

7.4   Distribution and Relationship Along the Distribution Chain

7.4.1   Argentinean Wine Markets

Of the 125 million cases sold in 2017 (Fig. 7.5), 80% were destined for the domestic market. In terms of revenue, this meant 64% revenue originating from the Argentinean market and 36% from export operations. This clearly shows the difference between export and domestic prices, the average export prices being much higher than the domestic ones. Argentina has been increasingly concentrated on producing wines for the medium- to high-end price ranges in global markets.

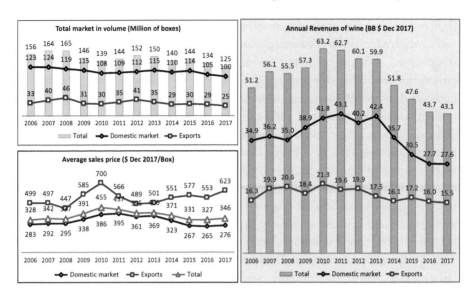

Fig. 7.5 Total market in volume (millions of cases), average sales prices (AR$ Dec. 2017/case), and annual revenues of wine (BB AR$ Dec 2017). (Source: Area del Vino)

When it comes to destination countries, the United States has been the most significant one in the last few years, importing 32% of Argentina's total bottled wine exports. The United States has been a steady and very dynamic market for Argentinean exports, especially due to Americans' preference for Malbec. In the second place, the United Kingdom accounts for 18% of the total export operations. Argentinean wines experienced a substantial change in focus in the UK market over the last decade. In the last years, efforts have been directed to importers with large participation shares of on-trade sales as well as off-trade chains with higher prices. After many years of continuous hard work, China has become a top market, joining Canada, Brazil, and the Netherlands.

7.4.2   Changes in the Domestic Market

The domestic wine market has followed behavioral patterns that mirror those of the global markets. For more than a decade, international discussions have ensued about the changes in consumer habits leaning toward higher-price wines, a phenomenon known as *premiumization*.

Several causes may help explain this change: firstly, older generations, with higher incomes, are slowly evolving into connoisseurs who are willing to pay higher prices for the wines they seek. Additionally, the 2008 crisis largely changed at a global scale the amount of wine that was consumed at home versus that which was consumed outside. Rather than paying high prices at restaurants, consumers prefer to buy wines on off-trade channels, which entails the possibility of purchasing higher-quality wines at lower prices when compared to hospitality establishments. This behavior, which started after the crisis in 2008, has remained valid until the present days.

In the case of Argentina, this process has been more accentuated, as the price pyramid started at a lower baseline than that of other countries. The total volume of wine consumption fell at an annual rate of 1% in the last decade. In this context, consumption of low-price wines, sold in Tetra Brik packaging, fell at an annual rate of 1.8%. However, bottled wine grew at an average of 1.2% annually, an early sign of *premiumization*. The phenomenon becomes increasingly evident when analyzing the evolution of bottled wines across different price ranges. Those at the bottom range (ARS 164 per case) fell at a rate about 5% annually, while the top price segment (ARS 835 per case) increased their volume at an annual average rate close to 19%.

It should be highlighted that sparkling wines and *frizzes* (sparkling wines typically aimed at a fun, young adult segment) have expanded greatly. This event not only signals a *premiumization* but also a change in consumers' behavior. Consumers seem to be shifting from still to sparkling wines, which additionally constitute a strategic introduction of a younger audience and of women into the wine market. This very marked change had a positive impact on those wineries leaning toward premium wine lines, as they could now improve their profitability. In turn, the wineries working in the lower price segments resorted to more aggressive strategies in order to maintain their position on the shelf, hoping for better consumption habits worldwide.

Despite the impressive sales growth volume evidenced by high-end wine lines, they still represent a small percentage of the total. In 2016, bottled wine accounted for almost 55% of the total volume, while higher price ranges, at ARS 422 per case, accounted for only 7.6%. The share of sparkling wines is about 4.6% of the total of volume. This market sector, it should be noted, represents 12.2% of the overall market that breaks down into 200 wineries that produce a total volume of 13.6 million cases, with an average of 68,000 cases per winery, figures obviously much higher for large wineries.

In the domestic market, the revenue derived from bottled wine represents 76% of the total revenue, and it has been growing at an average rate of 2% per year. The bottled wine market is clearly very attractive for investment, proudly showing considerable revenue both domestically and internationally. Due to their higher prices when compared to those available domestically, external markets have offered substantial investment opportunities.

7.4.3   Sales Channels in the Domestic Market

The current domestic wine market may be characterized as relatively saturated and highly competitive. A variety of elements serves to illustrate the said features:

Retraction from the Market   Over the past decade, the domestic wine market has been declining in volume. Given the projections for population growth, this scenario will ultimately create a market that becomes saturated with brands and competitive wineries.

Reorientation of Businesses and Wineries   Many wineries that became operational during the time of favorable exchange rates and that worked almost exclusively for international markets have to revise and change their strategy, which translated into a significantly increased competition in the domestic market.

Rise in the Commercial Chains' Negotiation Power   Commercial channels, especially large supermarkets, commercialize a relatively small portion of the total number of brands and wineries. The requirements for inventory rotation are essential for these sales channels, but few wineries have the capacity to comply with the said conditions. Many wineries do it to promote their brands, but as they begin to lose profits from a given channel, the endeavor becomes less appealing from a business perspective.

Discount Policies   With sales plummeting over the past few years, the business strategies designed by large retail alcohol beverage stores and wine shops aimed at offering discounts and special sale prices. These strategies are often devised by the stores themselves, in an attempt to attract new clients who will buy other products or who will contribute to product rotation. These strategies sometimes also include a variety of payment options, such as credit or debit cards, or the creation of a store club membership offering discounts to its members. Only large wineries with a large production volume, however, are able to take the impact of this type of deals, and very few can negotiate not being a part of them.

The current competitive climate is making commercialization costs grow significantly. According to a focus group covering 82 wineries, the reported commercial cost on their balance sheets was 18.9% of total sales in 2010 and rose to 21.7% in 2015. For promotional and discount-related activities, the cost for companies with a large domestic market share was about 7% of total sales.

Wineries in Argentina resort to various channels for sale. The proportion of on-trade wine sales (on-premise consumption) is about 17% of total volume, a figure similar to the worldwide average. Wineries will typically use distributors for the on-trade channel, while large-scale wineries will have their product transported directly.

Because of its promotional appeal, the on-trade channel is a very much coveted space. In fact, many wineries will seek to buy their own space into the wine lists. Beyond the type of customer visiting the hospitality establishment, measures need to be taken in order to preserve the wine properly. Additionally, wine-related sales skills are important. Furthermore, wineries should consider the risks associated with the sustainability of the hospitality business.

In the off-trade distribution channel (off-premise wine consumption), according to a survey conducted by Kantar Worldpanel in 2015, sales in large supermarkets represented 24% of the total volume and 30% of total revenue, similar to the global total. When including self-service or grocery stores with a format similar to that of small supermarkets, the proportion grew to 71% in volume and 72% in value, the difference being that self-service or grocery stores sell their products at higher average prices.

Although representing a smaller market share, alternative distribution channels are available. E-commerce stands as a very interesting option for businesses eager to sell their wine on this platform. This type of channel, albeit small, is growing at a rapid pace.

7.4.4   Winery Participation in Sales Channels

A huge challenge for many wineries in Argentina, the access to commercial venues from where to develop their winery's presence is key. Out of the 350 wineries participating in foreign markets with more than 2000 brands, only a reduced number are able to take active participation in the domestic market. The Argentinean supermarket distribution channel encompasses more than 60 companies. Of the total number of companies operating in the country, a reduced number, nonetheless, comprised by both national and international chains, represent a large percentage of total revenue.

Argentinean specialist stores, on their part, about 1000 establishments (some of these being more difficult to categorize as they sell other products as well), are scattered across the regions following the trends set by population and income distribution. However, a reduced number of specialist stores are currently working following a chain-like format, and, as such, they are running operations not only in main locations such as the city and province of

Buenos Aires but also in other regions of Argentina. Supermarkets have not been the only ones to develop online sale platforms for their customers, with leading specialist stores also developing their own, thus leading to a systematic and continuous growth in e-commerce.

With respect to winery presence in supermarkets and specialist stores, a small sample has been gathered, composed of the largest companies from each category, accounting for a total of 13 businesses, many of whom work jointly with chains throughout the country or have developed online platforms. These large chains, then, commercialize the wines from 189 wineries, a figure that represents half of the companies that export wines.

Fifty-five percent of all wineries have access to both supermarkets and large supermarkets. In other words, these establishments are responsible for selling the wines of only 104 wineries. In the case of specialist stores, on average, they sell the products from an increased number of wineries (139) and feature wines from smaller establishments that do not run business on larger channels. Only 54 wineries participate in both channels. Incidentally, these wineries are the largest ones in the country, many of them holding a dominant position in foreign markets as well. These figures, however, fail to reveal the fact that the supermarket with the most comprehensive winery list includes only 68 establishments, while the least comprehensive supermarket, with a modest domestic distribution, lists only 40. Specialist stores, on their part, cover 134 in the best-case scenario, while only 24 on the opposite end. This analysis clearly reveals not all wineries manage to be present across all channels.

It becomes clear, then, that the main off-trade sales channels leave aside a large number of wineries with their own wine brand. Many of these wineries have no participation in the domestic market as they only perform export operations. Others, however, will sell in small regional markets, while some have started to develop direct-to-consumer sales strategies as an alternative profitable option, in a scenario where wine tourism is of outmost importance.

Only 20 wineries (some of which belong to a single economic group) represent more than 85% of the total sales of wines from supermarkets. This shows that the said wineries focus on this channel in particular and hold the power to negotiate active participation on store shelves, in addition to maintaining rotation standards and margins that signify good business for commercial venues. The explicit nature behind the power of negotiation is evident in the ratio between the price paid by the customers and the price received by the wineries. On average, wineries receive 52% of what is paid by the consumer, which is much lower than many products with less added value.

7.5   Conclusion

The Argentinean viticulture sector has undergone striking transformations in the last quarter of the century, from the process of uprooting low-quality grapevines covering 72,000 ha (178,000 acres) to the plantation of highly demanded grapevines extending over 77,000 ha (185,000 acres), 30,000 ha (74,000 acres) of which correspond to Malbec. Additionally, production capacity has increased, combined with the arrival of national and international investments in the sector. Finally, two commercial developments are worth mentioning: wine *premiumization* in the domestic market and their export to the main international markets. The last five years have witnessed an adverse economic context in Argentina, which has slowed down the momentum for many wineries. In the next few years, lower inflation rates and a policy for remaining open to the world will allow the Argentinean wine industry to expand and evolve into an increasingly professional industry with an even sharper strategic focus, even, perhaps, with fewer companies operating.

References

Area del Vino – http://areadelvino.com
Bolsa de Comercio de Mendoza - https://bolsamza.com.ar
División Vinos Banco Supervielle - http://www.supervielle.com.ar
Euromonitor Internacional - http://www.euromonitor.com/
Instituto Nacional de Vitivinicultura (INV) - http://inv.gov.ar
Instituto Nacional de Tecnología Agropecuaria - https://inta.gob.ar
Kantar Worldpanel - https://www.kantarworldpanel.com/ar
Observatorio Vitivinícola Argentino - http://observatoriova.com
Organización Internacional de la Vid y del Vino - http://www.oiv.int
Nielsen Company - http://www.nielsen.com
Trade Map - https://www.trademap.org
Wines of Argentina - http://www.winesofargentina.org
Wine-Searcher - https://www.wine-searcher.com

8

The Chilean Wine Industry

G. Marcos Mora

8.1 Innovation, Production and Geographic Distribution of Chilean Viticulture and Wine

To successfully face the marketing of wines in the domestic and international markets, especially the latter, the Chilean wine industry has had to increase the quality of their products and conform to the requirements of target markets. This has involved major industry innovations, which occurred in the 1980s and 1990s (Alvarado 1999; Lima 2015). Some of the innovations were related to the use of stainless steel tanks and inert gases (Mora et al. 2014), pneumatic presses and oak barrels (French and American) for a limited number of years for the "aging" of the wines (Lima 2015). In this process, improving quality involved setting wines to market requirements. It needed high-quality grapes, which is consistent with that reported by Farinelli (2013) and Zago (2007), who stated that the quality is not only determined by the alcohol content of the grapes. In this sense, some vineyards are dedicated to producing super-premium wines and icons, usually made by their own production of grapes or on leased land, which can manage and/or select the grapes they use, in order to have quality control of the production. According to Farinelli (2013), from 1977 to 2011, most of the major vineyards in Chile incorporated the latest technology and a professionalization of the production process that allowed

G. M. Mora (✉)
Faculty of Agricultural Science, Department of Agricultural Economics,
University of Chile, Santiago, Chile
e-mail: mmorag@uchile.cl

© The Author(s) 2019   **177**
A. Alonso Ugaglia et al. (eds.), *The Palgrave Handbook of Wine Industry Economics*,
https://doi.org/10.1007/978-3-319-98633-3_8

them to generate higher-quality wines for the international market. According to Lima (2015), this was mainly due to foreign direct investment (in the form of joint ventures), which enabled local producers to quickly incorporate technology and know-how in the production of quality wines in exchange for better access to international markets. The super-premium brands that are produced in the country for export are usually the result of these joint ventures, but also full domestic investments currently exist. Moreover, it should be noted that for both domestic and international markets, there is a major proportion of low-end wines or streams. For the domestic market, nearly 50% are wines sold in box (bag in box), and about 70% of exports correspond to wines in bulk and bottled with prices below $30 a box.

Chile is a country with a great diversity of climates and soils allowing the development of a highly diversified viticulture. At the aggregate level, soils range from a basic in the north to more acid pH in the south; precipitation also increases from north to south, and thermal fluctuations are smoothed from east to west. Consequently, the situation described allows the expression of different varieties of grapes to reach the excellent potential if the variety-territory relationship is well chosen. Thus, the coastal areas of Chile are more appropriated for white grape varieties, such as Sauvignon Blanc and Chardonnay, and the inner areas favor red varieties, such as Cabernet Sauvignon. Below is a map with the different Chilean wine regions, which correspond to those indicated in the Agricultural Decree 464 of 1994, which established viticultural areas, and it provided rules for their use. Importantly, there are significant differences between the Chilean system designation of origin and employees in Europe. The Chilean system operates in an environment less regulated than the European. In Chile there is no figure of Regulatory Council with the powers it has in Europe; for example, Europe has the ability to set maximum production per hectare to ensure wine quality. In Chile, however, the responsibility for overseeing the procedure for granting certificates of designation of origin is carried out by private companies, previously the Agricultural and Livestock Service (AGS) has selected and authorized.

Of the 5.1 million hectares of arable land, viticulture represents approximately 137,000 hectares or 2.5% of the total. However, wine exports to 130 countries provide more than 1800 million dollars[1], and it generates more than 100,000 jobs, and it is expected that exports will reach 3 billion dollars in 2020 (ODEPA 2014), and if we add the domestic market, the wine sector would generate total sales of around 2500 million dollars. If you consider that the Chilean GDP, according to the World Bank, is around 277,200 million

[1] Exchange rate at 17 February 2016: 704.92 Chilean pesos per dollar. Source: Central Bank of Chile.

dollars, the share of the wine industry could be seen as marginal; however, it is necessary to take account of the contribution to GDP from other sectors involved in the wine business, such as transportation, logistics and communications, other manufacturing industries (glass, cardboard) and restaurants. Accordingly, it is an important sector for the Chilean economy for its capacity to generate productive linkages and its high added value, especially in the case of bottled wines.

According to Mora et al. (2014), the production of wine has an important impact on regional development, from the Coquimbo Region to the Araucania Region—it is one activity that takes place in much of the territory and has a strong impact on agricultural activities and labor employment as well as on demand of products and services. In recent times it has been extended to the regions of Atacama in the north and Lagos in the south. The wine industry is a cluster with a large capacity to generate added value, widely labor-intensive and of regional coverage; it involves a large number of industries related to suppliers and is involved in the exporting process, and it uses an extensive network of transport and communication for the development of its activities and has great potential to add value to their products.

Areas with vines intended for winemaking in the country are located between the regions of Atacama and Los Lagos, including the Metropolitan Region. According to the figures below, 74% of the vineyards correspond to red varieties and 26% of white varieties, mainly represented by Cabernet Sauvignon, Merlot and Carmenere for reds, and Sauvignon Blanc and Chardonnay for whites. Below is a chart with a greater number of varieties, highlighting Syrah and Carmenere, which have increased significantly in recent times.

Regarding the evolution of the vines, it is important to highlight the sustained growth of Carmenere, Syrah, Pinot noir, Cabernet Franc and Sauvignon Blanc (Table 8.1). However, it is necessary to pay attention to other grape varieties, which have also had a sustained and significant increase, and they approach 20,000 hectares. Behind this figure there is the incorporation of vines traditionally not produced in Chile such as Tempranillo, Viognier and Malbec.

In Chile, wine production is based mainly on a set of grape varieties of French origin and a local variety called Country (Pais), which currently accounts for about 5% of the total area of the Chilean vineyard. In 1985, the surface of this variety was nearly 30,000 hectares or approximately 25% of the current area, while Cabernet Sauvignon, the main cultivated variety at present, only reached just over 8000 hectares. Also, the first and largest change occurred between 1985 and 1994 with the increase from 245 to 4150 hectares

Table 8.1 Evolution of wine grape acreage by variety (ha)

	2010	2011	2012	2013	2014
Cabernet Sauvignon	38,425.7	40,837.0	41,521.9	42,195.4	44,176.4
Merlot	10,640.2	11,432.0	11,649.1	11,925.2	12,480.1
Chardonnay	10,834.0	10,970.4	10,570.9	10,693.9	11,633.8
Sauvignon Blanc	13,277.8	13,922.3	14,132.0	14,393.0	15,142.3
Chenin Blanc	55.8	55.8	55.8	55.8	56.0
Pinot noir	3306.8	3729.3	4012.5	4059.9	4195.9
Riesling	400.3	409.4	442.2	424.4	420.1
Semillón	929.7	959.0	920.9	902.5	968.1
País	5855.1	7079.2	7247.5	7338.7	7652.6
Carmenere	9502.0	10,040.0	10,418.1	10,732.5	11,319.5
Syrah	6886.8	7393.5	7744.6	7933.1	8432.2
Cabernet Franc	1345.0	1451.0	1533.3	1591.3	1661.5
Otros	15,371.7	17,667.6	18,389.1	18,116.2	19,453.9
Total	116,830.8	125,946.2	128,637.9	130,361.7	137,592.4

Source: Catastro vitícola de Chile 2014. SAG, 2014. División de Protección Agrícola y Forestal Subdepartamento de Viñas y Vinos, Inocuidad y Biotecnología Sección Viñas y Vinos

of Chardonnay, which was rigged to excellent commercial with the expansion of large vineyards near Aconcagua (Del Pozo 1998). Moreover, it should be noted that a number of hectares planted with vines still exist in the country that have not been declared to AGS because they correspond to micro farms (less than 0.5 hectares of planted vineyards), especially in the VIII region where Country is the main producing variety, also called Mission or Creole. However, according to vineyards registered by SAG 2014, there has been a sharp decline of this variety, which in 2006 approached 15,000 ha, and now it does not exceed 8000 ha.

In Chile the vast majority of wine grapes already use some irrigation system: 85% of cultivated hectares of white wine grapes and 90% of the hectares for wine grapes ink have some type of irrigation (micro-irrigation, drip, spray, gravitational, etc.) (Table 8.2). In the red varieties, the grape País is mainly grown in dry land. In this regard, rainfed vineyard is usually located in granitic and undulating topography, and soils show a marked water deficit, which translates into a vegetative weakening and low yield (1000–4000 kg per hectare). The variety País is a grape that records low prices, generally 50% less than the European varieties. However, in recent times there have been new products developed from this variety, and they are expected to contribute to added value; one of them is the foaming grapes and the other sour grapes, both having had the co-funding of the Foundation for Agrarian Innovation and the Ministry of Agriculture of Chile. Their yields are relatively low, on the order of 4000 kilos per hectare. The rest of white varieties and inks corresponding to fine strains are grown under some kind of irrigation.

Table 8.2 Cultivated area (ha) with grapevines in irrigated, rainfed and tended irrigation areas

Region	Water regime			Total
	Irrigated	Rainfed	Tended irrigation	
Tarapacá	5.00			5.00
Antofagasta	4.97			4.97
Atacama	117.42			117.42
Coquimbo	3371.67		11.90	3383.57
Valparaíso	10,137.29	18.40	6.50	10,162.19
Lib. Bdo. O'Higgins	46,610.97	679.20	91.90	47,382.07
Del Maule	46,385.52	6420.32	690.67	53,496.51
Del Bío Bío	2223.09	7052.06	292.90	9568.05
Araucanía	27.06	27.90		54.96
De los Lagos	19.00			19.00
Metropolitana	13,398.30	0.40		13,398.70
Total nacional	122,300.29	14,198.28	1093.87	137,592.44

Source: ODEPA

Regarding the vines-driven systems, it can be mentioned:

- In trellises: system was introduced in Chile in the second half of the nineteenth century by French technicians. Driving means consist of a frame and wires that support for lifting the vine at the approximate height of 1.2 to 1.5 meters, allowing better illumination of fruit and facilitating the work of care and harvesting. In addition, this technique allows the mechanization of vineyards, since it is currently one of the most commonly used forms of driving, mainly in vineyards intended for the production of preferably fine wines from the Central Valley (Table 8.3).
- In parronal: a driving system with heights of 1.8 to 2.0 meters, with horizontal trellis. It is widely used for the production of table grapes, although it is also used in some vineyards of Cabernet Sauvignon.
- In head or Gobelet: it was introduced by the Spaniards in the period of the conquest, so it is the oldest driving system; although this system is not suitable for the production of good-quality wines, it is still used in southern Chile and in dry vineyards.

8.2   Chilean Wine and Its Industrial Organization

Small vineyards in general are traditionally managed with low use of agrochemicals, facing greater technological backwardness, due to the lack of capital and poor access to financing, as well as other limitations related to soil fertility—low or excessive slope—and restricted access to water, thereby limit-

Table 8.3 Chile: surface area of vineyards according to conduction system (ha)

Region	Head	Double curtain	High trellises	Low trellises	Lira	Others	Parron	Scott Henry	Smart Dyson	Total
									Conduction system	
Tarapacá			5.0							5.0
Antofagasta			5.0							5.0
Atacama				24.4			93.0			117.4
Coquimbo	1.5		757.6	1310.7	8.9	109.8	1195.1			3383.6
Valparaíso	25.3		6627.1	3151.5	34.8	263.5	60.0			10,162.2
Lib. Bdo. O'Higgins	71.1	288.5	21,879.8	14,794.0	1116.6	988.7	8105.6	125.2	12.7	47,382.1
Del Maule	4753.1	668.9	15,604.5	23,107.4	610.5	853.2	7877.8	21.2		53,496.5
Del Bío Bío	6401.0		2053.7	782.1	69.4	97.7	16.4	147.9		9568.1
Araucanía	4.4		49.1	1.5						55.0
De los Lagos	0.2			18.8						19.0
Metropolitana	7.8	56.2	6849.5	5356.8	139.1	121.4	868.0			13,398.7
Total	11,264.4	1013.5	53,831.3	48,547.1	1979.3	2434.2	18,215.8	294.2	12.7	137,592.4

Source: Catastro vitícola 2014

ing opportunities for productive transformation. Its production is oriented to the local market of wine in bulk, and a significant percentage is marketed through informal channels. On the other hand, large traditional vineyards produce a wide range of wines for different consumers, both in domestic and foreign markets. They have large vineyards and have been pioneers in the opening and expansion of the export market. They achieve significant production and sales levels, and have a significant share of the domestic and foreign markets. In recent decades, there have emerged boutique vineyards and medium-sized export-oriented fine wines that have great capacity for innovation in the productive and commercial technology areas. They have generated direct distribution channels in different international markets, mainly, specialty shops and restaurants.

8.2.1 Investment Costs and Wine Grapes

According to Lima (2015), in the case of fine strains, the producer must incur a large initial investment to plant them (using a trellis system and drip irrigation). Also, you must wait at least two years to start production, which goes up to the fifth year just to achieve maximum production. When you consider the costs of planting and the first two years without production and fixed costs for the producer, who must incur mandatory cost to start production, which could eventually be recovered if he sells or leases the plantation to a third party, they represent between 16% and 21% of the total cost of production of the vineyard throughout their economic life (20 years).

Also, if you consider a return rate of 10% annually for the investment, which must be recovered in 20 years, the average total production cost per kg would rank between 0,15 and 0,33 dollars depending primarily on the level of production that can be achieved in the vineyard. Grape plantings, if properly maintained, can have a longer production than the usual 20 years (between 50 and 100 years); after recovering the initial investment, it becomes relevant to recover, at least, the annual costs of production, for which we take as a proxy for the average annual cost of production in the vineyard. This cost would be located between 0,12 and 0,27 dollars/kg produced.

Lima (2015) states that, with regard to the Country vine grape strain, whose production dates back to colonial times, it is important to know the average annual cost of production, which ranges between 0,10 and 0,21 dollar/kg, depending on the quantity produced. To estimate the average cost of production of the Country grape, as in the fine strains, yields are also important in the case of small winemakers (who have, on average, two hectares planted with wine grapes in the Bío Bio and four hectares in the region of Maule) having a large dispersion in unit production costs: for example, for low yields of 4000 kg/ha, the declared average costs range between 0,13 and 0,30 dollars/kg.

8.2.2   Prices Paid to Producers

In general, a steady decline of prices paid to producers is evident, irrespective of the grape variety and quality. This has been most pronounced in red varieties, which on average between 2011 and 2015 show a reduction of 65%, with the largest decline between 2014 and 2015. A similar situation occurs with white varieties, although somewhat with smaller magnitudes. Between 2011 and 2015, the prices paid for Sauvignon Blanc, Chardonnay and Semillon were reduced by 41%, with only a reduction in the last season which meant a decrease of 32% of the amount paid per kg. For a glimpse of the margin that could be presented in a vineyard, costs and prices of different varieties of wine grapes are presented (Table 8.4).

Moreover, it should be noted that prices for the Country variety, grown mainly in the upland of southern Chile, are historically recorded at least 50% lower than costs.

8.2.3   Land Tenure: Family Versus Corporate Enterprises

In Chile, for many years the wine-producing companies were mostly of family environment; the conversion of the Chilean industry entailed the develop-

Table 8.4 Costs and prices of wine grapes at producer level (dollars)

Costs and prices of wine grapes at producer level	Variety			
	Cabernet Sauvignon	Merlot	Carmenere	Country
Cost range(2012)	0.15–0.33	0.15–0.33	0.15–0.33	0.10–0.21
Average price, high quality (2012)	0.44	0.44	0.44	0.23
Average price, low quality (2012)	0.31	0.31	0.31	0.21
Average price, high quality (2015)	0.19	0.18	0.19	0.13
Average price, low quality (2015)	0.16	0.16	0.16	0.13

Source: ODEPA; Central Bank of Chile
Note: Exchange rate at 17 February 2016: 704.92 Chilean pesos per dollar

ment of the Chilean export model (mid-1980s) and the appearance of other legal properties. This is related to the foundations of the economic model applied in Chile since 1974, which favored large wine companies (Gilbert 2014). In this business environment, one of the most important was, and remains to be, Concha y Toro winemaking that was transformed from a family business into a company of a corporation type, which means that the traded value is known and therefore is subject to business performance. This transformation involved a more professional way of operating the technical and administrative management of the company. Today, Concha y Toro is one of the largest companies in the world, and the wine business investments have exceeded the borders with investments in Argentina and the USA, through the Trivento and Fetzer Vineyards companies, respectively (www.conchaytoro.com).

8.2.4 The Average Size Businesses and Wine Processors Types of Wines Marketed

In general, according to Mora et al. (2014), the Chilean wine industry has a significant concentration, as it shows about 50% of exports in value are attributed to almost ten companies, and only one of them is responsible for nearly 20% of Chilean wine exports value. This occurs in a context of an industry where more than 400 wineries spread between the Coquimbo Region and Bío Bío but with a high concentration in the Maule and O'Higgins Regions involved. It is also important to note that out of the total Chilean production, more than 75% of domestic is exported (Table 8.5).

Table 8.6 shows clearly that ten countries account for approximately 75% of Chilean exports, with five of them exceeding $100 million exported. In addition, it can be seen that there are countries from different continents, highlighting lately Asian countries like China and Japan.

With regard to the grape varieties used in the production of wines, the following are presented. The most important wines are blends, followed by monovarietal as Cabernet Sauvignon, Sauvignon Blanc, Chardonnay, Merlot and Carmenere, among others. It is important to relieve some unit values, such as wine with designation of origin, and some varieties such as Cabernet Franc and Pinot noir and sparkling wine. The latter wines have been an innovation in the field of exports, which have had a significant development in recent years.

Table 8.5 Chile: production of wines by type of wine and market (million liters)

Wine type and market	2013	2014
Domestic market (million liters)		
Popular wines (bag in box and others)	95.9	96.0
Low-end wines	7.3	6.7
Reserve wines	18.0	18.8
Great reserve wines	10.1	11.3
Sparkling wines	3.5	4.2
Others	81.7	91.9
Total domestic market	216.5	228.9
Export market (million liters)		
Bottled wines	435.8	451.8
0–20 dollars FOB/box	120.1	109.8
20–30 dollars FOB/box	169.4	186.4
30–40 dollars FOB/box	82.1	86.8
More than 40 dollars FOB/box	64.7	68.8
Others' packaging	26.5	26.7
Bulk	411.9	317.3
Sparkling wine	3.5	4.1
"Wine" with fruit	1.3	1.4
Total export market	879.0	801.3
Total	1095.4	1030.2

Source: ODEPA Y SAG, 2015

8.2.5 Types of Wineries: The Winegrowers' Farm Cooperatives and Industrial Enterprises

Chilean wineries generally are constituted as private companies, under different legal figures, the larger ones being open corporations and smaller companies with limited liability. There are more than 400 wineries in Chile. There are other types of legal constitution of the companies, but they are scarce, such as cooperatives, of which there is a record of 17 cooperatives with only 2 valid and active.

- Cooperative Wine Loncomilla was created on 14 January 1959, and it was formed by a group of visionary winemakers of San Javier and Villa Alegre. It acquired its legal personality by the Supreme Decree No. 13 dated 10 December 1959.
- Viña Lomas de Cauquenes was founded on 23 December 1939, under the name of Agricultural Cooperative Wine Cauquenes Ltda. (COVICA Ltda.), following the earthquake that destroyed most of the winemaking facilities owned by the winegrowers of the area. Today it is an important reference not only of the local economy but also of the regional economy. It currently has 240 members and a production of over 12 million liters of wine.

Table 8.6 Chile: exports of wines of denomination of origin in volume and FOB value

Countries	Volume (000 liters)				Value (000 USD FOB)				
	2014	January–November			2014	January–November			(%)
		2014	2015	Var. 2015/2014 (%)		2014	2015	Var. 2015/2014 (%)	
United Kingdom	57,319	54,089	53,538	−1.0	177,486	168,122	152,840	−9.1	11.7
China	31,880	28,599	43,755	53.0	110,577	99,451	144,533	45.3	11.0
USA	38,183	34,976	37,103	6.1	148,892	136,237	143,747	5.5	11.0
Japan	42,168	38,749	46,666	20.4	124,703	115,019	135,612	17.9	10.3
Brazil	33,852	31,944	34,806	9.0	109,207	102,721	103,736	1.0	7.9
The Netherlands	30,225	28,451	26,556	−6.7	98,637	93,215	76,786	−17.6	5.9
Canada	12,942	12,080	13,163	9.0	65,713	61,300	58,961	−3.8	4.5
Ireland	12,889	12,392	12,850	3.7	43,173	41,786	37,255	−10.8	2.8
Denmark	11,051	10,204	10,532	3.2	44,695	41,414	36,499	−11.9	2.8
Mexico	10,599	9953	12,135	21.9	32,438	30,385	33,888	11.5	2.6
Subtotal	281,108	261,437	291,104	11.3	955,521	889,650	923,857	3.8	70.4
Other countries	132,461	121,763	110,596	−9.2	466,728	427,551	387,972	−9.3	29.6
Total	413,569	383,200	401,700	4.8	1,422,249	1,317,201	1,311,829	−0.4	100.0

Source: ODEPA with information from the National Customs Service. Figures subject to review by further reports

- The Cooperative wine Curicó (ViñaRobles) was purchased by Concha y Toro in 2008.

8.2.6 Contractual Arrangements Between Warehouses and Distribution

There are generally arrangements or commitments and not proper contracts. In this regard, there are agreements between wineries and restaurants to sell their wines, and something similar happens between warehouses and supermarkets. Large wineries sell their products through distributors, which can be divided between those who are responsible for the internal market or external market. Some of the major wineries have offices in other countries, where sellers are directly related to various retailers who contact customers, either in the retail market (off-trade market) or hotels, pubs and restaurants (on-trade market). Small wineries have vendors who contact directly with distributors or sell directly to restaurants or other consumption locations.

In general, the most common of the great vineyards Incoterms (relative to the price paid for export) is Free on Board (FOB). At this price the vineyard exporters are responsible to leave the wine on the cargo ship; thereafter the buyer is responsible for the costs and risks incurred to deliver the wines at the port of destination. Finally, as suggested by Gilbert (2014), exporters need to deepen their knowledge about new changes taking place in the distribution, in which, in most countries, the power of retailers has been increasing. Consequently, the Chilean industry needs to be more closely linked to the retail channel (supermarket) and the consumer.

8.2.7 Contractual Arrangements Between Growers and Winemakers

Historically it has not been a practice to formalize the sale of grapes from growers to wineries. This situation has created problems between the actors in the chain of wine, because it has created problems of information asymmetry—misunderstanding in some cases between the parties taking advantage some of the wineries to pay less and even some moments below the cost of production. Currently, it has been regulated but not for intervention but rather for business sustainability, as international demand is requiring better quality and the wineries do not have enough grapes to cope with the demand and are used to buy from third parties under the technical assistance of the winery encouraging to produce grapes that allows making the required wine.

According to Lima (2015), in the Chilean market, three types of contracting grapes are considered by the winery:

1. Long-term recruitment. In this arrangement, the production of wine undertaking by the winery establishes a fairly detailed contract with the producer, where rather strict conditions are established for the management of the plantation during the grapes growth, such as maximum yields and handling requirements for the harvest. For such contracts usually a high price is set per kilogram of grapes. These contracts are generally used by producers whose land has exceptional conditions to produce good-quality grapes that can be converted into wines of high quality. Currently these contracts are used increasingly in the Chilean market.
2. Annual procurement. In this manner, intermediaries or wineries sign contracts with a base and a maximum price. These contracts are generally offered during the time between the grapes growing period and the harvest, and they are not renewed every year. This type of contract is currently being used by some small and medium grapes producers, dedicated to cultivate both traditional and fine varieties. According to what has been observed, middlemen made this contract with small producers, and wineries do the same with large producers. One of the frequent complaints of such contracts is that they are not always respected by the producer if he can get a better price for its produce.
3. Spot market. It is the market that exists throughout the harvest time. In this market the producer sells to a broker or grape vineyard in kilo format, regardless of probable alcohol levels or receiving an award for probable alcohol degree. In some cases brokers offer an initial base price for the grapes, which is subsequently adjusted upwards depending on whether the kilo of grapes ended trading at a higher price with large vineyards, which is not a common practice among all intermediaries. The price offered by intermediaries on the spot market is the same for all grape growers who want to sell, without additional quality considerations.

Then, with a focus on the value chain, activities and actors involved in the chain are presented. In this regard, the logic of a traffic light (red, critical; yellow, to be improved; and green, in good condition) can mean that small companies are the ones with the largest shortcomings in general (yellow and red) in both specific chain activities and the overall support. In general, large wineries have few shortcomings to stay and grow in this competitive market (Fig. 8.1).

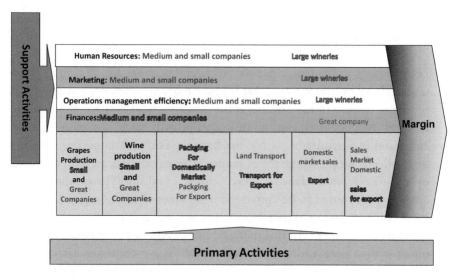

Fig. 8.1   Chile: value chain in the wine industry

8.3   Business Strategies for Marketing, Labeling and Communicating with Consumers

In the 1970s, buying wine in Chile was relatively simple, because it could be found in a liquor store or supermarket, bottled in 750 ml or 1 liter (at that time was the family wine) or larger format (5 liters of glass containers placed in a wicker mesh, which have now evolved to the package pet). There was no wine in boxes (bag in box), and the supply was very limited in terms of trademarks; there was no internet and promotion/advertising, which is why the source of information was the shop and talk to the clerk, something simple. Currently, the search for information is more complex, mainly due to the diversity of products both on shops and on virtual platforms. Moreover, the available supply has changed a lot, starting with the rapid development of supermarkets and high participation of food retailing (Reardon and Berdegué 2002). They have become the main shopping plaza wines. Along these lines, there are supermarkets oriented to sell differentiated products and others selling generic products. There are also specialty shops, which aimed at high-income segments of the market, where they offer a wide range of wines, including imported wines, and they are located in areas with residents who belong to a high socioeconomic status. With respect to the on-trade, the offer is available mainly at restaurants and hotels, which charge prices between 30% and 100% more than the off-trade channels (supermarket, specialty store, liquor stores).

In the past 30 years, the search systems of information have significantly changed not only for wine but for most food products, affecting especially younger consumers, who have a greater ability to master modern technology to obtain information on product characteristics. In this regard, the penetration rate of internet as a promotional space for wine or as a distribution channel is still small but steadily increasing with the passage of time. The internet is also widely used by wine consumers as a source of information. Other sources of information include journals, assistance from a salesperson at the shop and promotional events taking place at the end of the harvest and other events held throughout the year. However, a major source of information is the recommendations of friends and family.

8.3.1 Consumer Preferences

Undoubtedly, the scenario of purchase choice in the level of wine consumption in Chile has become more complex. In the 1970s, the choice was linked to the price, to the type (red or white) and to five existing commercial brands in the market at that time. The grape variety declared on the label, wines with lower alcohol content, the geographical area of production, prizes, carbon footprint and fair trade, among others, were not considered at that time. Today these attributes frequently appear in wines that are over $10 a bottle. The above reflects that the wine market in Chile has changed drastically. The price and brand are the only two attributes that customers consider while choosing a current or cheap wine, and even in these wines, the grape variety is declared on the label. Today, the main retail agent, the supermarket has on its shelves predominantly Chilean wines but also has imported wines. In the same vein, the specialty stores in Chile have both domestic and imported sophisticated wines, but in much greater diversity than supermarkets (Mora et al. 2013). When switching to bottled wine, attributes that the consumer considers in buying extend to four or six, and the price, the brand, the strain, the type of wine (reserve or varietal), the year of harvest and valley origin of the grapes are the attributes considered specifically; price is one of the most relevant variables in analyzing the marketing of wines, and results in many studies show a direct correlation between price and quality (Gneezy and Gneezy 2011; Schnettler and Rivera 2003; Mora 2004). It is also considered an important element when choosing a wine variable (Lockshin et al. 2006, 2009). This variable has also been analyzed from the standpoint of the demand price elasticity. In Chile, the prices of wine range between 80 and 100 dollars a bottle and have an inelastic price behavior, while the generic wines have a more elastic behavior, similar to those reported by Panzone (2012). The trademark has been analyzed as a choice criterion (Lockshin et al. 2006; Schnettler et al. 2012). In Chile, regarding the trademark, there have been established differences between supermarket own brands and trademarks, being this the last preference of consumers as they minimize the risk of dissatisfaction. As for grape varieties and geographical locations, the preferences are Cabernet Sauvignon in red wines produced in the valleys of Maipo, Colchagua and Maule (Mora et al. 2008). It is important to bear in mind that the Maule Valley is the largest in Chile (it comprises 40% of the total area of vineyards in Chile); however, it does not have the kind of national and international recognition that the Colchagua Valley has had. However, recently this valley has received some international awards and has developed a communication campaign, which have allowed it to position itself in the domestic and international markets. Moreover, in recent times other attributes involved in the decision buying process have begun to appear, such as alcohol, fair trade and carbon footprints. In this regard, Mora et al. (2012) identified the highest level of antioxidants (flavonols) for consumers' preferences in all segments analyzed of residents in Santiago de Chile tested. Some examples of "innovative" attributes observed in the Chilean market are presented.

Chilean consumer loyalty of wine in the off-trade channel is only expressed toward certain brands, such as wines with a strong position in the convenience segments (with bottled priced at $3–10), for example, Santa Rita Three Medals, Misiones de Rengo gray sticker, Santa Emiliana, Casillero del Diablo from Concha y Toro, Black Cat San Pedro and Carmen Margaux vineyard, where consumers reduce their risk by buying well-known brands which is consistent with the results obtained by Schnettler et al. (2012). For many other brands, there is no loyalty, also evidenced in part by the rejection of traditional brands in favor of supermarket own brands. There are also wines sold in bag-in-box packaging priced between $2 and 3 a liter. In this segment of wine, there is a loyalty linked to a low price and quality standard.

From the perspective of demand, linked to the attitudes and perceptions, the Chilean domestic market in several market segments are displayed, as described in Chile by Schnettler and Rivera (2003), Mora et al. (2010), Schnettler et al. (2012), Mora (2012a, b) and Mora et al. (2012). There are also some of them similar to those described in other countries like Spawton (1990) in Australia, Martínez-Carrasco (2002), Martínez-Carrasco et al. (2006) and Mora et al. (2004a, b) in Spain, Hollebeek et al. (2007) in New Zealand and Magistris et al. (2011) in the USA and Spain. Let us review the ones that are evident in Chile: "aspirational" tend to consume the same wines as those people who have a higher socioeconomic level; "ethnocentric" prefer their local products; "skeptic" see wine as an emblematic and different product but opt for healthy component of a wine; "modern millennium" review the available supply and pay attention to package design and labeling; "involved" appreciate the wine and buy larger quantities of wine; "basic or essential" buy ordinary wine, for low price and higher-frequency purchase and consumption; and "traditional baby boomers" are now more affluent, interested in the product, and looking for differentiation when there are special occasions. However, even when it was found, the existence of these segments in the Chilean market segments "involved" and "basic or essential" are those that concentrate more than 70% of this market, especially the latter.

Chilean wine consumers that belong to the millennium generation are similar to that described by Magistris et al. (2011) for the US millennium generation consumers, as people who are interested to try first and then buy and consume. It can be achieved through tasting and evaluating the aroma and flavor attributes, similar to that reported by Schmidt et al. (2013), who points out that these are the most important when choosing wine attributes. In studies conducted by Mora et al. (2008), Mora et al. (2010), Adasme et al. (2012) and Mora et al. (2012b), it is a segment that is characterized by its skepticism about wine, which could be associated with the millennium generation, according to age, since the people described are relatively young. Currently the younger generations of Chilean wine consumers are more demanding in terms of information. Consequently, people are increasingly buying reviewed wines from the available supply, and if there is something that appeals to them, they buy it.

8.3.2   Number of Brands, Price Positioning and Volume Segment

Lima (2015) makes an estimate of the domestic market share of the three largest wineries in Chile (Concha y Toro, San Pedro and Santa Rita), considering all their brands and subsidiaries, according to the sales reported (for both current and premium wines) on their balance sheets and reports to the authorities. It is estimated that these three vineyards accounted for 87% of the domestic market in 2014 (85% in 2013) and sales focused mainly on bottling and packaging formats. It should be noted that those three main vineyards indicated virtually no wine in bulk format sold in the domestic and international markets. Then, the information and prices listed are shown.

For Concha y Toro, one can say that it is a company facing all segments of the market, since the icon wines, led by Carmín de Peumo satisfying the ultra-premium segment on the top, are much above Tocornal boxed wines, Clos de Pirque and Fressco Cooler, which are placed at the bottom segment of popular wines (Table 8.7).

Table 8.7 Concha y Toro Winery: segment, brand and price of their wines

Segment	Brand	Price in dollars 2014
Ultra premium	Carmín de Peumo	133.3
	Gravas del Maipo	73.8
	Don Melchor	110.7
	Terrunyo	29.8
	Amelia	29.8
Super premium	Marqués de Casa Concha	16.3
	Gran Reserva Serie Riberas	10.3
Premium	Trío	7.4
	Casillero del Diablo	5.9
	Late Harvest	3.5
Sparkling	Subercaseaux	5.2
Varietal	Sunrise	3.1
	Santa Emiliana	2.8
Bi-varietal	Frontera	2.8
Popular	Exportación	1.9
	Exportación Selecto	2.1
	Clos de Pirque	1.9
	Tocornal	1.6
	Fressco Cooler	1.6

Note: Exchange rate at 17 February 2016: 704.92 Chilean pesos per dollar
Source: Central Bank of Chile

In contrast with Concha y Toro, Santa Rita vineyard produces wines in box. The most basic level is the wine "Santa Rita Three Medals", which is a varietal bottling wine (Table 8.8).

8.3.3   Commercial and Business Strategies of Chilean Wineries

According to a study undertaken by Lima (2015) for the Office of Agricultural Studies and Policies of the Ministry of Agriculture of Chile, some guidelines followed by the largest wine companies that supply the domestic market in Chile are presented.

In the "Premium" segment, it competes with large- and medium-sized wineries, mainly with Santa Rita, San Pedro Tarapaca, Santa Carolina, Undurraga, Errázuriz and Cousiño Macul wineries. It competes, albeit on a much smaller scale, with smaller wineries whose production and sales of wine in the "Premium" segment are focused mainly on exports. Sales in the "Popular" segment focus on packaged wine carton format (bag in box), which in 2014 represented approximately 45% of total sales volume in this segment. In this segment, Concha y Toro believes that foreign wineries find it very difficult to

Table 8.8 Santa Rita Winery: segment, brand and price

Winery	Segment	Brand	Price in dollars 2014
Santa Rita	Icono	Casa Real Santa Rita Reserva Especial Cabernet	132.4
		Bougainville Petite Sirah Santa Rita 2010	113.5
	Ultra premium	Pehuén Carménere Santa Rita	56.8
		Santa Rita Floresta Apalta Cabernet Sauvignon	43.8
		Santa Rita Floresta Cabernet Franc	43.8
		Santa Rita Triple C 2010	37.1
	Súper premium	Casa Real Carmenere Santa Rita	16.7
		Casa Real Cabernet Sauvignon Santa Rita	16.7
		Santa Rita Casa Real Cabernet Sauvignon	14.6
	Premium	Medalla Real Gran Reserva Cabernet Sauvignon	13.4
		Secret Reserve Red Blend Santa Rita	8.6
		Santa Rita Medalla Real Cabernet Sauvignon	7.9
	Varietal	Vino 120 3 Medallas Santa Rita	3.2

Note: Exchange rate at 17 February 2016: 704.92 Chilean pesos per dollar
Source: Central Bank of Chile

match the price-quality ratio that is offered by national wineries, especially in the "People" segment.

It is considered that Concha y Toro in order to remain competitive in the Chilean market has to keep their marketing in the "Popular" segment, which could be extrapolated to the dairy cows cell of the Boston consulting group matrix, that is, high share but low growth market.

Local market strategy. To increase the market share in the domestic market, Concha y Toro has focused its efforts on its strongest brands in terms of volume and acceptance. So they have sought to reinforce their participation in the "Popular" segment as well as an increasing presence in the "Premium" segment portfolio with Casillero del Diablo.

Concha y Toro considers that the distribution in Chile is essential. To increase growth in the domestic market, the company believes that it should distribute its wines in many retail locations with alcohol license sale, including bars, restaurants and wine shops, and also be leaders in the retail, especially given the growth experienced by sales of this channel in all territories.

Concha y Toro also indicates that it is constantly developing new formats and updating the presentation of the products that make up its portfolio. The methods of advertising and marketing strategies are different depending on the type of clients and their respective preferred product segment. During 2014, the company claims to have made great efforts in advertising their great reserve brands, Clos de Pirque, Casillero del Diablo and Marques de Casa Concha, through campaigns on radio, television and press, that is, wines that are below $12 a bottle.

8.3.4 Business Strategy

The strategy states that Concha y Toro seeks to sustain attractive growth rates and to achieve greater brand penetration and visibility in different markets. Therefore, it has developed a wide range of products seeking to participate in different market segments, offering good-quality wines at competitive prices. They have focused mainly on the growth of the "Premium" segment, which according to reports is attractive given its growth potential and prices, allowing them to improve their sales mix and increase its average sales price. Following this strategy, Concha y Toro has invested nearly $407 billion pesos in the last ten years in land, vineyards, infrastructure and other businesses to increase their own production. They also have constantly developed new products, research into new varieties and incorporate new production valleys. As for the commercial area, Concha y Toro notes that it has strengthened its global distribution network with the help of new own regional offices in key markets. At the same time, they indicate that in Argentina they have followed the same business model they have used in Chile since the Trivento winery has grown steadily in exports, taking advantage of the penetration of Argentine wines in major markets. The budget for 2015 is around US $50 million, which is planned to be allocated to support for future sales growth through the planting of new vineyards and expansion of productive capacity. Concha y Toro intends to continue planting new vineyards and the corresponding developing new infrastructure necessary on Chilean and the US grounds.

- Vineyards owned by the company. In 2014, approximately 46.8% (35% in 2013) of wine production corresponded to "Premium", "Varietal" and "Bi-Varietal" categories. These wines are produced from grapes from their own plantations or leases. However, the companies consider that their own grape production provides greater ease for cost control and enables obtaining raw material of better quality and reliability of their offer.
- Grapes from other vineyards. To satisfy its demand for production, Concha y Toro buys grapes from about 828 independent producers in Chile. The quantities purchased and the identity of those producers do

not vary substantially from one year to the next, since the list of producers remains the same for years. The criteria used to choose the producers are the geographical location, the grape variety and the agricultural methods. To guarantee quality, Concha y Toro offers technical assistance based on criteria similar to those used at its own vineyards. The company also aims to make purchases in small wineries that produce wine.

The winery San Pedro Tarapaca (VSPT) believes that it competes primarily against Concha y Toro and Santa Rita, and their competitive strength is based on a broad product portfolio, well-known brands and well-established distribution networks. In 2014, Concha y Toro and Santa Rita had a market share of approximately 27% and 31%, respectively. Along with these competitors, San Pedro Tarapaca considers that it also competes with Santa Carolina and medium wineries, such as Undurraga and Cousiño Macul, and small wine producers that make up the informal market of wine in Chile.

8.4   Conclusions

Chile is a major player in the wine world trade occupying the fifth place on worldwide exports with more than 1800 million dollars. There are more than 137,000 hectares of mainly French varieties, including Cabernet Sauvignon and Sauvignon Blanc. There are over 400 wineries, but just 10% account for more than 50% of total exports. The domestic market accounts for approximately 20% of the total selling, and the rest (80%) is gone to exports. The main international markets are the UK, the USA, China, Japan and Brazil. Exports of bottled wines with designation of origin and sparkling wines have had successful economic performance over the last five years. The vineyard area stretches from north to south along 900 km, and the areas of greatest wine importance are in the regions of O'Higgins and Maule, both located in the Central Valley.

Chile has achieved worldwide significant recognition. Every day the entire industry searches ways to improve competitiveness and makes progress in the development of the various components of the value chain. This requires further research, development and innovation, which require support, commitment and assessment of applied research by companies that are directly or indirectly related to the wine industry and also from the State. The search for a better value chain and production chains necessarily involves the generation of an accurate multidimensional knowledge that responds effectively to the solution of the problems of this industry making it increasingly competitive.

References

Adasme, C., M. Mora, and M. Sánchez. 2012. Segmentación del consumidor de vino orgánico en Talca, Chile. In: Marketing agroalimentario Aplicaciones metodológicas estudios de casos en el contexto global. Ed. Pearson, México.

Agricultural Decree N° 464, 1994, establishes viticultural zoning and sets standards for its use (official journal of May 26, 1995, last official daily modification n ° 38.268 of September 22, 2005).

Alvarado, R. 1999. Los caminos del vino. Ed. Universitaria. 131 pp.

Del Pozo, J. 1998. Historia del vino Chileno: Desde 1850 hasta hoy. Ed. Universitaria.

Farinelli, F. 2013. *Innovation and learning dynamics in the Chilean and Argentine wine industries.* AAWE working paper no. 145. Disponibleen: http://www.wine-economics.org/aawe/wp-content/uploads/2013/12/AAWE_WP145.pdf

Gilbert, J. 2014. Chile país del vino: Historia de la Industria Vitivinícola, 1492–2014. Ed. Universitaria. 300 p.

Gneezy A. and U. Gneezy. 2011. Price-based expectations, advances in consumer research, volume 38. Ed. Darren W. Dahl, Gita V. Johar, and Stijn M.J. Van Osselaer. Duluth: Association for Consumer Research. Disponible en: http://www.acrwebsite.org/volumes/v38/acr_v38_15794.pdf

Hollebeek, L., S. Jaeger, R. Brodie, and A. Balemi. 2007. The influence of involvement on purchase intention for new world wine. *Food Quality and Preference* 18: 1033–1049.

Lima, J. 2015. Estudio de caracterización de la cadena de producción y comercialización de la agroindustria vitivinícola: estructura, agentes y prácticas. Estudio encargado por Oficina de Estudios y Política Agraria del Ministerio de Agricultura de Chile. 209 pp.

Lockshin, L., W. Jarvis, F. d'Hauteville, and J.P. Perrouty. 2006. Simulations from discrete choice experiments to measure consumer sensitivity to brand, region, price, and awards in wine choice. *Food Quality and Preference* 17: 166–178.

Lockshin, L., S. Mueller, J. Louviere, L. Francis, and P. Osidacz. 2009. Development of a new method to measure how consumers choose wine. *The Australian and New Zealand Wine Industry Journal* 24: 35–40.

Magistris, T., E. Groot, A. Gracia, and L.M. Albisu. 2011. Do Millennial generation's wine preferences of the "new world" differ from the "old world"? *International Journal of Wine Business Research* 23 (2): 145–160.

Martínez-Carrasco, L., M. Brugarolas, F.J. Del Campo, and A. Martínez. 2006. Influence of purchase place and consumption frequency over quality wine preferences. *Food Quality and Preference* 17: 315–327.

Mora, M. 2004. Estudio de las actitudes y percepciones de los consumidores hacia los vinos de las Denominaciones de Origen de la Comunidad Valenciana. Tesis Doctoral. Departamento de Estudios Económicos y Financieros, Universidad Miguel Hernández de Elche, 270 p.

———. 2012a. Los grandes aportes de la agronomía en los últimos 20 años. In: Un siglo de compromisos con la innovación científica y tecnológica de la agricultura 1910–2010. Sociedad Agronómica de Chile, pp. 85–102.

———. 2012b. Conociendo al consumidor chileno de vinos para construir una relación comercial de mayor plazo relativo. Encuentro Nacional de Facultades de Administración y Economía – ENEFA 2012. Universidad de Talca, 21–23 de noviembre de 2012.

Mora, M., V. Padilla, and J. Espinoza. 2004a. Los países emergentes en el mercado mundial vitivinícola: el vino chileno, situación actual perspectivas y estrategia. Revista de Enología y Viticultura Profesional. N° 92:5–26. Año XV. Mayo – Junio. 2004.

Mora, M., M. Brugarolas, L. Martínez-Carrasco, and J. A. Espinoza. 2004b. Actitudes hacia los vinos de Denominación de Origen (D.O.) en la Comunidad Valenciana Revista ITEA (Información Técnica Económica Agraria). Asociación Interprofesional para el Desarrollo Agrario. pp. 119–123. Noviembre 2004. Número Extraordinario. Zaragoza. España.

Mora, M., C. Juri, R. Marchant, and N. Magner. 2008. Factores y atributos que explican la lealtad del cliente de vinotintoembotellado en las tres comunas de mayor ingreso de la Región Metropolitana, Chile. II Congreso Regional de Economía Agraria – XIII Congreso de Economistas Agrarios de Chile, 5 y 7 de noviembre de 2008 en Montevideo, Uruguay.

Mora, M., N. Magner, and R. Marchant. 2010. Segmentación de mercado de acuerdo a estilos de vida de consumidores de vino orgánico de la Región Metropolitana de Chile. *Revista IDESIA* 28 (3): 25–34.

Mora, M., S. Boza, Y. Aravena, and B. Schnettler. 2012. You can add functional value of an attribute on the label of a bottle of wine? 5th European Conference on Sensory and Consumer Research, Bern, Switzerland, 9–12, September 2012.

Mora, M., C. Adasme, and R. Escobedo. 2013. The Chilean wine market: Comparing wine sales at supermarkets and specialty wine shops. In: Wine case business case studies thirteen cases from the real world of wine business management. The Wine Appreciate Wild. Academy of Wine Business Research (AWBR), 97–108 p.

Mora, M., B. Schnettler, and G. Lobos. 2014. El gran crecimiento de la Industria Vitivinícola Chilena. In: La economía del vinos en España y en el Mundo. *Serie Economía* 23: 581–623.

Panzone. 2012. Alcohol tax, price-quality proxy and discounting: A reason why alcohol taxes may rebound. *Journal of Agricultural Economics* 63 (3): 715–736.

Reardon, T., and J. Berdegué. 2002. The rapid rise of supermarkets in latinamerica: Challenges and opportunities for development. *Development Policy Review* 20 (4): 371–388.

Schmidt, T., R. Bradley, and J. Taber. 2013. Consumer valuation of environmentally friendly production practices in wines, considering asymmetric information and sensory effects. *Journal of Agricultural Economics* 64 (2): 483–504.

Schnettler, B., and A. Rivera. 2003. Características del proceso de decisión de compra de vino en la IX Región de La Araucanía. *Ciencia e InvestigaciónAgraria* 30 (1): 1–14.

Schnettler, B., H. Miranda, J. Sepúlveda, N. Mills, M.J. González, M. Mora, and G. Lobos. 2012. Acceptance of national and store brands of wine by supermarket consumers in the south of Chile. *Ciência e Técnica Vitivinícola* 27 (1): 3–15.

Zago. 2007. The design of quality pricing in procurement settings via technology estimation, working paper, Universidad de Verona. Disponible en: http://idei.fr/sites/default/files/medias/doc/conf/fpi/papers_2006/zago.pdf

Websites

OFICINA DE ESTUDIOS Y POLÍTICAS AGRARIAS (ODEPA). Ministerio de Agricultura de Chile: http://www.odepa.cl

PROGRAMA DE DESARROLLO A LAS EXPORTACIONES (PROCHILE). Ministerio de Relaciones Exteriores de Chile: http://www.prochile.cl

Vinos de Chile.: http://www.vinasdechile.com/

WINES OF CHILE.: http://www.winesofchile.com

9

The South African Wine Industry

Nick Vink

9.1 Introduction

A number of aspects of the structure of the South African wine industry are of interest to any speculation about the likely futures of the industry. These include the structure of farm sizes, the relationship between what was traditionally called 'the trade' or producer wholesalers (brand owners) and the erstwhile cooperatives, the dominance of one firm in the market for branded wine, and the competitiveness of the industry as a whole, that is, including the upstream and downstream industries that service the sector. In this chapter, the origin and consequences of these are explained, to give a clearer picture of the likely future trajectory of the industry.

9.2 Historical Background

The South African wine industry, which marked its 360th vintage in 2018, has experienced only three long expansions throughout its history, and each of these was driven by export markets (Vink et al. 2018a). The first of these coincided with the establishment of the Dutch settlement in the Cape in 1652. This reliance on Europe and European geostrategic interests is summarized by Katzen (1982: 185) as follows:

N. Vink (✉)
Department of Agricultural Economics, Stellenbosch University,
Stellenbosch, South Africa
e-mail: nv@sun.ac.za

The new Cape always remained a genuinely colonial society, which could not achieve the autonomy and self-sufficiency of the San and Khoikhoi societies which preceded it. The settlers provided both the impetus for its growth and the measure of its dependence. The birth of the settler community was linked with the economic value to Europe of the Cape's resources, a harbour with fresh water where fresh vegetables and meat could be produced for passing ships. The existence of the 'Tavern of the Seas', the town of De Kaap [Cape Town] and its hinterland of corn and wine farming in the south-western Cape, was always dependent on its usefulness to Europe, expressed in the size of the Cape market constituted by the garrison and the visiting ships.[1]

Europeans knew about the Cape since 1488 when the Portuguese seafarer Bartholomew Diaz reached the Cape on his way to opening the Asian spice trade. However, the Portuguese had little interest in a settlement there because they (Katzen 1982: 187)[2]:

[C]rossed the Indian Ocean on the south-west monsoon on their voyages from Lisbon to Goa or Cochin, usually stopping at Mozambique on the way out, St Helena or the Azores on the way home.

In other words the Cape was too close to the origin of both outward and homebound journeys.

The Dutch and the English traveled around the Cape at the same time and with the same objective: to break the Portuguese monopoly of the spice trade (Terreblanche 2014). They both aimed at the weak point of the Portuguese monopoly, namely, South-East Asia rather than further north in China. The Cape was conveniently almost halfway on this new route (Katzen 1982)—thus the creation of the refreshment station on 6 April 1652 by the Dutch East India Company (the VOC). However, the settlement soon proved too expensive to run, so in 1657 the Company started to hand out land and cheap loans to free burghers to encourage settlement, in the process disregarding the land rights of the indigenous population (Terreblanche 2014).

Unfortunately, these free burghers also wanted to be free to take on slaves. Williams (2016) explains that Jan van Riebeeck, the first Commander of the settlement, took less than two months after his arrival to ask the company

---

[1] The total settler and slave population of the Cape remained lower than 1000 people through to around 1720, while the average number of sailors and soldiers aboard ships in the Cape Town harbor numbered more than 6000 per year, hence an export market (Boshoff and Fourie 2010).

[2] Katzen quotes from Boxer (2001). This is a translation (originally published in 1959) of a Portuguese publication by Bernardo Gomes de Bruto on famous Portuguese shipwreck stories.

authorities in Batavia (present-day Jakarta) for slaves 'to do the dirtiest and heaviest work in place of the Netherlanders'. As the production of wine constituted the largest source of revenue to the VOC for much of the first century, the wine farmers were politically influential. However, the VOC would not allow the enslavement of the indigenous 'free' Khoi, as they wanted to trade cattle with them. Slaves were, therefore, brought in, the first coming from what is now Angola, but most thereafter from the east. Thus, in the words of Williams (2016: 895) 'The elementary social and political relations of a slave economy and a slave society had been put in place –slaves and their masters producing wine and wheat under the authority of a merchant company'.

The second long expansion took place during the late 1700s and was also dependent on the strategic location of the Cape. In this case, Britain's competition with France for colonial possessions in Asia (specifically India) during the time of the Napoleonic Wars resulted in a French attempt to occupy the Cape. This was thwarted by Britain, which occupied the Cape in 1795 (and again in 1803) in order to keep their link to India open (Van Jaarsveld 1975). The resulting boost to the British economy spilled over to wine exports, which were given preferential access to the British market through to 1860 (Vink et al. 2018a).

The third long expansion in the South African wine industry coincided with the political changes of the 1990s that marked the end of *apartheid,* ushered in democracy, and resulted in growth in per capita income for the first time in decades. These changes marked a complete break from the past which, in the case of the wine industry, had been shaped by the Land Acts; by the establishment of a cooperative, the KWV,[3] in 1918 that eventually gained statutory power over the industry; and by a concerted effort among a small group of pioneering wine farmers to improve the quality of wine produced in the late 1960s and early 1970s.

Apartheid was introduced into South Africa as formal government policy after the National Party won the elections in 1948. With these elections, the government inherited a land dispensation that rested on two important laws, namely, the Natives Land Act of 1913 and the Native Trust and Land Act of 1936. These cemented the dispossession of land from black people that had occurred since the first settlement (Delius and Beinart 2013). They had two important implications for the industry, namely, that land ownership would

---

[3] 'Ko-operatieweWynboukundigeunie van Suid-Afrika' (later the 'Ko-öperatieveWijnbouwersVereniging van Zuid-Afrika, Beperkt' KWV, or Cooperative Wine Farmers' Association of South Africa, Limited).

be segregated (the 1913 Act stipulated that black people could only buy or lease land from other black people, and vice versa) and that the land rights of black people would be attenuated (e.g. their 'ownership' could not be used to secure a mortgage and did not qualify as property rights for the purpose of voting). Thus the Acts served as the basis for the suppression of black farming in an attempt to ensure a steady supply of (cheap) labor to the mines and to the farms of white South Africa (Greyling et al. 2018). At the same time, white farmers were supported in a myriad of different ways, including legislation to support the establishment and growth of cooperatives in the form of tax concessions as well as the principle of 'forced cooperation' as a means of countering free riding.

The KWV was established in 1918 against the wishes of 'the trade' (today's producer wholesalers[4]) (Van Zyl 1993). The aim was to counter the weaker bargaining power of grape growers (and their cooperatives where these existed). Members had to sell through KWV, which would in turn declare a surplus annually, which would be delivered free of charge and turned into spirits for disposal at the discretion of the organization. The restriction was that no produce could be sold on the domestic market at lower than the minimum price. The income would be used to finance the purchase of distilleries, vats, and buildings, and profits would be distributed to members on a pro rata basis. Ironically, the trade agreed to distill and store the surplus on behalf of KWV, and to purchase only from KWV. This was in exchange for an undertaking from KWV not to compete in the market with their products and not to deal directly with their clients. This agreement was eventually taken up in legislation in 1924 and formed the basis of a symbiotic relationship between the two parties until the 1990s.

However, the agreement proved to be ineffectual until KWV was granted statutory powers in a process that started in 1924, mainly because grape growers sold directly to the trade at less than the minimum price when it suited them (Van Zyl 1993). These statutory powers were expanded over time and eventually included the ability to set a minimum or floor price, to limit production by means of quotas, to force sales of all wine through the KWV, and to declare an annual wine surplus that had to be delivered to KWV free of charge. KWV also implemented production quotas in an attempt to gain control over the surplus even before it was produced. In the process, KWV

---

[4] The industry body that represents their interests is the South African Liquor Brand Owners Association (SALBA), earlier known as the Cape Wine and Spirit Institute (CWSI).

also gained a de facto monopoly on exports, as no one else took an interest in this market, especially after the advent of sanctions in the 1970s.

The main problem with the institutional arrangement was one of governance: the Board of Directors of KWV was elected by holders of quotas in the respective wine-producing districts, but each quota holder had a vote regardless of the quota size. The result was dominance by small-scale producers, most of whom produced wine grapes as an additional activity or held the quota mainly to get access to KWV products at a discount price, that is, they had an incentive to keep the minimum price as high as possible at the lowest possible cost of production, regardless of the fact that this encouraged an even greater surplus of inferior quality wine.

By 1990 the industry consisted of the KWV at the apex, with 70 cooperative cellars (now producer cellars) established by the grape growers, and who sold wine in bulk to KWV and to 'producer wholesalers', who established brands that were sold into the retail sector (both on and off consumption). There were also a small number (166) of private producers, some of whom were registered as wine estates (private cellars in today's nomenclature) who grew grapes and made wine on their own property and sold directly into the retail trade. This segment of the market was, however, largely unregulated and unexploited until the early 1970s when three estate owners pioneered the Stellenbosch Wine Route, just before the introduction of the Wine of Origin system in 1972, which formalized the definition of the different wine regions, and of the wine estates. This attempt to improve the quality of wine produced in the country was however dependent on the domestic market because increasingly effective boycotts and sanctions blocked access to export markets. However, by then the rapid growth in the post-WWII economy had turned into two decades of declining per capita income, starting in 1974. Growth in the super-premium and premium segments of the (white) domestic market was constrained, while the black middle class was still small (e.g. Southall 2004).

The end of the twentieth century therefore saw an industry that consisted of large numbers of relatively small-scale grape producers, relatively small cellars, only a handful of wine estates, and production that was dominated by Chenin Blanc grapes, planted mostly for volume rather than quality production. This was, in other words, the foundation upon which the post-apartheid boom in exports was built and explains to a large degree the idiosyncratic structural features of the modern industry. To this end, the next section provides an analytical description of the state of the industry in the early 1990s.

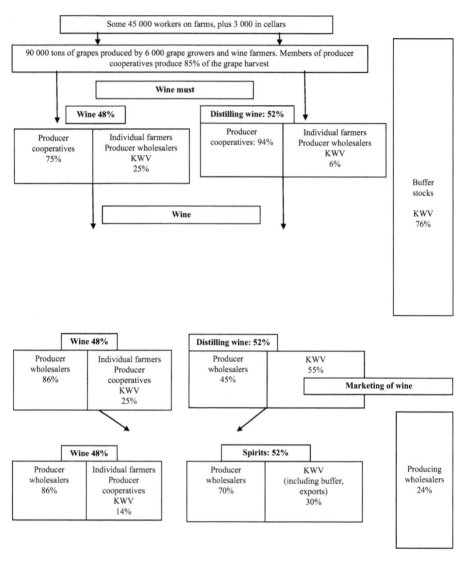

Fig. 9.1 The flow of product in the South African industry, 1982

9.3   The Industry at the Dawn of a New Era[5]

The institutional structure of the South African industry started to change almost as soon as the political changes of the first half of the 1990s took hold. The most important changes were to the role of the KWV, the structure of 'the trade' and of the cooperatives and lastly to the functioning of the wine estates and of the grape farms. The structure in 1982 is illustrated in Fig. 9.1.

Most of the grapes (85%) were delivered to the producer cooperatives, which were responsible for turning most of the grapes into grape must. More than half of the harvest (52%) was destined to be distilled, rather than turned into wine. At this stage, however, the producer wholesalers took over, turning 86% of the must destined for wine into wine, and 45% of the must destined to go to distilling into spirits. KWV was responsible for the rest of the distillate (55%). The producer wholesalers were responsible for marketing 86% of the wine (i.e. for the share that they processed) and for 70% of the distilled product, while KWV either 'marketed' 30% of the total as exports or kept as buffer stocks.

The impact of these changes can be seen in the structure of the modern industry. Therefore, the more recent history of each of these role-players is described in this section, as a precursor to an analysis of the modern structure of the industry.

9.3.1   The KWV

Under South African law, if a cooperative wanted to transform into a conventional joint stock company, it had to apply to the Supreme Court for permission. When KWV applied for such permission to the Western Cape Division, the Minister of Agriculture and Land Affairs, Derek Hanekom, approached the Court with information that he, as a representative of the public, had an interest in the matter and that it could not be allowed to go ahead until that interest had been recognized. As a result, a Ministerial Committee of Inquiry[6] was established in January 1997 and reported in February (RSA 1997). The core issue addressed by the Committee was which assets, acquired by the KWV to perform its statutory duties, belonged to the state or to various interested parties such as the producers. The report of the Committee recom-

---

[5] Data in this section are from the annual publication of South African Wine Industry Information and Systems (SAWIS) (http://www.sawis.co.za/info/annualpublication.php) unless otherwise specified.
[6] The author of this chapter was an independent member of this Committee.

mended deregulation of the industry, with remaining statutory powers (e.g. levies to collect information and fund research, maintenance of quality standards) to be placed under the control of a body that represented the whole industry. These recommendations were acceptable to the Minister.

At the same time KWV agreed to contribute R200 million[7] over 10 years and to provide services, valued at a further R227 million, for 5 years, to the South Africa Wine Industry Trust (SAWIT) (Business Day, 10 September 1997), a new institution whose Board was appointed by the Minister. Today these functions (information, generic promotion, research funding, transformation projects, etc.) are paid from statutory levies implemented under the Marketing of Agricultural Products Act and executed by four 'business units' that serve the industry (Vink et al. 2004). KWV became just another producer wholesaler in the industry. After changing hands a few times, the current controlling shareholder is non-listed UK-based investment group Vasari. The company has not done well compared to Distell, for example. In January 2005, Distell's share price was R26.00, while KWV's was R34.00 (Fin24 2005). By contrast, in 2016, at the time of the sale of KWV to Vasari, its share price was estimated at around R20 (Crotty 2016), compared to Distell at above R160 for most of October 2016.

9.3.2   The Producer Wholesalers

Numerically, the South African wine industry has always been dominated by grape growers, with never more than 20% of them having their own cellars on-farm to turn the grapes into wine. Their numbers ranged from some 6000 in the early 1980s to little more than 3000 today. Instead, most wine was made by the producer wholesalers (so-called because they also produced some grapes, but mostly bought in grapes, wine must, or wine, branded the product, and sold it into the retail market). The largest of these in 1990 were Stellenbosch Farmers Winery (SFW), Distillers Corporation, Gilbey's, and Douglas Green, all well-known purveyors of wine at that time. The current structure of these entities is, however, a product of the 'beer wars' of the 1970s (Mager 2008).

South African Breweries (SAB) was formed in the mid-1950s out of a number of smaller breweries. In 1960 it branched into the wine business by assuming control of SFW as a means of safeguarding its interests as an 'English'

---

[7]At a time when the exchange rate was in the order of $1 = ZAR4.50 – R4.70, that is, around $40 million.

company that had to keep on the right side of an Afrikaans government (Mager 2008). Shortly thereafter, Anton Rupert, a leading Afrikaner business figure, established the Oude Meester Group as a purveyor of fine wines and brandies. In 1972, the beer wars started when Louis Luyt, a fertilizer baron, established Luyt Lager and some other brands, together with Rupert, who took a 25% shareholding. However, neither the business nor the partnership flourished, so in 1975 Rupert bought out Luyt and established Intercontinental Breweries (ICB). By that time, SAB (with 131 stores) and the Rembrandt interests (with 180 stores) also had control over the retail market for liquor in South Africa (which consisted of 372 liquor stores) (Mager 2008).

However, ICB was losing money and SAB disliked competition. As a result, a deal was brokered between the two in 1979 (Mager 2008) and approved by Cabinet (Vink et al. 2004). First, SAB bought ICB in its entirety. In exchange, Rembrandt, SAB, and KWV formed Cape Wine and Distillers (CWD), the result of the merger of the three major players in the wine and spirits sector, SFW, Distillers, and Castle Wine. KWV purchased 30% of SFW and of Distillers and, together with Rembrandt, acquired the majority joint interest in CWD. The three principals each had a 30% shareholding, with SAB as a silent partner. The net result was that SAB was back to having a near monopoly of the beer market, while CWD had 75% of the turnover of the wine and spirits sector. Both eventually relinquished ownership over the retail sector, so the vertical integration of the two industries ended.

In 1982 the Competition Board interceded in this blatantly anti-competitive arrangement, condoning the beer monopoly, but declaring the rest of the arrangement to be illegal. However, it took little more than a meeting of a cabinet committee chaired by the Prime Minister (P.W. Botha), who had consulted Rupert and KWV and the Minister for Industry, Dawie de Villiers, to put an end to this interference. Subsequently, SFW and Distillers were again separated in 1988 but were amalgamated in 2000 to form Distell, the largest winemaker and liquor brand owner in the modern South African industry, with a large portfolio of imported and locally produced spirits, and beverages in the ready-to-drink (RTD) market, with ciders taking up the lion's share of these.

The unique position that Distell fills in the South African domestic market is evident from the data in Table 9.1, which shows the degree of concentration in domestic market share of the dominant companies globally. The upper panel shows market share, and the lower panel the Herfindahl-Hirsch Index (HHI), a measure of concentration—the lower the index, the more competitive the market. An index of below 1500 is usually regarded as a sign of healthy competition.

Table 9.1 Concentration in the market: a 'new world' comparison, 2014 (%)

	Argentina	Australia	Chile	New Zealand	South Africa	USA	World
			Market shares (%)				
Largest winery	27	16	31	23	31	23	12
Second largest winery	14	9	30	11	3	15	8
Third largest winery	12	9	29	10	2	13	6
Fourth largest winery	7	7	1	9	1	6	3
Combined share	60	41	91	53	36	44	30
All others	40	59	9	47	64	56	70
			Herfindahl-Hirsch Index (HHI)				
Largest winery	252.81	729.00	930.25	547.56	930.25	524.41	151.29
Second largest winery	86.49	198.81	876.16	129.96	6.25	210.25	67.24
Third largest winery	84.64	144.00	846.81	90.25	2.56	166.41	40.96
Fourth largest winery	49.00	43.56	1.96	75.69	1.96	31.36	10.24
Total	472.94	1115.37	2655.18	843.46	941.02	932.43	269.73

Source: Based on Anderson and Pinilla (2017)

In Chile (Concha y Toro) and South Africa (Distell), the largest enterprise has a market share of above 30%, far higher than their next competitors, New Zealand and the USA, with 23% each. However, large enterprises dominate the Chilean market, with the combined market share of the four biggest operators above 90%, which is in turn higher than any of the other countries, as shown by the HHI which shows that Chile's is the only uncompetitive domestic market among these countries. The South African market is unusual because, even though it has the lowest market share for the four largest enterprises at 36%, it has a higher HHI than all except Australia and Chile. Thus, in South Africa, one firm dominates the domestic market, given that the country imports less than 0.5% of domestic consumption.

9.3.3   The Producer Cellars

As mentioned, the current producer cellars started life as cooperatives, registered under a series of Acts of Parliament that protected this business form and supported its activities through most of the twentieth century. In keeping with the liberalization fashions of the past few decades, though, there are hardly any cooperatives left in South African agriculture and, where they have survived in the wine industry, it is more for convenience that out of any conviction that it is a superior business form.

Most of the cooperatives established under this legislation were in the field crop industries, that is, maize and wheat, and their main purpose was to supply inputs (including credit) to their farmer members. There were fewer cooperatives that took responsibility for processing farm products—these were prevalent in livestock products (dairy) and notably in wine, where wine grape farmers formed cooperatives to process the grapes into wine. There were 5 such cooperatives in 1915, 20 in 1945, and 69 by 1975, a number that remained through to 2000, that is, during the period when they started to change enterprise form from cooperatives to joint stock companies. These cooperatives handled 89.9% of the wine grape harvest in 1976.

The process of conversion of cooperatives to joint stock companies should be based on sound business principles: Sikuka (2010) summarizes the arguments that have been used, including the value of equity, corporate acquisition, the cost of equity, and the efficiency of the governance structure. Cook (1995) argues that cooperatives develop through different stages and come to a point where they have to choose between exit, continuation, or transition. However, as virtually all of South Africa's agricultural cooperatives (including the wine cooperatives) transformed at more or less the same time, it is clear that the driving force was rather the fear that the new government was going to relieve them of assets such as grain silos and cellar machinery that were built up with support from the former regime.

In many cases, the wine cooperatives are still operating in the same way as they did in the past, especially the operation of pool systems, whereby all wine of a certain type is pooled regardless of origin, and farmers are then paid out the average of the pool. This gives rise to familiar problems (Vink 2012), first of which is 'hiding in the pool' or adverse selection. In a pool system, the individual farmer has an incentive to deliver a product whose quality is below the average quality of the pool (and hence costs less to produce), and this works against all attempts to improve quality. Of course, the managers of a pool have to contend with fixed technology: they are operating a processing plant that may not be able to cater for small production runs, typically the case with higher-quality produce. There is also the problem that managers are tempted to overcompensate themselves when calculating the deductible cost of administering the pool.

9.3.4   The Private Cellars

The picture of a magnificent Cape Dutch homestead rising out of serried trellised ranks of green vines defines the image of itself that the industry has long propagated both domestically and overseas. The first of these wine farms was Groot Constantia, founded in 1685 and the oldest wine-producing farm in South Africa. These private cellars crush less than 25% of the total grape harvest in the country but capture an obviously larger proportion of the value of wine sold and exported (a statistic that is unfortunately not readily available). What we do know is that the off-consumption market is about 50–60% of the total domestic market and that the domestic market for basic wine is 56 times larger than the domestic market for ultra-premium wines in volume terms and 9 times larger in value terms. It is also three times larger in value terms than the market for super-premium and ultra-premium wines put together.

These wine farms were generally unregulated and without legal protection until the Wine of Origin system was introduced in legislation in 1973 in accordance with the Wine, Other Fermented Beverages and Spirits Act, 1957, largely because of the need to comply with EU regulations. It is in a sense a hybrid scheme, somewhere between the extremes of control found in Burgundy and Bordeaux and the much more relaxed rules found in the USA and Australia. It protects not only the geographic origin of a wine but also the cultivar and vintage.

The smallest demarcation is a 'single vineyard wine', where the vineyard may not exceed 6 hectares. This is followed by an estate wine, which has its own production cellar on the farming unit where the wine is produced: when this appellation is used, it means that the wine was produced from grapes grown on that unit. The next level is a ward, which describes a small demarcated area which may or may not fall under a district, which is the better known geographical description, and includes the well-known Stellenbosch and Paarl. Different districts then constitute a region, such as Klein Karoo and Coastal Region.

One of the more interesting changes over the past few decades since the introduction of this scheme is that most of the 'estates' have deregistered from this appellation (hence the more accurate 'producer cellars' because the constraint that grapes had to be produced on the farm itself meant that these enterprises could not fully exploit the value of their brands). Producers such as Beyerskloof and Kanonkop have made full use of this opportunity, using their brand image as super-premium wine producers to bring in high-volume second labels that sell at a premium in the market. So, for example, in 1991 there were 77 estates and 59 'non-estates' among the producer sellers, while by the year 2000 there were 92 estates and 185 'non-estates'. Today there are no more than a handful of estates left.

The producer cellars are even more geographically concentrated than the industry itself. Stellenbosch (which until 2017 included the Cape Town wineries around Groot Constantia and Durbanville) had 16.36% of the country's vines and 16.02% of the vineyard area, but 44% of all the private cellars.

9.3.5   The Wine Grape Farms

Most of the wine grapes grown in South Africa are grown on farms that produce grapes and not wine (and most of these farms produce grapes as one of a range of different enterprises, i.e. not many actually specialize in viticulture). The number of these grape growers has been declining quite rapidly: from more than 6000 registered growers in the 1970s to around 4600 in 1994 (and fewer than 3200 in 2016). However, most of these are small-scale growers. In 1997, for example, half of them delivered or pressed fewer than 100 tons of grapes, declining to 40% in 2016. At the same time grape producers were investing less: the area under vines has declined from above 103,000 hectares to some 95,000 currently. Furthermore, in a system where vines are kept on average for 20 years, the annual replacement should be 4%, that is, 20% of the national vineyard should be equal to or less than 4 years old. Instead, this proportion was 12.9% in 1997 and only 7.3% currently.

The cultivar composition of the South African industry also tells of the impact of the measures that KWV put in place to manage the surplus. The three most prevalent grape cultivars in the industry were the high-bearing Chenin Blanc, Palomino, and Colombar, represented 50% of the vineyard in 1975–1985, dropping to less than a third by 2005. By contrast, the plantings of Sauvignon Blanc, Chardonnay, Cabernet Sauvignon, Shiraz, Merlot, and Pinotage made up a derisory 5% of plantings in 1975 and were still less than 10% in 1990. Of course the Chenin Blanc planting of today is very different from that of the earlier era, while the area under Palomino and Colombar is now derisory.

9.3.6   Farm Workers

The policy environment for commercial agriculture in South Africa changed radically in the space of less than two decades, starting in the early 1980s with the withdrawal of a range of direct subsidies,[8] followed by accession to the Marrakesh Agreement and membership of the World Trade Organization (WTO) in early 1994, a few months later by a unilateral reduction in many tariff lines for agriculture to below the WTO bound rates, and in 1997 by deregulation of commodity markets when the Marketing Act of 1968 was replaced with the Marketing of Agricultural Products Act of 1996. Yet while the new government was deregulating commodity markets, it also started to intervene in resource markets (water, energy, land, and labor) (Vink et al. 2018b).

Until 1994, farm workers had never been protected in law: in fact the opposite, as a succession of 'masters and servants' Acts throughout the nineteenth century, in the aftermath of the abolition of the slave trade in 1808 and of slavery itself in 1838, skewed the common law in favor of their employers (Williams 2016). After the first democratic elections, the new government set about revising all of South Africa's labor laws, resulting in four major pieces of legislation, which all included farm workers for the first time. These laws included the Basic Conditions of Employment Act of 1997, in terms of which a Sector Determination could be promulgated to define minimum working conditions, including a minimum wage. This was introduced in agriculture in 2003. In 2013 the minimum wage was increased by more than 50% (Conradie et al. 2018).

Conradie et al. (2018) model the wage elasticity among wine grape farm workers, showing that even the 51% wage increase had a relatively small impact on permanent farm workers, because the long-run wage elasticity was only −0.58 to −0.70. Casual workers, many of them women, are not so fortunate, however, as in their case the long-run wage elasticity is −4.7, which means devastating losses when the wage rises. This also jeopardizes the prospects for viticultural practices such as canopy management and cover crops which have been introduced to better regulate the impact of drought and heat on the grapes (all symptoms of climate change). This makes it more difficult to produce quality wines, which in turn jeopardizes the international competitiveness of the industry.

However, the distinguishing feature of wine farm workers was the 'dop' or 'tot' system, whereby male workers were given wine regularly throughout the

---

[8] Note that the process started a decade before the first democratic elections in 1994.

day—in lieu of wages in the worst manifestation of the system or as partial remuneration. Williams (2016) traces the various attempts to make the practice illegal—this was already accomplished in 1809 but had to be supplemented with legislation at regular intervals (e.g. in 1928 and 1963). He also traces the origins back to the first settlement and the slave society that subsequently arose (Williams 2016). The results of this practice were predictable and devastating (e.g. Marcus 1989; London 1999; May et al. 2005), and persist to this day (e.g. Donald et al. 2017).

9.4   The Consequences

The origins of the particular structure of the South African wine industry have been described in some detail in the preceding sections. In this section the consequences will be investigated, with a focus on the efficiency of wine grape producers, the fragmentation of the industry, the shifting geography, and the competitiveness of the industry.

9.4.1   Efficiency of the Wine Grape Producers

Efficiency, based on technology and management, is central to international competitiveness. In a recent article (Piesse et al. 2018) the efficiency levels of wine grape farmers in the old established wine regions of South Africa (Stellenbosch and Paarl) is compared to that of farmers in the newer regions (the rest of the industry). Thus, the question whether experience plus first choice of location matters more than the follower's advantage of being able to use newer technology is addressed.

The results show that land area is the most important input into the amount of wine grape production, followed by labor and pesticides, while fertilizer, machinery, and electricity make smaller contributions. For the old regions, land area has a smaller impact on output than in the new (probably because of the lower yields of the cultivar portfolio), while labor has a bigger impact (probably because it is more skilled in the areas closer to the Cape Town metropolitan region). Inefficiency levels were reduced by expenditure on labor supervision in both regions, by a higher ratio of permanent to casual workers (permanent workers need less supervision) and by modern trellising in the old areas, but not in the new. More inorganic fertilizer increased inefficiency in both regions, increased drip irrigation reduced inefficiency in the new regions but not the old (in these areas irrigation infrastructure is intended for supplementary purposes, hence as insurance rather than to boost yields), while more dryland had a negative effect in the new areas but not the old. A higher proportion of red to white grapes reduced efficiency in the old regions but not the new. And finally, more old vines as a share of the total, suggesting low levels of replacement of the vine stock, only had a negative effect in the new regions. There is, therefore, evidence that farmers in the new regions have tended to go for higher yields at the expense of quality, whereas the old regions have tried to maintain their reputation for quality, a strategy that was wrong, at least in the short term.

There is also no real sign of an inverse farm size productivity relationship, a point made two decades ago by Townsend et al. (1998). For example, while the average vineyard increased by 55% between 1995 and 2015, the yield of wine grapes increased by 100% despite the shift to lower-yielding varieties, and the yield of wine increased by 75%.

9.4.2   Fragmentation of the Industry

South Africa is known for its highly sophisticated financial services sector. For example, the country was ranked 53rd out of 63 countries in the World Competitiveness Report of the World Economic Forum (2017), while the financial services sector ranked 31st (Schwab 2017). However, this was not always the case, and the wine industry more or less had to finance its own growth out of the devastation wrought by phylloxera (1886), tariff-restricted access to the market in Johannesburg in the period leading up to and during the Boer War (1899–1902) and the Great Depression (Vink et al. 2018a).

We have shown that one of the main instruments around this capital constraint was the producer cooperatives (aided by government loans and legislation that supported the cooperatives). However, because the cooperatives traded mostly in bulk wine, their main modus operandi was to manage a pool system, largely because their priority was quantity rather than quality. This became a self-fulfilling prophecy because the wineries themselves were built to deal with rapid throughput rather than with small batch production. As a result, the farmers' grapes were aggregated into pools with a wide range of qualities, and little differentiation in price, leaving individual producers with the age-old temptation to 'hide in the pool', as was shown earlier. Thus the solution to the problem of a lack of capital became the reason why farmers could not build up sufficient capital to produce higher-quality grapes.

One of the consequences of the export boom that commenced after the end of *apartheid* was the establishment of new grape production units in the industry, but this time with a difference: while the total number of producers was declining rapidly (and mostly among the smaller producers, as has been shown), the number of private cellars was increasing, and there was little substitution between these; in other words there has been no increase in the numbers of grape growers in the industry. While this does not change much in terms of fragmentation, it is interesting to speculate on its impact on those representative institutions that have the grape growers as their base membership, such as the industry body VinPro, and the relative influence of the producer cellars in industry initiatives.

What is evident currently, though, is a lack of leadership in the industry with regard to transformation, including land reform, even though a major initiative was launched more than a decade ago with the establishment of the South Africa Wine and Brandy Company (SAWB), an industry body whose main task was to influence government policy on behalf of the industry and in the process to support the work of the business units (SAWIS, Wines of South Africa (WOSA), and the Wine Industry Network for Expertise and Technology (Winetech)) with a focus on transformation of the industry. To this end, SAWB designed the Wine Industry Plan (WIP). Furthermore, a BEE program and scorecard were proposed, in accordance with the government's Broad-Based Black Economic Empowerment (B-BBEE program), but these initiatives came to naught when SAWB, which had just been transformed into the South African Wine Industry Council (SAWIC) was summarily terminated in 2008.

9.4.3   The Geography of the South African Industry

One of the unique features of the South African wine industry is its geographic concentration around Cape Town and the Cape Peninsular, with some 90% of the vineyards less than 200 km from downtown Cape Town. From a wine tourism perspective, the industry is even more fortunate, as the epicenter of good wine production is right on the city's doorstep, with the Durbanville Hills and Cape Town wards and the Stellenbosch and Paarl District all within an hour's drive. These four demarcations have a total of almost 300 private cellars, that is, some 60% of the industry total. Furthermore, while there are only about 50 old Cape Dutch farmhouses left, these are all in close proximity to Cape Town.

The geography of the wine industry has been changing globally over the past decades, arguably because of climate, a factor that has been prevalent in the wine business for a long time (Storchmann 2011), and more specifically because of climate change (Ashenfelter and Storchmann 2016). The South African industry, and specifically the Stellenbosch region, where the average maximum daytime temperature in the summer increased by 1.7 °C between 1961 and 2008, is no exception (Bonnardot and Carey 2008).

The diversity in wine styles that has always characterized the South African industry has come under threat from climate change—if the entire area is becoming hotter, for example, it is more difficult to retain a diversity of styles of wine (Vink et al. 2012). One way of dealing with this problem is to expand production into cooler areas, which has in fact been happening. For example, if one draws a line running east to west, and cutting through Vriesenhof farm in the Paradyskloof area of Stellenbosch, then there were 12 private cellars south of the line (i.e. toward the cooler coastal area) in 1991—now there are 31. Similarly, a north-south line that runs through Middelvlei farm gave 32 private cellars to the west of the line (also toward the coast) in 1991 and 72 in 2016. Other cool climate areas such as Elgin (24 private cellars), Durbanville (25), Cape Peninsula (21), and Hermanus and the southern Cape (40) have also shown the strongest growth in the number of private cellars. Diversity can, of course, also be enhanced by changes in viticultural and oenological practices and by changes in wine styles.

9.4.4   The Competitiveness of the Industry

Figure 9.2 shows the international competitiveness of the South African wine industry since 1985, measured in terms of the revealed comparative advantage

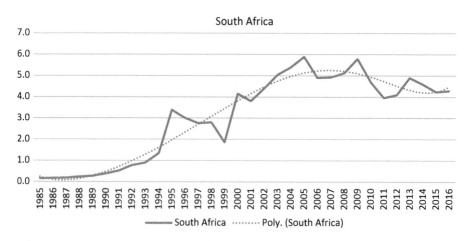

Fig. 9.2   South Africa's RCA in wine. (Source: Anderson and Pinilla 2018)

(RCA), an indicator that compares the growth in net exports of a product such as wine relative to a benchmark (in this case South Africa's net exports of all agricultural products) to that of global growth in wine exports relative to all agricultural exports. A ratio greater than one denotes competitiveness.

The first phase (Esterhuizen and Van Rooyen 2006) that can be identified from the data encompasses the era of regulation under the KWV and the subsequent transition to democracy, accompanied by the opening of export markets. However, competitive pressure from especially Australia and Chile soon brought the industry back to reality, while the new plantings of (mostly red) wine grapes had not yet come on stream.

The industry was able to weather these storms and posted an RCA of above five from 2003 to 2009, on the back of a weaker domestic currency, larger supplies of high-value grape cultivars, and rapidly growing exports into Germany. During this time the South African brand was being established with new initiatives such as the environmental (the Integrated Production of Wine and Biodiversity and Wine Initiatives) and social focuses. However, this era also came to an end, coinciding with the Great Recession that started in the USA in 2008/2009. The South African economy has yet to recover, thus exports are constrained by difficult trading conditions, and the domestic market shows few signs of growth. Furthermore, the industry has not fared well in terms of the prices that it can command on the global market: the average unit price of South Africa's wine exports is lower than that of any of its competitors.

9.4.5   Summary

There are a number of other aspects of the industry that should properly also be addressed in more detail, such as the lack of progress with land reform, the position of farm workers, and technology development and adoption, but space constraints preclude such discussion. In summary, then, the South African wine industry grew from the 17th largest wine producer by volume in 1910 to the 8th largest today. However, this relatively rapid growth in output was largely the result of growth in relatively low-quality high-yielding wine grape varietals.

At the same time, domestic wine consumption has been stagnant for the past five decades at a level of 8 to 10 liters per capita, excepting for a brief five years (1971–1976) after the establishment of the Stellenbosch Wine Route and the introduction of the Wine of Origin Scheme. The market for wine was clearly limited by the small middle-class market, which at the time consisted mainly of white people. However, per capita consumption has remained at these levels since 1990, an indication that the industry has failed to penetrate the rising black middle-class market.

The RCA of South Africa's wine exports was below one throughout most of the twentieth century, moving above one in 1994, increasing until 2008, and then remaining level. Thus, an industry with a low proportion of quality wine production, unable to grow its own domestic market, and highly dependent on the export market where it seems unable to improve the price points at which wine is sold.

9.5   The Future

If these are the origins and their consequences, then what does the future hold for the South African wine industry? While the future cannot be known, it is possible to envisage at least some important pointers for the industry:

1. Prosperity in the industry has always depended on its export performance. Given South Africa's position in the world economy, this means that the industry will, as now, be dependent on political stability to ensure exchange rate stability and on government performance to enhance market access.
2. The number of grape growers will continue to decline along with the area under vines until an equilibrium price can be reached where grape growing becomes more profitable. This will also mean that there has to be greater differentiation between wines of different quality, which in turn means investment in wine making and storage facilities. Therefore, these are not changes that will take place in the short term.
3. In this regard, however, the new phenomenon where brand owners from among the private cellars, rather than the producer cellars, are buying an increasing proportion of the high quality crop, will hasten this shift to premium prices for premium grapes.
4. The global market for wine has shifted from place as the most important descriptor (generally in the Old World countries, led by France) to culti- var, under the influence of the new world producers, especially Australia and the USA, and a new trend is now evident, namely, taste: people are drinking cheaper, blended wines (e.g. Morss 2017). This augers well for the South African industry, but only if the industry can convince the black middle class to drink wine. How an industry as fragmented as ours will succeed in this is, however, not clear.

5. The South African industry has hardly transformed in the 24 years since democracy, but the government has not sanctioned it for this lack of progress. The wine industry is no exception in this regard (nor is the agricultural sector as a whole) but industry expectations of government support must be tempered by realism about the ability of government to continually ignore this lack of progress.

References

Anderson, K., and V. Pinilla (with the assistance of A. J. Holmes). 2017. *Annual database of global wine markets, 1835 to 2015*, freely available in Excel at the University of Adelaide's Wine Economics Research Centre. www.adelaide.edu.au/wine-econ/databases.

Ashenfelter, Orley, and Karl Storchmann. 2016. Climate change and wine: A review of the economic implications. *Journal of Wine Economics* 11 (1): 105–138.

Bonnardot, V., and V.A. Carey. 2008. Observed climatic trends in South African wine regions and potential implications for viticulture. In *Proceedings of the VIIth international viticultural terroir congress* 19–23 May 2008, Nyon, Switzerland. 1, 216–221, AgroscopeChangins-Wädenswil.

Boshoff, W.H., and J. Fourie. 2010. The significance of the Cape trade route to economic activity in the Cape Colony: A medium-term business cycle analysis. *European Review of Economic History* 14 (3): 469–503.

Boxer, C.R. 2001. *The tragic history of the sea*. Minneapolis: University of Minnesota Press.

Business Day. 1997. Johannesburg.

Conradie, Beatrice, Jenifer Piesse, Colin Thirtle, and Nick Vink. 2018. Labour demand in the post-apartheid South African wine industry. *Journal of Agricultural Economics*, forthcoming. doi: https://doi.org/10.1111/1477-9552.12270.

Cook, M.L. 1995. The future of U.S. agricultural cooperatives: A neo-institutional approach. *American Journal of Agricultural Economics* 77 (5): 1153–1159.

Crotty, Ann. 2016. Battle looms over KWV sale. *Johannesburg, Business Day*. October 25. Available at https://www.businesslive.co.za/bd/companies/retail-and-consumer/2016-10-25-battle-looms-over-kwv-sale/. Accessed 8 May 2018.

Delius, Peter, and William Beinart. 2013. 1913 Land Act: A longer history of dispossession. *Mail and Guardian*, June 14. Available at https://mg.co.za/article/2013-06-14-00-1913-land-act-a-longer-history-of-dispossession. Accessed 23 April 2018.

Donald, Kirsten A.M., Anne Fernandez, Kasey Claborn, Caroline Kuo, Nastassja Koen, Heather Zar, and Dan J. Stein. 2017. The developmental effects of HIV and alcohol: A comparison of gestational outcomes among babies from South

African communities with high prevalence of HIV and alcohol use. *AIDS Research and Therapy* 14: 28.

Esterhuizen, D., and C.J. van Rooyen. 2006. An inquiry into factors impacting on the competitiveness of the South African wine industry. *Agrekon Volume* 45 (4): 467–485.

Fin24. 2005. Available at https://www.fin24.com/Companies/KWV-Distell-shares-at-highest-20050121. Accessed 8 May 2018.

Greyling, Jan, Nick Vink, and Emily van der Merwe. 2018. Gold: South African agriculture's transition from suppression to support (1886–1948). In *Agricultural development in the world periphery: A global economic history approach*, ed. Vicente Pinilla and Willebald. Cham: Palgrave Macmillan.

Katzen, M.F. 1982. White settlers and the origin of a new society, 1652–1778. In *A history of South Africa to 1870*, ed. Monica Wilson and Leonard Thompson. London: Croom Helm.

London, Leslie. 1999. The 'dop' system, alcohol abuse and social control amongst farm workers in South Africa: A public health challenge. *Social Science & Medicine* 48 (10): 1407–1414.

Mager, Anne Kelk. 2008. Apartheid and business: Competition, monopoly and the growth of the malted beer industry in South Africa. *Business History* 50 (3): 272–290.

Marcus, Tessa. 1989. *Modernising super-exploitation: Restructuring South African agriculture*. London: Zed Books.

May, Philip A., J. Phillip Gossage, Lesley E. Brooke, and Cudore L. Snel. 2005. Maternal risk factors for fetal alcohol syndrome in the Western Cape Province of South Africa: A population-based study. *American Journal of Public Health* 95 (7): 1190–1199.

Morss, Elliott R. 2017. *The future of the global wine industry: Boxes, bulk and blends*. Available at http://www.morssglobalfinance.com. Accessed 29 May 2018.

Piesse, Jennifer, Beatrice Conradie, Colin Thirtle, and Nick Vink. 2018. Efficiency in wine grape production: Comparing long-established and newly developed regions of South Africa. *Journal of Agricultural Economics* 49: 203–212.

RSA. 1997. *Report of the committee to investigate regulation of the wine and distillation industry*. Pretoria: Government of the Republic of South Africa.

SAWIS, various years. *Wine industry statistics*. Paarl: South African Wine Industry Information and Systems.

Schwab, Klaus, ed. 2017. *The global competitiveness report 2017–2018*. Geneva: World Economic Forum.

Sikuka, Wellington. 2010. The comparative performance of selected agribusiness companies and cooperatives in the Western Cape, South Africa. Thesis submitted in partial fulfilment of the requirements for the MScAgric (Agricultural Economics) degree, Stellenbosch University.

Southall, Roger. 2004. Political change and the black middle class in democratic South Africa. *Canadian Journal of African Studies* 38 (3): 521–542.

Storchmann, K. 2011. Wine economics: Emergence, developments, topics. *Agrekon* 50 (3): 1–28.

Terreblanche, Sampie. 2014. *Western empires*. Johannesburg: Penguin Books.

Townsend, Rob, Johann Kirsten, and Nick Vink. 1998. Farm size, productivity and returns to scale in agriculture revisited: A case study of wine producers in South Africa. *Agricultural Economics* 19 (1–2): 175–180.

Van Jaarsveld, F.A. 1975. *From Van Riebeeck to Vorster 1652–1974: An introduction to the history of the Republic of South Africa*. Perskor: Johannesburg.

Van Zyl, D.J. 1993. *KWV 75 Jaar/[KWV 75 years]*. Paarl: KWV.

Vink, N. 2012. The long-term economic consequences of agricultural marketing legislation in South Africa. *South African Journal of Economics* 80 (4): 553–566.

Vink, Nick, Gavin Williams, and Johann Kirsten. 2004. South Africa. In *The world's wine markets: Globalization at work*, ed. Kym Anderson, 227–251. London: Edward Elgar.

Vink, Nick, Alain Deloire, Valerie Bonnardot, and Joachim W. Ewert. 2012. Climate change and the future of South Africa's wine industry. *International Journal of Climate Change Strategies and Management* 4 (4): 420–441.

Vink, Nick, Willem H. Boshoff, Gavin Williams, Johan Fourie, and Lewis S. McLean. 2018a. South Africa. In *Wine globalization: A new comparative history*, ed. Kym Anderson and Vicente Pinilla. Cambridge: Cambridge University Press.

Vink, Nick, Johann Kirsten, Frikkie Liebenberg, Jan C. Greyling, and Ferdi Meyer. 2018b. Agricultural policies in South Africa. In *Handbook of International food and agricultural policies: Volume 1: Policies for agricultural markets and rural economic activity*, ed. Willi Myers and Thomas Johnson. Europe: World Scientific.

Williams, G.P. 2016. Slaves, workers, and wine: The 'dopsystem' in the history of the Cape wine industry, 1658–1894. *Journal of Southern African Studies* 42 (5): 893–909.

10

The Chinese Wine Industry

Linda Jiao and Shan Ouyang

10.1 Introduction

China is an emerging wine market experiencing rapid growth since the beginning of the 2000s. This market is also a market in evolution, in every aspect, from wine production to wine consumption. The cultivation of the vine in China can be traced back to ancient times, when people described their enjoyment of grape wine in poetry. Nowadays, China has come to be the world's second largest winegrower (by vineyard surface area), the sixth biggest wine producer, and the fifth most important wine consumer in terms of volume (OIV 2017). In addition, as we can observe from Fig. 10.1, the gap between wine consumption and production, which is filled by imports, has been expanding since the second half of the 2000s. Imported wine is a growing and developing part of the Chinese wine market, due to the evolving consumption behavior of Chinese wine drinkers. Regarding market size, according to International Wine & Spirits Research (IWSR), China is predicted to become the second largest wine market and the largest non-sparkling wine consumer by 2020.

The wine-production sector is highly concentrated in China with leading national wine groups providing a wide range of products which take over half

L. Jiao (✉)
University of Bordeaux, Pessac, France
e-mail: linda.jiao@u-bordeaux.fr

S. Ouyang
Beijing Artix Investment Company Co., Ltd, Beijing, China

© The Author(s) 2019
A. Alonso Ugaglia et al. (eds.), *The Palgrave Handbook of Wine Industry Economics*,
https://doi.org/10.1007/978-3-319-98633-3_10

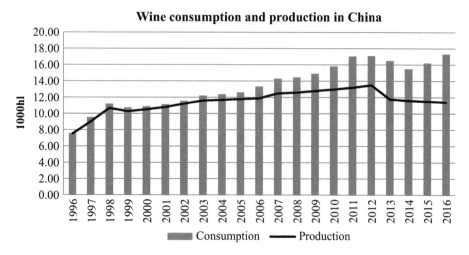

Fig. 10.1 Evolution of wine consumption and production in China. (Source: Cossllected from OIV annual reports of World Vitiviniculture Situation and OIV Statistics, 2013–2017)

of the entire market. However, the small wineries in Ningxia have gained the highest reputation among quality wine producers. In addition, the Chinese domestic wine industry is characterized by a high vertical integration along the value chain. Large groups and small wineries often have their own distribution channels. In particular, e-commerce and social network marketing have emerged over recent years, and the wine market is no exception to these trends.

Last but not least, it is worth mentioning that the intervention of the Chinese government is a key factor in the Chinese wine industry. The government released the first national standards and policies to regulate the domestic wine industry in the early 1990s and improved them during the 2000s. Then, in the "12th Five-Year Plan" for the Chinese wine industry (2012), the Ministry of Industry and Information Technology and the Ministry of Agriculture underlined the importance of government support in the domestic wine industry, especially in the development of the wine-production sector, the improvement of industrial structure, the innovation of science and technology, the guarantee of product quality and safety, and the promotion of domestic wine culture. Afterward, green development in the wine-production sector was highlighted in the "13th Five-Year Plan". Moreover, the government promotes wine as a healthier alternative to traditional spirits and encourages people to consume wine with moderation. During 2013–2014, the wine market, especially the fine-wine market, suffered significantly as a result of the crackdown on gifting and corruption, but it has been gradually recovering since 2015.

In order to have a global overview of the Chinese wine industry, we will introduce and analyze the main operators along the chain in this chapter.

10.2   Winegrowing and Winemaking Sectors in China

In China, the cultivation of the vine can be dated back to the fourth century BC. Poems like *The Song of Grapes* and *The Song of Liangzhou* in the Tang Dynasty recorded ancient people enjoying grape wine. Wine industrialization in China started in the late nineteenth century when European missionaries brought in vines and winemaking technologies. In 1892, Mr. Chang Bishi (1841–1916), a patriotic overseas Chinese, set up the Changyu Pioneer Wine Company. Four years later, Changyu imported quality grape vines in large quantities from Europe to Yantai, Shandong Province, and that is how the first wines in modern China were established. But the birth of Chinese wine culture should be dated to the 1980, thanks to China's reform, opening up to the rest of the world and the investment of foreign groups. Influential Sino-French joint ventures appeared during that time, such as the Remy Martin Group, which created the Dynasty Fine Wine Group in 1980, and Pernod Ricard, associated with the Beijing Winery, which created Dragon Seal in 1988. Later on, with the support and promotion of the Chinese government, wine production in China has been increasing gradually since the 1980s.

According to the report by the International Organisation of Vine and Wine (OIV) (2017), in China, the surface area under vine was 830,000 hectares in 2015 and forecasted to be 847,000 hectares in 2016, which accounts for about 1.5% of the entire national agricultural land. Most of the production is for table grapes and wine grapes account only for 15% of the total grape production. As regards wine production, the volume has been dropping slightly since 2012 from 13.5 to 11.4 million hectoliters, but China still remains in sixth position in the world. In fact, there are wineries in western China selling their bulk wine to be bottled in eastern China, and the production of wine is often double counted—the first time in the west and for a second time in the east. As a result, statistics on Chinese wine production are questionable.

10.2.1   Chinese Wine-Production Regions

Despite having huge geographical diversity, China has a rather unfavorable and extreme climate for viticulture. The vines are cultivated in various regions but under diverse climatic and soil conditions.

A specific challenge for grapes is that, in winter, the climate in certain wine regions is extremely cold and sometimes the temperature falls below −20 °C. To protect the grapes from the wind and cold, vines have to be buried in winter in order to keep them alive and then unburied in spring. Covering vines for the winter is undertaken by hand, which implies extra costs. This is the major reason why Chinese wine production has higher costs. Furthermore, vines generally need to be irrigated by river water or groundwater in most of the wine regions. Besides, Chinese wineries like hiring French winemakers and oenologists as consultants, as well as investing in advanced and expensive equipment.

Wine regions are dispersed throughout the country, but most of them are in eastern China. When it comes to wine regions, people usually talk about their administrative divisions, although those are insufficient to define certain wine regions (Li, 2016). It helps to have a first location of Chinese wineries. Geographically speaking, eight main wine regions can be considered: Shandong, Hebei-Beijing, Shanxi, Dongbei, Xinjiang, Ningxia, Gansu, and Yunnan (Fig. 10.2).

Regional official data concerning winegrowing and winemaking sectors are rarely available. In order to acquire more information, data on major wineries for each region were collected. These data are from online resources and not available for all considered wineries.

The eight main regions considered are:

10.2.1.1   Shandong

Shandong is the largest wine-production region in China, occupying the top place for market share by both volume (about 35% of the total wine production (author's calculation based on the China Brewing Industry Yearbook)) and value. This region has a long winemaking history and relatively advanced technologies. The vines here are mainly cultivated in the Shandong Peninsula, and the most famous region is Yantai (a protected geographic indication) where Changyu, the Great Wall, and Weilong are located. The climate in winter is moderate, so that vines can naturally survive without being buried. However, there are fewer sunshine hours in summer because of the rainy weather. The wineries in this region are mainly of around 150 hectares.

10.2.1.2   Hebei: Beijing

Hebei is another important wine region in China in terms of both volume (around 7% (author's calculation based on the China Brewing Industry

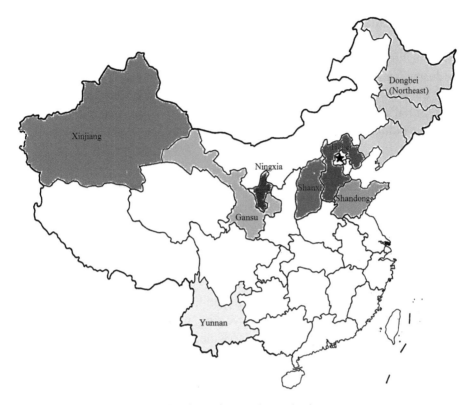

Fig. 10.2 Main wine regions in China. (Drawn by author)

Yearbook)) and value. The Hebei and Shandong regions represent nearly half of the total domestic wine production. The Hebei wineries are located in Shacheng (northwest of Beijing) and Changli (northeast of Beijing). The wines produced from these two regions are protected as geographical indications. The winter here is rather cold which means vines need to be protected artificially. The domestic grape variety Dragon Eye is widely planted in this region. The planting size of the wineries here is mainly from 100 hectares to over 500 hectares. There are also relatively smaller wineries such as Domaine Franco-Chinois, a Sino-French joint venture, which has 23 hectares of vineyards and 25 hectares in total.

Several relatively smaller wineries, with 70–100 hectares in plantation, are in the northwest and southwest of Beijing's outer suburbs, such as Dragon Seal and Changyu Aifeibao Winery. These wineries can be ideal for wine tourism thanks to their geographical location.

10.2.1.3 Shanxi

Winemaking is relatively small in Shanxi and its recognition in the wine industry is mainly due to the success of the Grace Vineyard. Grace Vineyard was the first family-owned winery in China, which was founded in 1997. It has a total of 133.33 hectares, of which 60 hectares are planted with vines with a production of 400,000 bottles per year.

10.2.1.4 Dongbei (the Northeast)

The Dongbei region consists of three provinces: Liaoning, Jilin, and Heilongjiang. Their production accounts for over 20% of the total production in volume (author's calculation based on the China Brewing Industry Yearbook). A domestic grape variety called *Vitis amurensis* is widely grown in the Changbaishan region of Jilin Province. This grape is highly resistant to extreme cold (Dongbei is the coldest region in winter in China), but its sugar content is often inadequate when harvesting, meaning it requires chaptalization. Besides, this region produces ice wine, and the most famous ice-wine region is Huanren County in the Liaoning Province. The wineries here are huge, from hundreds of hectares to thousands of hectares.

10.2.1.5 Xinjiang

Xinjiang is the largest grape-production region in China, and the cultivation of wine grapes has increased rapidly since the 2000s. The large wine companies are used to buying fresh grapes or grape juice from the independent wine-growers of this area. But also some wineries have been established here, have commercialized their own wines, and gained good reputations. Furthermore, Heshuo and Tulufan have officially become protected geographic indications since 2016. The wineries in Xinjiang are also huge, most of them occupying thousands of hectares in plantation.

10.2.1.6 Ningxia

Contrary to other provinces, "the wine industry occupies the most important position in the economic development of Ningxia" according to Pr. Li Demei, consultant of Ningxia Helan Qingxue Vineyard. Due to the Helan Mountain East Foothill appellation, the provincial wine bureau, and the winery classification system, Ningxia has gained the reputation as the producer of the highest-quality Chinese wines and is regarded as one of the country's most promising wine regions. The climate here is arid or semiarid with good conditions of sunlight and warmth. There are also convenient irrigation conditions thanks to the Yellow River. The vines have to be buried each winter to be protected from the cold and wind. There are 72 wineries with 34,000 hectares of vines for winemaking. More details about this region will be presented in the following sections.

10.2.1.7   Gansu

Gansu has a relatively long history of winemaking, but the wine industry hasn't taken an important position in this region, probably due to the inconvenience of transportation. The wine quality here has been barely satisfactory because of unfavorable climate conditions. Over the last few years, the wine industry has developed rapidly thanks to the support of the regional government, especially as regards organic wine production. In addition, the Hexi Corridor has become a protected geographic indication since 2012. The size of the wineries ranges from hundreds to thousands of hectares.

10.2.1.8   Yunnan

There is not a long winemaking history in this region, although the climate is relatively favorable for winegrowing. In a high-altitude but low-latitude geographical location, the sunlight is sufficient, the weather is not hot in summer and in winter, like the Shandong region, vines do not have to be protected as they can survive naturally. The vineyards are tiny, scattered all over the mountains in small plots with normally dozens of plots making up just 1 hectare. The difficulties and challenges of producing wine in Yunnan will be presented by the Ao Yun case in the section on foreign investment.

10.2.2   Grape Varieties

There are hundreds of grape varieties in China if we take into consideration both table and wine grapes. Red varieties dominate, representing 80% of the total. Among the main red wine varieties, Cabernet Sauvignon accounts for 80%, followed by Merlot representing 12.5%, Cabernet Gernischt (Carmenère) 5%, Shiraz, Cabernet Franc, Pinot Noir, and other foreign varieties in small quantities plus *Vitis amurensis*, which is a domestic variety. For white wine, Chardonnay accounts for over 61% of the total white-wine grape area, followed by Riesling representing about 36%, plus Chenin Blanc, Sauvignon Blanc, Gewurztraminer, Ugni Blanc, and so on. Dragon Eye is a celebrated domestic white variety (the Chinese Agricultural Year Book; Anderson and Aryal, 2013; Li, 2000).

The "12th Five-year Plan" indicates that strengthening winegrowing bases is a key factor to ensuring the quality and stability of winemaking raw materials. Local government should be in support of breeding high-quality imported-wine grape varieties that adapt well to the climate of Chinese wine regions.

Marselan, a hybrid variety of Cabernet Sauvignon and Grenache, is bred by INRA (French National Institute for Agricultural Research) and was first imported to China in 2001. Unlike in France where Marselan is cultivated little, this variety has spread across China during the last 15 years. Strongly structured and elegant wines are made from Marselan, and the result is that it is regarded as a grape variety which is highly adapted to the taste of Chinese consumers. Several Chinese wineries (such as Zhongfei Winery, Yiyuan Winery, and Huailai Amethyst Manor) present Marselan wines as their main product.

10.2.3 Big Wine Groups Versus Elite Wineries

There are about 450 wine producers in China but only 150 companies with a turnover of more than 5 million RMB registered in official statistics. The wine-production sector is highly concentrated in China with 5 leading groups taking more than 60% of total volume. The main groups are Yantai Changyu Group Co., Ltd.; Great Wall Wine Group Co., Ltd. of COFCO Ltd.; Dynasty Fine Wine Group Co., Ltd.; Yantai Weilong Grape Wine Co., Ltd.; and Dragon Seal Wines Co., Ltd. (Ubifrance 2012; IWSR 2015). According to the study by MarketLine, in 2015, in terms of market volume of domestic wine, the top 4 account for almost 60% of total volume and the remaining 40% is shared by hundreds of operators (see Fig. 10.3). However, since 2016, the degree of concentration has been diluted so that the top 4 account for less than half of the total volume. But, Changyu still holds the first position in China and takes around one fifth of the market.

Large companies provide a wide range of products from low-priced to high-end ones in large volumes. As a result, they need grape sources and grape juices from independent domestic growers or those worldwide. They buy

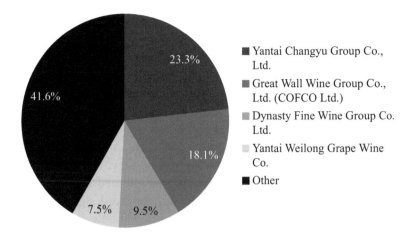

Fig. 10.3 China wine market share by volume. (Source: MarketLine 2015)

grape juices from New World producers such as Chile, Australia, and also from the Xinjiang Province. They mainly negotiate the price of grape juices without strict quality criteria. Therefore, in some cases, grapes produced by company-owned vineyards are often used for high-end products, while third-party grapes are for low-priced products. Besides, there are local producers who are used to importing bulk wine from Chile, Spain, or Australia and then mixing them with their own "grape juice" to improve their qualities, because their costs are lower than growing grapes themselves.

Wineries in the Ningxia region are the best representatives of elite Chinese wineries. All wines are produced by grapes cultivated in their own vineyards following certain requirements in quality in order to pinpoint their origin. "The idea was to change the current situation of the wine industry in China, which tended to 'industrialize wine production' and generate a 'massive amount of low-quality wines' according to a special consultant of the region's wine industry.

Most of the large companies and "small and fine" wineries operate vertically integrated businesses from growing grapes to making wine and then bottling. But there are some exceptions, and the bottling of bulk wine is described in the section entitled "Relationships along the chain".

10.2.4 Appellation Versus Brand

In China, there are seven protected geographic indications of grape wines: Changli, Shacheng, Helan Mountain East Foothill, Hexi Corridor, Yantai, Heshuo, and Tulufan.

The term "appellation" or "protected geographic indication" is rather new for Chinese wines. Helan Mountain East Foothill in Ningxia Province is the best-known appellation thanks to their gold medals in international wine competitions and their promotion in influential wine media. It is also as a result of the Ningxia government's effort. Other appellations are less well-known by consumers.

In 2011, Helan Mountain East Foothill became a protected geographic indication in China. In 2012, Ningxia became the first Chinese provincial wine region accepted as an official observer in the OIV. In the same year, the first provincial-level wine bureau in China was founded here. In 2013, the Ningxia government released the first local regulations designated for a wine region—"Ningxia Helan Mountain East Foothill Wine Region Conservation Regulations". And following the Bordeaux 1855 Classification, the government announced the introduction of a classification system to recognize and encourage Ningxia wineries producing high-quality wines. This is a classification system that divides the best wineries into five classes in accordance with strict conditions such as grape variety, yield (about 57.7–92.3 hl/ha by red wine), and wine quality. The classification system was officially implemented in 2016. Also a regulation aimed to protect the geographic indication of Helan Mountain East Foothill was released in the same year (Wu, 2016).

With the support of the local government and the cooperation of wineries, regional wine- industry associations sprang up in wine regions (Wu, 2014). There is no doubt that Ningxia is a pioneer and plays a guidance role for all the associations. The legal system, such as the protected geographic indication and the classification are frequently demanded by both wine producers and the Chinese government. Chinese wine regions are approaching international standards step by step.

As for the brands, Changyu has undoubtedly the highest market share, and it is also the brand with most consumer awareness, followed by Great Wall, Weilong, and Dynasty. From market share statistics, it is not hard to see that consumers have stronger brand awareness than appellation awareness.

Two quite different wine producers—Changyu and Helan Qingxue Vineyard—will now be described in order to have a better understanding of the characteristics of the Chinese wine industry.

10.2.5 Case Study: Changyu Versus Helan Qingxue Vineyard

Changyu is one of the oldest Chinese wineries. It has now been transformed into a big group which offers a wide range of products from wine to spirits produced from six production regions in China and eight chateaux from their properties in China and abroad. Their Pioneer International Chateau Alliance with several chateaux from France, Italy, Spain, New Zealand, and Australia produce their high-end wines with a very competitive image.

Changyu holds an important market share in almost every catalog in the Chinese wine market, with a very large range of products from cheap wine to high-end wine, cognac and brandy from their estates abroad, ice wine, and health-care liquor. Changyu still holds a positive status and keeps expanding its investment overseas in spite of the economic decline, the competition from imported wines and the downturn of wine consuming caused by the anti-corruption campaign from 2012.

By contrast, Helan Qingxue is not only at the opposite extreme to Changyu because of the size of the company but also in the building of the image of their products—100% Chinese ancestry. Founded in 2005, Helan Qingxue Vineyard is the first demonstration vineyard in Ningxia. It has about 13.33 hectares of vineyard with an annual production of 50,000 bottles, situated in Helan Mountain East Foothill. Its consultant, Li Demei, is a well-known Chinese winemaker trained in Bordeaux, as well as a professor in Beijing Agricultural College. This winery has built up its image and reputation gradually by the successful performance of their wines in several competitions. Their wines have won many awards in international contexts such as the Decanter World Wine Award and the "best Chinese wine" selected by the Revue du Vin de France (RVF) China.

10.2.6   Foreign Wineries and Joint-Venture Wineries in China

As mentioned before, Chinese wine industrialization was started by the Sino-foreign joint-venture wine companies, and, up until now, foreign capital has continued to invest in wineries in China. Among these foreign investments, there are wineries established by large groups such as Pernod Ricard which founded Helan Mountain Winery in Ningxia, the LVMH group which planted 66 hectares of vines in Ningxia for the production of its Chandon subsidiary in China, and the 25-hectare vineyard owned by Domaines Barons de Rothschild (Lafite) in Penglai, Shandong Province. In addition, there are also wineries established by wine enthusiasts like Dr. Karl Heinz Hauptmann, a financial-industry expert, who founded Chateau Nine Peaks in Shandong.

10.2.6.1 Moët Hennessy's Chinese Red Wine: Ao Yun

Ao Yun is the first luxury Chinese wine by Moët Hennessy produced in Yunnan Province. The history of producing Ao Yun is a vivid example to illustrate the surprisingly high cost of wine production in certain Chinese regions and also the challenges encountered by foreign investors. According to the president of Moët Hennessy Estates & Wines, Jean-Guillaume Prats, producing Ao Yun combines "a great human challenge and a logistical nightmare", which results in extremely high costs, even more than those to make Chateau Yquem (Schmitt, 2016). The logistics are very difficult since the vineyards are situated in the foothills of the Himalayas at an average altitude of 2500 m. Besides, when communicating with local farmers who speak only the local language, French managers are facing problems related to culture and the language barrier. Furthermore, electricity is not available on the farm, which means every winemaking procedure has to be done by hand. 2013 is the first vintage of this unique wine, with a small production of 24,000 bottles, priced at USD300 internationally.

10.3   Wine Distribution in China

10.3.1   Segmentation by Color and Grape Variety

As we can see in Fig. 10.4, still red wine dominates the market, accounting for 71% of the total wine sales in volume, followed by still white wine representing 23% of the total, complemented with small percentages of still rosé, sparkling wine, and Champagne. With an increasing popularity of Champagne, sparkling wines have gained some share but it is still limited. Among the grape varieties for red wine, Cabernet Sauvignon occupies the first place with around 35% of the total sales in volume, followed by Merlot with about 23%, Cabernet Franc 10%, Cabernet Sauvignon/Shiraz 10%, and others. For white wine, the top 3 most popular varieties are Chardonnay with 43%, Riesling 26% and Dragon Eye 8%, and others account for 23% of the total (author's calculation based on Euromonitor International (2011, 2015)). Rosé wines consumed in China are mainly made of Merlot.

10.3.2   Domestic Wine Versus Imported Wine

The majority of wine consumption is Chinese domestic wine that accounts for 77% of the total consumption. Imported wines make up the remaining

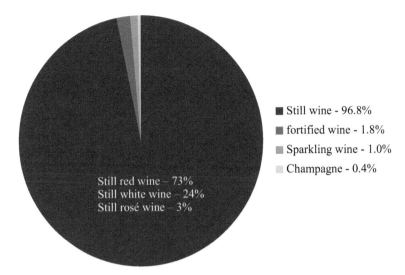

Still wine - 96.8%
fortified wine - 1.8%
Sparkling wine - 1.0%
Champagne - 0.4%

Still red wine – 73%
Still white wine – 24%
Still rosé wine – 3%

Fig. 10.4 Wine market share segmentation by color. (Source: MarketLine 2015 and author's calculation based on Euromonitor International 2011, 2015)

23% of consumption. With the evolving consumption behavior of Chinese wine drinkers, imported wine is a growing and developing part of the Chinese wine market with a high potential for the future. Among all the imported wines, France (36%), Chile (22%), Spain (12%) and Australia (11%), Italy (6%), and the USA (4%) are the top "countries of origin" (author's calculation based on Euromonitor International (2011, 2015)). French wine dominates the market but there is a significant growth of New World wines.

10.3.2.1 Export

Exports of Chinese wines are negligible and the main destination is Hong Kong. As the wine industry is still very young in China, only a few wineries sell their wines abroad. But with a good trend of development, it will not be long until we see Chinese wine all around the world as it is already possible to find Ningxia wines in California's wine cellars.

10.3.3 Wine Distribution

On-trade and supermarkets/hypermarkets are the leading distribution channels in China. According to IWSR (2015), Walmart, RT-mart/Auchan, Carrefour, Tesco (CRV), Metro, Parkson, and Lotus are the largest wine retailers in China (Fig. 10.5). Since 2016, on-trade has increased significantly in China. Meanwhile, e-commerce has contributed a significant share (MarketLine 2016, 2017).

10.3.4 Price Segmentation

Off-trade, the most common selling price range for all wines is 20–59.9 RMB (3–10 USD) per bottle. Nearly 80% of red wines are sold within that price range, and the same occurs for 71% of white wines, 78% of rosé wines, and 79% of sparkling wines (author's calculation based on Euromonitor International (2011, 2015)).

   When it comes to imported wines, the average spending per bottle ranges from 179 RMB for a casual drink to 260 RMB for a special occasion. On-trade, average spending per bottle varies from 219 RMB for an informal meal, to 296 RMB for a party or celebration, and up to 424 RMB for a business meal (Wine Intelligence 2015).

   The Chinese wine market is still in an hourglass structure (Fig. 10.6) with a mid-range market smaller than the low-priced and high-end markets. Domestic wine, along with low-priced imported wine, has gained the largest market share and still has potential. The top-end fine wines have been experiencing a decline over the last two years (2013–2015). While the mid-range market that includes mid-priced imported wines from a wide diversity of ori-

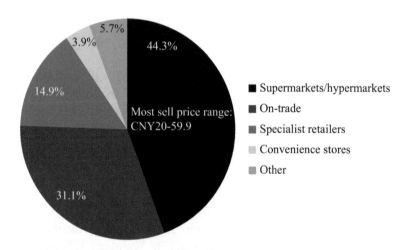

Fig. 10.5 Wine distribution in China. (Source: MarketLine 2015 and author's calculation based on Euromonitor International 2011, 2015)

Fig. 10.6 Hourglass structure. (Drawn by author)

gins—Old World wines as well as New World wines—is growing and is expected to continue that trend.

10.4 Relationships Along the Chain

10.4.1 From Winegrowing to Winemaking in China

According to the Chinese economic system, the ownership of land in China is public, which means that neither the winegrowers nor the wineries own the land. So, there are two common models of production among the wineries in China.

(a) Firstly, at the beginning of the development of the wine industry in China, wineries used to buy the grapes from independent winegrowers who rented land from the government to make their wines. They barely had any control during the viticulture productive process. Sugar and acid degrees after harvest are the only indicators to control grape quality. Independent winegrowers are numerous and hard to regulate, and they can also find alternative markets such as fruit-sugar production or switching to table grape varieties.

(b) During the past decades, the model of "wineries + independent winegrowers" has shown a lot of disadvantages, such as unstable quality and quantity of grape and unstable income for winegrowers. Recently, a growing number of pioneer wineries have tried to rent the land themselves and train their hired winegrowers.

Wineries choose either of these two explained models to cooperate with winegrowers depending on their size and their business strategy. Big wineries from more traditional wine regions, like Xinjiang, prefer to continue to buy grapes from winegrowers to ferment large quantities of cheap wines. The first model can't reach grape quality expectations of wineries aiming at making small production of high-quality wines.

The second model raises costs of production but it provides wineries with more innovation flexibility to create their own wines. Some wineries are also encouraged by government supports. In some regions, like in the Ningxia Province with the government subsidy, the rent of land is 100 times less expensive than in other regions.

Government supports have just extended to Xinjiang and Ningxia provinces. In other regions, government supports are still at municipal or district levels, like the Hengren County in Liaoning Province, Fangshan District in Beijing, or Penglai District in Shandong Province. For instance, from 2006 to 2014, the Penglai government allocated incentives and subsidies to encourage both the construction of wineries and the wine producers who own vineyards.

At the beginning, government supports were applicable from the land rent up to the distribution. But, since 2013, the distribution subsidy has diminished and market influence has begun to be more noticeable.

10.4.2   Market of Bulk and Bottled Wines

In China, wineries tend to be distributed geographically according to their size. According to the interviews with scholars and professionals, small wineries are concentrated in the eastern part of China, and big ones are often located in the western part.[1] Big wineries, often belonging to large groups and located in Xinjiang, send their bulk wines to other subsidiaries from the same group for bottling and distribution. Except for those kinds of wineries, most wineries in China are equipped with bottling and packaging pipelines. So, they often bottle in their wineries and sell their wine in bottles.

---

[1] Generally speaking, the wineries in the eastern part of China are relatively small compared to the wineries in the western regions such as Xinjiang and Gansu. Ningxia is a special case, though it is located in the western part of China.

10.4.3   Distribution of Chinese Wine

Viewed as a whole, Chinese wineries show a high degree of vertical integration. However, different wineries have different strategies to distribute and promote their wines.

10.4.3.1   Traditional Distribution Channels

Although distribution channels are improving gradually, *guanxi*[2] still plays a significant role in wine sales, which means that establishing a close relationship with distributors and with government, corporate, and private clients is a key factor for commercial success in China. The Chinese domestic wine industry is characterized by high vertical integration along the chain. Despite a huge difference in business models between large groups and small wineries, they often have their own distribution channels. Government and corporate clients are important buyers of Chinese wine. They purchase wine in a large volume for their staff or clients as a gift for national festivals such as the Mid-Autumn Festival, the New Year, and the most famous Spring Festival. In addition, the staff is often interested in getting discounts.

10.4.3.2   E-commerce

With the emergence of e-commerce and social networks, digital marketing has a very important role in the distribution of Chinese wine and is proving successful. There are distributors like Yesmywine.com which only sell wines on the Internet, and some multiple domestic importers/distributors use e-commerce to sell their wines such as JD (Jing Dong), Tmall (Alibaba Group), and GOME.

Chinese consumers can easily get lost in the middle of the wine shelves of a wine cellar or supermarket because of the lack of professional sales guidance. On the Internet, consumers can often get more information and also better advice from reading comments of other consumers, which helps them make their choices. In addition, delivery is fast and with very low prices. Buying wine online is appealing for young generations and for those who are interested

---

[2] Literally, guanxi means "go through the gate and get connections" or simply "relationships". In the business world, it is a Chinese term used to describe the network of relationships aimed to provide support and cooperation or exchange favors among the parties involved.

in bargains, although fake wine is a severe problem challenging consumers' trust.

For instance, on 9 September 2016, Tmall host edits first Global Wine & Spirits Festival online, bringing 100,000 wines and spirits from 50 countries of origin (including Chinese wineries) to Chinese consumers. Meanwhile, 5000 bars and pubs will provide free tastings and distribution services offline. It was a phenomenal event that showed the considerable influence of e-commerce on wine distribution in China. Besides, the Alibaba Group has expanded its activities to the Bordeaux region by acquiring wine estates and establishing a negociant company. The group intends to corporate with foreign wineries and exporters to retail wine to Chinese consumers through its Wine Direct platform.

Apart from the distributors, wine groups and large wineries also manage their own online platforms. Their wines are available from official online shops where consumers can acquire guaranteed authentic products. They promote their wine on social networks, in particular via Weibo (Chinese Twitter) and the official account platform of WeChat (a powerful app combining all kinds of existing social network apps, an essential of everyday life to make business). Also, they provide VIP services such as buying wine *en primeur*, enjoying exclusive member discounts, customizing products with special packing or whole barrel orders, and so on.

10.4.3.3   Promotion

Chinese wineries increasingly make high-quality wines with prices as expensive as imported wines. This brings some difficulty to consumers to choose between a Chinese wine and an imported wine. Thus, Chinese wineries use the same promotional methods as for imported wines. Master class and wine-tasting activities are organized by wineries cooperating with media such as *RVF* and *Decanter*. "Best Chinese wines" ranking competitions are also popular in building a good image to consumers.

10.4.4   Distribution of Imported Wine

There are not many barriers for foreign wine entering China. Unlike the three-tiered system in the USA, there are no particular regulations in China to prevent an importer distributing the wine on their own and even reaching end-buyers. *Guanxi* is also important for distributing domestic wine as well as imported wine.

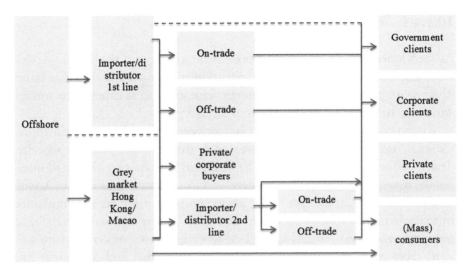

Fig. 10.7 Distribution chain of import wine in China. (Source: Wine Intelligence 2013). Dashed line represents significant relationship but with little volume

The distribution chain is somewhat vertically integrated without clear specialization or division of roles among the operators. Importers also play the distribution role or that of retailer, and so on. In addition, it is an advantage to establish a closer relationship with their clientele, especially with end-buyers, because retail stores with terminal clients are often the most profitable.

As presented by Fig. 10.7, there are five types of players along the imported-wine distribution chain: foreign suppliers, importers, distributors, interfaces, and final consumers. Foreign suppliers are foreign wine producers, merchants, or Chinese imported-wine brokers. They provide wine to first-line importers/distributors or to the gray market in Hong Kong or Macao.[3] Then, wine can be distributed from first-line importers to second-line importers/distributors, then to retailers, and so on. Another possibility is that importers distribute wine directly to retailers, restaurants, hotels, bars as well as to private or corporate buyers. Finally, wine reaches consumers. However, part of the wine in the gray market can flow directly to final consumers.

---

[3] Smugglers use the gray markets in Hong Kong or Macao to transfer imported wines into mainland China to evade import duties.

10.4.4.1   First-Line Importers/Distributors

As mentioned before, the border between importing and distributing activities is not clear. First-line importers/distributors import more than distribute. Their wine provisions are from foreign wine producers directly, or foreign wine merchants, or Chinese brokers of foreign wine.

We can consider five types of first-line importers/distributers: the historical national, the specialist, the super-regional, the regional, and the wheeler-dealer (Wine Intelligence 2013). The historical nationals are the small number of large groups like ASC, Summergate, C&D, Torres, and COFCO, with public or foreign capital, providing a wide range of products and implanted in major wine-consumption regions of China. The specialists are small and medium-sized organizations specialized in certain types or certain wine origins, most of them implanted in cities like Shanghai and Shenzhen. The super-regionals, successfully implanted in their regions, and the regionals are mostly in second- and third-tier cities of their region. The wheeler-dealers are opportunists looking for short-term profits, found at every level along the chain and in every region.

10.4.4.2   Second-Line Importers/Distributors

Second-line importer/distributors are essentially dedicated to the wholesale business. They are mostly private companies of different sizes, specializing in one region or one city and often successfully implanted in the second- and third-tier cities of their region. Their main supplies are from first-line importers/distributors, and many of them have also developed a direct import activity, but distribution remains as their main activity.

10.5   Conclusion

- China is an emerging wine market and has a young domestic wine industry. The market is characterized by its dynamism. The industry structure, especially the channels of distribution, has been evolving rapidly to adapt to changes in consumer behavior.
- The domestic wine industry is characterized by high vertical integration along the chain from winegrowing to winemaking and finally to distribution.

- Leading groups provide a wide range of products from low- to high-end prices and occupy about half of the total market of domestic wine. The degree of concentration has been experiencing a decreasing trend over the last two years. The large groups buy wine grapes from independent domestic winegrowers or import grape juice or bulk wine from the New World to obtain high volumes. Grapes produced by company-owned vineyards are used for high-end products.
- Independent winegrowers are numerous. They rent land from the government to grow vines and barely have control during the viticulture process. The quality of their grapes and grape juice cannot be guaranteed.
- Small wineries in Ningxia have a different business model to the large groups. Following the Bordeaux path, they have relatively strict regulations in terms of winegrowing and winemaking. All wines are produced from their own vineyards with high quality, and have gained an international reputation.
- There is a high cost in winegrowing because of extreme climates. In certain regions, vines have to be buried each winter in order to protect them from the cold and wind.
- The Chinese government has been playing a significant role in the development of the wine industry: government subsidies for winegrowing and winemaking sectors and also promoting wine as a healthier alternative to *Baijiu* (a strong Chinese distilled alcoholic beverage made from grains).
- Red wine undoubtedly dominates the market, followed by white wine. Rosé wine is scarcely consumed in China. Sparkling wine has started to gain in popularity, but it still has a long way to go.
- In China, *guanxi* (the network of relationships) is still a key factor of success in the wine business. Government and corporate manage a great number of clients but with high seasonality. The Chinese traditional festivals are the best occasions to make turnover.
- Domestic wineries, be they big groups or small wineries, often have their own channels to distribute wine. Online platforms are an effective way to promote their wines. E-commerce has been successfully operated in China by distributors as well as wineries themselves.
- Chinese consumers have become more open-minded and adventurous vis-à-vis novel products. Imported wine is growing and developing in China, thanks to the evolving behavior of Chinese wine consumers. Mid-price-ranged imported wines from the Old World as well as the New World have great potential on the Chinese market.

- There are not many entry barriers for imported wines. The border of the activities between importers and distributors is not clear. There is evidence of a vertical-integration trend along the imported-wine distribution chain.
- The export of domestic wine is negligible, although there is room for optimism because the quality of wine is improving.

References

Anderson, K., and N.R. Aryal. 2013. *Which winegrape varieties are grown where? A global empirical picture.* Adelaide: University of Adelaide Press.

Li, S.H. 2000. Grape production in China. FAO Corporate Document Repository. Available at: http://www.fao.org/docrep/003/x6897e/x6897e05.htm#TopOfPage.

Li, D. 2016. Defining the Chinese wine regions. *Decanter China.* Available at: https://www.decanterchina.com/en/columns/demeis-view-wine-communication-from-a-chinese-winemaker/defining-the-chinese-wine-regions.

Schmitt, P. 2016. Moët's Chinese wine 'a logistical nightmare'. *The Drink Business.* Available at: https://www.thedrinksbusiness.com/2016/06/moets-chinese-wine-a-logistical-nightmare/.

Wu, S. 2014. Ningxia wine region: We've got your back, says the government. *Decanter China.* Available at: https://www.decanterchina.com/en/knowledge/people/region-authorities/ningxia-wine-region-we-ve-got-your-back-says-the-government.

Wu, S. 2016. Ningxia announces wine classification system. *Decanter China.* Available at: https://www.decanterchina.com/en/news/ningxia-announces-wine-classification-system.

Audit de la distribution du vin en Chine. 2013. Wine Intelligence.

China Brewing Industry Yearbook. 2008–2011. China Alcoholic Drinks Association.

Le marché des vins et spiritueux en Chine Continentale. 2012. Ubifrance.

Portraits China. 2015. Wine Intelligence.

The IWSR/Vinexpo Report – The Wine World 2009–2019. 2015. International Wine and Spirit Research.

Wine in China. 2011, 2015. Euromonitor International.

Wine in China. 2015–2017. MarketLine.

World Vitiviniculture Situation. 2013–2017. International Organisation of Vine and Wine (OIV).

"12 Five-Year Plan" for Chinese wine industry. 2012. Chinese Ministry of Industry and Information Technology and Ministry of Agriculture.

"13 Five-Year Plan" for Chinese wine industry. 2015. Chinese Ministry of Industry and Information Technology and Ministry of Agriculture.

Part II

Regulations in the Wine Sector

Coord. by *Paola Corsinovi, Davide Gaeta*

11

Introduction: Regulations in the Wine Sector

Paola Corsinovi and Davide Gaeta

The European Union is the first wine-producing area with around 65% of world production; however, over the years the Europe's share of the world's vineyards has declined from 63% in 2000 to 54% in 2014 as the effect of EU policy as the permanent abandonment premiums ended in 2011 (OIV 2015). In the meantime, the share of all other world wine regions is increasing, in particular in Asia, which now accounts for 25% of the world's vineyards, and the international trade had a growth: which reached 20 million hl in volume in 2015; only 20 years before, in 1995, the export was about 11 million hl. Nowadays, wine has become one of the most globalized products in the world. A variety of factors have contributed to the process of globalization. Nevertheless, on the demand and consumers' side, social and religious culture, diet issues and alcohol policies have contributed to major changes in the geography of consumption with a reduction in the traditional EU wine countries versus outside the EU.

The EU domestic context and international scenes have (probably) played an important role in the design of wine strategies and interventions, since their inception in 1962. Wine policy is one of the most articulate laws of the Common Agricultural Policy (CAP) and the single Common Market Organization (CMO), and this is due to the complexity and heterogeneity of

P. Corsinovi (✉)
Centre of Economics, Hochschule Geisenheim University, Geisenheim, Germany

D. Gaeta
Department of Business Administration, University of Verona, Verona, Italy
e-mail: davide.gaeta@univr.it

© The Author(s) 2019
A. Alonso Ugaglia et al. (eds.), *The Palgrave Handbook of Wine Industry Economics*,
https://doi.org/10.1007/978-3-319-98633-3_11

the decision-making system, policy-makers, institutions and organizations involved in the process. The wine policy has gradually been established under the CAP; however, agricultural policy and both the EU domestic context and the international scenario have played an important role in designing the strategies of wine interventions. The new CAP and CMO's agreements 2014–2020 reached in 2013 are the results of three years of bargaining and intensive negotiation by the European member states that have different interests and level of economic support to reach.

The CAP is still the most integrated of all EU policies and accounts for the largest share of the EU budget and recognizes that its share of the budget has steadily decreased from about 75% of the total EU budget in 1985 to 38% by 2013. Recently, debates on CAP and the CMO have seen new decision-makers involved. The EU Parliament was involved under the co-decision procedure to the last CAP and CMO (including the wine sector) reforms for the period 2014–2020. After 46 years of implementation, the CAP and its CMOs are one of the most integrated EU policies and account for the largest share of the EU budget (38% by 2013).

The objective of this part is to investigate the multiple aspects of wine regulation and the actors (organizations) involved.

In details, this second part of the book is structured into three chapters (Chaps. 12, 13 and 14): Chap. 12 entitled "International Wine Organizations and Plurilateral Agreements: Harmonization versus Mutual Recognition of Standards" by Compés; Chap. 13, by Corsinovi and Gaeta, focuses on "The European Wine Policies: Regulations and Strategies"; and Chap. 14 by Mariani and Pomarici on "Barriers to Wine Trade".

Chapter 12 analyzes the international wine organizations and plurilateral agreements and the dialectic between harmonization and mutual recognition of standards. This part focuses on the role of the international organizations such as the International Organisation of Vine and Wine (OIV) and the World Wine Trade Group (WWTG). The first tries to promote harmonization and the second the mutual acceptance and recognition of standards. There are no formal relations between WWTG and OIV, although many WWTG members participate in the OIV. They don't compete, but their philosophies are very different. Through detailed analysis, this section highlights the different philosophies and goals of action. WWTG is smaller and more nimble because of the fewer members. It also has a direct link between industry practitioners and government, which is weaker in the OIV (principally government and researchers). The WWTG exists to facilitate trade and because of the unique partnership between industry and government can develop international trading agreements to facilitate trade. It also provides a strong link to the Asia-Pacific region due to well-developed relationships, which are lacking in the OIV. This one, despite its international nature, has a European focus, and its main activity is the establishment of standards and the development and approval of new practices. Perhaps a formal relationship with the European Commission could cause tensions with non-EU member states, pushing it toward the "Old World" and letting the WWTG as the "New World" institution (Raul Compés López, Chap. 12).

Chapter 13, on the "European Wine Policies: Regulations and Strategies" by Corsinovi and Gaeta, is organized into three parts. The first one describes the historical evolution of European wine policies and highlights the main drivers and outcome that have dominated the European Commission's aims since the first CMO in 1962, until the last reform in 2013. This section follows the evolution of the wine policies through three main phases: the first phase (Phase 1), referred to as "price and income support", has followed the objective of market equilibrium by reducing surplus wine quantities and guaranteeing the income stability of producers (such as distillations or aid for storage or buying alcohol). The second phase (Phase 2) could be identified as the "quality phase". It saw the introduction of a set of instruments to control production with the aim of adapting supply to market demand, improving production potential and management, and restructuring production potential in terms of quality and quantity (such as the aids for grubbing up and permanent abandonment, restructuring, green harvesting and harvest insurances). The third phase (Phase 3), starting mainly with the 2008 reform, marks officially the new policy orientation focusing on the "competitiveness" of quality wines. The second part of Chap. 13 analyzes the budget expenditure that has characterized the public interventions (and its three phases described) in 45 years (1970–2015). In the third part of the chapter, authors focus their analysis on the protection model for EU quality wines, based on a pyramid-structured project that is becoming more restrictive as they gradually move up the pyramid from the base to the peak, and its recognition at the international level and role of the international organization like World Trade Organization (WTO). The second section highlights the controversial aspects of the EU wine policy from financial expenditures to the requests of recognition and protection of quality wines in the international scenarios.

The dynamic growth of the wine traded and the increase of international trade have been driven by a number of external and internal factors including trade barriers. The understanding of which and how trade barriers operate in the wine markets is explained by the contribution of Chap. 14 on "Barriers to

Wine Trade" by Mariani and Pomarici that helps to interpret how the wine market evolved over time and to foresee how could it evolve in the future. Chapter 14 offers an updated analysis of tariff barriers and non-tariff measures and the free trade agreement relevant to wine trade. This chapter is organized as follows: in paragraph 2 the tariff barriers operating in the wine market are discussed, and an assessment of the impact of such barriers on the wine export flows is introduced; in paragraph 3 a general overview of non-tariff measures is offered, showing how these operate as barriers in the wine sector; in paragraph 4 an analysis is done of technical measures, which are the non-tariff measures more frequently resulting in trade barriers; in paragraph 5 it is shown how exporting and importing countries reduce the wine trade's barriers; and in paragraph 6, the events and processes which could modify trade barrier status in the wine market over the near future are presented. Some final remarks, in paragraph 7, conclude the chapter.

Reference

OIV. 2015. *World vitiviniculture situation*. Available at http://www.oiv.int/public/medias/2777/report-mainzcongress-2015-oiv-en-7.pdf

12

International Wine Organizations and Plurilateral Agreements: Harmonization Versus Mutual Recognition of Standards

Raúl Compés López

12.1 Introduction

Until the late 1980s, the European Union (EU) was the only real-world player in the global wine market because the new wine world was still in its infancy. The EU's wine policy was, and continues to be, different from the Common Agricultural Policy's rules and was largely influenced by the traditional philosophy of French regulation. At the time, the EU's policy was autonomous and independent of external influences. The only external institution of reference was the International Organisation of Vine and Wine (OIV), but its influence was very restricted in both technical and oenological standards.

Things started to change during the mid-1990s in several ways. First, the creation of the World Trade Organization (WTO) and the arrival of the current globalization era pushed the opening of markets. Second, the rapid and successful emergence of the new world wine countries changed the dynamics of international markets, increasing competition and leading to new business models and new forms of regulation. Third, the new entrants, at least some of them, wanted to promote a more liberal approach to issues related to the international markets. In the face of the European interventionist model—

The author thanks the comments made by Tony Battaglene

R. Compés López (✉)
Department of Economics and Social Sciences, Universitat Politècnica de València, València, Spain
e-mail: rcompes@esp.upv.es

© The Author(s) 2019
A. Alonso Ugaglia et al. (eds.), *The Palgrave Handbook of Wine Industry Economics*,
https://doi.org/10.1007/978-3-319-98633-3_12

created to monitor the supply and protect the origin in keeping up a main standard of quality—the new world model was based on self-governance and private coordination in order to reach common goals, mainly in the fields of innovation and in external markets (Castillo et al. 2014).

EU policy had to react to these changes, a reaction which took place on several levels: modifying internal changes of its wine's rules in 2008, pressing the WTO to defend geographical indications (GI), and strengthening the OIV's role in harmonizing standards. In the twenty-first century, a new paradigm in wine regulation began to spread.

Globalization increases interdependence among countries, and the wine sector is one of the paradigms of the globalization movement in the agrifood sector (Dubois 2013). In the field of policies, this pushes toward cooperation and the pursuit of convergence or, at the very least, coexistence of standards (Bingen and Busch 2006). This process is carried out in the frame of international organizations and through multilateral, plurilateral, or bilateral agreements (Dai 2007). One of the most relevant of all them is the WTO because it sets the framework for trade policies, internal policies that can distort trade, and, very often, other agreements.[1]

However, other specialized institutions also play an important role in the design of wine policies. The most important is the OIV, but the World Wine Trade Group (WWTG) must also be taken into account. Although there are clear differences between the two, they share the ultimate aim of promoting trade and facilitating business performance. In a global perspective, the OIV represents the search of convergence through harmonization (Juban 1994; Tinlot 2000) and the WWTG through recognition and mutual equivalence (Battaglene and Barker 2008). The OIV is a hard institution with European roots in which both new and old world countries participate, while the WWTG is a soft institution supported mainly by the United States and consisting of "new world" countries.[2] Even though the OIV and WWTG do not compete directly, they represent two ways of understanding interdependence

---

[1] WTO is the main influence in national—both internal and trade—policies. Some of the WTO agreements have direct influence over wine policies. It is a case of horizontal agreement for the Agriculture, SPS, and TBT and also for the TRIPS, who have specific provisions for protecting geographical indication of wines.

[2] From the emergence of "new" non-European producers after the Wine Tasting of 1976, also called the Judgement of Paris (Taber 2006), it is usual to divide wines into the new and the old worlds (Anderson 2003). This taxonomy is currently employed (Schirmer 2007), even if differences between the two are becoming weaker (Banks and Overton 2010), due to the bilateral and reciprocal influences in policies and management models.

policies in the framework of the WTO, and their philosophies fit the theoretical essence of the old and new worlds, respectively.

In this chapter we are going to analyze the role of the OIV and the WWTG in wine policies. This is an important topic because these institutions have received minimal attention throughout the analysis of wine's economic policy (Randelli and Dini 2013; Meloni and Swinnen 2013). The OIV has gained international recognition as the first source of technical harmonization in the wine sector (Hannin et al. 2006), and the WWTG is trying to go beyond this as a source of technical equivalence agreements.

12.2   The OIV[3]

12.2.1   Past and Present

The current OIV is the result of the evolution of several different actions of wine-producing countries in defending their common interests. The roots of this organization can be traced to the Congress held in Montpellier in 1874, where some European countries met to collaborate in the fight against phylloxera. Some years later, once the phylloxera challenge was overcome, in the Congress of Geneva, 1908, and Paris, 1909, the new common interest was in the prevention of fraud.

With these positive antecedents facing the international challenge of viticulture, in 1922 the *French Society for the Encouragement of Agriculture* suggested the creation of an international wine organization. The result was the creation of an International Wine Office (OIV) through an agreement dated November 29, 1924, between the governments of eight countries: France, Greece, Hungary, Italy, Luxembourg, Portugal, Spain, and Tunisia. It began its operations in Paris in 1928 (Peaslee 1974). On September 4, 1958, the organization's name was changed to the International Vine and Wine Office, in order to allow the incorporation of countries producing table grapes and dried grapes.

The International Vine and Wine Office was transformed into the International Organisation of Vine and Wine by decision of its General Assembly on December 5, 1997, in Buenos Aires (Argentina). Its mission was to modernize the resources of the office and to ease its adaptation to the world

---

[3] Most of the descriptive information on this point comes from the OIV website and from OIV documents and presentations.

context of the vitiviniculture sector. The agreement for the new organization was established on April 3, 2001, between 35 nations[4] and went into effect on January 1, 2004, based in Paris.

Today, the OIV has 46 member states throughout five continents, among which 21 are members of the European Union. It has also some territory and organization observers, most of them producers but also mainly consumers.[5] They account for about 85% of wine production and 80% of wine consumption worldwide. Its total budget, decided each year by the General Assembly and coming mostly from members' financial contributions, amounts to 1.5 million euros. The current president is the German Professor Dr. Monika Christmann, appointed during the 38th World Congress in Mainz, July 2015.

The United States is the only large producing country that is currently not an OIV member. In fact, it was previously a member as of 1984 but left the organization in 2001. The causes seem to be differences between the United States and European countries in matters of oenological standards and geographical indication protection and a representation system in which they were sometimes the minority.[6]

But in spite of US absence, the OIV is the most influential intergovernmental organization in the wine world. Its nature is scientific and technical, and its main role is setting standards for all products derived from the vine (vines, wine, wine-based beverages, table grapes, raisins, and other vine-based products). This involves drafting resolutions, recommendations, and proposals on various aspects of the production of and trade in wine products (i.e. oenological practices, product descriptions and definitions, labeling rules, marketing conditions, analysis and assessment methods, the protection of geographical indications, and the protection of varieties).

---

[4] Republic of Algeria, Federal Republic of Germany, Republic of Argentina, Australia, Republic of Austria, Republic of Bolivia, Federal Republic of Brazil, Republic of Chile, Republic of Cyprus, Kingdom of Denmark, Kingdom of Spain, Republic of Finland, Republic of France, Republic of Georgia, United Kingdom, Hellenic Republic, Republic of Hungary, State of Israel, Republic of Italy, Republic of Lebanon, Grand Duchy of Luxemburg, United Mexican States, Republic of Moldavia, Kingdom of Norway, New Zealand, Kingdom of the Netherlands, Republic of Portugal, Romania, Republic of Slovakia, Kingdom of Sweden, Swiss Confederation, Czech Republic, Republic of Tunisia, Republic of Turkey, Eastern Republic of Uruguay.

[5] AIDV (International Wine Law Association), Amorim Academy, AREV (Assembly of Wine-Producing European Regions), AUIV (International University Association of Wine), CERVIM (Centre for Research, Environmental Sustainability and Advancement of Mountain Viticulture), FIVS (International Federation of Wines and Spirits), OENOPPIA (Oenological Products and Practices International Association), UIOE (Union Internationale des Œnologues), VINOFED (World Federation of Major International Wine and Spirits Competitions), ASI (Association de la Sommellerie Internationale), WIM (Wine in Moderation), Yantaï (China), prefecture-level municipality and Ningxia Hui autonomous region, China.

[6] More information about this issue can be found in http://www.senat.fr/rap/l03-095/l03-0951.html

12.2.2 Functioning and Activities

The main body of the OIV is the General Assembly, composed of delegates nominated by members. It delegates some of its powers into the Executive Committee, which then entrusts some of its routine administrative powers to the OIV Steering Committee. The Office of Director General (who as of January 1, 2014, is Mr. Jean-Marie Aurand) is responsible for the internal administration of the OIV, which is composed of 14 members.

The OIV conducts its scientific and technical activity through expert groups, two sub-commissions and four commissions, coordinated by a Scientific and Technical Committee. This committee presents proposals to define the work and activity programs of the bodies of the organization.[7] Participating in the expert groups, sub-commissions and commissions are close to 1000 scientific representatives and experts that are appointed and managed by government authorities in OIV member states. They come from the scientific community and also, to a considerable extent, from the professional sector.

The resolutions of the General Assembly and the Executive Committee are adopted by general consensus and are usually incorporated, with no change to their legal scope, into more detailed standards—usually in the form of codes, periodically updated on the basis of the resolutions adopted by the organization.[8]

The main activities of the OIV are:

1. Contributing to international harmonization of existing practices and standards, in order to improve the conditions for producing and marketing vine and wine products and to help ensure that the interests of consumers are taken into account. The OIV resolutions are addressed to governments in the form of recommendations (Exhibit 12.1).

---

[7] The four commissions are Viticulture, Oenology, Economy and Law, Safety and Health; and the two sub-commissions Methods of Analysis and Table Grapes, Raisins and Unfermented Vine Products; with the expert groups to support their tasks.

[8] For instance, the International Oenological Codex, the Compendium of International Methods of Analysis of Wine and Must, the Compendium of international methods of analysis of spirited beverages, international standards for wine and spirit competitions, and the international standard for labeling wines and spirit drinks.

Exhibit 12.1 The Case of the EU

In the case of the EU, the standards and resolutions of the OIV are adopted automatically into their wine norms. Due to this, the Council Regulation (EC) No 479/2008 on the common organization of the market in wine stipulates that, in the matter of authorizing new oenological practices, the commission is to "base itself on the oenological practices recommended and published by the International Organisation of Vine and Wine (OIV)" and, on the subject of methods of analysis, "the methods of analysis for determining the composition of the products covered by this Regulation and the rules whereby it may be established whether these products have undergone processes contrary to the authorized oenological practices shall be those recommended and published by the OIV", and compliance with the standards recommended by the OIV for oenological practices also becomes a sufficient condition for marketing wines from third countries on the community market.

2. To assist other international organizations, both intergovernmental and nongovernmental, especially those that carry out standardization activities (Exhibit 12.2).

Exhibit 12.2 The Case of the Codex

The OIV collaborates with all intergovernmental and international organizations which are directly or indirectly concerned with vines and wine (WTO, FAO, Codex Alimentarius, WIPO, FIVS, AUIV, WCO, UPOV, OIML, and CIHEAM) in order to accomplish its aims. In particular, the OIV must guarantee that the codes of the OIV are coherent at an international level and that they are technically sound. In this framework of particular interest is the collaboration with the *Codex Alimentarius* because their norms, direct ices, and standards are a reference for the WTO (in particular the SPS Agreement) and therefore for international trade.

The OIV is a privileged partner of the Codex Alimentarius in the field of wine and wine products, in particular with regard to additives and processing aids. So, the Secretariat of the OIV participates in work on "acidity regulators" and "emulsifiers, stabilizers, and thickeners" electronic working group on food additives and submitted comments relating to the category "grape wine", although it lacks a cooperation protocol to confirm the OIV as technical and scientific organization of recognized competence in the field of vine and wine and a systematic strategy of member states aimed at consolidating relations between the two organizations with regard to wine products.

3. Compilation of global statistics such as area under vines, production (fresh grapes, raisins, wine), trade, and consumption, as well as economic and statistical analyses to influence decisions made.

4. Formation and training. The OIV establishes and coordinates the development of international research on emerging topics—impact of climate change, environmental issues, concern related to the consumption of wine—and training programs in the sector. It fosters contacts and scientific exchanges and training in countries throughout the world. This includes the OIV MSc in "Wine Management", created in 1986, and the World Congress of Vine and Wine, now in its 41st year.
5. Patronage and competitions. The OIV may grant patronage to international scientific conferences or national and international wine and spirits of vitivinicultural origin competitions, provided that their organization and internal rule procedures are in accordance with the international standards of the OIV.

12.3 WWTG[9]

12.3.1 Nature and Goals

Unlike the OIV, the WWTG is an informal plurilateral group of government and industry representatives from some wine-producing countries mainly of the "new world"—in fact, initially it was called the New World Wine Producers' Forum. It was founded in 1998 in Zurich by Argentina, Australia, Canada, Chile, New Zealand, South Africa, and the United States. The Republic of Georgia attended its first WWTG meeting in 2008 and became a full member, acceding to the WWTG agreements, in 2010. The WWTG members accounted for 29% of the global wine trade and 29% of wine exports in 2013.[10]

---

[9] The main sources of information for the above are the WWTG website (http://www.wwtg-gmcv.org/), the US Department of Commerce (http://ita.doc.gov/td/ocg/wwtg.htm), the US Department of Treasury/Alcohol and Tobacco Tax and Trade Bureau (http://www.ttb.gov/itd/world_wine.shtml), and Wine Institute (https://www.wineinstitute.org/). The Wine Institute is the voice for California wine and represents more than 1000 wineries and affiliated businesses. It works closely with several US official entities on tariff and trade barrier reduction, free trade agreements, and other negotiations to grow US wine exports globally.

[10] The WWTG welcomes participation in the group as observers of any national governments or members of the World Trade Organization interested in furthering these goals. Other countries that have participated in the meetings are China, Mexico, Paraguay, Uruguay, Brazil, and Moldova. In 2006, it set down principles derived from the WWTG agreements that could be applied in other international contexts. The most important extension initiative has been the development of the APEC Wine Regulators Forum (WRF).

The group has no formal membership, membership fees, and secretariat. The participants share the responsibility of chairing the WWTG, with the chair position rotating on an annual basis. The country that has the chair functions acts as secretariat and organizes the meetings of the group (one or two meetings per year). Meetings are attended by both government and wine industry representatives (in joint and separate sessions). During the Washington, DC-based WWTG meetings held in July of 2006, participants adopted the first industry section strategic plan, together with an integrated set of action plans to achieve the specified goals and objectives. WWTG also facilitates cooperation between their members to improve international markets.[11]

The main aim of the group is to facilitate international trade, to avoid trade obstacles, and to liberalize wine trade. For that, it promotes joint actions for the removal of trade barriers,[12] and instead of looking for harmonization, it searches for mutual acceptance of rules rather than imposing a single regulatory approach, given that it recognizes the unique characteristics of each regulatory system.

The reason for this emphasis in trade and mutual equivalence is that all of these countries integrated in the WWTG share an orientation toward external markets and have a great potential of growth production. They are very concerned with barriers to their exports, in particular the non-tariff barriers into the EU markets. They consider labeling requirements, tariffs, and appellation of origin or geographical indication as strong barriers.

12.3.2   Activities and Agreements

The main outputs of the WWTG have been two agreements which are at the core of their framework—a memorandum and a protocol—and two statements. Additionally, a January 2007 meeting included, for the first time, a Regulators Forum to provide regulatory bodies with an opportunity to discuss possible approaches to emerging regulatory issues. In 2008, the WWTG also

---

[11] Four WWTG members (Chile, Argentina, New Zealand, and South Africa) plus California formed the New World Wines Alliance. On March 10, 2010, they joined forces and put on an unprecedented combined show named "Down to Earth" at ProWein in Germany. ProWein is one of the leading trade fairs for the international wine and spirits industry (Source: The World Wine Trade Group And The Need To Promote Cooperation Among Wine Producers Of The New World, Marcela B. Knaup; *This article was first published by the International Trade Committee Newsletter of the American Bar Association, Section of International Law, Volume IV, No 3, 8-2010*).

[12] The decision to change the name of the group to World Wine Trade Group was to reflect the focus of the group on facilitating trade in wine.

represented the global wine industry, in conjunction with the CEEV (*Comité Européen des Entreprises Vins*, the representative professional body of the EU industry and trade in wines) at the WTO consultation on its strategy for reducing the harmful use of alcoholic beverages. In 2011, a joint meeting was held between FIVS[13] and WWTG on sustainability, which identified important synergies between WWTG and non-WWTG industries around this topic; finally, in 2015, a winegrowing report was produced.

The Mutual Acceptance Agreement (MAA) on Oenological (winemaking) Practices was signed in Toronto, Canada, in December 2001 by the United States and Canada, with Argentina becoming a signatory in December 2002. By 2005, all WWTG participants had ratified the MAA with the exception of South Africa, which ratified the MAA in 2011. Under that agreement, each country will permit the importation of wines from every other signatory country as long as these wines are made in accordance with the producing country's domestic laws, regulations, and requirements on oenological practices. The agreement recognizes that different countries use different winemaking practices due to local conditions, climatic variations, and traditions, and that grape-growing and winemaking practices are constantly evolving.[14]

The Agreement on Requirements for Wine Labelling (Labelling Agreement) was signed on January 23, 2007, in Canberra, Australia, by all participants with the exception of South Africa. It enables wine exporters to sell wine into WWTG markets without having to redesign all of their labels for each individual market. Under the Labelling Agreement, the WWTG participants have agreed to a *single field of vision* approach to wine labeling in order to ease the comparison of different wines for consumers, whereby four key common items of information (country of origin, product name, net contents, and alcohol content) are deemed to comply with domestic labeling requirements if they are presented together in any singular field of vision on the container. WWTG countries consider that these principles of clarity, consistency, and efficiency for wine labeling could provide the basis for a global standard if adopted by sufficient international bodies and countries—given that Codex Alimentarius Commission does not have an international standard for wine labeling.

On March 21, 2013, in Brussels, phase two of the Labelling Agreement was concluded through the Protocol to the Agreement on Requirements for Wine Labelling. This extends the earlier Labelling Agreement by providing

---

[13] Since 1951, is the International Alcoholic Beverage Federation, siege in Paris.

[14] A copy of the Mutual Acceptance Agreement is available on the US Department of Commerce website at:www.ita.doc.gov/td/ocg/eng_agreement.htm

for a degree of harmonization of rules regarding alcohol tolerance, variety, wine region, and vintage.

In October 2011, the United States, along with representatives from Argentina, Australia, Chile, Georgia, and New Zealand, signed a Memorandum of Understanding (MOU) on Certification Requirements, which aims to reduce barriers to international wine trade by encouraging the elimination of burdensome requirements and routine certifications of wine products and ingredients. The certification provides that routine certification of wine composition should not be required other than on health and safety grounds consistent with WTO rules, as well as requiring that any certification must be in line with Codex standards.[15]

In 2014, the WWTG governments approved the groundbreaking "Tbilisi Statement" of international principles for nations to use when establishing wine regulations. The "Statement on Analytical Methodology and Regulatory Limits" encompasses 11 science-based regulatory principles to help remove unnecessary obstacles in the international wine trade. These principles are a major step forward in bringing regulatory coherence to international wine trade.

12.4   Conclusions

The globalization of wine markets is pushed forward by several factors. On the institutional side, the most important are the broad liberalization caused by the WTO agreements and the soft wine rules created by the EU's reactionary reforms of 2008 toward new world wine countries model. This move is accompanied by the role of international organizations such as the OIV and the WWTG. The first attempts to promote harmonization and the second the mutual acceptance and recognition of standards, two different ways to facilitate trade and promote business. The OIV is stronger with a more global influence, but the fact that the United States is not included could be seen as a weak point.

There are no formal relations between WWTG and OIV, although many WWTG participant countries also participate in the OIV. While they don't

---

[15] Any countries require certification of compositional requirements for wine, which can act as an unnecessary barrier to trade, particularly when they do not relate to a health or safety issue in relation to wine or when the exporting country already has adequate systems in place to address such issues. Noting that the MAA already provided that routine certification should not be required between parties for oenological practices.

directly compete, their philosophies are very different. WWTG is smaller and nimbler due to having fewer members. It also has a direct link between industry practitioners and government, while the OIV have a strong influence from governments and from public and private researchers. The WWTG exists to facilitate trade and because of the unique partnership between industry and government can develop international trading agreements to facilitate trade. It also provides a strong link to the Asia-Pacific region due to well-developed relationships.

The OIV, despite its broad international nature, has a European focus, and its main activity is the establishment of standards and the development and approval of new practices. Perhaps a formal relationship with the European Commission could cause tensions with non-EU member states. However, even if some differences in regulation continue existing, and "new world" countries approach seems more liberal and trade oriented, the world of wine is every day more interconnected, and all big producers depend more and more on exports. In this situation, "new world" and "old world" trademarks seem every day less pertinent, which should drive to a convergence between WWTG and OIV.

References

Anderson, K. 2003. Wine's new world. *Foreign Policy* 136: 47–54.

Banks, G., and J. Overton. 2010. Old world, new world, third world? Reconceptualising the worlds of wine. *Journal of Wine Research* 21 (1): 57–75.

Battaglene, T., and J. Barker. 2008. Reconciling diverse approaches to regulation in the wine sector: Harmonisation, equivalence and mutual recognition. *Bulletin de l'OIV* 80 (920–922): 625–637.

Bingen, J., and L. Busch. 2006. *Agricultural standards*. Vol. 6. Amsterdam: Springer.

Castillo, S., R. Compés, and J.M. García. 2014. La regulaciónvitivinícola. Evolución en la UE y España y situación en el panorama internacional. In *Economía del vino en España y en elmundo*, coord. S. Castillo and R. Compés. CajamarCaja Rural.

Dai, X. 2007. *International institutions and national policies*. Cambridge: Cambridge University Press.

Dubois, S. 2013. Lecture géopolitique d'un produitalimentairemondialisé: le vin. *Revue internationale et stratégique* 1 (89): 18–29.

Hannin, H., J.M. Codron, and S. Thoyer. 2006. The International Office of Vine and Wine (OIV) and the World Trade Organization (WTO): Standardization issues in the wine sector. In *Agricultural standards*, 73–92. Dordrecht: Springer.

Juban, Y. 1994. Harmonization, standardization carried out by the OIV in the perspective of the World Trade Organisation. *Bulletin de l'OIV (France)*.

Meloni, G., and J.F.M. Swinnen. 2013. The political economy of European wine regulations. *Journal of Wine Economics* 8 (3): 244–284.

Peaslee, A.J. 1974. *International governmental organizations*. Vol. 1. Leiden: Brill.

Randelli, F., and F. Dini. 2013. Oltre la globalizzazione: le proposte della Geografia economica.

Schirmer, R. 2007. Les vins du Nouveau Monde sont-ils a-géographiques. *Bulletin de l'association des géographes français* 1: 65–80.

Taber, G.M. 2006. *Judgment of Paris*. New York: Scribner.

Tinlot, R. 2000. The risks of globalization and the necessary international harmonization carried out by the OIV. *Bulletin de l'OIV* 73 (827/828): 67–77.

13

The European Wine Policies: Regulations and Strategies

Paola Corsinovi and Davide Gaeta

13.1 Introduction

Over the years the European Union (EU) has introduced a number of measures/instruments designed to address the problems of income instability and supply control: until the middle of the 1980s, the principal goal of the EU wine policies was to ensure the development of productivity, create market stability, and provide income support (EU Commission 2002, 2006). Since the beginning, the context in which those reforms were forged has shifted significantly. In particular, the wine policy changed from a policy based on subsidizing production and the protection of domestic markets from non-European producers to a policy that aims to stimulate quality production and the competitiveness of the wine sector on the international scene. Many economists have been addressing wine policies and their effects (such as Anderson 2004, 2010, 2014; Anderson and Jensen 2016; Coleman 2010; Dal Bianco et al. 2016; Malassis 1959; Mariani et al. 2012; Montaigne and Coelho 2006; Corsinovi and Gaeta 2016, 2017; Meloni and Swinnen 2013, 2016; Niederbacher 1983; Pomarici and Sardone 2001, 2009; Spahni 1988).

This chapter is divided into three sections. Section 13.2 analyzes the main drivers that have characterized the EU wine policy from the first Common

P. Corsinovi (✉)
Centre of Economics, Hochschule Geisenheim University, Geisenheim, Germany

D. Gaeta
Department of Business Administration, University of Verona, Verona, Italy
e-mail: davidenicola.gaeta@univr.it

© The Author(s) 2019
A. Alonso Ugaglia et al. (eds.), *The Palgrave Handbook of Wine Industry Economics*,
https://doi.org/10.1007/978-3-319-98633-3_13

Market Organization (CMO) introduced in 1962 until the 2013 reform, followed by three main different public policy orientations and strategies that occurred in those years: phase (1) *price and income support*; phase 2, *quality of wine*; and phase 3, *competitiveness*. The policy analysis is supported by the analysis of budget expenditure (in Sect. 13.3) that has characterized the public interventions in 45 years (1970–2015). In Sect. 13.4, the authors focus the analysis on the protection model for EU quality wines, based on a pyramid-structured project that is becoming more restrictive as they gradually move up the pyramid from the base to the peak and its recognition at the international level and role of the World Trade Organization (WTO).

13.2   The Development of European Wine Policies: Objectives

Under the framework of the Common Agricultural Policy (CAP), the CMOs[1] were created with the scope to (1) implement a gradual convergence (agreement) of prices, (2) eliminate customs barriers, and (3) establish a single market for products under one common customs tariff for the rest of the world. From 1962 to 2007, 21 agricultural products were governed by their respective CMOs: from 2007 the CMO has incorporated within a single regulation all of the agriculture products (including the wine sector). The CMO of wine constitutes the legal and regulatory basis of the European wine market, covering all the rules from vineyards to wine production, from labeling to international trade.

The CMO of wine was initially established under the CAP in 1962 when the first legal text was created. Only in 1970 two formal regulations were published: one related to interventions on table wines (Reg. 816/1970) and the other concerning production of quality wines (Reg. 817/1970). During these years, the most important rules were adopted in 1987 (Reg. 822/1987), in 1999 (Reg. 1493/99), in 2008 (Reg. 479/2008), and in 2013 under the CAP reform (Reg. 1308/2013).

---

[1] The Common Agricultural Policy (CAP) is the main agricultural policy instrument of the EU. Today, it is organized in two pillars. Pillar I defines and funds market measure and it is founded by the European Agricultural Guarantee Fund (EAGF). Pillar II regards the Rural Development Programs (RDP), aimed to improve quality of life in rural areas, to support young farmers setting up a farm for the first time, and to introduce measures for investments and innovation in farms. Measures under Pillar II are financed by the European Agricultural Fund for Rural Development (EAFRD) and co-financed by EU Member States.

The objective of this part is to analyze the main drivers that have character-ized the EU wine policy from 1962 until the last reform in 2013. The latest wine reform adopted by the EU in 2008 and included in the 2013 single CMO had the following goals:

- Making EU wine producers even more competitive—enhancing the repu-tation of European wines and regaining market share both in the EU and outside
- Making the market management rules simpler, clearer, and more effec-tive—to achieve a better balance between supply and demand
- Preserving the best traditions of European wine-growing and boosting its social and environmental role in rural areas

As far as the wine sector is concerned, the 2013 CAP reform, in addition to its general goals to harmonize, streamline, and simplify the provisions of the CAP, maintains the fundamentals of the 2008 wine reform.[2]

The authors focus on the main public policy orientations that occurred in those years for the wine sector: the first, being referred to as *price and income support*, the second as *quality of wine*, and the third as *competitiveness*.

Table 13.1 summarizes three orientations—the main interventions in force, their period of implementation, and the outcome. The analysis of total wine expenditure will be presented in the following section: the impact of orientations on the total budget is shown in Fig. 13.2; Table 13.2 shows the main expenditure's line in millions of euros and % on the total budget (1970–2015).

Reflecting on the future of the wine policy strategies and monetary sup-port, Fig. 13.2 shows the financial scheme of the provision budget expendi-ture from 2014 to 2018 and published by the EU in the last reform in 2013 (Reg. 1308/2013). The data on expenditures has been collected from the European Agricultural Guidance and Guarantee Fund (EAGGF) and National Support Programs (annual financial report). The dataset created by the authors covers the CMO expenditures (included in the guarantee fund and EU own budgetary) but excludes the expenditures of the rural development funds and the co-financing from the Member States. The future amounts are available at EU Commission (Agriculture Direction) and published in the annex of Reg. 1308/2013 that establishes a common organization of the markets in agricul-tural products.

---

[2] https://ec.europa.eu/agriculture/wine_en

Table 13.1 The development of European wine policies

Orientations	Interventions	Implementation	Outcome
1. Price and income support	Distillation schemes[a]	1976–2012	– Market equilibrium by reducing surplus quantities
	Market withdrawals	1970–1999	– Income stability of producers
	Buying-in of alcohol from compulsory distillation	1970–1999	– Balancing enrichment costs
	Aid for concentrated grape must	1976–2013	– Export supports
	Aid for storage[a]	1987–2008	– Improving production potential management
	Export refunds	1987–2008	
	Regulatory measures[a]	2008–2013	
	Other intervention expenditures[a]		
2. Quality wines	Grubbing up/ abandonment	1976–2011	– Adapting vine supply to market demand
	Restructuring and reconversion	1979–2018	– Improving production potential management
	Green harvesting	2008–2018	– Restructuring production potential in terms of quality and quantity
3. Competitiveness	Promotion in third countries	2008–2018	– Improving development and competition of the wine sector
	Investments in enterprises	2008–2018	
	Innovation	2013–2018	

Source: Corsinovi and Gaeta (2017), European Commission (2002)

[a]The "aid for storage" included the aids for private and public storage and aid for re-storage of table wine. The "distillation schemes" covered the aids: obligatory distillation of table wine (1982); voluntary distillation (1976) of table wine; compulsory distillation of by-products of wine-making; crisis distillations (1999); potable alcohol distillation (1999); distillation of dual-purpose grapes (1987); preventive distillation (1987). "Regulatory measures" regard single payment scheme, harvest insurance, and mutual funds. The "Other interventions expenditures" is the sum of incentives/interventions linked to income and price support

13.2.1   The Era of "Prices and Income Support"

The first orientation strategy (Table 13.1) was identified as *price and income support*. Most of the interventions introduced between 1970 and 1979 were addressed to help and stabilize the income of the wine producers and defend the internal wine market of the EU.

More specifically three forms of distillations were implemented,[3] with the expectation to achieve market equilibrium by reducing surplus quantities. The objectives were twofold: to guarantee a fair price for producers while creating more effective measures to tackle growing market surpluses. As a consequence, market withdrawals and buying-in of alcohol from compulsory distillation were supported with the goal to remove wine and alcohol from the market. The aids for concentrated grape must[4] were meant to balance the increasing costs of producers in southern and northern wine-growing regions: in order to compensate for the competitive disadvantage suffered due to the higher cost of enrichment using must incurred by producers who were banned from using sugar to regulate alcoholic strength. The storage for table wine and grape musts should have encouraged producers to take surplus wine off the market, thus supporting market price stabilization. Export refunds were fixed by the difference between EU table wine prices (for wines to be exported) and the prices of these wines in the world market. The measure was implemented with the aim to establish a basis for commercial exports; however, it proved to be an instrument for helping to reduce and pay the EU's structural surplus of table wines.

From 2008, the EU introduced other market measures and direct payments to wine farmers with the aim to regulate wine markets and stabilize the income. In the regulatory measures (see note Table 13.1), the authors had

---

[3] (1) Obligatory distillation of wine from dual-purpose grapes, which originate from other grape wine varieties or dual-purpose grapes produced in excess of the normal verified quantity. (2) Obligatory distillation of by-products as wine lees and grape marc. (3) Voluntary distillation for table wine or distillation "with a guarantee of proper use" for those with long-term storage contracts. A few years later, with the reform in 1987, three distillations were voluntary and could be chosen by the producer: (1) distillation supplementary to long-term storage contracts, (2) preventive distillation, and (3) support distillation. Whereas the remaining three were compulsory: (1) distillation of by-products, (2) distillation of wines other than table wines, and (3) distillation of table wines. The 1999 (Reg. 1493/99) reform provided for two types of compulsory distillation, (1) wine obtained from dual-purpose grapes and (2) by-product distillation, and two types of voluntary distillation: (3) for the production of potable alcohol and (4) crisis distillation.

[4] Use of must for enrichment in order to compensate for the competitive disadvantage suffered due to the higher cost of enrichment using must incurred by producers who were banned from using sugar to regulate alcoholic strength.

Table 13.2 Total CMO wine expenditures, 1970–2015

	1970–2015		1971–1980		1981–1990		1991–2000		2001–2010		2011–2015	
	Million €	%	Million €	%	Million €	%	Million €	%	Million €	%	Million €	%
Distillation schemes[a]	9608.74	21.3	546.00	34.1	5131.99	38.4	2589.76	17.0	1043.52	12.9	297.48	4.4
Market withdrawals	6679.11	14.8	563.48	35.2	3494.62	26.1	2621.00	17.2	0.00	0.0	0.00	0.0
Buying-in of alcohol from compulsory distillation	4341.75	9.6	0.00	0.0	1176.73	8.8	1484.61	9.7	1680.40	20.8	0.00	0.0
Aid for concentrated grape must	3523.95	7.8	18.15	1.1	868.61	6.5	1328.23	8.7	882.82	10.9	426.14	6.3
Aid for storage[a]	3558.10	7.9	318.04	19.8	1221.59	9.1	1871.35	12.3	147.12	1.8	0.00	0.0
Export refunds	1046.64	2.3	36.92	2.3	270.51	2.0	540.71	3.5	198.50	2.4	0.00	0.0
Regulatory measures[a]	719.32	1.6	0.00	0.0	0.00	0.0	0.00	0.0	73.65	0.9	645.66	9.5
Other intervention expenditures[a]	2760.37	6.1	91.71	5.7	942.17	7.0	1726.00	11.3	0.00	0.00	0.00	0.0
Grubbing up/abandonment	3743.06	8.3	0.00	0.0	214.36	1.6	2330.92	15.3	939.03	11.6	258.76	3.8
Restructuring and reconversion	6167.34	13.7	26.88	1.6	40.02	0.3	743.73	4.8	2743.33	33.9	2613.38	38.6
Green harvesting	953.19	2.1	0.00	0.0	0.00	0.0	0.00	0.0	147.79	1.8	805.40	11.9
Investments and innovations	944.92	2.1	0.00	0.0	0.00	0.0	0.00	0.0	92.98	1.1	851.94	12.6
Promotion in third countries	980.83	2.1	0.00	0.0	0.00	0.0	0.00	0.0	122.39	1.5	858.45	12.7
Total expenditures	**45,027.31**		**1601.19**		**13,360.60**		**15,236.32**		**8071.53**		**6757.19**	

Source: Author's dataset (our elaboration from EAGGF annual expenditures), Corsinovi and Gaeta 2017)

[a]See notes in Table 13.1

included three interventions in accordance with the CMO Regulation 479/2008: single payment scheme (SPS) and harvest insurance.[5] Direct payments under the SPS were based on reference amounts of direct payments that were received in the past or on regionalized per hectare amount. The harvest insurance contributes to protecting the producer's financial status if affected by natural disaster, adverse climatic events, diseases, or pest infestation. Harvest insurance has absorbed a limited amount of resources partly due to the fact that it can be funded using other CAP measures (article 68, Health Check Reform).[6]

The policy orientation phase 1 *price and income support* has dominated the scene for more than 40 years. Due to the above description, European wine has suffered from issues relating to its recurring overproduction quantities, which was first developed in the 1970s, and worsened by the early 1980s. Among the interventions adopted in this orientation, the case of distillation scheme and buying-in of alcohol was significant. The distilleries continued to produce the alcohol because of the profit margin involved, and as for producers, it had become more convenient to produce wine solely for distillation. On the other hand, the distillery received support for the distillation, which was calculated in such a way as to compensate for the difference between the distillery's costs and the alcohol's market price. They paid the producer a minimum price, which varied depending on the quantity and type of wine or wine by-product to be distilled (Gaeta and Corsinovi 2014).

13.2.2 The Era of "Quality Wines"

CMO policies should have encouraged the wine sector to bring supply into line with demand in terms of both quantity and quality (EU Commission 2002). As a consequence of high costs and surplus quantities, EU recognized

---

[5] Among these, only the single payment scheme (SPS) and harvest insurance were financed in the wine sector between 2008 and 2015. Support for setting up mutual funds was created in order to provide assistance to producers seeking to insure themselves against market fluctuations. The measure is subject to national (and local) choices and covers the amounts paid by the mutual fund to holders of financial compensation.

[6] Article 68 allowed all Member States to retain up to 10% of their national ceilings for direct payments to provide support to specific sectors, for an expanded range of purposes: payments for disadvantages faced by specific sectors (dairy, beef, sheep and goats, and rice) economically vulnerable, support for risk assurance in the form of contributions to crop insurance premium, contributions to mutual funds for animal and plant diseases, and so on.

the need to focus on just quality of wines and consumer-oriented approach to production and development of quality wine policies.[7]

This was the basis of the second orientation (Table 13.1). The scenario was imagined to develop the *quality of wine* (phase 2) through rules designed to address the management of production potential with three main interventions on the vineyards: (a) the ban on planting and incentive of grubbing up, (b) restructuring and vineyards reconversion, and (c) green harvesting.

The EU introduced the ban on planting and the incentive for the grubbing up and permanent abandonment and developed the funds for the restructuring and vineyard reconversion with the outcome to adapt wine supply to market demand and restructure vineyard production in terms of quality and quantity on the other (Table 13.1).

The ban and grubbing up was introduced with the aim to create a wine sector adapted to market conditions by allowing less competitive vineyards to be permanently removed. Europe gave producers the possibility of reducing costs and permanently abandoning wine production in areas where that activity was no longer profitable, giving them the opportunity to abandon agricultural production altogether. From 1976 (Reg. 1162/1976) a ban on new planting and the obligation to distill the surplus production were introduced and toward the end of the 1980s financial incentives for voluntary grubbing up vineyards were increased (especially during the period 1991–2008).

This essentially withdrew the principle of the producer being free to plant and, for the first time, introduced a transitory ban on replanting or planting new varieties and created a regulatory system for planting and replanting rights. The existing ban on new plantings has been maintained and the provisions regarding replanting rights did not significantly change. When the system was first introduced, the ban of new plantings was considered a temporary measure but, since the CMO reform in 2013, has been continually extended.[8]

---

[7] In the political economy mechanism of quality wine regulation, Meloni and Swinnen (2013) provide interesting analyses of the expenditure distribution effects.

[8] The basic principle of the planting rights measures is that vines cannot be planted unless a right to replant or a right to make a new planting is held by the vine-grower. The CMO in 2013 abolished the total ban on the planting of new vineyards and replaced the transitional planting rights from 2016 to 2030 by a new system of authorizations for vine planting, for which Member States shall make available each year authorizations for new plantings corresponding to 1% of the total area actually planted with vines in their territory, as measured on 31 July of the previous year. Planting rights granted to producers, which have not been used by those producers, may be converted into authorizations as from 1 January 2016. Member States may decide to allow producers to submit requests to convert rights into authorizations until 31 December 2020. As a replacement, personal authorizations are granted free of charge, which are no longer transferable to the market.

Since 1980, restructuring and vineyard reconversion represents one the mosts import instrument impleneted to support the qualitywines (Orientation/ Phase 2). This measure has been implemented with the goal to increase the competitiveness of wine producers through paying compensation for the loss of revenue while a vineyard is being adapted and as a contribution to the costs of restructuring and conversion. The necessary restructuring of old vineyards was done on the basis of increasing production quality using machinery and introducing all the innovative processes.

Following the aim of supplying grape management and improving quality, the green harvesting measure was introduced from 2008. This provided for the total destruction or removal of bunches of grapes while still at an immature stage, therefore reducing the yield to zero. Restructuring and green harvesting represented the most expensive measures implemented during the phase 2 (*quality wines*), as shown in Table 13.2.

13.2.3   The Era of "Competitiveness"

While the EU debated on how to resolve the high budgetary expenditures and the consequences of overproduction and wine stock, the international competition was becoming ever stiffer.

In 2005 accumulated wine stocks represented the equivalent of one year of production and the structural surplus was estimated at approximately 14.5 million hl, equivalent to 8.5% of the total production. The EU wine producers were finding themselves at a disadvantage compared to those from third countries, who were often represented by a few restrictive production and market rules, large multinationals, and massive marketing operations. One of the greatest fears for the EU Agriculture Commission was the "attack" of new wine players on EU market: the imports from New World wine countries have increased substantially and the EU wine market was confronted with a reduction in the demand for domestic produced wines as overall consumption of wine has decreased especially in the most wine-procuring countries (EU Commission 2006). Although intentions were good, the problem was resolved too late. Among traditional European producer and/or consumer countries, the main EU producer countries (France, Italy, and Spain) show a negative average between 2000 and 2013. These values demonstrate the difficulty that EU countries have covering internal consumption (Gaeta and Corsinovi 2014).

After 38 years from the first CMO wine and less than 10 years from the reform 1493/99, a new CMO orientation identified by the author as orientation no. 3 (phase 3) (Table 13.1) geared to increase the *competitiveness* of the EU wine sector in a worldwide market and mainly against the growing of the third producing countries. This orientation was characterized by intervention linked to support the investments and innovation activities for the EU wine enterprises on hand and support the promotion of quality wines in third countries. These measures were introduced with the reform of 2008 (Reg. 479/2008). Analyses of these measures highlight a clear correlation between wine support programs on the one hand and rural development interventions (Pillar II of CAP) on the other. The EU firms cannot receive the support for the same topic from two sources of financing. This is most probably due to the nature of the measures themselves. For example, the investment measure essentially covers the same scope as the rural development (investment aid measures "modernization of agricultural holdings" and "adding value to agriculture and forestry products"). Furthermore, the obligation for the EU Member States to draw the dividing line between CMO and rural development has probably compromise the implementation of the investment measure. Here, different interests of wine lobby have probably played an important role in the distribution of support within the EU Member States.

13.3   Historical Expenditure and Provisional Distribution

The percentage of expenditures on the wine policy is represented in Fig. 13.1. The period 1970–2015 covers all of policy implementation period. During this time, orientation 1 *price and income support* represented the most important spending between 1970 and 2015 (almost 70% of the total); 24% of the total budget was designated for orientation 2 *quality wines*, and only 4% represented the amount for *competitiveness* (orientation 3).

In recent years, during the decade 2001–2010, half of the spending (47.5% of the total) occurred to support quality interventions. This value increased in the last six years of the decade while reaching 54.4% of the expenditure, followed by 25.3% in competitiveness and 20.3% for the price and income support.

Table 13.2 focuses on main expenditure cost line items in millions of euros and % of the total budget. As shown in the table, the spending for the distillation scheme was more than €9.60 billion in the period 1970–2015. Market withdrawals of wine, as political consequences of distillations schemes, has risen more than €6.6 billion in the same period. It represented more than one-third of all the wine budget costs used in 45 years (€45.027 billion). The buying-in of alcohol from compulsory distillation amounts more than 9% of the payments in the whole period with average cost around €1.5 billion (every ten years), while the aid for concentrated grape must was around €3.5 billion in 1970–2015 (7.8% of the total).

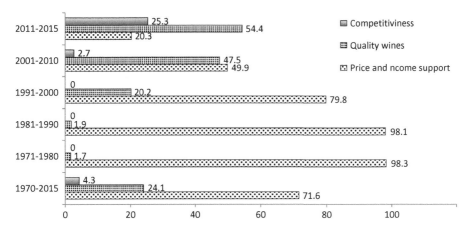

Fig. 13.1 Policy orientations through the % of budget expenditure. (Source: Author's dataset (elaboration from EAGGF annual expenditures), 2015)

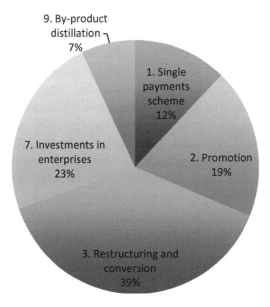

Fig. 13.2 National Programme Support 2019–2023: % of budget. (Source: Financial Report, European Commission—DG AGRI (https://ec.europa.eu/agriculture/sites/agriculture/files/wine/statistics/programming-2019-2023_en.pdf))

According to the budget expenditure, almost 8.3% (€3.75 billion) of the total EU wine expenditure (1970–2015) was designated to support the grubbing up/abandonment of vineyards. Restructuring of vineyards accounted for 13.7% of the total wine budget; €6.167 billion over the time 1970–2015 of EU resources have been designated with a pick in decade 2001–2010 of €2.7 billion.

Looking at the distribution of subsidies for orientations 3 "competitiveness", 12.6% of the budget (€851 million) was allocated from 2011 to 2015 for investments and innovation. Promotion in third country is the first largest expenditure category: between 2001 and 2010, €122 million of EU funding has been spent to subsidize promotion actions and almost €860 million (12.7% of the budget) in the last six years. The main beneficiaries were the appellation of origin (within the consortia organization) and the temporary associations of businesses and the producer groupings. For the most part, the resources were used by companies working in the US, Canada, China, and Japan to strengthen the markets. The majority of projects concentrated on joint participation in trade show events, contact with journalists from the countries of origin, and training activities for operators in the sector.

The wine reform adopted in 2008 brought major changes to the system of payments. With the CMO wine reform 479/2008, the CMO's financial resources were distributed via national envelope (National Programme Support, NPS), by transfer from rural development measures (Pillar II, see footnote 2). The regulation was based on measures that can be achieved through NPS managed directly by the EU Member States and activates at least one of the 11 measures.[9] Their implementation was voluntary and was left up to the individual Member State to decide. They are applied and managed according to objective criteria and take into account the economic situation of the producers concerned, as well as the need to avoid unjustified unequal treatment of producers (Gaeta and Corsinovi, 2014).

The financial distribution of each EU countries for national support measures is shown in Fig. 13.2. It highlights the latest percentage of financial

---

[9] (1) Single payment scheme, (2) promotion in third countries, (3) restructuring and reconversion, (4) green harvesting, (5) mutual funds, (6) harvest insurance, (7) investments, (8) use of concentrated grape must, (9) by-product distillation, (10) potable alcohol distillation, and (11) crisis distillation. The first nine measures were called definitive measures (2009–2013), which could be activated for the new CMO's entire programming period. The others (such as potable alcohol distillation, crisis distillation, and aid for the use of must for enrichment or concentrated musts) could be used for a maximum of four years (phasing-out measures) and are taken from the market support mechanisms provided for in the previous CMO.

scheme for the NPS programmed from 2019 to 2023. The 2013 CMO reforms introduce as a new measure innovation in the wine sector aiming at the development of new products, processes, and technologies concerning the wine products. Furthermore it opens promotion measures to information in Member States, with a view to informing consumers about the responsible consumption of wine and about the Union systems covering designations of origin and geographical indications. It also extends the restructuring and conversion of vineyards to replanting of vineyards where that is necessary following mandatory grubbing up for health or phytosanitary reasons. The regulation provides for more streamlined national programs with only 9 eligible measures rather than 11 of the 2008 wine policy: (1) SPS; (2) promotion; (3) restructuring and conversion (3) a, replanting of vineyards for health or phytosanitary reasons); (4) green harvesting; (5) mutual funds; (6) harvest insurance, (7) investments in enterprises; (8) Innovation; and (9) by-product distillation.[10] Looking at the distribution of funds, restructuring and vineyard reconvention represent the largest share of the future wine policy followed by the investments and promotion.

There can be no doubt that the move to eliminate and reduce the economic funds to market measures was well intentioned after more than 30 years, as it aimed to increase the efficiency and competitiveness of the European wine sector. The hope was for a future where wine makers would produce for the market and not for the distiller.

Who exactly had benefitted from these measures thus far? Undoubtedly, those with the biggest interest in obtaining aid for distillation were large-scale vineyards, which found themselves able to reallocate huge volumes of must and wine that would otherwise be in excess of market demand. Thus, in an anticompetitive manner, these aid payments rewarded those businesses not controlling production variables, safe in the knowledge that community subsidies would always be there.

During more than 45 years of wine reforms, both internal and international measures described in the previous three different phases represent an example of compromise between protectionist and liberalist policy, with obviously different effects on the market.

---

[10] The new programs no longer contain potable alcohol distillation, crisis distillation, funds for grape must, or funds for the use of concentrated grape must.

13.4   The EU System of Wine Classification

The first EU regulation for quality wines was created in 1970 (Regulation 817/1970). Up until this point, quality wine was only regulated at member state level and no EU rules existed. The first decrees were to be adopted by the France government in 1935.[11] Since the 1970s, the protection model for EU quality wines is based on a pyramid-structured project that is becoming more restrictive as they gradually move up the pyramid from the base to the peak (Corsinovi and Gaeta 2015).

The bottom section contains undifferentiated products (Table wine [TW], Vino da Tavola [Italy], Vin de Mesa [in Spain], or Vin de Table [in France]), which have no link to their place of origin and are therefore subject to significant legislative deregulation. Instead, they fall under generic legislation defining what the term "wine" means and how it should be marketed. The next tier in the pyramid is represented by the category or "Indicazione Geografica Tipica" (typical geographical indication, IGT). The production rules for these wines contain some basic regulations: production area and grape origin, types of vine that may be used, yield per grape/hectares (with a large range), and chemical-physical and organoleptic characteristics (such as color and taste). As we move up the pyramid and the production area is restricted, we find the category of appellation wines (DOC, AOVDQ). Here, the prerequisite of interaction, and therefore the relevant origin rules, plays a crucial role. The limits of the production areas represent real walls between quality territory and the undifferentiated world of production anarchy, which lies outside. A place name is thus used to identify the wine and its characteristics, which are in turn defined by the delimited geographic area and specific production criteria, the so-called production rules. Moving further up, there is another category represented by DOCG/AOC wines (controlled and guaranteed DO, Appellation d'Origine Contrôlée). The DOCG/AOC were reserved for wines already recognized DO for at least five years and are deemed to be of particular value. The DOCG/AOC are usually connected to a smaller area of production and more stringent rules. The top of the pyramid is made up of another peculiar aspect: subareas. These are more restricted areas within the appellation, with even more restrictive independent production rules and parameters. They are mentioned on the label and assume a homogeneous product,

---

[11] Among the wine literature, the political economy mechanism that created the existing set of European quality wine regulations is shown by Meloni and Swinnen (2013) and Gaeta and Corsinovi (2014); while other authors develop a political economy model of the size of geographical indications (Moschini et al. 2008; Deconinck and Swinnen 2014).

distinctive of the wider area. This is closely connected to the terroir as specific soils have a certain physical homogeneity, meaning that the nature of the soil can pass on a particular characteristic to its produce, notably to wine (Josling 2006). This term may thus be defined as the *terroir*, the place of production, and more specifically it is often used to indicate a specific name or legally defined vineyard and the vines that grow on that terroir. An example, or perhaps a model, of this is the French term *cru*. In reality, the stronger the link with the area of origin is, the richer the system is in terms of legislative specifications and production restrictions. Many restrictions are also imposed by producers' organizations or consortia in the production protocols such as prohibition of bottling the wine outside the geographical production area (e.g. Rioja; Chianti Classico, etc.); many wines cannot be exported in bulk (Corsinovi and Gaeta 2015). From 2008, the EU law for quality wine consists of two types of classification: (1) Protected Denomination of Origin (PDO) regarding *quality wines produced in a specified region* and (2) Protected Geographical Indication (PGI) regarding *quality wines with geographical indication*. PDO and PGI refer to the geographical names and qualifiers corresponding to the regions of production, used to designate the wines referred to in regulations, whose characteristics depend on the natural conditions, correlated to its viticulture characteristics (Gaeta and Corsinovi 2014).

13.4.1   The International Debate and the Role of WTO

The new EU wine regulations are largely inspired by the legislation applying to agricultural products and foodstuffs. At the international level, GIs are legally provided for by the WTO Agreement on Trade-Related Aspect of Intellectual Property rights (TRIPS).

In recent years the EU has held several bilateral negotiations for free trade agreements with third countries with the aims on one hand to reduce tariff and duties and open new markets and increase sales in both developed and emerging markets and provide on the other hand for the protection and recognition of specific quality production (Cogeca 2014).

Since 1994, the EU has developed specific agreements for protection of GIs for wines and spirits with other key producing countries, beginning with Australia (1994, renewed 2008), Chile (2002), South Africa (2002), Canada (2003), and the USA (2006, updated 2011).[12] However, such initiative has

---

[12] DG AGRI Working Document on international protection of GIs: objectives, outcomes, and challenges, 25 June 2012.

not made much progress due to opposition, in particular, from the USA, Australia, Chile, New Zealand, Argentina, Canada, and Japan. Until the TRIPS agreement will not offer adequate protection for European GIs, the EU is seeking this objective through different types of bilateral agreements (Cogeca 2014).

The EU wine sector has consolidated its market share in the last ten years as a first market destination for the top five EU wine-producing countries (Italy, France, Spain, and Portugal). The USA plays a key role for the EU wine business firms as the first market destination outside Europe in terms of value and volume (OIV 2016).

For these reasons the EU-US trade agreement—Transatlantic Trade and Investment Partnership (TTIP)—has taken on an important role among the EU trade policy. However, after three years of negotiation and with the new US President from November 2016, the negotiation seems to be far removed from to the final agreement. Its objective sought by policymakers is to remove trade barriers (tariffs, unnecessary regulation, restrictions on investment, etc.) to a wide range of economic sectors, including agriculture, in order to make it easier to buy and sell goods and services between the two partners. Rickard et al. (2014) have analyzed the impacts of the proposed EU-US free trade agreement on wine markets. They develop parameters to characterize the effects of tariffs and domestic regulations that affect production and consumption of wine between EU and the USA. The authors "show that reductions in tariffs would have relatively small effects in these wine markets, whereas reductions in EU domestic policies that affect wine grape production would have much larger trade and welfare implications".

The 2006 agreement between the EU and the USA on the marketing of wine did not resolve the issue and did not venture into who, prior to it being stipulated, had the possibility of using names, which at that point were considered to be "semi-generic" and were then promoted to "generic". As a consequence of this, American producers who in the past had marketed their wine under the names in question (such as Californian Chianti) could continue to do so. Looking back at where this all started, two important points arise.

The first is linked to the American classification system. The second is linked to the incomplete nature of the TRIPS agreement.

In relation to the first of these points as regards the American Classification system, the US Department of the Treasury, which is responsible for the Alcohol and Tobacco Tax and Trade Bureau (TTB) under the section of the Code of Federal Regulations (CFR) on labeling and promotion of wine products, created a classification system for geographically relevant symbols.

These symbols were then subdivided into "generic", "semi-generic", and "non-generic" and those corresponding to geographical designations.

The problem here lies in which category the symbol belongs to, as the level of protection available for the relevant DO in the USA varies depending on the category. This means that if a name is classified as generic (e.g. vermouth[13]), then it is not awarded any protection in the USA. The semi-generic category contains names with a geographical significance and which also specify a category of product, such as *Burgundy, Champagne, Chianti, Malaga, Marsala, Madeira, Porto, Sauternes,* and *Sherry.* According to US law, semi-generic names may be used as long as the true American origin of the wine is clearly declared to the consumer and the wine is in line with the quality standards laid down by the CFR.

The Internal Revenue Code defines each semi-generic name "as a name of geographic significance that is also a designation of class and type for wine. The IRC further states that a semi-generic name may be used to designate wine of an origin other than that indicated by its name only if there appears, in direct conjunction with the designation, an appropriate appellation of origin disclosing the true place of origin and the wine so designated conforms to the standard of identity."

This makes it possible to designate geographical names, such as Californian Chianti or New York Champagne, as the semi-generic name is accompanied by another designation of provenance (California, Napa Valley, New York, etc.) corresponding to the effective place of production. The USA justifies this by stating that this combination enables the American consumer to recognize where the wine comes from and how it is different to French Champagne or Chianti produced in Tuscany. However, names with a geographical significance belong to the non-generic category.

The prerequisite of recognition is paradoxically linked to the consumer protection.

US legislation recognizes the protection of a generic name if it is decided that at the point of purchase the consumer is capable of associating the wine with the geographical territory referred to in the name.[14] This means that names such as Bordeaux and Médoc are considered to be non-generic as the

---

[13] *Vermouth* is a type of aperitif wine compounded from grape wine, having the taste, aroma, and characteristics generally attributed to vermouth and shall be so designated.

[14] It *should be specified that* when the first European pioneer from the "old country" made wine in California from *Vitis vinifera* grapes that looked, smelled, and tasted like what they knew at home, they called it by old country names. By the early 1880s, names like Champagne, Burgundy, and so on were commonly used to describe wine similar to those grown in France (Muscatine et al. 1984).

origin on the product is clearly identified by the US consumer. It is easy to understand how the interaction between vine variety, territory, and production method, which is so important to European wine production, is not interpreted in the same way in the USA, where the reputation of a wine is mainly determined by the private brand (Appiano and Dindo 2007). It is therefore of little surprise that the majority of European DOs register their own brand as a trademark as well as the designation (collective brand).

The USA considered a trademark as "a word, phrase, or logo that identifies the source of goods or services" with the aims to allow consumers to "easily identify the producers of goods and services and avoid confusion". Trademark law protects on one hand and discourages on the other hand the businesses from adopting a name or logo that is "confusingly similar" to an existing trademark. This system generates a lot of confusion assimilating the trademark with GIs. A trademark can be assigned or licensed to anyone, anywhere in the world, because it is linked to a specific company and not to a particular place. Geographical Indications may be used by any persons, who produce the good according to specified standards only; if it is in the area of origin, a GI cannot be assigned or licensed to someone outside that place or not belonging to the group of authorized producers.

The second point arises due to the incomplete nature of the TRIPS agreement and the legislative gap which exists due to the incomplete nature (or perhaps carelessness) of the WTO TRIPS agreement, which introduced the issues relating to intellectual property rights (including geographical indications) and which was also accepted by the USA.

The key points can be found in article 22 of TRIPS on protection of geographical indications, article 23 on additional protection of geographical indications for wine and alcoholic drinks, and article 24 on international negotiations. The agreement in fact recognizes the link between product and territory in an indication or origin, but the human factor and the link with the place of origin are not included. Moreover, article 23 bans the registration of a brand representing wines with a GI when the origin stated is not the true origin of the product. In the case of homonymous geographical indications for wines, protection is accorded to each indication (article 23(3)). Article 23(4) states that "In order to facilitate the protection of geographical indications for wines, negotiations shall be undertaken in the Council for TRIPS concerning the establishment of a multilateral system of notification and registration of geographical indications for wines eligible for protection in those Members participating in the system".

13.4.2   The Protection of Traditional Wine Terms and Their Origins

The system described above has never been launched, and as the interpretation of the standards is done on the basis of national decisions, this has been the outcome. One the one hand, EU is calling for more protection for wines, and on the other, the USA is using strong arm tactics. It is precisely the protection of traditional terms that is an important issue being discussed in Brussels' European quarter and US wine departments. They are well and truly a characteristic specific to the wine sector. They provide (or perhaps "should provide") protection to certain designations traditionally associated with specific wines bearing a designation or indication of origin (Table 13.3). These terms are particularly complex as they face many problems and are of interest to a broad range of political actors (Member States and EU and non-EU wine organizations).

At EU level, two different types of traditional terms are included in the CMO. The first type is used for PDO or PGI. The second type is used for production or aging methods, quality, color, type of place, or for a particular event linked to the history of the product with a PDO or PGI. In addition to this, all terms and all new information connected to the protection of traditional terms are entered and updated in the EU's E-Bacchus database.[15] Traditional terms do not however constitute intellectual and industrial property rights like PDO and PGI but instead refer to production, processing, or aging details or to the quality, color, and type of place included and recognized on the label. In order to avoid discrimination between wines originating in the Union and those imported from third countries, terms traditionally used in third countries may obtain recognition and protection as traditional terms in the Union also where they are in conjunction with GIs and DOs regulated by those third countries.

In order to be able to use EU traditional terms (TTs) on the community market (see Table 13.3, bearing in mind that these terms include *Riserva*, *Brunello, Amarone, Vin Santo, Château, Torcolato*, and *Governo all'uso toscano*), third countries must demonstrate that the traditional terms in question are regulated by applicable standards, including those laid down by representative

---

[15] The E-Bacchus database is the register of EU PDOs and PGIs protected under the single CMO. This includes the list of GIs and DOs for third countries protected in the EU following the implementation of bilateral agreements on trade in wine and signed between the EU and the third countries concerned. E-Bacchus also includes the list of traditional terms protected in the EU under the single CMO Regulation.

Table 13.3 The main traditional terms as referred to EU Reg. 607/2009

States	Place of origin	Production and aging method	Quality characteristics	Historical wine typology	Color
Italy	Classico	Cannellino; Fine	Riserva; Superiore; Vendemmia Tardiva	Amarone; Cerasuolo; Garibaldi Dolce (or GD); Recioto; Sangue di Giuda; Sciacchetrà; Soleras; Torcolato	Ambra; Ambrato; Claret; Chiaretto
		Governo all'uso toscano	Vermiglio	Vin Santo or Vino Santo	Fiori d'Arancio; Rubino
		Occhio di Pernice			Oro
		Passito or Vino passito			
		Liquoroso Rebola; Scelto, Stravecchio; Superiore Oldo Marsala; Torchiato; Vecchio; Verdolino; Vergine; Vino Fiore; Vino Novello or Novello; Vivace			
France	Château, Clos	Vin jaune; Hors d'âge; Rancio	Cru artisan		Ambré; Clairet; Caret
		Sélection de grains nobles	Cru bourgeois		
		Sur lie	Cru classé, *whether or not supplemented by* Grand, Premier		
		Vendanges tardives	Grand, Deuxième, Troisième		
		Vin de paille	Quatrième; Cinquième; Grand cru; Villages		

(continued)/

Table 13.3 (continued)

States	Place of origin	Production and aging method	Quality characteristics	Historical wine typology	Color
Spain		Añejo; Chacolí-Txakolina; Clásico Criaderas y Solera; Crianza; Fondillón; Pajarete; Pálido; Solera; Sobremadre Gran Reserve; Lágrima; Noble; Oloroso; Vino Maestro Vendimia Inicial; Vino de Tea	Amontillado; Fino; Superior		Dorado
Portugal		Canteiro; Frasqueira; Garrafeira; Nobre; Solera; Leve; Làgrima	Fino; Superior; Super Reserva; Reserva velha (ou grande reserva); Vintage		Escuro; Ruby

Source: Author's creation from E-Bacchus database (2015) and EU Regulation 607/2009

professional organizations from the third country; that the terms enjoy a good reputation within the third country; that the terms have been used tradition-ally for at least ten years in the third country; and that the third country's regulations are clear enough so as not to mislead the consumer about the term in question. Many of these terms relate to famous wine countries or place or particular expressions. Table 13.3 tried to divide the main traditional terms according to their main characteristics like place of origin, production method and aging method, quality characteristics, historical wine typology, and color: Many of them identify both the quality characteristics that historical typol-ogy. For example, in France the traditional term "Château" refers to the historical expression related to a type of area and to a type of wine and is reserved to wines coming from an estate which really exists or which is called exactly by this word. "Cru artisan" and "bourgeois" are expressions related to the quality of a wine, to its history, and to a type of area evoking a hierar-chy of merit between wines coming from a specific estate (PDO "Médoc",

"Haut-Médoc", "Margaux", "Moulis", "Listrac", "Saint-Julien", "Pauillac", "Saint-Estèphe"). Traditional terms (TTs) like Premier and Grand Cru are expressions related to the quality of a wine but also are historical terms, reserved to wines with protected designations of origin defined by decree and when a collective use is made of this expression by incorporation to a designation of origin.

The right to use traditional terms is accorded to third countries subject to an evaluation carried out by the Commission and Member States of the requests submitted in this regard and only if all conditions have been met. The final condition for non-EU wines using terms recognized in Europe for European wines is that the product's importation to the EU must be preceded by a request from the non-EU country including the reason for the request and the information to justify the recognition of the terms (Appiano and Dindo 2007). Using a language other than the language spoken in the exporting country is permitted only if the use of such a language is provided for under national legislation and if the same language has been consistently used for the term in question for at least 25 years. The origin of the issue surrounding this lobbying case is twofold. Firstly, the EU has 359 traditional terms, 100 of which are synonyms of PDOs or GPIs (like *Vino de la Tierra* in Spain, *Appellation d'Origine Controlée* in France, and DOC or DOCG in Italy) and 259 of which are traditional terms that describe the quality of wine or particular production process. In Italy, for example, less than 58 traditional terms have been identified, but the term "Reserve" is present in 212 Italian PDOs, and the term "Novello" is in 187. In addition to these, there are also the terms "Sweet Wine", "Sweet Wine Fortified—Liquoroso", "Ripasso", and "Recioto". Secondly, the Commission is evaluating the changes to the standards for traditional terms with the aim of reducing their number in order to assure their protection at international level. Therefore, it intends to create two additional criteria to increase their validity. The first of these criteria relates to the distinctive characteristic of the traditional terms according to which general and non-specific terms could not be protected. The second criteria states that if a term is homonymous with a PDO/PGI or with a variety, then the Commission can automatically refuse it protection.

At the request of wine-producing countries, EU has always defended itself by stating that the conditions imposed on third countries for the use of traditional terms are a guarantee against possible abuse. It was made all the more difficult when the United States Trade Representative (USTR), the US government agency for development and control of trade policy, in the EU section of its 2013 Report on Technical Barriers to Trade strongly criticized the limits placed on the use of certain traditional terms on product labels. The

USTR stated that EU regulations on the use of terms such as Riserva, Rubino, Chateau, and Tawny restrict the ability of non-EU wine producers to use these terms on their wines sold in Europe: terms which the USTR considers to be common, descriptive, and commercially valuable.

It can be argued that rules for wine may acquire or lose relevance depending on the economic importance of other sectors covered by the agreements, as trade-offs between different types of traded goods (or services) are likely to occur.

Is it really a problem of international competition and protection for the European wine sector, or is it more a political and therefore lobbying debate?

13.5   Final Remarks

The EU wine sector has been characterized for decades by interventions linked to the income and price support. Covering the history of the wine CMO, we can identify three policy orientations.

The first orientation strategy (no. 1) is identified as *price and income support* program where most of the interventions were addressed to help and stabilize the income of the wine producers and defend the internal market of the EU. Orientation 1 has dominated the scene for more than 30 years. It represents the largest category of expenditure in the 1970/2015: more than 70% of the total.

CMO policies should have encouraged the wine sector to bring supply into line with demand in terms of both quantity and quality (EU Commission 2002). As a consequence, the EU recognized the need to adopt more quality wines and consumer-oriented approach to production and development of quality policies (orientation 2). The scenario of orientation 2 was imagined to develop the *quality of wine* trough rules designed to address the management of production potential: from 1976 introducing the ban on new planting, the planting rights system. This orientation has represented the 24% of the total financial expenditures.

The hope was for a future where wine makers would produce for the market and not for the distiller. Describing the possible new strategy is a very complex task. However, the last 15 years have shown an increase in the percentage allocated to the second and third orientations. During the decade 2001–2010, half of the expenditure (47% of the total—8 billion) was spent to support the quality interventions. This value increased in the last six years, reaching 54% of the expenditure, followed by 25% in competitiveness and 20% for the price and income support. An opposite trend: maybe something is changing. There can be no doubt after more than 30 years that the move to eliminate and reduce economic funds to market measures, like distillation, and which we called phase one, was well intentioned; it aimed to increase the efficiency and competitiveness of the European wine sector. This move may have been too late, with millions of euros thrown in the garbage basket of a privileged lobby made of cooperatives and farmers who survived without a real market and only with the holy help of their deputies in the EU Parliament in phase one.

There is no doubt also that a concrete forward step in international competitiveness was brought through quality policies that increased and fortified, with PDO and PGI production, the characteristics of the EU quality wine personality in the world market.

The EU is still moving from the administration of protection—quotas, tariffs, and subsidies—to the administration of precaution: security, safety, health, and environmental sustainability. This is the new version of the old divide between tariff and non-tariff barriers.

In summarizing the best and worst EU wine decisions, special evaluation of the EU international wine policy should be undertaken. Every phase described shows that it is still concerned with a strong protective action, both through tariff and non-tariff measures. International free trade agreements slowly keep on entertaining Brussels' bureaucrats without reaching a final agreement.

References

Anderson, K., ed. 2004. *The world's wine markets: Globalization at work*. Cheltenham: Edward Elgar.

———. 2010. Excise and import taxes on wine versus beer and spirit: An international comparison. *Economic Papers* 29 (2): 215–228.

———. 2014. *Excise taxes on wines, beers and spirits: An updated international comparison*. Working paper No. 170, American Association of Wine Economists, October.

Anderson, K., and H. Jensen. 2016. How much does the European Union assist its wine producers? *Journal of Wine Economics* 11 (2): 289–305.

Appiano, E.M., and S. Dindo. 2007. Le Pratiche Enologiche e la Tutela delle Denominazioni d'Origine nell'Accordo UE/USA sul Commercio Del vino. *Contratto e impresa/Europa, Cedam* 12 (1): 455–500.

Cogeca. 2014. Study on the competitiveness of European wines: Final report. http://ec.europa.eu/agriculture/external-studies/2014/eu-wines/fulltext_en.pdf

Corsinovi, P., and D. Gaeta. 2015. Managing the quality wines beyond policies and business strategies. *Review of Contemporary Business Research* 4 (1): 24–31.

———. 2016. *The EU wine policy orientations through the budget expenditure analysis (1970–2015)*. Annual American Association of Wine Economists (AAWE) June 21–25, 2016, Bordeaux (France).

———. 2017. EU wine policies and their consequences on the global wine trade. *Economia Agroalimentare/Food Economy* 19 (1): 59–88.

Council Regulation (EC) No. 1493/1999 of 17 May 1999 on the common organization of the market in wine.

Council Regulation (EC) No. 479/2008 of 29 April 2008 on the common organisation of the market in wine, amending Regulations (EC) Nos. 1493/1999, 1782/2003, 1290/2005, and 3/2008 and repealing Regulations (EEC) Nos. 2392/86 and 1493/1999.

Council Regulation (EC) No. 607/2009 of 14 July 2009 laying down certain detailed rules for the implementation of Council Regulation (EC) No. 479/2008 as regards protected designations of origin and geographical indications, traditional terms, labelling and presentation of certain wine sector products.

Council Regulation (EEC) No. 816/70 of 28 April 1970 laying down additional provisions for the common organization of the market in wine.

Council Regulation (EEC) No. 817/70 of 28 April 1970 laying down special provisions relating to quality wines produced in specific regions.

Council Regulation (EEC) No. 822/87 of 16 March 1987 on the common organization of the market in wine.

Council Regulation (EEC) No. 823/87 of 16 March 1987 laying down special provisions relating to quality wines produced in specified regions.

Dal Bianco, A., V. Boatto, F. Caracciolo, and F.G. Santeramo. 2016. Tariffs and non tariff frictions in the world wine trade. *European Review of Agricultural Economics* 43 (1): 31–57.

Deconinck, K., and J. Swinnen. 2014. *The political economy of geographical indications*. AAWE working paper No. 174, December.

European Commission. 2002. DG Agriculture Tender AGRI/Evaluation/2002/6: "Ex-post evaluation of the Common Market Organisation for wine". Available at: http://ec.europa.eu/agriculture/eval/reports/wine/fullrep_en.pdf

———. 2006. *Towards a sustainable European wine sector*. Communication from the Commission to the Council and the European Parliament.

Gaeta, D., and P. Corsinovi. 2014. *Economics, governance, and politics in the wine market: European Union developments*. New York: Palgrave Macmillan.

Josling, T. 2006. The war on terroir: Geographical indications as a transatlantic trade conflict. *Journal of Agriculture Economics* 57 (3): 337–363.

Mariani, A., E. Pomarici, and V. Boatto. 2012. The international wine trade: Recent trends and critical issues. *Wine Economics and Politics* 1 (1): 24–40.

Meloni, G., and J.F.M. Swinnen. 2013. The political economy of European wine regulations. *Journal of Wine Economics* 8 (3): 244–284.

Montaigne, E., and A. Coelho. 2006. Reform of the common organisation of the market. In Wine Study Requested by The European Parliament's Committee on Agriculture and Rural Development. Brussels.

Moschini, G., L. Menapace, and D. Pick. 2008. Geographical indications and the competitive provision of quality in agricultural markets. *American Journal of Agricultural Economics* 90 (3): 794–812.

Muscatine, D., A.M. Amerin, and B. Thompson. 1984. *Book of California wine.* Berkeley, Los Angeles/London: University of California Press/Sotheby Publications.

Niederbacher, A. 1983. *Wine in the European Community.* Office for Official Publication of the European Communities, Periodical 2/3-1983, Luxembourg.

OIV. 2016. *State of the vitiviniculture world market (April 2016).* Available at http:// www.oiv.int/public/medias/4710/oiv-noteconjmars2016-en.pdf

Pomarici, E., and R. Sardone. 2001. *Il Settore Vitivinicolo In Italia. Strutture Produttive, Mercati e Competitività alla Luce della Nuova Organizzazione Comune di Mercato.* Roma: Studi & Ricerche, INEA.

―――. 2009. *L'OCM Vino. La Difficile Transazione Verso una Strategia di Comparto.* Roma: INEA.

Rickard, B.J., O. Gergaud, S. Ho, and W. Hu. 2014. *Trade liberalization in the presence of domestic regulations: Impacts of the proposed EU-U.S free trade agreement on wine market.* AAWE working paper No. 173, November 2014.

Spahni, P. 1988. *The common wine policy and price stabilization.* Aldershot/Brookfeild: Avebury.

14

Barriers to Wine Trade

Angela Mariani and Eugenio Pomarici

14.1 Introduction

Wine has traditionally been traded goods, but only in the past two decades, the international wine trade has experienced a considerable growth: in the 1960s the exported share of global wine production was 10% and in 1990 this share had reached only 15%. However, by the year 2000 exported production had reached 25% of global production and more than 35% in 2017. More in detail, wine exports were in 2000 about 60 million hectoliters and 17 years later they are higher than 100 million hectoliters. This extraordinary growth suggests that the international wine trade was rather free to expand, without relevant hindrances; indeed, in 2010 the share of export from countries outside regional integrated areas was 60% in value and 52% in volume, with a 6-year increase of about 6 percentage points (in value and volume) (Mariani et al. 2014a).

Nevertheless, the international wine trade, like any other trade, is influenced by barriers which, even though they have not prevented the growth of

A. Mariani (✉)
Department of Economic and Legal Studies, University of Naples "Parthenope", Naples, Italy
e-mail: mariani@uniparthenope.it

E. Pomarici
Department of Land, Environment, Agriculture and Forestry, University of Padua, Padua, Italy
e-mail: eugenio.pomarici@unipd.it

© The Author(s) 2019
A. Alonso Ugaglia et al. (eds.), *The Palgrave Handbook of Wine Industry Economics*,
https://doi.org/10.1007/978-3-319-98633-3_14

wine export, have probably contributed to the openness of the different importing markets and to the competitive gaps among exporters, which have driven the complex evolution of international wine flows over last 40 years (Mariani et al. 2012; Morrison and Rabellotti 2017). It is likely that such gaps have derived from a different capacity to lower such barriers in a preferential manner. The understanding of which the trade barriers are and how they operate in the wine markets may, therefore, offer an interesting contribution to understanding how this market evolved over time and to anticipating how it could progress in the future.

Trade barriers result from customs tariffs, the so-called tariff barriers, or from policy measures that can potentially have an economic effect on international trade in goods, changing quantities traded, or prices or both, the so-called non-tariff measures (NTMs) (UNCTAD 2013). According to UNCTAD NTMs may be classified in technical measures, non-technical measures, and export measures.

In the context of a book which has the objective to present the structure of the global wine market, this chapter aims to offer an updated and comprehensive picture of how tariff barriers and NTMs contribute to the definition of the institutional setting of this market. This is done on the base of official documents and reports and of the scientific studies stimulated by the rise of the international wine trade.

This chapter is organized as follows: in Sect. 14.2 the tariff barriers operating in the wine market are discussed and an assessment of the impact of such barriers on the wine export flows is introduced; in Sect. 14.3 a general overview of NTMs is offered, showing how these operate as barriers in the wine sector; in Sect. 14.4 an analysis is done on technical measures, which are the NTMs more frequently resulting in trade barriers; in Sect. 14.5 it is shown how exporting and importing countries reduce the wine trade's barriers; and, in Sect. 14.6, the events and processes which could modify trade barriers status in the wine market over the near future are presented. Some final remarks, in Sect. 14.7, conclude the chapter.

14.2   Tariff Barriers

Tariffs are the most visible trade barrier: they cause an increase in import prices and reduce economic welfare for both wine consumers in the importing countries and wine exporters (Dunn and Mutti 2004). The level of tariffs is constrained by the World Trade Organization (WTO) rules: all members

Table 14.1 Types of tariffs in the international wine trade

Type of tariff	Description and examples
Ad valorem	One rate or different rates according to the import price of the product
	India, 150%; Nigeria, 30%; Argentina, 20%
Volume based	A single rate specified by volume unit (liter)
	Bermuda: US $2.63 per liter
Alcohol content based	One rate or different rates according to alcoholic strength
	Norway: NOK 4.31 (€0.51) per percent volume of alcohol per liter
Container based	Different rates according to the packaging of wine (bottled or bulk)
	Brazil: 27 % for bottled wine and 20% for bulk wine
	China: 14% bottled wine and 20% bulk wine
Wine type based	Different rates according to the type of wine (still or sparkling)
	Malaysia: MYR 7 (€1.56) per liter for non-sparkling wine and MYR 23 (€5.13) per liter for sparkling wine
Mixed	Ukraine: €0.3 per liter for still bottled wine, €0.4 per liter for bulk wine, and €1.5 per liter for sparkling wine (volume based by type of wine and container)
	Taiwan: still wine 10%, sparkling wine 20% (ad valorem by type of wine) Japan: 15%—up to a maximum of Yen 125 (€0.88) per liter but with a minimum customs duty of YEN 67 (€0.47) per liter—for bottled wine, YEN 45 (€0.32) per liter; for bulk wine, YEN 112 (€0.79) per liter; for fortified wines, YEN 182 (€1.28) per liter for sparkling wines

are committed to set tariffs at levels (most-favored-nation tariff) above which they cannot be raised any more without compensation to the other countries. Currently the WTO-bound tariffs are the result of the Uruguay Round, seen that the new negotiations, the Doha Round, were considered unsuccessful in 2015 (Financial Times 2015). Applied tariffs may be (and usually are) lower than the bounds, since tariffs may be reduced or cleared in the framework of preferential agreements.

Tariffs on wine may be defined in various ways, as wine is a much differentiated product and may be traded in different container types. Therefore, depending on the importing countries, tariffs on wine could be expressed as ad valorem, with one rate or different rates according to the price level of the product; specifically volume based (per liter); specifically alcohol based (alcoholic strength); and a mix of ad valorem and specific rates. In addition, tariffs can differ by the type of wine (still bottled or bulk, sparkling wine). Specific tariffs based on volume are the most popular in Europe and North America, whereas ad valorem tariffs are the norm in the Asia-Pacific region, with the exception of Japan and Malaysia (Anderson 2010). Table 14.1 shows some examples of tariffs on wine imports.

Table 14.2 EU most favored nations import duties

MFN import duties on wine	€ per liter
Bottled still wine, < 13% alc.	0.154
Bottled still wine, 13–15% alc.	0.181
Bottled still wine, 15–18% alc.	0.219
Bulk still wine, < 13% alc.	0.116
Bulk still wine, 13–15% alc.	0.142
Bulk still wine, 15–18% alc.	0.181
Sparkling wine	0.375

Source: Our elaboration

Due to the presence of specific tariffs, evaluating and comparing the level of market protection for wine require complex estimates and specific tariffs should be transformed into the so-called ad valorem equivalent (Babili 2009).[1]

Overall, tariff protection is quite low in countries which have long been involved in the wine trade such as the European Union (EU), the USA, Canada, Australia, and New Zealand (with the notable exception of Japan). By contrast, the tariff level is high in countries which have recently experienced growing wine imports, that is, mainly Asian markets (Anderson 2010; Anderson and Nelgen 2011).

Table 14.2 shows the import duties defined according to the principle of most favored nations for EU. The highest is that applied to sparkling wine, €0.37/liter, while the lowest, which would be applied to low alcohol bulk wine, is only €0, 12/liter.

All in all, the impact of tariff barriers on the international wine trade is rather small, but not negligible. Anderson and Wittwer (2018) simulated changes in the global wine flows (production, consumption, international trade) from 2014 to 2015 under various scenarios; in the scenario in which all import tariffs on wine were to be removed multilaterally, the value of world wine trade would be 7% greater in 2025 compared to a baseline solution which includes the likely effect of the UK leaving the EU.

14.3 Non-tariff Measures as Trade Barriers: An Overview

A wide and heterogeneous range of policy interventions other than border tariffs could affect trade costs incurred from producers to final consumer and/ or alter conditions of international trade, including policies and regulations

---

[1] According to the WTO rules, tariffs should be ad valorem.

Table 14.3 Non-tariff measures classification

Import: technical measures
A   Sanitary and phyto-sanitary measures
B   Technical barriers to trade
C   Pre-shipment inspection and other formalities
Import: non-technical measures
D   Contingent trade-protective measures
E   Non-automatic licensing, quotas, prohibitions, and quantity-control measures other than for SPS or TBT reasons
F   Price-control measures, including additional taxes and charges
G   Finance measures
H   Measures affecting competition
I   Trade-related investment measures
J   Distribution restrictions
K   Restrictions on post-sales services
L   Subsidies (excluding export subsidies under P7)
M   Government procurement restrictions
N   Intellectual property
O   Rules of origin
Export
P   Export-related measures

Source: UNCTAD (2013)

that restrict trade and those that facilitate it. NTMs have the potential to distort international trade, whether their trade effects are protectionist or not, and could be applied to imported and exported goods.

For practical purposes, as shown in Table 14.3, NTMs have been categorized by UNCTAD depending on their scope and/or design in 16 chapters (A to P), with each individual chapter divided into groupings with up to three layers of subcategories (UNCTAD 2013). The last chapter includes all the relevant export measures. While the import measures are broadly distinguished as:

- *Technical measures* (sanitary and phyto-sanitary measures, technical barriers to trade and pre-shipment inspections) that could serve a legitimate purpose as they are put into place for valid concerns such as food safety and environmental protection
- *Non-technical measures*, some of those are manifestly employed as instruments of commercial policy (e.g. quotas, subsidies, trade defense measures, and export restrictions)

The WTO provides guidelines for the application of NTMs. Overall, focusing on the import measures, the WTO rules indicate that they must be transparent, not overly restrictive to trade or applied arbitrarily. These rules help distinguish legitimate policy regulations and procedures from protectionist measures that may impede trade. In other word, a NTM may be WTO-inconsistent and act as a barrier to trade.

With regard to the wine trade, as well as for all agricultural and food products, sanitary and phyto-sanitary measures (SPSs) and technical barriers to trade (TBTs) are considered those of major concern (Disdier et al. 2007; for a review UNCTAD 2013), and they will be discussed in the next section.

Among the other NTMs, it is worth mentioning for wine, under category F, the internal taxes and charges levied on imports (that have domestic equivalent)—such as consumption taxes (value-added tax [VAT]), excise taxes, and taxes or charges for sensitive products categories (such as tax on packaging for environmental purposes).

Internal taxes on wine are quite different among countries worldwide, as they are implemented for several different aims, such as protectionism of locally produced alcoholic drinks (beer, spirits, etc.), prevention of alcoholism, or environmental reasons (taxation on recycling).

In theory, the level of internal taxes should not generate competitive advantages for wines of different origin and type, as it should only have an effect on the demand size and growth, especially in the lower-income segments of the population, even if for the higher income segments who consider wine as a "status symbol" the opposite may be true (in accordance to Veblen effect, wine demand grows with increasing consumer prices).

In fact, with reference to *excise taxes,* as they could be implemented in different way (i.e. on volume or on value), the picture is more complex and a competitive advantage could result for certain types of wine. In countries where the excise is applied to volume unit, its incidence is higher for low-priced wines (compared to high-priced/quality wines). Therefore, in these countries the market for low-priced/quality wines could shrink, and both exporters and consumers (low-income segments) of this wine are penalized.

According to the estimate by COGEA (2014), considering the main wine-importing countries, excise duty on volume are particularly high in Singapore, Norway, Australia, and the UK. In contrast, excise duties are on value in China and are not applied in countries such as Hong Kong and Germany. When considering VAT Denmark and Norway apply the highest rate, compared to Japan, the USA, and Singapore, where rates are relatively low (zero in Hong Kong). Finally, Norway and Denmark have implemented a *tax on packaging,* differentiating respectively in accordance to the type of packaging (bottles or bag-in-box) or the volume (increasing with cl volume).

Finally, it is worth mentioning that other measures such as state trade enterprise (under category H—measures affecting competition) and restriction on resellers (under category J—distribution restrictions) could affect internal market growth, price, and product availability. In some countries like Finland, Norway, Sweden, and Canada, retail sale on wine and liquor is restricted to government-controlled monopoly. Within the monopoly, a procurement board identifies importers and wholesalers for products on the basis of quality, ability to deliver, and price.

In particular, Canada operates under a system of provincial government-controlled liquor control boards (LCBs), and the operation of these monopolies differs from province to province. These LCBs have been contested by the USA as they frequently provide direct and indirect subsidies to Canadian producers. As a matter of fact, British Columbia and Ontario regulations favor the sale of domestic wine by providing additional retail locations, including farmers' markets and dedicated areas in grocery stores (Wine Institute 2015).

In the USA, there exist two types of state-specific regulations, some even county- or municipality-specific, that are widely considered to be responsible for the demand in domestic and imported wine. The first set of regulations affects the retail availability of alcoholic beverages (whether grocery stores are allowed to sell alcoholic beverages). The second set of regulations affects the distribution—in particular, interstate sales of wine (Rickard et al. 2017).

14.4 Focus on Main Technical Measures (SPS and TBT)

The most pervasive technical measures affecting wine trade are related to categories A and B, that is, the TBTs and the SPSs. SPS and TBT measures are comprehensive of a wide array of regulations which are different by scope and vary considerably by type (Table 14.4). SPSs include regulations and restrictions to protect human, animal, or plant life or health. TBTs address all other technical regulations, standards, and conformity assessment procedures imposed with a non-trade objective (i.e. to ensure safety, quality, and environmental protection, etc.).

Regardless of whether they are imposed (or implemented) with protectionist intent or to address legitimate market failures, those measures can affect trade, hindering market access or causing an increase in costs and time lost.

In this contest the measures which concern most the wine trade, according to the literature, are the following (Wine Institute 2013, 2015; WFA 2010,

Table 14.4 Import measures: technical measures

A—Sanitary and phyto-sanitary measures	A1 Prohibitions/restrictions of imports for SPS reasons
	A2 Tolerance limits for residues and restricted use of substances
	A3 Labeling, marking, and packaging requirements
	A4 Hygienic requirements
	A5 Post-harvest treatment
	A6 Other requirements on production or post-production processes
	A8 Conformity assessment related to SPS
	A9 SPS measures, n.e.s.
B—Technical barriers to trade	B1 Prohibitions/restrictions of imports for objectives set out in the TBT Agreement
	B2 Tolerance limits for residues and restricted use of substances
	B3 Labeling, marking, and packaging requirements
	B4 Production or post-production requirements
	B6 Product identity requirement
	B7 Product-quality or product-performance requirement
	B8 Conformity assessment related to TBT
	B9 TBT measures, n.e.s.
C—Pre-shipment inspection and other formalities	C1 Pre-shipment inspection
	C2 Direct consignment requirement
	C3 Requirement to pass through specific port of customs
	C4 Import-monitoring and import-surveillance requirements and other automatic licensing measures
	C9 Other formalities, n.e.s.

Source: UNCTAD (2013)

2018; European Commission 2016; USTR 2018; ICE 2010; Battaglene and Milton 2010; Battaglene 2014):

- Maximum residue limits of agrichemicals—differing between countries both in level and for approved use on products.
- Oenological practices—in many countries wine production is regulated by oenological rules. This means that it is possible to produce wine using a country-specific set of practices and substances compared to what should be allowed by the *Codex Alimentarius*.
- Certification and testing procedures—to access the markets, many importing countries require a complex set of certificates and certification forms, which may not always be justified by the intention of protecting people's health. Such certification requires considerable effort, resulting in an increase in costs and time lost.
- Wine labeling regulations—this is an issue of growing concern due to the lack of consistency in standards between countries. As different health warnings and list of ingredients are required, producing a label unique to each country adds a significant additional cost to wine exporters.

14.4.1   WTO Regulation: SPS and TBT Agreements

SPS measures and TBTs are subject to WTO regulation under two agreements: the *Agreement on Technical Barriers to Trade* and the *Agreement on Sanitary and Phyto-Sanitary Measures*. In brief:

- Sanitary and Phyto-Sanitary Measures Agreement provides rules on how governments can apply food safety and animal and plant health measures. It applies to essentially all measures taken by WTO members to protect human, animal, or plant life or health from certain risks within its territory and which may affect international trade. In seeking to protect health, WTO members must not apply sanitary or phyto-sanitary measures that are unnecessary, not science-based, and arbitrary or which constitute a disguised restriction on international trade.
- Agreement on Technical Barriers to Trade is designed to ensure that technical regulations and conformity assessment procedures (testing and certification) do not create unnecessary obstacles to trade.

The main principles behind the regulation of such agreements are summarized in Table 14.5 (WTO 2010, 2014).

Implementation of WTO regulations has given rise to some critical issues for the wine trade. The main issue is that few standards have so far been defined by the *Codex Alimentarius*, recognized by the WTO as a standard-setting organization while the International Organisation of Vine and Wine (OIV), though an intergovernmental organization committed to establishing technical and commercial standards for wine, is not recognized by the WTO.[2]

It should be noted that the problem of non-tariff barriers could further intensify as some new fast-growing wine-importing countries are setting up wine market regulations. Furthermore, in some of these countries (including China, India, and Brazil), growing interest in domestic wine production could lead to maintaining (or raising) protectionist policies and stepping up support for local producers.

14.4.2   Plurilateral Initiatives

WTO principles of equivalence and mutual acceptance of rules have been successfully applied by the World Wine Trade Group (WWTG) to ensure an

---

[2] The OIV has applied to become observer at the WTO but the request has not yet been discussed.

Table 14.5 Key elements in SPS and TBT agreements

	EU	USA	Canada	Others in America	R-K-B	GCC	China (#)	India	Japan	South Korea	AFTA
EU		WA	WA	FTA (Mexico)				N	FTA	FTA	N (Singapore, Malaysia, Vietnam, Thailand, Philippines, Indonesia, Myanmar)
USA	WA		FTA (NAFTA)	FTA (Mexico-NAFTA) FTA (Peru, Colombia, Panama, and CAFTA-DR)						FTA	
Chile	FTA	FTA	FTA	FTA (MERCOSUR)			FTA	FTA	FTA	FTA	FTA (Singapore, Thailand, Vietnam)
Australia	WA	FTA		FTA (Perù) N (Mexico, Colombia, and Chile)		N	FTA	N	N	FTA	FTA (Singapore, Thailand, Philippines) N (Indonesia) FTA (AANZFTA)
New Zealand	WA				N		FTA			FTA	FTA (Singapore, Thailand, Philippines) FTA (AANZFTA)

Source: Our elaboration

Explanatory notes:

WA wine agreement, *FTA* free trade agreement, *N* negotiation ongoing for FTA, *M* member

CAFTA-DR Dominican Republic-Central America FTA (Costa Rica, El Salvador, Guatemala, Honduras, Nicaragua, and the Dominican Republic)

NAFTA North American FTA (USA, Canada, and Mexico)

MERCOSUR South American FTA (Argentina, Brazil, Paraguay, Uruguay, and Venezuela)

R-K-B: FTA among Russia, Kazakhstan, Belarus

GCC Gulf Cooperation Council (Bahrain, Kuwait, Oman, Qatar, Saudi Arabia, and United Arab Emirates; Jordan and Morocco have been invited to join)

AFTA ASEAN FTA (Brunei, Indonesia, Malaysia, Philippines, Singapore, Thailand, Vietnam, Laos, Myanmar, and Cambodia). Unlike the EU, AFTA does not apply a common external tariff on imported goods

AANZFTA FTA among ASEAN, Australia, and New Zealand

(#) Since 2008 wine imports to Hong Kong and Macao have not been subject to tariffs and there are no certification requirements

effective reduction of TBTs among the participating countries.[3] The main achievements of the WWTG can be summarized as follows:

1. The Mutual Acceptance Agreement on Oenological Practices—this agreement eliminates barriers to trade based on differences in oenological practices by establishing that signatory countries will accept that wine made in another signatory country should be allowed to be sold in its market, despite different cross-border winemaking practices. Market access is conditional upon compliance with WTO obligations to protect the health and safety of consumers and prevent deception of consumers. The agreement is a landmark in the development of international trade because it is the first multilateral Mutual Acceptance Agreement, in any field, fully compliant with the WTO's TBT Agreement.
2. The Agreement on Requirements for Wine Labeling—this agreement addresses barriers to the wine trade by harmonizing labeling requirements, enabling the sale of wine in WWTG markets without having to redesign labels for each individual market. Under the agreement, labels must contain four items of mandatory information, anywhere on a wine bottle label in a single field of vision, such as country of origin, product name, net contents, and alcohol content.
3. The Memorandum of Understanding on Certification Requirements—this aims to reduce trade barriers by encouraging the elimination of burdensome requirements and routine certifications of wine products and ingredients. According to the memorandum, signatories' certifications regarding wine composition, free sale condition, or analytical reports about the components of imported wines will no longer be required. However, those certifications will still be required if needed to protect human health or safety (like SPS Agreement requirements). Certifications on vintage, grape variety, and appellation will only be needed if there are reasonable doubts about the truthfulness of label representations.

Another important initiative is going on within the Asia-Pacific Economic Cooperation (APEC), the Pacific Rim economic forum made up of 21 members.[4] In 2008 the Wine Regulatory Forum (WRF) of government

---

[3] The WWTG is presented in Chap. 12 (The International Wine Organisations and Plurilateral Agreements and The Dialectic Between Harmonisation and Mutual Recognition of Standards Raúl Compés López).

[4] Australia, Brunei Darussalam, Canada, Chile, People's Republic of China, Hong Kong, Indonesia, Japan, Republic of Korea, Malaysia, Mexico, New Zealand, Papua New Guinea, Peru, the Philippines, Russia, Singapore, Chinese Taipei, Thailand, the USA, Vietnam.

officials and stakeholders dedicated to regulatory cooperation and facilitation of the wine trade was launched. The WRF has the following mission: examining options to simplify and harmonize wine regulation across the APEC region, reduce technical barriers to trade, and protect consumers and sharing information and building capacity in wine regulation across the APEC region.

Up to now the WRF has realized five main goals (https://www.wineregulatoryforum.org):

1. *To bring transparency to import requirements for wine exporters*—the WRF completed five compendia outlining wine-related requirements in APEC economies covering the following topics: export certificates, food safety and composition, pesticide maximum residue limits (MRLs), labeling, and methods of analysis.
2. *To provide regulators with examples of best practices to consider when revising regulations*—the WRF partnered with FIVS-Abridge[5] to provide access to the database for wine regulators so they can compare and contrast their requirements against other economies when considering regulatory changes.
3. *To reduce the number of required export certificates*—as a follow-up to the 2011 WRF dialogue on certification, in 2014 the USA and China developed a consolidated wine export certificate that resulted in a significant reduction of unnecessary certificates issued for trade between those economies. Based upon this work, in 2016 the WRF created a consolidated APEC Model Wine Export Certificate. Chile was the first economy to implement this certificate (which also has become a model in the dairy sector).
4. *To educate non-producing APEC economies about wine as a unique food product*—the WRF brought regulators to wineries and wine testing laboratories in the USA, New Zealand, Australia, and Vietnam.
5. *To increase the accuracy of testing of wine in regulatory laboratories*—the WRF is in the third round of wine ring tests and labs are getting hands-on support to help increase precision and accuracy.

---

[5] FIVS-Abridge is a comprehensive, up-to-date, and interactive database of international regulations and trade agreements covering wine. FIVS-Abridge consists of a database of national regulations and relevant international agreements for markets around the world, covering topics such as certification, composition, labeling, marketing, packaging, production, promotion, tariffs, taxation, and transportation (http://fivs-abridge.com/index.htm).

14.5 Free Trade Agreements Relevant to Wine Trade

Over the last decade, in response to the difficulties of the Doha Round negotiations, export-driven countries have chosen the path of bilateral/regional free trade agreements (FTAs) to phase out barriers to trade among the signatory countries. Such agreements facilitate trade but, unlike multilateral agreements, have a discriminatory and trade-distorting effect. On the one hand, these agreements are a way to phase out tariff and non-tariff barriers to trade (thus facilitate trade, the so-called trade creation effect); on the other hand, they create a comparative advantage for those signing them to the detriment of other countries, so-called trade diversion effect (Dunn and Mutti 2004).

There are currently many ongoing negotiations and several trade agreements already signed and it is interesting to analyze those who are most relevant to wine, where there are agreements with countries that have put up high barriers to trade and with the greatest growth potential of imports. Beside the benefits gained from expanding exports, being first on the market and being able to consolidate market position may also allow such countries to drive the evolution of consumer preferences. (This is a major side effect for exporters in new wine-importing markets.)

The scenario is quite complex and in continuous development, with a plethora of different agreements in some way relevant to the wine trade. A glance to the main agreements signed or in discussion (under negotiation) by the main exporters with both traditional wine-importing countries and new emerging markets is given in Table 14.6. To build this general portrait, the primary sources were national government websites, updating previous research (Mariani et al. 2014a, b).

Taking into consideration the different types of agreements and the participating countries shown in Table 14.5, some aspects should be highlighted.

The EU has followed a unique approach to the wine sector, signing specific trade agreements with its main trade partners, which are in some cases also competitors (USA 2006; Canada 2004; Mexico 2004; Chile 2002, new 2013; Australia 1994, new 2009; South Africa 2002), with priority being given to protecting geographical indications. Indeed, in these agreements the EU has offered several concessions regarding the reduction of technical barriers (such as recognition of oenological practices and simplified import procedures) in exchange for the protection of GIs.

From 2006, following the strategy outlined by European Commission in its communication *Global Europe: Competing in the World* (European

Commission 2006), the EU has stepped up its efforts in trade negotiations to create free trade areas with regions or countries assigning a central role to the protection of GIs for wines, spirits, and food products (Ahearn 2011). Such efforts have resulted in several trade agreements (European Commission 2018).

As regards traditional importing countries, the EU signed in September 2017 an FTA with Canada, the Comprehensive Economic and Trade Agreement (CETA). In this market the USA, according to the North American Free Trade Agreement (NAFTA), and Chile still have a preferential access. For EU exporters, beside the phase out of tariff and the protection of GIs, other advantages should be related to the new rules of transparency and simplification applied by liquor control board (European Commission 2014). While the negotiations with the USA on the Transatlantic Trade and Investment Partnership (TTIP) were stopped until further notice at the end of 2016. The USA, Chile, and Australia still have preferential access.

In December 2017, the EU-Japan Economic Partnership Agreement was finalized and on 18 April 2018 it was submitted for approval to EU Member States. According to the agreement, Japan's tariff on wine imports from the EU will be fully eliminated when the agreement comes into force, thus allowing the erosion of the competitive advantage of Chile that has an FTA in force since 2007 and also to gain a competitive advantage over Australian export that has a more limited preferential access since 2015.[6]

With regard to new emerging markets in Asia, in 2011 the EU signed a FTA with the *Republic of Korea* of great importance for wine (immediate duty-free access) (European Commission 2010). In this market Chile, the USA, Australia (2014), and New Zealand (2015) also have negotiated a preferential access. Very close to ratification are the agreements signed with *Singapore*, where Chile, Australia, and New Zealand already have preferential agreements *and Vietnam* where Australia and New Zealand already have preferential agreements (but with limited commitments to reducing tariffs for wine). However, the negotiations between the EU and India are still in progress, and India's market protection policy for wine is a major issue between the two parties. In the meantime, India has already signed an FTA with Chile and negotiation is ongoing with New Zealand.

---

[6] Japan-Australia Economic Partnership Agreement (JAEPA) entered into force on 15 January 2015. The bulk wine tariff (> 150 liters) was eliminated on entry into force of the agreement. The tariff for wine in containers (> 10 l < 150 l) will be eliminated over ten years. The wine tariff for bottled (and bag-in-box < 10 liters) wine will be eliminated on 1 April 2021.

Table 14.6 Wine exporter's main free trade agreements (FTA)

Sanitary and phyto-sanitary (SPS) measures agreement	
Risk assessment	WTO members are required to base their SPS measures on a risk assessment, as appropriate to the circumstances, and to take into account risk assessment techniques developed by relevant international organizations
Harmonization	WTO members are encouraged to base their SPS measures on international standards, guidelines, and recommendations, where they exist[a]. Governments are allowed to choose their own standards. However, if the national requirement results in a greater restriction of trade, it is required a scientific justification that the relevant international standard would not achieve the appropriate level of health protection
Equivalence	WTO importing members should accept the SPS measures of exporting WTO members as equivalent if the exporting country objectively demonstrates to the importing country that its measures achieve the importing country's appropriate level of protection. Typically, recognition of equivalence is achieved through bilateral consultations and the sharing of technical information
Transparency	Governments are required to notify other countries of any new or changed sanitary and phyto-sanitary requirements which affect trade and to set up offices (called "enquiry points") to respond to requests for more information on new or existing measures
Agreement on technical barriers to trade	
Harmonization	Where international standards exist or their completion is imminent, WTO Members shall use them (or the relevant parts), as a basis for their technical regulations except when such international standards would be an ineffective or inappropriate means for the fulfillment of the legitimate objectives pursued, for instance because of fundamental climatic or geographical factors or technological problems
Equivalence	WTO Members are encouraged to accept foreign technical regulations and conformity assessment procedures as "equivalent" to their own (even if they differ) provided that they fulfill the same objectives or offer an assurance of conformity with standards equivalent to their own procedures
Mutual recognition	WTO Members are encouraged to enter into negotiations for the Mutual Recognition (Acceptance) of the results of conformity assessment procedures
Transparency	Governments are required to notify other members, through the WTO Secretariat, of proposed measures that may have a significant effect on other members' trade and that are not based on relevant international standards. To facilitate the exchange of information, each member must put in place an "enquiry point" that is able to answer all reasonable enquiries from other members

Source: Our elaboration

[a]The three international standard-setting bodies specifically mentioned are the International Plant Protection Convention, the World Organisation for Animal Health, the Codex Alimentarius Commission

Over time, Australia and New Zealand have negotiated FTAs that phase out tariffs on wine with other Asian countries, such as Thailand and the Philippines. A FTA is in force with the Association of South-East Asian Nations (ASEAN) countries (AANZFTA), overall with limited tariff reduction for wine (or total exclusion for religious or cultural sensitivities such as for Malaysia).

In the Chinese market Chile and New Zealand have got an important advantage over competitors, as both countries (Chile in 2005 and New Zealand in 2008) have signed FTAs. Tariffs on wine imports (14% for bottled wine and 20% for bulk wine) have been progressively reduced, to reach zero in 2012 for New Zealand and, in 2015, for Chile. As a result, Chile and New Zealand have been able to enjoy a significant advantage over competitors (ABARES 2012). Later on, Australia signed a FTA in 2015 where tariffs on wine will be eliminated within four years (from 14% to 11.2% and then by a further 2.8% on January 1 every year until it reaches zero in 2019).

The EU and China, inside the "EU-China 2020 Strategic Agenda for Cooperation", have concluded in 2017 a bilateral agreement that will result in the protection, against imitations and usurpations, of 100 European geographical indications (of which more than half related to wine) in China and 100 Chinese geographical indications in the EU. Cooperation between the EU and China on geographical indications began over ten years ago, leading to the protection in 2012 of ten geographical indication names on both sides ("10+10" project).

Currently no country has agreements with Russia. (Negotiations were ongoing with New Zealand; however, they were suspended in 2014 following events in the Ukraine.) Russia joined the WTO in late 2011, and while its high wine tariffs are likely to decrease over time, a complex and non-predictable assortment of non-tariff barriers (mainly certification and customs procedures) continues to be the biggest obstacles to entering this market. Recently trade relation between Russia and the main Western countries has become very controversial, as trade sanctions (embargo on imports) have been used for political reasons by western countries supporting the Ukraine, all this in response to Russia's occupation of Crimea. Starting in 2014, Russia banned some major food products (pork, poultry, fish and seafood, vegetables and dairy products), from the EU, the USA, Canada, Australia, and Norway. After, the embargo was extended to include Albania, Montenegro, Iceland and Liechtenstein, the Ukraine, and Turkey (in October 2016 the embargo on Turkish food was relaxed slightly). Wine up to now has been excluded from retaliation against major exporters,[7] but Russia has first banned wine imports from Georgia, between 2006 and 2013, and recently (2017) from Montenegro.

The emergence of an increasing number of FTAs between wine-producing countries and emerging consumer markets could change the mid- to long-term dynamics of the global wine market.

Overall it is to be stressed that, among the New World wine countries, Chile has focused much of its marketing strategy on wine export opportunities (Wehner 2009). As a result of its success in negotiating FTAs, it has obtained preferential market access to the top developed and emerging wine markets around the world. In contrast another important Latin-American wine-producing country like Argentina, after joining the Mercado Común del Sur (MERCOSUR), lost the possibility to sign any FTA on its own. This lack of openness toward international trade, according to Del Bianco et al. (2017), contributes to explain the country's weak export performance. In addition, it is to be mentioned that Argentina is the only major wine producer to have imposed a 5% tax on the value of exported wines.

Australia and New Zealand have also been very active in negotiations to reach agreements with emerging wine-importing Asian countries. In particular Australia has been able to bridge the gap with other competitors in two major markets such as South Korea and China even though these competitors had already obtained improved access to those markets through their own FTAs (Anderson and Wittwer 2015).

In this scenario, EU exporters without a preferential access to China could continue to face a disadvantage as New World producing countries, thanks to existing trade deals, would be able to consolidate their positions. Overall, the EU has been able to sign several FTAs that allow better access to markets and an increase of GIs' protection for wines.

14.6   Elements of Change

The current scenario of barriers to international wine trade could undergo some remarkable changes in the near future which could be the result of changes in (i) the international trade policy of some major player on the world

---

[7] However, wine imports to Russia in the period 2015–2016 have been significantly lower than in the previous two years; imports then rose to the pre-crisis levels (2013, 5 million hl for €920,000; 2017, 4.7 million hl for €880,000).

scene, or (ii) a more general decision concerning the international positioning of the country, as is the case of Brexit, or, finally, (iii) changes concerning additional requirements that companies have to satisfy, beyond legal requirements, which derive from new consumers' sensibilities and from retailers' requests.

14.6.1   Globalization Process and US "America First"

The world economic globalization process has been governed for a long time by the paradigm of multilateral liberalization following the WTO's rules. The failure of the Doha round, together with the increase in the economic and political weight of the major developing countries on the international scene, mainly in the Asia-Pacific region, and, more recently, the US President Trump strategy called "America first", led to more complex and less predictable international relations.

In particular the USA seems to propose moving away from multilateral or regional arrangements with multiple trade partners to bilateral agreements where they can stress more their negotiation strength. Up to now, the USA has withdrawn from the Trans-Pacific Partnership and has requested to renegotiate the North American Free Trade Agreement (NAFTA). Furthermore, they intend to rebalance trade with those countries that experienced the most commercial surplus in respect to the USA, such as China and Germany (ISMEA 2017), and start to increase tariff on some products (steel and aluminum).

In such context, the USA runs a significant deficit in food and agricultural trade with the EU. The threat to apply protectionist measures could have a major impact on EU exports of food products and in particular wine, given its great importance in trade with the USA: EU countries export wine for €10 billion, of which one third is exported to the USA.

Furthermore, the USA contests that the EU's GI system contributes to the asymmetry (trade deficit) in US-EU trade in agricultural products for products subject to the EU's GI regime.

The Special 301 Report of the annual review of the state of intellectual property protection and enforcement in US trading partners around the world states that "The United States is working intensively through bilateral and multilateral channels to advance U.S. market access interests in foreign markets and to ensure that GI-related trade initiatives of the EU, its Member States, like-minded countries, and international organizations, do not undercut such market access" (USTR 2017, p. 22).

The EU GI agenda remains highly concerning for the USA, for several reasons. In the first place, the EU GI system raises concerns regarding the extent to which it impairs the scope of trademark protection, including a respect to prior trademark rights. Secondly, some troubling aspects of the EU GI system influence access for the USA and other producers to the EU market. Lastly, EU continues to seek to expand its GI system beyond its border, through bilateral trade agreements and in multilateral and plurilateral bodies as well (such as the WIPO Lisbon Agreement) which impose the negative impact of the EU GI system on market access and trademark protection in third countries.

The USA is trying to fight the EU's aggressive promotion of its exclusionary GI policies through FTAs negotiation, as well as in international forums, including APEC, WIPO, and the WTO. "In addition to these negotiations, the United States is engaging bilaterally to address concerns resulting from the GI provisions in existing EU trade agreements, agreements under negotiation, and other initiatives, including with Canada, China, Costa Rica, Ecuador, El Salvador, Indonesia, Japan, Malaysia, Morocco, the Philippines, South Africa, and Vietnam, among others" (USTR 2017, p. 23).

14.6.2   UK Brexit

Brexit, the parting of the UK from the EU, is going to modify the international wine trade scenario as the UK is one of the most important players in the wine market. The UK currently represents the first wine consumer market among non-producing countries, the second wine importer in value and volume, and it is also an important re-exporter. Such wine-related trading activities make the UK the home of a flourishing wine business, which is worth about £17 billions. When it quits the EU, the UK will leave a wide regional integrated area and will lose the preferential import and export channels represented by the preferential agreements arranged by EU with several partners. As a consequence, wine imports in the UK (13.5 million hectoliters) and wine exports (about 880,000 hectoliters for a value of €615 million) from the UK will be exposed to barriers higher than today. How this will happen will depend on how the UK will define trade relationship with the EU and other partners. Rollo et al. (2016) suggest that the most practical trade policy for the UK to adopt when leaving the EU is the EU's tariff schedules previously agreed at the WTO. On the base of this assumption, and under the hypothesis that negotiations for preferential arrangement will take years, Anderson and Wittwer (2017, 2018) have simulated Brexit effects. They forecast that between 2014 and 2025 the growth (in value) of the UK's wine consumption and import will be 9% instead of 24%, warning, though, that it will be the slower income growth to make a smaller wine market in the UK in 2025 than would otherwise have been the case. As a matter of fact, the import duties applied in their simulations are the small ones indicated in Table 14.2, which can play only a minor role.

Anderson and Wittwer's simulations assume a smooth transition in the technical aspects of trade between the UK and the EU. But this is a worrying issue for the wine business community. In October 2017 the most important bodies representing traders and producers in the UK and Europe signed a joint declaration[8] urging "the EU and the UK to agree to a gold standard agreement that preserves wine and spirit tariff-free trade and fair competition" and calling "for predictable, pragmatic, non-disruptive transitional implementation arrangements, allowing businesses to continue trading in the knowledge that the rules will not change at all without a phase-in period". Indeed, the joint declaration highlights several matters that may endanger trade flows between the UK and the EU after the transition period, generating relevant trade barriers, which involve rules concerning oenological practices, labeling, intellectual property rights protection and in particular GI protection, custom practices, and people movements. Also in the case of Brexit, therefore, NTMs will be the true variables which will determine trade flow evolution.

14.6.3   Private Standards

Last but not least, it should be stressed that the international wine trade is constrained not only by national technical regulations resulting in non-tariff barriers but also by private standards. In the last decade there has been an intense development of private standards, mainly targeting, initially, food safety (often exceeding requirements established in international standards developed by the *Codex Alimentarius*) and in recent years mainly related to social and environmental aspects. Such standards can be set by individual firms (usually large retailers), collective national organizations, or international standards organizations. Private standards are voluntary, but if required by large retailers and/or large companies they become de facto mandatory for suppliers. Such standards do not fall within the rules of the WTO. Indeed, these standards area matter of increasing concern for all the effects that they

[8] Joint paper about Brexit published by spiritsEUROPE, Comité Européen des Entreprises Vins, Scotch Whisky Association, Wine & Spirit Trade Association, October 2017.

may have upon access to international markets, especially for small businesses (Henson and Humphrey 2009). Private standards, therefore, may operate as barriers which will discriminate not among countries but among types of firms or supply chains.

Concerning social and environmental standards, in most wine-producing countries specific initiatives were developed to measure, communicate, and, in some cases, certify the compliance of wineries with principles of sustainable development, that is, environmental, social, and economic sustainability (Flores 2018; Merlo et al. 2018; Mariani and Vastola 2015). The scope was to make available to wine producers a simpler and more focused standard compared to ISO standard as ISO 14001 (environmental management) or ISO 26000 (corporate social responsibility). Despite the lower administrative burden of such wine-specific standards, the compliance with their prescription could be difficult for some actors and, in some circumstances, for all actors in specific areas resulting in relevant trade barriers (Pomarici et al. 2015; Jourjon et al. 2016). Moreover, the compliance with such standards, in case of not-integrated supply chains (bottlers purchasing wine or winery purchasing grape) may have serious consequences on the overall chain's governance and on the linkages among the participants (Cafaggi 2016). As a matter of fact, in order to guarantee final product compliance with the desired set of requirements, the lead firms have to apply a strict control upon the whole upward supply chain. Therefore this compliance asks for specific contracts between participants to the supply chain, sometimes international,[9] which may influence both the forms and the functions of the chains, and that may result in new barriers to trade. As a matter of fact, regulatory provisions related to social responsibility and sustainability expand the scope of contracting along the chain from the exchange (of products or services) to the regulation (of the process) and produce changes in the contractual relationships between participants, that is, the leader chains and the suppliers and eventually their subcontractors.

14.7   Final Remarks

Previous paragraphs show that the international wine trade has to overcome a complex variety of barriers, deriving from import duties and, more often, from NTMs. As a matter of fact, wine exports to some markets are still hampered

---

[9] The importance in the wine industry of de-integrated supply chains emerges in many chapters of this book and with quantitative details in Chap. 23 (Conegliano Valdobbiadene Prosecco case). The increasing relevance of de-integrated supply chains with an international extension is demonstrated by the rise of international trade of bulk wine, which accounts for near 40% of total export (+ 88% on 2000).

by high tariffs and regular wine export faces a variety of technical barriers related to the particular characteristics of this alcoholic product, which is obtained with production practices often subject to rules and regulated by specific labeling systems.

In this scenario, the object of negotiations is a push to negotiate bilateral agreements, to reduce the impact of tariff and non-tariff barriers which affect wine trade. In negotiating these agreements, each exporting country targets specific issues to protect the distinctive elements of their offer and, in so doing, distorting and diverting effects are generated. It is not easy to assess the effects of preferential access to the markets on export flow changes, because the competitive performance is determined by many factors (e.g. exchange rate, marketing effort) but scientific studies demonstrate the discriminatory effect of preferential agreements (ABARES 2012) and the heterogeneous impacts on trade of technical measures (Dal Bianco et al. 2016).

Considered the elements of change discussed in Sect. 14.6, in the future the impact of tariff and non-tariff barriers could become even stronger and in such perspective it would be useful to renovate the commitment for a non-discriminatory reduction of non-tariff barriers at the very least. As *Codex Alimentarius* does not cover many relevant concerning issues (and it is not likely that something will change), it would be desirable to increase the role of OIV, eventually with an official recognition of this organization by WTO.

Concluding, what looks worth highlighting is that the rules concerning the wine's international trade act as barriers but also, as far as NTMs are concerned, act as drivers of specific behavior, which are relevant elements of the global wine market's institutional settings. As a matter of fact, such rules, beyond the discriminatory effects that may operate locally, are likely to support the consumers' trust, which is the key element of a fair progress in a globalized wine market.

References

ABARES – Australian Bureau of Agricultural and Resource Economics and Sciences. 2012. *Consultation with the Australian wine sector on barriers to trade in wine markets*. Report to client prepared for the Grape and Wine Research and Development Corporation.

Ahearn, R.J. 2011. *Europe's preferential trade agreements: Status, content, and implications*. Congressional Research Service, 7–5700. www.crs.gov, R41143, 1–41.

Anderson, K. 2010. Excise and import taxes on wine versus beer and spirits: An international comparison. *Economic Papers* 29 (2): 215–228.

Anderson, K., and S. Nelgen. 2011. *Global wine markets: A statistical compendium, 1961 to 2009*. Adelaide: University of Adelaide Press. www.adelaide.edu.au/press.

Anderson, K., and G. Wittwer. 2015. *Impact of Australia's free trade agreements with China, Japan and Korea: The case of wine, Wine Economics Research Centre*. Working paper No. 0415.

———. 2017. U.K. and global wine markets by 2025, and implications of Brexit. *Journal of Wine Economics* 12 (3): 221–251.

———. 2018. Brexit, follow-on FTAs, and global wine trade, University of Adelaide: Wine Economics Research Centre, *Wine Policy Brief No. 19*.

Babili, M. 2009. *Ad valorem equivalent in the WTO, NAPC-TPD*. Working paper n. 43.

Battaglene, T. 2014. An analysis of ingredient and nutritional labeling for wine. In *BIO Web of Conferences*. Vol. 3. EDP Sciences.

Battaglene, T., and C. Milton. 2010. Potential impacts of organic wine regulation as a technical barrier to trade. In *Proceedings of the 33rd World Congress of Vine and Wine*, Tbilisi, Georgia, June 20–27.

Cafaggi, F. 2016. Regulation through contracts: Supply-chain contracting and sustainability standards. *European Review of Contract Law* 12 (3): 218–258.

COGEA. 2014. *Study on the competitiveness of European wine*. Brussels: European Commission.

Dal Bianco, A., M.J. Estrella-Orrego, V.L. Boatto, and A.J. Gennari. 2017. Is Mercosur promoting trade? Insights from Argentinean wine exports. *Spanish Journal of Agricultural Research* 15 (1): 8.

Dal Bianco, A., V. Boatto, F. Caracciolo, and F.G. Santeramo. 2016. Tariffs and non-tariff frictions in the world wine trade. *European Review of Agricultural Economics* 43 (1): 31–57.

Disdier, A.C., L. Fontagné, and M. Mimuni. 2007. *The impact of regulations on agricultural trade: Evidence from SPS and TBT agreements*. CEPII Working papers n. 04.

Dunn, R.M., Jr., and J.H. Mutti. 2004. *International economics*. New York: Routledge.

European Commission. 2006. *Global Europe: Competing in the world*, communication COM (2006) 567.

———. 2010. *EU-South Korea free trade agreement: A quick reading guide*. Available at: http://trade.ec.europa.eu/doclib/docs/2009/october/tradoc_145203.pdf.

———. 2014. *CETA – Summary of the final negotiating results*. Available at: https://trade.ec.europa.eu/doclib/docs/2014/december/tradoc_152982.pdf.

———. 2016. *Report from the commission to the European Parliament and the council on trade and investment barriers*. Available at: http://trade.ec.europa.eu/doclib/docs/2017/june/tradoc_155642.pdf.

———. 2018. *Overview of FTA and other trade negotiations*. Available at: http://trade.ec.europa.eu/doclib/docs/2006/december/tradoc_118238.pdf.

Financial Times. 2015. *The Doha round finally dies a merciful death*. Available at: https://www.ft.com/content/9cb1ab9e-a7e2-11e5-955c-1e1d6de94879.

Flores, S.S. 2018. What is sustainability in the wine world? A cross-country analysis of wine sustainability frameworks. *Journal of Cleaner Production* 172: 2301–2312.

Henson, S., and J. Humphrey. 2009. *The impacts of private food safety standards on the food chain and on public standard-setting processes.* Paper prepared for FAO/WHO. Available at www.fao.org.

ICE. 2010. *Raccolta delle documentazioni necessarie per l'esportazione del vino.* Verona.

ISMEA. 2017. *L'America first di Trump scenari globali per il commercio agroalimentare.*

Jourjon, F., H.C. Chou, A. Gezart, A.E. Kadison, L. Martinat, E. Pomarici, and R. Vecchio. 2016. Wineries evaluation of costs and benefits of sustainability certification program: The case of Terra Vitis in France, recent patents on food. *Nutrition and Agriculture* 8 (2): 138–147.

Mariani, A., and A. Vastola. 2015. Sustainable winegrowing: Current perspectives. *International Journal of Wine Research* 7: 37–48.

Mariani, A., E. Pomarici, and V. Boatto. 2012. The international wine trade: Recent trends and critical issues. *Wine Economics and Policy* 1 (1): 24–40.

Mariani, A., F. Napoletano, E. Pomarici, and R. Vecchio. 2014a. Tariff and non-tariff barriers to wine exports and initiatives to reduce their effects. *Agricultural Economics Review* 15 (1): 5–24.

Mariani, A., F. Napoletano, R. Vecchio, and E. Pomarici. 2014b. European wine exports: The key role of trade policy. *EuroChoices* 13 (3): 46–53.

Merli, R., M. Preziosi, and A. Acampora. 2018. Sustainability experiences in the wine sector: Toward the development of an international indicators system. *Journal of Cleaner Production* 172: 3791–3805.

Morrison, A., and R. Rabellotti. 2017. Gradual catch up and enduring leadership in the global wine industry. *Research Policy* 46 (2): 417–430.

Pomarici, E., R. Vecchio, and A. Mariani. 2015. Wineries' perception of sustainability costs and benefits: An exploratory study in California. *Sustainability* 7 (12): 16164–16174.

Rickard, B.J., O. Gergaud, S.T. Ho, and F. Livat. 2017. Trade liberalization in the presence of domestic regulations: Public policies applied to EU and U.S. wine markets. *Applied Economics* 50 (18): 2028–2047.

Rollo, J., I. Borchert, K. Dawar, P. Holmes, and L.A. Winters. 2016. *The World Trade Organization: A safety net for a post-Brexit UK trade policy?* Briefing paper 1. UKTPO, University of Sussex. Available at: http://blogs.sussex.ac.uk/uktpo/files/2017/01/Briefing-paper-1-final-1.pdf.

UNCTAD. 2013. *Non-tariff measures to trade: Economic and policy issues for developing countries for developing countries.* Geneva.

USTR (Office of the United States Trade Representative). 2017. Special 301 Report. Available at: https://upload.wikimedia.org/wikipedia/commons/thumb/4/41/US-TradeRepresentative-Seal.svg/1200px-US-TradeRepresentative-Seal.svg.png.

———. 2018. *National trade estimate report on foreign trade barriers.* Available at: https://ustr.gov/sites/default/files/files/Press/Reports/2018%20National%20Trade%20Estimate%20Report.pdf.

Wehner, L. 2009. *Power, governance, and ideas in Chile's free trade agreement policy, German Institute of Global and Area Studies (GIGA).* Working papers No 102.

WFA (Winemakers' Federation of Australia). 2010. *Submission on the trans-pacific partnership agreement submission to DFAT.*

———. 2018. *Trade and market access report.*

Wine Institute. 2013. *International trade barriers report for U.S. wines – 2012.*

———. 2015. *International trade barriers report for U.S. wines – 2015.* Available at: https://members.wineinstitute.org/files/TB/CalWine.TradeBarriersReport2015.V07Web.pdf.

WTO. 2010. *The WTO agreements series – Sanitary and phytosanitary measures.* Available at: https://www.wto.org/english/res_e/booksp_e/agrmntseries4_sps_e.pdf.

———. 2014. *The WTO agreements series – Technical barriers to trade.* Available at: https://www.wto.org/english/res_e/publications_e/tbttotrade_e.pdf.

Part III

Diversity of Organization in the Wine Industry

Coord. by *Adeline Alonso Ugaglia*

15

Introduction: The Diversity of Organizational Patterns in the Wine Industry

Adeline Alonso Ugaglia

Part I showed the extreme diversity of the wine industries worldwide, diversity which is particularly interesting from an industrial economics point of view for further analyses. These different industries show an important diversity in the major actors constituting the core of the industry, the role(s) they are playing in the industry and in the production process, plus the strategies they set for the future. The diversity of the players, the length of the value chain and the complexity of the organization depend on the status of the wine countries (Fig. 15.1). The wine industries of the Traditional producing countries (also called Old wine countries) are known to be more atomized and fragmented than the wine industries of the New producing countries. In this chapter, we present the different organizational patterns for grape and wine production and the strategies developed by key players in the Old wine countries to distribute and sell wine. These strategies are not only basic business models, but also a way to face their recent loss in trade shares and to catch demand from emerging consuming countries, that is to survive and sustain on the world wine market.

A. Alonso Ugaglia (✉)
Bordeaux Sciences Agro, University of Bordeaux, Gradignan, France
e-mail: adeline.ugaglia@agro-bordeaux.fr

© The Author(s) 2019
A. Alonso Ugaglia et al. (eds.), *The Palgrave Handbook of Wine Industry Economics*,
https://doi.org/10.1007/978-3-319-98633-3_15

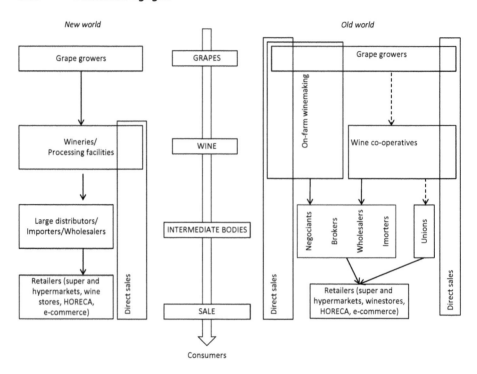

Fig. 15.1 Simplified representation of wine industries for Old and New world countries. (Source: Author; Note: The dashed arrows reflect the potential financial contract to buy fresh grapes between producers and co-operatives or between co-operatives and commercial unions depending of the law status of the co-operative)

15.1 Producing Firms: From Producing Grapes to Selling Wine

The production of grapes and wine rely on different actors according to the status of the country (Old/New), but it can also vary within a wine industry, especially in the Old world. For grapes (or must) production, it is possible to observe simple grape-growing farms in both types of countries. The farms are producing fresh grapes and sell or deliver them to the following actor in the chain. But in the Old world, these farms can also be the ones processing, distributing and/or selling the wine directly to the consumer. They are in this case very different from the basic grape-growing farms, especially from those in the New world. This difference has some consequences on the economic performance of these firms. Regardless of how it is measured, the winemakers' income has a great variability. This variability is related to differences in size (area) of farms (economies of scale in the New world) but also in productivity and costs of the labor force. The winemakers bottling and selling their wines also have to support the cost of vinification and commercialization. The price also plays an important role in the differentiation of winegrowers' income levels. But the main difference for winegrowers from Old and New wine countries relies on yield. The appellation regimes dominating the Old world constraint yields to preserve quantity and quality of wines on the market, while yields are not limited in the New world. It means that the production costs are higher in the Old than in the New world, relative to the quantity produced per ha. As might be expected from the product differentiation and market segmentation in France, income differences are quite clearly related to geographic division into regions (Delord 2011). Wine bottling can be considered as an alternative element of income differentiation. The appellation system is certainly an essential factor to explain the differences in the economic performance of grape-growing farms, but the collective and individual aspects of this differentiation should also be distinguished.

15.2   The Strategies of Downstream Wine Firms

Many different players are concerned by wine distribution in the Old wine countries compared to the New world where the organization at this stage is less complex with large intermediate bodies. In the Old World, the downstream players are diverse, including winegrowers producing wine from their own grapes as seen above, but also wine co-operatives, negociants, wholesalers and importers are concerned. They faced a huge success during the twentieth century, growing in volume and value while benefiting from the rapid growth of world trade flows. But the context has changed, the consumption decreases in Europe, and these countries have to compete with the wines from the New world. Facing such changes, the players in distribution channels have set some different strategies to survive.

This diversity is more or less represented according to the countries and the wine industries concerned. The number and the diversity of companies that make up the downstream sector reflect the wealth and importance of this sector in France for example. It is synonymous of richness in terms of market adaptation but can also be perceived as a weakness that could explain the loss of market shares of the Old world countries. Indeed, too much diversity in the number of actors involved in the wine industry can lead to long chains and too much fragmentation, preventing the emergence of very large firms that alone would be able to provide high volumes in the markets to position themselves competitively. While the heterogeneity of downstream companies has been shown in particular in France (Couderc 2008) (except in Champagne), other studies also show the huge capacity that players can develop to group and grow together via mergers and other processes of concentration. For example, some wine co-operatives formed commercial unions in order to strengthen their market power (Cadot et al. 2016). These commercial unions are co-operatives of wine co-operatives and are responsible for the marketing and sales of the wines processed by their members (wine co-operatives). They can also adapt their strategies according to their situation and merge with other wine co-operatives or stay small and autonomous if they benefit from a niche market (Corade and Lacour 2015). Mergers allow to manage the value all along the chain, when forming commercial unions is focused on supply concentration. Combined with the type of management and governance they choose, the authors show that they can develop a positive autonomy (autonomous co-operatives, types 1 and 2) or an autonomy leading to marginalization (autonomous co-operatives, type 3). A strategy based on the autonomy of the co-operative can result in positive as well as in negative trajectories. Therefore their resilience and sustainability depend on the strategy they choose (Fig. 15.2).

Even if the atomization of still wine supply remains the norm in the Old wine countries compared to New ones, it also seems that SA companies (e.g., wine merchants or negociants) started the process of concentration in the Old producing countries. Martin (2008) shows that negociants are also developing different types of strategies in addition to the concentration process. They can either adapt but keep the link to appellation regimes (weakening the terroir by the dilution of the geographical reference: e.g., creation of brands with a light reference to the location, or providing some technical advice to the growers in order to claim for their wine typicity) or they can conduct local

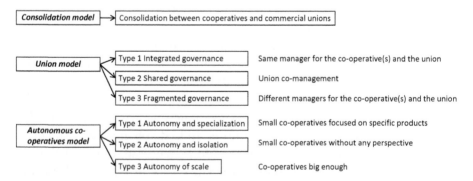

Fig. 15.2 Diversity of strategies for wine co-operatives. (Source: Corade et Lacour 2015)

bypass operations to develop similar strategies to those of the New world countries (developing branding and varietal wines). Pesme et al. (2010) compare two of the main players in the Aquitaine wine sector according to the strategies they develop: the co-operatives and the wine merchants. They analyze the nature of strategic operations from the point of view of the concentration process taking place in the Bordeaux-Aquitaine region. Their results provide both qualitative and quantitative evidence to prove that a number of collaborative approaches have been adopted in the region. They highlight the fact that these players are more willing to respond to the conditions of a new competitive environment and consequently to consider new strategic approaches. The wine value chain is undergoing deep restructuring process. With the spotlight focused on producing a size effect on the sector through concentration, they examine in greater detail what this process really is. It is not limited to size objectives as it commits the players to thorough production and market changes. This led to concentration operations analyzed in terms of strategic changes, notably with regard to the flexibility of the strategies that the players are meant to design and develop. All of these results from different studies ultimately result in a heterogeneous performance of these downstream firms, but which does not only depend on the size of the firms. Some strategies set by these firms well manage to value the factors of competitiveness which have made the success of the sector a long time ago, based on the valuation of concepts as terroir, origin and reputation. Other strategies are not successful and the downstream firms struggle to survive. However, there are only few exits from the market.

The chapter is dedicated to further analyses of the organization of vineyards and wineries and the strategies of wine co-operatives and negociants. Thanks to case studies (mainly from France), these contributions provide a better understanding of the organizational patterns in the Old world wine industries. The chapter organized as follows:

Chapter 16 uses the Allen and Lueck (2002) transaction cost framework to examine the organization of vineyards and winemaking. The authors focus on three important organizational features of worldwide wine production: limited contracting, small vineyards producing high-quality grapes and the separation of wineries from vineyards in the nineteenth century.

Then, Chap. 17 shows that the widespread assumption that mergers are the best way for co-operatives to break free from their "natural" territorial anchoring (perceived to be a strong impediment to their global insertion) is questionable. Observation of the recent merging processes of wine co-operatives shows a more subtle phenomenon at work. On the one hand mergers do indeed loosen their constitutive territorial anchoring. On the other hand, they also come together with new geographical and organized proximities, prone to the re-dimensioning of the territorial scale of the co-operative action. These findings were supported by a round of thorough interviews with most of the managers of the Aquitanian co-operatives created by merger between 1994 and 2006.

Chapter 18 deals with the diversity as a specificity of the wine market. There are an extremely large variety of wines, as well as producers who make them. What is important to understand about this diversity is that it is organized. Diversity is embedded in a complex set of social relationships and is governed by various institutions. From this perspective, the organization of this level of variety can be seen as a historical process. The actors involved constantly seek to ensure their business models are coherent with the current production and market environment. To achieve this, they do not simply adjust their own strategy or the way they implement it but also try to change the environment, where it is needed, by interacting with other decision makers. In the wine industry this manifests itself as the power game between wine-growers and merchants. The wine region of Bordeaux is a striking example of how historically organized diversity can be transformed into the basis of success on the wine market. At the same time, this example shows the fragility of a regional production system which is only temporarily coherent.

References

Cadot, J., A. Alonso Ugaglia, B. Bonnefous, and B. Del'homme. 2016. The horizon problem in Bordeaux wine co-operatives. *International Journal of Entrepreneurship and Small Business* 29 (4): 651–668.

Corade and Lacour. 2015. Les trajectoires d'évolution des coopératives vinicoles girondines. *Canadian Journal of Regional Science* 38 (1/3): 29–37.

Couderc, J.P. 2008. Manifeste pour un aggiornamento commercial dans la filière vin en France. In *Introduction, Bacchus 2008*, 336p. Paris: Dunod.

Delord, B. 2011. Faits et chiffres : La forte dispersion des revenus dans la viticulture française. *Économie rurale* 324 (juillet-août): 60–70.

Lueck, D. 2002. *The nature of the farm: Contracts, uncertainty, and organization.* Cambridge: MIT Press.

Martin, J.C. 2008. Terroir et stratégies du négoce dans la filière vitivinicole : une approche historique. In *Bacchus, 2008*, 19–38. Paris: Dunod.

Pesme, J.O., M.C. Bélis-Bergouignan, and N. Corade. 2010. Strategic operations and concentration in the Bordeaux-Aquitaine region. *International Journal of Wine Business Research* 22 (3): 308–324.

16

The Organization of Vineyards and Wineries

Douglas W. Allen and Dean Lueck

That the vineyard, when properly planted and brought to perfection, was the most valuable part of the farm, seems to have been an undoubted maxim in the ancient agriculture, as it is in the modern through all the wine countries. … The vine is more affected by the difference of soils than any other fruit tree. … vineyards are in general more carefully cultivated than most others, …. In so valuable a produce the loss occasioned by negligence is so great as to force even the most careless to attention.
[Adam Smith, *Wealth of Nations*, Book One, Chapter 11].

16.1 Introduction

It is not surprising that Adam Smith would include a discussion of wine in his great treatise—after all, wine has been in the hearts of poets and at the center of civilization since the beginning of cultivation. Nor is it surprising, indeed almost predictable, that Smith would also focus in on the critical economic aspects of wine. Although most of his discussion relates to the political economy of old vineyard interests, as opposed to the planting of new vines in an effort to protect their rents, there is mention of three critical features. First, wine is a valuable commodity. Second, wine output and quality are heavily

D. W. Allen (✉)
Department of Economics, Simon Fraser University, Burnaby, BC, Canada
e-mail: allen@sfu.ca

D. Lueck
Indiana University, Bloomington, IN, USA

© The Author(s) 2019
A. Alonso Ugaglia et al. (eds.), *The Palgrave Handbook of Wine Industry Economics*,
https://doi.org/10.1007/978-3-319-98633-3_16

influenced by Nature in a complicated way. Third, wine production is subject to necessary meticulous care by the grower and vintner. These three fundamental economic features still remain part of the wine story and are important in understanding the organization of vineyards and wineries.

This book contains chapters on the wine industry from all over the world. Each chapter contains a general description of the industry within a given country, concentrating on quantities, varieties, values, and overall industry structure. Our purpose is to consider a selected number of organizational issues of wine production, and in doing so we rely on these chapters as well as the limited studies found in the literature for institutional detail. Although there are many aspects to wine organization, and exceptions everywhere, in this chapter we focus on three stylized facts that are present across all of the chapters. These issues include matters of contracting at the vineyard (the use of labor contracts, the scarcity of tenancy contracts), the inverse relationship between vineyard size and wine quality, and the historical vertical disintegration of the vineyard from the winery in the nineteenth century (and the recent reintegration for boutique wineries).

In general, we rely on the framework of farm organization articulated in Allen and Lueck (2002). Indeed, the organization of wine was not examined in that work and now provides an out-of-sample test of that model. Like other crops, we show below that the organization of vineyards and wineries is best explained by the specific transaction costs that arise in the context of growing grapes and producing wine. This industry produces an interesting case study because of the asymmetric advances in science for producing wine compared to growing grapes and because transaction costs play such a large role in production.

We begin with a brief review of Allen and Lueck (2002), followed by a discussion of grape and wine transaction cost issues. We then explain the various organizational features and close with a discussion of how grapes and wines relate to other crops and their organization.

16.2   The Allen and Lueck Framework of Agricultural Organization

Allen and Lueck (2002) created a general framework for examining farm organization that relied on three key features. First, all parties involved choose the organizational structure that maximizes the expected value of the productive relationship. Second, Nature plays an important twofold role: creating uncertainty in the year-to-year outputs that masks the actual inputs used in production and creating predictable seasonal stages of production through crop cycles, stages, and timeliness. Third, all parties are risk neutral, concerned only with the expected net value of production. These three features allow the development of simple models within the context of a specific crop that depend mostly on the transaction cost constraints of the crop in question. Difficulties that arise over strategic behavior or risk aversion are avoided, and straightforward comparative statics are forthcoming.

In the Allen and Lueck framework, output is: $Q = h(l, e, k) + \theta$, where Q is the observed harvested output which is assumed to have a unit price and l is land attributes, e is labor effort, k is other capital, and $\theta \sim (0, \sigma^2)$ is the randomly distributed composite input of Nature. Any given input can only be measured with error or might even be unobservable. Because the human actions $h(l, e, k)$ and the actions of Nature θ cannot be separately identified, the conditions for transaction costs are present. The logic then is for the parties to choose the form of organization that maximizes the value of this output subject to the transaction costs that are created with any given type of organization.[1]

Allen and Lueck stressed that in agriculture the critical transaction costs result from conditions "close to the ground" or "at the field level." Thus, the ability of farmers to exploit the difficult-to-measure land attributes, underreport the crop output, over-report crop inputs, or shirk their labor duties to their advantage act as major constraints to contracting and vertical integration. Likewise, land and other capital owners can exploit the labor inputs of farmers or shirk on the application of their capital inputs. The role Nature plays at the field level varies by crop, time of year, and over time. When it comes to the organization of vineyards and wineries, our focus is on the specific features of grapes and fermentation that allow parties to exploit one another.

16.3   The Transaction Costs of Grapes to Wine

Wine is the final product of an agricultural-manufacturing process, not unlike bread, cheese, or salami. And yet, the transaction cost conditions of wine production are often so extensive that wine is somewhat of a unique farm

---

[1] "Organizations" can be thought of as a collection or distribution of property rights. Transaction costs are defined as the costs of establishing and maintaining a distribution of property rights (Allen 1991).

product. Wine comes (mostly) from grapes through a process of natural fermentation. If ripe grapes are placed in a container, they begin to break down,
and the natural yeast on the skin interacts with the sugars in the juice to produce an enzyme to initiate the chemical reaction into alcohol. The fermentation process stops when all the sugar is converted or the alcohol content is
high enough to kill the yeast. Thus, unlike other so-called processed foods,
wine almost produces itself.[2]

Unlike most agricultural commodities where the quality range is quite narrow, with wine there is an enormous quality dimension, and only the highest
end is fit and desired for human consumption. Thus, although most wine
comes from just one vine species (*Vitis vinifera*), these produce hundreds of
thousands of wines.[3] These various wines differ in appearance (color, clarity),
aroma (intensity, types such as earthy or floral), and taste (sweetness, body,
acidity, tannins, flavors). These in turn are determined by the location of vineyard, terrain, viticulture, vinification, storage, and transport. Each of these
general inputs is the result of hundreds of decisions, some of which are
observable.

16.3.1   Vineyards

Unlike other fruits and vegetables, grapes do not like nutrient-rich soils, and
they do well on steeply sloped hillsides due to the enhanced drainage and
sunshine.[4] The limited locations for growing grapes fit for wine increase the
scarcity and price of wine land.[5] For a given location, the soil fertility, acidity,
heat retention, and soil type determine the best variety, vine density, row
direction, spacing, vine training, pest control, and winter protection. Many of
these decisions are made at the start of the vineyard, but many, like canopy
management, pruning, and timing of harvest involve ongoing on-the-spot
decisions.

Vines, if properly looked after, can produce for 50–100 years. Much of the
processes of layering to fill in gaps and pruning are done by hand and are
almost art forms based on skill and knowledge. Pruning too much can reduce

---

[2] Thornton (2013) has a detailed description of the science of fermentation.

[3] Thornton (p. 55, 2013) notes there are many varieties, perhaps in the thousands using a narrow definition of variety.

[4] Thornton (p. 60, 2013).

[5] As noted in several chapters of this book, across the world wine is one of the most valuable crops per
acre. The high value of wine land means that the costs of abusing such land are also high.

yield, while too little pruning can lower the fruit quality. Likewise canopy management is critical: too little sun prevents grape growth and composition, but too much can burn and dehydrate the grapes. Thinning, another hand process, removes some immature grapes during the growing season to improve the quality of remaining grapes. Every vineyard manager must decide on the optimal quantity-quality trade-off. As grapes ripen the acid content starts to fall, but the sugar content increases, creating another trade-off that has to be managed to produce the appropriate sugar-acid balance. Grape tasting, another difficult-to-measure skill, is still the best way to determine the optimal time to harvest.

In each stage of grape production, the conditions for rather large transaction costs exist. Vineyards are location-specific firms that rely on critical natural ingredients that vary from location-to-location, year-to-year, and day-to-day. These measurement problems (Barzel 1982) allow costly actions to hide behind the random inputs of Nature. Vineyards also produce a grape whose value depends on its quality, and although the quality of the grape can be measured at some cost, the human inputs required to produce high quality are difficult to measure.[6] When difficult to measure, suppliers of high-quality inputs have moral hazard incentives. Finally, the grapes themselves are small and costly to divide at the vineyard and are therefore easy to hide or steal.[7]

16.3.2   Wineries

Once the grapes are picked, they begin to decay immediately. Because of this perishability, it is important for them to be crushed soon so fermentation starts within a proper window. Wine quality at this stage depends heavily on the ability to manage yeasts, bacteria, sugars, and other chemical elements. In contrast to the vineyard side of production, where grapes are still grown under natural conditions similar over the past few centuries, a technical revolution has taken place in wineries.

Prior to 1850 almost all vineyards were integrated with the winery—the wine being produced in the farmer's cellar. Knowledge of the fermentation process was weak, control of temperature was difficult, and the role of natural elements was enormous. The result: much of production was not palatable.[8] Wine quality

---

[6] Goodhue et al. (2003) note the difficulty of measuring these qualities.

[7] Simpson (p. 4, 2009), notes "But transaction costs in viticulture were higher than with most other forms of agriculture, because nature influenced considerably both the size and quality of the harvest."

[8] Simpson (pp. 5–7, 2009).

was so variable and difficult to verify that fraud was common as various impos-
ters sold products under the guise of noted or reputable producers.[9]

By 1900, technological changes in the form of thermometers, refrigerators,
continuous presses, aero-crushing turbines, sterilizers, and pasteurizers altered
wine production and organization.[10] Further innovations came in the form of
cultured yeasts, which are more predictable than the natural yeasts present on
the grapes. Cultured yeasts produce wine with a smaller variance in output
quality. Likewise, the introduction of stainless steel tanks allowed for better
control of temperature, oxygen exposure, and speed of fermentation, reducing the variance in the flavor of the wine. These innovations not only created
elements of economies of size but drastically reduced the role of Nature in
production. Although the fermentation process remained complicated and
continued to require extreme monitoring, these processes could be directly or
indirectly measured for most qualities of wine.

Because of these technological changes, there has been an interesting organizational difference between vineyards and wineries. Whereas, at one time
they were both stages of wine production in which Nature (and therefore
transaction costs) played a large role, in the mid-nineteenth and early twentieth century technical innovations occurred that reduced the transaction cost
environment at the *winery* stage, but not at the level of the vineyard. In the
next section we show how the presence and transformation of transaction
costs have shaped the organization of the wine industry.

16.4   Explaining Organizational Features

In this section, we examine how organizations involved in producing wine grape
and wine have varied over time and location. We use the transaction costs framework just described and merge it with the data from other chapters in this volume
and other studies. In particular, we examine the use of contracting, the relationship between quality and vineyard size, and the evolution of the winery.

16.4.1   Contracting in the Wine Industry

Vineyards have historically been family farm operations. Even today, vineyards remain relatively small compared to the dramatic increases in farm sizes

---

[9] Simpson (p. 11, 2009) notes that in the late nineteenth century artificial wines made from raisins mixed
with water and sugar accounted for one-sixth of French and one-quarter of Spanish wine consumption.
[10] Simpson (p. 9, 2009).

for grains and other important crops. Also as the quality of grape produced at a given vineyard increases, so does the likelihood of family organization on that vineyard. In modern times there are large vineyards, often organized along corporate lines, but they mostly produce low-quality grapes.

In Allen and Lueck (2002), contracting arises when labor, land, and other capital is owned by different parties and can be combined in low transaction cost settings. In agriculture, land (and the assets attached to the land) is often combined with labor through cash rent or share contracts. In a cash rent contract, the labor owner (the farmer or grower) uses the attributes of the land assets in exchange for some fixed dollar rent per acre. At the margin, the price of any given attribute, such as moisture or canopy size, is zero. This means that when cash rent contracts are used, they provide the farmer with an incentive to exploit the landowner's land attributes to increase output and income to the farmer. Hence, for a grain crop under conventional tillage, the farmer might cultivate the cash-rented land in such a way that excessively uses the moisture and soil nutrients to increase the short-run harvest at the long-run expense to the landowner. If a landowner is able to measure or monitor this exploitation, this moral hazard could be eliminated. In agriculture, this transaction is simply the cost of doing business with the cash rent contract.

The most common alternative to cash renting is a share contract, in which the farmer pays his rent in a fraction of the output rather than in cash. In a share contract, farmer moral hazard is reduced compared to a cash rent. Even though the farmer uses the land attributes at a zero marginal price, the marginal returns of this exploitation are now lowered by the "tax" of the share. This "tax effect" also reduces the labor effort incentive of the farmer and creates an incentive to underreport the crop. The potential for underreporting can be a serious problem for share contracts when the output is easy to hide and valuable.[11]

In cases in which crop production has just one major transaction cost problem: either soil exploitation is important, farmer labor is vital, or crop theft is critical. When there is just one particular problem at hand, then one of these two—contracts cash rent or crop share—is often sufficient to manage the contracting arrangement. For example, alfalfa is a hay crop that is planted (often not annually), cut periodically throughout the year, baled or stacked, and sold. For alfalfa, soil exploitation is limited because the farmer has limited

---

[11] Umbeck (1977) noted that the problem of underreporting in gold mining made share contracts were highly unlikely on the gold fields during the California rush.

access to the soil nutrients, but crop theft is possible given the size of bales. Under these conditions, a cash rent contract works well, and virtually all alfalfa contracts are cash rents. On the other hand, sugarcane grants the farmer full access to the soil but is impossible to steal given coordination and industrialization required to harvest and process it. For sugarcane, there is also just one major transaction cost problem (soil exploitation) and virtually all sugarcane contracts are crop-share contracts.

In some situations, like the production of grapes, all of the transaction cost effects are present: land attributes can be exploited, farmer labor easily shirks, and outputs can be stolen. In these cases the simple one- or two-dimensional contract used in most agriculture becomes incomplete and incapable of managing the transaction costs at hand. In these cases, contracting is unlikely.

Consider a vineyard available for contracting with a viticulturist-farmer. The viticulturist's incentives are not incentive compatible with the long-term maintenance of the vines and grape stocks, and moral hazard results. To enhance the short-term goals, the farmer will engage in pruning, canopy management, tilling, and pest control that will increase the short-term crop yield but harm the long-term viability of the vine stock and lead to years of recovery. Indeed, it is hard to imagine another crop where the cost of mis-attention and poor incentives are higher—as noted above long ago by Adam Smith. Any use of (short-term) cash rent contracts in the leasing of vineyard land would adversely affect the longevity of the vines.

Crop sharing also has substantial transaction costs. As noted, grapes are highly sensitive to the quality of labor effort applied during the growing season. When crops are shared, the viticulturist has an incentive to lower his quality and quantity of labor input, including the maintenance of the vines. There also is the potential for grape theft. Grapes are small and vary in quality across the entire crop. Given their high value, a farmer working on a share contract would have a strong incentive to collect those grapes of high quality for himself and leave the poorer grapes for the landowner.

With both cash rent or crop-share contracts in there remain are potentially large transaction costs. These costs include the resource costs and deadweight losses arising from measuring the timeliness and quality of farmer effort and the hidden land attributes. These costs also include the resource costs and deadweight losses arising because Nature contributes to variation in the volume and quality of the harvest. Given that vineyards are subject to so many types of transaction cost problems, it is not surprising that contracting over the vineyard stage of production was rare historically and today.[12] Vineyards are mostly operated by owner-operated family farms.

Interestingly, on these small family run vineyards, the use of wage labor, especially during harvest, is common. Wage workers are paid by time and have an incentive to slow down and work with reduced efforts. Wage labor is used for simple tasks where output is highly correlated with time and effort reasonably easy to monitor. These tasks bear little in common with the viticulture tasks of the owner. During harvest, the use of wage labor for high-quality grapes has two major benefits. First, workers who slow down and "take their time" are not "dirty pickers" who pick just the low-hanging visible fruit. The slow wage picker is more likely to pick all of the grapes on the vine. Second, the wage picker has no incentive to mishandle and bruise the fruit out of haste. Thus, as grape quality increases, more harvest workers on the vineyard are used and paid by the hour.

16.4.2   Vineyard Size and Grape Quality

In almost every discussion of wine-growing regions, one relationship stands out: high-quality grapes tend to be grown on small vineyards. The chapters in this volume find this relationship as well, although Chile (Mora this volume) seems to be an exception. In his discussion of the American wine industry, Thornton observes:

> Large wine-grape growers tend to specialize in producing low-quality grapes for bulk commodity wines, while smaller vineyards often concentrate on growing higher-quality grapes for premium and luxury wines. (p. 61, 2013)

Allen and Lueck note that the size and organization of the farm is determined by some fundamental trade-offs. On the one hand, the random role of Nature raises the costs of monitoring and measuring such inputs as labor effort, land use, and capital exploitation—leading to small firms controlled by a single residual claimant. In addition, the predictable seasonal elements of agriculture often prevent any gains from specialization found in large-scale operations—

---

[12] Carmona and Simpson (2012), mostly relying on our theory laid out in *The Nature of the Farm*, do an excellent job in describing the problem of underreporting grape quantity and quality and use this as a base for explaining why sharecropping was so little used historically. They also go into considerable detail in terms of how contracts were modified away from the standard simple share contracts to accommodate the special circumstances of grapes.

again, leading to small firms. When a farmer has to change tasks every few weeks due to the changing seasons that drive the biological aspects of production, there is little point in specializing in any given task. Large roles of Nature, on both the random and seasonal dimensions, encourage small family farms. On the other hand, whenever Nature can be removed from production, then some type of larger firm often emerges. When random elements are eliminated, then contracting over labor, land, and other inputs becomes routine. When the seasonal elements of production are reduced or eliminated, then larger scales of operation are common with corporate structures.

Consider the facts noted above in the production of high-quality grapes. These grapes tend to be produced on steep hillsides where machinery has a difficult time operating. They are produced in regions that rely on natural weather patterns and not irrigation.[13] They rely on hand pruning, thinning, and picking. Each stage requires care and attention which are difficult to monitor.[14] Under such circumstances, the moral hazard problems are so great, and the gains from specialization of a given task are so small that each farm is limited by the capabilities of a single residual claimant. High-quality vineyards will be small farms operated mostly by one family.

In most wine regions, there are a small number of vineyards that make up large fractions of the total acreage used and tonnage produced. For example, in California these vineyards tend to be located in the central valley where the land is flat, the vines irrigated, and the pruning and picking are mostly done by machine.[15] The flat land allows for the use of machines and for certain types of irrigation, both of which reduce the role of Nature and allow for large numbers of wage employees to be used. Since wage employees cannot be expected to take extreme care of the grapes, these large vineyards tend to produce a lower-quality, lower-variance grape. Taken together, the reduced measurement costs allow corporate structures to exist, with wage labor and larger plantation-style organization.

---

[13] Indeed, in France the high-quality grapes are not allowed (by law) to be irrigated, (see Ugaglia, Cardebat, and Jiao, this volume). Irrigation reduces variance in both yields and quality. Hence, other things equal, increased irrigation should also be correlated with vertically integrated wineries and vineyards.

[14] In the chapter on Chinese wines (this volume), Jiao and Ouyang note that in the Ningxia region of China the climate is such that the high-quality vines must be covered each winter to prevent damage from the cold.

[15] Lapsley, Alston, and Sambucci (this volume). They also note that in the US just three firms (Gallo, Wine Group, and Constellation) produce or import 50% of wines consumed. The 20 largest firms in the US have a market share of 90%, dominated by the low-priced segment of the market (Thornton, pp. 2–3, 2013). Albisu et al., in this volume, note that in Spain 84% of wineries are small, with less than ten workers, while four large firms do the bulk of exporting, most of which is considered low-quality cheap wine.

16.4.3 The Evolution of the Winery

The second phase of wine production involves the winery, the place where the harvested grapes are converted into wine. Historically the winery was also a family run affair (indeed, it was the same family) with no contracting.[16] The Allen and Lueck framework provides an explanation for this historical vertical integration. Prior to the mid-nineteenth century, the role of Nature in the fermentation process was enormous and mostly misunderstood by those in the industry. The grapes were perishable and fermentation starts almost immediately after harvest, and any delays in production could mean a vast reduction in wine quality.[17] During this era, wine making was *by guess and by God*, depending on Nature and ill-defined skills associated with experience and personalized knowledge.

As noted above, a series of innovations throughout the nineteenth century, including increased understanding of the biochemistry of fermentation, allowed for better control and actual measurement over the fermentation process. The result was a great reduction in the role of Nature in the winery. What had at one time been a mysterious process became understood and controllable. At the same time, the efficient size of a modern winery increased, both in terms of physical and human capital. This increased fixed physical and human capital resulted in falling average costs. Large wineries were able to exploit the economies using hired wage labor, which could be more cheaply monitored given the reduced role of Nature. Even in the sensitive areas of blending and timing, low monitoring costs allowed for high-quality wage labor to be engaged.

Beginning in the mid-nineteenth century and carrying on for the next 100 years, wineries vertically *disintegrated* with vineyards.[18] Once produced, high-quality grapes could be measured (unlike the inputs used to produce them), and so it was possible for vineyards to supply wineries with grapes—especially for medium- to low-quality grapes. As a result, large wineries are

---

[16] Fernandez-Olmos et al. (2008) explain this by focusing on the asset specificity of grapes and vines. Presumably either side of the vineyard/winery transaction could conceivably hold the other side hostage given the importance of asset and timing specificity. However, given the repeated nature of wine production, the importance of reputation, and the ease of the law in regulating such behavior, this seems an unimportant transaction cost source to explain the vertical integration. It also seems unable to explain the vertical disintegration we explain below.

[17] Franken and Bacon (p. 107, 2014).

[18] Knox (1998) argues that in Europe it was the rise of wine cooperatives that separated the vineyard from the winery to increase marketing and transfer rents. This fails to explain why the separation took place in other parts of the world where contracts between vineyards and wineries were used instead of cooperatives. Simpson (pp. 1–2, 2009) has a discussion of the relationship between family vineyards and cooperative wineries in Europe.

able to contract with many small vineyards.[19] In Europe, cooperatives formed at the winery level, while in North America corporate wineries contracted with the vineyards, but the fundamental forces were the same in both cases.[20]

Interestingly, the emergence of high-end "boutique" wines over the past 30 years has seen a move toward vineyard and winery reintegration in this sector.[21] These wineries develop a reputation for a very specific, complex wine, and often this results from the reintroduction of Nature into the process. For example, these wineries often use the natural yeasts found on the grapes, rather than use cultured yeast; they often hand-select grapes for a specific acid/sugar/taste balance.[22] The reintroduction of Nature into the wine-making stage and the requirement for grapes with potentially difficult-to-measure qualities means that the transaction costs of market relations between the vineyard and the winery are higher. Not surprisingly then, these boutique firms reintegrate back to have the vineyard and winery within one firm under the control of a single residual claimant.

16.5   Conclusion

The organization of vineyards and wineries can understood using the transaction costs framework of Allen and Lueck (2002).[23] These transaction costs arise when individual farmers and capitalists to alter their inputs in ways that enhance their own wealth at the expense of each other. In agriculture, the variability of Nature introduces random elements into production and prevents the parties from deducing the inputs of others and the seasonal aspects of Nature that limit the ability to exploit gains from specialization.

---

[19] Thornton (p. 66, 2013) notes that 90% of California grapes are sold by contract to wineries.

[20] Dramatic reductions in transportation costs have allowed the expansion in world trade, but it is not clear how this change has effected wine and vineyard organization. Unsurprisingly, it has increased the size of the industry.

[21] Even in China, where the wine industry is the youngest, the best wines have integrated vineyards and wineries. Jiao and Ouyang state:

When it comes to the elite Chinese wineries, the wineries in Ningxia are best representatives. All wines are produced by the grapes cultivated in their own vine-yards with certain requirements in quality thus to reflect of its origin. [this volume]

[22] Robinson (p. 779, 2006).

[23] Simpson (2011) examines related issues, stressing path dependence, and political economy forces.

Although most of the chapters in this volume are concerned with the fundamentals of quantity and price of wines around the world, each chapter contains some information on the organization of the wine industry. We have used these studies to examine three common features of wine production around the world: the limited role of contracting, the negative correlation of vineyard size with grape quality, and the general separation of vineyards from wineries over the past 150 years. In each case the observed behavior is well explained by an understanding of the transaction costs involved, and a recognition that the organization of the industry results from an attempt to mitigate these transaction costs.

References

Allen, Douglas. 1991. What are transaction costs? *Research in Law and Economics* 14 (Fall): 1–18.

Allen, Douglas, and Dean Lueck. 2002. *The nature of the farm: Contracts, uncertainty, and organization.* Cambridge: MIT Press.

Barzel, Yoram. 1982. Measurement costs and the organization of markets. *Journal of Law and Economics* 25 (1): 27–48.

Carmona, Juan, and James Simpson. 2012. Explaining contract choice: Vertical coordination, sharecropping, and wine in Europe, 1850–1950. *Economic History Review* 65 (3): 887–909.

Fernandez-Olmos, M., J. Rosell-Martìnez, and M. Espitia-Escuer. 2008. Quality and governance mode choice: A transaction cost approach to the wine industry. *Research in Agricultural & Applied Economics* 1–6.

Franken, J., and K. Bacon. 2014. Organizational structure and operation of the Illinois wine industry. *Agricultural and Resource Economics Review* 43: 104–124.

Goodhue, Rachel, Hyunok Lee DaleHeien, and Daniel Sumner. 2003. Contracts and quality in the California Winegrape industry. *Review of Industrial Organization* 23: 267–282.

Knox, Trevor. 1998. *Organization change and vinification cooperatives in France's Midi.* Working paper 7-1, University of Connecticut.

Robinson, J., ed. 2006. *The Oxford companion to wine.* 3rd ed. Oxford: Oxford University Press.

Simpson, James 2009. *Old world versus new world: The origins of organizational diversity in the international wine industry, 1850–1914.* Working papers in economic history, 09–01, Universidad Carlos III de Madrid.

———. 2011. *Creating wine: The emergence of a world industry, 1840–1914.* Princeton: Princeton University Press.

Thornton, James. 2013. *American wine economics.* Berkeley: University of California Press.

Umbeck, John. 1977. A theory of contract choice and the California Gold Rush. *Journal of Law and Economics* 20 (2): 421–437.

17

Wine Co-operatives and Territorial Anchoring

Marie-Claude Bélis-Bergouignan and Nathalie Corade

17.1 Introduction

Since the beginning of the 2000s, the French wine sector has been facing a brutal crisis, in sharp contrast to the euphoria of the 1990s. The nature of its problems is twofold as the underlying fall in French domestic demand, whose fragility has been observed near unanimously, is coupled with a decline in external markets, this within a context of global market oversupply. Producers, unions or inter-branch organizations have reacted[1] and have begun to develop a response. Generally speaking it involves two strategic orientations focused on future penetration of external markets: total or partial reorganization of production models directed simultaneously toward rejuvenating supply and improving attractiveness via efforts on quality and marketing and incitement from regulatory and administrative bodies to increase groupings in production areas and institutional territories of reference, in other words the AOC (Appellation d'Origine Contrôlée).

---

[1] Reports from Berthomeau (2001), César (2002) and Pomel (2006).

M.-C. Bélis-Bergouignan (✉)
Bordeaux University, Bordeaux, France

N. Corade
Bordeaux Sciences Agro, Gradignan, France
e-mail: nathalie.corade@agro-bordeaux.fr

© The Author(s) 2019
A. Alonso Ugaglia et al. (eds.), *The Palgrave Handbook of Wine Industry Economics*,
https://doi.org/10.1007/978-3-319-98633-3_17

Table 17.1 Co-operative mergers (1968–2006)

	No. of mergers	No. of co-operatives involved	Names of co-operatives involved
1968	2	4	Bourg and Tauriac
			Vic Bilh and Madiran
1989	1	5	Labatut + Orthevielle + Pouillon + St-Cricq + Mugron
1990	1	2	Bergerac and Le Fleix
1992	1	2	Montravel and Sigoulès
1996	1	2	Gensac and Graves de Vayres
1998	2	4	Landerrouat and Duras
			Francs and Gardegan and Tourtirac
2000	1	2	Mugron and Geaune
2001	1	2	Gan and Bellocq
2002	2	6	Vertheuil and St-Estèphe
			Prignac, Queyrac, Begadan and Unimédoc
2004–2005	4	10	Cocumont and Beaupuy
			Carsac-de-Gurson and St Vivien
			Ordonnac and Unimédoc
			Anglade, Générac, St Gervais and Marcillac
2006	1	2	Landerrouat/Duras and Cazaugitat

Co-operatives are not exempt from these trends with the recent Pomel report (2006, p. 23) highlighting the need for mergers. These recommendations reflect a process which has long been observable. Indeed, in Aquitaine where the wine co-operative, an important element at the "heart of the wine sphere" (Doucet 2002), represents 45% of farms and 28% of volume produced; grouping processes (most of which are mergers) have already started and their number has increased over the last decade (Table 17.1). Thus, of the 17 mergers carried out since 1968, 9 have been completed since 2000: they have involved 22 co-operatives, reducing the total number from 77 in the 1990s to 64 in 2006.

As they have triggered a noticeable change in the co-operative system, these mergers are frequently analyzed as the destructive vector in their constitutive territorial attachment (Chiffoleau et al. 2005). Undeniably, wine co-operatives are deeply rooted in their territory due to both their locally based mutual governance and their products' characteristics. It is also undeniable that territorial attachment can represent a constraint on their global integration. We believe that this analysis is questionable because the opposition between territorial attachment and a globally oriented merger strategy is excessive. A priori, the logic behind merger processes involves loosening rather than transcending a co-operative's territorial constraints. This problem has influenced our analysis of merger processes in which Aquitaine wine co-operatives have been actively involved.[2]

We have therefore conducted a series of semi-directive interviews with managers of organizations who have participated in grouping operations, most of which being mergers carried out from the 1990s onward in the Gironde (33) and Dordogne (24) departments, in other words 7 of the 11 mergers completed between 1990 and 2006[3] as well as a grouping in the form of a commercial union.[4]

These thorough interviews, carried out with managers of merged organizations, were built around an analytical framework designed to collect the following information, notably as regards the loosening of the territorial constraint: the history of the merger and/or the grouping; the objectives governing its implementation; the view of the players concerning the ineluctability of merger processes in the Aquitaine wine-growing region; the methods used in these processes; the real effects, that is to say the results in economic, structural and even human terms and the interviewed players' evaluation of these real effects compared to those expected; the driving elements as well as those that hinder the success of these processes.

Based on the analysis of these answers, the present article aims to show that while playing on global dimensions linked to the need to adapt to market conditions, and despite the prevailing opinions of the subject, these mergers are neither motived by, nor respond to, the need to break free from a founding territorial attachment. With reference to the proximity economy, we will show that even if it generates obstacles to global adaptation, this need is not excluded from merger processes which do not omit territorial links. Indeed, these processes represent specific coordination mechanisms which, through new forms of expression, bring together spatial proximity with other forms of non-spatial proximity (Pecqueur and Zimmermann 2004).

---

[2] This work was carried out with the financial participation of the Aquitaine region within the framework of research projects attached to the Institut des Sciences de la Vigne et du Vin de Bordeaux.

[3] The studies, having been carried out in January 2006, with the latest merger to date, between the co-operatives of Landerrouat/Durasand of Cazaugitat, having taken place in March 2006, we did not study it as such but we were informed of the project by the Landerrouat Director, who explained the reasons for its creation and its future methods.

[4] Among the seven mergers studied, there is one which concerns two co-operatives initially belonging to the same commercial union and whose manager is also director of the commercial union. This particular case provided the opportunity, at the same time, to study the grouping that union toward co-operative constitutes.

Thus, *geographical proximity*, which focuses classically on the spatial distance separating economic players, prevails, a priori, in the co-operative merger operations we have observed. But it is not necessarily an efficient support for coordination between these merged co-operatives. The groupings we have seen are based upon different forms of logic to those of *organized proximity*, which Rallet and Torre (2004) express in terms of proximity of similarity and proximity of belonging. First of all, proximity of similarity governs groupings between co-operatives.[5] Nevertheless, the latter have neither identical interests, despite possessing objectives which have become common ones, nor the same working rules. Proximity of belonging, a supplementary dimension to organized proximity, therefore has to take over in order to complete the merger process. With reference to the fact that interactions between the members of the same organization are facilitated by their recourse to the same rules, we can, via the creation of new co-operative rules in the merged structures, highlight the re-dimensioning of the territorial scale of co-operative action. The article therefore shows that if co-operative mergers represent ways to loosen them from territorial constraints (1), they trigger a re-dimensioning of the territorial scale of co-operative action (2).

17.2 The Merger: The Favored Way to Loosen Territorial Constraint

The merger, whether it be a merger-acquisition or a pure merger,[6] is the operation by which two or more companies bring their assets and liabilities together to create a new structure with the commitment of each party being irreversible, contrary to that which characterizes a simple strategic alliance. In Aquitaine, more than 60 years after their creation and following a path marked by the creation of commercial unions or alliances—frequently leading to a later merger—mergers are, to the detriment of alliances, the favored response of co-operatives to the shocks generated by the recent globalization of the wine market. These mergers can be interpreted as the co-operative's way to loosen its territorial attachment, which is seen as a constraint in the global context of the sector where organizations with less dependency on a territorial logic are shown to be efficient.

[5] The logic of similarity refers to the fact that the players share the same representation system, the same beliefs and the same knowledge, independently of their affiliation to a specific organization.
[6] In the last case, the two organizations disappear to rebuild a new one.

17.2.1   From Crisis Diagnosis to Spatial Lock-In

A priori, we can only be struck by the similarity of situation which led to the creation of wine co-operatives in Aquitaine in the 1930s and their mergers in recent years. The crisis is the common denominator of both movements. Thus, wine co-operatives were created to respond to a double problem: a technical problem since wine-making requires heavy investment (in winery equipment) and a capacity to innovate in the technological and oenological fields and a commercial problem because with the slowdown in sales opportunities and overproduction, concentrating the supply is a means to increase both their bargaining power and their ability to adapt and innovate (Hinnewinkle and Roudié 2001).

Moreover, the crisis, as an upheaval in market conditions and a danger to their existence, seems as accurate a description of the wine-making situation in the 1930s as in the 2000s. The need to unite seems to have been simply reactivated by the current context. This substantiates the idea put forward by Draperi (Draperi and Touzard 2003, p. 77) that "the market place is central to explaining changes in co-operatives". Subsequently nevertheless, the comparison made between these two movements suggests the existence of fundamental differences, with globalization leading toward market re-dimensioning strategies linked to the need for diversification and greater supply flexibility. Thus, a merger expresses less the need to lighten the costs uniting geographically close entities and more that of reaching a "critical" size in order to position one's product on a global market and break free from a territorial constraint which hinders competitive efficiency.

17.2.1.1   Responding to New Market Configurations

The current wine crisis originates in the redefinition of the rules governing competition. Formerly, the competitiveness of French wines, and notably those with an AOC, suffered little on world markets, but now it is being challenged by the success of wines coming from traditionally non-producing countries. These so-called New World countries or new producing countries (Australia, South Africa, United States, Chile, New Zealand) have doubled both their production between 1990 and 2000 and their exports between 1980 and 2000. During the same time period, traditional producer countries have only seen their exports rise by 20%. If, as regards world exports, Europe and countries such as France and Italy have confirmed their domination, this is nevertheless being eroded little by little by countries on the American continent and countries such as South Africa and Australia (Onivins 2002).[7]

As these new countries originally consumed small quantities of wine, they directed their strategies toward the world market from the outset. As a result, the latter, already highly segmented, underwent massive repositioning toward mid-market and upmarket segments, the traditional ones occupied by French production and in particular production in Aquitaine which is 98% based on AOC products. For the last 20 years, these New World countries have combined this market positioning with a downstream strategy which is deliberately directed toward the consumer and in particular toward the world consumer. This strategy is based upon differentiation via private commercial brands supported either by worldwide groups with diversified product ranges (Diageo, LVMH, etc.) or by national groups with an international dimension concentrating almost exclusively on wine (Gallo, Southcorp, Mondavi, etc.) (D'hauteville et al. 2004). The product is not defined according to *terroir* but by brand and grape variety. Henceforth, the vineyard structuring associated with these products is different to that found in AOC systems which is generally more fragmented, more piecemeal and less integrated (D'hauteville et al. 2005; Garcia-Parpet 2001). Effectively, brand promotion requires significantly higher financial resources.

The changes in supply resulting from the rise of these new producing countries is taking place in a context of stagnant world consumption due to the combined effect of a drop in consumption in the traditional producing countries (e.g., French consumption fell from 160 liters/year/person to 56 between 1960 and now) and an increase in other parts of the world. This double phenomenon has created innovation opportunities in the wine field as a response to consumers with little drinking experience (in the countries where consumption is increasing). Secondly, consumption habits have changed in the traditional countries with wine evolving from having a nutritional status to being a leisure product. These innovations have been bolstered by an absence of rules (outside those of the OIV[8]) managing production modes equivalent to those prevailing in the AOC system.

The study we have carried out confirms that the merger of wine cooperatives is perceived both by institutional actors as an ineluctable process

---

[7] "The market share in volume of New World countries in trade exchanges increased from 4% in 1990 to 14% in 1997 and 19% in 2001."

[8] OIV: Organisation Internationale de la Vigne et du vin, in charge of defining international norms in order to protect producers and consumers.

(Pomel 2006), certainly in order to survive but, above all, to respond to the demands, defined as such, of the world wine market.

17.2.1.2 Territorial Attachment as a Spatial Lock-In Factor

The competition exerted by brand strategies on *terroir* strategies undermines the productive organizations supporting the latter. Henceforth, the close link with the territory induced both by the co-operative organization and the belonging to an AOC is criticized when it is considered as a limiting factor to the competitive efficiency of these organizations.

This means the near-exclusive affiliation of Aquitaine's production to AOC could limit its capacity to adapt to the changing consumer demands. Indeed, a *terroir* strategy (Rastouin and Vissac-Charles 1999) is distinct from brand differentiation initiatives by its reliance on the value it gives to a specific resource, that is to say a comparative advantage "naturally" attached to a given territory (production methods inherited from tradition, the intrinsic characteristics of a territory, know-how, etc.). By making exclusive reference to specific territorial resources, AOC wine production systems generate a specific asset (Colletis and Pecqueur 2004)[9]: the *terroir* becomes the basis of a market strategy.

For their part, brand strategies applied in the wine sector are based upon a generic asset: the grape variety, whose characteristic is not to be attached to a place or to a territory, while not being associated with a localized or localizable production method either. This is effectively an asset which is easily transferable.[10] On the contrary, strategies linked to the AOC base their effectiveness upon strong territorial attachment. Thus, for Benkala and Boutonnet (2004), "AOC strategies, by basing product positioning on a specific territorialized asset, thereby resist standardization and homogenization, even production relocation" (p. 1).

From an economic perspective, associating territorial attachment with AOC affiliation has many disadvantages. Firstly, it generates diversity and heterogeneity in the same time space and between different temporalities. An AOC product only possesses the characteristics attributed to it by the *terroir* at instant *t*, and in contrast to a grape variety or brand product, its room for

---

[9] According to Colletis and Pecqueur (2004, p. 4): "By asset we mean factors 'in activity', whilst by resources it is a question of factors to exploit, organise or still to be revealed."

[10] "A generic factor is independent of the 'spirit of the place' where it is produced" (Colletis and Pecqueur 2004, p. 4).

maneuver concerning these characteristics is rather limited as the AOC strictly defines production rules. Moreover, the AOC limits productive capacities since production quantity is limited through defined maximum yields per hectare and the demarcation of vine-planted surface areas. This hinders internal growth strategies based upon extending wine plantations.[11]

Secondly, the co-operative structure itself limits growth strategies. Territorial division which defines the territorial area on which the co-operative can draw its resources (surfaces) limits the extension capacity of the wine-growing area due to two phenomena: the non-elasticity of the surface area of a given territory and the competition between several co-operatives on the same territorial area. Indeed, in areas featuring a high level of wine-making activity, which is the case of the Gironde, for example, it is not unusual for the same space to be shared by several co-operatives. Moreover, they often have to face competition from private cellars or even great chateaux with well-established reputations. Added to this are the classical risks incurred by co-operatives, that of the departure of members tempted to go it alone as this decision is frequently seen as more rewarding and more closely associated with value.

Thus, the low or even inexistent capacity to increase yields, to increase the number of members and to develop production are all hindrances to the implementation of growth strategies. As regards the co-operatives we studied, before their merger, most experienced a significant loss of members (sometimes as high as 20%) in a context of near-stagnation of wine-growing surface area and production volume. The reduction in the number of members, the consequence of both the difficulties encountered and the attempt to overcome them by reducing the productive structure, revealed their inadequacies in the new demand context.

These co-operatives have therefore suffered the same classical fate as agricultural activities in general and *terroir* activities in particular, of detrimental links to the land and to a geographical origin. Henceforth, their territorial attachment has turned into a confinement close to genuine spatial lock-in (Rallet and Torre 2004). With Boschma (2005), we can note that this lock-in is not only cognitive, since access to new markets involves acquiring previously unknown skills and aptitudes, but also organizational ones since going beyond it implies a transformation of the co-operative organization. Nevertheless, it does not seem that this situation is irretrievable as mergers can potentially help to overcome it. The interviews carried out with the managers of merged organizations support the idea that in a first case, mergers are a means to release the spatial lock-in, at least partially. In particular, this is

---

[11] We know of current thinking (2006) concerning merger projects in the l'Entre-Deux-Mers region.

because they can increase the scale of the partnership networks, be they client and distribution networks or ones with suppliers.

17.2.2   Matching the Market, the Mergers' Primary Objective

If groupings are not a new phenomenon in the world of co-operatives, it seems nevertheless that the form (of a merger) these groupings have taken these last few years reflects a stronger will to break free from territorial constraint. Indeed, excepting the mergers carried out in 1968, explained in essence by the wish not to segment a wine-growing heritage, the wave of more recent mergers, completed since the 1990s, is a response to a different logic: that of the market's re-dimensioning.

17.2.2.1   From a Grouping to a Merger: From Connective Forms of Logic to Additive Ones

In Aquitaine, the grouping of wine co-operatives is recurrent. From the years 1950–1960 onward, they have been based upon commercial unions for the most part and packing unions for others. In this way, we have seen the creation of:

- In 1966, UNIMÉDOC, the commercial union of co-operatives from the Médoc area, today merged with these same co-operatives.
- In 1967, PRODIFFU, created in the form of a SICA (Société d'Intérêt Coopératif Agricole, French for collective interest agricultural society) and transformed into a co-operative union in 1984. It sells bottled wine made by five cellars which are its members.
- In 1974, UNIVITIS, created in the form of a SICA and transformed into a co-operative union ten years later, today grouping four co-operatives focused on selling bulk and bottled wine.
- In 2004, Bergerac Vins, the most recent organization, bringing together two co-operatives and a union selling bulk wine.

Along with these unions, other forms of commercial grouping have appeared. In 1959, for example, SOVICOP, an open joint stock company, was formed by the grouping of seven co-operatives (four in Dordogne and three in Gironde). Today it sells 250,000 hl of bulk or bottled wine, the different appellations produced by 24 co-operatives in Gironde, Dordogne and Lot-et-

Garonne, to *négociants*, large-scale retailers and specialized wine shops both in France and for export. Similarly, there is PRODUCTA, created in 1949 as a public limited company by three co-operatives. Other wine co-operative unions exist for packing: UNIDOR in the Bergerac area which was created in 1961 and l'Union Saint-Vincent in 1981 in the Entre-Deux-Mers region.

The development of commercial unions has led to a diversification of the commercial circuits used by co-operatives in Aquitaine (Couret 1999). In Gironde and in Dordogne, which geographically cover the co-operatives we have studied, French *négociants* represent 49.8% of sales outlets, of which 11.7% are for export, 17.8% for unions, 9% for individuals, 7.1% for large- and medium-scale retailing and 4% for wholesalers. This diversification alone does not respond to what is currently at stake: on one hand because it does not grant enough room for maneuver or bargaining power to the co-operatives regarding the networks on which they depend, especially with *négociants* and large retailers, and on the other hand because it does not provide access to the building of common mechanisms which would enable them to break free from spatial, cognitive and organizational lock-ins.

Thus the process in current use is very different because groupings, especially commercial ones, have been substituted by the most extreme form of alliance: a merger. This movement, for which we can anticipate an extension, therefore no longer involves a simple connective logic of interfirm relations but a real additive logic which is irreversible and which implies a heavy commitment from the partners (Douard and Heitz 2003) enabling them to make decisive steps forward in this direction. The interviews conducted with the co-operative managers who have carried out these restructuring processes help us appreciate the stakes and the perspectives.

17.2.2.2 Mergers: Between Defensive Strategies and Offensive Ones

The answers to the first three questions on our interview grid indicate that the groupings, and more precisely the mergers, are effectively perceived as means to eliminate the territorial constraint described above—at least partially. Indeed, thanks to the first question, we can identify the initial causes which led to the merger. By grouping these causes, linked to the history of the organizations concerned and of the objectives finally put forward at the time of the merger (question 2), we can show that today, mergers have become the favored route (question 3) to break free from territorial constraint, hindering co-operative development (Table 17.2).

Table 17.2 Mergers' initial causes and final objectives (number of answers to these items/number of co-operatives studied)

Merger cause	Merger type	Objectives
Difficulties to sell: 7/7 Difficulties linked to quality and technical problems: 4/7 Difficulties linked directly to volumes (insufficient size to sell well on markets): 2/7 Difficulties linked to the absence of reputation: 1/7	Defensive: due to the demand of structure(s) in difficulty, 4/7 Offensive: initiated by a structure anticipating difficulties to come, 1/7 Mixed: meeting between structures having difficulties and those anticipating future difficulties, 2/7	Save a co-operative: 5/7 Increase volumes to tackle large- and medium-scale retailers or penetrate the international market: 3/7 Develop the bottled-wine market: 3/7 Widen the range with the extension to new AOCs: 2/7 Rationalize the link between production site/product: 1/7 Decrease the number of competitors: 3/7 Reach a sufficient size to develop quality and integrate traceability: 2/7

The mergers we studied are mostly justified by the will to "save" an organization in difficulty or in need of support. The current context is an important lever in the decision to implement these mergers. Indeed, it forces the organizations to consider productive and commercial strategies with the potential to stand together in the face of current market conditions. Thus, it is always the emergence of a problem which leads to the thinking process and then to the triggering of the merger process, with the "crisis" making the idea of a merger more obvious and more immediate.

If the notion of crisis implies a difficult situation, be it experienced or anticipated, it is noticeable that all the cases we studied came under this logic. Even when the merger appears as more "natural", like in those cases between commercial unions and their affiliated co-operatives, it is the "crisis" which triggers the "enactment".

Henceforth, mergers or groupings appear as survival operations where "ill" organizations lead "healthy" ones to consider a merger. Indeed, we have only found one example of a co-operative seeking a merger partner before a co-operative in difficulty came to see it first. The result of this is a majority of merger-acquisitions, even if most of the production sites are preserved.

In all circumstances, the economic difficulties are defined as difficulties to sell: they are directly or indirectly related to problems of size and/or production volumes. Indeed the commercial problems are generally associated with difficulties to improve the quality of products, which translates either into items unsold or sold at very low prices or low bargaining power on the market linked to weak negotiable volumes, themselves leading to low valuation of the products. Mergers are therefore considered as a means to "bypass" the obstacle of size which was generated in part by territorial constraint.

Thus the examples studied show that mergers are carried out to rationalize the organization of the co-operative fabric rather than to go on the offensive. Notwithstanding, these mergers are an opportunity to define or redefine strategic choices, notably for the "acquiring" organizations. Thus, if the principal causes of mergers stem from a crisis situation, one that needs to be addressed or anticipated, little by little, during the merger process, they transform into more offensive strategic objectives.

Equally, the merger (or the grouping) is always justified by the will, experienced as a necessity, to reach a size considered more satisfactory to be "better" from a commercial point of view. In fact, it ends up being seen as a genuine opportunity to commit to more offensive commercial strategies. It is therefore less a question of achieving internal economies of scale in the strict sense than reaching a "critical" size enabling the acquiring companies to embark upon actions which they would never have been able to perform alone.

On this point, the co-operatives' managers are unanimous: a merger does not generate economies of scale per se. On the contrary, it first of all feeds into the development of new functions and new actions, and even when redeployments of activities are put into place, this implies extra costs. However, after a while, the learning effects can lead to co-operatives benefitting from economies of scale. A priori, these propositions are confirmed in the cases we analyzed by the improvement of merged co-operatives' performances in terms of volumes and turnover. The recovery in productive performances, whether it be attributable to the mergers we studied or also the result of processes put in place before the merger, still leaves strong disparities between merged co-operatives, either in terms of member numbers (an order of 1–5), areas cultivated (of 1–13), in crop volumes (1–11) or turnover (1–18).[12]

Increase in volumes and rationalization of the co-operative organization, in particular regarding the link between production site and product, enabling diversification, eventual broadening of the product range, development of sales in bottles and development of quality are therefore the key words of the mergers we observed in Aquitaine. Thus, according to Christensen et al.

---

[12] The qualitative approach carried out here does not allow us to go beyond the highlighting of stylized effects that a later quantitative approach should lend support to.

(2002), *in fine*, merger strategies in Aquitaine are less about the search for economies of scale and to a greater extent concern the will to adapt to market conditions which are sometimes volatile and within which New World producers have triggered genuine ground-changing innovation.[13]

For this reason, reaching a "critical" size is considered as a means to grow by uniting the co-operatives' bargaining power against large retailers whom they now wish to deal with directly. These strategies to increase size very often involve the association of a large organization with one (or many) much smaller ones. Increase in size is therefore not exclusive of composition effects. The merger seemingly grants leadership to the largest organization, probably considered as the best placed to energize the others without incurring the risk of power struggles which are too symmetrical and therefore destabilizing for the merged structure.

The elimination of competitors and the anticipation of an improvement in the competitive position are also arguments put forward in favor of a merger, with the expected beneficial results being seen ex post in reality. De facto, a merger is preferred to an alliance or a commercial union because by eliminating structures, it is reputed to reduce the level of competition between co-operatives, which, a priori, according to merger managers, a simple commercial union cannot achieve. From this point of view, competition on the wine market and competition for control of resources are linked. Indeed, a merger is a means to reach these objectives by building upon a tighter control of the vineyard, tipping the balance on whether to merge or not in its favor. Obviously, it cannot guarantee there will be no competition at all as co-operatives must still compete with independent organizations. However, it does minimize competition between co-operatives which is not the case of a commercial union since the latter brings together entities which remain autonomous. Thus, accessing a broader market or at least being better armed to compete in a more aggressive market is seen as the major stakes for mergers.

Moreover, as major problems in co-operatives stem from their size which is considered too small, a merger is the means to preserve sufficiently high

---

[13] A groundbreaking innovation puts a product onto the market which can be seen as intrinsically "less good" than certain products dominating the market at present. Therefore, for this reason, it cannot be sold to the usual consumers. But it is simpler and more approachable and therefore establishes itself in a part of the market which, up to then, did not reveal demand. Subsequently, the product improves to overlap the preoccupations of the more demanding segments of the market and by doing so, helps to remodel the whole market, thereby triggering an upheaval in it.

volumes in order to have the resources to carry out a number of actions without which it would now be difficult to be well positioned on the market and, at a minimum, maintain the bargaining power to sell products at a reasonable price. A merger is also associated with a search for resources to fight back against new, aggressive, commercial strategies. Indeed, co-operatives often do not possess the financial resources to invest in quality, commercial communication and promotion. By merging, they can be more efficient in this field than by a simple gathering of means through a strategic alliance.

A merger is therefore considered as a way to compensate for the obstacle of spatial lock-in. As it is irreversible compared to the connective logic of the commercial-alliance type, by gathering agents with potentially different interests under a single structure, it minimizes, a priori, problems of opportunism induced by a simple alliance. Nevertheless, certain risks remain as mergers between co-operatives or, otherwise, lead to "organizational upheavals" (Samuel 2003).

Thus, in a first approach, we can bear witness to the role of territorial constraint in the decision to merge. As it limits the growth and development potential of co-operatives' activities in a context where size effects are crucial, the territorial link forces organizations to go beyond an alliance logic and seek a merger. This explains the unanimity of merged organizations' managers we interviewed regarding this ineluctability of the processes. Two of the managers, even if they represent co-operatives positioned on very different products, went as far as to say that mergers represent "the future in the wine-co-operative world". A more refined analysis shows that this loosening does not rhyme with a disappearance of the territorial constraint: in reality, it is more a question of a re-dimensioning of the territorial scale of a co-operative's action.

17.3   Dimensioning the Territorial Scale of the Co-operative Action

Mergers are co-operatives' favored way to recover room for maneuver hindered by territorial constraint. However, in spite of the fact that they are justified by the will to break free of this constraint, the underlying logic reaffirms their attachment to the territory. The re-dimensioning of the territorial scale of the co-operative action is seen first of all in the complementarity of geographical and organized proximities during the choice of the right partner to merge with. This re-dimensioning is then seen in the efforts engaged by the merged co-operative to maintain and rebuild itself as a territorialized unit.

17.3.1 Complementarity of Geographical and Organized Proximities in the Choice of the Merger Partner

On one hand, a priori, geographical proximity intervenes in the choice of the partner chosen to enter a merger with and this helps to maintain the territorial attachment. On the other hand, the mechanisms used to prepare the merger show that organized proximity is an essential complementary determinant in the decision to commit.

17.3.1.1 A Priori, Geographical Proximity Underlies the Choice of the Partner

All cases of the mergers we studied are characterized by a unification of geographically close partners. This particularity stems from the fact that the co-operatives in difficulty who initiate the search for a partner first turn to the nearest co-operative except if there are historical enmities. Two reasons explain this phenomenon. First, geographical proximity is a core element to relations which are sometimes economic, like belonging to the same co-operative union or the exchange of know-how (e.g., the same wine technician working in both co-operatives), but also these relations are informal, linked to a family of neighborly relations between members and, sometimes, between managers. These relations, preexisting the merger, make it "natural" to seek a partner nearby.

Second is the more "economic" reason: geographical proximity reduces potential costs generated by the existence of several delivery and production sites and simplifies relations, notably between members and managers. A merger must minimize extra costs and even deliver economies of scale. Thus, at the outset, the nearest co-operative appears to be the "natural" merger partner de facto. Nevertheless, geographical proximity in the strict sense is not a sufficient condition to unite since many mergers will not take place between "the closest" organizations.

Admittedly, in the Aquitaine vineyards with a low co-operative density (Landes, Pyrénées-Atlantiques), geographical proximity prevails as the factor to choose a partner. In these cases, geographical proximity is the determining element in the merger. In other cases, especially in Gironde and in Dordogne, geographical proximity has played an important role but not a sufficiently important one to explain the mergers. Other factors have come into play in their completion.

Ultimately, we cannot deny that geographical proximity plays an important role since the mergers carried out in recent years fulfill this condition. Nevertheless, distance alone cannot adequately explain these mergers.

17.3.1.2 Proximity of Similarity at the Heart of the Commitment to a Merger Process

The reasons given by the managers to explain the choice of a given merger partner are in reference to the dimensions of organized proximity. The commitment to the merger process is mostly determined by the existence of proximity of similarity between the potential partners. A priori, it comes into play from the moment the merger is envisaged but also during the merger process itself via respective learning phases put in place to guarantee the success of the operation (Table 17.3).

Firstly, in the Aquitaine co-operative context as in the co-operative world in general, mergers take place between co-operatives. They have in common their way of working which characterizes their status: de facto, belonging to the co-operative *milieu* itself constitutes an element of proximity. Thus, at least for the moment, they do not consider merging with non-co-operative organizations. Moreover, with the exception of a merger between a wine co-operative and a co-operative supplying cereal farms, the only mergers completed have been between wine co-operatives.

This last statement is less trivial than it may seem if we consider the heterogeneity of the organizations sharing the co-operative status, whether they

Table 17.3 The determinants of a commitment to merger

The initial partner envisaged becomes the final partner	Geographical proximity influences the choice of partner	The final determinant
Yes: 6/7	Yes = 4/6	Co-operative members of the same commercial union
		Proximity of products: co-operatives making the same AOC
	No = 2/6	Better personal relations than with the nearest co-operative
		Co-operatives members of the same commercial union
No: 1/7	No	Initial partner chosen according to geographical proximity but merger not completed, choice of partner made because of long-standing relations

belong to the same sector or not. In this respect, the exception described above is instructive. Despite a common co-operative culture, the organizations, beyond the fact that they belong to different sectors, had neither the same structures nor the same internal working procedures, which certainly caused difficulties. Thus the merger triggered a cultural transformation since it implied moving from a "family way of working to one whose management methods are inappropriate to the way small wine co-operatives operate".

A contrario, belonging to the same sector strengthens the similarities but does not guarantee that the union between wine co-operatives "goes without saying". The numerous merger projects between wine co-operatives which never saw the light of day attest to this. Thus, belonging to the co-operative world, and moreover to the wine co-operative world, most probably facilitates mergers but it still remains that proximity of similarity does not suffice in predicting with certainty whether the merger will go ahead or not.

A priori, proximity of similarity is a necessary condition to begin the merger process. Nevertheless, the cases we studied show that it does not become a sufficient condition, once the risks of "unnatural" partnerships have been minimized. Indeed, the merger project only appears possible or worth consideration when the "cultural" gaps are narrow, which confirms the idea that across a merger, breaking free from spatial lock-in goes together with a loosening of cognitive obstacles too.

Consequently, many mergers are the result of a series of meetings enabling the parties to know each other better and a number of test appointments to "feel" whether there is affinity with the intended partner. It is the reason why mergers are not completed with the geographically closest potential partner as the geographical proximity does not compensate for cultural or organizational distance. Thus, we have frequently been told that "knowing one another", and for that, often "learning to know one another", is a vital pre-requisite for a merger approach. In the same way, "very different ways of working" are enough to break the desire to become partners and move to the final step: a merger.

Henceforth, procedures which lead to most of the mergers we studied are relatively heavy. With the exception of two cases (Table 17.4), the mergers were preceded by audits and the setting up of commissions to analyze the ways of working and the company's results. Each of these procedures brings together all the members of each organization, co-operative members and employees, which results in making the grouping mechanisms slower and more complex.

In our case, when the approach procedures did not take place, the reciprocal ignorance of the partners, and the absence of transparency which resulted

Table 17.4 Similarity, learning processes and success conditions for merger

Processes prior to merger	Success/ failure	A posteriori analysis of the difficulties encountered	A posteriori analysis of the conditions for success
Audits, commissions, organized working groups: 5/7	Success: 4	Difficulty to make those who are doing well—or who think they are—understand the benefits. Difficulty to convince the other party that no site will close. Fear of being put far from the center of decisions	Prior existence of common ways of working (e.g., commercial union). Do not join a structure which is too "ill". Do not pass a limit, in terms of volumes, beyond which the structure becomes too complex to manage. Generates strong communication tools
	Failure: 1	Problems financing the project. Departures of co-operators	Do not make alliances with partners too distant in their way of working
No audits, simple situation analysis: 2/7	Failure: 1	Poor reciprocal knowledge. Discovery once the merger was made of differences in working methods and of problems. Departures of co-operators	Carry out an audit. Get to know one another. Establish transparency regarding decisions and strategy. Have the same ways of doing things and of thinking about the product
	Success: 1	None	Approval from members necessary. Generate strong communication tools

from this, was analyzed a posteriori by the current managers as the essential reason for the failure to merge. For examples we studied, even when the organizations know each other well, analysis and thinking procedures were put in place to finalize the merger. Even when the thinking took place after the action, and where, we were told, "you must not think too much as you risk taking no action", several meetings were set up.

Common "ways of doing things", close working methods (such as work times and salary systems) and similar viewpoints on the product therefore appear as minimum guarantees to establishing confidence between the potential partners, activating learning processes with the goal of building the merger process.

These journeys are often described as being chaotic: between those which begin with the idea of a simple grouping and end up with a merger; those which begin with the idea of a partnership with the co-operative which seems the most natural fit, because the closest geographically, and which conclude with co-operatives that were not considered at the outset; those which develop from a heavy process and those which are completed without too much thought; and those which are carried out with a precise idea and others which are done a little by a non-choice; the journeys leading to a merger are diverse.

If the choice of partners appears guided by a combination of forms of geographical and similarity proximity, mergers are also the opportunity to rebuild a territorialized co-operative entity structured around the proximity of belonging.

17.3.2   The Merger, the Opportunity to Rebuild a Territorialized Co-operative Entity

The success of a merger requires going beyond prior learning, even if this is thorough. The proximity of belonging therefore comes into play to analyze the manner in which mergers favor the emergence of a new territorialized co-operative entity: they bring about a redefinition of the rules and the local compromises since from this belonging to a new entity, they reorganize the proximity between actors who were historically distinct.

17.3.2.1   Rendering the Co-operative Organization Viable Through a Rebuilding of Rules

By associating organizations which are often geographically near to each other and which are frequently similar, but nevertheless with specific company cultures, a merger provokes a redeployment of organizational resources. Merged co-operatives have to (and will have to) go as far as an organizational homogenization in order to meet the performance objectives assigned to the merger.

Resource redeployment involves rules which, at least in the short term, will ensure stability for the new structure: salary rules, quality management and so on (Table 17.5).

In the examples we studied, several scenarios are ongoing: adopting the rules of one of the partners, taking rules from each of the structures, redefining "as if starting from scratch"[14] rules which for some will be new and for others not. For some, that translates into a redefining of working methods: new salary rules, new quality framework, setting up a profit-sharing scheme for members, an incentive policy to take part in trade events, redefining employees' social status, creating an internal newsletter run by the employees

---

[14] Term borrowed by a person interviewed.

Table 17.5 Observable organizational changes post-merger

Production sites	Specialization of sites by function: 5/7
	Specialization in terms of production: 1/7
	Site closures: 2/7
Salary rules	Establishment of a new quality framework: 2/7
	Establishment of a new rule via conciliation between the different preexisting ones: 2/7
	Extension of a specific working rule from one co-operative to the partners: 2/7
Quality	Quality and traceability development: 3/7
Employees	Social status harmonization: 1
	Redirecting employees' positions (movement from administrative to commercial): 2
Supervisory board	Imbalance in favor of the most important co-operators (% of volumes): 1/7
Miscellaneous	Member involvement in the commercial activity via payment for participation in trade events. Establishment of sales-based profit-sharing schemes. Establishment of a company social committee (Christmas party, internal newsletter, etc.)

and so on. For others, it was a question of taking what was good from each co-operative according to the principle that "not all is good in an organisation doing well and not everything is to be discarded from one doing badly".[15]

The solution, if it does not always seem easy to put in place, resides nevertheless in conciliating differentiated forms of company culture, with varying degrees of success and conflict. Moreover, this has led certain authors to say that "mergers form 'tests' which reveal sustainability criteria, because it is necessary to rebuild a collective project and the rules associated with it" (Chiffoleau et al. 2005).

In all cases, mergers translate into a necessity to rebuild around a new entity, securing a specific common adherence in order to establish a new territorial attachment.

17.3.2.2 Mergers Lead to a Rebuilding of Co-operative Territorial Legitimacy

Mergers between co-operatives translate into an extension of their territorial area. To a certain extent, this new spatial scale forces participants to redefine their territorial legitimacy. If this redefinition leads to a rethinking of certain co-operative governance rules, it does not put the co-operative pact into question.

---

[15] Expression borrowed by a person interviewed.

Firstly, in the co-operative framework, the changes inherent to a merger take place in a collective decision-making and action-taking context where respect for all the members' representativeness is expressed. Most probably, the latter is skewed by the influence of the key or dominant players, knowing that a leadership role is generally well accepted since it is seen as being dynamic. Respect for this principle implies (re) structuring the supervisory board which must be done in a way that is not seen as unfair, knowing that mergers, as highlighted in the first part, are carried out between organizations with different human and economic weights. In some of the cases we studied, the supervisory boards were at first seen as very unequal as regards the representative weight of each co-operative in the new structure. Most of the time, the flexibility granted during the formation of the supervisory boards led to compromises which in turn ensured the merger was adhered to.

Secondly, the reconfiguration involves structural reorganizations with an underlying issue of the future of the production sites. Their preservation may be questioned, notably when one of the co-operatives is in an unmanageable technical situation and/or their functional role in the new organization is put into doubt. Because of the size effects it seeks, a merger is often accompanied by the development of new functions (commercial or service functions) alongside those of the traditional wine co-operative. Henceforth, questions concerning the sharing and distribution of these functions must be tackled. In the context of a merger, there is a great risk that certain production sites will take "power" over the others, not so much in terms of the preservation or disappearance of sites as in the concentration of functions. Indeed, we can suppose that distances can be an obstacle to the closure of sites as they will engender extra costs in transport, for example, or in capital assets which are inherent to the lack of appreciation of the investments undertaken. However, this argument is modulated according to the spatial distances separating the two partners and according to the type of strategy favored by the new structure. For the moment, the mergers carried out have only led to a small number of closed production sites in Aquitaine.

On the other hand, a merger can translate into a concentration of strategic functions in one site or in just a few. This question is fundamental to the place of each co-operative in the merged organization and to the distribution of functions between each site. Thus, in the cases we studied, we find particularly strong attention given to the distribution of functions over the sites. Some mergers have led to a specialization of sites, whether it be by product (each site specializing in the production of a particular AOC wine) or by function (a site specializing in production while another focuses on sales and administration).

Other mergers have not modified their initial structural organization. Still others in longer-established mergers have ended up abandoning production sites.

Thirdly and finally, reconfiguring resources involves relationships with members. What happens to these members in the new organization? Ruffio et al. (2001) identify two types of organization. A first type is based upon a plan where the member is seen as means to achieve a certain level of economic efficiency, provoking a change in the nature of the link with the member. On the contrary, a second type builds on a strengthening of the co-operative's interface role between the co-operator and the market. "In this model, the co-operative ... is at the centre of a network built on a double organisation, relational (with the member) and economic, whose relations with the territory are different. The first level maintains the local level while the second operates in a larger territorial context (regional or inter-regional)."

While it is difficult to classify the mergers observed into one of the two models, especially because the groupings are recent, the second form seems to prevail. However it is established in different ways. For some, the distribution of functions or at least the internal reorganization of the structure is done with the will not to lose links with the co-operators. In others, the reorganization induced by the merger was not seen by the co-operators as a way to cement relations between them and the structure and this led to co-operators leaving. For still others, the question of the link with the co-operator was not addressed in this way, either because the structure that was built did not fundamentally change the link with the co-operator or because the link was considered above all in terms of a capacity to pay the members better and that henceforth, the efficiency of the structure (whose effectiveness cannot be predicted in advance) is the essential condition in the preservation of the link. Henceforth, the departure of members following a merger does not seem to result from a deliberate choice on the organization's part and therefore do not fall under logic of exclusion.

17.4   Conclusion

Thus, contrary to an image which is too widespread, mergers of wine co-operatives are far from signing a death warrant to co-operative territorial attachment. If this attachment turns out to be a constraint, it nevertheless remains a significant and positive element in co-operative strategy. Admittedly, this significance can be altered according to the vineyards studied. Thus, when the co-operative has a near monopoly of the AOC, which is the case of a few co-operatives in Aquitaine, the strategy of loosening the ties can lead to their elimination, all the more so as it is easier to carry out in the absence of "close", competitors in all the senses of the term. A contrario, mergers with companies which are better equipped from a commercial point of view but further away in terms of organized proximity can, once a learning process has been successfully completed, lead to a strengthening of the territorial attachment.

All these elements lead us to qualify the restrictive dimension of the attachment, with our analysis showing that via mergers, co-operatives rebuild their links to the *terroir* through an effective expression of the co-operative interest with those of their members. The analysis of the merger processes in terms of geographical and organized proximity allows us to appreciate the permissive character of geographical and similarity proximities insofar as the proximity of belonging alone can release the spatial, cognitive and organizational lock-ins which threaten the sustainability of the co-operative structure. This confirms the idea that, to a certain extent, the proximity of belonging dominates the other forms of proximity with which it combines in the merger process.

The "right merger", enabling co-operatives to increase their influence and position themselves in a better way cannot, for all that, free co-operatives from ongoing issues of territory (maintaining small-sized farms or balancing power with *négociants*) and trade (competitive positioning of the whole sector in Aquitaine). If merging with close players solves certain problems, the question of the limit of these strategies remains. Will the predictable strengthening of the globalization movement in the wine sector force co-operatives to envisage alliances with players further away if their strategies move closer and closer toward the world market? Therefore, in a context of increased concentration in the wine sector, the question regarding the direction of change for these co-operative organizations remains open.

References

Benkala, A., and J.-P. Boutonnet. *Proximité et signalisation de la qualité, approches croisées pour l'étude d'une AOC, le cas de Pellardon*, 4e Journée de la proximité, 06-18-2004, 14 p.

Berthomeau, J. 2001. *Comment mieux positionner les vins français sur les marchés d'exportation?* Rapport remis au Ministre de l'Agriculture, juillet.

Boschma, R. 2005. Proximity and innovation: A critical assessment. *Regional Studies* 39 (1): 61–75.

César, G. 2002. *L'avenir de la viticulture française*, rapport d'information, Sénat, n° 349.

Chiffoleau, Y., F. Dreyfus, M. Filippi, J.-M. Touzard, and P. Triboulet. 2005. "Réseaux d'entreprises et réseaux sociaux dans le développement des coopératives agricoles: enseignements des recherches PSDR en Midi-Pyrénées et Languedoc-Roussillon", Communication pour le *Symposium international "Territoires et enjeux du développement régional"*, Lyon, 9–11 mars 2005.

Christensen, C.M., M. Verlinden, and G. Westerman. 2002. Disruption, disintegration and the dissipation of differentiability. *Industrial and Corporate Change* 11 (5): 955–993.

Colletis, G., and B. Pecqueur. Révélation de ressources spécifiques et coordination située, Colloque international sur *L'économie de proximité*, Marseille, 8–9 juin 2004, 18 p.

Couret, F. 1999. Compte rendu de l'enquête 1999 sur l'efficacité des coopératives vinicoles d'Aquitaine, Les ateliers de la coopération vinicole Aquitaine, FCVA, Bordeaux.

D'hauteville, F., J-P. Couderc, H. Hannin, and E. Montaigne. 2004. *Bacchus 2005, enjeux, stratégies et pratiques dans la filière vitivinicole*, édition La Vigne, Dunod, Paris, 298 p.

———. 2005. *Bacchus 2006, enjeux, stratégies et pratiques dans la filière vitivinicole*, édition La Vigne, Dunod, Paris, 301 p.

Douard, J.-P., and M. Heitz. 2003. "Une lecture des réseaux d'entreprises: prise en compte des formes et des évolutions", *Revue Française de Gestion*, n° 146, pp. 23–41.

Doucet, C. 2002. "Activités viticoles et développement régional", *thèse pour le doctorat ès sciences économiques*, Université Montesquieu Bordeaux IV, 343 p.

Draperi, J.F., and J.M. Touzard, eds. 2003. *Les coopératives entre territoires et mondialisation*, 375 p. Paris: L'Harmattan.

Garciet-Parpet, M.-F. 2001. *Le terroir, le cépage et la marque*, Cahiers d'ESR, n° 60–61, pp. 149–180.

Hinnewinkel, J.-C., and P. Roudié. 2001. *Une empreinte dans le vignoble: XXe siècle: naissance des vins d'Aquitaine d'Origine Coopérative*, LPDA éditions.

ONIVINS. 2002. Stratégie et rentabilité des entreprises de négoce de Bourgogne, ONIVINS-Infos, n 97, octobre, 37p.

Pecqueur, B., and J.-B. Zimmermann. 2004. Chapitre introductif. In *Économie de proximités*, 13–41. Paris: Hermès-Lavoisier.

Pomel, B. 2006. *Réussir l'avenir de la viticulture de France*.

Rallet, A., and A. Torre. 2004. "Proximité et localisation", *Économie Rurale*, n° 280, mars-avril 2004, pp. 25–41.

Rastouin, J.-L., and V. Vissac-Charles. 1999. Le groupe stratégique des entreprises de terroir. *Revue internationale des PME* 12: 171–192.

Ruffio, P., R. Guillouzo, and P. Perrot. 2001. Stratégies d'alliances et nouvelles frontières de la coopérative agro-alimentaire. *Économie rurale*, 264–265, juillet–octobre.

Samuel, K.-E. 2003. Prévenir les difficultés post-fusion/acquisition en utilisant la gestion de crise. *Revue Française de Gestion* 145: 41–54.

18

Diversity and a Shifting Power Balance: Negociants and Winegrowers in Bordeaux

Sofya Brand

18.1   Introduction

In the beginning of the new millennium, the ways to make French wines more competitive were at the center of debate as the industry was losing its place on global markets. Concentration and integration of the very fragmented wine sector was widely seen as the most efficient way to cut costs, to gain economies of scale and scope and, more globally, to follow the lead of main foreign competitors (Berthomeau 2001; César 2002; Pomel 2006). Since then some companies merged, some have been acquired, others gone bankrupt. However, many companies not only managed to survive but also preserved their independence. After all, as we will discover in this chapter, winemaking in France has its traditions and particularities.

Bordeaux is one of the most notable examples. Diversity is the key word when describing the winemaking industry of this region. "Bordeaux as a territory created a platform for the generation of variety on an unprecedented scale. … Bordeaux's territorial identity depends more on an integration of variety than in homogeneity" (Patchell 2011, pp. 41–42).

Diversity in Bordeaux manifests itself through wide range of products but also various actors involved in making and marketing them. All those actors have different strategies, internal organizations and complex relationship. The very complex nature of regional's wine sector is imminently rich of divisions: professional, qualitative and territorial. Professional division—between grape

S. Brand (✉)
Département MMS, Institut Mines Télécom – Business School, Paris, France

© The Author(s) 2019
A. Alonso Ugaglia et al. (eds.), *The Palgrave Handbook of Wine Industry Economics*,
https://doi.org/10.1007/978-3-319-98633-3_18

growers and merchants, while very present throughout the whole history of Bordeaux as a wine region—helps in a manner to overcome two other ones.

In this chapter, we aim to focus on the essence of negociants' profession and its evolution. Given that nowadays some factors, which have played a fundamental role in shaping wine production systems as well as relationships between their actors, are no more that crucial (e.g. transport costs), we try to understand why the value chain structure split between grape growers and negociants persists and is presumably a part of Bordeaux's performance.

Our analysis belongs to the tradition of historical institutionalism. Thus, to understand the existing value chain structure in Bordeaux, we begin with a brief historical review focused on merchants' role in developing the industry, then we dress a picture of what Bordeaux wine region actually is and finally we focus on the different types of merchants present these days in Bordeaux.

18.2   Brief Historical Review

The modern history of Bordeaux as a wine territory has its roots in the Middle Ages when in 1152 Eleanor, duchesse of Aquitaine, married Henry Plantagenet, who two years later became King of England, and Aquitaine subsequently became dependent on the English Crown. "Marriage and politics rather than consumer demand first brought the wines of Bordeaux to England" (Colman 2008, p. 10). Bordeaux's port was instrumental for the opening up of export routes. "Geographic advantage put the Bordeaux wine producers in the unusual position of enjoying greater renown abroad than at home" (Colman 2008, p. 11).

As all commerce was going through the port, it is the city and not the region that gave its name to the wine. Merchants played a vital role in developing exports from Bordeaux. At times when goods mostly traveled by sea, producers could not sell their wines directly and needed merchants to assure the logistics. From the thirteenth century up to the French Revolution, the development of the wine industry in Bordeaux was driven by the sea commerce first with Britain, then with Holland and after that with Antilles Islands.

During almost 500 years, the dependence on the English Crown not only provided Bordeaux wines with a huge market but also assured preferential treatment vis-à-vis main competitors from other ports (e.g. La Rochelle) and wine producers from neighboring regions.[1] And that is even despite that for a

[1] Tax and Privilège de Bordeaux.

long period of time wines from Bordeaux, the so-called clarets, were not of high quality, hence they could not be stored or transported for long distances. Merchants even had to blend them with wines from neighboring regions to improve their quality bypassing protectionist measures lobbied by Bordeaux vineyards' owners.

In 1453, after the Hundred Years war was over, France got the Aquitaine territory back and restored its rule over wine market in Bordeaux. As a result, wine trade with England declined and British merchants gave way to Dutch, Hanseatic and Breton ones. These new buyers needed different types of wine: whites for distillation, sweet whites and reds fit for transportation on long distances. Merchants from Holland settled in Bordeaux in order to oversee operations and prospect supply market for better deals. They also introduced new production techniques, and "new French clarets", more quality wine, which could also be stored for longer time, appeared in the seventeenth–eighteenth century. The move brought fame to the region as a whole but also to the separate local crus, that started gaining reputation. From now on some wines originated from Medoc and Graves were identified by the name of vineyard's owner or cru. The eighteenth century also saw Bordeaux and its wine prospering, thanks to massive colonial trade traffic with Antilles Islands.

The French revolution marked a new period for the regional wine industry. All tax advantages, which Bordeaux enjoyed for many years, were abolished. As if this was not enough of the challenge, the cancelation of Privilège de Bordeaux meant the region's opening up to wines from neighboring vineyards and other parts of France. Now, merchants were officially free to buy wines from wherever they like. Merchants, who are usually quick to adapt to new realities, used non-Bordeaux wines for their blends in order to improve quality, ensure consistency and adjust quantity. They were selling their branded wines under Bordeaux name regardless of real origin of wines. Merchants' warehouses were full of wine, even Grands crus were bottled in those warehouses until the middle of the twentieth century.

After the Revolution Bordeaux continued to develop its territorial identity distinguishing itself from other wine regions by building up a qualitative image of its wines. Three major factors contributed (Réjalot 2007). First, after the revolution Bordeaux regional vineyard got precise delimitation. After France has been divided into departments, Bordeaux wine region began to be strongly associated with Gironde. Secondly, the concept of "chateau"—a wine-producing estate using exclusively its own grape—started to spread in Gironde from 1850s. Last but not least, Bordeaux Wine Official Classification of 1855 of chateaux in Medoc and Sauternes that was drawn up for the

Exposition Universelle on request of Napoleon III contributed to individualization of Bordeaux and to its glory.

After defeating powdery mildew—the reason for the crisis in Bordeaux in 1850s—the second half of the nineteenth century was full of success for the wine industry. The new railway linked Bordeaux to Paris and the Midi region, and the arrival of a railroad to Gironde meant a huge improvement for local infrastructure and logistics. It was also the time of big technical improvement in grape growing and winemaking (Roudié 1994). Bordeaux wine industry grew in terms of both exports and domestic sales, and it exported its winemaking savoir faire to other parts of the world—a real proof of fame and recognition. Bordeaux also signed bilateral tax agreements with many countries, something that was restricted before because of the legacy of the protectionist policy of Colbert's government.

In the last quarter of the nineteenth century, a pest called phylloxera put abruptly an end to the prosperous business. It devastated vineyards causing dramatic drop in local production, the whole French wine industry declined. Bordeaux felt the impact immediately: wine commerce stalled, producers and merchants were next to be ruined. As merchants were not able to get enough wine from producers in Gironde, they brought them from other regions and countries, which have not yet suffered from phylloxera (Spain, Portugal, Algeria, Italy, etc.). Bordeaux thus became a large port importing wines. During the crisis, merchants once again proved to be ready to go to great lengths to avoid bankruptcy and so they used every possible way to make a product that could be sold as wine. Produced using various techniques available at that time, very often this final product had nothing in common with traditional winemaking. This was the time when wine could even be produced without grapes at all (Stanziani 2003).

The solution to protect vineyard from phylloxera was found by grafting local vine with the aphid-resistant American species. The vineyards have been replanted progressively and very quickly the situation changed dramatically from limited supply to overproduction. This was due to several reasons (Réjalot 2007): local production level was restored while the wine imports did not stop; merchants continued to use artificial techniques to fabricate wine; finally, during the crisis some markets have been lost as for example Argentina which started producing its own wine.

This crisis came as a blow to winegrowers, putting them in a very tough financial condition and opposing to merchants. As merchants were to blame for overproduction and fraudulent techniques used to produce wines, the power balance shifted once again. Winegrowers used the opportunity to construct a legal foundation to protect their interests. That is how the controlled designation of origin system was initiated. As a first step, in 1911 Bordeaux wine region was officially confined to Gironde, only wines produced in the department could bear the name of Bordeaux. The process was not quick and it is only in 1935 (after years of debates and intermediate laws[2]) that the French Senate approved the bill submitted by Joseph Capus, senator from Gironde. This law created the "Appellation d'Origine Controlée" (AOC), a complex set of rules governing quality wines production in parallel to "Statut viticole" regulating table wines segment at those times. For merchants new legislation has changed a lot: they lost control of the product which passed in the hands of winegrowers. It has also impacted Bordeaux as a region—the law placed the production problems in the field of collective action rather than individual one.

Times of turbulence continued as in 1929 the Great Depression gripped the world economy. Demand of Bordeaux's fine wines declined and in order to keep the industry afloat wine producers increased production of cheaper red wines and focused on domestic market instead. The strategy proved to be challenging, as the segment was occupied by ordinary Languedoc wines. To reduce risks an important part of Bordeaux's vineyards was replanted in whites, less affected by the crisis. From 1932 winegrowers who were earlier reluctant to participate in cooperative movement started joining their efforts, and in 1940 the region counted 51 cooperatives producing 15% of wine in Bordeaux (Roudié 1994).

During the World War II, wine trade was hardly perturbed by German occupation. After the liberation many merchants were questioned regarding their collaboration with Nazis and the Vichy government. After the War Bordeaux had to restore its wine industry in new conditions. The inter-professional body—Conseil interprofessionnel du vin de Bordeaux (CIVB)—was officially created in 1948, consolidating producers' and merchants' syndicates. New Grands Crus were classified in 1953 (Graves) and in 1955 (Saint-Émilion). This period also saw acceleration in cooperative movement: the number of members continued to grow until 1970s. Progressively wines of Bordeaux returned to the export markets, but sales recovery on national market was more important with confirmed regional specialization in whites. After having outlived another crisis in 1956, terrible freeze this time, Bordeaux region continued its development switching to origin wines and improving production techniques. Things went more or less smoothly until 1970s when abrupt speculative price jump followed by considerable price decline caused serious financial difficulties. The chock was

---

[2] Law of 1 August 1905; Law of 6 May 1919; Law of 22 July 1927.

aggravated by growing competition from imported wines coming from the European Union. This was a moment that changed a lot in winegrowers' and merchants' relationship, as former once again saw the latter as the cause of their trouble. The CIVB splitted because members representing winegrowers quitted considering that the organization was incapable to manage the industry and to solve the crisis. Later in 1976 the CIVB was reformed with establishment of parity in representation of winegrowers and merchants; its power and functions were extended.

The lack of trust that poisoned the relations between main actors on the market was fueled by a largely politicized and mediatized "Cruse scandal", which made headlines in 1973. Twelve merchants were accused in fraud and fakery including upgrading of table wines into origin wines (AOC). This scandal made some chateaux owners bypass merchants and start direct sales. Also, it valued bottling in chateau instead of merchants' warehouses—a move to sideline the merchants from the production process and guarantee quality. However, in practice quite often it meant mobile bottling lines belonging to merchants traveling from one châteaux to another. Merchants' positions were undermined with the raise of "chateaux" popularity. Many unknown "petit chateaux" came on the market replacing wines produced under merchants' brand names. In 1970–1980 the merchants' profession changed from blending and maturing wines to distributing different chateaux already finished and bottled in the estates. The production of wines under merchants' brands declined.

However, in the 1990s facing the raising competition of the New World branded wines on the export markets and raising demand for branded wines from retail distributors, some merchants returned to their traditional role. They started to invest more in their own brand production or in supplying private labels to retailers. This activity needs stable relationships between merchants and grape growers in order to assure constant quantity and quality supply. However, actors of wine industry in Bordeaux do not usually frame their collaboration by a written contract, as long-term relationships without explicit contract engagement are very common.

The reason for the existence of institutions that regulate wine economy in Bordeaux is the need to secure the shifting balance between winegrowers and merchants as both parties were struggling to have an upper hand on the market. Preserving balance between those factions was a key for the whole system to compete with other territories and producers.

18.3   Diversity and Divisions in Bordeaux Vineyard Now: Products, Actors, Performance

With its 111,000[3] hectares (ha), Bordeaux is the biggest wine region producing AOC wines. It represents 1.5% of the worldwide vineyard, 15% of the total French vineyard and 25% of country's AOC vineyard. It is planted mostly with Cabernet Sauvignon, Merlot and Cabernet Franc in reds and Sauvignon Blanc and Semillon in whites. Wine is fundamental for region's economy representing 78% of its agricultural production. Bordeaux produces about 769 millions of bottles yearly, mostly red wines, which is 85% of its total production. The region counts 65 appellations.

Bordeaux sells its wines in 150 countries all over the world for €3.65 billion a year. It exports 42% of its production volume mostly in Europe (43%), Asia (35%) and Northern America (12%). The wines exports from Bordeaux represent over one third of total French wine exports. Its five top destinations are China, Belgium, the United States, the United Kingdom and Germany. In France 46% of Bordeaux wines are sold in supermarkets, 9% in hard discounts and 45% in wine shops, on-trade market, online and so on.

Bordeaux wine production industry is a very fragmented one: it counts 6300 winegrowers with an average farm size of 17.6 ha, 33 cooperatives with 3 unions, 300 merchants and 82 brokers. Twenty-five organizations for defense and management (ODG) represent the interests and self-govern the 65 appellations. As seen above, the CIVB, created in 1948, is a central regulation body of wine industry in Bordeaux. It has the role to unify and balance divergent interests of all actors. It has four missions: economic, marketing, technical and representation of Bordeaux's interests on national and international political arenas (Smith et al. 2007). CIVB is the biggest inter-professional board in French wine industry with its total budget reaching almost €36 million (including member's fees and EU subsidies).

Bordeaux wine industry has several divisions that are mediated by various institutions. The industry needs institutional mediation firstly to balance the power between winegrowers and merchants who have always struggled for control on markets, margins, product, influence and so on. They also represent two opposed product concepts: chateau wines versus branded wines. As mentioned above in 1970s chateau concept prevailed over the traditional

---

[3] 2016, source: Conseil Interprofessionnel du Vin de Bordeaux.

approach when merchants used to sell the majority of wines under their own names. Currently, only few Bordeaux brands are known internationally, with Mouton Cadet being the most known example. The brand owes its popularity to its elder brother—Chateau Mouton Rothschild. On the national market Castel is an undisputed leader with the brands such as Roche Mazet, Cambras, Ormes de Cambras, Baron de Lestac, Vieux Papes, La Villageoise and so on. During the last 25 years Bordeaux wine industry undergoes concentration process on both sides. Winegrowers have seen their number to divide by more than twice and the average farm size to grow from 7 to 17 ha. Merchants and cooperatives have been also consolidating over this period (Pesme et al. 2010). However, the industry remains very fragmented and thus the coordination between winegrowers and merchants is a very critical issue.

Another notable feature of the industry is the quality split: Bordeaux is mostly known for its top wines that only represent a tiny part of regional wine production. These luxury wines are able to find their clients almost at all market condition. However, most of the industry winegrowing estates are occupied producing ordinary wines, which are heavily dependent on market fluctuations. According to Jean-François Moueix,[4] one of the most influential merchant in Bordeaux: "The difference was such big that I couldn't see what could allow normal coexistence in the long term. The palaces cannot prosper nearby favelas." At the same time the whole region takes profit from the aura of these wines. The quality division is represented by different kinds of categorization and hierarchization of thousands of different wines produced in Bordeaux. Different types of product identification juxtapose: AOC, brand, chateaux and so on. Three main classifications represent the region's patrimony: Bordeaux Wine Official Classification of 1855, The Graves Classification and The Saint-Émilion Classification. All three together unite over 100 estates. These top wines are mainly distributed internationally—80% exported, according to the Union of Grands Crus, which is much above the average Bordeaux wine exports figures.

Finally, Bordeaux is divided into many wine-producing territories. Bordeaux is actually represented by 65 appellations grouped together in 6 regions: le Medoc, Blaye et Bourg, le Libournais, l'Entre-Deux-Mers, Les

---

[4] Interview, Christian Seguin "Bordeaux partout, voilà la Vérité" in the newspaper *Sud-Ouest*, Thursday 14 June 2007, p. 7. Original version: "Le fossé était tel que je ne voyais pas ce qui pouvait permettre une cohabitation normale, de longuedurée. Les palais ne peuvent pas s'épanouir à côté des favelas. Cet état de fait était intolérable. La comparaison entre lesdeux mondes de Bordeaux avait quelque chose d'indécent, d'inacceptable. Alors je me dis qu'il y a toujours un canyon, mais au moins, de l'autre côté je vois une vie à l'endroit où l'on entrevoyait la désertification. Je trouve qu'il est bien queles grands crus puissent servir d'exemple, de référence à un territoire qui a échappé à la fossilisation."

Graves et Sauternais. The biggest and most powerful appellations are Bordeaux and Bordeaux Superieur; they represent about a half of the total vineyard area and can be produced all over Bordeaux wine region.

These self-governed wine territories are very heterogenic in terms of reputation, production volume and type, organization, aspirations and market success. Vineyard prices and their evolution in diverse appellations reflect differences between them. Vineyards priced above €200,000/ha (Saint-Émilion, Pessac-Léognan, Pomerol, Margaux, Saint-Estèphe, Saint-Julien and Pauillac) regroup 10% of the vineyard surface but 75% of its value (compared to only one third in 1991). Average appellation vineyard price in Gironde has grown by one quarter between 2000 and 2016. While top wines are experiencing a price hike, some appellations were trading at much smaller price in 2016 as opposed to 2000 (Table 18.1). Sauternes, for example, suffered a lot from road safety legislation: drivers started sacrificing aperitifs and digestives (Sauternes is usually consumed as such), hence creating a sharp fall in demand.

The diversity of Bordeaux wines can be considered as a market advantage as it is satisfying the demand for diversity and penetrates all market niches. On the other hand, it does not always aid the clear positioning and commercial strategy. Moreover this quite complicated hierarchized offer, which is not necessarily expressed by clear price positioning, cannot always be easily decrypted by consumer because it requires specific knowledge.

Is complicated Bordeaux system performant? Do the institutions in place assure its longevity? There are no standard indicators for measuring performance knowing that a wine-producing region cannot be considered from a pure economic point of view only but is a complex social organism having different challenges in front of it. The answer is probably yes, but not for everyone. Some less renowned appellations had to join their efforts creating associations (Cotes de Bordeaux or sweet wines) to compete on the national and international markets and improve their bargaining power vis-à-vis

Table 18.1 Vineyard price in Bordeaux rouge equivalent

AOC	1991	2000	2016
Bordeaux rouge	1	1	1.0
Bordeaux blanc	0.8	0.7	1.0
Pauillac	9.2	7.8	125.0
Fronsac	3.1	2.3	2.2
Saint-Émilion	6.5	4.8	14.4
Medoc	2.5	1.8	3.1
Sauternes	7.3	2.5	2.2
Gironde total	**2.2**	**1.7**	**6.4**

Source: Safer

buyers, supermarket chains. The diversity, which is an important asset of Bordeaux, lacks strategic dimension. The same conclusion can be drawn while reading "Plan Bordeaux Demain", Bordeaux wine industry development plan launched by CIVB in 2010.[5] Without contesting the fundamental principles of Bordeaux vineyard functioning, this document points out major failures of Bordeaux wine industry: missed opportunities on national and global markets and weakening of the brand "Bordeaux". As a main remedy the plan proposes to focus on promising markets and quality segments and to dispose of entry-level wines, creating at the same time conditions for effective interplay between actors.

18.4   La Place de Bordeaux: How Does Market Function Between Winegrowers and Merchants

The process of winemaking, which turns grapes from a vineyard into a bottle on a shop shelf or a restaurant table, can be divided into five stages: vine growing, winemaking, blending and aging, packaging and marketing. This process is complex and involves a large scale of expertise and knowhow. Traditionally in Bordeaux the division between these steps has been quite net: first two were under grape growers' responsibility and the rest belonged to merchants. Nowadays the division between two professions has started to blur due to the ongoing backward and forward integration process. Moreover, family ties in the wine industry in Bordeaux are very strong and mix the interests of many businesses. Nevertheless, the traditional way of dealing with each other is still in place: Place de Bordeaux.

What is the famous "Place de Bordeaux"? It is a "market place where, with the brokers' mediation, the variety produced by winegrowers is exchanged into the merchants' hands" (Patchell 2011, p. 54). Merchants play a central role in integrating Bordeaux's variety. According to the Association of Bordeaux Wine Merchants, the Union des Maisons de Bordeaux (UMB), 300 merchants sell about 2/3 of wines produced in Bordeaux. On the one hand, merchants collect different wines to produce their own blends under their brand names or private labels. On the other, they create more or less large portfolios of different estate wines and appellations and distribute them

---

[5] New strategic plan "Bordeaux, ambitions 2025" has been launched in 2018.

globally. This core merchants' competence consisting of selling a range of competing products representing diverse estates of the region makes difference between Bordeaux market place and most other wine regions.

As we have seen above, there is a quality divide between products produced in Bordeaux, so there are two different markets, each of them involving wine-growers, brokers and merchants. The key element of the Bordeaux market place is its well-established futures market—another unique feature of Bordeaux in regard to the value chain. This is a complex social mechanism based on reputation and market evolvement expectation which makes Bordeaux merchants and brokers inherent component of Grands Crus distribution. Wine futures are a purchase of wine 18–24 months before release while it is still aging in barrels. Futures market actually concerns approximately 250 to 500[6] chateaux depending on the quality of the year and market condition (Chauvin 2009), mostly Grands Crus Classés, but not exclusively. Patchell (2011) proposes the acceptance to the futures market as criteria to distinguish modern Grands Crus from "small chateaux". The "en primeur" campaign is held in the spring several months after harvest. It starts by professional tastings organized by producers' associations where the wines are noted by critics, journalists and market professionals (Hadj Ali et al. 2010). After tastings, producers fix prices (Chauvin 2009), communicate them to merchants via brokers and make them proposals in terms of quantity. These quantities are allocated taking into consideration the hierarchy of the merchants on the market and the past relationship between producers and merchants. Based on the notes, expectations regarding price evolution and the estimated demand from their clients, merchants place their orders paying them often more than a year in advance. Some most exclusive Grands Crus release their wines in several tranches especially when demand is particularly high selling successive tranches for a higher price. There are several advantages for both sides, producers and merchants, in the wine futures (Chauvin 2009). Producers benefit from fixing the price more or less autonomously (release price and recommended price), from advance payment and from the merchants distribution net that they use without any cost. For merchants it is an opportunity to secure their stocks, especially of the rare and most valued wines and to make profits, more or less important depending on price evolution. In some years when the market price is lower or equal to the release price, they make a loss. Lately with the development of online sales, private customers got an easier access via merchants to the wine futures promoted as an alternative financial

---

[6] In 2012 Pauillac first cru Chateau Latour left the en primeur system.

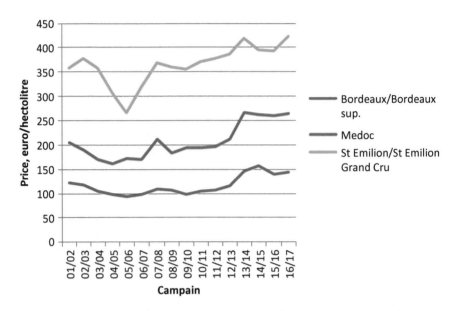

Fig. 18.1 Bulk wine price fluctuations in Bordeaux. (Source: FranceAgriMer)

investment. This guise of Grands Crus fuels this traditional practice. Futures market is a key element of the existence of the Bordeaux wine market: "if the 'en primeur' market ceases to be, then Grands crus brokers will disappear. Campaign brokers will remain but they will not arbitrate mechanisms fundamentally. In Bordeaux all is judged and done in relation to the purchase. Futures market is consubstantial to merchants' existence itself. Middlemen are its lever. This is an ancestral system that could seem closed, but which shouldn't be dismantled."[7]

The quite specific futures market of Grands Crus Classés does not exist autonomously; it is tightly related to the overall Bordeaux wine market in a sense that merchant's position in Grands Crus business can influence its overall market power and potential investment attractiveness. Although en primeur market plays a very significant role, the majority of Bordeaux wines are not sold over this system and pass through different value chains. Firstly,

[7] J.-Fr. Moueix, interview with Christian Seguin "Bordeaux partout, voilà la Vérité" in the newspaper Sud-Ouest, Thursday 14 June 2007, p. 7. Original version: "Si les ventes en primeur disparaissent, les courtiers des grands crus disparaîtront. Il restera des courtiers de place qui feront de la vente de place, mais qui n'arbitreront plus les mécanismes en profondeur. Or, à Bordeaux, tout se juge et se réalise par rapport à l'achat. Les primeurs sont consubstantiels à l'existence même du négoce de place de Bordeaux. Les courtiers en sont le levier. C'est un système ancestral qui peut sembler fermé, mais qu'il ne faut pas démonter."

grape growers can act independently and market their wines directly. They can also sell their harvest to a cooperative, which can also market wines on its own. However, more often they all sell their wines to merchants. In this case the wines they supply can be either contracted or sold on the spot market (in bulk or bottled). Bordeaux wines offer vary considerably from year to year in terms of quality and quantity. If on the futures market the price is fixed by the producer, on the spot market it is regulated by the balance of the offer and the demand. The variability of quality, quantity and price affects the relationships between actors, making them quite tight in the situation of overproduction or scarcity. The following chart (Fig. 18.1) shows bulk wine price fluctuations of some AOC in Bordeaux:

The price fluctuations which have a direct effect on the grape growers' and merchants' income can be so important that they can provoke serious confrontation between actors. In such cases CIVB or appellation syndicates have to intervene. The inconsistency of the spot market deals is a main preoccupation of all actors and governing structures.

18.5   Typology of Bordeaux Merchants

Bordeaux's merchants control about 70% of wines produced in the region. Despite the fact that there are about 300 merchants, only 46 of them perform 94% of the total business and the list of who is really in charge can be narrowed down further (Table 18.2). Only two merchants (Castel and Johanès Boubée) contributed over one-third to the total Bordeaux merchants' turnover in 2014, making over €700 million each (even more if we consider Castel together with the merchants that the firm controls (Oenoalliance, Barton & Guestier, Barriere)).[8]

Table 18.2 Merchants' concentration in Bordeaux

Turnover, million euros	Number of firms	% of total turnover
>75	10	50
35–75	20	31
15–35	16	13
Total	46	94

Source: CIVB "Vin de Bordeaux: repères économiques", June 2014

---

[8] Unlike the majority of merchants in Bordeaux, the portfolio of these two companies is much diversified and the wines from Bordeaux represent less than a half of it.

All these firms represent a much heterogeneous community in many aspects. Many of them are long-established dynasties (Butel 2008) with British (Barton, Johnston, Lawton, etc.), German (Schröder et Schyler, Eschenauer, Kressmann, etc.) or Dutch (Beyerman, Mahler-Besse, Quien, etc.) origins. Others represent families with wine commerce traditions from Corrèze (Borie-Manoux, Moueix, Horeau-Beylot) which entered Bordeaux wine business mostly in the beginning of the twentieth century; there are some more recent entries with no family wine tradition at all—Castel that has become an international giant is one of the most important examples—and finally there are some recently appeared companies trying to occupy available niches.

The difference lies not only in the origin of these firms of course but also in their size, market strategy, relationships with winegrowers, financial and organizational structure and so on. They can present different level of backward integration. Total backward integration when merchants produce wines form their own vineyards or buy grapes from grape growers is very rare in Bordeaux. Some merchants own vineyards via their wine-producing estates, but their production is not used to produce merchants' commercial brands. More often merchants buy bulk wine and then blend and age it or they buy already bottled wine and distribute it as it is.

Table 18.3 Typology of negociants in Bordeaux: variables

Domain	Variables
Size, structure and value chain positioning	Turnover, number of employees
	Number, type and geography of sites and subsidiaries
	Backward or forward integration
	Grands Crus Classés proprietors
	Added value, Stock rotation
Distribution	Main clients: large retailers or HRC (hotels, cafés, restaurants) or wholesalers or specialized stores or private customers
	National market or export
Product portfolio	Specialization in Grands Crus Classés, chateaux, brands or private labels; bulk or bottled
	AOC or table wines
	Bordeaux or other regions, other products in portfolio
Finance	Shareholders number, type (cooperative, private, wine and spirits or other industry, institutional) and geography
	Participation in mergers and acquisitions
	Gross profit margin, net profit margin, current ratio, gearing, acc. receivable, acc. payable, financial autonomy ratio, return on capital employed
Supply	Grapes, bulk or bottled wines
	Suppliers: independent grape growers, cooperatives, own vineyards; long-term contract practice

Considering all these differences, we tried to classify merchants in order to identify their business models. Our typology is based on the database that joins quantitative and qualitative data we produced by our own survey (questionnaire and interviews), open sources and financial data from Diane and Zephyr databases by Bureau van Dijk. Based on the data availability, 92 merchants have been analyzed; the majority of them are members of UMB.[9] The typology was made using data analysis techniques: multiple correspondence analysis and hierarchical cluster analysis. The variables we used characterize the relationships between merchants and their resource suppliers. We consider four main types of resources (Jullien and Smith 2008): demand, wine, finance and labor.[10] The following table summarize the variables used (Table 18.3).

One company has been excluded from data analysis because of its specificity. Maison Johanès Boubée, merchant acquired in 1999 by Carrefour group, its unique shareholder and client, all in one. So it cannot be correctly compared to other merchants and represents a class in itself. With headquarters in Bordeaux, this is one of the three biggest actors on the French wine market. In 2014 its turnover amounted to €772 million and the volume sold was 300 million liters. For Carrefour group, it exercises several roles: wine sourcing, bottling, central buying service for bulk and bottled wines, wine logistics in France. Oriented on private labels production, Johanès Boubée has seven sites all over France and deals with all French wines, Bordeaux wines representing 28% of the total volume. It also produces spirits and syrups, which represent about 5% of the total volume. It has a quite low export activity. This is not a classic representative of the Bordeaux merchants and it is not directly involved in competition among them. Its competition field lies more on national level between other distribution chains' central buying services.

Other 91 companies have been distributed between 7 groups (Table 18.4).

It is interesting to compare this typology with "winning models" identified by CIVB in its strategic plan of industry development discussed above. The plan identifies three main models:

1. Big operators having large diversified portfolio in "fun" (€2–6/bottle shelf price) and "exploration" (€6–20/bottle) segments with the turnover over €500 million.

---

[9] We excluded three companies' members or former members of UMB because spirits and not wine represent their main focus.

[10] Considering the unavailability of the employees' related data for the majority of analyzed firms, it was not included in data analysis.

Table 18.4 Typology of negociants in Bordeaux: results

Group	Number of firms	Description
1	5	Large merchants of Bordeaux, with the turnover more than €50 million, belong to this group. These companies are specialized in their own brands or private labels production. They are often backward integrated, some own vineyards. Their product range offers not only Bordeaux wines but also wines from other regions. They are present on national and international markets. Some of them have good financial performance, some more modest. However, the majority of them have a little resort to bank credits in order to finance their growth
2	3	The companies of the second group are of important size and superior financial results. They are specialized mostly in distribution of higher-range wines, including Grands Crus Classés. They sell them on the global market: France and export. These companies have very little production activity but important stock. They own renowned chateaux or are their subsidiaries
3	15	This group unites quite big merchants with no specialization, often subsidiaries of other merchants. They have a mixed product range—own brands, petits châteaux and sometimes Grands Crus—and important production activity. They are present in all distribution channels. Their financial performance is not stunning. The use of bank credits is quite important among these firms
4	9	This group represents financially successful merchants of important size. They have significant production facilities, often multiple sites, proceed by external growth strategy. Their product portfolio is diversified and they are proactive on the market. Export market oriented, on national market they are present in different distribution channels
5	28	In this class little but financially stable companies appear. In terms of structure, they are independent and family owned. They do not have a large stock. They offer "small chateaux" to wholesalers on national market
6	9	These are very little companies owned by wine producers and they specialized in marketing of their own products
7	22	This last group represents outsiders among merchants. Mostly little family owned companies with high level of bank debt and poor financial results

2. Companies of more modest size but still big with the turnover over €100 million dealing with "exploration" category and having more focused portfolio than the previous group.

3. Grands Crus specialists with the turnover €20–100 million, financially healthy in terms of capability to finance important stock, having good

clients portfolio to whom they offer high standard services and range of products.

Obviously, actual state of things identified by our typology is far enough from these profiles. Some companies indeed meet perfectly these "winning models" profiles, but a lot just survive. At the same time other competitive models look promising, such as some little companies dealing with niche markets. Given the rise in popularity of modern distribution channels, such as online sales for example, as well as easier and targeted access to consumers, there is a room for various models able to distribute variety that Bordeaux produces.

18.6   Conclusion

To conclude we would like to cite again Jean-François Moueix[11]: "Diversity makes the wealth of Bordeaux. Willing to proceed by concentration would be an enormous mistake. It would kill the distribution. Omnipresence of product all over the world is an imperative. Bordeaux, Bordeaux, Bordeaux everywhere." This point of view can be questioned of course. Nevertheless, Bordeaux wine region represent a very complex production system with many divisions to settle. It is populated by much atomized though concentrating actors on both sides—production and distribution. They propose on the global market an heterogeneous product portfolio with rather complex identification juxtaposing several attributes: appellation, brands, classifications and so on. While generally producers control the product, they do not control distribution and on the contrary merchants who control distribution do not control production. Therefore, coordination between them and the whole production system governance remain the issue of critical importance. While divide between grape growers and merchants is still on the agenda, it has started to blur, as many grape growers set up their own commercial companies as well as merchants acquire vineyards. Also, socially these two professional groups are often linked by family or financial ties.

---

[11] J.-Fr. Moueix, interview with Christian Seguin "Bordeaux partout, voilà la Vérité" in the newspaper *Sud-Ouest*, Thursday 14 June 2007, p. 7. Original version: "C'est la diversité qui fait la richesse de Bordeaux. Vouloir procéder à des concentrations constituerait une énorme erreur. Ce serait nécroser une distribution. L'impératif c'est l'omniprésence du produit dans le monde. Bordeaux, Bordeaux, Bordeaux partout."

References

Berthomeau, J. 2001. Comment mieux positionner les vins français sur les marchés d'exportation? Rapport remis au ministre de l'agriculture.

Butel, P. 2008. *Les dynasties bordelaises: splendeur, déclin et renouveau*. Paris: Perrin.

César, G. 2002. L'avenir de la viticulture française entre tradition et défi du Nouveau Monde. Rapport d'information n° 349 (2001–2002) de M. Gérard CÉSAR, fait au nom de la commission des affaires économiques, déposé le 10 juillet 2002. Sénat.

Chauvin, P.M. 2009. *Le marché de réputations. Cadres, chiffres et entrepreneurs de réputation sur le marché des Grands Crus bordelais LAPSAC*. Bordeaux, Université Victor Segalen Bordeaux 2. Doctorat en sociologie.

Colman, T. 2008. *Wine politics: How governments, environmentalists, mobsters, and critics influence the wines we drink*. Berkeley: University of California Press.

Hadj Ali, H., S. Lecocq, and M. Visser. 2010. The impact of gurus: Parker grades and en primeur wine prices. *Journal of Wine Economics* 5 (1): 22–39.

Jullien, B., and A. Smith, eds. 2008. *Industries and globalization: The political causality of differences*. Basingstoke: Palgrave Macmillan.

Patchell, J. 2011. *The territorial organization of variety: Cooperation and competition in Bordeaux, Napa and Chianti Classico*. Farnham/Burlington: Ashgate.

Pesme, J.-O., M.-C. Belis-Bergouignan, and N. Corade. 2010. Strategic operations and concentration in the Bordeaux-Aquitaine region. *International Journal of Wine Business Research* 22 (3): 308–324.

Pomel, B. 2006. Réussir l'avenir de la viticulture de France. Propositions présentées par Bernard Pomel, préfet, chargé de la coordination nationale des comités de bassin viticole pour la mise en oeuvre d'un plan national de restructuration de la filière vitivinicole française, mars 2006.

Réjalot, M. 2007. *Les logiques du château: filière et modèle vitivinicole à Bordeaux, 1980–2003*. Pessac: Presses universitaires de Bordeaux.

Roudié, Ph. 1994. *Vignobles et vignerons du Bordelai: 1850–1980*. Talence: Presses universitaires de Bordeaux.

Smith, A., J. de Maillard, and O. Costa. 2007. *Vin et politique: Bordeaux, la France, la mondialisation*. Paris: Sciences Po, Les Presses.

Stanziani, A. 2003. La falsification du vin en France, 1880–1905 : un cas de fraude agro-alimentaire. *Revue d'histoire moderne et contemporaine* 50 (2): 154–186.

Part IV

Backward Vertical Integration

Coord. by *Georges Giraud*

19

Introduction: Outsourcing Versus Integration, a Key Trade-Off for Wine Companies?

Georges Giraud

In all European wine-producing countries, with a long history of winemaking, the wine industry is composed of numerous, highly skilled actors applying outsourced or integrated business models according to their individual experience and know-how. The factors of success and profitability are multidimensional and the principal scientific challenge is to disentangle such factors, as far as it is possible (Maumbe and Brown 2013). Among European wine producers, French and Italian estates achieved the best profitability ratios from 2002 to 2008, regardless of the indicator used (Pappalardo et al. 2013). Available European data sources do not provide breakdowns at the regional level, and profitability may vary from one wine-producing area to another according to the notoriety of the terroir.

Although outsourcing is generally considered, within the management science literature, as a useful tool for increasing efficiency by reducing the agency costs, it has been found that companies processing top-quality products are more likely to integrate the stages of working out (Kremic et al. 2006; Fill and Visser 2000). Other factors to be considered are the risk of loss of core knowledge and increased transaction costs (Kremic et al. 2006). The main reason in favor of integration is that it allows at keeping quality under control along all stages of processing from raw material to sales. Quality control is acting as a key factor in meeting the expectations of the market's premium segment. In the wine sector both practices occur in various countries and vineyards. Two

G. Giraud (✉)
AgroSup, Graduate School of Agronomy and Food Science,
University Bourgogne Franche-Comté, Dijon, France
e-mail: georges.giraud@agrosupdijon.fr

© The Author(s) 2019
A. Alonso Ugaglia et al. (eds.), *The Palgrave Handbook of Wine Industry Economics*,
https://doi.org/10.1007/978-3-319-98633-3_19

main categories of wine grape growers exist: those who focus on grapevine cropping alone and those who also integrate the winemaking, whom we will refer to here, respectively, as viticulturists and winemakers. Several recent publications found that profitability increases with winemaking process integration (Cadot 2013; Castriota 2018; Corsi 2013).

The effect of terroir is based on pedo-climatic conditions (Atkinson 2011; Gade 2004) in combination with local winemaking practices and traditions. We can thus assume that terroir acts on firms' strategies not at the parcel level but at the appellation's one. In the forthcoming case studies, the contributors will investigate whether the choice between integrating winemaking process versus outsourcing depends upon the land availability where the wine estate is located. This assumption is supported by the findings of Cross et al. (2011), who found that the influence of terroir on vineyard prices (in the Willamette Valley of Oregon) was more strongly related to appellation designations than to locational attributes such as slope, aspect, elevation or soil type.

The bond between terroir and high-quality wine is not always well established through the appellation labeling scheme. With respect to grape procurement, brokers are said to be key and efficient substitutes for merchants in monitoring the winemaking process on the estates (Fares 2009). These findings suggest that, both upstream and downstream from the winemaking stage, outsourcing may be a factor of improved efficiency within the wine industry, especially for those among the companies employing a strong branding strategy.

Dilger (2009) found that in Germany, winegrowing estates led by salaried managers are more likely to bottle and sell wines of higher quality at higher prices and in lower quantities than estates led by their owners themselves. As a corollary to this finding, we may expect to find small winegrowers producing grapes of medium quality more prone to contract with external winemakers, whereas small growers who are able to produce top-quality wine should integrate added value through bottling on their own estates.

Visser and de Langen (2006) have pointed out that, in the case of Chile, the efficiency of a wine sector, within a given district, is strongly related to close networking and cooperation between that district's companies. This means that the outsourcing dilemma is not a simple to make or to sell decision for the core producers focused on winemaking but also includes R&D facilities, training facilities, the providers of dry materials, distribution channels and wine tourism activities (Visser and de Langen 2006).

These findings are congruent with those of Amadieu and Viviani (2011) who have demonstrated that a high level of intangible expenses has a positive impact on wine companies' performance by increasing expected profit and reducing variance risk. In addition, the authors indicate that, when R&D expenses are low in the wine industry, intangible expenses are mainly related to promotion and marketing and tend to be outsourced to independent marketing agencies (Amadieu and Viviani 2011).

Between integrating winemaking process in the estate and outsourcing to traders, a medium business model is provided by the cooperative scheme. The winegrower members of a cooperative delegate the winemaking process to this cooperative winery, in which they are collectively owners. They can focus on vine growing and use contractual commitment to sell their harvest to the cooperative as fresh grape or must. Cooperatives are key actors in the wine industry.

Market access for small grape-wine growers is often considered by literature through the case of cooperative wineries (Del Campo et al. 2009). Cooperatives are an alternative business model between small independent estates, making their own wine, and grape-wine growers selling fresh harvested grape or must to traders. This medium position between integration and outsourcing of winemaking seems to perform well for medium-range wines and innovative wines but does not fit with top-quality wines such as *premiers crus* or *grands crus* (Chiffoleau et al. 2007).

The literature review carried out here points to the fact that while outsourcing is considered to be a basic principle of good management for modern companies, it is sparsely applied in the wine industry with respect to the core stage of winemaking, although it is likely to be used for peripheral activities. Given that the majority of wine estates are not loss-producing, our goal is to study whether outsourcing or vertical integration of the wine companies is a factor of growth and profitability.

This objective will be achieved thanks to the oncoming four case studies. The case study made by G. Giraud and A. Diallo focuses on the effect of terroir on integration versus outsourcing strategies adopted by winemakers in Burgundy region, where the mosaic of vine parcels, so-called Climats de Bourgogne, is quite salient. The authors indicate that choosing between staying winegrower versus becoming a winemaker mainly depends on the terroir where the wine estate is located and influences its profitability. Clustering of wines based on *Appellation d'Origine Contrôlée* leads to village-based wine segmentation and also depends on export capability and distribution strategy at estate level.

The second case study explores the strategies chosen by cooperative companies in order to secure wine or grape procurement and analyzes how these choices influence the wine industry organization and profitability, since land regulation often aims at preserving the already existing winegrowers, instead of facilitating the incoming of new players, through planting rights scheme. The text from A. Alonso Ugaglia and J. Cadot pays special attention to the effect of financial constraints and strategies on vertical integration in wine French cooperatives. The authors clearly indicate that the proneness to alleviate risk and keep costs under control leads to vertical integration, whereas the literature review, as seen before, argues toward outsourcing.

The third case study from Pomarici, Barisan, Boatto and Galletto depicts the Prosecco wine industry structure. The production chain of this Italian well-known sparkling wine is deciphered in terms of integration, or not, of the winemaking process. Consistency with demand, production flexibility and cost efficiency are found as related to outsourcing orientation of the most important companies of the Prosecco industry. However, further investigation is needed in order to assess the effect of outsourcing on profitability.

The last case studied by A. Coelho and E. Montaigne gives insights from the vertical integration backward in the international wine industry. The authors pinpoint the influence of land availability, including land regulation, on large wine companies' growth pathways. According to land availability or scarcity, worldwide companies select different ways of growth. International wine brands need to ensure a stable quality of wines and volume to supply. Sourcing of wine and grape becomes a major stake into a market led by overall scarcity. Consequently, the companies act in order to secure wine or grape procurement chain. When land availability for vineyard is good, say in Chile or Australia, the growth of wine companies is based on greenfield investments (vineyard planting). However, given the scarcity of vineyards available for purchase in other places, such as Europe or the USA, making the procurement chain secure is achieved via brownfield investments which include mergers and acquisitions of already existing wine companies.

Finally, the common trait of these four case studies is land. Land for vineyard is available, or not, at worldwide level. Land is managed individually or collectively through cooperatives for viticulture and/or winemaking. Land is acting as terroir for quality-based segmentation of wines and consequently designs the wine industry organization at each level: worldwide, country or village.

References

Amadieu, P., and J.L. Viviani. 2011. Intangible expenses: A solution to increase the French wine industry performance? *European Review of Agricultural Economics 38* (2): 237–258.

Atkinson, J. 2011. Terroir and the Côte de Nuits. *Journal of Wine Research 22* (1): 35–41.

Cadot, J. 2013. Agency costs, vertical integration and ownership structure: The case of wine business in France. In *AAWE 7th Annual Conference*, Stellenbosch, June.

Castriota, S. 2018. Does excellence pay off? Quality, reputation and vertical integration in the wine market. AAWE Working paper, 227, March, 46 p.

Chiffoleau, Y., F. Dreyfus, R. Stofer, and J.-M. Touzard. 2007. Networks, innovation and performance, evidence from a cluster of wine cooperatives in Languedoc, France. In *Vertical markets and cooperative hierarchies*, ed. K. Karantininis and J. Nilsson, 35–59. Dordrecht: Springer.

Corsi, A. 2013. To make wine or to sell the grapes: Determinants of on-farm winemaking in Piedmont. In *AAWE 7th Annual Conference*, Stellenbosch, June.

Cross, R., A.J. Plantinga, and R.N. Stavins. 2011. The value of terroir: Hedonic estimation of vineyard sale prices. *Journal of Wine Economics 6* (1): 1–14.

Del Campo, F.J.G., D.B. López Lluch, and F. Vidal Jiménez. 2009. Corporate and farmer objectives in the wine business: The key to success of failure. *International Journal of Wine Research 1*: 27–40.

Dilger, A. 2009. In vino veritas: The effect of different management configurations in German viticulture. *Journal of Wine Research 20* (3): 199–208.

Fares, M. 2009. Brokers as experts in the French wine industry. *Journal of Wine Economics 4* (2): 152–165.

Fill, C., and E. Visser. 2000. The outsourcing dilemma: A composite approach to the make or buy decision. *Management Decision 38* (1): 43–50.

Gade, D.W. 2004. Tradition, territory, and terroir in French viniculture: Cassis, France, and appellation contrôlée. *Annals of the Assoc. of American Geographers 94* (4): 848–867.

Kremic, T., O.I. Tukel, and W.O. Rom. 2006. Outsourcing decision support: A survey of benefits, risks, and decision factors. *Supply Chain Management: An International Journal 11* (6): 467–482.

Maumbe, B.M., and C. Brown. 2013. Entrepreneurial and buyer-driven local wine supply chains: Case study of Acres of Land Winery in Kentucky. *International Food and Agribusiness Management Review 16* (1): 135–157.

Pappalardo, G., A. Scienza, G. Vindigni, and M. d'Amico. 2013. Profitability of wine grape growing in the EU member states. *Journal of Wine Research 24* (1): 59–76.

Visser, E.J., and P. de Langen. 2006. The importance and quality of governance in the Chilean wine industry. *Geojournal 65* (3): 177–197.

20

To Make or to Buy? A Managerial Trade-Off of Winemaking Process in the Burgundy Vineyards

Georges Giraud and Abdoul Diallo

20.1 Introduction

Located between the cities of Paris and Lyon, in the northeast quarter of France, the Burgundy wine-grape growing area occupies 31,470 hectares (ha) and includes 3430 wine estates employing 11,300 farmers and other workers. It produces 1.5 million hectoliters (hl) of wine, selling for €1.2 billion in 17 million cases, of which 48% are exported. Burgundy is a small wine-producing region in terms of geographic area but produces great wines, highly priced. From 2000 to 2010, the share of the total harvest sold as fresh grapes, grape must or juice increased from 10% to 16% (Bruley 2011). This new trend toward outsourcing pertains to the core stage of business for wineries, since winemaking outsourcing can lead to a loss of control for the wine-grape growers. Questions arise as to how wine-grape growers are coping with this new business model and conversely how winemakers can keep the quality of their raw materials under control when buying freshly harvested grapes or must on the open market.

The present study explores the strategies of wine estates with respect to outsourcing versus integration of the winemaking process through an analysis

G. Giraud (✉)
AgroSup, Graduate School of Agronomy and Food Science,
University Bourgogne Franche-Comté, Dijon, France
e-mail: georges.giraud@agrosupdijon.fr

A. Diallo
AgroSup, Dijon, France

© The Author(s) 2019
A. Alonso Ugaglia et al. (eds.), *The Palgrave Handbook of Wine Industry Economics*,
https://doi.org/10.1007/978-3-319-98633-3_20

of original and recent data from the Burgundy wine industry. The data analysis seeks to establish well-identified clusters among wine estates with respect to their choice of outsourcing versus integration.

Our research questions are: (i) does the choice of business model, between staying a viticulturist and also becoming a winemaker, matter with respect to profitability? (ii) Does terroir act on firms' strategies? Such hypothesis suggests that wine estates' strategies will be different from one vineyard to another and not only among estates of different sizes. We will investigate these questions within the mosaic of the vineyards in Burgundy.

20.2   Dataset and Analysis

The dataset used covers all 3430 estates producing grapes or wine in Burgundy in 2011 (Table 20.1). Variables are based on data gathered by the Burgundy Wines Board from each company via their cellar registers, including white, red or sparkling wine; regional appellation, *village* appellation, *premier cru* or *grand cru*; and selling bottled wine, in bulk or freshly harvested grapes or must (Appendix 1).

A hierarchical ascendant classification (HAC) was applied to winegrowers' data for the identification of clusters, using the Ward algorithm for maximization of intercluster variance (Gordon 1999). A principal components analysis (PCA) was then applied to the clusters so identified in order to extract the most important variables and to analyze the structure of the observations with respect to these (Abdi and Williams 2010). Finally, the ratios of efficiency and profitability were compared according to the size and status (viticulturists vs. winemaker) of the wine estates.

The overall turnover of Burgundy wines is estimated at €1.2 billion per year, of which 48% is exported. Within the domestic market, 23% is sold in mass-distribution outlets (supermarkets), 14% by direct sales, 12% via bars or restaurants and 3% in specialist urban wine shops (Brivet 2013). With respect

Table 20.1 Number of wine estates according to the wine-grape-growing area, Burgundy 2011

Côte & Hautes Côtes de Beaune	1137
Mâconnais	633
Côte & Hautes Côtes de Nuits	627
Chablis	413
Côte Chalonnaise	361
Grand Auxerrois	259

Source: Bruley (2011)

to the winemaking process, 55% of grape production is harvested, transformed into wine and bottled on the same holding; the remainder is harvested and sold as fresh grapes, grape must or juice to the cooperative wineries or traders. The 1600 year-old tradition of winemaking in Côte d'Or[1] is still vivid: 72% of the grapes harvested in this area is made into wine by the wine-grape growers themselves; only 21% is collected by means of mechanical harvesting. In the newer vineyards in Burgundy, where winemaking traditions are a mere century old, 47% of the harvest is used as grapes or must by the cooperative wineries, and 71% is collected by mechanical means.

The Burgundy region accounts for 0.4% of worldwide wine production and represented 2.8% of global wine sales in 2010 (Cadilhon et al. 2011). The share of Burgundy wines' export value is thus seven times higher than their share of volume or growing area. Burgundy produces 1.5 million hl of wine, of which 60.5% is white wine, 31.5% is red and 8% is sparkling. At 54 hl per ha, average yields are among the lowest in France; average production per estate is 395 hl, the smallest scale of production after Champagne and Alsace. Within its 31,470 ha (amounting to 3.6% of the total area planted to vines in France), Burgundy holds 84 *appellations d'origine* (23.5% of the total number of French wine appellations). A *grand cru* appellation is held by 1.5% of the wine produced in Burgundy, while 47.5% bears a *premier cru* or *village* appellation. The remaining 51% of wine bears the regional appellation. The 200 million bottles produced yearly in Burgundy account for 3.2% of overall French wine output in volume and 18.5% in value, indicating an average price six times higher than the French average.

Notwithstanding this high price average, the range of prices for Burgundian wines is broad. In 2010, in mass-distribution channels in France, 15% of wines were sold for less than €3.50 per bottle (excluding value-added tax [VAT]), and 41% were priced between €3.50 and €6, while 33% were priced from €6 to €12 and 11% were sold for more than €12 per bottle. The lower the price, the higher the frequency of the regional appellation within the segment; the reverse is true for *premier cru* and *grand cru* appellations. Still, in urban wine shops in 2010 prices ranged from €7 for a white (chardonnay) regional appellation to €665 for a red (pinot noir) Gevrey-Chambertin Village appellation. Pricing policies in export countries are obviously dependent on importers' practices according to local price levels and thus do not allow for meaningful comparisons.

---

[1] The oldest wine-grape-growing area within the region of Burgundy.

This high pricing situation applies for prestigious, elegant and top-ranked wines such as Chablis, Meursault or Pommard. Some of these wines come from small- or medium-sized wineries, and others are issued by traders who are in some cases less inclined to brand their wines under the *appellation d'origine* labeling policy, preferring instead to promote their own brands.

Benefiting from deep-rooted traditions based on more than a millennium of know-how in the pristine mosaic of *Climats de Bourgogne*, the top-ranked wines bearing *premier cru* or *grand cru appellation* are both exported and sold on the highly demanding domestic market. These wines are made according to a long process in which quality control and the specifications attached to the appellation are extremely strict. This means that winemakers must tightly control every stage of the process via integration. At the other end of the market range, wines from the regional appellation face strong competition on both the export and domestic markets and have to contend with price pressure on large volumes. Consequently, keeping costs under control is more important for those winegrowers who are more oriented toward large-scale production. Efficient processing and modern management approaches, including outsourcing, are used in order to maintain profitability.

20.3   Main Results and Discussion

The HAC analysis carried out found that the strategies of Burgundian wine estates with respect to selling bottled wine versus harvested grapes/must or wine in bulk differ according to the color of the wine and the level of *appellation d'origine* (Appendix 1). Results obtained with data from the vineyards of Chablis, Côte de Nuits, Hautes Côtes de Nuits, Côte de Beaune and Hautes Côtes de Beaune are shown in order to illustrate our findings.[2] In Chablis, 98.5% of winegrowers produce white wine; in Côte & Hautes Côtes de Nuits, 82.6% of the estates produce red wine; and in Côte & Hautes Côtes de Beaune, 52.2% produce red wine.

Four clusters within the 413 winegrowers in Chablis were clearly identified by means of the HAC (Fig. 20.1). Not surprisingly, no difference based on wine type (red or white) appears among these clusters, since in Chablis nearly everybody produces white wine. The dominant business model consists of selling the harvest in bulk as fresh grapes or must to local cooperative wineries, merchants or traders.

---

[2] The results from the other wine-grape-growing areas (Mâconnais, Côte Chalonnaise and Grand Auxerrois) are rather similar.

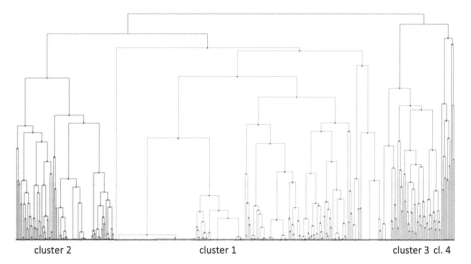

cluster 2   cluster 1   cluster 3 cl. 4

Fig. 20.1 HAC dendrogram of wine business models in Chablis. (Source: Authors)

The business of cluster 1—the largest cluster, including 54% of Chablis winegrowers—is relatively specialized, with 87% of wines bearing the *village* appellation (Appendix 1). Fully 92% of the wine produced by cluster 1 is sold as fresh grapes or must, primarily to cooperative wineries. The winegrowers of cluster 2 are 100% white winemakers and sell 68% of their wine in bulk to traders. The winegrowers of cluster 3 are the most diversified: although 64% of the wine they produce bears the *village* appellation, a sizeable 22% of this cluster's production is sold as *premier cru*, while a smaller portion (12%) is sold under the regional appellation. Cluster 3 is the only one with estates selling 78% of their production in bottles. The winegrowers of cluster 4 are also 100% white winemakers but are more strongly oriented toward the premium Chablis segment, with 63% of wine sold under the *premier cru* appellation and 13% as *grand cru*. Though working with these very stringent levels of *appellation d'origine*, 93% of the harvest from cluster 4 is sold as fresh grapes or must. Cluster 4 is also the smallest cluster, with winegrowers working with specialized small traders rather than with large cooperative wineries or larger traders.

It is worth considering whether the choice of wine business model operates under specific conditions in Chablis. The land there is principally devoted to cereal cropping and cow breeding. Even when they own some blocks of vine, the farmers in the Chablis area are most often breeders and mixed farming oriented. Vine growing is not their primary activity. As farmers, they are able to pay attention to wine-grape growing, but they are inclined to delegate winemaking to other actors. This dominant scheme does not cover the whole spectrum of wine production in Chablis. Some farmers have wine as their main business. This is at least the case of the 16% of the winegrowers from Chablis belonging to cluster 3.

Within the five clusters identified as significant by HAC among the 627 winegrowers from Côte & Hautes Côtes de Nuits, cluster 1 includes 50% of the observed estates (Fig. 20.2). The main business model of clusters 1 and 5 is based on bottling wine on the estate (Appendix 1). However, a notable share of wine produced in this area is sold as fresh grapes or must (clusters 2 and 3), and cluster 4 is differentiated by selling wine in bulk.

Although producing red wine is their dominant feature, the winegrowers of cluster 2 are the most diversified, with 44% of their production in white wine and 18% in sparkling wine. Cluster 2 provides wine for the regional appellation with 78% of its production. The winegrowers of other clusters are also diversified with respect to the level of *appellation d'origine* they use. Those of cluster 3 sell 94% of their production as fresh grapes or must. Two-thirds of their production is for the *village* appellation and 26% for the regional one. The winegrowers of cluster 4 sell wine in bulk and provide 30% of their production to *premiers crus* and *grands crus*. Cluster 5, the smallest one, bottles 67% of its production and produces mostly (81%) *grands crus*.

Almost two-thirds of the winegrowers from Côte & Hautes Côtes de Nuits are also crop farmers. This may explain why the dominant business model is to sell freshly harvested grapes and must or wine in bulk for three of the five clusters.

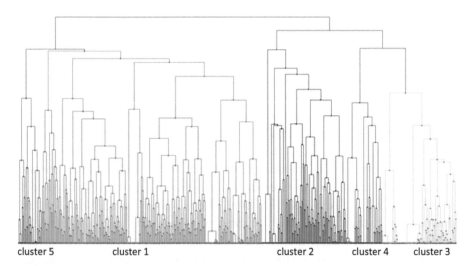

cluster 5   cluster 1   cluster 2   cluster 4   cluster 3

Fig. 20.2 HAC dendrogram of wine business models in Côte & Hautes Côtes de Nuits. (Source: Authors)

Among the 1137 wine estates established in Côte & Hautes Côtes de Beaune, HAC analysis allows us to distinguish five meaningful clusters (Fig. 20.3). The winegrowers of clusters 1 and 5, accounting for 45% of the estates, bottle their own wine, mostly red, and notably for *premiers crus* (Appendix 1). Those of cluster 3 (16% of the estates) also make primarily red wine, selling it in bulk for any level of *appellation d'origine*. The estates of clusters 2 and 4 sell, respectively, 90% and 87% of their production as freshly harvested grapes or must and make white wine for 55% of their output. The winegrowers of cluster 2 (25% of the estates) supply the regional appellation with 55% of their production, whereas those of cluster 4 (14% of the estates) are oriented toward *premiers crus* for 57% of their output.

The estates in Côte & Hautes Côtes de Beaune are the most focused on wine-grape growing among the farmers belonging to the Burgundian wine sector. They are also the least specialized in terms of the type of wine they produce, making both red and white wines (Appendix 1).

In each of the three wine-grape-growing areas described above, no significant correlation exists between the business model with respect to outsourcing versus integration of the winemaking process and the appellation profile of the clusters. The propensity to bottle one's own wine on the estate seems to be higher for the *premiers crus* and *grands crus*. However, some clusters working with regional or *village* appellations also bottle their own wine.

The choice of business model does seem to be related to the color of wine produced. Among the winegrowers making red wine from 60% to 99% of

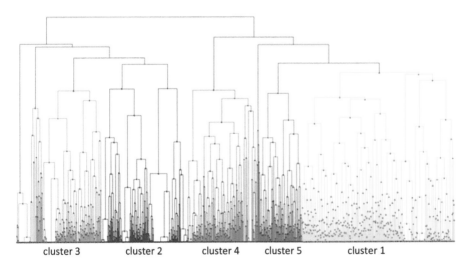

cluster 3   cluster 2   cluster 4   cluster 5   cluster 1

Fig. 20.3 HAC dendrogram of wine business models in Côte & Hautes Côtes de Beaune. (Source: Authors)

their production, 56% bottle their own wine. For the winegrowers making white wine from 66% to 100% of their production, 50% sell their harvest as fresh grapes or must. This is surprising with respect to certain financial implications. While white wine is usually sold within two years after harvest, red wine can be kept for longer and can benefit from cellaring. One consequence of this is that producing white wine may be considered as more favorable in terms of cash flow. There is thus a kind of paradox in red wine-grape growers bottling their own wine: by doing so, they tie up capital and create a cash-flow requirement for their estates. White wine-grape growers, on the other hand, can be seen as facilitating the raising of easy cash for the traders and the cooperative wineries by selling their production prior to the winemaking stage.

Another salient relationship found was between the bottling process and the rate of direct export. Of the winemakers bottling their own wine, from 69% to 93% had a rate of direct export ranging from 6% to 62%. This does not mean that the other winegrowers were unable to export. By outsourcing the bottling stage, however, these wine-grape farmers have to export indirectly by means of agents, most often the traders who buy their harvest or wine in bulk.

Within each Burgundian wine-producing area, winegrowers who bottle their own wine achieve noticeable rates of exportation. This means that bottled wine has been the standard for foreign shipping, in accordance with traceability requirements from distant markets. This situation may change in the near future given the cost of shipping glass with weight and no value, compared to shipping wine in bulk. The decision to ship bottled wine is easy to understand for top-ranked wines with premium prices such as *premiers crus* or *grands crus*. At high price points, the weight sensitivity of shipping is low. The trade-off between bottles and bulk for foreign shipping may be less clear for medium-range wines, which make up the majority of business today, especially for distant markets such as Asia.

Overall, the HAC employed identifies the differences among clusters within each wine-producing area. A more complete perspective is needed for deeper analysis.

Carried out with data from the previously identified clusters across all of Burgundy, a PCA yields interesting results (Fig. 20.4). The three most important factors extracted, with Eigen value > 1.5, explain 67.6% of the overall variance, which is strongly significant (Appendix 2).

The first acting factor, explaining 28.1% of the overall variance, is composed of winegrowers making red wine versus white wine. Red wine is generally bottled on-estate, whereas white wine is more often sold as fresh grapes or must. The second factor differentiating winegrowers explains 22.7% of the variance and is made up of winegrowers making sparkling wine bearing the regional appellation (such as Crémant de Bourgogne) versus those producing

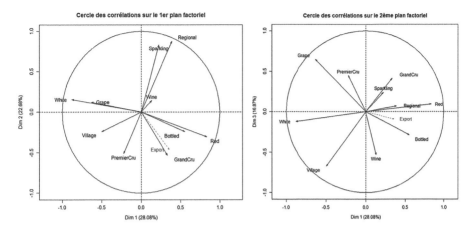

Fig. 20.4 Principal Component Analysis of winegrowers' business models, Burgundy 2011. (Source: Authors)

grands crus or *premiers crus*. The third factor differentiating winegrowers explains 16.9% of the overall variance. It opposes those winegrowers selling their harvest as fresh grapes or must versus those selling wine in bulk under the *village* appellation.

These results are congruent with the previous findings indicating that a variety of business models are found within the Burgundian wine sector. Not strictly linked to a specific level of *appellation d'origine*, the choice between outsourcing and integration of winemaking seems more closely tied to red versus white winemaking. Our next question is: does it interfere with estates' efficiency and profitability?

The results obtained through data analysis indicate that important differences exist among the estates (Table 20.2). Size of operation has an impact on efficiency and profitability, but it is not the only factor: winemakers and viticulturists do not have the same efficiency or profitability, whatever their size. Those who integrate winemaking are more profitable than those who focus only on viticulture.

On average, annual income is 10% below expenses for the 25% smallest viticulturists (first quartile) and exceeds expenses by 15% for the 25% biggest ones (last quartile) (Brivet 2013). For winegrowers making wine, annual income is 6% below expenses for the smallest quartile and 22% above expenses for the largest quartile. For the viticulturists, the rate of return is −3% for the smallest quartile and +6.5% for the largest. This translates into a ratio of +3.5% for the smallest quartile of winemakers and +14% for the largest quartile. In terms of both efficiency and profitability, in other words, the magnitude of ratios increases with size of operation, although the difference between viticulturists and winemakers is also noticeable.

Table 20.2 Efficiency and profitability of wine estates according to size and business model

Burgundy 2011	Turnover/expenses			Rate of return of assets		
	Viticulturists	Winemakers	Δ	Viticulturists	Winemakers	Δ
1st quartile	−10%	−6%	4	−3%	+3.5%	6.5
Last quartile	+15%	+22%	7	+6.5%	+14%	7.5
Δ	25	28		9.5	10.5	
Wine estates	μ size	μ yield		μ sales	Income/ working unit	
1st quartile	8 ha	47 hl/ha		5700 cases	€57,000	
Last quartile	34 ha	62 hl/ha		14,100 cases	€47,000	

Source: Author's elaboration from Brivet data (2013)
Δ = |x−y| is the difference of value between the categories or the quartiles, that is, 4 = |−10% − (−6%)| and 25 = |−10% − 15%|

The estates belonging to the last quartile have an average size of 34 ha, produce 62 hl/ha and sell 14,100 cases of 12 bottles each. The average size of estates from the first quartile is 8 ha; they produce 47 hl/ha and sell 5700 cases. Surprisingly, estates in the first quartile earn €57,000 per working unit, whereas large estates earn €47,000. The ability to address niche markets and to export directly may be determining factors with respect to profitability among Burgundian wine producers.

The range of efficiency and profitability is sensitive to the size of the estates, but it also depends on the business model. The difference (Δ) is larger according to size within the same business model than it is between business models within the same size category.

20.4   Limitation

The first limitation of such results is based on the way data are defined. Extracted from wine cellar registers, the data employed here do not include the final destination of the merchandise. Fortunately the location of the company is given, allowing an analysis of the effect of appellation on business strategy in the wine industry in Burgundy.

Another limitation is the absence of records indicating the financial links between wine companies. As a result of local land pressures, expected incomes from wine in Burgundy and the funds needed to run a wine business with important stocks of (usually red) wine for long-term cellaring, it is prudent for winegrowers to clearly separate their different ownerships. It is now common to have two or three different companies operating within the same estate: one owns and manages the vineyard, a second oversees winemaking in a dedicated building, separate from the owners' home, and a third one manages the wine cellar and handles the marketing and selling of the wine. Some of the exchanges recorded in the dataset thus represent contracts between different companies within the same holding rather than genuine outsourcing.

A similar limitation relates to the close relationships between some traders and estates. Formerly distinct, these businesses are nowadays more strongly interrelated. In order to secure high quality and minimum quantities of grapes at harvest, it is now common to find traders who own parcels of vines in part or in full. In this case, the sales of fresh grapes or must and the shipping of wine in bulk to the trader cannot be seen as pure outsourcing practices. They are internal sales within different titular ownerships of the same wine company. The reverse situation occurs as well. Some winemakers, in addition to bottling their own wine, also buy fresh grapes or must from other viticulturists in order to produce a broader portfolio of different wines. In doing so, they become traders in their own right.

20.5   Conclusion

Instead of identifying the best way to manage a profitable business in the Burgundy wine industry, our study highlights the diverse possible ways of doing so. Our results indicate that the diversity of wines and the mosaic of small and large estates are not limiting factors for making excellent wines and running a viable business simultaneously. Within this diversity, the *terroir* of origin is a key factor in the choice of business models according to the long experience of the winegrowers.

The more prestigious the wine is and the higher its price, the better integrated the winemaking process is likely to be. This correlation is stronger for the red wine sector than it is for the white wine sector, where the relationships are a bit more complex. In any case, this indicates that outsourcing, although used occasionally, is not the dominant path to business profitability within the French wine industry, at least for top-quality wines such as the *grands crus* and *premiers crus* of Burgundy.

Although congruent with previous studies and a good depiction of the mosaic of wine businesses in Burgundy, the results found here suggest the need for further investigation and additional data in order to arrive at a better understanding of wine-grape growers' business model decisions. A more complete dataset based not only on cellar registers but supplemented by a specific survey would be useful in order to confirm or refute the present findings. It would also be interesting to carry out similar surveys in wine-producing areas other than Burgundy.

Appendix 1: Sales' Breakdown of 3430 Wine Estates According to Clusters and Wine-Grape-Growing Areas

| Burgundy, 2011 | Packaging | | | Color of wine | | | Appellation level | | | | Direct | Estates |
Cluster	Bottled (%)	Grape (%)	In bulk (%)	Red (%)	White (%)	Sparkling (%)	Regional (%)	Village (%)	Premier cru (%)	Grand cru (%)	export (%)	number
Auxerre 1	87	4	9	60	33	7	73	27	0	0	6	96
Auxerre 2	5	84	11	10	90	0	38	53	9	0	1	67
Auxerre 3	31	22	47	30	66	4	82	16	2	0	5	52
Auxerre 4	7	93	0	2	4	94	99	1	0	0	0	44
Beaune 1	80	15	5	64	34	2	30	42	27	1	11	398
Beaune 2	6	90	4	27	55	18	55	42	3	0	0	284
Beaune 3	26	13	61	73	26	1	45	37	17	1	3	182
Beaune 4	9	87	4	45	55	0	6	19	57	18	3	159
Beaune 5	93	5	2	52	47	1	20	41	37	2	62	114
Chablis 1	2	92	6	0	99	1	2	86	11	1	0	223
Chablis 2	19	13	68	0	100	0	2	85	11	2	4	91
Chablis 3	78	9	13	2	97	1	12	64	22	2	34	66
Chablis 4	1	93	6	0	100	0	21	3	63	13	0	33
Chalon 1	79	10	11	63	32	5	35	44	21	0	9	152
Chalon 2	19	28	53	70	20	10	85	11	4	0	1	112
Chalon 3	4	91	5	5	6	89	98	1	1	0	0	54
Chalon 4	6	77	17	24	75	1	34	28	38	0	0	43
Macon 1	20	43	37	12	77	11	82	18	0	0	3	247
Macon 2	5	70	25	0	100	0	8	91	1	0	1	196
Macon 3	89	5	6	13	85	2	48	52	0	0	20	190
Nuits 1	79	9	12	91	8	1	28	46	21	5	27	315
Nuits 2	27	64	9	38	44	18	74	16	8	2	5	120
Nuits 3	3	95	2	96	4	0	26	65	7	2	0	108
Nuits 4	8	1	91	97	3	0	18	52	23	7	1	52
Nuits 5	69	27	4	99	1	0	2	12	5	81	42	32

Note: breakdown of wine sold (%) as bottled/fresh grape/wine in bulk; red/white/sparkling; regional/village/premier cru/grand cru appellation; number of estates in the cluster

Appendix 2: Results of PCA, 3430 Wine Estates, Burgundy 2011

Component	Eigen value	Percentage of variance	Cumulative % of variance
Comp 1	2.808	28.084	28.084
Comp 2	2.268	22.681	50.765
Comp 3	1.687	16.874	67.639
Comp 4	1.296	12.958	80.597
Comp 5	0.967	9.673	90.270
Comp 6	0.696	6.963	97.233
Comp 7	0.275	2.749	99.982
Comp 8	0.001	0.009	99.991
Comp 9	0.001	0.007	99.998
Comp 10	0	0.001	99.999

	Coordinates and correlation			Cos^2			Contribution		
	Dim 1	Dim 2	Dim 3	Dim 1	Dim 2	Dim 3	Dim 1	Dim 2	Dim 3
Red	0.8357	−0.3034	0.0949	0.70	0.09	0.01	24.87	4.06	0.53
Sparkling	0.2246	0.8325	0.2396	0.05	0.69	0.06	1.80	30.55	3.40
White	−0.8807	0.1576	−0.1203	0.78	0.02	0.01	27.62	1.10	0.86
Regional	0.3903	0.8752	0.0701	0.15	0.77	0.00	5.42	33.77	0.29
Village	−0.4977	−0.2392	−0.6721	0.25	0.06	0.45	8.82	2.52	26.77
Premier cru	−0.2224	−0.5092	0.4481	0.05	0.26	0.20	1.76	11.43	11.90
Grand cru	0.3335	−0.5313	0.4108	0.11	0.28	0.17	3.96	12.45	10.00
Bottled wine	0.5532	−0.239	−0.2884	0.31	0.06	0.08	10.9	2.52	4.93
Grape/must	−0.6318	0.1243	0.6449	0.40	0.02	0.42	14.22	0.68	24.65
Wine in bulk	0.1343	0.1443	−0.5303	0.02	0.02	0.28	0.64	0.92	16.67

References

Abdi, H., and L.J. Williams. 2010. Principal component analysis. *Computational Statistics 2* (4): 433–459.

Brivet, H. 2013. *Résultats économiques 2011 des vignerons bourguignons*. CER 71, Vinomarket, BIVB 28 janvier, 19 p.

Bruley, S. 2011. La viticulture en Bourgogne, RGA 2010. *Agreste Bourgogne* 125, 6 p.

Cadilhon, J., O. Catrou, and A. Renaud. 2011. Strong geographical identities, Census agriculture 2010, Wine industry. *Agreste Primeur* 271, 4 p.

Gordon, A.D. 1999. *Classification, monographs on statistics & applied probability*. 2nd ed. London: Chapman & Hall/CRC.

21

Vertical Integration and Financial Performance of French Wine Farms and Co-operatives

Adeline Alonso Ugaglia and Julien Cadot

21.1 Introduction: Benefits and Costs of Vertical Integration

Most studies and policymakers state that vertical integration is required to create value, such as Bijmanet al. (2012) who observe that, on the European scale, the most sustainable wine co-operatives are those which have implemented vertical integration or Couderc et al. (2010) who consider that the Languedoc-Roussillon wine firms should maintain control of their bottling and branding activities to capture more value on the regional scale. Moreover, Cadot (2015) observed that vertical integration significantly increases the margin of all wine firms but that it depends on the ownership structure of the firm. This reveals that vertical integration implies internal costs related to the relationship between the ownership and the management of the firm.

Therefore, the choice of vertical integration can be seen as a trade-off between a decrease in transaction costs and an increase in internal costs. Vertical integration requires an upper-skilled management which should

A. Alonso Ugaglia (✉)
Bordeaux Sciences Agro, University of Bordeaux, Gradignan, France
e-mail: adeline.ugaglia@agro-bordeaux.fr

J. Cadot
Institut Supérieur de Gestion (ISG), Paris, France and Department of Agricultural and Applied Economics at Virginia Tech, Blacksburg, USA
e-mail: juliencadot@vt.edu

A. Alonso Ugaglia et al. (eds.), *The Palgrave Handbook of Wine Industry Economics*,
https://doi.org/10.1007/978-3-319-98633-3_21

403

develop a specific human capital through learning by doing (Couderc et al. 2010). This changes the relationship between the owners of the firm and the managers (Cadot 2015). The management benefits from an informational advantage which could lead to agency costs.[1] In other words, because of their dominant position, the managers could adopt a behavior and an investment policy which do not strictly optimize value for the firm's owners. This mechanism should be different according to the ownership structure of the firm. Indeed, there should be no agency costs when the manager is also the owner of the firm. And, following the Jensen and Meckling (1976) approach, the level of these costs should be inversely related to the proportion of ownership held by the manager. The agency costs of certical integration should not affect farmers, but the issue can be critical for co-operatives, because of their "vaguely" defined ownership structure (Cook 1995) due to the double quality of the members, who are user-owners, and other principles of the co-operative structures such as the "one member one vote". Cadot (2015) shows that vertical integration implies agency costs[2] for outsider-managed firms but the overall impact of vertical integration remains positive. Unexpectedly, the agency costs associated with vertical integration do not increase in the case of co-operatives. However, co-operatives show the lowest overall impact of vertical integration on performance. Cadot and Viviani (2013) observe that the downstream structures related to Languedoc-Roussillon wine co-operatives, either a union of co-operatives or a subsidiary, stated that they are financially constrained, while the first-tier co-operatives are not. This could reveal that the co-operatives are reluctant to allocate sufficient resources to support their strategies of vertical integration.

In this chapter, we gather results about vertical-integration strategies of wine farms (and especially co-operative members compared to the others) and wine co-operatives in France to explore wine farms' performance in relation to their vertical-integration level. In the following section, we present the samples used for two studies, one focusing on vertical integration by wine firms, and the other by wine co-operatives. Then, we present the results.

---

[1] This is the concept of "entrenchment" of managers, formalized by Shleifer and Vishny (1989).
[2] This result is in line with D'aveni and Ravenscraft (1994).

21.2   Description of the Samples: French Wine Farms and Bordeaux Wine Co-operatives

21.2.1   French Wine Farms

The Farm Accountancy Data Network (FADN) in Europe provides representative data on farms according to three criteria: region, economic size and type of farm (ETO[3]). Here we used the data of the ETO viticulture for France over three years (2010, 2011 and 2012) on a constant sample. Insofar as this database does not differentiate between co-operative members and wine farms selling bulk wine (not registered in the database that refers only to the product sold) (Delord 2011), we coupled this data with the CVI.[4] We use the information on the destination of sales of wine farms to differentiate (Cadot et al. 2017):

- The co-operative members who deliver their grapes to a co-operative (over 75% of volumes). Then the co-operative processes and sells the wine on behalf of its members.
- The wine farms called "bulk" that produce wine from their grapes and sell more than 75% of their volume in bulk.
- The wine farms called "mixed", producing and selling wine in bulk and in bottles, each representing 25–75% of the volumes.
- The wine farms called "bottle", producing and selling wine in bottles for more than 75% of the volumes.
- The others, using several of these distribution channels and possibly selling fresh grapes and which do not fit in any of the categories proposed above.

The pairing of the FADN and the CVI allows us to create a file with 801 winegrowers. We exclude the farms with less than three registered years and the wine farms from the Champagne and Poitou-Charentes[5] (mainly Cognac) regions, to set a sample of 684 wine farms, including 258 wine co-operative members, 108 wine farms selling mainly bottled wine ("bottle"), 137 wine farms selling bulk wine ("bulk") and 111 "mixed" wine farms (Table 21.1). Thirty-eight percent of the wine farms deliver most of their grapes to a wine

---

[3] ETO: economic and technical orientation.

[4] CVI: computerized vineyard register in France.

[5] The financial characteristics of Champagne and Cognac farms are fundamentally different from the average French wine farms in terms of strategy.

Table 21.1 Number and wine farms' allocation

	Number of farms	Distribution (%)
Co-operative members	258	38
Bulk	137	20
Mixed	111	16
Bottle	108	16
Others	70	10
Total	684	100

co-operative. Fifty-two percent process wine and sell the wine in bulk or in bottles, by themselves or through intermediaries (negociants or wholesalers). The remaining 10% are composed of a variety of models and it is difficult to classify them (fresh harvest as the main activity or as an addition to wine selling). We do not present the results for this latest category which is very heterogeneous.

Appendix shows the distribution of these wine farms by wine region.

21.2.2   Bordeaux Wine Co-operatives

In 2010, the Bordeaux wine region encompasses 7400 farms cultivating vineyards, with 5700 farms specialized in wine growing. The vineyard covers 124,000 ha (about 50% of the agricultural area of the Gironde department) and generates 90% of this area's agricultural value. Two thousand four hundred and sixty winegrowers are co-operative members. They operate 24,279 ha, that is, 20% of the wine area in this department. The 39 Bordeaux co-operatives process about 36% of the 5.8 million hectoliters (hl) of the wine produced. The average size of farms exclusively making wine through the co-operatives is about 10 ha (DRAAF 2011).

There is no official database about co-operatives in France, so we used a survey to extract economic and financial information on all the Bordeaux wine co-operatives. This original database includes accounting data and information on the distribution channels and the volumes (both from the *déclaration de récolte*), the number of co-operative members and the area they operate in. Some questions (such as investment or winemaking costs per hl) are directly answered by the co-operative accountants. As a result, we are able to compute the sales per hl as well as the price paid to producers per hl and to make the link with the distribution channel, general co-operative features and financial ratios for the 2005–2010 period.

Our approach relies on the distinction of co-operatives according to their downstream strategy: "traditional", "union" or "vertical integration" following and adapting Cook (1995). We consider that the downstream strategy is:

– "Traditional", when co-operatives have implemented neither a union nor a vertical-integration strategy (12 co-operatives in 2010).
– "Union", when more than 30% of turnover is made up of sales thanks to a union of co-operatives for the commercial part (10 co-operatives in 2010).
– "Vertical integration", when bottled wine represents more than 30% of the turnover (15 co-operatives in 2010).

The "traditional" and "union" co-operatives are comparable in size considering the number of producers (Table 21.2). However, the size of the producers' farms is higher for producers who belong to a co-operative in "union". We observe that sales of co-operatives in "union" are also, on average, higher than sales of "traditional" co-operatives. This may be a direct consequence of the average size of producers' farms. The vertically integrated co-operatives seem to be more heterogeneous than the others in terms of size. Indeed, they encompass both the co-operatives with the highest number of producers and those with the lowest number. We make the same observation for the total area operated by co-operative members. It seems that the vineyard of each winegrower is smaller for these co-operatives than for co-operatives in "union".

Table 21.2 Size, sales and distribution channel

		Number of members	Area (ha)	Sales (€)
Traditional	Obs	57	76	76
	Mean	69	524	3,147,210
	Min	30	125	416,569
	Max	185	1935	14,600,000
Union	Obs	29	35	35
	Mean	77	785	4,351,052
	Min	33	100	466,085
	Max	208	2560	15,200,000
Vertical integration	Obs	73	102	102
	Mean	134	647	7,170,552
	Min	12	30	462,991
	Max	549	3671	25,400,000
Total	Obs	159	213	213
	Mean	100	626	5,271,695
	Min	12	30	416,569
	Max	549	3671	25,400,000

Note: Observations are co-operative-year, for example, 37 co-operatives over a five-year period (2005–2010)

Indeed, the average number of producers is higher for "vertically integrated" co-operatives, but the average area operated by each co-operative is smaller. The wine price (sales per hl) is closely comparable for "traditional" and "union" co-operatives.

In France, some co-operatives are specialized in the first stage of processing and sell the wine in bulk as a raw material to private companies (negociants) which will blend and market the product—the bottle of wine—to retailers. Traditionally, the main activity of Bordeaux wine co-operatives is to process the wine grapes produced by the co-operative members and to sell bulk wine to negociants, who blend, bottle and market the wine to retailers. This is what we consider as the "traditional" co-operatives. Others have chosen to blend and market their own wines to retailers, the "vertically integrated" co-operatives. They have successfully entered niche markets through vertical integration, that is, bottling and branding their own wine, such as the co-operatives of Saint-Émilion and Listrac in the Bordeaux wine region. Some other co-operatives have chosen to constitute a co-operative with other co-operatives, called a "union", specialized in the blending and marketing of wine. These co-operatives—the co-operative "unions"—have chosen to federate into second-tier co-operatives which directly compete with negociants.

The distinction between the first-tier co-operatives and the union of co-operatives is made in only a few studies. Cadot et al. (2016) collected data for the Bordeaux wine industry and show that 32% of Bordeaux wine co-operatives sell more than 75% of their wine in bulk, 27% sell more than 75% of their wine through a co-operative union and 40% sell more than 75% of their wine in bottles.

21.3 Wine Farms' Performance and Vertical-Integration Level

21.3.1 Ratios

Wine farms' performance is analyzed considering economic indicators but also financial performance ratios. The FADN provides the income generated by farms, taking into account the specificities of the farm: rents and distinction between employment and family work. Here, we present the production of the year[6] and, following Delord (2011), two specific balances in the financial analysis of farms, total income and family income for farms according to their degree of vertical integration.[7] The most relevant and operational measure of family income is the current income before tax (Chassard and Chevalier 2007; Delord 2011). The current income before tax, the sum of operating income and the financial result of the firm, corresponds to the benefit that can be assigned to the remuneration of the manager and self-employed caregivers who work on the farm. It is useful to analyze the ability of farms to generate income for all permanent workers, paid or unpaid, through the total income registered with the FADN. It is the amount of family income (not employees) and all expenses for employees, salaries and benefits, expressed per annual work unit (Delord 2011). The annual work unit represents the number of hours for a person employed full time for one year on a farm.

To explore the financial structure, we then propose an analysis of simplified average operating balances by wine farm category. We present, on one hand, the economic assets, defined by the consideration of two aggregates, fixed assets and working capital requirements (WCR).[8] Secondly, we present the financial liability which includes equity and net debt.[9] We propose to analyze financial performance by type of operation from average financial characteristics. To this end, we decompose the profitability of the activity depending on the margin and capital turnover, following a fairly standard approach in financial analysis, which can be applied to the analysis of farms (Barry and Ellinger 2012). We present an analysis of WCR in days of turnover[10] and debt ratios by measuring the amount of debt to equity and the debt ratio on the result. Finally, we look at two ratios that approximate the maturity of the debt to that asset: the medium- and long-term debts on the amount of assets and short-term debt on WCR.

---

[6] The production of the year is the aggregation of production sold, inventory variations, capitalized production, production and own consumption of various products from inseparable secondary activities, less purchases of animals. Production for the year does not include subsidies.

[7] We are interested in co-operative members as a reference, bulk, mixed and bottled private cellars. "Other" farms represent a minority and are not considered in the analysis of the degree of vertical integration.

[8] The need for working capital is the sum of trade receivables and payables less stocks. This is the amount necessary to fund the business operating cycle, that is to say, the gap between cash expenses incurred for the production and receipts from sales of products.

[9] Net debt is the sum of financial debt less cash operating assets (cash and securities). Debt allows us to consider only the debts that cannot be repaid immediately by farms.

[10] As seen above, the working capital is a highly dependent variable of the position of the companies in their sectors. Considering vertical integration leads us to attend to this aggregate.

21.3.2 Economic Performance

Table 21.3 shows the average data for four aggregates of the farm balance sheet. Co-operative members correspond to grape farms that combine the least assets (€250,000 against €440,000 for the entire sample). In particular, they have a much lower WCR compared to the amount of capital assets, while WCR is roughly equivalent to the amount of capital assets for all farms. The co-operatives are also the farms for which the net debt is the lowest since it only represents 13% of the financial liability (Fig. 21.1). At first reading, we see that the wine farms are well capitalized since the amount of equity is higher than the average capital assets (balance sheet analysis above), indicating that the working capital is necessarily positive. The debt level is generally low; it is generally less than one third of the total economic record.

The balance sheet of private cellars bottling their wine ("bottle") is over three times that of co-operative members (€870,000 against €250,000 on average). WCR represents 52% of total assets and 320 days of sales, which is higher than the average of the sample. Net debt represents 30% of the balance sheet, which is higher than that observed for all other wine farms. The balance sheet of wine farms processing and selling bulk wine ("bulk") is closer to the one of co-operative members. Fixed assets are higher (€213,915 against €152,567) and WCR as well (€156,355 against €94,490). The share of assets (58%) is also higher than the WCR in the economic assets (42%). Net debt is also quite low: 16% of the financial liability. "Mixed" wine firms have an amount of assets which is quite close to the one of private cellars processing and selling bulk wine ("bulk"), but the WCR is much higher. It represents 57% of the balance sheet and in days of turnover,

Table 21.3 Economic balance by level of vertical integration

	Economic assets (€)			Financial liability (€)		
Co-operative members	Fixed assets (€)	152,567	61%	Equity (€)	215,890	87%
	WCR (€)	96,490	39%	Net debt (€)	33,594	13%
Bulk	Fixed assets (€)	213,915	58%	Equity (€)	312,590	84%
	WCR (€)	156,355	42%	Net debt (€)	59,530	16%
Mixed	Fixed assets (€)	231,179	43%	Equity (€)	405,854	76%
	WCR (€)	302,238	57%	Net debt (€)	129,867	24%
Bottle	Fixed assets (€)	450,424	52%	Equity (€)	613,966	70%
	WCR (€)	420,964	48%	Net debt (€)	260,014	30%
Total	Fixed assets (€)	223,477	51%	Equity (€)	327,869	78%
	WCR (€)	196,614	49%	Net debt (€)	93,684	22%

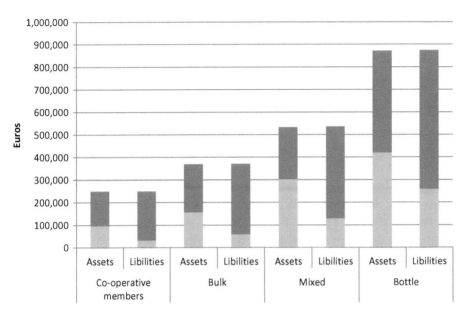

Fig. 21.1 Economic balance by level of vertical integration. (In dark gray, "high balance" on the asset and liabilities, respectively, corresponds to fixed assets and equity. In light gray, the "low balance" to match assets and liabilities, respectively, in WCR and net debt)

Table 21.4 Vertical integration and profitability ratios

	Margin (%)	Capital turnover	Working capital requirements	Profitability (%)
Co-operative members	25	0.48	290	11.82
Bulk	15	0.57	267	8.74
Mixed	17	0.66	309	11.96
Bottle	19	0.64	271	12.42
Total	20	0.60	282	11.41

and it is equivalent to the "bottle" wine farms' (318 against 320 days). The level of debt, 24% of the balance sheet, is as close to these same wine firms bottling the wine.

21.3.3   Financial Performance

The analysis of the production, the results and the financial structure allows us to calculate financial ratios. For the total sample, the average margin (family income over production) is 20% (Table 21.4). The capital turnover ratio is

0.60 (1 active euro is required to achieve production of €0.60), which positions the wine farms in the capital-intensive businesses (Vernimmen et al. 2015): this ratio of capital turnover is close to that of Eutelsat, whose business model is based on the ownership of a fleet of satellites. The profitability of operating assets is 11%. This result should be interpreted with caution. However, this return does not take into account the income of the farmer. Considering a minimum income of €20,000 per year, the economic profitability drops to 7.20% which is rather low, given the risk of the activity. Under these conditions, the return on average equity is 9.26%. Financial liabilities represent 28.3% of equity and less than twice the result of the company (financial debt/income = 1.95) (Table 21.5). Fixed assets are funded at 47% by medium- and long-term debts (medium- and long-term debts/assets) and short-term debt represents 11% of the WCR, which is rather low. The wine farms are profitable and have a low debt level, whether in the long or the medium term (see Tables 21.4 and 21.5).

21.3.3.1 Co-operative Members: A Significant Working Capital Requirement and Very Limited Bank Financing

The margin obtained by co-operative members is higher than the margin of wine farms that have chosen to integrate downstream activities. This margin indicates a capital-intensive behavior, with a turnover ratio of assets of 0.48, much lower than the average farm (0.60). These characteristics are typical of companies whose business is centered on production (grape production in this case).

The WCR represents 290 days of sales, which is higher than the one of private cellars bottling the wine (271 days) and private cellars processing and selling bulk (267 days). This significant amount reflects the relationship between the co-operative and the co-operative members. The producer brings

Table 21.5 Vertical integration and financial risk

	Financial debt/equity (%)	Financial debt/ income	Medium- and long-term debts/assets (%)	Short-term debt/ working capital requirements (%)
Co-operative members	15.56	3.56	28.18	5.81
Bulk	19.04	4.82	36.86	12.15
Mixed	32.00	2.96	56.51	14.18
Bottle	42.35	1.29	62.66	11.54
Total	28.57	3.35	47.46	11.24

his production to the co-operative and his income is smoothed over the whole year, usually with a delay of three months. Conversely, the farmer gets the amount of production sold in the weeks following the transaction if the wine sold by the co-operative is bulk wine. Ultimately, the efficiency obtained is 11.82%, which is greater than for the entire sample. This result, however, is relative: if we take into account an income of €20,000 for the farmer, the economic profitability drops to 4% and the return on equity would be only 4.82%, which seems very low to cover the risk associated with the activity.

The debt level is low, with net debt representing 15.56% of equity. It represents a little more than the result of a year. But if we take into account an income of €20,000 for the farmer, it represents 3.56 times the result, which is not negligible. Net assets are financed for less than a third of the debt in the medium and long term, and short-term debt represents only 5.8% of the WCR. These figures can be explained in two ways: a low level of investment, which can be alarming for the future of the co-operative system whose base is the competitiveness of co-operative producers, or a limited banking support. Note that members do not present short-term financial risks. The analysis shows that they have a short-term debt margin in the eventuality of temporary difficulties.

21.3.3.2 The Wine Farms Selling Bulk: Low Profitability and Low Debt

The margin obtained by "bulk" wine farms is lower on average than the one obtained by the "bottle" wine farms, with a capital turnover that is not better. Economic profitability falls to 8.74% but amounts to only 3.12% when considering an income of €20,000 for the farmer, which is not nearly enough to offset the economic risk on the activity. Thirty-six percent of the capital is financed by medium- and long-term debts which are slightly higher than the amount observed for co-operative members but very far from wine farms bottling the wine. However, the debt represents 1.82 times the family's income and 4.82 times the adjusted result, which is by far the highest ratio.

21.3.3.3 The "Mixed" Wine Farms: An Interesting Profitability but a Risk on WCR

The margin of "mixed" private cellars is between that of "bulk" private cellars and "bottle" ones. However, the capital turnover ratio is higher than that of these two categories of wine farms, which is explained both by the value added by the integration and the relatively small amount of assets (closer to "bulk" wine farms than "bottle" ones). Therefore, the "mixed" private cellars have an economic profitability of 11.96%, which is close to the profitability achieved by the "bottle" wine farms. The total debt level is 32%, which is just in between the "bulk" and the "bottle" wine farms. One point must be noticed: these wine farms are those with the highest WCR, with 309 days of production, and working capital financing rate of short-term debt is the highest (14.18%). Among the various types of wine farms observed in the sample, "mixed" private cellars are those that are most at risk of short-term failure. Note, however, that by correcting the result of a minimum income of €20,000 for the farmer, the result net debt ratio of these operations is better than the ratio for "bulk private" cellars or co-operative grape growers.

21.3.3.4   The Wine Farms Bottling and Selling the Wine: An Interesting Profitability and a Reasonable Debt

The valuation induced by bottling production improves the capital turnover ratio, but the cost of labor relative to the co-operative members reduces their margin. The "bottle" wine firms have the highest economic return of 12.42%. Net debt represents 42% of equity, against 28% for the entire sample. This debt can result in more favorable investment dynamics for these operations: the medium- and long-term debts account for almost two thirds of the assets. Despite this, the average debt represents 1.18 times the result (and only 1.29 times when we take into account the minimum income for the farmer), which is really reasonable. Similarly, the short-term risk is on average very limited since the short-term debt financing represents less than 11.5% of WCR.

From the co-operative members to the wine farms that sell bottled wine on the market, the producing firms have different degrees of vertical integration. It should be noted that the intermediate degrees of vertical integration have weaknesses, which are consistent with the bipolarization tendency of wine farms toward specialization or total integration observed by Traversac et al. (2007). According to our results, integrating the winemaking activity can lead to an increase of production, in value, by wine farm and by unit of work or area, but the expenses associated with the integration result in a lower income per unit of work and per area than the one obtained by co-operative members. The profitability of the capital employed on these farms is low and insignificant when we take into account the need for a minimum income for the farmer. The situation of "mixed" private cellars is different: the integration of the bottling activity improves the income of the wine farms and the profitability of the farm. But they face difficulties to manage their WCR. As a result, these farms are the ones facing the highest risk of bankruptcy. In this context, supply is an important issue for wine co-operatives and trading companies (negociants), not only in a long-term development perspective but also to avoid facing production overcapacity. Our analysis shows that co-operative members have a large debt capacity, probably due to lack of investment dynamics. The positive point is that this debt capacity makes it possible to finance their development if co-operatives are able to provide attractive growth prospects. Co-operatives can adopt strategies involving a partnership with trading companies, where one of the sources of supply, the "bulk" private cellars, is drying up.

21.4 Vertical Integration by the Wine-Processing Firms: Economic and Financial Performance in Bordeaux Wine Co-operatives

21.4.1 Descriptive Statistics

To go further with the vertical-integration process, we focus on the relationship between the price paid to co-operative members and the downstream strategies of co-operatives (Cadot et al. 2016). We analyze the trade-off between co-operatives' current payments to members relative to their investment, that is, a larger cash payout. When the co-operatives prioritize the price paid to producers, putting short-term decision-making ahead of the value of the firm, they tend to weaken the long-term strategy of the co-operative (through underinvestment). As a result, the horizon problem is a threat to the co-operatives' sustainability, especially when facing a crisis on the wine market. We propose to explore the relationship between the horizon problem of co-operatives and their downstream strategies. This should help us reveal the real long-term commitment of producers (co-operative members) to their co-operatives, according to the strategies chosen, and through this the sustainability of the different types of co-operatives.

Within the Bordeaux wine co-operatives, we observe that the wine price (sales per hl) is closely comparable for "traditional" and "union" co-operatives (Table 21.6). Both types of co-operatives deliver the same price to the producers per hl on average. However, the lowest value, for one "traditional"

Table 21.6 Product price and price paid to producers

		Sales per hl (€)	Price paid to producers (€/hl)
Traditional	Obs	71	71
	Mean	105	73
	Min	30	45
	Max	189	132
Union	Obs	29	35
	Mean	105	74
	Min	62	43
	Max	170	123
Vertical integration	Obs	29	50
	Mean	131	105
	Min	91	46
	Max	255	223
Total	Obs	129	156
	Mean	111	83
	Min	30	43
	Max	255	223

Note: Observations are co-operative-year, for example, 37 co-operatives over a 5-year period (2005–2010)

co-operative, is far below the lowest value observed for co-operatives in "union". Moreover, a striking point is that the minimum price paid to producers is higher than the output price. It can be interpreted as an extreme case of the horizon problem. As expected, the output price is higher for vertically integrated firms (+€26/hl for the average price). The price paid to producers is also higher (+€31/hl for the average payment).

Then, the margins (before the payment to producers), the obsolescence ratio and the leverage are, on average, highly similar for each type of co-operative (Table 21.7). The level of obsolescence is high for all categories of firms. These levels are far above the 50% which would represent the average obsolescence of a firm regularly renewing its assets.

21.4.2   The Co-operatives and Vertical Integration: Alone or Through a Union?

The results obtained confirm that the payment to producers is significantly higher in "vertically integrated" co-operatives (Cadot et al. 2016). The additional output price (sales per hl) largely explains this additional payment as the surplus due to belonging to a union is no longer significant and decreases by about €16/hl (from 23.76 to 8.00) for "vertically integrated" co-operatives when we introduce the sales per hl in the regression. If we introduce the margin, we do not see a difference: the output price explains most of the surplus.

Table 21.7 Margins, obsolescence and leverage

		Margins	Obsolescence	Leverage
Traditional	Obs	70	69	71
	Mean	76%	64%	0.45
	Min	48%	0%	0.02
	Max	97%	94%	1.41
Union	Obs	29	35	35
	Mean	70%	71%	0.37
	Min	44%	4%	0.00
	Max	94%	94%	1.35
Vertical integration	Obs	29	35	102
	Mean	70%	67%	0.48
	Min	48%	47%	0.00
	Max	91%	90%	2.11
Total	Obs	128	139	208
	Mean	73%	66%	0.45
	Min	44%	0%	0.00
	Max	97%	94%	2.11

The margin is the difference between the price paid to producers and the winemaking costs; the asset obsolescence is the ratio of asset amortization on the gross value of assets; and the leverage is the ratio of medium- and long-term debts on equity

However, when considering the interaction terms of margin with the downstream strategies, we observe that the premium for "vertically integrated" co-operative members disappears, which means that the surplus obtained by these producers is directly related to them. The price paid to producers is highly sensitive to the margin for co-operatives in "union" and less for "traditional" co-operatives. This may reveal a stronger connection between the co-operatives' capacity and the cash transfer to producers for co-operatives in "union", explaining why these latter are less risky than "traditional" co-operatives. For "vertically integrated" co-operatives, the more comfortable margins may provide a slack, making the price paid to producers independent of the yearly variations of margin.

There is an almost negligible difference between the price paid to producers in "traditional" co-operatives, that is, those which sell bulk wine to negociants, and the price paid to producers in co-operatives which have chosen to federate into a "union". By contrast, the "vertically integrated" co-operatives are able to offer a significantly better price for the production of the co-operative members. This research shows that "traditional" co-operatives prioritize payment to producers over renewal of assets, while co-operatives in "union" seem to anticipate the need for investment by a decrease of the price paid to producers when the capital obsolescence reaches a certain level. This mechanism would reveal a form of financial constraint which is not observed for "vertically integrated" co-operatives. It would come that the "traditional" co-operatives are prone to short-termism, while co-operatives which have chosen vertical integration throughout a "union" preserve their future financial capacities and the co-operatives which have chosen full vertical integration are able to provide a better price to the producers. However, it is hard to disentangle these effects of the co-operative strategy from those of the geographical indication that the wine co-operative can use to brand its wines.

21.5 Conclusion

Altogether, these results show that vertical integration for wine-grape producers can be carried out at the farm level or collectively via co-operative membership. In both cases, it seems that operating on the bulk-wine market is not profitable. Indeed, bulk-wine producers display low financial performance, and "traditional" co-operatives seem to be affected by short-termism, by prioritizing the payment to producers over the co-operative's sustainability. As such, vertical integration appears an efficient way to create value for wine-grape producers, but it should not stop at the bulk-wine production stage. They should rather bottle the wine. Moreover, vertical integration requires a full consideration of costs and investments necessary to perform well. In our view, this implies specific learning and presents wine-grape producers with new challenges, whether they choose to perform vertical integration alone or within a wine co-operative.

Appendix: Number of Wine Farms by Level of Vertical Integration for the Main Wine Regions (France, Viticulture)

	Co-operative members	Bulk	Mixed	Bottle	Others	Total
Alsace	13	0	11	8	10	42
Val de Loire Centre	1	14	14	10	12	51
Bourgogne-Beaujolais-Jura-Savoie	8	9	15	28	27	87
Bordeaux Aquitaine	31	51	39	26	5	152
Sud-Ouest	6	9	5	1	3	24
Vallée du Rhône-Provence	94	18	17	14	6	149
Languedoc-Roussillon	100	32	6	12	7	157
Corse	5	4	4	9	0	22
Total	258	137	111	108	70	684

References

Barry, P.J., and P.N. Ellinger. 2012. *Financial management in agriculture*. 7th ed, Boston: Prentice Hall, 408p.

Bijman, J., C. Ilopoulos, K.J. Poppe, C. Gijselinck, K. Hagedorn, M. Hanish, G. Hendrikse, P. Kühl, P. Ollila, P. Pyykönen, and G. Van der Sangen. 2012. Support for farmers' cooperatives – Final report, European Commission, 127pp.

Cadot, J. 2015. Agency costs of vertical integration—The case of family firms, investor-owned firms and cooperatives in the French wine industry. *Agricultural Economics* 46 (2): 187–194.

Cadot, J., and J.L. Viviani. 2013. Contraintes financières et ordre de financement hiérarchique des entreprises agroalimentaires: une approche par données d'enquête. *Economies et Sociétés – Systèmes Agroalimentaires* 11–12: 1909–1929.

Cadot J., A. Alonso Ugaglia, B. Bonnefous, and B. Del'homme. 2016. The horizon problem in Bordeaux wine cooperatives. *International Journal of Entrepreneurship and Small Business*, Special Issue on Wine 29(4): 651–668. https://doi.org/10.1504/IJESB.2016.10000526.

Cadot, J., Ugaglia A. Alonso, and J.P. Serra. 2017. Les effets de l'intégration verticale sur els revenus et les performances financières en viticulture française. *Economie rurale, Faits et chiffres* 360: 85–104.

Chassard, M., and B. Chevalier. 2007. Un large éventail de revenus agricoles. In *L'agriculture, nouveaux défis*, 2007th ed., 31–45. Paris: INSEE.

Cook, M.L. 1995. The future of US agricultural cooperatives: A neo-institutional approach. *American Journal of Agricultural Economics* 77 (5): 1153–1159.

Couderc, J.P., G. Giordano, and H. Remaud. 2010. Les entreprises de la filière vin. In: La vigne et le vin: mutations économiques en France et dans le monde, Les études de la documentation française, 99–156.

D'Aveni, R.A., and D.J. Ravenscraft. 1994. Economies of integration versus bureaucracy costs: Does vertical integration improve performance? *Academy of Management Journal* 37 (5): 1167–1206.

Delord, B. 2011. Faits et chiffres: La forte dispersion des revenus dans la viticulture française. *Économie rurale*, n 324, juillet-août, 60–70.

DRAAF. 2011. Modernisation, valorisation, restructuration, October [online] http://draaf.aquitaine.agriculture.gouv.fr/IMG/pdf/ DRAAF-Vitietats_generaux_signatures_cle4dc613-1.pdf. Accessed 22 Dec 2014.

Jensen, M.C., and W.H. Meckling. 1976. Theory of the firm: Managerial behaviour, agency costs and ownership structure. *Journal of Financial Economics* 3: 305–360.

Shleifer, A., and R. Vishny. 1989. Management entrenchment, the case of manager-specific investments. *Journal of Financial Economics* 25: 123–139.

Traversac, J.-B., M. Aubert, J.-P. Laporte, and P. Perrier-Cornet. 2007. Deux décennies d'évolution des structures de la viticulture française. Chapitre supplémentaire (web). In Couderc J.P., Hanin H., d'Hauteville F., Montaigne E. (dir.), Bacchus 2008, Dunod 2007, 32p.

Vernimmen, P., P. Quiry, and Y. Le Fur. 2015. *Finance d'Entreprise 2016* « le Vernimmen », Dalloz, 1 199p.

22

The Prosecco Superiore DOCG Industry Structure: Current Status and Evolution over Time

Eugenio Pomarici, Luigino Barisan, Vasco Boatto, and Luigi Galletto

22.1 Introduction

In the international wine market, Prosecco is known as the wine produced in a delimitated area located in Northeastern Italy using at least 85% of Glera grapes.[1] Such area includes nine provinces in the Veneto and Friuli-Venezia Giulia regions, and the concerned area under vines covers about 28,000 hectares.

According the EU regulation, Prosecco is a wine with a protected designation of origin (PDO),[2] so named because the delimited production area includes the village of Prosecco (near Trieste), from where the Glera production spread out over part of the Veneto and Friuli-Venezia Giulia areas. Prosecco is produced as sparkling (spumante), semi-sparkling (frizzante) or still wine; currently nearly all the production is sparkling. The sparkling wine is obtained

---

[1] Other local varieties commonly used are Bianchetta, Verdiso and Perera.

[2] According to Reg. 1308/2013, a PDO wine is a wine named with a geographical name identifying the production area, produced complying with a product specification (*disciplinare di produzione* in Italian), that is, a set of rules concerning the production area and grape varieties, yield per hectare and analytical parameters in wine.

E. Pomarici (✉) • L. Barisan • V. Boatto • L. Galletto
Department of Land, Environment, Agriculture and Forestry, University of Padua, Padua, Italy
e-mail: eugenio.pomarici@unipd.it; luigino.barisan@unipd.it; vasco.boatto@unipd.it; luigi.galletto@unipd.it

© The Author(s) 2019
A. Alonso Ugaglia et al. (eds.), *The Palgrave Handbook of Wine Industry Economics*,
https://doi.org/10.1007/978-3-319-98633-3_22

by the Martinotti (or Charmat) method; the still wine is obtained by a primary fermentation (base wine) which then undergoes a secondary fermentation in pressure tanks, after which it is bottled with an isobaric filling machine (De Rosa 1987).

Prosecco sparkling wine is one of the most interesting success cases in the wine business of recent years (Boatto et al. 2016; Rossetto et al. 2011). The Prosecco success is witnessed by the dramatic increase in supply: the aggregate supply of sparkling Prosecco wine was about 512 million bottles in 2016, a fivefold growth compared to 2000.

In the production process of the sparkling Prosecco, it is possible to recognize three main phases technically separable: grape production, processing (primary fermentation) of grapes to produce base wine, second fermentation of wine and bottling.[3] A production process thus structured allows for the existence of two intermediate markets for the intermediate outputs: grape market and base wine market.

Currently the Prosecco production involved 14,500 grape-producing farms, 1700 plants producing base wine and 600 plants performing second fermentation and bottling. Likewise in the whole Italian wine industry, the connection among all these technical units displays a wide variety of forms of production organization. These are allowed by the existence of some production phases which can be performed by independent agents and by the interaction between market segments and not uniform constraints determined by production technology in general and economies of scale in particular (Pomarici et al. 2008; Schamalensee and Willig 1989).

The whole Prosecco production is split into two categories: Prosecco with *denominazione di origine controllata* (Prosecco DOC) and Prosecco with *denominazione di origine controllata e garantita* (Prosecco DOCG), which, in the sparkling version, is named *Conegliano Valdobbiadene Prosecco Superiore DOCG* (from here CVPS DOCG). DOC and DOCG are the two categories laid down by Italian wine law[4] in order to establish a distinct hierarchy among Italian PDO wines. DOCG wines include wines of particular value, whose product specification must fulfill particularly severe requirements. The Prosecco DOC product specifications require a maximum yield per hectare equal to 18 tons of grape and in sparkling wine a total acidity content of not less than 4.5 grams per liter. The CVPS DOCG product specifications

---

[3] Secondary fermentation and bottling are virtually not separable.
[4] Law 238/2016.

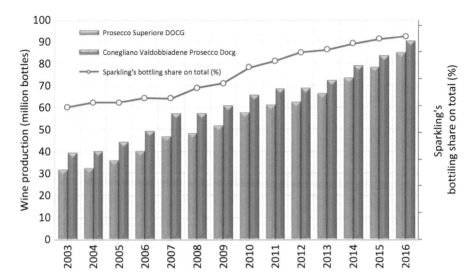

Fig. 22.1 Conegliano Valdobbiadene Prosecco DOCG: trends in sparkling wine market (bottles), 2003–2016. (*Sparkling: Prosecco Superiore DOCG and Superiore di Cartizze DOCG; Source: Data processing C.I.R.V.E., Conegliano, 2018)

require that grape production is carried out in a particular area inside the larger DOC production area, corresponding to the Conegliano Valdobbiadene hills; moreover, it requires a maximum yield per hectare equal to 13.5 tons of grape and, in sparkling wine, a total acidity content of not less than 5 grams per liter.

Currently the CVPS DOCG's production (about 90 million bottles) represents a share over the total Prosecco supply of about 18%; such relatively small share represents the top-quality Prosecco, which is rooted in a specific tradition, terroir and landscape. Also the CVPS DOCG's production has grown dramatically in the recent past (Fig. 22.1) being supplied both to the domestic market (60% in 2016) and to foreign markets (40% in 2016) (Fig. 22.2).

As part of whole Prosecco industry, the Prosecco Superiore DOCG's supply involves a smaller number of actors. Referring to 2016 are operating: 3387 grape-producing farms[5] (with 7549 hectares), 433 plants producing base wine, 181 plants performing second fermentation and bottling. Such hierarchy of figures reflects that existent in Italy, and the plants working at the end of the supply chain are connected to the upper echelons through different organization models.

---

[5] Specialized firms in grape production linked to private and cooperative wineries.

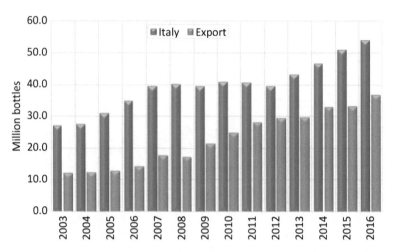

Fig. 22.2 Conegliano Valdobbiadene Prosecco DOCG: trends in sparkling wine sales on domestic and foreign markets, 2003–2016. (Source: Data processing C.I.R.V.E., Conegliano, 2018)

The aim of the current chapter is to analyze the evolution and the current structure of the Prosecco Superiore DOCG's industry, giving qualitative and quantitative evidence to the role of the different models of supply chain illustrated in Chap. 3 and shedding light on the interaction connecting the different supply chains via the intermediate markets of grape and base wine.

Already in 1976, Merlo and Favaretti offered a framework for understanding the Prosecco DOCG's supply chain, raising a number of research questions (Merlo and Favaretti 1976). Later, starting in 2003, the organization of the Prosecco production in the Conegliano Valdobbiadene area was continuously monitored in order to give an informative support to the activity of the local producer consortium (Consorzio di Tutela Vini Conegliano Valdobbiadene Prosecco DOCG).

22.2 Data and Methodology

The analysis of the CVPS DOCG's industry is carried out by integrating data (2010–2016) coming from three sources:

(a) AGEA (national agency in charge of monitoring the wine market), for data concerning official declaration about harvested grapes and wine production

(b) Valoritalia (certification body in charge of CVPS production control),[6] for data about the exchanges of grape and wine across agents involved in the Prosecco Superiore supply chain

(c) The Conegliano Valdobbiadene Prosecco District Observatory, offering a database built up by the yearly survey on wineries bottling Prosecco Superiore DOCG[7]

The analysis of the last database lets us classify the CVPS DOCG bottling wineries according to one of the supply chain models existing in the Italian wine industry, as identified in Chap. 3:

The agricultural supply chain or wine growers chain, which represents an integrated vertical coordination model based on bottlers directly controlling the whole production process and delivering to the final market wine obtained mainly from self-produced grapes.

The cooperative supply chain, which represents an integrated vertical coordination models led by the wine cooperatives with bottling facilities controlling the whole production process and delivering to the final market wine produced from grapes harvested by cooperative members.

The *industrial supply chain or transformer-bottlers' chain*, which represents a de-integrated vertical coordination model characterized by actors performing mainly grape processing and sparkling wine production, with no or rather small vineyards. *Transformer-bottlers are supplied by specialized* grape growers or even by firms belonging to the agricultural supply chain.

The *bottlers' supply chain or plain bottlers' chain*, which in the case of the CVPS DOCG's industry represents the de-integrated vertical coordination model characterized by actors performing mainly second fermentation and bottling. Plain bottlers are mostly supplied by vintners or by wine growers and wine cooperatives.

The association to the different supply chains of private wineries was carried out considering the main source of grape and wine. Only wineries bottling wine coming exclusively or mainly from grape of own production were classified as typical agricultural firms.

Data coming from AGEA and Valoritalia allowed the understanding of the quantitative consistency and the role in terms of production of the upward agents: grape growers and base wine producers (vintners).

---

[6] According to EU and Italian legislations.

[7] The Interdepartmental Centre for Research in Viticulture and Enology (CIRVE) of the Padova University is in charge of the survey.

The analysis of data concerning wineries associated to the considered supply chain allowed to trace the flow of grape and base wine inside each supply chain and the exchanges between the supply chains. In particular, analysis of data concerning wineries belonging to the non-integrated supply chains allowed to quantify the input (grape or wine) they receive from upward agents (grape growers or vintners) or from agents belonging to the integrated supply chains.

22.3   The Conegliano Valdobbiadene Prosecco Superiore DOCG Industry Structure in 2016

22.3.1   Firm Models in the Industry

As the CVPS DOCG production chain is the combination of three separate phases, potentially it may involve six possible firm models. Besides the fully integrated model, where the three production phases are performed by the same firm, three different specialization models for each production phase and two partially integrated models (namely grape production and production of base wine or production of base wine and secondary fermentation and bottling) are technically possible.

In the CVPS DOCG's production only five out of six possible firm models are present, since actors specialized in base wine production from purchased grape are not present. On the other hand, the fully integrated model is present in the two different forms of agricultural private firm and cooperative firm. The supply of the Prosecco Superiore DOCG's industry is, therefore, the combined output of both the integrated and the de-integrated supply chains.

Figure 22.3 offers a pictorial description of the structure of the industry and, to start with, the figures concerning the quantitative consistency of firms representing the different models in terms of number of production phases performed by the same firm. Among firms that perform the whole process, there are 111 private producers and 7 cooperatives. Farms specialized in grape production (grape growers) represent a rather widespread model, nearly 824 followed by about 250 firms performing only grape production and processing to obtain the base wine (vintners). Firms specialized in secondary fermentation and bottling and firms producing the sparkling wine purchasing grape are relatively few, about 30 for each model, but with an important role in the industry.

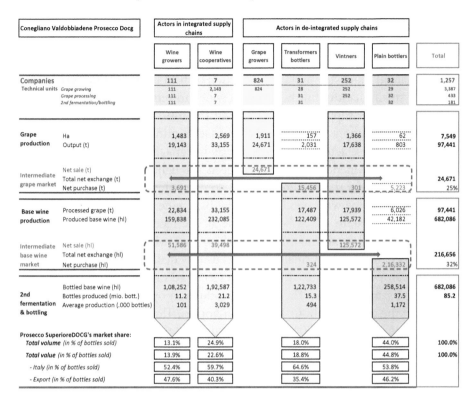

Fig. 22.3 Conegliano Valdobbiadene Prosecco DOCG' supply chains, 2016. (*Prosecco Superiore DOCG Sparkling; ⋯⋯= Production linked to the related own firms; Source: Data processing C.I.R.V.E., Conegliano, 2018.)

22.3.2 Supply Chains' Features and Contribution to Industry Supply

Figure 22.3 highlights the contribution to the Prosecco Superiore DOCG production by the four supply chains.

Wine growers contribute to supply 13% in volume (the lower share) and 14% in value. The average production by firm is about 100,000 bottles, also the lowest in the industry. Their bottling plant is, on average, rather small. Not all the firms in this supply chain exploit their whole production potential on the final market and supply the de-integrated supply chains with 24% of the base wine they produce.

Wine cooperatives contribute to supply one-fourth in volume and one-fifth in value (second share). The average production by firm is the largest, about three million bottles. Wine cooperatives process grapes produced by about 2200 associated grape-producing farms which control 2570 hectares. Some of the wine cooperatives transfer a share of the base wine to other wine cooperatives or to the de-integrated supply chains.

Transformer-bottlers contribute to supply nearly one-fifth in volume and a higher share in value. The average production by firm is about 500,000 bottles, a relatively small quantity but higher than wine growers. Anyway, some wineries belonging to this supply chain are among the top bottlers. Specialized grape growers mostly supply transformer-bottlers (accounting for 91% of their needs) and therefore these actors lead a partially de-integrated supply chain, where the coordination of wineries and grape producers is sought after by the grapes intermediate market. In the bottling process, some of the actors integrate the self-produced base wine with purchases on the base wine intermediate market; but others are not able to sell as bottled wine all the base wine they produce and, consequently, sell wine on the intermediate base wine market. Transformer-bottlers own, in few cases, small vineyards, usually dedicated to special products.

Plain bottlers contribute with the larger share to supply 44% in volume and almost the same in value. The average production by firms is quite large, the second in the industry, about 1.2 million bottles. They are mostly supplied by vintners (accounting for 70% of their needs) and therefore these actors lead a de-integrated supply chain where the coordination of bottling wineries with upward actors or actors belonging to other supply chains is sought after in the intermediate market of base wine. Also plain bottlers own in few cases small vineyards and grape processing, usually dedicated to special products.

The analysis of average prices for direct sales and sales to commercial channels reveals some differences in product differentiation strategies of the considered supply chains, which are more evident in direct sales (Table 22.1). The transformer-bottler wineries appear more oriented to high prices, while wine cooperatives show lower prices.

Table 22.1 Prosecco Superiore DOCG price differentiation by type of supply chain, wine destination and size[a] on domestic market, 2016

		Total	Very big	Big	Medium	Small
Wine growers	Direct sale	6.14	7.35	6.74	6.20	5.89
	Wholesales	5.31	5.28	5.32	5.37	5.21
Cooperatives	Direct sale	5.60	5.71	–	–	4.50
	Wholesales	4.55	4.55	–	–	–
Transformer-bottlers	Direct sale	7.11	8.73	6.33	6.52	5.49
	Wholesales	5.31	5.44	5.09	5.31	5.09
Plain bottlers	Direct sale	7.06	7.24	6.02	7.32	5.22
	Wholesales	5.17	5.13	6.04	4.98	4.42

[a]Bottling sizes (bottle × 1000 by year): very big > 1000; big 1000–500; medium 500–150; small < 150
Source: Data processing C.I.R.V.E., Conegliano, 2018

All the supply chains contribute to the delivery to domestic and foreign markets but with some differences. Plain bottlers are more oriented to export, while transformer-bottlers are more oriented to the domestic market (Fig. 22.3).

A last element of differentiation among supply chains is the share of production bottled for third parties (large retailer or other traders), which deliver to the market the wine with their own brands. Wine growers and plain bottlers in the interest of third parties contribute a relatively small share of their production, respectively, 20% and 12%, while wine cooperatives and transformer-bottlers in the interest of third parties contribute a larger share of their output, about 60%.

22.3.3   Intermediate Markets in the Industry

Since the de-integrated supply chains contribute to the final output of the industry by 62%, the intermediate markets assume a structural role in the CVPS DOCG's industry. In fact, as already indicated, they allow not only vertical relations but also transfers between firms belonging to different supply chains or the same supply chain. Anyway, in spite of the fact that exchange flows among individual actors have many trajectories, flow analysis shows that the integrated chains are net suppliers of actors operating in the non-integrated production chains as transformer-bottlers and plain bottlers.

The *grapes intermediate market* relies largely (93% of the net exchange) on the supply of 824 simple grape growers. Minor suppliers are farms belonging to the wine grower chain; their contribution as suppliers varies every year according to price evolution and the quantity of their harvest. Main purchasers are the transformer-bottlers (62% of the net exchange), while minor purchasers are firms belonging to the wine grower chain looking for grapes in case the customers' demand exceeds their own grape availability, and, in a few cases, plain bottlers, owners of pressing facilities, intervene as grape buyers. Total net exchanges represent about 25%[8] of the whole grape production, while total exchanges are near 30%. Transactions are of on-the-spot ones or, in many cases, based on long-lasting contracts or informal agreements. Intermediaries play a relevant role.

The *base wine intermediate market* is supplied by different types of actors. The largest suppliers are vintners followed by wine growers, while wineries belonging to the plain bottlers' chain are the main purchasers. The most important marketplace is at the *Camera di Commercio* in Treviso. Exchanges of grapes

---

[8] Grapes delivered by cooperative members to the cooperative processing facilities are kept out of this estimation.

and wine are negotiated there each Tuesday. Some brokers are recognized as the most influential in the base wine market. Total net exchanges represent about 32% of the full production, while total exchanges are likely near to 50%.

22.3.4 Supply Concentration and Analysis by Winery Dimension

The Prosecco Superiore DOCG supply is rather concentrated (Fig. 22.4), as it appeared to be also ten years ago (Galletto and Bianchin 2009). About two-thirds of the total production is delivered to the market by 20 wineries, 11% of the population, and the larger four wineries produce 30% of the total output (Table 22.2).

Very big wineries (yearly production over one million bottles) are present in all supply chains, but their number is rather small among wine growers; however, wine growers represent 90% of small wineries and one-fourth of medium wineries (Table 22.3). One-half of the very big wineries belong to the plain bottlers' supply chain and one-half of the big wineries belong to the transformer-bottlers' supply chain.

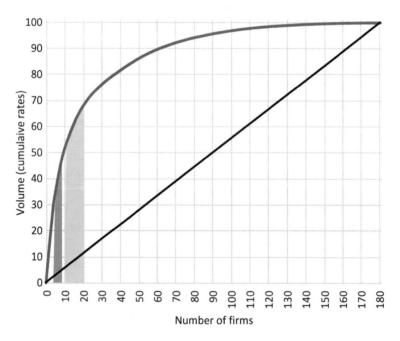

Fig. 22.4 Conegliano Valdobbiadene Prosecco DOCG: concentration index, 2016. (Source: Data processing C.I.R.V.E., Conegliano, 2018)

Table 22.2 Conegliano Valdobbiadene Prosecco's companies: concentration index, 2008–2016

Year	Concentration index[a]				
	HHI	CR_4	CR_8	CR_{10}	CR_{20}
2008	316	26.9	42.0	47.3	66.8
2016	346	29.9	45.7	51.4	67.8

[a]HHI, Herfindahl-Hirschman's index; CRx, concentration ratio for the top X firms
Source: Data processing C.I.R.V.E., Conegliano, 2018

Table 22.3 Prosecco Superiore DOCG producers' distribution by type of supply chain and bottling size[a], 2016

		Total	Very big	Big	Medium	Small
Wine growers	N.	111	3	6	21	81
	%	61.3%	10.0%	28.6%	52.5%	90.0%
Cooperatives	N.	7	6	0	0	1
	%	3.9%	20.0%	0.0%	0.0%	1.1%
Transformer-bottlers	N.	31	5	10	10	6
	%	17.1%	16.7%	47.6%	25.0%	6.7%
Plain bottlers	N.	32	16	5	9	2
	%	17.7%	53.3%	23.8%	22.5%	2.2%
Total	N.	**181**	**30**	**21**	**40**	**90**
	%	**100.0%**	**100.0%**	**100.0%**	**100.0%**	**100.0%**

[a]Bottling sizes (bottle × 1000 by year): very big > 1000; big 1000–500; medium 500–150; small < 150
Source: Data processing C.I.R.V.E., Conegliano, 2018

22.4 Evolution of the Industry over Time (2010–2016)

The output of all supply chains increased substantially over the period 2010–2016, but with a different rate (Table 22.4). The production of wine growers and transformer-bottlers shows a higher increase than average (47%), while the wine growers' expansion was lower than average. Anyway, these differences in the growth rate caused only small changes in the share of the four supply chains on total production, with only a slight increase of transformer-bottlers and decrease of plain bottlers and wine growers.

The number of wineries belonging to the four supply chains changed differently. Wineries belonging to the wine growers and plain bottlers' supply chains increased (respectively, by 16% and 14%), while wine cooperatives decreased by one unit and transformer-bottlers by 9%. The interaction between changes in aggregate production and number of wineries of the supply chains determined different changes in the average production of wineries. The average production of wineries belonging to plain bottlers' supply

Table 22.4 Prosecco Superiore DOCG industry structure: evolution over the period analyzed, 2010–2016

	2010	2011	2012	2013	2014	2015	2016	Changes (%) 2010–2016[a]
Data concerning whole industry:								
Prosecco Superiore DOCG production (million bottles)	57.8	61.2	62.7	66.5	73.4	78.4	85.2	47.4%
Prosecco Superiore DOCG wineries (units)	166	168	168	170	183	187	181	9.0%
Wine growers:								
Prosecco Superiore DOCG wineries (units)	96	99	101	104	111	115	111	15.6%
Volume sold (million bottles)	8.3	9.7	8.9	10.7	12.3	12.7	11.2	34.9%
Grapes processed (%)	19.3%	18.9%	19.5%	20.7%	21.1%	19.4%	23.4%	4.1%
Bottled market share (%)	14.4%	15.8%	14.2%	16.1%	16.8%	16.2%	13.1%	−1.3%
Average Prosecco DOCG sold per winery (0.000 bottles)[a]	87	97	88	102	111	110	101	16.1%
Bottling under contract (%)[a]	12.9%	13.1%	7.0%	9.4%	7.2%	19.9%	6.70%	−6.2%
Wine cooperatives:								
Prosecco Superiore DOCG wineries (units)	8	8	8	7	7	7	7	−12.5%
Volume sold (million bottles)	14.4	14.1	15.4	16.3	17.3	19.6	21.2	47.2%
Grapes processed (%)	30.7%	31.4%	32.4%	30.8%	28.1%	30.5%	34.0%	3.3%
Bottled market share (%)	25.0%	23.1%	24.5%	24.6%	23.6%	25.0%	24.9%	−0.1%
Average Prosecco DOCG sold per winery (0.000 bottles)[a]	1862	1677	1877	2324	2372	2816	3029	62.7%
Bottling under contract (%)[a]	12.4%	18.5%	21.5%	33.8%	41.8%	60.7%	65.9%	53.5%
Transformer-bottlers:								
Prosecco Superiore DOCG wineries (units)	34	28	27	28	28	30	31	−8.8%
Volume sold (million bottles)	8.3	8.1	9.8	10.5	10.5	12.2	15.3	84.3%
Grapes processed (%)	15.1%	13.7%	16.1%	17.0%	14.9%	13.6%	17.9%	2.8%
Bottled market share (%)	14.40%	13.2%	15.7%	15.8%	14.4%	15.5%	18.00%	3.6%
Average Prosecco DOCG sold per winery (0.000 bottles)[a]	243	291	364	373	375	403	494	103.3%
Bottling under contract (%)[a]	5.7%	15.9%	12.8%	16.5%	56.4%	64.2%	34.6%	28.9%
Plain bottlers:								
Prosecco Superiore DOCG wineries (units)	28	32	32	30	36	35	32	14.3%
Volume sold (million bottles)	26.7	29.3	28.7	29.0	33.2	34.0	37.5	40.4%
Grapes processed (%)	4.1%	4.7%	3.3%	4.4%	5.1%	4.3%	6.2%	2.1%
Bottled market share (%)	46.3%	47.8%	45.7%	43.6%	45.2%	43.3%	44.0%	−2.3%
Average Prosecco DOCG sold per winery (0.000 bottles)[a]	946	903	908	955	912	958	1172	23.9%
Bottling under contract (%)[a]	5.3%	9.4%	6.1%	10.1%	8.0%	11.6%	14.4%	9.1%

[a]Share on total bottles of Prosecco Superiore DOCG sold without own brands
Source: Data processing C.I.R.V.E., Conegliano, 2018

chains remained unchanged, while production increased for those wineries belonging to other supply chains. The higher increase is shown by transformer-bottlers.

The current high share of production supplied to third parties is the result of a dramatic increase which occurred over the last six years. Such increase has been particularly high among wine cooperatives and transformer-bottlers.

22.5 Final Remarks

The CVPS DOCG's industry, which shows a remarkable complexity in its structure, reflects, despite some peculiarities, the general structure of the Italian wine industry. The multiple forms of production's organization appear consistent with demand differentiation and the varied intensity of economies of scale at diverse levels of the production process (Silvestre 1987). The result is the availability of a production with competitive costs, despite the fragmentation in the grape production phase. Moreover, the intense interrelation between different types of actors plays a relevant role in making the supply of final markets (Lambert and Cooper 2000) effective and flexible. Such features of the industry are, together with the quality of the product, key elements of the CVPS DOCG's competitiveness and can be considered representative of the competitiveness of Italian wine supply as a whole.

Although non-agricultural actors play the major role on the final market of the CVPS DOCG, and one-fourth of the final output relates to the wine cooperatives, wineries belonging to the wine grower chain have a quite relevant share of the aggregate output in volume, equal to 13%. Nevertheless, such share is lower than at national level (20%), while lower is also the relative price positioning of wine growers with respect to the Italian production as a whole.

The minor role of wine growers and their lower average price positioning is therefore a peculiarity of the CVPS industry and is consistent with the nature of the product, sparkling wine, which usually requires very expensive branding strategies to command high prices. Up to now transformer-bottlers have been more successful (the same happens in Champagne). Anyway, the intertemporal analysis (2010–2016) demonstrates that the increase of the CVPS DOCG's production has affected all supply chains, keeping almost unchanged their shares over the aggregate output, while there is some evidence that wine growers are progressively learning how to manage the relationship with this peculiar type of wine market. A further specificity of the CVPS DOCG's industry is the production share sold to third parties, which apply their own brands to the product. If the interest of large retailers is growing in the Italian wine industry as a whole, their growth rate has been particularly high for all brands of Prosecco, as a consequence of the exceptional success of this wine, which relies on the fact that the Prosecco name is working as a brand on the market.

The CVPS DOCG's industry appears to be, today, in excellent condition and represents, together with the Prosecco DOC, the most dynamic element of the Italian wine industry. Nevertheless, the likely evolution of the market in the next future will cause significant stress to this industry. The availability of grapes and wine will be a crucial element in Prosecco Superiore DOCG's business as the competition among bottlers will increase. In addition, the extremely high cost of vineyards entitled to produce CVPS DOCG and the difficulties to obtain the authorizations for planting new vineyards make almost prohibitive the establishing of new large fully integrated wineries.

In this scenario the crucial element for large players will be the ability to further develop the current network of loyal suppliers (grapes, base wine or sparkling wine), motivating them with adequate contracts and incentives. In this perspective, a key factor of success will be the possibility to enjoy economies in the distribution and marketing phases. This would determine sufficient added value to share with suppliers and the possibility to assist suppliers in delivering particular types of Prosecco.

References

Boatto, V., L. Barisan, and E. Pomarici. 2016. Posizionamento rispetto al mercato. In *Rapporto Annuale 2016. Dalla Denominazione al mondo: il successo internazionale del Conegliano Valdobbiadene Prosecco Superiore Docg*, 34–71. Pieve di Soligo (Treviso): Conegliano Valdobbiadene Prosecco DOCG.

De Rosa, T. 1987. *Tecnologia dei vini spumanti*. Brescia: Aeb.

Galletto, L., and F. Bianchin. 2009. Le aziende vitivinicole del Distretto del Prosecco DOC di Conegliano Valdobbiadene: un'analisi campionaria delle innovazioni, dei rapporti distrettuali e del posizionamento strategico. *Economia e Diritto Agroalimentare* 14 (1): 77–97.

Lambert, D.M., and M.C. Cooper. 2000. Issues in supply chain management. *Industrial Marketing Management* 29 (1): 65–83. https://doi.org/10.1016/S0019-8501(99)00113-3.

Merlo, M., and G. Favaretti. 1976. Effetti economici della legge sulla denominazione d'origine dei vini. Il Prosecco di Conegliano e Valdobbiadene. *Agricoltura delle Venezie XXX* (4): 122–164.

Pomarici, E., S. Raia, and R. Tedesco. 2008. Dimensione ottimale delle imprese nel mercato vitivinicolo: riflessioni su alcuni casi di studio. *Bulletin de l'OIV* 81 (926): 261–268.

Rossetto, L., V. Boatto, and L. Barisan. 2011. Strategies and interpreting models of a reformed DOC: The prosecco case study. *Enometrica* 4 (1): 57–77.

Schamalensee, R., and R.D. Willig. 1989. *Handbook of industrial organisation.* Amsterdam: North-Holland.

Silvestre, J. 1987. Economies and diseconomies of scale. In *The New Palgrave: A dictionary of economics*, 80–84. London: The Macmillan Press Ltd.

23

International Perspectives on Backwards Vertical Integration

Alfredo Coelho and Etienne Montaigne

23.1 Introduction

This chapter provides a broad understanding of the motivations and debates related to vertical integration backwards, through concrete examples or practical cases. Vertical integration backwards in the wine industry was extensively discussed in the literature (see, e.g. Sidlovits and Kator 2007). However, those contributions focus on one region or country or a particular type of firm (e.g. wine co-operatives).

Without pretending to cover all the dimensions of vertical integration, we introduce hereafter, through several examples, the causes or consequences that lead firms to practice vertical integration.

Conceptual approaches to vertical integration were already discussed elsewhere. Briefly, the literature on vertical integration of firms points out two main explanations for the adoption of such a strategy. Noneconomic theories—mainly institutional theory and the theory of the dependency of the resources (DiMaggio and Powell 1983; Pfeffer and Salancick 1978)—state that organizations engage on vertical integration without taking into account the efficiency criteria. By contrast, theories on economics argue that

A. Coelho (✉)
Bordeaux Sciences Agro, Gradignan, France
e-mail: alfredo.coelho@agro-bordeaux.fr

E. Montaigne
Department of Agricultural Economics, Montpellier Supagro, Montpellier, France
e-mail: etienne.montaigne@supagro.inra.fr

© The Author(s) 2019
A. Alonso Ugaglia et al. (eds.), *The Palgrave Handbook of Wine Industry Economics*,
https://doi.org/10.1007/978-3-319-98633-3_23

organizations adopt the structures maximizing firms' efficiency (Nelson and Winter 1982; Williamson 1975). As we will see hereafter, these contrasting views are also part of the debate on vertical integration backwards in the wine industry.

This chapter is structured in two parts. The first part discusses the different paths of vertical integration backwards among international wine firms. The second part highlights the constraints wine firms face in Europe, particularly in France, to vertically integrate the upstream of the wine chain. Those constraints are not directly related to the existence of a mechanism to regulate the grape-growing potential but more due to the way a particular country translated the European legislation on the vine planting rights scheme to the national environment.

23.2   Vertical Integration Backwards in the Top International Wine Firms

Vertical integration is a common practice among international wine firms. Integration strategies are not new phenomena in this industry because historically most wine firms always tried to control the production potential (sourcing of wines or grapes). For example, Geraci (2004) explains the trend toward vertical integration in Californian vineyards and wineries since the 1970s as a means to improve firms' efficiency—all sizes concerned—and firms' resilience toward production cycles.

This chapter will address only the strategies of vertical integration backwards concerning grape growing and other vineyard-related operations; however, vertical integration at the upstream of the value chain may involve other operations, substituting some of the activities involving suppliers and services outsourced. Among the most well-known examples, we can point out the case of E&J Gallo who built a glass factory at Modesto (California) to produce glass bottles close to the winemaking and bottling facilities. Other examples include wine firms acquiring shareholdings in oak barrels manufacturers, nurseries, or cork manufacturers.

The comprehension of vertical integration strategies backwards can be achieved through the analysis of the motivations for the restructuring of the leading wine firms in the last three years. Those motivations can be synthesized as follows (see, e.g. Coelho and Rastoin 2004):

- Securing wine or grapes in quantity and quality
- 'Scale' and 'scope' effects

- The acquisition of wine brands, namely, in the premium segments (popular premium, premium, super-premium, and ultra-premium)
- The access to distribution networks, particularly in the export markets

Securing wine or grapes procurement in quantity and quality is therefore one of the main motivations for restructuring the leading international wineries.

With respect to grape supply, it is first necessary to distinguish between firms practicing (partial or full) vertical integration from those who buy directly from third parties. Firms that do not practice full vertical integration backwards (i.e. firms do not directly own vineyards) may opt to buy grapes or wine in the spot market or, in alternative, to establish contracts with suppliers as grape growers and bulk wine providers (see, e.g. Montaigne et al. 2007).

Firms can buy grapes or wine through medium- to long-term contracts. The establishment of grape contracts is not so widespread in Europe but in some regions contracts may be a typical way of ensuring supplies (quality and volumes) (e.g. Alsace, Champagne, and Vin de Pays des Sables du Lion) (see, e.g. Goodhue et al. 2002; Franken 2012; Longbottom et al. 2013; Montaigne and Sidlovits 2003). Therefore, in some circumstances, grape contracts may be useful to reduce the risks and ensuring grape quality levels required by the buyers as those grapes may not be available in the spot or open markets. In Argentina, New Zealand, Hungary, and California, the wineries introduce alternative mechanisms of coordination to source quality grapes adapted to the segments of the market (super-premium, ultra-premium, etc.) (see Codron et al. 2013; Montaigne et al. 2005).

Most of the leading wineries across the world need to establish contracts with grape growers or other suppliers to meet their needs in terms of volume and quality. Grape contracts may range from informal (i.e. 'handshake') to formal and detailed agreements. Contracts may include more than 30 pages of clauses, including technical practices, supervision, bonuses, and penalties. Unfortunately for the growers, most of the formal contracts do not precise the prices to be paid for the grapes. Likewise, concentration of wine firms increases the power of the leading wineries and the dependency of the grape growers from those firms.

Other 'hybrid' agreements include the (total or partial) sale of vineyards owned by a major winery to a real estate investment trust (REIT) followed by a 'lease-back' agreement of the same vineyards. This strategy is convenient for wine firms planning to reduce the amount of tangible assets on their own balance sheets and benefiting from the leverage effect of the financial costs paid during the lease-back period. As an example, Diageo Château & Estate

Wines sold more than 800 hectares of vineyards in California in 2010 to the real estate investment firm Realty Income and then signed a 20-year lease-back deal (with an option to extend it to more 80 years).

Among the major wine firms, firms focus primarily on the management of the wine brands and establish long-term contracts with key and high quality wine suppliers in different geographies to ensure icon wine, variety and secure the sourcing. In the USA, E&J Gallo adopted this strategy for some of its core brands. Among the wines imported by E&J Gallo from third countries, it includes the following brands owned by Gallo: Italy (Ecco Domani, Bella Sera, Da Vinci, etc.), France (Red Bicyclette and Pont d'Avignon), Chile (Viña Chilcaya), Australia (Black Swan), and so on. This strategy provides more flexibility and a focus in the management of the brands as the companies do not need to ensure the management of the vineyards, which are managed by third parties (costs and risks related to the management of the vineyards are shared or transferred to partners).

Mergers and acquisitions are also a means for diversifying grape supplies beyond firms' home country. For example, when Foster's Group (Australia) bought Beringer in California (Château Saint Jean, Chateau Souverain, Meridian Vineyards, Beringer Vineyards, Stag's Leap, and St. Clement Vineyards) (2000), it became less dependent on the supplies of grapes and wine produced in Australia through its own wine branch (Mildara Blass). The new entity was renamed Beringer Blass and became the world's largest premium wine company. In an opposite move, Constellation Brands (USA) acquired BRL Hardy (Australia) in 2001 creating at the time the largest wine company in the world.

The supply of wines from third parties is a strategic choice helping firms to expand on emerging markets. For example, the case of a Chinese leading firm who has signed two partnerships: one in Canada for the export of ice wine to China and, in another case, in New Zealand for the export of wines to China. This strategy entails some constraints such as transportation costs and national or regional excise duties (e.g. in the case of the states of Karnataka and Maharashtra in India) which may reduce margins considerably.

Vertical integration upstream is an important issue in some protected designated areas (PDOs) (e.g. Champagne). The cases of the Lanson International and Taittinger illustrate this issue. Grapes in Champagne are a unique and relatively scarce resource. Initially, when the champagne house Lanson International was put on the market for sale in 2005, it attracted many potential bidders. However, Lanson International did not directly own any vineyards (grapes were sourced through contracts). At the same time, another champagne house was put on the market for sale—Taittinger—

which controlled more than 60% of the volume of grapes needed for its own production. Therefore, most potential buyers for Lanson International moved away as the size of the vineyard owned by the competitor Taittinger represented an exceptional and unique opportunity to control a vineyard in Champagne. Vineyard control in Champagne is of particular interest as beyond the constraints related to the scarcity of vineyards available for purchase, both the price of grapes (roughly around €5/kg) and the prices of land with vineyards (average prices reaching more than €1.2 million/hectare in 2016) are extremely high.

In the case of a champagne maker, the non-integration of grape production decreases investments (in vineyards) and ensures flexibility, but it becomes a risky strategy whenever harvests are low. Moreover, the absence of direct ownership over the grapes can prevent firms' expansion plans.

Buying wine from the vineyards of New World producing countries or from traditional producing countries and the transportation of those wines to major importing markets (USA, UK, Germany), supplying the main brands, particularly for the entry-level still wine ranges, translate into an emerging of international wine sourcing.

These two examples—vertical integration upstream and sourcing regionally and globally—illustrate two types of strategies, often interlinked, characterizing today's global wine industry:

- Strategies for controlling resources (focus on the vertical integration backwards)
- Strategies of flexibility (focalization on brands and distribution channels)

The first strategy is based on the acquisition of unique and irreversible physical assets (land, vineyards, farm equipment, winemaking, and storage facilities). Rather this pattern corresponds to an institutional and cultural environment typical of PDO wines; that is, firms are strongly embedded in the territories. In the second case, efforts are market-oriented with a focus on finding new customers and maintaining the customer/buyer basis. Therefore, this illustrates a dichotomy between, on the one hand, a strategy based primarily on tangible investments (i.e. a 'supply-driven strategy') and, in the second case, a strategy based on intangible investments (i.e. a 'marketing-driven strategy') (see Gereffi 1999).

Vertical integration lowers transaction costs and assures regular and constant supply of grapes. Coordination issues may encourage integration backwards. Vertical integration of the vineyards also protects against price increases. For example, in recent years grape growers in the South of France were involved in strong protests (voiding tanks containing foreign wines in the facilities of French importers, stopping Spanish trucks in the highway carrying bulk wine, etc.) against the important price gap between French and Spanish entry-level wines. By integrating the vineyards, wineries may be able to avoid fluctuations on prices in the open market.

23.2.1 Backward Vertical Integration: Lessons from the Top 40 World Wine Firms

Among the top 40 world wineries (see Coelho and Rastoin 2004; Coelho 2013), we identified the top 12 vineyard owners. The top holders include a second-tier French co-operative (Vinadeis) and three Italian three-tier co-operatives (Caviro, Cavit, Riunite & Civ + GIV). Co-operatives are 'hybrid' organizations and their vineyards tend to be directly owned by members, not by the co-operatives themselves. However, in the last few years, the advanced average age and retirement of members (lack of successors and new young grape growers) and major grubbing-ups of vineyards in Southern European countries (France, Spain, and Italy) (shrinking of the sourcing potential) led these co-operatives to purchase or lease land with vineyards. The direct involvement of wine co-operatives in the control of vineyards is a growing movement, but at the very beginning. The vertical integration backwards by wine co-operatives is still influenced by strong legal, institutional, and financial constraints (Fig. 23.1).

Concerning other leading wine firms (i.e. non-co-operatives), the above table suggests a link between vineyard ownership and the internationalization of firms. At first, the internationalization of wine firms through the ownership of vineyards contributes to diversify the supply of wines from different geographies and origins. At the international level, Cavit (Italy) is the only wine co-operative owning wine-related assets outside the home country, which owns a major shareholding in the German sparkling wine producer Kessler (Württemberg).

International wine brands need to ensure a stable quality of wines and volumes to supply buyers. Most of the international wine firms are not completely autonomous as they need to purchase grapes or bulk wine through contracts or in the spot market.

Vertical integration backwards also allows companies to diversify the geographies of the vineyards through different varietals, soils, and microclimates. This strategy is particularly developed by the leading Chilean wine firms (Concha y Toro, Viña San Pedro Tarapacà Wine Group).

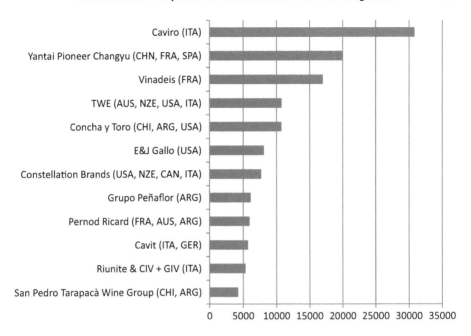

Fig. 23.1 The 12 leading world wine producers by vine surfaces in 2016 (ha). (Source: Annual Reports, International press)

23.2.2 Expanding Vertical Integration: Greenfield Investments or Mergers and Acquisitions?

International wine firms have the opportunity to integrate vertically the vineyards through two main strategies, either greenfield (ex nihilo) investments or mergers and acquisitions (brownfield investments). Both strategies are suitable and can be successful for the world leading wineries; however, mergers and acquisitions tend to be more expensive and risky. Among the top world wine firms, Constellation Brands (USA) and Treasury Wine Estates (TWE) (Australia) expanded their vineyard surfaces through major mergers and acquisitions of wineries in different locations (see hereafter).

> **Exhibit 23.1 Vertical Integration Backwards Through Mergers and Acquisitions: The Example of TWE (Australia)**
>
> **2001**: Southcorp (Australia) merges with Rosemount (Australia)
>   Southcorp owned 6070 hectares of vineyards and joint ventures in Languedoc (France) and California.
>   Rosemount held 2023 hectares of planted vineyards and a joint venture with Robert Mondavi Winery.

2005: Foster's Group (Australia) acquires with Southcorp (Australia)
Southcorp owned 8063 hectares of vineyards planted in Australia. The target main brands included: Penfolds, Rosemount Estate, Lindeman's, Wynns Coonawarra Estate.
2011: Demerger of the Foster's Brewing (Australia) beer and wine activities
The wine activities of the new 'pure player' were renamed Treasury Wine Estates (TWE).
2015: Treasury Wine Estates (Australia) acquires Diageo (UK) wine operations
The acquisition of Diageo Château and Estate operations from Diageo helped TWE to increase 'masstige' (i.e. wines positioned as prestigious and affordable in the mass-market segment) and 'luxury' supply of wines. Diageo Château and Estate operations include vineyards and wineries in the USA (Beaulieu Vineyards, Sterling Vineyards, Acacia, Provenance, and Hewitt) and the UK (Blossom Hill).
2016: Treasury Wine Estates (Australia)
TWE is one of the top 3 world wine multinationals and owns more than 14,000 hectares of vineyards (Australia, New Zealand, USA, and Italy). The last operations show a clear link between vineyard ownership and vineyard location/quality and brand building in the premium and luxury segments.

Due to the absence of vine planting rights schemes similar to the one in the European Union (EU), leading Chilean wine producers expanded their vineyard plantings through different investments in Chile and Argentina. Concha y Toro expanded in the home country and in Argentina mainly through the planting of new vineyards. This strategy enables to company to have a 'complete control of the productive process and supply chain' (Concha y Toro 2015) (cf. Exhibit 23.2).

Exhibit 23.2 Vertical Integration Backwards Through Greenfield Investments: The Example of Concha y Toro (2002–2018) (Chile)

Concha y Toro is the leader of wine production and exports in Chile. It is also one of the top three Argentinean wine exporters (Trivento subsidiary). Vineyard surfaces increased at an average growth superior to 9% year-on-year in the last 10 years.

'Our business model is to make Concha y Toro, the most vertically integrated company of the wine industry' (*in* Concha y Toro, Annual Report, 2015). The company sources grapes and bulk wine from third parties mainly for entry-level wines—such as Casillero del Diablo—(50% of the wines in the popular, varietal, and premium segments) and other low-priced wines (almost 76% of the volumes) (source: Concha y Toro, Annual Reports). Wine brands in the higher-end segments are exclusively from grapes sourced from the vineyards of the company.

Grapes represent approximately 30% of Concha y Toro's direct costs and the company buys 65% of its grapes or bulk wine from third parties. Therefore, the company's gross margin is highly sensitive to fluctuations in the prices of the grapes during the harvesting period and of the bulk wine for the rest of the year.

The expansion of the company included a partnership with Baron Philippe de Rothschild (France) to produce Almaviva (US $80/bottle).

In 2011, Concha y Toro acquired the vineyards and winemaking facilities of the main organic wine producer in the USA (Fetzer Vineyards and Bonterra). This acquisition was the first major investment of the company outside Latin America. In 2015, the company established an R&D center dedicated to viticulture and winemaking in Chile.

Chilean wine production is highly dependent on Cabernet Sauvignon. The diversification of vineyard plantings allows Concha y Toro to diversify the tasting profiles for this varietal but also to find the most suitable locations for new grape varieties (e.g. Gewürztraminer, Riesling, and Syrah) (Tables 23.1 and 23.2).

Table 23.1 Concha y Toro: expansion of vineyard surfaces 2002–2018 (ha)

Locations	New plantings 2002–2005	Vineyard surfaces (ha) 2005	2010		2018	Change 2005–2018	Strategy for vertical integration
Chile	1189	4545	8445	9717	10 valleys, 55 vineyards	113%	Greenfield
Argentina	349	433	1068	1140	3 valleys, 9 vineyards	164%	Greenfield
California	–	0	–	468	2 valleys, 14 vineyards		Acquisition

Source: Own elaboration based on annual reports

Table 23.2 Concha y Toro: expansion of vineyard surfaces in Chilean valleys 2005–2015 (ha)

Chilean valleys (ha)	2005	2010	2015	Change 2005–2015
Limarí	313	896	965	186.3%
Casablanca	339	415	424	22.4%
Leyda	–	130	130	–
Aconcagua	–	–	100	–
Maipo	620	974	853	57.1%
Cachapoal	611	1306	1463	113.7%
Colchagua	636	1757	2163	176.3%
Curicó	442	666	683	50.7%
Maule	1584	2300	2413	45.2%

Source: Own elaboration based on annual reports

The two examples above illustrate the main paths undertaken by leading wine firms around the world to expand vertical integration backwards.

In contrast with the Chilean example, the major wine firms in the EU, particularly in France (see Montaigne et al. 2012, about the restrictions of the mechanism for the distribution to structure the vine planting rights scheme in France), tend to expand dominantly through mergers and acquisitions in order to expand the vineyard basis.

23.3   The Planting Rights Scheme: A Look into the European Constraints to Vertical Integration Backwards

As we discussed in the previous part of the chapter, at the international level, the access to raw materials—wine grapes—is a key point for firms' success across the wine chain. However, over time firms need to redefine their boundaries through a proactive and intentional approach as a reaction to changes in the competition environment.

In the EU, vine planting rights were a means adopted by legislation to help industry to better manage the production potential (i.e. grape growing) and regulate the supply of wines. The wine common market organization (CMO) framework, established in 1970, introduced this policy measure in 1976 to better regulate the wine production by limitation of the potential, after two 'wine wars' between Italy and France. This legislation applies to the firms operating vineyards within the EU. However, even if the planting rights scheme concerns all vine-producing countries, the transposition of European rules into national legislations diverges across countries (see Montaigne et al. 2012).

The case of the transposition of European rules into French vineyards illustrates how the system blocked the distribution of sizeable areas of vine planting rights among vine producers. The transposition of the European rules of vine planting rights to France is unique. For example, in the last 30 years, in the Languedoc-Roussillon—the largest French vineyard region—there was not any greenfield investment to establish a single vineyard above 3 hectares. In contrast, many studies document many greenfield investments to establish large vineyards above 50 hectares in other European countries (e.g. in the Douro valley or Hungary) (see Delord et al. 2015). Those cases illustrate the influence of the French legislation, creating barriers preventing firms to increase vertical integration backwards. Firms planning to extend the vineyard surfaces could only purchase each year a tiny amount of vine planting rights in the open ('spot') market. As an alternative, firms could vertically integrate vine production—at a significant cost—through mergers and acquisitions. In the most prestigious protected designated areas such as Champagne, Bordeaux, and Burgundy, land prices and the scarcity of the grape supply were two of the main barriers for investors.

23.3.1   The Vine Planting Scheme in France: An Atypical Case of Redistribution

Most often, vineyard extension in France requires grape growers use the most traditional approach, that is, the purchase of plots already planted (brownfield investment). The decision to acquire vineyards depends not only on vine planting rights but it also took into account the location (closeness to grape farms), the value of land in the land market, the value of the products into consumer markets, and the patrimonial approach characterizing the behavior of grape growers. The availability of vine plantings influenced the price but the French national reserve set up a common price for the planting rights sold through the reserve. In protected designation areas, the scarcity of land is the main factor explaining the price of vine planting rights.

In France, there was an important wine crisis at the early start of the twentieth century. As a consequence, France introduced a vine planting rights scheme in 1931. Six decades later, French legislation adapted to the most significant wine reform at the European level in 1999 by introducing the 'reserve' mechanism for vine planting rights. The national reserve for the management and distribution of vine planting rights became a tool of the public policy under the supervision of the Ministry of Agriculture.

By law, all vine plantings should be justified through proprietorship. Changes in the wine policy created two types of planting rights in France: those originated from the uprooting vine plots and those distributed through the national reserve. Growers who uprooted vine plots or the entire vine surfaces on a wine estate could sell the planting rights on the open market during eight years.

In this case, the national reserve was a tool to administer vine planting rights originated through the uprooting of vine planting rights not replanted within the eight-year lifespan. The reserve also hosted new planting rights, granted by the EU to each individual country within the framework established through the CMO for wine reform in 1999.

The national reserve provided free planting rights for young farmers. The remaining grape growers could acquire planting rights from the national reserve at a cost. In the spot market, transactions for vine planting rights could proceed directly, that is, between two grape growers or through the intermediation of a broker.

The price for the sale of vine planting rights derived from the national reserve was established at approximately €1750/ha in the first four campaigns (2002/2003–2005/2006). Prices decreased to €1500/ha in the following four campaigns and reached €1000/ha in the campaign of 2011/2012. As each grape grower could sell his planting rights to the national reserve, the main consequence was those prices became also the key reference for the prices of vine planting rights in the free market. The main outcome of this process was the complete disconnection between the amount paid for planting rights and market prices for land. Champagne was the most striking example, as the prices of vine planting rights were completely insignificant when compared to the price of land.

Therefore, whenever French grape grower plans to increase the vineyard surfaces of his own estate, he needed to acquire a planting right to plant vines in the free plot. In addition, the proprietorship of vine planting rights was not the only necessary condition to be allowed to plant a vine. The scheme also required an 'authorization' to plant vines. In practice, with the exception of wines without geographic indications (i.e. the former 'table wines') excluded from the planting rights scheme from 1999 to 2015, the two other European categories of wines (PDO and Protected Geographic Indications (PGI)) were able to control their production potential through a board—*Organisme de défense et de gestion (ODG)*, that is, *syndicats de cru*—governing each PDO and each PGI. The board (ODG) established an annual quota of authorization for each PDO or PGI in order to prevent excessive growth of the production potential not in line with the specific PDO or PGI market demand. The ODG (board) distributed the quota in proportion to the individual demands of grape growers. In addition, there was a maximal cap of three (five for collective programs) hectares/farmer/year for each area producing wines under PGI and one hectare/farmer/year for wines under PDO. This maximum annual expansion was the source of major controversies among the wineries wishing to establish ex nihilo vine projects. Major wineries recognized the planting rights scheme in France as a barrier to vertically integrate the vineyard. The greatest controversy concerned the American Mondavi company undertaking to create a 50-hectare vineyard in Aniane, a typical tiny village in Languedoc (Torres 2005).

What is the economic rationality behind the French scheme? The planting rights scheme involves three different levels among decision-makers. The first level concerned is the national level of decision-makers. Decision-making is established in close relation with rules set up at the European level. Those rules consider the balance of the global wine market and no differentiation among vineyards. The main purpose of the regulation is to control the vine surfaces in each European country and limit their expansion. Therefore, the organization controls the European wine production potential and shares vine planting rights between all European countries, smoothing the competition between countries. The traditional objective of this regulation is to limit the overproduction (i.e. 'the wine lake') for a perennial plant and to reduce the King effect which leads to a collapse in prices and income.

The second level of decision-making concerns regions. Here, the main factor concerns the definition of the rules for the production of PDO and PGI wines. Those rules impact French vine plantings and other European countries. The purpose of those regulations is to differentiate the wines according to quality, originality, *terroir and tradition*. At the regional level, producers face reduced yields in vineyards and an increase in the costs of production due to supply constraints. This explains why the ODG is managing the scarcity preventing a potential oversupply crisis. This level-playing field creates a real motivation for investors and large firms to vertically integrate backwards.

The third level of decision-making concerns individuals. Following the expansion of the European vineyards, within the framework introduced in the European wine legislation (CMO) by 1999, appeared the global anticipated oversupply in 2014 with 50 million hectoliters above the average world production. All the vine-producing countries were impacted by the wine lake. A large part of wine estates and firms got into financial distress or went bankruptcy. The wine lake also impacted New World wine producers, particularly Australia. EU implemented in 2007, a large subsidized uprooting program for 175,000 hectares. The new subsidized program impacted all the vine regions in Europe. The more significant share of the vines removed were located in wines without PDO and PGI regions. Those regions were the most impacted by the crisis. PDO and PGI regions were also impacted, but the grubbing-up scheme concerned mainly old vines or old grape growers.

The purpose of vertical integration backwards was to increase benefits in the long run through the construction of a set of rules, differentiation, increasing profitability, and reaching affordable prices for PDO and PGI. In the absence of vine planting rights, firms would have to pay only the cost of establishing of a new vineyard, independently of market prices for land (€30,000 on average in Bordeaux compared €1.2 million/ha in Champagne). The main political argument promoted by the tenants of the liberalization of vine planting rights of Europe relied on the possibility granted to large firms reach economies of scale. This argument was clearly refuted in the literature (Delord et al. 2015). The planting rights scheme privileges already established vineyard owners and their successors. The scheme requires an authorization for extending the surfaces through a 'democratic' approach limiting the vine surfaces distributed to each individual.

The decision-making process for the allocation of vine planting rights was a major constraint for the establishment of ex nihilo vine projects among French vineyards. Major French wine firms (Castel, Grands Chais de France, Boisset, Baron Philippe de Rothschild, Advini, etc.) perceived the planting rights scheme as a barrier for expansion and for the integration of the upstream of the wine chain. A close look into the strategies of the leading French wine firms shows the expansion and progressive integration backwards of vineyards was achieved essentially through mergers and acquisitions.

23.4   Conclusion

This chapter discusses the motivations and strategies followed by the leading international wine firms to vertically integrate the vineyards. We compare the approaches used by the wineries in the New World—where there is no legal system or institutional system to manage the production potential—and the vine planting rights in Europe, particularly in France. These two contrasting situations explain how institutional rules may shape the strategies of firms to integrate the vineyards. The above reflection suggests how important it would be to integrate the different approaches and constraints into the public debate to raise the competitiveness of European vineyards.

References

Codron, J.M., E. Montaigne, and S. Rousset. 2013. Quality management and contractual incompleteness: Grape procurement for high-end wines in Argentina. *Journal on Chain and Network Science* 13 (1): 11–35.

Coelho, A. 2013. Concentration des grandes firmes vitivinicoles. *Le Progrès Agricole et Viticole* 12: 11–18.

Coelho, A., and J.-L. Rastoin. 2004. Stratégie des grands groupes internationaux: vers l'émergence d'un oligopole mondial du vin? In *Bacchus 2005: enjeux, stratégies et pratiques dans la filière vitivinicole*, ed. F. D'Hauteville, J.-P. Couderc, H. Hannin, and E. Montaigne, 79–99. Paris: Dunod.

Concha y Toro. 2015. Annual reports, several years.

Delord, B., E. Montaigne, and A. Coelho. 2015. Vine planting rights, farm size, and economic performance: Do economies of scale matter in the French wine sector? *Wine Economics and Policy* 4 (1): 22–34.

DiMaggio, P.J., and W.W. Powell. 1983. The Iron cage revisited: Institutional isomorphism and collective rationality in organizational fields. *American Sociological Review* 48 (2): 147–160.

Franken, J.R.V. 2012. *Quality considerations for coordination of the California wine-grape supply chain, American Association of Wine Economists*. AAWE Working Paper, No 99, February.

Geraci, V.W. 2004. *Salud! The rise of Santa Barbara's wine industry*. Reno: University of Nevada Press.

Gereffi, G. 1999. *A commodity chains framework for analyzing global industries*. Durham: Duke University.

Goodhue, R.E., D.M. Hejen, H. Lee, and D. Sumner. 2002. Contract use in wine grape industry. *California Agriculture* 56 (3): 97–102.

Longbottom, M., C. Simos, M. Krstic, and D. Johnson. 2013. Grape quality assessments: A survey of current practice. *Wine & Viticulture Journal* 28: 33–37.

Montaigne, E., and D. Sidlovits. 2003. Long term contracts and quality in the wine supply chain: Case of the Appellation "Vins des Sables du Golfe du Lion". In *Budapest, ISNIE, 7th Annual Conference of the International Society for New Institutional Economics*, September 11–13, 20p.

Montaigne, E., D. Sidlovits, and G.G. Szabó. 2005. Examination of contracting relationships in the Hungarian Wine industry. In *Budapest, Hungary: 2nd International Conference on Economics and Management of Networks*, September 15–17, Corvinus University of Budapest, 27p.

Montaigne, E., S. Rousset, and J.-B. Traversac. 2007. *Quelles perspectives pour les contrats en raisin entre production et négoce? in Bacchus 2008: enjeux, stratégies et pratiques dans la filière vitivinicole*. Paris: Dunod, Chap. 3.3.

Montaigne, E., A. Coelho, B. Delord, and L. Khefifi. 2012. *Etude sur les impacts socio-économiques et territoriaux de la liberalization des droits de plantations viticoles, Rapport d'étude*. Presented at the international board of the Association of European Vine and Wine Regions (AREV), Brussels.

Nelson, R.R., and S.G. Winter. 1982. *An evolutionary theory of economic change*. Cambridge, MA: Belknap Press.

Pfeffer, J., and G.R. Salancik. 1978. *The external control of organizations: A resource dependence perspective*. New York: Harper & Row.

Sidlovits, D., and Z. Kator. 2007. *Characteristics of vertical coordination in the Hungarian wine sector*. Paper presented at the joint IAAE – 104th EAAE Seminar Agricultural Economics and Transition: "What was expected, what we observed, the lessons learned." Corvinus University of Budapest, Budapest, September 6–8, 28p.

Torres, O. 2005. *La guerre des vins: L'affaire Mondavi. Mondialisation et terroirs*. Paris: Dunod.

Williamson, O.E. 1975. *Markets and hierarchies: Analysis and antitrust implications*. New York: Free Press.

Part V

Efficiency of the Business Models in the Different Wine Industries

Coord. by *Jean-Marie Cardebat*

24

Introduction: Does a National Model Exist Which Favors Trade Performance?

Jean-Marie Cardebat

The previous parts (Parts I and III) reveal the multiplicity of organization models existing in the wine sector. Choosing the degree of vertical integration therefore appears as a crucial factor for these organization models (Part IV). At present we need to appraise the efficiency of these models. The key question to be asked revolves around the existence of a model which will dominate the others in terms of efficiency and economic performance, a model toward which all wine companies should eventually converge. This question is particularly relevant in Europe where the global model is heavily based upon the collective management of the company's reputation through the Protected Designation of Origin (PDO), small-scale properties and upstream rather than downstream integration. This model has been, in part, challenged by New World competition which relies on strong brands free of PDO constraints, large estates which are able to exploit economies of scale and tight control of sales via downstream rather than upstream integration. We therefore introduce the hypothesis that a difference exists here, on average, between the Old and the New World concerning the elements just specified above. The New World's commercial success since the 2000s has led to the Europeans questioning their organization model. However, is the Manichean opposition occasionally made between the two models founded? Must the Old World move toward a brand model to preserve its world-leader status in the wine sector?

J.-M. Cardebat (✉)
University of Bordeaux, Pessac, France
INSEEC Bordeaux, Bordeaux, France
e-mail: jean-marie.cardebat@u-bordeaux.fr

A. Alonso Ugaglia et al. (eds.), *The Palgrave Handbook of Wine Industry Economics*,
https://doi.org/10.1007/978-3-319-98633-3_24

Answering these questions is not easy as the concept of economic performance is multifaceted. It differs especially according to the focus of analysis: are we speaking about companies, sectors, a region or a country? At the company level, the traditional ratios of financial profitability remain predominant for measuring performance, but they are increasingly challenged in favor of nonmonetary value creation linked to the mind-set of corporate social responsibility. For example, we can oppose a company's environmental performance with its financial performance. At the sectorial level, the same questions can be asked regarding performance indicators: from simply aggregating the financial performances of companies within this sector to considering nonfinancial factors such as its territorial impact (local employment, landscape function, tourist impact, etc.). To measure the economic performance of a sector we will also take account of its contribution to the country's trade position. On a national scale, the economic performance of a sector will, essentially, be seen from this trade-balance angle. A high-performing sector is one which runs a positive trade balance, involving a net currency surplus entering the country.

There therefore exists a wide panel of approaches to performance ranging from the microeconomic, at the company level, to the macroeconomic, on a sectorial and national scale. Given that notions of performance and efficiency are difficult to grasp, our study cannot claim to be exhaustive, yet we will strive to address these two aspects in this part. The present chapter focuses on international trade. It addresses the question of the trade performance of wine-producing countries according to two of their strongest characteristics: Old or New World and a system directed toward PDOs or one toward brands with a simple indication of origin. The following chapter will also consider the PDO versus brand debate, but from an angle which is clearly more microeconomic. It will discuss the best way for wine producers to manage reputation and therefore their future sales, either individually through a brand or collectively through a PDO. This approach will go beyond the Manichean and partisan framework which frequently encroaches upon the public debate of such issues. Finally, the last two chapters of this part will present diametrically opposed national case studies of economic success in the wine sector. Indeed, Chile and Switzerland have both enjoyed great success but by following completely different trajectories. These chapters perfectly illustrate the cautious approach one must take when addressing questions of efficiency, performance and economic models. The major lesson to be learnt from this part is that there is no miracle recipe for success in this sector at a national level but that different strategies are possible according to the micro- and macroeconomic characteristics governing the country.

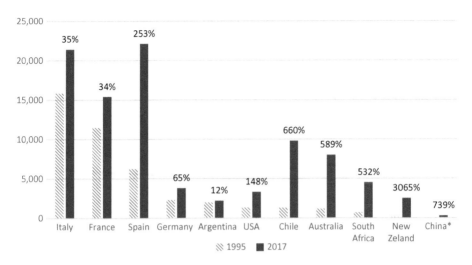

Fig. 24.1 Change in exports in volume between 1995 and 2017. (Source: OIV [Wine International Organization] statistics. Note: the percentages reported correspond to growth rates between 1995 and 2017. (*) For China, the data are from 1995 to 2014)

Table 24.1 Average export price in 2017 (in € per liter)

Country	Average export price €/l
France	5.84
New Zealand	4.22
USA	3.88
Argentina	3.24
Italy	2.74
Portugal	2.69
Germany	2.52
Australia	2.16
Chile	1.78
South Africa	1.30
Spain	1.27

Source: OIV statistics

A simple analysis of major wine-producing countries' export figures reveals a significant rise in the volume of exports between 1995 and 2017, for both Old and New World countries. Figure 24.1 highlights two major pieces of information. The first is that the Old World still leads wine exchanges. This is all the more true when we consider the value of exports where France remains the leader with nearly €9 billion of exports in 2017. In Old World countries, only Spain has had difficulties to increase the average price of its exports (Table 24.1) and it is ranked last in this classification of major exporters. This clearly shows that there is no opposition between the New and the Old World as regards value creation, according to which the New World exports high volumes of low-value wine while the Old World exports high-value wines.

The second piece of information from Fig. 24.1 is that the New World is catching up given the strong increase of its countries between 1995 and 2017. The growth of exports in volume from Chile or Australia is spectacular. The export growth rate is even more impressive from countries which were only minor exporters in 1995. This is especially the case for New Zealand which has, in the space of two decades, established itself as a significant exporter on the same level as Argentina or the USA. Moreover, New Zealand exports high-value wines. The average price of its exports places it in second position behind France's (see Table 24.1). The cases of Chile (New World leader in volume) and New Zealand (leader in average price) are clearly the most significant to indicate how the New World is catching up with the Old.

A flat analysis of the wine-producing countries' export statistics therefore provides a contrasted outcome and does not allow us to identify one model as more efficient than another. Indeed, a weaker progression in volume was in part compensated by increased added value (i.e. average price) of the wines exported.

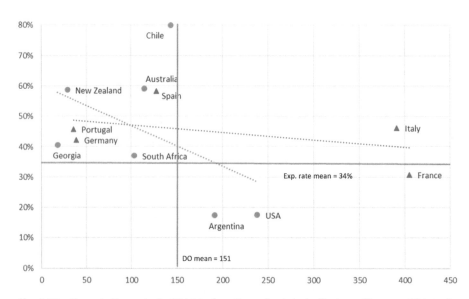

Fig. 24.2 Exportation rate in 2014 in function of origin indicators. (Source: OIV statistics. Note: on the x-axis we find the number of PDOs (for the European countries) or that of simple origin indicators (DO for New World countries). The triangles indicate European countries (except Georgia) and the circles represent New World countries (including Georgia))

To go deeper into the analysis of trade performance, Fig. 24.2 presents the exportation rate of the major producers (a country's exports in volume divided by its production volume). This exportation rate is cross-referenced with the number of origin indicators per country recorded by the OIV. These are the PDOs for the European countries and simple Denominations of Origin (DO) for the New World. The PDO system is historically linked to the European agricultural regulation (Meloni and Swinnen 2014). Most of the other countries and notably those of the New World use a simple origin indicator which is nonrestrictive from the technical point of view. A linear trend can be added for each of the two groups of countries (European and New World) which shows the global link between the origin indicators and the exportation rate.

Figure 24.2 provides different information to the previous graph. Indeed, this time, the New World countries dominate the Old World. The leading country is Chile which exports 80% of its production. Next come Australia and New Zealand with an exportation rate close to 60%. The European countries, with the exception of Spain, lag behind on this measure with the majority of their production being sold on their national market, even if the latter has continued to shrink since the 1960s. Regarding the linear trends expressed by dotted lines on Fig. 24.2, the other lesson concerns the negative relation between the origin indicators and the exportation rate, although the low number of points does not allow us to draw a statistically significant conclusion. The vertical and horizontal lines appearing in Fig. 24.2 represent, respectively, the averages of the number of DOs (151) and of the exportation rate (34%). These lines allow us to isolate four quadrants. Among the major wine-producing countries, those having the lowest number of DOs (lower than the average on the left side) have the highest exportation rate (higher than the average at the top). With the exception of Italy, all the countries are in fact located either in the northwest or in the southeast of these quadrants. However, the Old World and New World countries fall into each of these two quadrants and are therefore not polarized. Once again we need to note, however, that this type of analysis does in no way lead us to a conclusion concerning the causality between these variables.

Figure 24.3 provides supplementary information. It no longer simply considers the exportation rate but the trade balance relative to national production, still cross-referenced with the number of PDOs and DOs. It also shows changes in this ratio between 1995 and 2014. Between these two dates we can observe a significant progression of the New World countries with the exception of the USA. New Zealand's performance appears the most impressive. On the contrary, Germany is the country whose trade performance has worsened the most followed by the USA. As above, it is not possible to isolate a

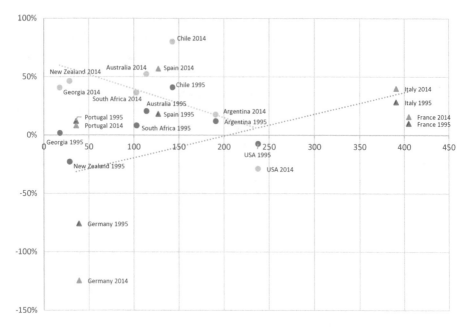

Fig. 24.3 Trade balance relative to production volume (y-axis) in function of the number of PDOs and DOs (x-axis) for a selection of countries between 1995 and 2014. (Source: OIV statistics. Note: the ratio is calculated on the basis of the trade balance divided by the production of each country, with all the variables expressed in volume. On the x-axis we find the number of PDOs (for the European countries) or that of simple origin indicators (DO for New World countries). The triangles indicate European countries (except Georgia) and the circles represent New World countries (including Georgia). Linear trends are given for the year 2014)

model which seems more efficient than another. Old and New World countries have had very diverse trajectories within each group of countries. Similarly, there is no clear relation between the number of origin indicators and trade performance.

This simple statistical analysis of international trade in wine points therefore appears to conclude that there is no link between business models—approximated by belonging to the Old or New World or by the number of origin indicators—and trade performance, approximated by very simple indicators of exportation and trade balance. We must remain cautious given the limits of this study which remains highly descriptive. Nevertheless, this work probably invalidates the Manichean idea, according to which the New World is outperforming the Old in terms of export performance. In the same way, as regards the average price of exported wines, it is difficult to support the idea that the Old World remains the bastion of value creation compared to the

New. This analysis of the statistics of international exchange sends us back a complex and contrasting image. This image will be confirmed in the following chapters.

Reference

Meloni, G., and J. Swinnen. 2014. The rise and fall of the world's largest wine exporter-and its institutional legacy. *Journal of Wine Economics* 9 (1): 3–33.

25

Individual and Collective Reputations in the Wine Industry

Florine Livat

25.1 Introduction

At first glance, the wine world seems characterized by two different models of reputation that reflect varying cost structures, wine technologies, and wine styles. The so-called New World[1] (Argentina, Australia, Chile, New Zealand, South Africa, and the United States) is known to promote private brands and non-blended wines with varietal labeling that are easy for buyers to recognize. The Old World (European and Middle Eastern countries with a long-established history of wine production, since at least Roman times) produces wines characterized by a profusion and even proliferation of geographic indications (GIs) and appellations of origin (AOs). GIs and AOs have some common attributes. Wines with this kind of identity are owned and marketed collectively by unions, associations, trade bodies, or other kinds of coalitions.

---

[1] According to Banks and Overton (2010), the Old World–New World dichotomy, which structures much of the thinking about the wine industry, is not relevant anymore. Indeed, this segmentation neither represents the complexity of production and marketing in these broad regions, which are not homogenous, nor takes into account the rapidly expanding wine production and consumption in China and India, and even Brazil. These authors suggest the addition of a "Third World" category. Some other authors recommend creating a new niche in the global wine markets, a "Historic World," which is dedicated to wine-producing countries using mostly indigenous grape varietals, such as Armenia, Georgia, or Israel (Keushguerian and Ghaplanyan 2015).

F. Livat (✉)
Kedge Business School, Bordeaux, France
e-mail: florine.livat@kedgebs.com

A. Alonso Ugaglia et al. (eds.), *The Palgrave Handbook of Wine Industry Economics*,
https://doi.org/10.1007/978-3-319-98633-3_25

463

On the contrary, branded wines aim to distinguish themselves among competing products and have an individual owner. As such, these two seemingly opposite reputation models appear to coexist in the wine industry, but such a categorization might be simplistic. Reputation is not supported by a unique model in the Old World or the New World, and this is what we will illustrate in this chapter.

Reputation, which is defined by economists as a perception of quality,[2] emerges in situations of incomplete information. In wine markets, where a typical experience is usually shared, reputation becomes a key asset, as summarized by Fombrun and Shanley (1990, p. 233): "by signaling consumers about product quality, favorable reputations may enable firms to charge premium prices, attract better applicants, enhance their access to capital markets, and attract investors." Castriota and Delmastro (2012) identify three different sources of reputation for wine:

- International, national, regional, or local institutional reputation results in wine classifications that guarantee a minimum level of quality. The European Union (EU) wine laws imply that wines produced within the EU are divided into two quality categories, each with different rules for winemaking practices and labeling: Table Wines (TW) and Quality Wines Produced in Specified Regions (QWPSR). In the United States, the Alcohol and Tobacco Tax and Trade Bureau provides the American Viticultural Area (AVA) system; every AVA is a US winegrape-growing region with well-defined boundaries and distinguishable by geographic features. There is no regional- or quality-based hierarchy, and some larger AVAs contain smaller ones within their boundaries (known as sub-AVAs). Both systems support institutional reputations.
- Coalitions of producers define production rules. Castriota and Delmastro (2012) talk about collective reputation, which can be associated with AOs and/or with groups of AOs when several appellations coexist within a single regional vineyard. These coalitions are funded through fees—compulsory or not—provided by producers. The Wines of Chile Association, which represents the viticultural producers of Chile, is in charge of promoting Chilean wine in national and international environments. As such its mission is to develop a collective reputation. In Italy, the Consorzio Del Vino Brunello Di Montalcino is an association of producers that aims to

---

[2] "The term 'reputation' expresses what is generally said or believed about the abilities and/or qualities of somebody or something" (Belletti 2000, p. 239).

enhance the image of wines produced in the Tuscany wine region benefiting from the Brunello di Montalcino denominazione di origine controllata e garantita (DOCG), a local AO.

– Single wineries provide individual reputations. Quite often, individual reputation is conveyed and even incarnated by the brand name. Yellow Tail is one of the biggest wine brands; Shalauri Cellars is another one, produced in the Kakheti region of Eastern Georgia. A single winery can provide several individual brands, each with a specific blend or varietal.

Examples of the three sources of reputation in the wine sector can be drawn from Old and New World countries, suggesting a strong interpenetration of both reputational models.

In this chapter, we focus mainly on institutional and collective reputation, given that the role of brands is extensively analyzed in the marketing literature: how it emerges and which effects are produced. Considering reputation effects, origin and brands can be conciliated. In Sect. 25.2, we present briefly some historical elements to understand why appellations and brands and varietals prevail in, respectively, the Old and New Worlds. In Sect. 25.3, we present how appellations act in wine markets. In Sect. 25.4 we discuss how origin can be seen as a brand, and in Sect. 25.5 we present some failures of collective reputation. We conclude our thoughts in Sect. 25.6.

25.2 Brief History of the Wine Industry

Two distinct models of the wine industry have evolved since the eighteenth century: the Old World, which is highly fragmented, grounded in certification of origin and the official classification of wines as a vehicle for collective reputation, and the New World, which is more concentrated and based on individual brands as a vector for individual reputation.

25.2.1 Old World and Appellation of Origin: A Review

France created the first European label of origin systems—the appellation d'origine controlee (AOC)—which was conceived of as a protected designation of origin (PDO), that is, a geographic indication certified by the government: "Products covered by AOC labels are controlled by the state to ensure both their territorial origin and their conformity to precise rules for production and processing that guarantee their 'typicity,' or distinctive character"

(Barham 2003, p. 128). This designation occurred in a specific industrial and institutional context. Indeed, the economic features of winegrowing as well as the intrinsic uncertainty of winemaking come from the fact that traditionally in Europe, winegrowing and winemaking are integrated in a single, small family business, whereas marketing and trade are carried out by merchants in charge of domestic and international distribution (Simpson 2011a). This specific organization of the French wine industry resulted from the market instability produced by the mid-eighteenth-century phylloxera crisis and other vine diseases (powdery mildew), which have weakened the position of most winemakers and strengthened the position of the merchants in the commodity chain. It has also provided incentives for the emergence of a regulatory framework allowing for the creation of appellations of origin, thanks to the lobbying of winemakers in a context of wine fraud and adulteration.

In the late 1780s, Young (1794, pp. 24–25, quoted in Simpson 2011b, p. 44) noted that in France, the cultivation of vine depended "almost entirely on manual labour … demanding no other capital than the possession of the land and a pair of arms; no carts, no ploughs, no cattle." Low entry costs, little capital expenditure apart from planting the vineyard, and the ability to use small plots of land to grow vines competitively compared with other crops were attractive, but there were some negative aspects, such as few economies of scale, huge weather effects, and risks of pests and vine diseases. As summarized by Simpson (2011b, p. 44), "grapes had to be processed quickly because they were easily damaged or diseased, and therefore family growers also made their own wine." Using wage labor or some form of rental arrangement was inappropriate due to a classical moral hazard problem: workers or tenants treat the vines with less care than the owners, given that wages were not sufficiently high to ensure good-quality work, and the vines could be permanently injured if different viticultural operations were poorly carried out, even for a single year. Some exceptions were found in Bordeaux, where fine-wine producers developed a contract that provided good working conditions and wages to ensure that workers returned each year, developing know-how and increasing their level of care and time devoted to vines to improve the harvest quality (Simpson 2011a).

By the end of the eighteenth century, after the 1789 French Revolution, winemakers and wine merchants had to deal with counterfeiting. Words such as *Bordeaux* or *Champagne* were generic names used by foreign traders to sell wine from a different origin. If in the Bordeaux region certain châteaux and individual brands were successful, elsewhere traders exerted increasing control over the producers. This occurred in Champagne, where negociants dominated the market because they manufactured the products and mixed them.

Simpson (2011a) notes that blending provides numerous opportunities for fraud and adulteration.[3] In Bordeaux, some new comers among wine estate owners also sold low-quality mixed wines, creating division among winegrowers themselves. Even if unions and professional associations were created, the conflicts remained, and local lobbies tried to influence every regulation (Stanziani 2004). As summarized by Stanziani (2004, p. 158), "during all the 19th century judicial interpretations guaranteed the protection of individual trade-marks and brands but they refused to take in consideration collective marks and generic names." Information for the consumer was unclear, the average quality decreased, and generic names suffered from a loss of reputation. At that time, reputation already played a major role in markets. If fine wines were sold under brand names, and commodity wines were sold to merchants for blending, "consumers might not be able to tell exactly what had been added to the wine they were drinking or where it had been produced, but they could make a choice of which retailer to frequent, being influenced no doubt by that person's reputation for fairness, quality, price, or good company" (Simpson 2011a, p. 23). The instability of quality from one harvest to the next made it impossible to create brands, and thus the retailer's reputation was crucial.

From the late 1850s to the mid-1870s, the phylloxera disease, transmitted by an aphid, destroyed most of the French vineyard. The American vines were aphid-resistant, so the task of reconstituting the French vineyards by means of grafting traditional French vines onto American rootstock began by the end of the nineteenth century. This redevelopment of winegrowing areas drove merchants to misuse denominations of origin and even poison consumers with fake products (Marie-Vivien 2010). The phylloxera crisis also forced merchants to search for alternative supplies: in foreign countries or by adding sugar to grapes. But "the subsequent recovery in domestic production was not accompanied by a marked reduction in these supplies, and growers had to stand by and watch prices, and their profits, fall steeply from the turn of the twentieth century, leading to demands that the government intervene" (Simpson 2005, p. 528). At the same time, the combination of falling transport costs, urbanization—implying that consumers no longer knew the origin of the wine—and rising real wages led to consumption per capita increasing

---

[3] "Fraud involved selling wine under the label of a private brand such as Moët & Chandon, or collective regional brands (Bordeaux or Champagne) when it had been produced elsewhere. Adulteration, by contrast, consisted of adding ingredients that were considered illegal or 'unnatural' to wine and the winemaking process like resin, honey, herbs but also lead and lead compounds" (Simpson 2011a, p. 7). For a series of examples, see Holmberg (2010).

from 76 liters in 1850–1854 to 168 liters in 1900–1904 (Nourrisson 2013). As a result, "as the distance between the producer and consumer increased, so did the economic power of the merchants, who were able to purchase their wines over an increasingly large area" (Simpson 2011b, p. 45).

At the beginning of the twentieth century, many producers were encouraging a state intervention. Former professional representatives were excluded and new commissions were organized with technicians and agronomists. Vine diseases forced governments to invest in research and new winemaking technologies to improve wine quality (Simpson 2011b), even if scientific progress made it easier for potential fraudsters. In several wine regions, winegrowers pointed out that consumers required information and a guarantee of quality, especially if they were willing to pay more to avoid drinking fraudulent and/or adulterated wines. Despite the oppositions of merchants and conflicts in establishing geographic boundaries, as winegrowers and rural workers became more organized, their political influence increased (Simpson 2005) and several laws were enacted in 1905, 1908, 1919, 1927, and 1935 to allow for the creation of the French appellation system.[4] According to Stanziani (2004, p. 149), this system is required "when neither the market alone nor the individual marks provide efficient information on the quality of goods." For Jacquet (2009), who studies the appellation system in Burgundy, the regulation associated with the AOC labeling also aimed to avoid rural depopulation and promote the republican order. Nowadays there are more than 350 AOCs in France. Spain and Italy have followed this trend. In Spain, the denominación de origen (DO) appellation system was first developed in the Rioja wine region in 1926. The denominación de origen calificada (DOC), or denominació d'origen qualificada (DOQ) in Catalan, is a higher category of Spanish wine, reserved for regions with the highest grape prices and stringent quality controls. Rioja was the first Spanish region to be awarded DOC status in 1991. The Italian government introduced the system in 1963 with currently three levels: DO (designation of origin, seldom used), DOC (controlled designation of origin), and DOCG (controlled and guaranteed designation of origin). To reinforce the effect of certification, wines are tasted by government-licensed professionals before being bottled, and DOCG wine bottles are then

---

[4] Simpson (2005) shows that if establishing regional appellations has helped growers in winning back market power in the Bordeaux and Champagne vineyards, another response was shown in the Midi region (Languedoc area): the creation of producer cooperatives, better equipped than merchants to classify wines and guarantee quality for consumers, has provided incentives to plant quality vines and allow growers to capture the growing economies of scale in wine production and marketing. This creation occurred because the sector was united (small and large growers and even merchants also affected by low prices) and mass demonstration in 1907, previously unknown in France.

sealed with a numbered governmental seal across the cap or cork, which results in a paper strip if torn out during opening. For a presentation of the EU wine classification, see Delmastro (2005, p. 2).

The economic and institutional features of the European wine industry, generated at least partly by some natural constraints, have allowed for the emergence of the appellation system as a support for collective reputation and to provide information about the products. The New World history is different.

25.2.2 New World: Brands and Varietals

Simpson (2011b) studied the exogenous changes that occurred in the wine industry between 1870 and 1914 in California, Australia, and Argentina, which evolved from a traditional viti-viniculture to a new organization of the commodity chain. By the beginning of the twentieth century, this chain was dominated by large industrial wineries producing wines that could be branded. In the New World, grape production was a specialist activity whereas wine-making and marketing were integrated into a single business.

In the 1850s, the New World wine industry was small scale. By 1900, in Australia, California, and Argentina, grape growing was a specialist activity and grapegrowers sold their grapes to winemakers, who also made a business of wine. Indeed, in the New World, climatic conditions made the vines much easier to grow than in the Old World. Harvest failures and diseases were far less frequent, and grape quality was more stable and less heterogeneous from one harvest to the next than in the Old World (Simpson 2011b). As depicted by Simpson (2011b), New World grapegrowers met with few problems, needing little capital to create new vineyards and other employment opportunities. Wineries need winemaking facilities, and their investments are linked to credit availability. When the market downturns, low prices do not allow for capital-intensive wineries to purchase grapes from independent grapegrowers who, as a consequence, crush the grapes themselves: the wine supply is not diminished but at the same time quality declines as independent grapegrowers are not necessarily skilled in winemaking. This increased separation between grape growing and winemaking has led to unbalanced growth between grape growing and winemaking.

In California by the end of the nineteenth century, facing falling prices and fraud, winemakers and wine dealers established collective associations to agree on prices and quantities. After several conflicts, the winemakers' corporation disappeared and horizontal consolidation as well as vertical integration allowed the wine dealers' trust (the California Wine Association) to control distribution and guarantee non-adulterated wines, while the political climate was relatively permissive toward big businesses and trusts. This provided the conditions to develop a mass market for wines and to invest in brand names. This market is characterized by limited competition, given that investments in production facilities and brands raise entry costs for potential newcomers.

Australia was the only New World country with a significant export trade, with a fifth of its national production sold in the United Kingdom. Australia's high internal tariffs as well as the narrowness of the domestic market provided an incentive to export even with high freight costs. But a long sea travel, some extreme temperatures during it, and a necessary rest of several months on the arrival of wines caused major quality problems for the wine trade. Simpson (2011b, p. 55) summarizes that "trusted agents were required at both ends of the chain: in Australia to check that only well-made wines were shipped; and in London to determine the appropriate remedies to correct the wines on their arrival." Two major London houses dominated trade. They specialized in Australian wines; invested in vineyards, winemaking facilities, European methods for viticulture and vinification; and bought large quantities of grapes, hired agents, and invested in modern techniques of advertising such as point-of-purchase communication, all necessary conditions to create a standardized product that could build consumer recognition. Even as the South Australian government tried to compete, providing incentives to plant vines and creating a vine depot in London, it failed to improve quality, and by 1911, three big players dominated the exports from Australia to the United Kingdom and were able to develop major brands.

A lot of European immigrants moved to Argentina before 1914. They were accustomed to drinking wine, so wine producers competed on price rather than on quality. By the end of the nineteenth century, there was a rail connection between Mendoza and Buenos Aires to take advantage of the good growing conditions for grapes, the winemakers who learned the needed skills to produce wines properly in the hot climate and use the upgraded winemaking equipment (Blanchy 2010). Grape growing is a specialist activity and grapes were sold to wine producers, who could sell large quantities of ordinary wines to agents, intermediaries, and/or retailers. Wine had been a basic beverage in the Argentine diet, and leaders such as Peròn as well as the military dictatorship encouraged the supply of plentiful cheap wines.

But during the twentieth century, the growth of the wine industry was very slow due to isolationist and protectionist policies enacted during the 1950s and, as a result, the Argentinian wine industry lacked innovation (Townsend and Tiefenbacher 2011). Facing a falling demand, the Argentinian wine sector destabilized, and in the 1980s, 36% of all vineyards were eradicated (Pont and Thomas 2011). The modernization of the wine industry started in the 1990s with the replacement of traditional varietals such as Criolla with Malbec. The focus of production has shifted from low-cost quantity to quality. The opening of international markets; some technology transfers; foreign investments by big, recognized players such as Mondavi, Lurton, and Chandon; the arrival of maverick winemakers; as well as the peso devaluation in 2002 (Mount 2012; Pont and Thomas 2011), even if disadvantageous to most citizens, made wines highly competitive in foreign markets and enabled the recognition of Malbec to become the emblematic variety of Argentina. If Malbec is not a brand, it has a strong economic and emotional connection to Argentina, where 70% of the world's Malbec vineyards are now planted.[5]

25.2.3   Two Different Models

Because of natural, institutional, and economic conditions, wineries from the New World mainly rely on "individual brand advertising" (BA) to promote quality perception and develop an individual reputation; European wineries use geographical indications (GIs) as a quality signal that allow them to share the costs of promotion and to develop a common reputation (Yue et al. 2013, p. 1). For Bureau and Valceschini (2003, p. 72), "the appellation of origin has proved successful in allowing even small producer groups to benefit from a well-established reputation." On the contrary, as studied in the marketing literature, a brand is a vector for individual reputation (see Lockshin et al. 2000).

In Sect. 25.3, we focus on geographic indications as a vehicle for collective reputation.

25.3   Geographic Indications and Collective Reputation

A DO is used traditionally to suggest specific production practices or look for natural endowments to positively affect wine taste. In the wine sector, emphasizing the place of origin as an indicator of quality is one way to differentiate products (Stasi et al. 2011), especially for connoisseurs (Atkin and Johnson 2010).

---

[5] See https://historyandwine.com/2014/07/02/cahors-france-the-french-malbec-story/; retrieved September 15, 2016.

25.3.1 Coalition of Economic Agents and the Collective Reputation Effect

"Wine denominations are a perfect example of coalitions of economic agents who share a common reputation" (Castriota and Delmastro 2011, p. 9). An appellation can be seen as a coalition of producers who operate within the same local area (Delmastro 2005). This coalition emerges because the wine industry is characterized by information asymmetry and is highly fragmented. Indeed, even if that sector has experienced consolidation recently, a lot of small and family-owned vineyards remain, especially in Europe (Roberto 2011). Sometimes, the owner is the sole full-time employee and has to be simultaneously a vine grower, winemaker, purchasing officer, salesperson, and so on (Edwards 1989). Moreover, these actors are often constrained by small marketing and advertising budgets (Yuan et al. 2004) or are not aware of contemporary marketing concepts to increase sales (Spawton 1986). With the creation of AOCs, there is the underlying idea that members of that coalition will benefit from the group image—as suggested by the collective reputation theory proposed by Tirole (1996)—and that belonging to a higher reputation group generates higher rents. However, Gergaud et al. (2017) show in the case of Bordeaux wines that collective reputation does not systematically offer net benefits to producers. Following Tirole's collective reputation theory (1996), Delmastro (2005) reminds us that an appellation's reputation depends on the rules that the coalition members have adopted, on their past and present behavior, and on the effectiveness of monitoring procedures. In the wine sector, the coalition exists at two different levels: (1) at every AO and vineyard, thanks to a wine commission if the vineyard is composed of several different appellations and (2) in a wine commission that is in charge of promoting the vineyard as a whole thanks to an umbrella, such as Bordeaux, Burgundy, or Toscana (Tuscan wines). According to Fig. 25.1, the umbrella can be seen as a geographical indication. Some producers do not use such umbrellas to avoid what they consider a declassification of their wines, especially when their brand has achieved recognition on the market and enjoys a high individual reputation.[6] As such, in some cases, appellations and brands are conceived as two models generating opposite effects.

---

[6] A great growth, such as Château Mouton Rothschild in Bordeaux, indicates the Pauillac appellation in the label, but it doesn't make any explicit reference to Bordeaux as a collective umbrella.

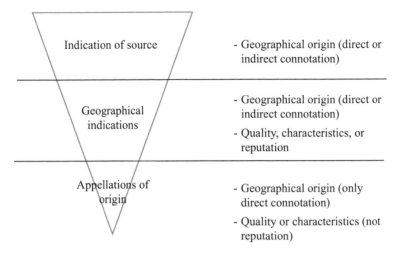

Fig. 25.1 Denominations of origin. (Source: Addor and Grazioli 2002, p. 870)

25.3.2 A Regulation to Increase Welfare and Efficiency that Generate Profits

Wine is a typical experience product, and wine markets exhibit imperfect information. In many countries, the public sector provides a certification of origin to solve at least partly the information problem. When this origin is certified by the government through an appellation of origin (AO), it becomes a collective quality signal. For instance, the European Commission has introduced legislation to guarantee that the product is produced in the mentioned region and allows producers to market their product with a label stating a PDO.

Stanziani (2004), who studies the emergence of the AO in France (called AOC), considers them to be collective marks that appear when neither the market alone nor the private individual quality signals provide efficient information on the quality of goods. For Meloni and Swinnen (2013), given that consumers have imperfect information and high ex ante monitoring costs about wine quality, regulations such as the AO guarantee a quality level or reduce information costs, which can improve welfare. Menapace and Moschini (2011) have shown that this kind of credible certification scheme reduces the cost of establishing reputation, compared to a situation in which only private brands are established, and improves the reputation mechanism to ensure quality.

For wine, in addition to origin, several restrictions, such as grape varietals, maximum yields, practices in the vineyard and in the cellar, and alcohol level, also apply before obtaining an AOC designation. Since 2008, the system is similar to that of taxes: winemakers must declare that their wine has been produced in accordance with AOC requirements; to assure this, wines are subject to random tests by an expert from a public agency. A given wine can lose its appellation status for a given vintage if it doesn't achieve the appellation criteria.[7]

Geographic indications (GIs) are viewed as public goods (Schamel and Anderson 2003) because they are used simultaneously by many firms that are free to enter and exit the market, provided that all the requirements are met (Moschini et al. 2008). Rangnekar (2004) views them as "club goods," non-rival, congestible, and excludable, and producers are free to decide the size of the club. Binding a brand to a territory also generates a profit for some groups of producers who have access to key assets or skills required to get the certification or the AOC, such as land and a vineyard that can't be delocalized or will damage owners of land and vineyards in neighboring areas where less reputed and less expensive wines are produced (Meloni and Swinnen 2013). Castriota and Delmastro (2014) notice that using a well-known geographical group brand enables small producers to get the benefits of a reputation profit. But Winfree and McCluskey (2005) show that when a collective reputation becomes a public good, there is an incentive to free ride, and the provision of quality decreases as the size of the group increases.

25.3.3   Translating Terroir and Protecting Traditions

Economists usually view certifications of origin as collective quality signals (Bramley et al. 2009). But AOC labeling can also be seen as a way to translate terroir (Barham 2003), which refers to natural qualities of a geographic area (soil, microclimate, slope, exposure, etc.) blended with human factors (know-how or particular techniques) perceived as confined to that area and history (such as public knowledge of a product originating in that area and recognition of the association between product and place). Behind AOCs and terroir there is the idea that unique values are, at least partly, generated by local places. Said differently, "to talk about terroir, it is necessary that the origin of

---

[7] See, for instance, Bordeaux producer brand Les Hauts de Pontet-Canet, which is usually awarded with a Pauillac appellation but didn't get it for the 2012 vintage:

http://www.decanter.com/news/wine-news/587659/pontet-canet-second-wine-loses-aoc-status?utm_source=Eloqua&utm_medium=email&utm_content=news+alert+link+24102014&utm_campaign=Newsletter-24102014

the production is clearly defined and that the peculiarities of the place are the guarantee of a minimum of typicality" (Mora 2016, p. 43). Several agricultural products can benefit from that certification of origin: wine, cheese, meat, lavender, lentils, honey, ham, butter, spirits, and so on. The number of products benefiting from a protected designation of origin is increasing in Europe (Profeta et al. 2010). Broude (2005) also views GIs as tools to protect cultural heritage and preserve traditional methods of production or to establish and preserve an identity. Addor and Grazioli (2002) also note that GIs are based on collective traditions. Vogel (1995) notices that some people attach value to regional traditions and are willing to pay a premium for it.

25.3.4   Origin Effect and Reputation

The promotion of a region of origin has a long history in the wine industry. Schamel (2006) has shown a trend toward more regional differentiation. On the academic side, origin has often been used as a vector for collective reputation used in empirical analysis. Indeed, several applications of a hedonic pricing method for wine refer to appellation, which includes group reputation (see, among others, Delmastro 2005; Landon and Smith 1997; Schamel and Anderson 2003).

An extensive body of literature has addressed the issue-of-origin effect[8] on wine perception, evaluation, and purchase decisions. Yue et al. (2013) show that region of origin, specifically geographical indicators, is an efficient tool to signal good quality. They cite examples such as the Champagne region of France in which well-known brands have invested in quality and advertising over a lengthy period, thus building and maintaining a successful collective reputation for the vineyard as a whole. In research by Batt and Dean (2000), the origin of wine was found to be a key variable affecting consumer purchase decisions. An argument for promotion of the region is also given by Hong and Wyer (1989), who demonstrate that origin has a direct influence on evaluation of a product and in addition encourages stronger consideration of the other attributes of the product. Consumers possess stereotyped beliefs about the quality of products from a country of origin (Samiee 1994). This is known as the "halo effect," suggested by Maheswaran (1994). Huber and McCann (1982) also demonstrate that origin can provide product quality signals when consumers are not able to ascertain or are not familiar with the actual quality

---

[8] For a review of the country-of-origin effect on perceived quality, see Verlegh and Steenkamp (1999). For an analysis of the region-of-origin effect, see Van Ittersum et al. (2003).

of the product. This is backed up by research from Elliot and Cameron (1994), who find that country of origin may be used as a quality indicator when the product cannot be assessed by objective criteria. As such, the link between origin and reputation seems obvious: origin is a means to enhance reputation and its vehicle.

According to Bruwer and House (2003), the image of a region of origin can be used as a point of differentiation if it can take advantage of the positive associations consumers have with that region. In some ways, origin acts like a brand and considering the two models as opposite isn't really accurate anymore.

25.4   Origin and Branding

More and more, GI and individual brands are used simultaneously in the wine world. As an example, as noted by Rasmussen and Lockshin (1999), since the early 1990s, many Australian wine companies have indicated regional brand names on their labels.

The brand notion is also meaningful in the French context with its use of AOCs. According to Viot and Passebois-Ducros (2010), managerial practices reveal three major types of brand strategy in the French wine industry:

- The merchant brand: usually blended wines that are made, bottled, and packaged by merchants and maintain a stable quality.
- The producer brand: any wine estate that grows vines and has winemaking facilities can create its own brand name, including using the word *château* traditionally in the Bordeaux vineyard or the word *domaine* in Burgundy.
- The retailer's brand: wine that is available only in the outlets of a single retailer.

At this point, origin and brand cannot be considered as two opposite models. They are often used jointly. Origin also has some dimensions of brands, as shown in the next section.

25.4.1   Regionality and Territorial Brands

Origin can also affect the concept of a collective brand. Moulard et al. (2015) show that origin affects consumers' perceptions of a wine's authenticity and their willingness to pay for it, with a positive effect in the case of Old World wines. Consumers can be emotionally attached to a place, based on previous visits to the wine region (Cardinale et al. 2016). Similar to brands, place can generate attachment and loyalty. And similar to any collective brand, place may act as a quality signal through spillovers that create reputation linkages among various products or individuals (Choi et al. 1995). Cardinale et al. (2016) identify that producing a good in a quality geographical area generates a competitive advantage for those goods, and that name becomes a place-based brand, because the area of origin is inimitable by competitors. And because it is collective, it reduces the marketing costs for every single winery.

Regionality is a concept that reconciles origin and brand and has been defined as the reputation a wine region has for producing wines with a particular style (Easingwood et al. 2011). When a wine region lacks regionality, it must compete on price, what is not easy given the huge supply in the wine world. Similar to brands (Lockshin et al. 2000), regionality is a differentiation device that forms a kind of contract between the producer and the consumer to obtain a consistent style of wine. Also similar to brands, regionality requires uniqueness. Developing the notion of territorial brands, Charters and Spielmann (2014) show that GIs have to be managed like brands. Territorial brands must have a natural link to a place, resulting in something that cannot be produced elsewhere, and it must be overarching, that is, encompassing all individual corporate brands in the territory. Champagne is an emblematic example of a territorial brand. It also illustrates the coexistence of brands and appellations (Charters and Spielmann 2014).

The effects of origin can be the same as that created by individual brands. At the same time, appellations have spread all over the world and can be used jointly with brands.

25.4.2 Appellations in the New World

Easingwood et al. (2011) note that there is now a plethora of denominations of origin in the New and Old Worlds. The US AVA that began in 1979 was inspired by the French AOC model. Geographical indicators in the EU delineate a certain region and in addition provide parameters on growing methods, yields, winemaking, aging, and more, all supposedly leading to higher-quality wines. By contrast, an AVA in the United States is defined solely as a geographical unit that possesses characteristics unique from the surrounding areas. The rules are less restrictive than in Europe, stating that 85% of the grapes must be grown in that AVA. There are no parameters for growing, winemaking, and other factors such as that seen in the EU. Thus, there is no "objective" assurance of quality. Blanchy (2010, p. 30) notes that a system of DOC was created in Argentina in 1999 but that in Mendoza few producers use it, even if it begin to capture consumers' attention (Defrancesco et al. 2012). Nevertheless, for export, most wineries do include non-protected geographical names on the label (Defrancesco et al. 2012) to generate an origin effect in consumers' minds. In Chile, the system is still in its infancy, but some regulations of denominations of origin have been evolving since 1995. For Schamel (2006), the trend toward regional differentiation is reinforced by the better protection of geographical indications in many countries, raising the rates of return on investments in regional promotion and suggesting that "marketing" a region can be rewarded even in the New World. Schamel (2009) also shows that in New Zealand high-quality brands rely heavily on overall regional reputation, and in California some highly reputed brands lose their strength and start to rely on regional reputation.

Using denominations of origin appears to be a trend in the wine industry, even in the so-called New World. But in some cases, it fails to improve reputation through a collective mechanism, as discussed in Sect. 25.5, and individual strategies remain relevant, at least jointly with collective ones.

25.5   The Failures of Denominations of Origin

25.5.1   Credibility of Certification and Proliferation of Information

The AOC system provides a product certification that acts to transform unobservable experiences, but it also gives credence to elements such as origin as observable search attributes (Auriol and Schilizzi 2003). Auriol and Schilizzi (2003, p. 3) define certification "as a process whereby an unobservable quality level of some product is made known to the consumer through some labeling system, usually issued by a third independent party." Considering that consumer confidence associated with certification is a major concern, these authors show that the sunk costs of certification enable the achievement of credibility and that certification is better accomplished by an independent body, either a private firm or a public agency. One specificity of GIs is that their recognition, administration, and control are shared by public and private bodies, depending on the system of protection (Addor and Grazioli 2002). But frauds still exist. Indeed, mixing wines from several appellations and mislabeling bottles regarding their origin are some common types of fraud (Holmberg 2010). Some winemakers also try to ridicule the appellation system: in the 1990s,

Didier Dagueneau, a producer of outstanding Pouilly-Fumé AOC wines in France, got an AOC for his worst production, made with bad-quality grapes and branded "Quintessence of My Balls" (Doward 2005).

Meloni and Swinnen (2013) notice that government decision-making can be influenced by political pressures related to regulation-induced prices, which reduces overall welfare and efficiency, and that the AOC system is the result of efficient lobbying from wine producer organizations that put pressure on the French government. Teil (2010) note that since their creation AOCs have been suspected of not conveying reliable information. Nevertheless, their use is expanding in the world, and they coexist with many other strategies to reveal quality. As a consequence, the wine market has become complex, hosting hundreds of thousands of brands and other quality signals. The certification of origin can be associated with a brand (Lockshin et al. 2006), sometimes with a medal (Orth and Krška 2001), a back label (Mueller et al. 2010), or some other typical quality signals in the wine sector. The consumer can also use some other sources of information, such as grades and comments published by experts (Dubois and Nauges 2010), public opinion[9] (Ashenfelter et al. 2007), specific press, or even movies (Cuellar et al. 2009). This proliferation and even redundancy of information, labels, and appellations can produce distortions including consumers' lack of attention or trust and even misunderstanding (Anania and Nisticò 2004; Marette 2005). Viot and Passebois-Ducros (2010) show that there is confusion, in the consumer's mind, between the brand and the appellation of origin. Livat et al. (forthcoming) show that consumers cannot decipher the quality attributes that the different DOs are meant to signal, which questions the optimal number of AOs. In such a context, some producers, aware of the potential inefficiency of certification of origin to improve their reputation, question the role of coalitions as well as their own membership in such groups.

25.5.2 Coalitions are Challenged

In January 2013, the Loire appellation Montlouis-sur-Loire, a grouping of 72 wineries, broke away from the official Loire wine commission, named InterLoire, and decided to be responsible for its own marketing and promotion, withdrawing its funding contribution to the wine commission of only €70,000 for the whole group. They believe and hope to be more efficient individually and to improve their reputation. Another member, the Bourgueil appellation, decided

---

[9] Such as in 2003 with the US consumers' boycott of French wines.

to go it alone in 2009 (see Anson 2013). In the case of Bordeaux wines, in 2004 four appellations created their own subgroup: Côtes de Bordeaux is the umbrella for Premières Côtes de Blaye, Premières Côtes de Bordeaux, Côtes de Castillon, and Bordeaux Côtes de Francs appellations, all of whom share "the idea of creating a common sign of recognition." They consider that recognition is not provided by their single AOs, but they remain members of the regional wine commission (see their website bordeaux-cotes.com).

The AOC, as a coalition, is in charge of generic advertising, thanks to funds provided by the members. A return on investment is expected because of spillover effects from the collective reputation toward the individual reputation of the winery. In Bordeaux, a breakaway group emerged in 2010 because non-voluntary (i.e., compulsory) fees are not legal, and they felt that the regional wine commission was not working in the interests of those who compulsorily support it financially (Anson 2010). But in 2012, the court ruled that winemakers must pay the fees. Hence, in France at least, some actors consider challenging the coalitions. In US wine regions, Rickard et al. (2015) highlight that individual reputation outside of the umbrella region can be affected by a collective reputation, even if these individual producers don't contribute financially to the promotional efforts, through a reputation-tapping phenomenon. In the case of Bordeaux wines, Gergaud et al. (2017) show that if collective reputation generally provides some benefits to individual group members, the gains obtained from generic promotion by the wine commission do not always compensate for the costs of mandatory membership.

25.6   Conclusion

The wine market exhibits several different quality signals: individual and collective, private and public. The number of wines benefiting from a protected designation of origin is increasing in the Old World (Profeta et al. 2010) as well as in the New World (Easingwood et al. 2011). Similar to brands, AOs aim to signal quality. If brands support individual reputation, denominations of origin are a vehicle for collective reputation. Both coexist more and more frequently on the same label, suggesting in some way a convergence of both reputational models. Reputation is not supported by a unique model, neither in the Old World nor in the New World.

Reputation is a key variable in wine markets. The prolific literature on hedonic pricing highlights its positive effect on price. Livat (2007) has shown that consumers substitute Bordeaux appellations with the same level of reputation. Livat et al. (forthcoming) show that they substitute them according to semantic elements, that is, similar names as carriers of reputation, not according to intrinsic characteristics of wines associated with the production process (location, climate, and technology). If such a result pacifies appellations and brands by highlighting the power of names, it also suggests that the appellation system is not understood by consumers and is currently too complex to address informational needs in wine markets. Simplification and a lower degree of horizontal differentiation might be a better option.

References

Addor, F., and A. Grazioli. 2002. Geographical indications beyond wines and spirits. *The Journal of World Intellectual Property 5* (6): 865–897.

Anania, G., and R. Nisticò. 2004. Public regulation as a substitute for trust in quality food markets: What if the trust substitute cannot be fully trusted? *Journal of Institutional and Theoretical Economics 160*: 681–701.

Anson, J. 2010. "Cronyist" CIVB to be sued by breakaway group. *Decanter*, December 10.

———. 2013. Montlouis-sur-Loire cuts itself loose from InterLoire. *Decanter*, January 9.

Ashenfelter, O., S. Ciccarella, and H.J. Shatz. 2007. French wine and the US boycott of 2003: Does politics really affect commerce? *Journal of Wine Economics 2* (01): 55–74.

Atkin, T., and R. Johnson. 2010. Appellation as an indicator of quality. *International Journal of Wine Business Research 22* (1): 42–61.

Auriol, E., and S.G. Schilizzi. 2003. *Quality signaling through certification: Theory and an application to agricultural seed markets*. IDEI Working Paper, 165. Toulouse: Institut d'Economie Industrielle (IDEI).

Banks, G., and J. Overton. 2010. Old world, new world, third world? Reconceptualising the worlds of wine. *Journal of Wine Research 21* (1): 57–75.

Barham, E. 2003. Translating terroir: The global challenge of French AOC labeling. *Journal of Rural Studies 19* (1): 127–138.

Batt, P.J., and A. Dean. 2000. Factors influencing the consumer's decision. *Australian & New Zealand Wine Industry Journal 15* (4): S34–S41.

Belletti, G. 2000. Origin labelled products, reputation and heterogeneity of firms. *Actes et Communications: Institut National de la Recherche Agronomique. Economie et Sociologie Rurales 17* (1): 239–259.

Blanchy, G. 2010. La construction des vins argentins à travers l'affichage. *Sciences de la Société 80*: 60–75.

Bramley, C., E. Biénabe, and J. Kirsten. 2009. The economics of geographical indications: Towards a conceptual framework for geographical indication research in developing countries. *The Economics of Intellectual Property*, 109–141. Available at http://www.wipo.int/export/sites/www/ip-development/en/economics/pdf/wo_1012_e.pdf

Broude, T. 2005. Taking trade and culture seriously: Geographical indications and cultural protection in WTO. *University of Pennsylvania Journal of International Law* 26: 623.

Bruwer, J., and M. House. 2003. Has the era of regional branding arrived for the Australian wine industry? Some perspectives. *The Australian & New Zealand Grapegrower & Winemaker*, December 1.

Bureau, J.C., and E. Valceschini. 2003. European food-labeling policy: Successes and limitations. *Journal of Food Distribution Research 34* (3): 70–76.

Cardinale, S., B. Nguyen, and T.C. Melewar. 2016. Place-based brand experience, place attachment and loyalty. *Marketing Intelligence & Planning 34* (3): 302–317.

Castriota, S., and M. Delmastro. 2011. *Inside the black box of collective reputation (No. 89/2011)*. Perugia: Università di Perugia, Dipartimento Economia.

———. 2012. Seller reputation: Individual, collective, and institutional factors. *Journal of Wine Economics 7* (01): 49–69.

———. 2014. The economics of collective reputation: Evidence from the wine industry. *American Journal of Agricultural Economics 97* (2): 469–489. https://doi.org/10.1093/ajae/aau107.

Charters, S., and N. Spielmann. 2014. Characteristics of strong territorial brands: The case of champagne. *Journal of Business Research 67* (7): 1461–1467.

Choi, C.J., S.H. Lee, and D. Oh. 1995. The strategy of grouping and reputation linkage in clubs and multi-product firms. *European Journal of Political Economy 11* (3): 521–533.

Cuellar, S.S., D. Karnowsky, and F. Acosta. 2009. The *Sideways* effect: A test for changes in the demand for merlot and pinot noir wines. *Journal of Wine Economics 4* (02): 219–232.

Defrancesco, E., J.E. Orrego, and A. Gennari. 2012. Would 'New World' wines benefit from protected geographical indications in international markets? The case of Argentinean Malbec. *Wine Economics and Policy 1* (1): 63–72.

Delmastro, M. 2005. An investigation into the quality of wine: Evidence from Piedmont. *Journal of Wine Research 16* (1): 1–17.

Doward, J. 2005. French bitter over wine study. *The Guardian*, March 20.

Dubois, P., and C. Nauges. 2010. Identifying the effect of unobserved quality and expert reviews in the pricing of experience goods: Empirical application on Bordeaux wine. *International Journal of Industrial Organization 28* (3): 205–212.

Easingwood, C., L. Lockshin, and T. Spawton. 2011. The drivers of wine regionality. *Journal of Wine Research 22* (1): 19–33.

Edwards, F. 1989. The marketing of wine from small wineries: Managing the intangibles. *International Journal of Wine Marketing 1* (1): 14–17.

Elliott, G.R., and R.C. Cameron. 1994. Consumer perception of product quality and the country-of-origin effect. *Journal of International Marketing 2* (2): 49–62.

Fombrun, C., and M. Shanley. 1990. What's in a name? Reputation building and corporate strategy. *Academy of Management Journal 33* (2): 233–258.

Gergaud, O., F. Livat, B. Rickard, and F. Warzynski. 2017. Evaluating the net benefits of collective reputation: The case of Bordeaux wine. *Food Policy 71*: 8–16.

Holmberg, L. 2010. Wine fraud. *International Journal of Wine Research 2010* (2): 105–113.

Hong, S.T., and R.S. Wyer. 1989. Effects of country-of-origin and product-attribute information on product evaluation: An information processing perspective. *Journal of Consumer Research 16* (2): 175–187.

Huber, J., and J. McCann. 1982. The impact of inferential beliefs on product evaluations. *Journal of Marketing Research* 19: 324–333.

Jacquet, O. 2009. *Un siècle de construction du vignoble bourguignon: Les organisations vitivinicoles de 1884 aux AOC*. Dijon: EUD, Collection Sociétés.

Keushguerian, V., and I. Ghaplanyan 2015. Carving out a new market niche: Historic world of wines. *BIO Web of Conferences, 5,* 03002.

Landon, S., and C.E. Smith. 1997. The use of quality and reputation indicators by consumers: The case of Bordeaux wine. *Journal of Consumer Policy 20* (3): 289–323.

Livat, F. 2007. Mesure des interactions de prix: Une analyse des modalités de substitution parmi sept vins de Bordeaux. *Economie & Prévision 4*: 127–145.

Livat, F., J. Alston, and J.-M. Cardebat. forthcoming. Do denominations of origin provide useful quality signals? The case of Bordeaux wines. *Economic Modelling*. https://doi.org/10.1016/j.econmod.2018.06.003.

Lockshin, L., M. Rasmussen, and F. Cleary. 2000. The nature and roles of a wine brand. *Australian & New Zealand Wine Industry Journal 15* (4): S17–S24.

Lockshin, L., W. Jarvis, F. d'Hauteville, and J.P. Perrouty. 2006. Using simulations from discrete choice experiments to measure consumer sensitivity to brand, region, price, and awards in wine choice. *Food Quality and Preference 17* (3): 166–178.

Maheswaran, D. 1994. Country of origin as a stereotype: Effects of consumer expertise and attribute strength on product evaluations. *Journal of Consumer Research 21* (2): 354–365.

Marette, S. 2005. *The collective-quality promotion in the agribusiness sector: An overview*. Ames: Center for Agricultural and Rural Development, Iowa State University.

Marie-Vivien, D. 2010. The role of the state in the protection of geographical indications: From disengagement in France/Europe to significant involvement in India. *The Journal of World Intellectual Property 13* (2): 121–147.

Meloni, G., and J. Swinnen. 2013. The political economy of European wine regulations. *Journal of Wine Economics 8* (3): 244–284.

Menapace, L., and G. Moschini. 2011. Quality certification by geographical indications, trademarks and firm reputation. *European Review of Agricultural Economics 39* (4): 539–566.

Mora, P. 2016. *Wine positioning: A handbook with 30 case studies of wine brands and wine regions in the world*. Cham: Springer.

Moschini, G., L. Menapace, and D. Pick. 2008. Geographical indications and the competitive provision of quality in agricultural markets. *American Journal of Agricultural Economics 90* (3): 794–812.

Moulard, J., B.J. Babin, and M. Griffin. 2015. How aspects of a wine's place affect consumers' authenticity perceptions and purchase intentions: The role of country of origin and technical terroir. *International Journal of Wine Business Research 27* (1): 61–78.

Mount, I. 2012. *The vineyard at the end of the world: Maverick winemakers and the rebirth of Malbec*. New York: W. W. Norton & Company.

Mueller, S., L. Lockshin, Y. Saltman, and J. Blanford. 2010. Message on a bottle: The relative influence of wine back label information on wine choice. *Food Quality and Preference 21* (1): 22–32.

Nourrisson, D. 2013. *Le buveur du XIXe siècle*. Paris: Albin Michel.

Orth, U.R., and P. Krška. 2001. Quality signals in wine marketing: The role of exhibition awards. *The International Food and Agribusiness Management Review 4* (4): 385–397.

Pont, P.C.M., and H. Thomas. 2011. The sociotechnical alliance of Argentine quality wine: How Mendoza's viticulture functions between the local and the global. *Science, Technology & Human Values 37* (6): 627–652.

Profeta, A., R. Balling, V. Schoene, and A. Wirsig. 2010. Protected geographical indications and designations of origin: An overview of the status quo and the development of the use of regulation (EC) 510/06 in Europe, with special consideration of the German situation. *Journal of International Food & Agribusiness Marketing 22* (1–2): 179–198.

Rangnekar, D. 2004. *The socio-economics of geographical indications*. UNCTAD-ICTSD Project on IPRs and Sustainable Development, Issue Paper, 8.

Rasmussen, M., and L. Lockshin. 1999. Wine choice behaviour: The effect of regional branding. *International Journal of Wine Marketing 11* (1): 36–46.

Rickard, B.J., J.J. McCluskey, and R.W. Patterson. 2015. Reputation tapping. *European Review of Agricultural Economics 42* (4): 675–701.

Roberto, M.A. 2011. The changing structure of the global wine industry. *International Business & Economics Research Journal (IBER) 2* (9): 1–14.

Samiee, S. 1994. Customer evaluation of products in a global market. *Journal of International Business Studies 25* (3): 579–604.

Schamel, G. 2006. Geography versus brands in a global wine market. *Agribusiness 22* (3): 363–374.

———. 2009. Dynamic analysis of brand and regional reputation: The case of wine. *Journal of Wine Economics 4* (01): 62–80.

Schamel, G., and K. Anderson. 2003. Wine quality and varietal, regional and winery reputation: Hedonic prices for Australia and New Zealand. *Economic Record 79* (246): 357–369.

Simpson, J. 2005. Cooperation and conflicts: Institutional innovation in France's wine markets, 1870–1911. *Business History Review 79* (03): 527–558.

———. 2011a. *Creating wine: The emergence of a world industry, 1840–1914*. Princeton: Princeton University Press.

————. 2011b. Factor endowments, markets and vertical integration. The development of commercial wine production in Argentina, Australia and California, c1870–1914. *Revista de Historia Económica/Journal of Iberian and Latin American Economic History (Second Series) 29* (01): 39–66.

Spawton, T. 1986. Understanding wine purchasing: Knowing how the wine buyer behaves can increase sales. *The Australian and New Zealand Wine Industry Journal 1* (2): 54–57.

Stanziani, A. 2004. Wine reputation and quality controls: The origin of the AOCs in 19th century France. *European Journal of Law and Economics 18* (2): 149–167.

Stasi, A., G. Nardone, R. Viscecchia, and A. Seccia. 2011. Italian wine demand and differentiation effect of geographical indications. *International Journal of Wine Business Research 23* (1): 49–61.

Teil, G. 2010. The French wine "appellations d'origine contrôlée" and the virtues of suspicion. *The Journal of World Intellectual Property 13* (2): 253–274.

Tirole, J. 1996. A theory of collective reputations (with applications to the persistence of corruption and to firm quality). *The Review of Economic Studies 63* (1): 1–22.

Townsend, C.G., and J.P. Tiefenbacher. 2011. Spatial change in South American viticulture: Static factors and dynamic processes in past, present, and future Chilean and Argentinean land use patterns and varietal choices. In *Proceedings—International Geographical Union 2011 Regional Geography Conference*, Santiago, Chile.

Van Ittersum, K., M.J. Candel, and M.T. Meulenberg. 2003. The influence of the image of a product's region of origin on product evaluation. *Journal of Business Research 56* (3): 215–226.

Verlegh, P.W., and J.B.E. Steenkamp. 1999. A review and meta-analysis of country-of-origin research. *Journal of Economic Psychology 20* (5): 521–546.

Viot, C., and J. Passebois-Ducros. 2010. Wine brands or branded wines? The specificity of the French market in terms of the brand. *International Journal of Wine Business Research 22* (4): 406–422.

Vogel, D. 1995. *Trading up: Consumer and environmental regulation in a global economy*. Cambridge, MA: Harvard University Press.

Winfree, J.A., and J.J. McCluskey. 2005. Collective reputation and quality. *American Journal of Agricultural Economics 87* (1): 206–213.

Young, A. 1794. *Travels during the years 1787, 1788 and 1789, undertaken more particularly with a view of ascertaining the cultivation, wealth, resources, and national prosperity, of the Kingdom of France*. Vol. 2. Bury St. Edmunds: W. Richardson.

Yuan, J., A.M. Morrison, S. Linton, R. Feng, and S.M. Jeon. 2004. Marketing small wineries: An exploratory approach to website evaluation. *Tourism Recreation Research 29* (3): 15–25.

Yue, C., S. Marette, and J.C. Beghin. 2013. How to promote quality perception: Brand advertising or geographical indication? *Non-tariff measures with market imperfections: Trade and welfare implications 12*: 73.

26

The Chilean Wine Cluster

Alfredo Coelho and Etienne Montaigne

26.1   Introduction

In a few years, the Chilean wine industry became an example of success and a serious competitor for the European and international wine producers. The success of the wine industry can be explained by the way it is organized as a 'cluster', through horizontal and vertical linkages, where the main stakeholders in the industry are simultaneously in competition and cooperation, that is to say, 'coopetition' (Nalebuff and Brandenburger 1996). Contrary to the dominant organization of the European wine industry, the Chilean model is more 'relational' (i.e. driven by relationships across the cluster).

The Chilean wine industry achieved unexpected performances in the last few decades. The industry demonstrated an extraordinary capacity to produce, export, and compete in international markets. Those achievements are related to natural conditions (quality of the soils, climate, land, water availability, etc.) but also to the way the industry is organized. Following the pioneering work of Alfred Marshall in 1890, in the last few years there was a

A. Coelho (✉)
Bordeaux Sciences Agro, Gradignan, France
e-mail: alfredo.coelho@agro-bordeaux.fr

E. Montaigne
Department of Agricultural Economics, Montpellier Supagro, Montpellier, France
e-mail: etienne.montaigne@supagro.inra.fr

© The Author(s) 2019
A. Alonso Ugaglia et al. (eds.), *The Palgrave Handbook of Wine Industry Economics*,
https://doi.org/10.1007/978-3-319-98633-3_26

prolific literature about the organization and success of 'cluster' organizations.[1] Despite such important number of publications, there is not a unified theory allowing to explain the diversity of those institutional arrangements (Bell et al. 2009). In this perspective, the success of the Chilean wine industry has been described in the professional publications as 'the Volvo of the wine industry' and attracted a considerable amount of academic research (cf. Visser and Langen 2006; Giuliani and Bell 2005).

This chapter is structured in three parts. The first part describes and explains the organization of the wine cluster as an institutional arrangement and introduces the uniqueness of public-private partnerships in Chile. The second part introduces the key elements of the cluster architecture: trust, the role of the leading firms, intermediaries, and the capacity of the cluster to solve problems related to collective action. Finally, the third part presents some performance achievements and risks and discusses resilience of the wine cluster.

26.2 The Wine Cluster as an Institutional Arrangement

26.2.1 On the 'Cluster' Concept

Clusters are 'geographic concentrations of interconnected companies and institutions in a particular field' (Porter 1998, p. 78). The pioneering work of Marshall (1890) introduced the concepts of agglomeration economies and positive externalities induced through a collective organization in clusters. Clusters include a mix of linkages (knowledge, inputs, competencies, resources, etc.) and supporting institutions (financing, standard setting, education, etc.) within a wine region or country (Porter 1998). Clusters are collective projects focused on the long-term survival and development of an industry or region. Inter-firm cooperation in wine clusters is essential to ensure long-term focus and competitiveness. The main elements describing the anatomy of a cluster are the following: trust, the leadership of the main wine firms, the ability to solve collective action problems (CAPs), and the availability of efficient intermediaries (grape and wine brokers, importers, distributors, etc.). Porter applied this concept to the Californian wine cluster (Porter and Bond 1999).

---

[1] Frequently used as a synonym of 'industrial district'.

Another stream of literature on 'business models' describes 'clusters' as valuable intangible assets (Teece 2010). This concept is also discussed in the literature on industrial economics as the 'third Italy' (Becattini 1992).

The literature on international business and economics also identifies other wine clusters in Latin America and highlights the importance of government-sponsored institutions such as Mendoza (Argentina) (McDermott 2007; McDermott et al. 2009), Serra Gaucha (Brazil) (Fensterseifer and Rastoin 2013), and Baja California (Mexico) (Trejo-Pech et al. 2012).

26.2.2 The Role of Public-Private Partnerships to Promote Efficiency

Public-private partnerships have been pointed out as essential arrangements to explain the success of several industries and countries.

Innovation priorities in the cluster are decided by common agreement between firms, associations, public bodies, and other stakeholders. Those priorities integrate the national innovation system. Innovation priorities and goals were defined through *Strategic Plan 2020* (a new strategic plan that sets up directions for 2025) for the Chilean wine industry. The strategic plan sets up targets at $3 billion in exports by 2020, through an average interannual growth rate of 9.2%.

The four main pillars defined in the strategic plan include diversity and quality, sustainable development, innovation, and country image.

Clonal and sanitary selection of varieties illustrates this strategy. A close partnership between ENTAV (*Etablissement national technique pour l'amélioration de la vigne*), a French institution in charge of improving the quality of vine plants, and the University of Talca was promoted for the benefit of Chilean nurseries.

26.2.3 A National Innovation Strategy Adapted to the Regions

In recent years, Chile implemented projects and programs to reinforce the participation of the regions in the definition of regional innovation and economic development policies. An example of these programs was the creation of Regional Development Agencies (ARDP). In 2005–2007, the Chilean government established regional agencies to foster development in production in an integrated manner. This process was promoted through Corfo, the Chilean Economic Development Agency. Corfo is the state agency for the advancement of economic and regional development in Chile. The agency finances innovation projects—including wine—through a branch dedicated to innovation (InnovaCorfo).

Corfo was also involved in the attraction of foreign investments—greenfield, mergers and acquisitions, and joint-ventures—related to wine and supporting industries (suppliers, tourism, etc.). Such actions included the organization of an international forum targeting overseas investors. Several editions of the forum were quite successful as it attracted a diversity of investors (Italy, Spain, the USA, China, etc.) to strengthen cluster activities: grape nurseries, barrel makers, and so on.

A key role of regional ARDP consisted in the implementation of a bottom-up approach to facilitate regional innovation agendas and the development of new projects and programs to enhance competitiveness—Programs for Modernization and Competitiveness (PMCs)—based on regional assets, strengths, and opportunities. PMCs defined agendas for the local development in each subregion. Three main regions were concerned by those wine-related programs (see list in Table 26.1 hereafter).

In the programs, the region and stakeholders—public and private organizations, universities, and civil society—became responsible for defining and implementing a long-term strategic vision. The ARDP is an important example on how to strengthen the participation of regions and implement private-public partnerships in Chile.

Another major initiative consisted in the allocation of funds for innovation at the regional level through the Innovation Fund for Competitiveness (FIC) and regional science and technology centers of CONICYT, the national agency in charge of R&D projects.

The FIC was established in 2006 as a fund created on the basis of the resources built on a percentage of sales of copper worldwide (note: Chile is the world's largest copper producer). The FIC is the main instrument to allocate new and more significant resources to the efforts of the Chilean State agencies in innovation. The two main agencies that benefit from the Chilean State

Table 26.1 Main wine-related Programs for Modernization and Competitiveness (PMCs)

Region	Program	Goals
Coquimbo	PMC Pisco Spirit (grape wine, spirits)	Grape vines, distilled spirit
O'Higgins	PMC Vitivinicola del Valle de Colchagua	Quality wine
	PMC de Turismo Valle de Cachapoal	Wine tourism
Maule	PMC Vinos de Maule	Carmenère grape
	PMC Turismo, Vino, Gastronomia	Wine and food tourism

Source: Corfo

resources are Corfo (InnovaCorfo) and CONICYT. The Foundation for Agrarian Innovation (FIA) is also responsible for the implementation of projects in viticulture, agriculture, and food.

FIC management is allocated through performance-based agreements involving the discussion, consultation, and implementation through various stakeholders of the wine cluster (public and private). This instrument aligns the priorities of the agencies with the strategic objectives defined by the Council of Ministers.

26.2.4 An Innovation Strategy Driven by the Wine Industry

Beyond the architecture of the national innovation system extended to the regions, the Chilean wine industry has established its own innovation system through the foundation of innovation consortia. The joint work between producer associations, research centers, universities, and suppliers included the creation of innovation consortia for the agriculture and food sector (including wine).

The creation of consortia initiative began in 2004 under the leadership of CONICYT and support of the World Bank, Corfo, and FIA agencies. Initially, 11 consortia were established in Chile with public resources of approximately 25 million pesos (2200 million pesos/consortium).

Among those consortia, the wine industry founded two consortia dedicated to the cluster—Vinnova and Tecnovid (Santelices et al. 2013). Funding is usually shared between public and private operators. The first projects financed (five years) reached $10 million and were financed by public (60%) and private (40%) sectors and universities. Later, the industry launched a new wave of medium-term projects co-financed in 2012. These research initiatives were supported by the Chilean State, moving to a more proactive engagement in the development of the economy.

In order to develop strategic innovation projects, the industry established two consortia dedicated to research and development. Both consortia consist in a public-private partnership whose goal was to bring together industry and universities to meet the challenges of exporting. The consortium brings together about a 100 wineries. Close collaboration with UC Davis (California) and the Australian Wine Research Institute (AWRI) was developed.

Both consortia were grouped into a new entity called *I+D Vinos de Chile S.A.* in charge of managing the new wave of projects approved in 2012. This new consortium is in charge of improving the competitiveness of Chilean wines in particular through the efforts of quality and sustainable development. It brought together various R&D initiatives dedicated to improving the competitiveness of the wine cluster and is integrated with the national association of Chilean wineries (*Asociación Gremial Vinos de Chile*). The governance of the consortium is administered by a dozen members from the industry and Chilean universities.

This entity complemented R&D efforts made by individual firms. This consortium has inter-institutional cooperation with universities and research centers as well as public agencies and private organizations in Chile and abroad (UC Davis, Liquor Control Board of Ontario (LCBO), Société des Alcools du Québec (SAQ), Vinmonopolet, etc.).

The main R&D programs endorsed by the consortium cover the following areas:

- A quality program dedicated to the vineyard (genetic improvements).
- A sustainable development program (wine conservation, *terroir* and vineyard zoning, climate change, disease in the vineyard, biodiversity, irrigation, energy and greenhouse gas emissions, social responsibility, codes of good practice, suppliers). In 2016, more than 60 vineyards and producers have been formally certified as *Sustainable wine of Chile* (www.sustentavid.org).
- A technology transfer program (positioning and differentiation, absorptive capacity).

Both government-sponsored initiatives combine an approach connected to the national innovation system (region-based) and another one associated to the consortium of *I+D Vinos de Chile S.A.* stimulates innovation and promotes the creation and transfer of knowledge within the cluster. These public-private partnerships complement the efforts of wineries dedicated to R&D and innovation.

In general, Chile's innovation system is often cited by international organizations (The World Bank, OECD) as a model for other developing countries. This is a third-generation public-private partnership and includes the joint participation of members from the private sector and public agencies. Third-generation partnerships raise new problems for the Chilean State as it does not have a direct control over the assets covered by the partnerships.

26.2.5   An Inter-organizational Structure

The Chilean wine cluster appears as an inter-organizational arrangement that contributes to a better coordination and boosts competitiveness. Relations between stakeholders are characterized simultaneously by situations of competition and cooperation. Clusters include public and private institutions and horizontal, vertical, and transversal relationships. The frequency and intensity of the relationships define the strengths of the linkages.

These arrangements and their advantages were described by Porter (1998), in particular increasing productivity, processing and structuring of innovation efforts, stimulating new projects, and contributing to the development of entrepreneurial projects. The Chilean wine cluster is represented synthetically in Fig. 26.1.

The cluster structuring objectives are defined in conjunction with those defined in *Strategic Plan 2020*. The pattern of inter-organizational relationships within the cluster goes beyond the wine cluster itself because relationships with other clusters are possible (e.g. cluster of tourism, food processing cluster). It should be noted that for several years Chile established a new food policy *'Chile: food power'* (*Chile, Potencia Agroalimentaria*) and actions on export promotion and attraction of foreign investments, which include the wine cluster. Those actions integrate the strategic objectives defined in this policy framework.

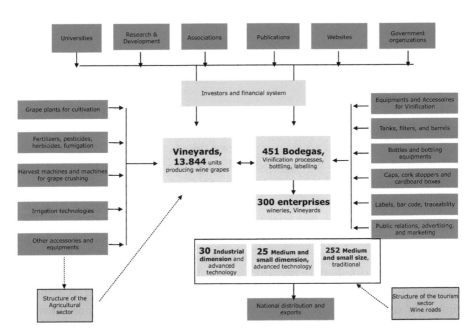

Fig. 26.1 An overview of the Chilean wine cluster. (Source: Adapted from Wines of Chile)

In recent years, efforts have been made to strengthen the weak links in the cluster through innovation and R&D projects (Vinnova, Tecnovid, CONICYT), an active policy to attract foreign investments to meet the needs and overcome the weaknesses of the cluster (Prochile, Corfo).

26.3   The Architecture of the Wine Cluster

26.3.1   Trust and the Ability to Solve Collective Action Problems

A set of trust relationships between the stakeholders stimulates cooperation in the cluster. Trust relationships limit opportunism, facilitate coordination, and contribute to solve CAPs (see, e.g. Visser and Langen 2006). Social capital and trust are two essential elements for the implementation of a third generation of public-private partnerships.

Leading firms may contribute to solve CAPs because they have a direct control over strategic resources and incentives. On the other hand, the quality of cluster governance and the resolution of CAPs depend on the institutions, such as associations, the availability of public or private institutions, and the pressure exerted by the dominant stakeholders ('voice' and 'exit').

26.3.2   New Firms Entering into the Industry

Over the last few decades, the cluster attracted a great number of new firms, particularly new wineries and grape nurseries (see Fig. 26.2). The number of new wineries increased particularly in two decades (1990–2009). The establishment of new firms was significant during the expansion of Chilean wine exports backed through government initiatives.

A significant number of grapevine nurseries were established after 2001. Twenty-two new grape nurseries were established after 2001 to supply *Vitis vinifera plants*. According to ODEPA (2015), the volume of *Vitis vinifera* plants marketed in Chile (7.2 million plants in 2014) is considerably higher than the plants supplied for the production of table grapes (approximately 3.3 million of plants in 2014). The establishment of a new wave of wineries increased the needs for the supply of certified vine plants. Therefore, the number of domestic and international grape nurseries expanded likewise.

Some of the main leading wineries established their own grape nurseries in the early 2000s: Viña Concha y Toro (Lourdes, 2000) and Viña Santa Rita

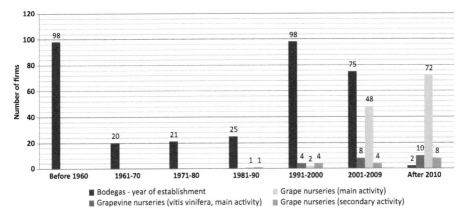

Fig. 26.2 Establishment dates of grape nurseries and *bodegas* in Chile. (Note 1: new wineries include both the bodegas producing more than 300,000 liters and the bodegas with an export activity. Data includes established wineries until 2011 (Source: INE); Note 2: grape nurseries include the suppliers of *Vitis vinifera* plants and the suppliers of table wine plants. Some of the grape nurseries supplying plants for table grapes may also supply *Vitis vinifera* plants. Data includes established firms in 2015 (Source: SAG))

(Santa Rita, 2000). Other wineries launched their own nurseries in a later phase: Viña Undurraga (La Rioja, 2009), Viña Almaviva (2009), and Viña Santa Carolina (2014). The cluster attracted foreign grape *Vitis vinifera* nurseries quite early. Two French nurseries established production facilities in Chile: Pepinières Guillaume in 2001 and Pepinières Richter in 2009.

26.3.3 Concentration and Role of the Leading Wine Firms

Leading firms must ensure leadership and demonstrate a capacity to adapt and innovate (R&D efforts, etc.). In export markets, leading firms may act as entrepreneurial 'icebreakers' creating opportunities for small and medium firms in the cluster (e.g. the penetration of distribution networks and marketing channels).

Further, the leading wine firms are members of a national association of wine producers accounting for more than 95% of the country's wine production. Within the public-private partnership, the main public agencies provide support (technical, financial, administrative, legal, etc.) to the wine cluster either at the regional, national, or international levels.

The Chilean wine industry is highly concentrated, with the four leading firms accounting for more than 88% of volumes sold on the domestic market.

Table 26.2 Concentration of the market shares in the domestic market of the leading wine firms in Chile (% of the total volumes)

	2005	2008	2010	2013	2015
Concha y Toro	27.1	29.7	30.7	28.5	28.1
Santa Rita	24.4	28.7	29.4	29.5	31.6
San Pedro Tarapacà	21.7	23	24.4	27.3	28.4
Santa Carolina	3.2	2	1.8	1.4	0.6
Others	23.6	16.6	13.7	13.4	11

Source: Concha y Toro

In addition, concentration of leading firms increased over time (see Table 26.2 hereafter). For example, one of the major operations concerned the merger of San Pedro Wine Group with Tarapacà in 2008 to establish one of the top four leading firms in the cluster.

The Chilean leading wineries are all publicly listed in the stock exchange and the founding families own significant shareholdings in the firms. For example, Concha y Toro has been listed in the Santiago Stock Exchange in Chile since 1933, but it is also listed on the New York Stock Exchange. These leading firms are also important wine producers and investors in Mendoza (Argentina). Concha y Toro operates through Trivento, its Argentinean-owned subsidiary and one of the top three leading wine exporters in Argentina.

The degree of concentration reflects greater bargaining power for the purchase of wine grapes and bulk wine. Despite the expansion of vineyard surfaces directly controlled by the leading Chilean firms, those firms are not completely self-sufficient.

Further, concentration facilitates investment, particularly in intangible assets and overall guidance of the Chilean industry. For example, the CEO of Concha y Toro, Rafael Guilisasti, has long been the chairman of the main Chilean wine association—*Asociación de Viñas de Chile*—and a Corfo advisor. Mr. Guilisasti was one of the main negotiators of the Free Trade Agreement between Chile and the European Union (EU). Following the agreement, Chilean wine exporters benefit from a unique tax advantage among New World wine producers (0% taxation for wine exports to the EU).

Corfo provides financing for product, process, and organizational innovation at the different levels of the wine cluster. The main mission of the agency is to transform Chile in a global innovation and entrepreneurial hub. The agency has representative offices in the Chilean regions but also a dedicated branch to attract foreign investors (nurseries, wineries, equipment suppliers, etc.). Corfo promotes investment and coordination among stakeholders in different areas, particularly in the less competitive linkages of the wine cluster.

Another government agency—Prochile—acting as Chile's trade facilitator and promotion agency includes 15 regional offices and representatives in over 55 offices worldwide. The main activities of Prochile include boosting the Chilean export basis by engaging new firms in export activities. Further, the agency helps firms to foster the internationalization processes and promotes wine tourism. Wines of Chile are in charge of the wine promotion of Chilean wines. Promotions are co-founded through wine producers associations. The Chilean government contributes with 15% of the total amount, through Prochile. This agency also provides logistics and market information to wineries and sponsors other generic market campaigns such as 'Taste of Chile' (Hennicke 2015).

The main wine firms have the ability to absorb knowledge. Those firms are active in the acquisition, creation, and transfer of knowledge. Firms differ on their cognitive capacity (Giuliani and Bell 2005). The financial strength and strategic objectives facilitate investments in R&D. For example, in early 2015, Concha y Toro has invested $5 million for the opening in Chile of a research facility dedicated to R&D in viticulture and oenology. Concha y Toro's R&D partnerships include, among others, joint activities with UC Davis (California) and Mercier nurseries (France).

Further, those firms also influence coordination and control. This phenomenon is of particular interest when transaction costs are low and coordination is exerted through non-market-based mechanisms.

Intermediaries (grape and wine brokers, etc.) also play an important role in strengthening the relationships between stakeholders and in lowering transaction costs (Montaigne and Coelho 2012; Baritaux et al. 2005). Wine brokers are important in revealing information (volumes, stocks, prices) not publicly available, particularly when prices and volumes for entry-level wines are quite important. Intermediaries can also play an important role in financing small and medium companies and reducing transaction costs.

26.3.4   The Influence of Strategic Alliances and Foreign Investments

Since the first foreign investment in the Chilean wine production by Miguel Torres (Spain) in 1979, many foreign investors were attracted by the Chilean wine cluster. These investments have taken two main forms: greenfield investments in production and strategic alliances (or joint-ventures).

Chile's strengths as a wine producer are numerous: low disease pressure in the vineyard, diversity of climates and soils, lack of constraints for extending vineyard plantings, a favorable ecosystem for innovation, and differentiation through the production of a high-potential grape variety Carmenère (red wine). However, it seems important to note the international image of Chile is of an international producer of entry-level varietal wines, at very competitive prices. For example, Cabernet Sauvignon is the most widespread grape variety, occupying nearly a third of the vineyard surfaces. The price for Cabernet Sauvignon in bulk can reach as low as 35 cents/liter on European markets. This price is below the average market prices for bulk wine in Castilla-La Mancha. This region is the lowest cost producer in Southern Europe. Chilean wine tends to be a good 'value for money' and a quite popular supplier among international bulk wine buyers. Those conditions necessarily attract foreign investors to the Chilean wine cluster.

Chile is not only a low-cost producer, but it also produces wines at different price ranges. In the country, many international joint-ventures were established with the objective of producing high-quality premium wines. For example, in 1997, Concha y Toro has signed a cooperation agreement with the Bordeaux-based winemaker Baron Philippe de Rothschild for the joint production of a Chilean wine—Almaviva—exported at an average price of $80 per bottle.

Inter-firm cooperation agreements in the alcohol beverage industries are essential to improve efficiency and upgrade products and processes. These agreements facilitate sharing resources among partners (Coelho and Rastoin 2004). Thus, the 'partners' in the alcoholic beverages sectors can benefit from leverage effects and reinforce their strengths as well as limit their weaknesses. In addition, by putting together a pool of resources, raw material suppliers and wine producers in the cluster can benefit from the economies induced through the cluster ('size' effects). In the alcohol industries we can identify, at least, four types of inter-firm agreements:

- Agreements whose main motivation is to obtain raw materials (wine grapes, a specific type of grape or a particular geographical origin, bulk wine, etc.)
- Inter-firm agreements where the primary goal is to increase the crushing or processing capacity
- Inter-firm agreements where the main motivation is to get access to distribution networks
- Inter-firm agreements where the main objective is to target advertising and promotional objectives or a specific marketing goal

According to Torres et al. (2008), during the period 1998–2004, the average price of wine exported for wineries involved in international joint-ventures projects (US $4.9/bottle) was higher than average prices for the wines produced through foreign-owned subsidiaries (US $1.6/bottle). Moreover, exports of wines associated with joint-ventures accounted for price ranging from 23% to 30% of the market for super-premium wines, while the same segment accounted only for 9% to 17% of the subsidiaries of foreign-owned firms.

Farinelli (2012, p. 204) explains the main interests of inter-firm agreements in the Chilean wine cluster:

- Joint-ventures were a combination of unique resources, combining local and international knowledge, and a learning opportunity for partners.
- Local partners see the joint-venture as a quick way to access international markets and to make fast technology changes. Local partners perceive inter-firm agreements as a way to reduce time and effort necessary to access to knowledge related to soils, climates, and grape-growing practices.
- This is a 'win-win' situation. It brings mutual benefits for partners as it is specific to the Chilean wine industry and cannot be replicated into the international wine industry. Joint-ventures are a set of unique factors related to the industry and include institutional benefits.

The main strategic alliances and foreign investments in the Chilean wine cluster are detailed hereafter (Fig. 26.3).

- **1970: Miguel Torres S.A. (Espagne) (the pionnier)** ➜ **Miguel Torres (Chile)**
- Gonzalez Byass (Esp.)   ➜ Conde de Aconcagua (JV c/ Estampa)
- Guelbenzu (Esp.)   ➜ Guelbenzu
- Bodegas y Bebidas (Esp.)   ➜ Selentia (JV c. grupo San Pedro)
- Antinori (Ita.)   ➜ Haras de Pirque
- Francesco Marone Cinzano (Ita.) ➜ Reserva de Caliboro
- Baron Philippe Rothschild (Fra.)   ➜ Almaviva (JV c/ Concha y Toro)
-   ➜ Los Vascos (JV c/ grupo Santa Rita)
- Bruno Prats (Fra.)   ➜ Aquitania (JV)
- Château Dassault (Fra.)   ➜ Altair (JV c/ grupo San Pedro)
- Marnier Lapostolle (Fra.)   ➜ Lapostolle
- Boisset (Fra.)   ➜ Gracia (JV c/ grupo Corpora)
- Château Larose Tritaudon (Fra.)   ➜ Casas del Toqui
- Laroche (Fra.) (*JEANJEAN since OCT. 2009 – Languedoc*)   ➜ Araucano
- Billington (EUA)   ➜ Billington
- Kendall Jackson (EUA)   ➜ Calina
- Robert Mondavi (EUA)   ➜ Caliterra (JV c/ grupo Errazuriz)
- Beringer Blass (EUA)   ➜ Domaine Conte (JV c/ Santa Carolina)
- Franciscan Vineyards (EUA)   ➜ Veramonte
- Odfjell (Norvège)   ➜ Odfjell
- Sogrape (Portugal)   ➜ Los Boldos
- Accolade Wines (Australia)   ➜ Anakena

Fig. 26.3 Main joint-ventures and foreign investments in the Chilean wine cluster (1979–2018). (Source: World Wine Data 2018)

26.3.5   Penetrating International Markets Through Free Trade Agreements and Generic Promotion

Like New Zealand, Chile is an economy oriented toward agro-exports. The signing of free trade agreements with strategic trading partners offers the country a comparative advantage unmatched by the main international competitors.

The development of Chilean exports at the international level is ensured through reduction or elimination of trade barriers. Over the years, the Chilean government engaged on a trade liberalization process and signed many bilateral and multilateral agreements, including free trade agreements with the EU, the USA, China, and Japan. In the last decades, Chile signed 20 cooperation agreements, involving 57 countries.

Free trade agreements provide considerable advantages for bottled and bulk wine exporters to penetrate international markets. For example, following the free trade agreement between China and Chile, starting on 2015, Chile stopped paying any duties (0%) to export their wines to China. Also, Chilean bulk wine exporters do not pay any duty to export their wines to the EU. This provides a competitive advantage to Chilean wine producers when compared to other New World wine producers. Bulk wines being quite price-sensitive, it makes international free trade agreements a key advantage for the industry.

Generic promotion of Chile is also one of the strategic orientations for the competitiveness of the cluster in international markets. Three organizations are highly active in promoting the image of the country: Chile Foundation, Prochile, and Wines of Chile. Generic promotion of the country's image is also co-financed. *Strategic Plan 2020* forecasts a considerable increase in funds dedicated to the promotion of wines, starting on US $7.50 million in 2010 to reach US $19.02 million by 2020. This strategy will raise investments in promotion from US $0.17/case to US $0.24/case by 2020 (Cogea 2014, pp. 91–92).

26.4   Performances, Risks, and Resilience in the Chilean Wine Cluster

Collective management of the wine cluster offers significant competitiveness advantages. We can point out many indicators justifying the success of the Chilean wine cluster: expansion of production potential, increasing market shares in key export markets (the USA, Canada, the UK, Japan, Brazil, etc.), international recognition (medals, green awards), attractiveness of the cluster to foreign investors, financial performance of the wine companies, offering quality wines at very competitive prices—particularly in the entry-level segments—and adaptability and innovation among industry firms.

In the past, grape plantings in Chile have been steady for many decades as the legislation established on 1974 banned grape plantings and replanting. Changes operated in the legislation in 1985 suppressed the barriers to new plantings and extended the possibility to produce wines from table grapes (González et al. 2014). In the following years, Chilean wine expanded considerably the surfaces planted with *Vitis vinifera* grapes. Nowadays, the production in the country remains highly dependent on the surfaces of Cabernet Sauvignon (see Fig. 26.4).

The expansion of surfaces did not spread homogeneously. The main wine regions remain Maule and O'Higgins, but on an attempt to diversify the supply of wines and adapt to climate change, the industry also expanded to new Northern in Southern non-traditional wine regions but which provide a potential to grow grapes adapted to the palates of international wine markets (e.g. the production of Riesling and sparkling wines) (see Table 26.3).

The particular case of the Bío Bío region contrasts with the general trend in Chile as the region shrank by 30.5% its grape surfaces between 2000 and

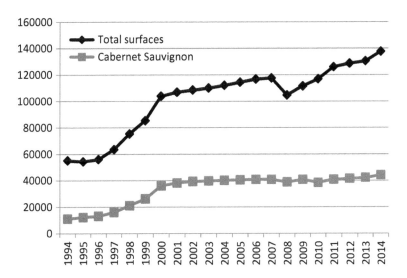

Fig. 26.4 Evolution of wine grape plantings in Chile (ha) (1994–2014). (Source: Elaborated by authors based on data from ODEPA)

Table 26.3 Evolution of wine grape plantings in the main regions in Chile (2000–2014) (ha)

	2000	2005	2010	2014	Var. 00–05	Var. 10–14	Var. 00–14
Maule	45,050	49,335	45,850	53,496	9.5%	16.7%	18.7%
O'Higgins	29,041	32,553	38,517	47,382	12.1%	23.0%	63.2%
Metropolitana	9450	10,783	12,432	13,398	14.1%	7.8%	41.8%
Valparaiso	4782	5524	9050	10,162	15.5%	12.3%	112.5%
Bío Bío	13,744	13,970	8085	9568	1.6%	18.3%	−30.4%
Coquimbo	1804	2197	2766	3383	21.8%	22.3%	87.5%
Other regions	60,630	67,307	79,557	87,469	11.0%	9.9%	44.3%
Total surfaces (ha)	103,876	114,445	122,641	137,582	10.2%	12.2%	32.4%

Source: SAG

Table 26.4 Evolution of grape variety plantings, wine production, and exports in Chile (2000–2015)

	2000	2005	2010	2015	Var. 00–05	Var. 10–15	Var. 00–15
Surfaces *Vitis vinifera* (ha)	103,876	114,448	116,831	135,582	10.2%	16.0%	30.5%
Cabernet Sauvignon (ha)	35,967	40,441	38,426	44,176	12.4%	15.0%	22.8%
Carmenère (ha)	4719	6849	9502	11,319	45.1%	19.1%	139.9%
País (ha)	15,179	14,909	5855	7653	−1.8%	30.7%	−49.6%
Production (million hl)	6419	7894	8844	12,867	23.0%	45.5%	100.5%
Wine exports (million hl)	2.65	4.14	7.25	8.75	56.2%	20.7%	230.2%
Wine exports (billion $US)	0.569	0.872	1533	1826	53.3%	19.1%	220.9%

Source: ODEPA, SAG

2014. This region concentrates the highest percentage of small grape producers owning less than 1 ha (accounting for 70% of all Chile) and producers face considerable changes in competitiveness and bargaining power in the market for grapes.

Grape producers also showed an increasing interest for Carmenère, a traditional Bordeaux red variety with a high potential to target international markets (+139.9%). At the opposite, the surfaces of traditional País variety were cut but half (−49.5%) as it showed little interest for export markets. Therefore, Chilean wine producers adapted their production potential to the international wine demand (see Table 26.4).

In addition, the exports in volume and value—in line with the goals defined in *Strategic Plan 2020*—had a strong increase (+230% in volume and +220% in value). These indicators demonstrate how successful Chile was in penetrating international markets.

In the long run, firms look to increase the average price per case of wine exported; however, wine exports remain concentrated in the price bracket US $20–29.9/case (Fig. 26.5). Despite of an internationally attractive bulk wine market, it does not seem to be a priority for the industry as the average prices and margins in this market remain low. The bulk wine market is often an adjustment factor to help the industry to reach market balances (production, domestic consumption, stocks, volumes exported).

Based on studies on the perception of the actors, Lobos and Viviani (2010) and González et al. (2014) identified the main sources of risks in the wine cluster. Those sources include the exchange rate, wine prices, climate change, and the variability on the profit rates. According to the above authors, small vineyards attribute more importance to the following factors: wine prices, climate change, yields (productivity), and food security risks. Small vineyards attribute less importance to legal and environmental risks as well as the price of grapes. The coverage of agricultural risks in Chile through insurance or other derivatives is rare in the country.

Risk is included in the resilience scope (Bhamra et al. 2011). The concept of resilience was first introduced in the literature by Holling (1973) and led to an extensive literature (Coutu 2002; Hamel and Valikangas 2003; Bhamra et al. 2011). We can define resilience as 'the capacity to continuous reconstruction' (Hamel and Valikangas 2003). Sudden changes in the business environment—turbulences and discontinuities—may impact considerably the long-term performances of the Chilean wine cluster. Major disasters, such

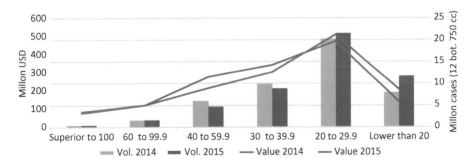

Fig. 26.5 Exports of bottled wine from Chile per price bracket (US$/case) (2014–2015). (Source: ODEPA)

as the Chilean earthquake on February 2010, or institutional, economic, or political negative shocks may disrupt the wine cluster. Wine clusters are constantly exposed to external disruptions due to changes in the industry and in the market. The ability to adapt to these changes—that is, resilience—determines the evolution of the wine cluster after such disruptions (maintain momentum, cooperation among stakeholders, etc.). Over the last years, the Chilean wine cluster was able to adapt to external disruptions (e.g. political cycles, earthquakes, etc.) and to introduce minor and major changes without losing its own identity.

The Chilean wine cluster also demonstrated it is able to adapt in the long run. Indigenous and foreign-owned firms brought new knowledge to the industry. The leading Chilean wine firms filled institutional voids by creating an intra-firm market for innovation (Castellaci 2015).Collective initiatives and the interconnection of public-private partnerships reinforced the resilience of wine cluster (Castellaci 2015).

26.5   Conclusion

The Chilean wine cluster is an institutional arrangement that promotes competitiveness and strengthens firms' adaptability and resilience during wine and economic crises. The Chilean model is unique and difficult to reproduce due to conditions related to agro-export orientation, concentration of firms, and public-private partnerships in the cluster. This model is similar to the New Zealand wine cluster. Nevertheless, beyond the socioeconomic embeddedness and the specialization in typical grape varieties (Sauvignon Blanc and Pinot Noir), New Zealand has the highest world average prices for wines exported.

In recent years, Chile achieved significant progress in competitiveness. Substantial improvements are still needed to ensure the sustainability of the wine cluster in the long run (Lima 2015).

Efficiency and dynamic institutional arrangements are strongly influenced by the national and regional political cycles. The financing of innovation and R&D activities depends largely on the availability of funds provided by international sales and copper prices.

The asymmetry of power in the negotiations for the payment of wine grapes or bulk wine frequently challenges small- and medium-sized producers. Overproduction leads to market imbalances, national wine prices are subject to high variability, and the domestic demand is unable to absorb the excess of wines on the market. Those are some of the common challenges the wine cluster should address in the future.

References

Baritaux, V., M. Aubert, M. Remaud, and E. Montaigne. 2005. Matchmakers in wine marketing channels: The case of French wine brokers. *Agribusiness* 22 (3, Summer): 375–390.

Becattini, G. 1992. *Le district marshallien: une notion socio-économique*. In *Les régions qui gagnent*, ed. G. Benko and A. Lipietz, 37–39. Paris: PUF.

Bell, S.J., P. Tracey, and J.B. Heide. 2009. The organization of regional clusters. *Academy of Management Review* 34 (4): 623–642.

Bhamra, R., S. Dani, and K. Burnard. 2011. Resilience: The concept, a literature review and future directions. *International Journal of Production Research* 49 (18): 5375–5393.

Castellaci, F. 2015. Institutional voids or organizational resilience? Business Groups, Innovation, and Market Development in Latin America. *World Development* 70: 43–58.

Coelho, A., and J.L. Rastoin. 2004. Vers l'émergence d'un oligopole sur le marché mondial du vin? In *Bacchus 2005: enjeux, stratégies et pratiques dans la filière viti-vinicole*, ed. F. D'Hauteville, E. Montaigne, J.-P. Couderc, and H. Hannin. Paris: Dunod/La Vigne.

Cogea. 2014. *Study on the Competitiveness of European Wines*. Luxembourg: Publications Office of the European Union.

Coutu, L.D. 2002. How resilience works. *Harvard Business Review* 80 (5): 46–55.

Farinelli, F. 2012. *Natural resources, innovation and export growth: The wine industry in Chile and Argentina*. Maastricht: Maastricht University.

Fensterseifer, J.E., and J.-L. Rastoin. 2013. Cluster resources and competitive advantage: A typology of potentially strategic cluster advantages. *International Journal of Wine Business Research* 25 (4): 1751–1062.

Giuliani, E., and M. Bell. 2005. The micro-determinants of meso-level learning and innovation. *Research Policy* 34: 47–68.

González, M.M., G.L. Andrade, and B.S. Morales. 2014. El gran crecimiento de la industrial del vino chilena. In *La Economía del Vino en España y en El Mundo*, Capitulo 17, ed. R.C. Lopez and S. Castillo-Valero, 581–623. Cajamar.

Hamel, G., and L. Valikangas. 2003. The quest for resilience. *Harvard Business Review* 81 (9): 52–63.

Hennicke, L. 2015. Chile wine production 2015, *Gain report*, no CI 1502, USDA Foreign Agricultural Service, Santiago de Chile, March.

Holling, C.S. 1973. Resilience and stability of ecological systems. *Annual Review of Ecology and Systematics* 4 (1): 1–23.

Lima, J.L. 2015. *Estudio de caracterización de la cadena de producción y comercialización de la agroindustria vitivinícola: estructura, agentes y prácticas, Oficina de Estudios y Políticas Agrarias (ODEPA)*. Santiago de Chile: Ministerio de Agricultura.

Lobos, G., and J.-L. Viviani. 2010. Description des perceptions des sources de risque des producteurs vitivinicoles. *Economie Rurale* 316: 48–61.

Marshall, A. 1920. *Principles of economics*. 8th ed. London: Macmillan (First edition, 1890).

McDermott, G.A. 2007. The politics of institutional renovation and economic upgrading: Recombining the vines than bind in Argentina. *Politics and Society* 35 (1): 103–143.

McDermott, G.A., R.A. Corredoira, and G. Kruse. 2009. Public-private institutions as catalysts of upgrading in emerging markets. *Academy of Management Journal* 52 (6): 1270–1296.

Montaigne, E., and A. Coelho. 2012. Structure of the producing side of the wine industry: Firm typologies, networks of firms, and clusters. *Wine Economics and Policy* 1: 41–53.

Nalebuff, B., and A. Brandenburger. 1996. *La Co-opétition, une révolution dans la manière de jouer concurrence et coopération*. Paris: Village Mondial.

Oficina de Estudios y Políticas Agrarias (ODEPA). 2015. Actualización de la Comercialización de Plantas Frutales, Vides y Plantines de Hortalizas en Chile, Ministerio de Agricultura, Asociación Gremial de Viveros de Chile, Santiago de Chile, Diciembre.

Porter, M. 1998. Clusters and the new economics of competition. *Harvard Business Review* 76 (6): 77–90.

Porter, M.E., and G.C. Bond. 1999. The California Wine Cluster, Harvard Business School Case 799–124, June 1999 (Revised February 2013).

Santelices, B., F. Lund, T. Cooper, and J.A. Asenjo, eds. 2013. *Innovacion basada en conocimiento científico*. Santiago de Chile: Academia Chilena de Ciencias.

Teece, D.J. 2010. Forward integration and innovation: Transaction costs and beyond. *Journal of Retailing* 86 (3): 277–283.

Torres, J.P., J.B. Salvagno, and M. Willington. 2008. Joint-ventures y especializacion productive en la industria del vino en Chile. *Estudios Publicos* 109: 225–266.

Trejo-Pech, C., R. Arellano-Sada, A.M. Coelho, and R.N. Weldon. 2012. Is the Baja California, Mexico, wine industry a cluster? *American Journal of Agricultural Economics* 94 (2): 569–575.

Visser, E.-J., and P. de Langen. 2006. The importance and quality of governance in the Chilean wine industry. *GeoJournal* 65: 177–197.

27

Producing and Consuming Locally: Switzerland as a Local Market

Philippe Masset and Jean-Philippe Weisskopf

27.1 Introduction

To date the wine economics literature has almost completely neglected Switzerland and its wines, unlike its neighboring countries France, Italy and Germany, which have been subject to numerous research papers. There are several reasons which may justify this lack of interest in Swiss wines. Switzerland is a small player on the global wine market as it ranks only 24th in terms of volumes produced (Wine Institute 2014b). Moreover, given its high consumption of wine per capita (about 40 liters per year and per inhabitant, Wine Institute 2014a), the local production is not sufficient to satisfy the demand. Thus, exports of Swiss wines are negligible (less than 1%, Bundesamt für Landwirtschaft 2015). As a consequence, the reputation and visibility of Swiss wines outside the country itself remain very limited.

Switzerland, nevertheless, displays specificities that warrant a deeper analysis. First, the structure of the Swiss wine industry and the business models adopted by most wine producers are particular. A large number of small and family-run wineries, which predominantly sell their wines directly to final customers, coexist with a few cooperatives and large wineries, which sell most of their wines through retailers. Second, the production conditions are distinctive due to both the geography of the country and its high labor costs. Switzerland's vineyards spread along Alpine valleys, rivers and lakes and tend

P. Masset (✉) • J.-P. Weisskopf
Ecole hôtelière de Lausanne, HES-SO // University of Applied Sciences
Western Switzerland, Lausanne, Switzerland
e-mail: philippe.MASSET@ehl.ch; Jean-Philippe.WEISSKOPF@ehl.ch

© The Author(s) 2019
A. Alonso Ugaglia et al. (eds.), *The Palgrave Handbook of Wine Industry Economics*,
https://doi.org/10.1007/978-3-319-98633-3_27

to be very sloping in nature, thereby making it difficult to mechanize the wine-growing process. The presence of a large mountain range in the middle of the country further leads to the existence of multiple microclimates characterized by diverse weather patterns and soil types. This variety allows Swiss producers to offer a great diversity of wines,[1] which is both an opportunity—as it allows a better match with customers' taste—and an additional source of complexity, especially for foreigners. Wages and land prices, which are among the highest in the world, push up the prices of local products including wines. Third, the market is characterized by low trade barriers and the presence of numerous wine merchants, which result in aggressive pricing of foreign wines. Thus, local producers have to remain competitive in comparison to foreign wines and are not in a position to raise their prices in order to exploit the demand-supply imbalance. Overall, these elements result in a complex situation, which is best summarized by two quotes, which may appear contradictory at first: "entry-level Swiss wines are the most expensive in the world",[2] while "the best Swiss wines are still a bargain for the quality".[3] The costs of production result in high prices *on average*, while the pressure from imports and the lack of visibility of Swiss wines prevent the best producers from increasing their prices to the level of their peers from more reputed regions.

The remainder of this chapter discusses and analyzes the elements introduced above in detail. We devote particular attention to the business models adopted by Swiss wineries and their fit with the conditions of production and the organization of the wine market in Switzerland. This chapter proceeds as follows: the next section (Sect. 27.2) discusses wine production in Switzerland. Section 27.3 examines the market for local and foreign wines in Switzerland. In Sect. 27.4, we present the various business models that are encountered in Switzerland and analyze their respective performance. Section 27.5 concludes.

27.2   Wine Production in Switzerland

27.2.1   History of Wine in Switzerland

Switzerland has a long history of wine growing. Vine plants dating back to the Iron Age (around 800 BC) have been found in Valais. Under the Roman

---

[1] Switzerland hosts more than 50 indigenous grapes in addition to international varieties.
[2] Philippe Bovet, quoted in Mathez de Senger (2015).
[3] José Vouillamoz, quoted in Laird (2013).

Empire, the production of wine rapidly increased. During the Middle Ages, abbeys and monks further fostered the production of wine in Switzerland, notably in the regions of Neuchâtel (Carthusian monastery of La Lance), Vaud (Abbeys of Aucrêt and Montheron in the Lavaux) and Valais (Abbey of Saint Maurice, Monastery of Notre-Dame de Géronde). At that time, wine was mostly produced to satisfy one's own needs and not for sale. The situation evolved and, following the 1847 Sonderbund War, entrepreneurs took over wine production from the monks and turned it into a flourishing business.[4]

In 1850, vineyards covered 35,000 hectares (ha), more than twice today's surface (Swiss Wine 2015). The decline in acreages after 1850 can be attributed to natural, demographic and economic factors. The natural factor takes the shape of a deadly foe for vines, the phylloxera. It was first identified in 1854 in New York State and rapidly proliferated. By 1861, it had reached Europe. In Switzerland, the arrival of the destructive insect is reported a few years later (Forel 1874). Despite desperate actions from Swiss authorities, it eventually destroyed much of the existing vineyards (Dumartheray 2012). During the first half of the twentieth century, the acreages devoted to vines continued their decline and never recovered from the phylloxera outbreak. Various demographic and economic factors are partially responsible for explaining this stagnation (Virieux 1947). The rapid urbanization of Switzerland and the small surface of the Swiss Plateau (which is both the most densely inhabited region in Switzerland and also where the vast majority of the vineyards are located) limit the space available for wine growing. Insufficient profitability and increased competition from foreign wines put additional pressure on the Swiss wine industry. Another factor that contributed to the sluggishness of the Swiss wine sector relates to old succession laws, which favored the parceling of land. As most wineries in Switzerland are family-owned, the enforcement of this law has made it difficult for wine producers to ensure the financial viability of their operations over the long term. This law also provides some justification for the relatively small size of wineries in Switzerland. According to Emery (2001), the 5259 ha of wine growing in Valais are represented by 119,500 parcels owned by about 23,000 proprietors. More than half of these proprietors cultivate wine on less than 1000 square meters and only 250 own more than 2 ha.

More recently, the trend of reducing wine-growing areas has not only receded but has even started to reverse with a timid increase of 4% between the mid-1980s and 2014. The quantity of wine produced has nevertheless

---

[4] Zufferey (2010).

decreased by about one third over the same period (Bundesamt für Landwirtschaft 2015). This lower productivity per hectare reflects a shift from a mostly quantity-oriented production toward a more qualitative approach. At the same time, the decline in productivity also induced an increased demand for foreign wines, which has led to a more competitive environment. The progressive liberalization of wine imports has accentuated this phenomenon. The past decades have been characterized by a desire by more and more Swiss producers to boost the quality of their wines. This trend finds its origin in Valais, the largest wine-producing region in Switzerland, but has since spread over the whole country. In Valais, Louis Imhof, Simon Maye and Charles Caloz have played an important role in this evolution. In 1966, they founded the Saint Théodule Guild, whose primary objective was to foster the production of high-quality wines in Valais.[5] Since 1966, the Guild has seen a dramatic increase in size, with more and more producers willing to become members, thereby reflecting their eagerness to provide the market with wines of high quality. Producers from other parts of the country have also started to recognize the potential offered by their terroir and some of them (e.g. Daniel and Martha Gantenbein, Luigi Zanini, Jean-Michel Novelle) have acquired a strong reputation, not only in Switzerland but also on foreign markets.[6]

27.2.2   Geography, Climate and Classification System

Switzerland is a fairly small country (41,285 square kilometers) with a mountainous landscape. From a geographical viewpoint, the country can be subdivided into three parts: the Alps (around 60% of the surface), the Jura (a mid-altitude mountain range that accounts for about 10% of the surface) and the Plateau, which stands in-between the Jura and the Alps and is densely populated (close to 400 people per square kilometer, about 30% of the surface). As a result, only a small part of the country can be considered as suitable for wine production. Most of the acreage available for growing wine can be found on the Plateau (especially in its Western part) and in Alpine valleys such as the Valais (which corresponds to the northern tip of the Rhone Valley) or Graubünden (the southern tip of the Rhine). As such, the production of wine in the country remains modest (around 115 million liters in 2013) when compared to France (4200 million liters) or Italy (4400 million liters). It

---

[5] Feuille d'Avis du Valais (1966).

[6] For instance, Daniel and Martha Gantenbein export about two thirds of their production and have made it into Fallstaff's list of the 100 best wines in the world.

nevertheless ranks Switzerland 24th in the world in terms of production (Wine Institute 2014a, b).

Switzerland is located in the middle of Europe and is surrounded by three of the world's most important wine-producing countries: France, Italy and Germany. Famous wine-growing regions such as Burgundy (Côte de Beaune and Côte de Nuits), the Rhone Valley (Côte-Rôtie, Hermitage, Châteauneuf-du-Pape) and Piedmont (Barolo and Barbaresco) lie within a less than 200 kilometer radius from Switzerland. The climate on the Swiss Plateau is continental and is close to climatic conditions in Burgundy and home to rather cooler grape varieties. In the Valais, on the other hand, we observe an arid climate with low precipitations and high average temperatures but cool nights due to the mountains and altitude. In Ticino, a third, distinct, more Mediterranean climate is discernible. Sunshine is longer and rain is common in spring. The soil in which wine is grown varies quite widely as well. The Plateau is primarily gravelly, the Valais has soil ranging from granite to schist and limestone, and Ticino is composed of granite in the North and limestone in the South. Overall, the elements for producing high-quality wines are present in several of the largest wine-producing areas in Switzerland (e.g. Valais, Ticino or Graubünden).

The country still lacks a clear and homogeneous classification system such as the ones encountered in Piedmont, Bordeaux or Burgundy. Not being in the European Union, Switzerland is not required to implement the same regulations as its neighboring countries. Until recently it was therefore up to the vintners to decide what to put on the label. The situation started to change about two decades ago when Appellation d'origine contrôlée (AOC) systems, similar to those used in France, were progressively put in place. However, as a federal country, Switzerland grants considerable autonomy to the cantons responsible for implementing these new regulations. This decentralized organization impedes a unified brand appearance of Swiss wines, as the various wine-producing regions of the country follow different rules and have different marketing strategies. As an example, the terminology "Grand Cru" is used in Vaud and Valais, while the terminology "Premier Grand Cru" is encountered in Geneva and Vaud. The conditions for a wine to obtain this title are, however, different in all three cantons (which together represent 75% of the production in Switzerland) leading to an incomprehension by customers (Thomas 2014). This situation results in an additional source of complexity, which makes it difficult for customers to understand different terroirs or historical status and their impact on wine quality and pricing.

27.2.3   Wine Regions and Wine Styles

The Alps and differences in altitudes, soil composition, exposures and hygrometry result in a variety of terroirs and, thus, a surprisingly large number of wine types can be encountered in Switzerland.

Swiss wine is produced on 14,883 ha of vineyards, mainly located in the west and in the south of Switzerland. Switzerland is further subdivided into six wine-growing regions. The canton of Valais (5000 ha) represents the largest wine-growing surface followed by Vaud (3800 ha), the German-speaking part of Switzerland (2600 ha), Geneva (1400 ha), Ticino (1100 ha) and the three-lake region (950 ha).[7] Some "terroirs" benefit from an especially strong reputation. This is the case for the canton of Vaud whose Chasselas from Calamin or Dézaley are well-known. In Valais, the villages of Fully and Chamoson are well-known for their Petite Arvine and Syrah, respectively. The cantons of Graubünden and Ticino are recognized for the quality of their Pinot Noir and Merlot, respectively.

Red wine varieties account for 58% of the total surface and white varieties for the remaining 42%, with a mixture of international and local varieties, some of which have been created by the Swiss oenological research center. The most common international grape varieties include Cabernet Franc, Cabernet Sauvignon, Gamay, Merlot, Pinot Noir and Syrah for red, and Chardonnay, Marsanne, Müller-Thurgau, Pinot Gris and Sauvignon Blanc for white. The country is also home to a variety of "specialties", that is, indigenous varieties such as Carminoir, Cornalin, Diolinoir, Gamaret, Garanoir and Humagne Rouge for red, and Amigne, Chasselas, Humagne Blanche, Païen, Petite Arvine and Johannisberg for white. Over the past two decades, wines produced from these varieties have seen their market share increase. These varieties possess the potential to produce wines of great interest but generally require a lot of attention and are production-wise not always as efficient as international varietals.

27.3   The Wine Market in Switzerland

Since 1980, the wine supply from the Swiss market has always been lower than domestic consumption. As shown in Table 27.1, the breakdown of consumption between Swiss and foreign wines remains stable over time with

---

[7] All data in this section is taken from BLW (2015).

Table 27.1 Consumption, imports and exports (2008–2013)

	2008	2009	2010	2011	2012	2013
Consumption	293.0	303.0	297.9	302.3	291.5	269.4
Imports	187.6	193.6	196.9	192.5	192.8	187.3
Production	107.4	111.4	103.1	112.0	100.4	83.9
Exports	2.0	1.9	2.1	2.2	1.7	1.8

Notes: Quantity in million liters
Source: GTIS, Euromonitor International

39.2% and 60.8%, respectively, for 2013. Switzerland thus has to resort to wine imports (1.85 million hl) and is only able to export a marginal fraction of its production (17,000 hl).

Consumers primarily buy wine in supermarkets, followed by direct purchases from producers and specialty shops. While the latter two remain at a relatively constant market share, supermarkets have managed to increase their market share gradually and this distribution channel now represents 42% of total sales.[8] However, wines sold at supermarkets come mostly from abroad or from large domestic wine producers. Smaller or more renowned producers tend to sell their production directly to customers, often based on a reservation system, with a limited quantity that each customer may purchase. In this section, we first examine the situation of foreign wines in Switzerland and then move to the analysis of the market for local wines.

27.3.1 Specificities of the Market for Foreign Wines in Switzerland

As domestic production is not sufficient to cover demand, 60% of wines have to be imported to cover total consumption. Switzerland has established rules and quotas on imports of agricultural products and therefore on wine through time. Until 1995 it was thus only possible to import red wine. This rule has been softened and white wine imports have been allowed since 1996. Since 2001, accompanied by the adoption of the General Agreement on Tariffs and Trade (GATT)/World Trade Organization (WTO) rules of the Uruguay round, Switzerland merged the quotas on red and white wines to obtain a general quota on wine imports of 170 million liters a year. Over the past few years this quota has more or less been completely exhausted with imports oscillating between 152 and 168 million liters (Bundesrat 2012). This historic rule may explain how, until this day, 70% of red wine consumption consists

---

[8] Association suisse du commerce du vin.

of foreign wines, while 60% of white wine consumption emanates from domestic production (Swiss Wine Promotion 2014). These rather low trade barriers have been further facilitated with the signing of bilateral agreements with the European Union, making wine imports attractive and relatively easy for foreign producers. The different agreements have also maintained taxes and import duties at a low level, which is coupled with a low value-added tax (VAT) of 8%.

Due to their relatively high income and wealth, the Swiss population is willing to spend more money on wine than people in other countries are. For example, the average price of a bottle bought in Switzerland lies at 7.95 Swiss Francs (CHF)[9] (Observatoire des vins en grande distribution en Suisse 2015), while in France it stands at 3.80 CHF (€3.17) (FranceAgriMer 2012). Switzerland thus constitutes an attractive market for foreign wine producers as pricier products can be sold more easily. This is coupled with a historically and culturally strong interest for wine in Switzerland. Consumers are willing to inform themselves before buying wine and take the visibility and notoriety of foreign wine producers into account in their purchase decision. Wine knowledge is therefore rather high and reinforced by travel to neighboring wine regions.

As a consequence, there are a large number of wine shops catering to this strong demand for foreign wines. This competition among wine shops puts price pressure on foreign wines and has led to a situation in which some of the most prestigious foreign wines can be obtained more easily and cheaper than in their home countries. Furthermore, the proximity to some of the best wine regions in the world renders the direct sourcing and importations from domains easy. In recent years, the strong appreciation of the Swiss franc with respect to the euro has further reinforced the attractiveness and good value of foreign wines. This constellation creates price pressure on Swiss producers due to the low production costs in foreign markets and the relatively easy and cheap possibility for these to import to Switzerland.

27.3.2 Specificities of the Market for Local Wines in Switzerland

According to the Swiss Wine Promotion (2014), Switzerland has around 4000 professional winemakers who, on average, cultivate wine on a surface of 1.5–10 ha and produce around 20,000–50,000 bottles per vintage. This

---

[9]This number probably underestimates the true average price as it is solely based on prices from supermarkets which tend to sell at cheaper prices.

average hides a contrasting reality: while most wine estates can be considered as rather small, it is a few larger wineries that retain a substantial market share. For instance, the Provins cooperative accounts for close to one fourth of the overall production in Valais (Emery 2001).

The market structure appears to be adapted to the specificities of Swiss wines. The primary market is relatively homogenous with most small producers selling the majority of their wines directly to consumers. More popular, smaller-quantity wines are predominantly sold directly to consumers through a reservation system which is similar in spirit to the allocation system in Burgundy. This leads to a situation in which customers remain loyal to winemakers. This phenomenon is further enforced by producers who reward loyalty in various ways (e.g. by increasing allocations on specific wines or outright refusing to give the most sought-after wines to customers just ordering these). Larger producers tend to sell a major part of their harvest through supermarkets or specialized wine shops. The distribution is, however, more complex as larger producers tend to cover the full spectrum of quality levels. They sell entry-level wines through dedicated brands via hard discounters or supermarkets and turn toward a more direct distribution to consumers for high-end wines (Thomas 2014). On the secondary market, Swiss wines are nearly non-existent as in general wines are bought to drink and not to sell at a later period.

Another important attribute of Swiss wines is related to its price. As mentioned, Swiss wine is perceived as expensive. This can mostly be attributed to high production costs and more specifically high labor costs. With minimum wages starting at around 20 CHF per hour, it is very difficult to produce cheap wine. This high labor cost is accompanied by legal and geographical constraints of the vineyards. Due to complex succession laws, parcels are divided and thus remain very small. Moreover, parcels may often be quite dispersed and build on hillsides as terraces. This leads to a loss of time when moving from one parcel to another and makes the use of mechanical equipment nearly impossible. The repair and construction of stone walls needed to maintain the soils on hillsides further increases costs. According to Emery (2001), this leads to a production cost of 35,000–55,000 CHF per hectare. The high purchase power of customers, however, allows vintners to sell their wines at prices which more or less cover their costs. According to a recent survey, a majority of customers are ready to spend on average 10–20 CHF for a bottle of wine (M.I.S. Trend 2013). Interestingly, this amount is quite similar to the average price at which Swiss producers sell their wines and corresponds to a classic pricing strategy in a competitive market in which marginal costs are relatively equal to selling prices.

Even though prices have largely remained stable in nominal terms and cover production costs, their positioning compared to foreign wines has varied substantially over the last five years. The 40% appreciation of the Swiss franc toward the euro has made local wines look relatively more expensive when compared to foreign wines. At the same time, prices from nearby wine-producing regions (Burgundy, Piedmont, Rhône and Bordeaux) have strongly increased over the last decade. These two phenomena result in a market structure in which Swiss entry-level wines look extremely expensive when compared to their foreign counterparts. On the other hand, prices of the best Swiss wines have become increasingly attractive to customers as they offer good quality at a very competitive price when compared to good French or Italian wines. Thus "as Swiss wineries are less competitive compared to foreign ones with respect to price levels and topographical conditions, they are forced by the market to differentiate themselves by creating better value for customers" (Fueglistaller et al. 2014). This focus and evolution from quantity to quality allows Swiss wines to enjoy a relatively good level of notoriety within the country. In fact, only French and Italian wines are better known than local ones by Swiss wine consumers (M.I.S. Trend 2013). In general, Swiss customers have a good opinion of "their" wines, with only 5% of people thinking that foreign wines are of better quality, while 46% strongly disagree with this statement (M.I.S. Trend 2013).

27.4 Business Models in Switzerland and Their Respective Performance

The business model applied by Swiss wineries is to a large extent influenced by two constraints. On the one hand, the historical and geographical context implies that most wine estates are forced to be of small size. On the other hand, the strong presence of foreign wines on the market puts pressure on wine producers and influences their strategies. Generally, two business models are encountered in Switzerland: small/family wineries which sell most of their production directly to final consumers and cooperatives/larger wineries which sell to final consumers mainly through supermarkets and specialty shops. In the following paragraphs, we present four small examples illustrating different cases which are representative of the Swiss wine business.

Denis Mercier Since 1982, Denis Mercier has cultivated 7.2 ha situated mainly around the town of Sierre (Valais) and produces on average around

40,000 bottles per vintage (Mémoire des Vins Suisses 2015b). He has specialized in varieties that are typical for his region and has achieved a considerable
reputation for his Cornalin. He has been following a traditional approach to
wine-making and reaches for the highest quality standards. His wife takes care
of the distribution and welcomes clients picking up their wines at the winery,
which is the norm. The couple is now helped by their daughter and employs
additional personnel for the harvest only. Most clients go to the winery to
collect their wine order and take the opportunity to have a discussion with
one of the three family members to learn more about the wines they purchase
and wine-making in general. Due to his reputation and small-scale production, about half of the ten varieties Denis Mercier has on offer are available in
limited quantities only. Prices have somewhat increased with inflation through
time but remain at a very reasonable level considering the quality and work
put into its production. This approach is representative of many small, successful Swiss wineries. Family businesses with a direct distribution channel
and warm welcome, rather stable prices through time and a limitation of
quantities, ensure that loyal customers receive at least one bottle of their
desired wine.

Domaine Louis Bovard Louis-Philippe Bovard took over the family domain
in 10th generation in 1983. He cultivates 16 ha and produces around 180,000
bottles annually (Mémoire des Vins Suisses 2015c). His wines are distributed
either directly to visiting consumers or through specialty shops throughout
Switzerland. This is possible due to the segmentation of his wine range which
goes from cheaper entry-level wines to more expensive and prestigious cuvées.
His winery is located in the middle of the Lavaux (Vaud), which is now a
UNESCO World Heritage site and famous for its Chasselas cultivated on
ancient stone terraces. Mr. Bovard is known for his curiosity and innovative
spirit. This has led him to try out different international varieties next to the
classic Chasselas and Pinot Noir grapes of the region. He can build on his
ownership of one of the best known appellations of Switzerland (Dézaley
Grand Cru) which grants him immediate recognition on the Swiss market.
He, furthermore, was mentioned favorably after a recent visit by Stephan
Reinhardt of TWA which granted him visibility at home and abroad (Moginier
2015). Even before this recent acclaim and for the last 15 years, Mr. Bovard
has exported some of his wines, following the trend set by German and
Austrian wineries. He also took part in recent trips to Japan to reinforce his
position there, hoping to sell at least 5000 bottles on this market (Buss 2013).
This example illustrates a willingness to increase exports through more

international visibility built on a strong domestic presence for wineries with a medium-sized annual production. This is reinforced by the creation of different product lines to play on price discrimination. In many respects, Mr. Bovard incorporates the direction Swiss wineries aim to pursue in the future.

Provins Provins has been the cooperative of the Valais region since 1930. Its 4400 members cultivate around 1100 ha and produce 13–15 million bottles a year, which corresponds to 23% of the harvest in Valais or 10% of the harvest in Switzerland as a whole (Mémoire des Vins Suisses 2015a). Their members are compensated per square meter, not kilo, to encourage cooperators to strive for quality versus quantity. A priori, it may seem as if such a large company may not be able to produce high-quality wines; however, quite the opposite is true. Provins has decided to strongly segment their market and diversify into different lines according to quality and customer. They introduced an entry-level line of wines in supermarkets and for hard discounters at affordable prices. They further created a "Maitre de Chais" line of wines which are labeled as premium wines and consist only of the best grapes of exceptional parcels. These wines can also be found in supermarkets, specialty shops and Provins shops and go for about 75% more than the entry-level line. Finally, it distributes a "Crus des Domaines" line which fetches double the price of the "Maitre de Chais" line and aims to compete with the world's top wines (Provins 2015). In 2014, Provins introduced an iconic wine, named "Electus" (sold at 190 CHF), to compete with the best wines in the world. In a tasting by Jancis Robinson in 2014, it reached a good position when opposed to very good wines from France and Italy (Guertchakoff 2014). This constitutes one of the first attempts at competing at a high price and quality level with neighboring wine-growing regions. The election of Provins as winemaker of the year 2013 and of its oenologist Miss Gay in 2008 further shows the commitment to follow, even as a cooperative, a qualitative path.

Obrist Obrist has taken a different form of expansion and service. This company started as a wine merchant in Vevey (Vaud) in 1854 but soon understood that having its own vineyards could be beneficial. It therefore started buying some up in 1896. Since the 1960s, it collaborates with a winery in Valais to be able to source wines from that region and sell them in their shops. Nowadays, Obrist is one of the largest wine merchants and producers in Switzerland with parcels ranging from Lavaux to Valais and covering a total of 55 ha. It sells its wines to restaurants, through specialty shops, its own shops and directly to individuals (Obrist 2015). This more diversified approach of doing business is followed by some Swiss producers. A few, such as Obrist, try to create a value chain from production to distribution while also diversifying in the sale of other domestic or foreign wines. Others have expanded abroad (e.g. Georg Fromm to New Zealand) or have opened a smaller-scale wine bar or restaurant (e.g. Weingut Bad Osterfingen).

27.5   Conclusion

The wine market in Switzerland is saturated. Local winemakers face several internal constraints (conditions and costs of production) and external challenges (proximity to the world's most reputed wine-growing areas, strong competition from foreign wines). Consequently Swiss winemakers have no choice but to focus on quality and rely on a differentiation strategy. There is no place for mediocrity and no excuse for producing wines of bad quality. In this context, small wineries seem well armed. But it is crucial for Swiss wines to improve on their visibility and notoriety, not only to reach foreign markets but also to remain successful on their own local market. The following eight points summarize this situation:

1. **A saturated market**: In general and as noted by Fueglistaller et al. (2014) "The Swiss wine market [...] can be characterised as a saturated market which is comparable to a zero-sum game where additional gains of one market participant can only be realised to the detriment of another". Thus, wining market share is only possible on the back of other producers or foreign wines. To be able to compete with foreign wines, a differentiation or pricing approach can be pursued (see Catry 2009).
2. **Quality over quantity**: Over the last 20 years, most wine producers have opted to switch from quantity to quality and revert back to traditionalism. This hints at the fact that a product differentiation approach yields better results than aggressive pricing campaigns when producers face high production costs. The success of the most qualitative producers has driven more and more producers to pursue this direction.
3. **Niche products**: In line with a product differentiation strategy, winemakers have been planting indigenous grape varieties on an increasing surface area. As it is difficult to compete with foreign wine producers and their international varieties, this allows Swiss producers to reduce competition and propose a niche product which may also bear fruit in a future internationalization strategy. Both the higher-quality perception of these specialties

and the difficulty in growing some of them (e.g. such as Cornalin) justify higher prices.

4. **Small is beautiful**: Concentrating on small wineries is a direct response to growth problems which emanate from two distinct sources. First, high labor costs impede growth. Up to a certain size, the reliance on cheap (or free) labor from family members allows winemakers to reduce costs. Many have understood that growing larger and having to employ one or two workers may lead to financial difficulties. Second, the difficult succession laws and high land costs render the purchase of additional parcels complicated. It therefore appears that having small family wineries is the most efficient way to contain costs.

5. **No place for mediocrity**: Many producers are having a difficult time since the Swiss franc surged against the euro. As a consequence, in 2012, the Swiss Parliament decided to declassify ten million liters of AOC wines to simple table wines (Herminjard 2013). These difficult times have further been reinforced by a drop in alcohol consumption on the national market. As prices of Swiss wines are relatively inelastic due to costs and the desire to keep loyal customers, a response to these two phenomena has been difficult. It thus appears that wines of lesser quality or which do not have a distinctive positioning have difficulties being sold.

6. **No excuse for bad quality**: The geographical and geological particularities of Switzerland offer good to excellent conditions for wine growing. Like some of its closest neighbors (Burgundy and Alsace in France, Mosel and Nahe in Germany), Switzerland used to have a relatively cold climate. This made it difficult to ensure a good and qualitatively homogeneous crop from one vintage to another. Global warming has changed this situation and has transformed a former weakness into strength. Since the mid-1990s, very few years have suffered from bad weather, while a number of vintages have benefited from outstanding conditions (1995, 2000, 2005, 2009, 2010, 2013 in some parts of the country, 2015).

7. **Visibility and notoriety**: The difficulty in sourcing many wines has led to a lack of visibility as many are very difficult to obtain or taste. This low visibility is reinforced by a variety of factors. A unique and clear AOC system is yet to be developed. Moreover, there is currently a quasi-absence of wine experts on the market. Hopefully, the situation has started to change. Vaud and Valais, the two leading cantons in terms of quantity produced, are now working on classification systems. The recent advent of expert wine tastings and winery rankings shows that Swiss wines have evolved qualitatively and are now in a comparable position to good-quality foreign wines. Especially the favorable mention of the Chasselas grape and

several producers in Robert Parker's Wine Advocate (TWA) has increased awareness of Swiss wines at home and abroad.[10]

8. **Exports**: An increase in notoriety and visibility should facilitate the export of Swiss wines. It has become a necessity to grow abroad in order to diversify output and reduce complete reliance on the home market for some producers. As in other Swiss industries, the choice to go for niche products and varieties is the best.

Overall, it appears that the idea of producing and consuming locally has worked for Swiss winemakers. However, the positive developments thus far should continue to evolve in the future for producers to remain competitive and profitable.

References

Bundesamt für Landwirtschaft (BLW). 2015. *Das Weinjahr 2014 Weinwirtschaftliche Statistik*. Bern: Schweizerische Eidgenossenschaft.

Bundesrat. 2012. *Contingents d'importation de vins*. Retrieved October 8, 2015, from http://www.parlament.ch/d/suche/Seiten/geschaefte.aspx?gesch_id=20123482

Buss, P.-E. 2013. L'avenir des vins suisses se joue à l'étranger. *Le Quotidien Jurassien*, September 14: 38.

Catry, B. 2009. *Viti 2015 – stratégie vitivinicole valaisanne à l'horizon 2015*. Lausanne: Université de Lausanne.

Dumartheray, P. 2012. 1886: très vilain phylloxéra. *24 heures*, June 28. Retrieved from 24 heures: http://www.24heures.ch/vaud-regions/1886-tres-vilain-phylloxera/story/12015090

Emery, S. 2001. *Enquête sur l'avenir de la viticulture dans les régions alpines et*. Sion: Etat du Valais.

Feuille d'Avis du Valais. 1966. Fondation de la Confrérie des Vignerons. *Feuille d'Avis du Valais*, May 9: 1.

Forel, F.-A. 1874. Le phylloxera vastatrix dans la Suisse occidentale jusqu'au 31 Décembre 4874. *Bulletin de la Société Vaudoise des Sciences Naturelles* 13 (74): 661–683.

FranceAgriMer. 2012. *Achats de vins tranquilles par les ménages français pour leur consommation à domicile*. Paris: FranceAgriMer.

---

[10] David Schildknecht, a journalist at TWA, has put four Swiss vintners in his best of 2012 list and, in 2015, Stephan Reinhardt, another journalist of the TWA team, wrote two articles fully devoted to Swiss Chasselas and Pinot Noir, with many scores close to or larger than 90.

Fueglistaller, U., A. Fust, D. Burger, J. Varonier, and F. Welter. 2014. How SMEs differentiate from others in the Swiss wine market with respect to their market orientation and entrepreneurial orientation. In *Rencontres de St.-Gall*, 1–21. St. Gallen: KMU-HSG.

Guertchakoff, S. 2014. L'Electus, ce vin ambitieux qui secoue le vignoble suisse. *Bilan*, November 3.

Herminjard, P. 2013. L'économie vitivinicole suisse peine à maintenir ses parts de marché. *Patrons* (7–8), p. 7.

Laird, M. 2013. *Les vins suisses gagnent une reconnaissance mondiale.* April 4. Retrieved from swissinfo.ch: http://www.swissinfo.ch/fre/economie/dans-le%2D%2Dwine-advocate%2D%2Dde-robert-parker_les-vins-suisses-gagnent-une-reconnais-sance-mondiale/35375216

M.I.S. Trend. 2013. *Étude sur le marché du vin en Suisse 2013: notoriété, habitudes de consommation et d'achat, image.* Swiss Wine Promotion.

Mathez de Senger, C. 2015. Quelles sont les conséquences du franc fort pour les vins suisses? *Bilan*, January 28.

Mémoire des Vins Suisses. 2015a. *Producteurs Valais.* Retrieved October 8, 2015, from http://www.mdvs.ch/fr/producteurs/valais/provins.html

———. 2015b. *Producteurs Valais.* Retrieved October 8, 2015, from http://www.mdvs.ch/fr/producteurs/valais/anne-catherine-denis-mercier.html

———. 2015c. *Producteurs Vaud.* Retrieved October 8, 2015, from http://www.mdvs.ch/fr/producteurs/vaud/domaine-louis-bovard.html

Moginier, D. 2015. L'envoyé de Parker a apprécié les chasselas. *24 heures,* March 3.

Obrist. 2015. *Notre histoire.* Retrieved October 8, 2015, from https://www.obrist.ch/fr

Observatoire des vins en grande distribution en Suisse. 2015. *Situation au 31 mars 2015.* Sion: Etat du Valais.

Provins. 2015. Retrieved October 8, 2015, from http://www.provins.ch/fr/index.php

Swiss Wine. 2015. *Swiss wine history.* Consulté le September 15, 2015, sur http://www.swisswine.ch/: http://www.swisswine.ch/en/wine-tourism/swiss-wine-history

Swiss Wine Promotion. 2014. *Key figures.* Retrieved October 8, 2015, from http://www.swisswine.ch/en/vineyard/the-figures-of-the-swiss-wine

Thomas, P. 2014. Vins suisses: les sept questions qui fâchent. *L'Hebdo*, April 12: 12–16.

Virieux, R. 1947. De l'économie viticole en Suisse. *Revue économique et sociale: bulletin de la Société d'Etudes* 5 (4): 264–271.

Wine Institute. 2014a. Per capita *wine consumption by country.* Retrieved September 3, 2015, from Wine Institute: http://www.wineinstitute.org/resources/statistics

———. 2014b. *World wine production by country.* Retrieved September 3, 2015, from Wine Institute: http://www.wineinstitute.org/resources/statistics

Zufferey, A.-D. 2010. *Histoire de la vigne et du vin en Valais: Des origines à nos jours.* Sierre: Musée valaisan de la Vigne et du Vin.

28

Conclusion: What's Next?

Adeline Alonso Ugaglia, Jean-Marie Cardebat, and Alessandro Corsi

This book offered a broad overview of the different business models in the wine industry worldwide. It showed the diversity of this highly fragmented and extremely diverse sector. Above all, the different chapters showed that there is no dominant model and no guarantee of success at national scale in whatever we are talking about Old, New or New World wine countries. In particular, this book refutes the idea, however widespread in the Old World, that the model of the large, vertically integrated industries relying on one or more strong brands sold internationally would be the unique way for success in wine-producing countries. Different models coexist at national and international levels and they are constantly evolving according to the challenges they already face. Many chapters showed that the actors operating in the wine industries as the wine industries themselves already adapt their strategies. Whether the actors within a particular industry or the wine industries grouped

A. Alonso Ugaglia (✉)
Bordeaux Sciences Agro, University of Bordeaux, Gradignan, France
e-mail: adeline.ugaglia@agro-bordeaux.fr

J.-M. Cardebat
University of Bordeaux, Pessac, France
INSEEC Bordeaux, Bordeaux, France
e-mail: jean-marie.cardebat@u-bordeaux.fr

A. Corsi
University of Turin, Turin, Italy
e-mail: alessandro.corsi@unito.it

© The Author(s) 2019
A. Alonso Ugaglia et al. (eds.), *The Palgrave Handbook of Wine Industry Economics*,
https://doi.org/10.1007/978-3-319-98633-3_28

523

in national or international institutions, all players, in order to compete and perform on the wine market, use different tools to differentiate (mergers, vertical integration, clustering, designation of origin, brands, combination of origin and branding, etc.). At a micro level, the observation is similar. *Grands Crus* in the Old World or large and vertically brand companies in the New World are far from being the only destinies for a wine estate to exist. Reality is more complex. The importance of localization, proximity with consumers, the existence of a community sharing strong societal values and new forms of financing or sales, in connection with the evolution of the sociology of the consumer, are all factors that can allow small estates and wineries to achieve success. It is even possible that the latter are more resilient to the changes that will probably be imposed on the wine industry in the next decade.

We identify four mutations that could reshuffle the cards in the global hierarchy of wine-producing countries in the coming years. They are as many challenges as these countries, industries and companies in the sector will have to face in the future. They concern:

- the production of grapes and wine, in a context of climate change for most of the major producing countries;
- international wine trade, against the backdrop of possible trade wars and of de-globalization;
- the new geography and the new sociology of wine consumption that are beginning to upset demand;
- new ways to sell wine and communicate to reach the new consumers.

Thus, producing, exchanging, selling and consuming wine are likely to evolve very significantly in the next 10–15 years. These developments could be at the origin of an upheaval in the hierarchy of wine-producing and exporting countries. What could the world of wine and the wine industries worldwide look like by 2030 according to the expected changes? Rather than providing uncertain predictions, we will try to identify the most important trends that may affect the future of the wine industry.

28.1   Climate Change

A first important determinant of changes is the environmental context of the current wine production that is changing due to shifts in climate patterns already observed for the past and predicted for the future. These changes in temperature and air humidity are already modifying different elements as grape characteristics (sugar, acidity). The production challenges and the strategies to ensure a sustainable product need to be adapted accordingly (Schultz 2016). Wine production could therefore evolve along two directions.

– First, the reduction of wine supply in certain regions facing climate change. In the latter case, the Old World (mainly France, Italy and Spain), the other countries of Southern Europe, but also Australia, Argentina, South Africa or California (United States) could appear as the future big losers of global warming. In addition to global warming, the European countries are particularly subject to extreme events such as late frost or hail storm as shown in particular by the 2017 vintage in the Bordeaux wine region. The evolution of viticultural techniques can limit these negative evolutions, for example, through the emergence of resistant grape varieties to water stress to reduce the impact of the high temperatures but also to diseases as powdery and downy mildew. The costs of these techniques, together with the needed organizational changes, the risk aversion of the winegrowers and their willingness to change, could then be decisive. As to the consequences of climate change in traditionally producing areas, a possible adaptation is the change in the variety mix. Grape varieties traditionally produced in each area of the Old World are the result of a secular selection of the best fit to the particular local natural (soil and weather) conditions. There is a wide dispersion in the optimal weather conditions for the different varieties (Ashenfelter and Storchmann 2016); hence, a rational adaptation strategy could be changing the varieties choosing the best fit to the new conditions. Nevertheless, such a path does not go without difficulties. Apart from the needed investments, the main problems could arise from two sides. One is the difficulty in changing the institutional setting of the regulations concerning appellation wines. For instance, in Italy and France, many Protected Designation of Origin (PDO) regulations dictate the varieties that can be used or not according to the area and the type of wine. Even though regulations can obviously be changed, some producers may be reluctant to do so, and conflicts on this issue can arise within the community. A second problem might be the consumers' acceptance of a change in taste of traditional wines and, more generally, in the characteristics they associate with those particular wines. Nevertheless, also consumers' tastes and preferences may change, either because of the different availability of wines or because of simply following new fashion trends. The changing preferences of English consumers for different wines across time (Ludington 2018) are an example of such a change. The evolution of wine production since the 1960s in the Bordeaux wine region from white to red following the evolution of consumers' taste is a second one.

– Second, the exploration of new terroirs in non-producing regions at the moment, reinforced by the evolution of viticultural techniques. Vine growing in tropical or semitropical areas, as in India or in certain areas of China or Brazil, is expected to grow. The growth of wine consumption in Asian countries is such that these terroirs will receive strong incentives to develop either from local companies or from foreign investors. Climate change is likely to have a positive impact on some parts of Northern Europe. England is increasingly considered as a terroir with a high potential for wine making. It is therefore already possible to observe pioneers planting vines in England. Germany or even the Scandinavian countries could also see their wine production—already important in Germany—increase. Canada or the North of the United States could follow the same evolution.

The economic impact of these changes is difficult to assess but has to be considered. An in-depth analysis is necessary to build relevant scenarios and to provide risk analysis for individual regions and to quantify the costs and/or benefits of regional climate developments. It is nevertheless clear that climate change and technical developments associated with it will disrupt the mapping of global wine production. New challengers will certainly emerge. China is one of the favorites because this country has already begun to move on toward a large-scale wine production and already proclaims itself an important wine-producing country. This change in production mapping should also be reinforced by the upcoming difficulties in international wine trade.

28.2   International Wine Trade and De-globalization

The hardening trade war between the United States, China and Europe in the wine market presumably foreshadows a new world order in which international trade will be much more limited. What we can call a form of deglobalization begun with the slowdown in trade flows since the 2009 economic crisis and the rise of socio-environmental concerns related to globalization. The wine sector will not escape this trend. By the symbolic nature of wine, because it is attached to regions and therefore to countries, of which it often bears the name, wine appears as an ideal good to overtax in the context of a commercial war. In the past, it has already been the target of this type of practice (especially French wines during the second Iraq War). It is all the easier to hit the wine as it is an alcoholic beverage and therefore carries negative societal externalities. Non-tariff measures, including health measures, therefore appear to be obvious instruments of protectionism. Here we underline once again the importance of regulations and public interventions on the setting of the wine industries.

We can expect the protectionism to favor, by nature, local consumption and domestic markets. The incentive to produce and consume locally is becoming stronger and stronger. The large, export-oriented firms are presumably the more exposed ones, in particular those which export wines with low unit value. This could be reinforced by the rise of local consumption relative to oenotourism (with the mapping of new wine routes and the opening of the estates for visits and wine tastings, e.g. in the Old producing countries such as France and Italy). Successful business models of local and short distribution channels for wine sales have already and successfully been developed for several years by the *Grands Crus*, models that could also be adopted by smaller estates.

The restriction of trade should therefore favor the emergence of new vineyards and a fragmentation of world production. In this, it is linked to the climatic evolution which will impact the world production. It should also encourage more local consumption and ultimately new forms of sales. The way to sell the wine could change significantly in the years to come. In a world where the "local" food concept is gaining importance and tells a story about the product, where the distance becomes expensive, it will be necessary to retain a more local clientele. Many vineyards are already aware of that. But for the most famous brands and for the most spread in the world, the local market is not enough. The extent to which production and consumption will shift to local wines is nevertheless constrained by natural conditions and by consumers' habits. While global warming, for instance, favors wine production in the United Kingdom, its production is undoubtedly insufficient to meet the present British demand for wine, and it will presumably also be in the future, unless deep changes in consumption habits occur.

28.3   Changes in Wine Consumption

Reactions at the global scale to the changes induced by global warming are also possible through changes in consumption habits and, hence, in the demand for wine. Nevertheless, they are only possible in the long run. Copying with these trends would imply an increase in wine consumption in Traditional producing countries and a decrease in New consuming countries. This contrasts with the trend toward converging drinking habits between different beverages (Holmes and Anderson 2017) and would require a huge change in many countries' marketing outlets. Just to give an example, the share of exports over the Italian production, which was around 5 percent in 1950, is now around 50 percent (Corsi et al. 2018). A strong reconversion toward domestic consumption is hardly conceivable. But an increase in the competitive pressure in the international markets is easily predictable, because most of the changes induced by the changing trade flows will presumably take the form of trade-diversion effects rather than of a direct substitution of domestic production for imports.

At micro level, these trends could have different impacts on the different operators of the chains, depending on the structure of the wine sector in each country and on the strength of the changes they could have to face. The distribution of the gains and of the losses from climate change as well as from trade shrinking will be linked to the organization of the industrial chain and on the market power of the operators. The more concentrated the wine processing, the more it has some market power vis-à-vis the pure grape growers and hence the possibility to pass the negative effects to them. This is nevertheless less obvious when wine cooperatives are important players in the wine processing. Wine estates producing grapes and wine are more common in the Old wine countries and on the higher-quality segment. As such, they will suffer more the consequences of climate change (that will affect quality) and less those of the trade reduction, as compared to the other operators (because of the lower price elasticity of these wines).

28.4   Distribution and Relation to the Consumers

Two further main issues seem central trying to forecast the future of wine sales. The first concerns the use of the Internet in the relationship with the end customer and the second questions the relevance of traditional distribution channels. These two issues are closely linked. The Internet allows easy direct sales and thus doing without traditional intermediaries. Having a commercial website is however far from enough to organize a direct sale commercialization system. The estates would have to be able in the future to create a "community" around their name, their brand. Crowdfunding as an innovative financial tool constitutes an interesting vector for building a community of customers actively participating in the life of the property (Bargain et al. 2018). More and more vineyards are using it to finance new equipment or new plantings or even the development of a new product or marketing strategy. A refund of the funds poured in the context of a crowdfunding campaign in the form of bottles of wine is both a new way of financing and, perhaps above all, a new form of selling (eventually, since it is the bottles of future vintages that are sold). It is a way to bring new consumers to the product of a specific estate. In addition, we look at community management as being able to become an essential communication tool for building such a community of customers, even more than other forms of communication. It is in this context that we can imagine a gradual decline in the number of sales via conventional distribution channels compared to direct sales, interrogating once again the organization of the wine industries and the relative power that some actors have. The rise of an expanded wine tourism offer will also go into this direction.

These types of sales closer to the consumer (direct sales) should be in line with the evolution of sociology of wine consumers. From a rather old, European, masculine, not interested in social medias and high-income consumer, the typical wine consumer is becoming (and it will be even more true tomorrow) younger, international (American and Asian in particular), more feminine and more connected (Cardebat 2017). Once again, it appears that social networks and the exchange of information between consumers on the Internet concerning the quality of wines are likely to become increasingly important. The notion of community will be all the more affirmed, giving more importance to the new opinion-makers such as "the wine community" and the other consumers, much more than the traditional opinion-makers like newspapers, guides or famous experts. The notion of community does not necessarily refer to purely local customers in geographic terms but to customers sharing common values that wine conveys (typical characteristics, societal and environmental commitments, for landscape preservation or social purposes, etc.). Of course, these trends are not at the same stage everywhere in the world, much depending on the tradition of drinking wine and on the country status according to wine production, since the tradition of drinking local wines is deeply rooted in Old wine countries and can help in facilitating the creation of wine communities. Though, customers can now be everywhere in the world, even if a rise in the obstacles to exports can be anticipated. We are not describing here the end of exports, but an evolution in the way of doing business at the international level. If exports become more costly, operators will have to think about how to reach foreign consumers, especially new consumers from New wine countries. Two strategies emerge. The first one is related to product differentiation: building a strong brand and creating a strong community that will make consumers willing to pay more for a product that represents a strong added value for them. The second strategy is about the "tariff jumping". If there are barriers to trade, then the players must produce closer to consumers, as Japanese car companies did in the United States in the 1980s. Absurd as it may seem to some experts for which a wine is attached to a terroir, this strategy can pay off for generic wines, produced by leading brands used to using grapes from different terroirs to produce their wines. This model will be similar to that of the big brewers who produce their beer locally in the United States, for example (local and craft breweries). We can therefore anticipate a future growth of foreign direct investments in the wine sector: greenfield investments, corresponding to the purchase of land and the pure creation of a new vineyard, but also brownfield investments when brands buy existing vineyards or create alliances with local brands.

It is therefore self-evident that many variables will affect the future evolution of the wine industry worldwide, so that an exercise of prediction of the potential future directions of the wine industry is inherently imperfect and partial and potentially totally wrong. This is the risk of such an exercise. But our effort has been to present the most likely evolutions and some hints on the interplay among the different actors of the industry and to offer a perspective in terms of breaks of tendency rather than of a plain extension of past trends. The wine industry is very likely to know several breaks of tendency in the next 10–15 years and the actors of the industry will need to make strategic choices.

References

Ashenfelter, O., and K. Storchmann. 2016. The economics of wine, weather, and climate change. *Review of Environmental Economics and Policy* 10 (1): 25–46.

Bargain, O., J.M. Cardebat, and A. Vignolles. 2018. Crowdfunding in the wine industry. *Journal of Wine Economics* 13 (1): 57–82.

Cardebat, J.M. 2017. *Économie du vin*. Paris: La Découverte.

Corsi, A., E. Pomarici, and R. Sardone. 2018. Italy post 1938. In *Wine globalization. A new comparative history*, ed. K. Anderson and V. Pinilla, 153–177. Cambridge: Cambridge University Press.

Holmes, J., and K. Anderson. 2017. Convergence in national alcohol consumption patterns: New global indicators. *Journal of Wine Economics* 12 (2): 117–148.

Ludington, C.C. 2018. United Kingdom. In *Wine globalization. A new comparative history*, ed. K. Anderson and V. Pinilla, 239–271. Cambridge: Cambridge University Press.

Schultz, H.R. 2016. Global climate change, sustainability, and some challenges for grape and wine production. *Journal of Wine Economics* 11: 181–200.

Index[1]

A

Acquisition, 140, 211, 342, 349, 376, 386, 439–441, 443–447, 450, 490, 497

Agreement, 10, 59, 72, 97, 126, 150, 153, 164, 188, 204, 250–263, 266, 279, 280, 282, 283n15, 287, 288, 293, 299–301, 302n5, 303, 304n6, 306–310, 312, 366, 429, 439, 489, 491, 496, 498–500, 514

Alliance, 35, 141, 260n11, 342, 348, 351, 352, 356, 361, 497–499, 530

AOP
  Australia, 45
  Chile, 45
  France, 43, 44
  Spain, 43
  United States (US), 43, 45

Appellation d'origine controlee (AOC)
  Argentina, 477
  Australia, 343
  Chile, 343, 477

China, 369

France, 19, 24–27, 29–33, 39, 43, 44, 343, 369, 465, 468, 473, 479, 480, 511, 520

Italy, 343, 468

South Africa, 343

Spain, 43, 468

United States (US), 343, 369, 477, 480

Area, 18, 20–22, 24–26, 27n3, 28, 43, 47–52, 54, 54n3, 56, 57, 62, 64, 66–68, 72, 75, 78–81, 84, 86, 87, 89, 99–101, 106, 106n1, 108, 110, 111, 117, 123, 132–136, 141–147, 156–163, 165, 167, 171, 178, 179, 183, 186, 190, 196, 197, 212, 213, 215, 216, 218, 220, 225, 227, 230, 232, 258, 266n1, 267, 272, 272n8, 278, 279, 282, 285, 291, 297, 304, 309–311, 320, 335, 339, 346–348, 350, 358, 371, 389–391, 391n1, 392n2, 393–396, 399–401, 406–408,

---

[1] Note: Page numbers followed by 'n' refer to notes.

© The Author(s) 2019

A. Alonso Ugaglia et al. (eds.), *The Palgrave Handbook of Wine Industry Economics*, https://doi.org/10.1007/978-3-319-98633-3

414, 421, 421n2, 423, 424, 440,
446–448, 464, 467, 468, 468n4,
472, 474, 477, 492, 496, 509,
511, 519, 525, 526

Argentina/Argentine
distribution, 174
domestic market, 155, 166, 169,
170, 173, 174, 176, 470
revenue, 9, 168, 170, 174
size, 163, 166
technology, 8, 157, 161, 163, 463,
471
varieties, 156–163, 169, 471, 525
vine area, 163
winemaking sector, 9, 169
Australia/Australian
emergence and cyclical growth,
132–136
features in grape growing, 9,
142–148, 469, 470
future, 8, 132, 237
structure of the wine industry,
136–142
wine distribution and retailing,
148–151

B

Barriers, 10, 236, 242, 246, 252,
259n9, 260, 262, 262n15, 266,
280, 288, 291–312, 446–448,
450, 500, 501, 508, 514, 529
tariff, 252, 292–294
Bordeaux/Bordeaux wines, 8, 11, 26,
28, 37–39, 42, 151, 212, 234,
235, 242, 245, 281, 324,
363–379, 405–408, 415–418,
447, 449, 466, 467, 467n3,
468n4, 472, 476, 480, 502, 511,
516, 525
Bottle/bottle of wine, 19, 36–39, 42,
45, 58, 59, 65, 67, 70, 88, 89,
93, 97, 100, 101, 112, 113,

115–121, 126, 164, 169, 171,
172, 179, 191, 196, 197, 238,
240, 301, 306, 347, 349, 372,
376, 377, 384, 390–392, 395,
396, 405–408, 410–414, 418,
428, 431, 445, 498, 499, 503,
514, 515, 517
bottling, 4, 38, 48, 54n3, 55,
58–60, 70, 72, 193, 194, 233,
240, 279, 321, 368, 377, 384,
394, 396, 399, 403, 408,
410–415, 422, 423, 425–428,
431, 432, 438
Brand, 205
Argentina, 6, 174, 463, 469
Australia, 5–7, 140, 151, 386, 440,
443, 444, 463, 469, 470
branding, 12, 64, 323, 384, 403,
408, 433, 476–478, 524
Chile, 5–7, 12, 178, 191, 193, 197,
440, 456, 463, 464, 478
China, 6, 90, 233
France, 5, 8, 38, 40, 365, 408, 440,
443, 473, 479, 511
Italy, 56, 64, 68, 440, 442, 444, 464
South Africa, 6, 209, 219, 463
Spain, 90, 99
United States (US), 5–7, 90, 117,
282, 463, 477
Brexit, 308–310
Broker, 29, 35, 37, 39, 41, 42, 189,
243, 244, 369, 373, 374, 384,
430, 448, 488, 497
Brownfield investments, 386, 443, 447,
530
Bulk/bulk wine, 4, 6, 12, 19, 23,
36–38, 42, 58, 66–68, 70, 83,
88, 89, 93, 94, 97, 99, 100, 108,
113, 115, 117, 119, 120, 126,
145, 148, 149, 164, 166, 169,
178, 183, 193, 205, 216, 227,
233, 240, 245, 293, 294, 306,
333, 347, 374–377, 390,

392–397, 399, 400, 405, 406,
408, 410–415, 417, 418, 439,
442, 444, 445, 496, 498, 500,
503, 504
Burgundy/Burgundy wines, 5, 8, 11,
12, 26, 42, 44, 145, 161, 212,
281, 385, 389–399, 447, 468,
472, 476, 511, 515, 516, 520
Business model, 11, 113, 196, 241,
245, 253, 324, 377, 385, 389,
390, 392–395, 397–399, 412,
444, 460, 489, 507, 508,
516–519, 527

C

Certification, 262, 262n15, 298–302,
302n5, 306, 425, 465, 468,
473–475, 478–479
organic, 30
Champagne, 19, 23, 24, 26, 27, 30,
34, 35, 37, 42–44, 63n8, 236,
281, 281n14, 322, 391, 405,
405n5, 433, 439–441, 447–449,
466, 467n3, 468n4, 475, 477
Chile/Chilean
brand, 5–7, 178, 191–195, 440
consumer, 5, 183, 188, 192, 478
contracts, 189
costs and prices, 5, 183–184, 188,
192, 233, 440, 444, 497, 498
cultivated area, 180, 181
denomination of origin, 187, 478
domestic market, 178, 192–195,
210, 495, 496
export, 3, 5, 6, 45, 92, 178, 183,
185, 187, 194, 196, 197, 259,
307, 343, 444, 458, 459, 478,
487, 489, 493, 494, 497, 498,
500–503
industrial companies, 5, 13, 62, 178,
181–190, 194, 195, 197, 386,
440, 444, 445, 501

land tenure, 184–185
marketing, 5, 6, 151, 177, 190–197,
307, 478, 495
varieties, 160, 161, 178–180, 184,
185, 192, 197, 489, 498, 504
wine co-operatives, 9
China/Chinese
appellations–brands, 233–234, 276
distribution, 90, 236–244
grape varieties, 229–232, 234, 236
groups–wineries, 228, 232–235,
242, 245, 336n21
joint-ventures, 227, 229, 235–236
wine consumption–production,
225, 226, 244, 256
wine regions, 232, 234, 240
Classification, 49, 52, 230–231, 234,
278–279, 295, 365, 370, 379,
457, 464, 465, 469, 510–511,
520
Climate change, 18, 152, 214, 218,
259, 492, 501, 503, 524–526,
528
Cluster, 5, 12, 45, 179, 377, 390,
392–396, 400–401, 487–504
Collective, 12, 43, 64, 72, 282, 286,
310, 321, 358, 359, 367, 448,
463–481, 488, 494, 500, 504
Common Market Organization
(CMO), 10, 18, 84, 249–251,
265–267, 270–274, 276, 276n9,
277, 283, 283n15, 287, 446,
447, 449
Community management, 529
Company, 5, 11, 12, 28, 38, 39, 51,
55, 55n5, 60–63, 65, 67, 68, 74,
86–88, 90, 94, 95, 97, 122, 123,
136, 140–142, 162, 165–168,
170, 173–176, 178, 184–186,
189, 193–197, 202, 203,
207–209, 211, 232, 233, 235,
242, 244, 276, 282, 308, 310,
321, 322, 342, 347, 348, 350,

355, 357, 358, 360, 363, 375n8,
376–379, 377n9, 383–386, 390,
398, 399, 408, 409n10, 412,
415, 431, 440, 442, 444, 445,
448, 456, 476, 488, 497, 501,
518, 524, 526, 530
  wine, 11, 12, 38, 61–63, 67, 86,
  136, 141, 185, 194, 230, 235,
  383–386, 398, 399, 440, 476,
  501
Competitiveness, 2, 4, 6, 10, 22, 44,
  45, 94, 101, 151, 152, 169, 197,
  201, 214, 215, 218–219, 251,
  265–268, 273–274, 276
Concentration, 3, 9, 11, 26, 48, 59–63,
  69, 86, 114, 139, 150, 163, 170,
  185, 209, 210, 217, 232, 245,
  322, 323, 359, 361, 363, 370,
  375, 379, 379n11, 430–431,
  439, 488, 495–497, 504
Consumer/wine consumer, 2–5, 9, 22,
  23, 35–37, 39, 41, 44, 58, 63,
  64, 67, 86, 89, 93, 94, 96,
  99–102, 105, 106, 118,
  123–126, 150, 152, 155,
  160–162, 168, 169, 171, 172,
  175, 183, 188, 190–197, 225,
  232, 234, 241–245, 256, 257,
  261, 272, 273, 281, 282, 285,
  287, 292, 294, 296, 301–303,
  307–309, 312, 320, 344, 344n8,
  345, 351n13, 364, 371, 379,
  447, 464, 467, 468, 468n4, 470,
  473, 475–481, 479n9, 513–517,
  524, 525, 527–530
Consumption/wine consumption, 6,
  18, 20–22, 39, 43–45, 54, 58,
  66–68, 66n11, 70, 73, 74, 85,
  85n3, 86, 90–92, 94–98, 100,
  101, 106, 113–121, 124, 126,
  131, 132, 141, 148, 156, 162,
  172, 174, 188, 193, 210, 219,
  220, 225, 226, 236, 237, 256,

258, 259, 273, 277, 280, 294,
296, 310, 321, 328, 330n9, 344,
409n6, 463n1, 467, 503, 507,
512–514, 520, 524, 526–528
Contract, 23, 33, 42, 48, 59, 71–72,
  99, 112, 113, 132, 145, 188,
  189, 269n3, 311, 320, 326, 331,
  331n11, 332, 333n12, 335n18,
  336, 336n19, 368, 376, 384,
  399, 429, 432, 434, 439, 440,
  442, 466, 477
Co-operative
  member, 12, 33, 34, 354, 355,
  404–408, 409n7, 410–415, 417,
  418
  France/French, 348, 404, 406
  wine, 9, 11, 33–35, 41, 42, 44,
  321–323, 339–361, 403–418,
  437, 442
Cost
  opportunity, 272, 508
  production, 5, 9, 27, 32, 36, 44, 65,
  169, 183, 184, 188, 205, 236,
  240, 321, 386, 449, 508,
  514–516, 519
  transaction, 11, 323, 326–332,
  329n7, 335n16, 336, 337, 383,
  441, 497
Crisis, 2, 18, 20, 21, 63, 85, 86, 90,
  92, 94, 95, 132, 171, 172, 268,
  269n3, 276n9, 277n10, 339,
  343–347, 349, 350, 366–368,
  415, 447, 449, 466, 467, 526
Crowdfunding, 528
Cybercommerce, 40–41

D

De-globalization, 524, 526–527
Demand, 11, 22, 44, 45, 94, 101, 116,
  120, 126, 132, 133, 158, 161,
  162, 164, 165, 168, 169, 179,
  188, 191, 192, 251, 267, 268,

271–273, 277, 287, 296, 297,
339, 345, 346, 349, 351n13,
364, 367, 368, 371, 373, 375,
377, 386, 429, 433, 448, 467,
470, 502, 504, 507, 510, 513,
514, 524, 527

Denomination of origin, 8, 25n2, 99,
467, 473, 477–480

Direct sale, 35–37, 39, 42, 67, 68, 95,
125, 368, 390, 428, 528, 529

Distribution
distribution chain, 9, 41, 170–175,
243, 246
distribution channel/channel of
distribution, 18, 35–41, 48, 63,
67, 68, 94–96, 99, 100, 174,
183, 191, 226, 237, 241, 244,
321, 378, 379, 384, 405–407,
441, 513, 517, 527–529
sale channel, 35, 67, 173–175, 407
supply chain, 48, 55, 73, 100, 431

E

Economics, 2, 21, 52, 84, 106, 152,
162, 183, 202, 230, 255, 276,
292, 320, 325, 341, 369, 405,
437, 456, 466, 489, 507, 526

Estates, 8, 11, 12, 33, 38, 42, 44, 113,
141, 163, 164, 205, 207, 212,
213, 235, 242, 285, 365, 368,
370, 372, 373, 376, 384, 385,
389–401, 439, 440, 444,
447–449, 467, 476, 515, 516,
524, 527–529

European regulation, 33

Europe/European Union (EU), 10, 18,
21, 36, 39, 43, 45, 49, 52, 54n3,
56, 64, 73, 90, 139, 140, 142,
145, 147, 149–152, 178, 201,
202, 212, 227, 249–251, 253,
254, 256, 258, 260, 261,
265–267, 266n1, 269, 271–274,

276, 278–280, 284–288, 293,
294, 303, 304, 306–310, 321,
335n18, 336, 343, 368, 369,
386, 405, 421, 438, 439, 444,
446, 447, 449, 450, 464, 466,
469, 472, 475, 477, 496, 498,
500, 509, 511, 514, 525, 526

Exporter, 3, 10, 19, 43, 77, 93, 100,
151, 153, 188, 242, 261, 292,
296, 298, 302–305, 307, 444,
457, 458, 496, 500

Exports, 2, 18, 47, 77, 106, 131, 155,
178, 201, 237, 252, 259, 268,
291, 343, 364, 385, 391, 400,
429, 439, 457, 470, 487, 507, 527

F

Farm size, 9, 48–52, 74, 81, 111, 201,
216, 330, 369, 370

Firm, 9, 11, 12, 39, 45, 48, 55, 57–60,
62–65, 67, 68, 73–75, 82,
86–89, 95, 97, 99, 100, 106,
110–113, 117, 118, 123, 132,
136, 139–141, 148, 156, 201,
210, 274, 280, 310, 311,
320–324, 329, 333, 334,
334n15, 336, 375, 376, 377n10,
378, 384, 390, 403, 404,
409–411, 414–418, 423n5,
425–429, 437–443, 446, 447,
449, 450, 464, 474, 478, 488,
489, 492, 494–497, 499, 501,
503, 504, 527

France/French
consumption, 21
cybercommerce, 40, 41
distribution channels, 36–39
export, 19, 20
import, 18–20
mass distribution, 40, 391
negociants, brokers, 29, 39, 41
organic, 28, 29, 33, 36

France/French (*cont.*)
  PDO/PGI/AOC, 25
  performance, 43, 404
  production, 33, 344
  varieties, 147, 197
  wine co-operative, 11, 35
  winemaker, 228
  wine regions, 23–24
  yields, 43, 45, 391

G
Geographic indication (GI), 19, 24, 39,
    54, 56, 69, 73, 100, 234, 254,
    282, 308–310, 448, 463, 465,
    471–476
  Argentina, 279, 280, 307–309
  Australia, 279, 280, 304, 307, 476
  Chile, 279, 280, 304
  China, 228, 233, 234, 279, 280,
    304
  France, 39, 279, 280, 465
  South Africa, 279, 280, 309
  Spain, 279, 280, 286
  United States (US), 279, 280, 282,
    304
Germany, 3, 6, 7, 17, 19, 21, 36, 100,
    124, 147, 219, 296, 308, 369,
    384, 441, 459, 507, 511, 520,
    526
Globalization, 2, 6–9, 145, 148, 163,
    253, 254, 262, 308–309, 342,
    343, 361, 526
Grands Crus, 8, 39, 44, 365, 373, 374,
    378, 385, 394–396, 399, 524,
    527
  France, 8, 39, 44, 378, 399
Grape, 7, 22, 48, 78, 106, 131, 156,
    177, 225, 255, 269, 301, 320,
    326, 344, 366, 384, 389, 405,
    422, 438, 466, 488, 511, 524

Grape grower, 27–29, 34, 52n2, 58,
    112, 120, 136, 189, 204, 205,
    208, 213, 217, 220, 363, 364,
    368, 372, 375, 376, 379, 384,
    414, 425, 426, 428, 429, 439,
    441, 442, 447–449, 528
  grape producer, 111, 112, 205, 213,
    215–216, 428, 502
Grape growing, 9, 11, 18, 22–31, 33,
    34, 43, 48, 51, 52, 72, 73, 82,
    88, 110, 112, 117, 142–148,
    220, 261, 320, 321, 366, 438,
    446, 469, 470, 499
Greece, 7, 17
Greenfield investment, 386, 443–446,
    497, 530

H
History, 8, 10, 17, 18, 24, 63, 78, 201,
    207, 228, 231, 236, 283, 285,
    287, 341, 348, 364, 463,
    465–471, 474, 475, 508–510
Hypermarkets, 35, 37, 39–41, 96, 237

I
Importer, 3, 19, 23, 39, 44, 68, 105,
    114, 119–123, 171, 241–244,
    246, 297, 309, 321, 391, 442,
    488
Imports, 3, 10, 66, 68, 106, 113, 117,
    119–121, 142, 148, 151, 171,
    210, 225, 233, 243–245, 243n3,
    252, 273, 292–296, 298,
    302–304, 306, 307, 307n7,
    309–311, 334n15, 366, 441,
    508, 510, 513, 514, 528
Industry
  industrial organization, 8–11, 13,
    22, 132, 181–190

structure, 152, 226, 244, 326, 386, 421–434

Innovation, 5, 18, 44, 45, 73, 94, 163, 177–181, 183, 185, 197, 226, 240, 254, 266n1, 274, 276, 277, 330, 335, 344, 351, 351n13, 470, 489–494, 496, 498, 501, 504

Institution, 10, 11, 208, 217, 250, 251, 253–255, 324, 368, 369, 371, 488, 489, 493, 494, 524

International
  market, 4, 18, 22, 72, 85, 86, 89–92, 100–102, 156–158, 173, 176–178, 183, 193, 197, 253, 260, 311, 349, 371, 378, 471, 487, 499, 500, 502, 503, 528
  trade, 4, 6, 7, 10, 12, 18, 43, 45, 251, 258, 260, 266, 292, 294, 295, 299, 301, 307, 311n9, 312, 456, 460, 526
  wine firms, 438–446, 450

International Organisation of Vine and Wine (OIV), 10, 18–22, 21n1, 77, 114, 225, 227, 234, 250, 251, 253–259, 262, 263, 299, 299n2, 312, 344, 458–460

Investments, 2, 7, 11, 63, 78, 84, 100–102, 132, 151, 152, 157, 158, 161–164, 168, 170, 172, 176, 178, 183–185, 208, 220, 227, 231, 235, 266n1, 274, 276, 276n9, 277, 280, 343, 359, 374, 404, 406, 413–415, 417, 418, 441, 444, 445, 469–471, 478, 480, 493, 494, 496–500, 525

Italy/Italian
  distribution, 48–52
  farm size, 48–52
  land tenure, 51
  marketing, 17, 19, 58, 64, 72, 280

relationships along the chain, 68–73
supply, 52, 60, 67, 68, 70, 433
wine production organization, 55–60

L

Land tenure
  Italy, 51
  Spain, 81

Local
  consumer, 58, 516
  consumption, 527

M

Market
  domestic, 45, 64, 90, 94–96, 121, 140, 150, 152, 153, 155, 156, 166, 169–176, 178, 193, 195, 197, 204, 205, 209, 212, 219, 220, 265, 367, 390, 392, 423, 428, 429, 470, 495, 496, 527
  local, 71, 86, 89, 90, 101, 183, 195, 507–521, 527
  niche, 63, 166, 322, 379, 398, 408
  wine, 2, 4, 6–8, 10, 17, 21, 23, 26, 38, 40, 43, 45, 70–72, 90, 121, 124, 151, 155, 164, 170–173, 225, 226, 235, 237, 238, 244, 251–253, 262, 266, 269, 273, 280, 292, 299, 307, 309, 310, 312, 324, 342, 345, 351, 365, 374, 377, 421–424, 428, 430, 433, 449, 463n1, 464, 465, 473, 479–481, 501, 503, 507, 508, 512–513, 519, 524, 526

Merchant, 11, 23, 35, 38, 40, 203, 243, 244, 322–324, 364–370, 372–379, 384, 392, 466–468, 468n4, 476, 508, 518

Merger, 11, 123, 140, 209, 322–324, 340–361, 341n3, 341n4, 376, 386, 440, 443–447, 450, 490, 496, 524

Model, 7–13, 29, 40, 43, 48, 55, 75, 82, 112, 122, 185, 214, 239, 240, 251, 254, 262, 266, 278, 278n11, 279, 326, 327, 339, 360, 377, 379, 406, 423–427, 455–461, 463–465, 471, 472, 476, 477, 480, 487, 492, 504, 527, 530

O

OECD, 492

Oenology, 257n7, 497

Offer, 40, 43, 44, 78, 124, 125, 151, 164, 166, 189, 190, 234, 252, 280, 292, 305, 312, 371, 375, 378, 379, 417, 426, 472, 500, 508, 516, 517, 520, 529, 530

Old world/old producing country/ traditional producing country (TPC), 2, 5–11, 17, 43, 91, 145, 220, 239, 245, 251, 254, 254n2, 263, 319–323, 344, 441, 455, 457–460, 463–469, 463n1, 476, 477, 480, 523–525, 527

Organic
certification, 30–31
wine, 19, 28, 33, 35, 36, 138, 231, 445

Organization
agricultural, 326–327
industrial, 8–11, 13, 22, 132, 181–190

Origin, 4, 12, 25, 25n2, 34, 39, 50, 52, 54n3, 63, 74, 83, 90, 99, 100, 145, 147, 168, 178, 179, 185, 191, 197, 201, 202, 205, 211, 212, 215, 220, 233, 238, 242, 244, 254, 259–261, 276–279, 281–287, 296, 301, 323, 336n21, 346, 365, 367, 376, 399, 442, 456, 458–460, 465–469, 471, 473–480, 524
denomination of, 8, 24

Outsourcing, 12, 58, 383–386, 389, 390, 392, 395–397, 399, 438

P

Performance, 5, 6, 8–13, 41–44, 65, 84, 85, 185, 197, 220, 235, 254, 307, 312, 320, 321, 323, 350, 357, 364, 369–372, 378, 384, 404, 408–418, 455–461, 487, 488, 491, 500–504, 508, 516–519

Planting rights, 272, 272n8, 287, 386, 438, 444, 446–450

Plurilateral
agreements, 10, 250, 253–263, 301n3
trade agreements, 10

Policy, 10, 21, 23, 43, 64, 72, 73, 119, 120, 122, 152, 156, 161, 168, 169, 173–174, 176, 203, 214, 217, 226, 250, 251, 253–255, 254n1, 254n2, 265–284, 292, 294–296, 299, 304, 307, 309, 357, 366, 391, 392, 404, 446, 447, 470, 489, 493, 494
wine, 10, 73, 249–251, 253, 265, 267, 274, 277, 288, 447

Price, 2, 4–6, 9, 10, 19, 36, 39–41, 45, 60n7, 62, 64, 65, 67–69, 71, 72, 74, 79, 85, 87, 88, 90, 93, 96–101, 106–108, 110, 111, 117, 118, 120–122, 124–126, 132–136, 140, 142, 150, 153, 156, 161, 162, 164, 168–175, 178, 180, 184, 188, 189, 191, 193–196, 204, 205, 208, 216, 219, 220, 233, 236, 238–239, 241, 242, 245, 251, 266, 268–271, 274, 287, 292, 293,

296, 297, 321, 327, 328, 331,
337, 350, 352, 367, 371,
373–375, 377, 384, 391, 392,
396, 399, 406, 408, 415–418,
428, 429, 433, 439, 441, 442,
445, 447–449, 457, 458, 460,
464, 467–470, 468n4, 477, 479,
480, 497–499, 501, 503, 504,
508, 514–518, 514n9, 520, 528
Prosecco, 4, 12, 66, 386, 421–434
Protected designations of origin (PDO)
  Argentina, 8
  Australia, 8, 49, 440, 459, 525
  Chile, 8, 456, 459
  China, 8, 19, 440, 526
  France, 8, 19, 24, 25, 78, 100, 286,
    448, 459, 465, 525
  Italy, 8, 19, 48, 50, 69, 73, 421, 525
  South Africa, 8, 525
  Spain, 8, 78, 80, 82, 89, 92, 99, 286
  United States (US), 8, 90, 525
Protected geographical indication
    (PGI)
  Argentina, 8
  Chile, 8
  China, 8
  France, 8, 19, 24, 25, 27, 33, 42,
    448, 449
  Italy, 8, 52, 54n3, 64, 69, 73
  South Africa, 8
  Spain, 8, 78, 82
  United States, 8
Proximity
  geographical, 342, 353–355
  organized, 342, 352–357, 361

Q
Quality
  grape, 11, 51, 56, 57, 71, 72, 99,
    156, 157, 176, 177, 189, 216,
    227, 331, 333–335, 334n13,
    439, 479

wine, 56, 64, 71, 73, 74, 82, 83,
  87–91, 93, 94, 96, 99, 100, 151,
  152, 163, 172, 178, 181, 196,
  205, 214, 220, 226, 240, 251,
  266, 268, 271–274, 272n7, 278,
  278n11, 279, 287, 288, 296, 365,
  367, 384, 385, 399, 440, 464,
  477, 490, 501, 510, 511, 518

R
Regulation, 8, 10, 24, 26, 33, 38, 44,
  64, 72–74, 106, 122, 145, 152,
  153, 156, 212, 219, 234, 242,
  245, 250, 253, 258, 261–263,
  265–284, 294, 296–299, 302,
  302n5, 305, 310, 311, 369, 385,
  386, 421, 449, 459, 467, 468,
  473–474, 478, 479, 511, 525,
  527
Reputation, 8, 10, 12, 18, 24, 44, 57,
  64, 94, 148, 151, 226, 230, 231,
  235, 245, 267, 282, 285, 323,
  335n16, 336, 346, 349, 365,
  371, 373, 456, 463–481, 510,
  512, 517
  collective, 12, 64, 463–481
Restaurant, 35, 36, 41, 66n11, 68,
  100, 101, 118, 172, 179, 183,
  188, 190, 195, 243, 372, 390,
  518, 519
Retail, 9, 57, 64, 65, 67, 68, 95, 96,
  99, 112, 117, 118, 121, 122,
  125, 137, 140, 145, 148–151,
  173, 188, 190, 191, 195, 205,
  208, 209, 242, 243, 297, 308,
  348, 351, 368, 408, 429, 434,
  467, 470, 476, 507
Risk, 10, 84, 133, 174, 188, 192,
  271n6, 299, 305, 327, 346, 351,
  352, 355, 356, 359, 367, 383,
  385, 386, 412–415, 439, 440,
  466, 488, 500–504, 525, 526, 530

S

South Africa/South African
  competitiveness, 343
  efficiency, 211, 215–216, 261
  farm workers, 214–215, 219
  fragmentation, 215–217
  geography, 215, 217–218
  industry structure, 201–221
  KWV, 203–205, 207–209, 213, 219
  private cellar, 205, 212–213, 217, 218, 220, 346
  producer cellar, 205, 210–213, 217, 220
  producer wholesalers, 201, 204, 207–210
  wine grape farms, 211, 213–215
Spain/Spanish
  distribution, 83, 86–87, 89–100
  domestic market, 90, 94–96
  employment, 82, 86
  exports, 77, 86, 87, 90, 92–94, 100, 101
  farm net income (FNI), 84–85
  farm size, 81
  grape varieties, 79, 83, 98
  land tenure, 81
  marketing strategies, 89–90
  relationships along the chain, 97–100
  vineyard, 4, 77–85, 87, 100–102
  wineries, 86–90, 94, 95, 98–101, 168
  wine sector, 77–102
Spirits, 17, 19, 25, 26, 38, 40, 44, 63, 122, 131, 151, 152, 204, 207, 209, 226, 234, 242, 257n8, 259, 260n11, 279, 296, 304, 310, 376, 377, 377n9, 475, 490, 515, 517
  eaux de vie, 32
Standards, 10, 81, 98, 175, 192, 208, 226, 234, 250, 251, 253–263, 281–283, 286, 297–299, 305, 310–311, 333n12, 371, 379, 396, 409, 488, 517
Store/wine store, 35, 39–41, 96, 121, 124, 173–175, 190, 191, 204, 209, 243, 297
Strategy, 4–13, 45, 57, 63–66, 74, 89, 93–95, 97, 101, 102, 151, 168, 172, 173, 175, 190–197, 216, 240, 241, 249, 250, 258, 261, 265–284, 303, 307, 308, 321–324, 340, 343–346, 348–352, 356, 359–361, 363, 367, 371, 376, 378, 384–386, 389, 390, 392, 398, 403–418, 428, 433, 437–445, 450, 456, 476, 478, 479, 489–492, 500, 511, 515, 516, 519, 525, 528–530
Supermarket, 35, 39–41, 64, 67, 96, 140, 150, 173–175, 188, 190–192, 237, 241, 369, 372, 390, 513, 515, 516, 518
Supply, 8, 12, 22, 48, 52–68, 70, 71, 73, 74, 94, 97–101, 125, 132, 133, 140, 145, 190, 193, 194, 204, 211, 219, 244, 251, 254, 265, 267, 268, 271, 272, 287, 311, 311n9, 322, 335, 339, 343, 344, 365, 366, 368, 375, 376, 386, 395, 415, 422–431, 433, 439–442, 444, 446, 447, 449, 467, 469, 470, 477, 494, 495, 501, 512, 525
Surface, 21–25, 27n3, 29–31, 34, 51, 77, 81–84, 156–163, 179, 225, 227, 346, 371, 443–445, 447–450, 496, 498, 501, 502, 509, 510, 512, 514, 519
Switzerland, 12, 456, 507–521

T

Territory/territorial, 11, 18, 23, 48, 49, 73, 78, 178, 179, 195, 256, 272n8, 278, 281, 282, 299, 323, 324, 339–361, 363–365, 368, 370, 371, 441, 456, 465, 474, 476

Terroir, 8, 10, 17–19, 25, 34, 37, 43, 74, 279, 322, 323, 344–346, 361, 384–386, 390, 399, 423, 449, 474–475, 492, 510–512, 526, 530

Tourism
  oenotourism, 527
  wine, 73, 96, 175, 217, 229, 384, 490, 497, 529

Trade
  barriers, 10, 251, 252, 259n9, 260, 280, 292, 294–297, 301, 310, 311, 500, 508, 514
  wine, 2, 3, 5, 6, 8, 10, 18–19, 101, 251, 252, 258–260, 262, 291–312, 365, 367, 470, 524, 526–527

Tradition, 8, 43, 47, 56, 58, 93, 261, 267, 345, 363, 364, 376, 384, 391, 392, 423, 474–475, 529

Typicity, 322, 465

U

United Kingdom (UK), 3, 5, 19, 120, 124, 138, 140, 149, 150, 171, 197, 208, 256n4, 294, 296, 309, 310, 364, 365, 369, 441, 444, 470, 501, 526, 527

United States (US)
  distribution, 106, 110, 112, 117, 121–126
  domestic, 114–119, 126
  farm size, 9, 48–52

imports–exports, 106, 119–121, 334n15

production regions, 107, 108, 117

varieties, 107–110, 119

wine production–consumption, 106, 113–121, 126

V

Varietal, 7, 8, 25, 52n3, 54, 87, 93, 108, 110, 117–119, 145, 147–149, 151, 153, 158, 162, 165, 191, 194, 219, 323, 442, 444, 445, 463, 463n1, 465, 469–471, 473, 498, 512

Variety/grape variety
  cepage, 8, 19
  wine grape, 48–51, 52n2, 52n3, 73, 79, 83, 84, 157, 163, 180, 183–184, 205, 211, 213–216, 219, 227, 230, 231, 245, 280, 330, 333, 384, 389–391, 393, 395, 396, 399–401, 408, 418, 446, 496, 498, 501, 502, 504

Vertical integration, 11, 12, 74, 88, 209, 226, 241, 244, 246, 327, 335, 335n16, 385, 386, 403–418, 437–450, 469, 524
  backward, 437–450

Vine, 7, 21, 23, 24, 26–28, 32, 34, 43, 48–52, 54, 62, 78, 106n1, 111, 123, 131–136, 142, 145, 156, 158, 162, 163, 179–181, 183, 212, 213, 216, 220, 225, 227–231, 235, 245, 256–258, 272n8, 278, 279, 282, 325, 328, 332–334, 334n14, 335n16, 366, 372, 385, 391, 393, 399, 421, 438, 443, 446–450, 466–470, 468n4, 472, 476, 489, 494, 508, 509, 526

Vineyard, 2, 4, 7, 11, 20, 21, 23, 24, 26–28, 32, 34, 38, 43, 47–52, 52n3, 54n3, 55, 59, 75, 77–85, 87, 100–102, 106, 110–113, 126, 133, 134, 140, 142–145, 147, 148, 153, 155–157, 161, 163, 164, 168, 170, 177, 179–181, 183, 184, 188, 189, 193, 196, 197, 212, 213, 216, 217, 225, 229, 231, 233, 235, 236, 240, 245, 266, 272, 272n8, 273, 277, 279, 323, 325–337, 334n13, 335n16, 335n18, 336n20, 336n21, 344, 351, 360, 365–367, 369–372, 376, 378, 379, 383, 384, 386, 389–399, 406, 407, 425, 428, 434, 438–450, 464, 466, 468n4, 469–475, 492, 496–498, 503, 507, 509, 512, 515, 518, 527, 528, 530

W
Wholesaler, 42, 44, 67, 68, 71, 74, 121–123, 126, 205, 208, 210, 297, 321, 348, 376, 378, 406
Wine
  sparkling wine, 42, 54, 65, 66, 68, 72, 74, 80, 93, 101, 138, 141, 160, 161, 172, 185, 197, 236, 238, 245, 293, 294, 386, 390, 394, 396, 421–426, 433, 434, 442, 501
  winegrower, 11, 72, 186–188, 225, 230, 239, 240, 245, 321, 324, 363–379, 384, 385, 390, 392–399, 405–407, 467, 468, 525
  winemaker, 8, 9, 24, 29, 33–38, 42, 55, 71, 143–144, 170, 183, 186, 188–190, 209, 228, 235, 320,

321, 384, 385, 389, 390, 392, 393, 396, 397, 399, 466, 469–472, 474, 478, 480, 498, 514, 515, 518–521
  winemaking, 7–9, 11, 12, 18, 23, 29–35, 38, 39, 42–44, 52n3, 58, 106, 113, 133, 134, 141, 147, 150, 156, 157, 165–170, 179, 185, 186, 227–236, 239–240, 244, 245, 261, 301, 323, 363, 366, 372, 384–386, 389–399, 406, 414, 417, 438, 441, 445, 464, 466, 468–470, 476, 477
  winery, 9, 11, 54n4, 55–57, 59, 63n8, 64, 65, 68–71, 69n13, 75, 86–87, 89, 90, 94, 95, 98, 99, 106, 110, 112–114, 116, 117, 119, 122, 125, 126, 132, 136, 137, 139–141, 145, 149–151, 153, 155, 158, 160, 162, 164–170, 172–176, 185–189, 193–197, 216, 226–237, 239–242, 240n1, 245, 259n9, 302, 311, 323, 325–337, 334n13, 334n15, 335n16, 335n18, 336n21, 343, 385, 389, 391–393, 396, 425, 426, 428–431, 433, 434, 438, 439, 442–444, 448, 450, 465, 469, 471, 477–480, 491, 492, 494–498, 507–509, 515–520, 524
World Trade Organization (WTO), 214, 251, 253–255, 254n1, 258, 259n10, 261, 262, 266, 279–282, 292, 295, 299, 301, 305, 306, 308–310, 312, 513
World Wine Trade Group (WWTG), 10, 250, 251, 254, 255, 259–263, 299, 301, 301n3
WTO, *see* World Trade Organization
WWTG, *see* World Wine Trade Group

Printed by Printforce, the Netherlands